Elizabeth

The Celluloid Sacrifice: Aspects of Sex in the Movies
Stardom: The Hollywood Phenomenon
Stanley Kubrick Directs
Hollywood, England: The British Film Industry in the Sixties
Rudolph Valentino
Double Takes: Notes and Afterthoughts on the Movies
Superstars
The Shattered Silents: How the Talkies Came to Stay
Garbo
Peter Sellers: The Authorized Biography
Joan Crawford
Dietrich
No Bells on Sunday: Journals of Rachel Roberts (as Editor)
National Heroes: British Cinema Industry in the Seventies and Eighties
Bette Davis
Vivien: The Life of Vivien Leigh
It's Only a Movie, Ingrid: Encounters On and Off Screen
Woody Allen: Beyond Words (trans. Robert Benayoun)

ALEXANDER WALKER

Elizabeth

The Life of Elizabeth Taylor

GROVE WEIDENFELD
New York

Published by Grove Weidenfeld
A division of Grove Press, Inc.
841 Broadway
New York, NY 10003-4793

First published in Great Britain in 1990 by George
Weidenfeld & Nicolson Limited, London.

Library of Congress Cataloging-in-Publication Data

Walker, Alexander.
    Elizabeth / Alexander Walker.
        p.   cm.
    Includes bibliographical references and index.
    ISBN 0-8021-1335-4 (alk. paper) : ~~$21.50~~ #22.95
    1. Taylor, Elizabeth, 1932–   . 2. Motion
picture actors and actresses—~~United States—~~
~~Biography.~~ I. Title.
    PN2287.T18W25 1990
    791.43′028′092—dc20
BIO
TAYLOR [B]   90-21610
                                                 CIP

Manufactured in the United States of America

Printed on acid-free paper

First American Edition 1991

10 9 8 7 6 5 4 3 2 1

Frontispiece: As Gloria Wandrous, greeting the day
with a Jack Daniel's in *Butterfield 8*. She resisted making
it, but the film won Elizabeth Taylor her first Oscar.

4/91   BIO
            TAYLOR

CONTENTS

Part Four: Surviving

FOR RICHARD SCHICKEL

ILLUSTRATIONS

· · ·

Between pages 270 and 271

'Turn on the siren,' said the bride-to-be,
'and let them know I'm coming.'

PART ONE

· · ·

Sara and Elizabeth

LIKE FATHER, LIKE MOTHER

Elizabeth Taylor always had a pretty good idea of what might have happened to her had there been no war, no films and no need to leave the country where she was born: 'Probably if there hadn't been a World War Two, I would have been a debutante, lived in England and married someone very secure and staid. I never would have become an actress. I would have had as many children as I could physically have had...'

It is one of the few times in her life that she looked back. Rarer still was one of the few times she went back – back to her birthplace. Fifty years into her restless life, she suddenly appeared on the doorstep of the house where she was born, and offered to buy it back. The owners, a banker and his wife, appropriately enough, were surprised but gratified and invited her in. She had little trouble remembering her old nursery, her parents' bedroom, the back staircase used by the manservant and the maid to get between the kitchen and their quarters. But her memory for other parts of the house was more vague: she had barely turned seven when she left England. She might have recognized one of the road signs, though: dating from the 1930s, it portrayed a little girl in silhouette on a plumpish pony warning motorists of the nearby riding school and of 'Horses Crossing' – a piquant omen for a girl who first found fame in the saddle. Local folklore points out the bridlepath along the side of the road – still unbuilt – in which the Taylors' house stood, where venerable beeches divide it from pastureland that has since become a golf course. 'That's where she learnt to sit on a horse ... That's where they taught her to ride for that film.'

It wasn't, of course. But that's one of the more harmless fictions about Elizabeth Taylor that have been seeded by those who never knew her, but, due to her star status, feel they do intimately.

That she was British by birth is no fiction. She was also American. She took one nationality from the country where she was born, the other, from her parents.

The house was called Heathwood, and stood in Wildwood Road in what was then a semi-rural pocket on London's northern edge, where the 'old money' of Hampstead Heath encountered the newer settlers of Golders Green. Names like 'Heathwood' and 'Wildwood' reflected the suburban dwellers' dream of a countryside that was reachable and afford-able, and much of it remains as it was in Elizabeth's impressionable childhood. Blackberry brambles and red-berried rowans in autumn, cel-andines and dog-daisies in spring and summer, and, close by, the wooded acreage of Hampstead Heath. Foxes now come down to nose out the dustbins; voles are often sighted, too. One couldn't have had a more English environment in which to grow up.

Elizabeth's parents were taken to be British, too – by quite a few people in the 1930s, and even by some in the 1980s, including one of Elizabeth Taylor's lovers. 'He dressed like an Englishman,' says one London art dealer of Francis Taylor, who was in that line of business before the war. 'She spoke with an English accent,' says one New Yorker who had encountered Sara Taylor, Elizabeth's mother, while he and her daughter were enjoying an affair in Beverly Hills. The importance of being English was not exactly a fantasy on her parents' part, but a part of the life-style they had adopted and grown to value by the time Elizabeth came along. They are good examples of folk who were transformed by fortune, accident and aspirations quite as much as their famous child would be. Like her, they exchanged one world for another and assumed quite different identities according to their needs, talents and opportunities.

Both Francis and Sara Taylor came originally from a part of America where it was deemed prudent to retain a plain style of living until you had earned the right to flaunt your pretensions. Francis Taylor was born in Springfield, Illinois, on 18 December 1897; Sara Viola Warmbrodt in Arkansas City, Kansas, on 21 August 1896.

The Taylors were Presbyterians (Francis's father was also a Mason), who had English and Scottish blood and probably also Ulster connections. Good looks ran in the family. Present-day Londoners who remember Francis all remark immediately on what a handsome man he was. His father had been a clerk in a general store who worked his way up to management level but still never lost a chance for a handshake with clients. Francis, too, had a concern for a good appearance and good manners. 'He was a gentleman in every sense of the word,' says Sir Hugh Leggatt, the influential London art dealer, 'and to a young man [like me at the time] he was kind, courteous and helpful . . . always elegantly dressed.' Another thing everyone remembers about Francis Taylor: his sparkling blue eyes.

How the young man rose to become a star in his own profession – admittedly a star of lesser magnitude than his daughter, but, to his own clients, every bit as dazzling – is something that would have interested F. Scott Fitzgerald. Already, it has a hint of Hollywood fatefulness about it.

A tantalizing glimpse is to be found in an unexpected place – in the private files of Hedda Hopper, the movie colony gossip columnist, a feared personage, a sycophant to those who toadied to her, the scourge of those who didn't. At the time she was laying her public flail on Elizabeth Taylor for her brazen impiety, as Hopper alleged, in snatching Eddie (Fisher) from Debbie (Reynolds) before Mike (Todd) was cold in his grave. Hopper received approving mail by the sackful from readers whose indignation she had whipped up against Elizabeth. Among them was a letter from a Florida reader of her syndicated Hollywood column. This lady had been to school in Cherokee, Oklahoma, with Francis Taylor's father. The Taylors moved to Arkansas City, 'not long after cars became a common thing and a way of life', she wrote to Hopper. 'All the girls thought [young Francis] marvellous, but he seemed not to notice.' The writer then recalled how 'Francis's uncle from New York City came to take him to New York where he was buying and selling art.' By chance, she ran across the young man a few years later in Newman's store, where his father was clerking. Francis was 'back from Europe and New York, looking Ivy League or Cottontail ... We recognized each other, but you know how it is after so long, you just don't speak ... He still looked like he was a nice lad.'

Howard Young, the husband of Francis's aunt, didn't have the good looks or charm of his nephew, but he had something more immediately negotiable – wealth (and no children of his own). He was from St Louis, where he had made money early on from his business retouching and tinting family photographs. Then he made much more money through a lucky oil-well investment. Howard Young in person was no wildcatter, but he was a thruster. He had energy for business and an eye for the main chance. He discovered he had a gift for opening and closing deals – not in oil, but in oil paintings. He probably lacked the patient temperament needed to manage an art dealer's business, but he found an apt pupil in his nephew Francis. By comparison with his ebullient uncle, he was a shy boy, but one with taste, manners and above all charm. By the time his uncle had finished with him, Francis had been given a good grounding in the international art market that was catering for the demand of discerning Americans – and some less discerning – for good eighteenth-century European, and especially English, portraits. The experience of St Louis and New York had also given him an easy manner with the rich and famous. He was, as they would have said in his home-town, a good catch.

'He married a girl from Arkansas City who had done some "local theater",' wrote Hedda Hopper's correspondent, 'and had gotten bitten by the bug, and later my in-laws felt she had driven Liz to be the actress she [herself] could not have been.'

Sara Warmbrodt's family origins are more widely scattered than Francis Taylor's own well-defined WASP background. Her father was a German immigrant, an engineer by trade, who worked as foreman-manager at a laundry. Her mother had the artistic talents that the daughter inherited, including the ability to play piano and violin. By all accounts, Sara was a spirited girl. She was among the first in town to get her hair bobbed. And she took the route out of town quite as early as Francis Taylor, but into art of another kind – the theatre. Adopting the stage name Sara Sothern, she quickly worked her way on to the stock-company circuits. Friends she had in later life recall her saying that she could play any role offered her, 'once I set my mind to it'.

'Setting her mind to it' was deeply ingrained in Sara by her upbringing and religion. Her mother practised Christian Science, a faith that gives its servants a powerful sense of individual worth and just as powerful a belief that you can gain whatever you want if your convictions are strong enough. In short, who you wish to become is inherent in who you already are. The plays Sara appeared in were useful practice-pieces for such positive thinking. She was rapidly promoted from 'utility parts' to leading roles. And those people who couldn't see into Sara's soul and witness her commitment to whatever characters she was playing had the consolation of her vivacious beauty to look at.

Sara Sothern's strength of will repays study. Later she applied it to shaping every detail of Elizabeth's early life, and her own stage triumph in the early 1920s was created out of the same act of faith in an individual's power to reshape reality by spiritual and emotional conviction. Sara really only played one part of distinction in her life; but she played it four years running, and so well that it took her from Los Angeles to Broadway and London's West End. It was in a four-act play called *The Fool* written by the stage illusionist Channing Pollock, and Sara's role, though minor, was crucially placed and dramatically effective. It was a story of faith-healing. Sara played Mary Margaret, 'a poor cripple girl', who, when the sceptical mob are forcing their way into the mission hall to attack the man they consider a false evangelist, falls on her knees and begins reciting the Lord's Prayer. As 'the friend of the people' is attacked by the intruders, she suddenly springs to her feet and runs to his aid. 'Mary Margaret, where are your crutches?' a woman screams. 'I kin walk!' cries Sara. The mob takes fright: 'God's in this room.'

In short, *The Fool* had just the sort of fundamentalist conviction that

Mary Baker Eddy and Aimee Semple Macpherson had popularized in America. Faith was answered and desire achieved. It also possessed a tempting sense of short-cut, just as prevalent in the film industry as it is in fundamentalist religion, where a unique individual can convert her stardom into real power by concentrating on what she wants and not minding too much how she gets it: 'I want' ... FADE OUT ... FADE IN ... 'I got'. In Act Four, the miraculously cured Sara gives her benefactor a coloured print of 'Mama's Treasure' and he, in turn, gives her a muff and a neckpiece in beaver. (Sara's daughter was destined to exact more prodigious tribute from her admirers.) And as the curtain comes down, she slips her arm possessively into his and both turn their gaze up at a putative Star of Bethlehem, Sara secure in the more worldly radiance of the stage spotlight. It was a thrill she could never forget.

Sara Sothern played the part opposite James Kirkwood on Broadway, where they opened in October 1922, and did so well that she was taken across the Atlantic and co-starred with Henry Ainley at the Apollo Theatre, London, in September 1924. Photographs of that production depict her as a plausible fifteen-year-old (though she was actually twenty-eight) with an urchin haircut and astonishingly large and staring eyes that singled her out from among the stiff and staid English players. Despite a sniffy notice in *The Times* – 'a religious orgy of a type very popular in the United States' – *The Fool* had a respectable run in London, helped by its stars and its religious uplift. Sara's personal success in it gave her an easy entrée into fashionable London life and so-called 'fast' society. Sara Sothern may have been solidly Victorian in matters of faith, but she also had the all-night energy of a Twenties' flapper girl. One of the stage directions in the play read: 'The conspicuous feature of [Mary Margaret's] costume is a pair of soiled gold slippers that once set off a ballgown.' After the show, Sara frequently saw the night out in newer dancing shoes.

She was back in New York in 1925, unsure of what she should do next. Like most Broadway players, she had made a film test. But although her good looks were an attraction on stage, something about them prevented the camera from falling in love with her – and, at nearly thirty, she was too old for any of the ingenue heroine roles of the silent era. While she waited for work, she ran into Francis Taylor and his Uncle Howard in a Manhattan nightclub. She and Francis were married the following year.

Their temperaments were radically different, their wills of unequal strength, but they had a lot in common. The speed of their engagement and marriage perhaps signifies that they recognized this. Both had quit high school without a thought of going on to college; but the worlds of art dealing and the theatre, both international pursuits, had put a cosmopolitan polish on them. They had charm, too, in plenty. Moreover, when together,

Sara and Francis made heads turn: they were a strikingly handsome couple. Though Francis was shy compared with his wife, she had ambitions for both of them and the conviction that if God wanted them to do well, then do well they would. To Howard Young, it looked a safe, steady combination. After hearing Sara swear that her stage career lay behind her, he sent the newlyweds off to Europe to buy art for his American clients.

The next three years were like a working honeymoon. Through Howard Young's generous funding, and their own talent for turning social connections into business opportunities, the Taylors explored the art markets of London, Paris, Berlin and Vienna, buying pictures from other dealers or people of wealth (or, as it happened, people suddenly without wealth due to the raging German inflation) which they sent back to the New York gallery. They mixed business and pleasure, always staying in the top hotels, leading a nomadic but very comfortable cosmopolitan life, rather like that of film stars. What brought their 'grand tour' to a halt was the decision to start a family.

'We knew that when the time came to settle down and have a family,' Mrs Taylor wrote later, 'of all the places in Europe we would choose England.'

Both of them were Anglophiles, as much by sympathy as business sense. Gainsborough, Reynolds, Romney and lesser artists of that genre always sold well in Howard Young's New York gallery, but the Taylors liked nothing better than being in London. They already had a large client list there, and the social life, entertainment and a standard of living that was a cut above what they could expect in America all appealed to them. Embassy records show that Mrs Taylor arrived before her husband, possibly to house-hunt. She registered as an American citizen on 5 February 1929 (her passport number was 313, a token of simpler days of travel). Her husband followed on 2 April 1929 (passport no. 492). By then, Sara had found a 'dream house' for them. It had not been an easy search. She had constructed the home she wanted in her mind before she found it on the property agents' lists. Sara had been brought up on the improving narratives of Victorian storytellers in which family mansions abounded, as well as on the Edwardian pastoral fantasies that Kenneth Grahame's children's books embodied. Her imagination was coloured by the latter's *Dream Days* and *The Golden Age*, and by her favourite book of all, Frances Hodgson Burnett's *The Secret Garden*. Eventually, at 8 Wildwood Road, Hampstead, she found a place that fulfilled the craving of her imagination. The house itself was solid enough, and modern, too, built two years earlier for a Mr Kadesh: it was imposing-looking at the top of its tiered front garden, with a porticoed entrance. Mrs Taylor saw it first in early spring. It looked to her as if a film studio had planted it out with all the flowers the scene needed: 'tulips almost three feet high, forget-me-nots, yellow and lavender violas, flaming snapdragons, rich red wall-flowers, and a formal rose garden that terraced down to [the] heath'. The garden today still has its slightly 'out of this world' look: but now three thirty-foot-high magnolia trees, probably planted by the Taylors, edge its otherwise unfenced border with the footpath. Behind the house were a tennis court, more herbaceous beds, and something that sealed Sara's immediate attraction to it. A tiny wooden gate let into the hedge gave access to a semi-private wild wood, 'all fenced in with iron railings', containing a brook, a pond and a rich variety of wildlife and birdsong. It was called 'The Sanctuary', or, more prosaically, 'Turner's Wood'. It was a wonderful place ... for children to play, Mrs Taylor thought.

Her first child arrived in 1929, a boy who was named Howard, as a compliment to his wealthy uncle. Sara's mother had been writing to her from America, impressing on her daughter the Christian Science tenet that beautiful thoughts produced beautiful consequences ... and beautiful babies. In Howard's case, the recipe worked spectacularly well. He was a striking infant, golden-haired, with a well-defined face that inside a few years made him look like a budding Rupert Brooke – a comparison he grew to hate. By this time, the Taylors had moved into Heathwood, clinching the house purchase with an on-the-spot cheque, so certain was Sara that good omens were already in residence.

A little over two years later, at 2.30 a.m. on 27 February 1932, a cold and foggy morning, with a Dr Huggenheim in attendance, Sara gave birth to her second child.

After thanking God for a girl, the mother fell into a deep sleep of exhaustion and contentment. But on awakening, she discovered things had not gone so smoothly this time. The child looked, well, 'funny' – in the sense of peculiar, not droll. Quite alarming, in fact. Her eyes were screwed tight shut, though that was commonplace among the newborn. But across her shoulders and upper arms was a thin down of black hair. Hypertrichosis, said the doctor reassuringly, a chromosomal variant: it would soon disappear. In fact, it was to recur at intervals for years. Mrs Taylor blamed herself for this deficiency in the baby; she had not been imbibing beautiful thoughts of the requisite strength. From then on, she prayed strenuously that her baby be restored to normal. It cost her an effort of faith as strong as the one she had so successfully simulated in *The Fool*. The miracle wasn't as dramatic as throwing away her crutches and walking, but, when it came, it was gratifying. After ten days or so, during which the doctor occasionally prised the infant's eyelids open but found only the whites visible, the child was being held in Sara's arms when she suddenly snapped open her eyes and looked straight up at her parent's face. A delighted Sara found herself gazing into two pools of deep violet fringed by thick black lashes. She remembers – with the sharpness of a film close-up – that the baby then smiled. A nurse of an unromantic nature put this down to wind – babies at that age, you know, can't show emotions. But Mrs Taylor remained convinced of her daughter's very special greeting for her. The child's birth was noted in *The Times* and registered at nearby Hendon – for the Taylors' address was actually in Golders Green, rather than smarter Hampstead, though Sara glossed over this. She was given the names Elizabeth Rosemond, the latter after her aunt.

'Just pink skin and no feathers,' Elizabeth wrote, much later on, when she came across a dead fledgling that had dropped out of the nest. She picked it up and cosseted it, uselessly of course. Mrs Taylor, in the months ahead, fussed over an infant who looked just as vulnerable and pathetic. At the age of sixteen months, Elizabeth's babyhood chrysalis began peeling away and a dazzling child slowly emerged. Dark hair, those double-lashed eyelids, seed teeth where, at one time, bare gums had suggested to Sara the awful likelihood of her baby needing dentures! Soon she was the 'dark angel' to the 'Botticelli angel' of her fair-haired brother: prayers had been abundantly answered. Elizabeth was slow to walk; but when she started toddling, her family found there was no stopping her.

2

'A MARVELLOUS FEELING'

'What a podge!' Elizabeth exclaimed years later, seeing a family snapshot of herself aged two, a big head set on a dumpy body, but with hair already luxuriantly drooping over those eyes of hers that drew compliments even from passing strangers. She was an unusually active and enquiring child and her parents' life encouraged this. The Taylors loved exploring their adopted country: they had the American zeal for discovering the new and something of the pioneers' boldness. Trailer caravans that could be hooked on to the family car had become a craze in the 1930s, and the Taylors bought one for their Buick. Into the two vehicles they packed (as well as themselves) a maid, a temporary nurse for Elizabeth, their cook, a golden retriever, tents, a folding pram and plenty of wet-weather wear.

Off they would go on excursions to the Norfolk Broads and later, when the rains came, to milder Devon. Mrs Taylor wrote of these trips with an exuberance that displays her pragmatic romanticism. Clearly, she was living out the English family fantasies of the children's books she had read – and was to re-read to her children. In her published accounts, only a scattered reference to 'Old World charm' or a barbecue built of rocks betrays an American approach to the English pastoral adventure. 'First we put up the gay yellow and red tents. One for the two maids and one for a dressing room. Our bright green caravan had two bedrooms: one for daddy and me and one for the children, plus a dining room and kitchen combined. The Buick was red and the clothesline, hanging from the trees with our many-coloured bathing suits dangling in the breeze, made us look and feel like a band of romantic gypsies. Only the scale of the operation as described here is un-English; the mother's relish for order and purpose shows a woman well able to manage her dreams and bring illusion to life. The energy, too, is American, even if it is exercised not on the plains of Kansas but in English farmers' fields and sheltered inlets where blackberrying, home-made stews, fresh-laid eggs and a visit to the harbour to buy cockles and mussels for high tea filled a well-planned day.

Mrs Taylor was a vivid writer as well as a keen recorder of detail: characteristics echoed by Elizabeth when she took up her classroom pencil to compose her first literary work.

In later years, what fascinated Elizabeth most about her uncle Howard Young was his directness of approach. He knew what he wanted and went out to get it. His appearance helped. 'He was a great bear of a man, a bit like George Shultz, the former US Secretary of State,' Sir Hugh Leggatt recalls, 'but scrupulously honest and not ruthless unless he was crossed.' One story told about Howard Young suggests the same sort of fearlessness that Elizabeth herself was to show in public and in private.

Coming over to England on the boat one summer, he found that a fellow dealer who specialized in fine silver had stolen a march on him by approaching a client of his with a satisfyingly direct sale.

'Do you mind if I borrow these?' Young asked the client. Parcelling up the Georgian plate, he went straight to the maverick dealer and emptied the contents out in front of him with a clatter. 'Now if you ever interfere with one of my clients, you'll never have any more dealings with me. Do you understand?' The chastened man said he did. 'Very well ... Now I know what he paid you for all this. I am going to give you $500 more.' The lesson was rubbed in so that it would be remembered without rancour – but it was remembered.

On another occasion, having discovered that the Romney he had bought from an aristocratic English owner and unwittingly sold to a client was a copy – a story the rival dealer Duveen was putting about with glee – Young located the original, bought it and sold it to the same client as before. 'It shows you how Howard could recover from a knockout,' says a present-day London art dealer, Sidney Sabin. Howard Young's reputation for boldness and resilience wasn't lost on Elizabeth as she grew up.

It seems, though, that Francis Taylor found the presence of his uncle a bit of a strain. Whenever they were together in London, the nephew maintained a self-effacing air. Some dealers never even knew that they were related: they simply accepted Francis as the junior partner. Left to himself, however, Francis could be considerably more enterprising than his conservative uncle allowed. Howard mistrusted any English art that was later than Landseer. Francis, however, began forming friendships with contemporary artists, some of whom had homes or studios near the Taylors. The metropolitan art colony had been steadily moving from its late-Victorian base in Chelsea 'up the hill' to St John's Wood and

Hampstead. Among the contacts Francis made were Laura Knight and Augustus John. The latter's work was to assist the Taylors at a crucial moment in their personal fortunes. Francis also extended his private purchases to the Continent, and a French Impressionist or two began appearing on the living-room walls at Heathwood. Elizabeth was to inherit her father's taste in art and, in time, much of his collection.

A passion for fine art was only one of the links between the Taylors and Victor Cazalet, the man who more than anyone else, perhaps, encouraged them to think of England as their permanent home and themselves as an upper-class English family. Consciously or not at first, Sara set her heart on that ambition. Not out of snobbery: 'Englishness' was what she adored, not rank or title, though if these came with it, they only rounded out her romantic illusion. The old theatrical drive to transform herself into the part she'd been assigned had never really left her, in spite of her sincerity in giving up her stage career. It was a natural reflex of hers to look around at the Taylors' growing number of friends and acquaintances and assimilate many of their characteristics and social values. Her own accent was witness to this: it had become more 'English'. Though it wouldn't have fooled the natives (not that she ever tried), it came to be accepted, then and later, as an English accent by quite a few Americans.

From their earliest years, Sara strove to give her children a feel for the life she herself had read about as a child, tasted briefly during her successful season on the London stage, and now was well placed to acquire and enjoy. In short, Sara was bent on inventing other selves for herself and her children, pushing them ever closer to the desirable norm of the social classes she perceived to possess charm, influence, respect and a good life. The prime agent of this aspiration was Col. Victor Cazalet.

Victor Cazalet had connections everywhere: a Member of Parliament, a landowner, a sociable bachelor, a London clubman with the time (and money) to play confidant and act as go-between for a variety of influential people in and out of politics. Then in his late thirties, he was a crony of Winston Churchill (who was out of office at this period and a Tory rebel), and he counted Anthony Eden, Churchill's protégé, among his intimate friends. Cazalet was known as a man for all causes. Prominent among them was the campaign for a Jewish homeland and the movement for world unity. He was also a Christian Scientist and a lay preacher: another of the links between this worldly yet spiritual man and Sara Taylor. The probability is that she had met and got to know him before her marriage to Francis, for it is almost inconceivable that Cazalet should not have attended the London production of *The Fool*, with its evangelizing message, or thereafter made it his business to meet the actress, Sara Sothern, who provided its emotional *coup de théâtre*. Cazalet later became

Elizabeth's unofficial godfather, since the fairly austere faith of Christian Science made no provision for official ones. Victor's mother Maud (called 'Auntie Molly' by Elizabeth) and his sister Thelma, also an MP, and a campaigner for women's rights, 'took up' these charming Americans who did all the English things; in her turn, Sara Taylor diverted her formidable energy to some of the charities, including Zionism, that the Cazalets sponsored. It is likely that Elizabeth's later conversion to the Jewish faith, and her life-long support for Israel, owes something to the sympathetic views she heard being expressed at home in these formative years.

Victor Cazalet fitted neatly into Sara's mythology. He was more than a little like the benevolent godfather of Victorian literature: a rich, kindly, well-connected bachelor who radiates his own happiness among the less fortunate, or else is rescued from some secret sorrow of his own by the love of an innocent child. An incident that happened just before Elizabeth's third birthday reinforced her mother's view of their friend and patron. It is also the first account of one of those overwhelming illnesses that intermittently struck at Elizabeth in later years, turning some seemingly trivial affliction into a major crisis and creating its own all-involving drama.

On this occasion, a throat infection had spread to Elizabeth's ears, causing abscesses that called for lancing and hot poultices day and night for weeks. Elizabeth had to try to sleep propped up, since even a down-filled pillow pressing on her ear was agony. As Mrs Taylor tells it, with an art that shows how well she had assimilated the sickbed sentiment of the High Victorian writers, the strain showed on her and Francis to the extent that Elizabeth begged her parents to get some rest, and said, 'Mother, please call Victor and ask him to come and sit with me.' The inspirational overtone deepens with the arrival of Cazalet and his mother, who had driven ninety miles from their country estate in Kent through thick fog to reach Elizabeth's bedside. 'Victor sat on the bed and held [Elizabeth] in his arms and talked to her about God. Her great dark eyes searched his face, drinking in every word, believing and understanding. A wonderful sense of peace filled the room. I laid my head down on the side of the bed and went to sleep for the first time in three weeks. When I awakened, she was fast asleep. The fever had broken.'

Even allowing for artful retouching, this picture indicates how strongly the mother and daughter – to say nothing of their spiritual benefactor – believed in the strength of the will to overcome temporary woes of mind or body. Think healthy thoughts. Don't dwell on illness. Never look back with regret or remorse. To do so is in vain and only gives negative powers a chance to insinuate themselves into one's well-being. Such were the lessons Elizabeth learned from the annealing illness of early childhood and the spiritual comfort of saving herself through will-power: and such was the mechanism for continuous salvation she was to adopt throughout her life.

Mrs Taylor's favourite children's authoress, Frances Hodgson Burnett, put it succinctly in *The Secret Garden*. 'Thoughts – just mere thoughts – are as powerful as electric batteries – as good for one as sunlight is or as bad for one as poison. To let a sad thought or a bad one get into one is as dangerous as letting a scarlet fever germ get into your body. If you let it stay there after it has got in you may never get over it as long as you live.' The amazing resilience of the mind – and, even more, of the body – stiffening at times into a stubborn resistance to the world and a total conviction in one's own rightness: the crucial part of Elizabeth Taylor's adult personality owed much to the Victorian certainties of Frances Hodgson Burnett, though it might never have occurred to Elizabeth to acknowledge the connection.

Elizabeth was brought up to believe in the sort of heavenly perfection that more prudent or less committed mothers would have warned their children against accepting as a goal in life.

Even the wild woods of 'The Sanctuary' yielded moral lessons that were drilled into the little girl. On her almost daily walks beside its brook and through its dells, Elizabeth used to pluck a posy of flowers. Disappointingly, she found they wilted in the heat of her tight little fist. Mrs Taylor cheered her up. God made the flowers, she assured her. 'He makes them perfect and keeps them perfect, doesn't he?' her precocious child is supposed to have answered. Maybe she did answer so, or in words to that effect. But the point is, Sara dinned into Elizabeth the lesson that spiritual reality transcends the appearance of things. It doesn't matter how the rest of the world views a thing; if you see it differently, and know in your heart of hearts that you are right, then that is how it is. Most people learn by later experience that this is how it is *not*. Elizabeth Taylor always seemed to be able to maintain the comforting alternative.

As Elizabeth grew slightly older, she reached the age when she might have had another kind of fantasy presented to her as a treat, if not exactly as a moral lesson. But the cinema didn't figure at all in her upbringing. Mrs Taylor adopted the view of many upper-class English mothers of the time that the cinema was a vulgar, working-class entertainment, not to be preferred to Christmas pantomimes or children's plays like *Peter Pan*. Elizabeth doesn't recall a single visit to the movies all the time her family lived in London, and her mother confirms this, authoritatively, by saying that she didn't take her.

Instead, the treats that Sara gave Elizabeth and her brother Howard were more in line with those that might occur to a metropolitan English mother bringing up her children the way that, say, Christopher Robin had been brought up by Nanny. The first of A. A. Milne's books for children had been published in 1924, when Sara was acting in London, and *Winnie the Pooh* was the talk of the town when the newlywed Taylors reached London on their honeymoon in 1926. Royalty-worship figured largely in the excursions of Sara and the children. At the pomp and ceremony they were, thanks to their friendship with the Cazalets, frequently to be found in the front row. A few months after her illness, Elizabeth was watching King George V's silver jubilee procession through London. A month later, Thelma Cazalet got the family invited to 11 Downing Street, then the official residence of Neville Chamberlain, Chancellor of the Exchequer, and they saw the Trooping of the Colour on Horse Guards Parade. Elizabeth, aged three and a half, wore a Paris-made organdie frock appliqued with tiny felt flowers. Her mother's gaze was riveted on the women of the Royal Family standing in the open windows of Admiralty House when she heard a piercing cry from her daughter: 'Oh, mummy, do look at the King's horse.' The future star of *National Velvet* was giving early warning of her first love affair.

On another occasion, Queen Mary's birthday, 'Auntie Molly' Cazalet commissioned Elizabeth to take a gift on her behalf to Buckingham Palace. Brother Howard had performed the same loyal duty a year earlier, but with less grace, since he was already showing incipient rebellion against the constricted English upbringing that his parents imposed on him and his sister. The visit was made memorable for him only by his knitted shorts – then general wear for well-bred middle-class English children – slipping down on the palace doorstep due to the perished elastic in the waistband. Boys are quick to pin the blame on mother for such humiliations. Howard's resistance to Anglophilia seems to have intensified when he was sent to Arnold House, a prep school for day boys in St John's Wood, where his frustrations made a good pubescent boxer out of him.

Discipline at home was stricter than it might have been in a family not subject to Mrs Taylor's overly zealous concern with correctness and appearances.

When Elizabeth did something wrong, she wasn't simply chided. She was totally ignored, not spoken to, in short 'sent to Coventry': a punishment historically meted out to Royalist prisoners in the jails of that Midlands city by their Cromwellian captors and, later, adapted by English parents to make their disobedient children properly remorseful. Ignoring Elizabeth was found to be an efficacious way of bringing her to heel. Of course, in those days, it didn't cost a film company millions to ignore Elizabeth Taylor.

Her worst fault was untidiness. Sometimes, she was stubborn over this 'to the point of mulishness'. Moreover, when her nanny was trying to dress her for some event or other, she would begin to play games with the patient woman, skipping about this way and that so that the clothes couldn't be put on her jiggling little body. The game ended only with the arrival of Mrs Taylor, scolding Elizabeth for making them all late. Penitence was expressed (when the child could write) in a note to mother, slipped under her pillow for discovery at bedtime. Elizabeth kept up this act of contrition until well into her teens, though it probably contributed to her loathing, later in life, for writing any notes whatsoever.

Mrs Taylor was to say later that one of her biggest difficulties was teaching Elizabeth the difference between 'Can I?' and 'May I?' – not a difficulty that many mothers would have worried over. It never struck her that perhaps the child's confusion wasn't to do with grammar at all, but could be put down to stubbornness. For Elizabeth, there was no difference between 'can' and 'may'. She watched her brother's efforts to assert his own identity with instinctive approval. But the little sister wasn't ready to emulate him, yet.

The first time that Elizabeth tasted the exhilaration that came from catching other people's attention and winning their love and applause came at a charity event in London. Various versions have entered movie mythology. One has Elizabeth dancing for King George V and Queen Mary at a Command Performance. Occasionally, the story has a sentimental variation, and the reigning monarchs' two little grandchildren, Princess Elizabeth and Princess Margaret Rose, Elizabeth's near contemporaries, are the royals present. Neither version is accurate, though both seek to imply a predestined link between throne and screen, or between the two Elizabeths, that is manna to gossip columnists. The encounter was more in the nature of a lucky accident, though a revealing one.

Elizabeth was about four at the time. She had been taught a few rudimentary dancing steps – the kind every little girl acquires, along with dolls and prams. Just where she was taught, though, is still a mystery, for the prestigious dancing school in South Kensington run by Madame Vacani, dance tutor in her time to royalty, continues to deny the story that Elizabeth Taylor, film star, was ever a pupil of theirs. It's quite likely Elizabeth picked them up for amusement, maybe watching her brother learning his own steps on some visit or other to his prep school. In any case, she was included in the benefit recital put on by the Vacani pupils in the presence of the Duchess of York (the future Queen Elizabeth the Queen Mother) and the two young princesses. Perhaps Auntie Molly, nudged by Sara, used her influence. Mrs Taylor's account of the occasion loses the details in the haze of proud memory that her daughter, costumed as a butterfly, should be given the chance to curtsey to royalty. Elizabeth seized her chance – and then refused to let go. She continued fluttering around the stage of the Hippodrome, doing an improvised *pas seul* to the enjoyment of understanding mothers and, possibly, to the welcome relief of Royalty, to whom any mild departure from routine is a gratefully received respite. Before her mother retrieved her from the wings, she had taken several curtain calls.

In 1964, the performer of this unscheduled interlude nearly thirty years earlier published a slim, highly selective fragment of autobiography which at least showed that subsequent, more momentous events in her life hadn't diminished the captivating spell of that tiny moment of power. 'It was a marvellous feeling on that stage – the isolation, the hugeness, the feeling of space and no end to space – and then the applause bringing you back into focus, and noise rattling against your face.' To Mrs Taylor, too, the incident was a revelation. Hearing the no doubt ironic but warm-hearted applause ring out for her daughter's impulsive bit of limelight-stealing revived an aching regret for the night when a reputedly staid British audience called 'Bravo, bravo, bravo!' as the curtain came down on her at the Apollo Theatre almost ten years earlier. Not all the king's horses and all the king's men could persuade her to resume her career, she vowed, favouring a royal metaphor even here, 'but I knew from the benefit recital that Elizabeth had inherited a certain amount of "ham"'.

But if she had any presentiment that the daughter might one day resume the stage career her mother had abandoned, Mrs Taylor did nothing to encourage it. English mothers of a certain social standing – and Sara by now could surely count herself one of them – did not put their daughters on the stage.

Around 1936, the Taylors acquired the other asset that well-off Londoners were learning to enjoy in the period between the wars. They already owned a car: now they found themselves a country cottage. Victor Cazalet had purchased an estate near Cranbrooke, in Kent, with a large manor house called Great Swifts. He invited his friends down for a weekend. It was on a walk through the beech woods – by a path they imaginatively named Cathedral Walk, for Sara was, as usual, playing romantic games with her children – that mother and daughter found their own 'enchanted house' and 'secret garden'. It had been the gamekeeper's lodge. Now it lay empty and dilapidated. They discovered that it was known locally as the Haunted House, and that it had figured in Jeffery Farnol's novel *The Broad Highway*. Sara's romantic nature needed no better reference. She claimed it for the family's use – 'our home' – and Cazalet, on the spot and with typical generosity, made them a gift of the use of it.

With true American 'can-do' confidence, the Taylors worked throughout the summer, pulling the place apart, cleaning, painting and refurbishing it, planting flowerbeds, a laburnum and almond blossom trees.

From country auctions they fetched period furniture – a washstand, brass beds, a table that opened out to seat twenty, a stone fireplace that they converted into a barbecue pit. Fearlessly they killed off the rats, turned a dairy into a bathroom and brought piped water from miles away. Sheer American energy solved problems as quickly as they arose. A new use was found for even the old coal cellar: it became an English pub with a sign that said, 'Ye Olde Rat Hole'. For seats, they used beer kegs cut in half. Their labours over, there was only the name to think of; and Sara, echoing the grander Cazalet mansion, called it Little Swallows. She had had a perfectly marvellous time bringing her Frances Hodgson Burnett story to life. For her account makes it clear that like Mary Lennox, the orphan who regenerates her own walled-in bit of neglected greenery in *The Secret Garden*, Sara felt 'it was almost like being shut out of the world in some fairy place.'

Elizabeth was not yet five; but the days she passed at Little Swallows were almost the last ones of freedom and safe seclusion that she was to know in her life. Though she often tried to rediscover some 'fairy place', or some fantasy of her own inducement, she would never again be able to shut out the world so well.

3

TROUBLE IN EDEN

Elizabeth's mother had created Little Swallows out of her own romantic attachment to the stories of Victorian childhood. Now she made it a place of instruction as well as a home and a pleasurable retreat from London. On the Wedgwood-blue floor of the tiny bathroom, she made Howard and Elizabeth paint the letters of the alphabet. Bath-time and teeth-brushing were occasions for putting the scattered letters together into words. Elizabeth got a good – and literal – grounding in basic communication even before she started school.

It was at the country cottage, too, that Elizabeth acquired one of her earliest skills and longest-lasting attachments. Victor Cazalet presented her with a pony for Easter 1937. 'Betty' was the little mare's name: she came from the New Forest, another of Sara Taylor's oft-quoted literary locations. She had read Captain Marryat's tale, *The Children of the New Forest*, to her own brood: now she was able to involve them directly in one of its pleasures. Elizabeth and Betty took to each other as if there was a natural bond between them, though not before the animal had mildly rebelled when brother and sister mounted her together for a preliminary trot round the estate. She shook Elizabeth off, into a nettle bed. 'But they made me get right back on,' Elizabeth said. Pain was thus associated with persistence: another lesson learned. Visitors to Little Swallows were frequent and often distinguished: either Victor Cazalet's political friends or Francis Taylor's business clients like the Sassoon family, whose vast connections had opened many doors – and private picture galleries – to the dealer. Neville Chamberlain, the future Prime Minister, came to a barbecue; and Anthony Eden, who would become Churchill's wartime Foreign Secretary, tried out Betty: but the mare, loyal to her fond little owner, shook herself vigorously. Eden slid off.

'Betty,' said Elizabeth, 'I'm your new mistress and I love you very much.' Thousands of children have said that to a pet. But Elizabeth, aged five, added a condition that was to be part of the bargain she made with life: 'I want you to love me.'

Mrs Taylor noted, with the pride of someone who had drawn so many moral lessons from nature, that there seemed to be a symbiotic tie between the pony and her tiny owner. Animals had souls, too, she had told Elizabeth; her daughter carried this pantheistic sentiment to the extreme. Not only did she talk to Betty, like the child Dr Dolittle might have had, but, if we're to credit it, even saved the chickens on the home farm from having their necks wrung for the family meals. Fowl for boiling or roasting had to be bought at the local market already dead; presumably their souls were beyond saving. Elizabeth's colony of pets grew: baby lambs, guinea pigs, tortoises, kittens, puppies. She was never to lose the habit of assembling large numbers of animals around her, as many a hotel was later to testify to its cost – or, rather, hers.

Elizabeth looked on Royalty a second time at George VI's coronation in 1938. Mrs Taylor had actually been invited to it, by Thelma Cazalet, the two of them discreetly brunching on sandwiches along with other VIPs in Westminster Abbey. Elizabeth and the rest of the family viewed the procession from the American Embassy, the former Dorchester House. In later years, on her return to London, she nearly always stayed at the Dorchester Hotel, which took its name from the other, now demolished, town house. It was a second home to her.

Wherever else her later career took her, England remained the country of Elizabeth's happy childhood. She never dreamed at that age that such a childhood would soon be lost to her forever.

It is impossible to establish precisely when Elizabeth's formal schooling began, for Byron House, a co-ed kindergarten and prep school in High-gate, no longer exists. Its records have been lost and it doesn't figure in Elizabeth's admittedly very random reminiscences, perhaps because she was there for only about a year and a half.

It's likely that she was enrolled, aged five-and-a-half, for the autumn term of 1937. Byron House was 'a rather posh little place', as one of her schoolmates, Susan Ritchie, calls it today. It had enough social cachet to get a fond mention from one of its old boys, the Poet Laureate John Betjeman, when it closed its doors. Sara would have selected it with some care to accord with her own strict view of bringing out a child's personality: instruction followed the Montessori system, based on individual activity and free expression. Sara bought her daughter the recommended school uniform from Peter Robinson's, then in Oxford Circus, consisting of a summer frock of green silk – 'very 1930s', says Susan Ritchie, who hated hers – to which shirts and jumpers were added in winter. Elizabeth had a medical check-up from one Mrs Colville Barrington MB, BS, and her general condition was, unsurprisingly, pronounced satisfactory, though she was considered somewhat on the small side.

Elizabeth's nanny, a nice old-fashioned lady called Frieda, left her at school – a short bus journey from nearby Hampstead – in time for 9 a.m. lessons, and returned for her at about 2.30 p.m. Sometimes she was delivered and collected by Culver, the family chauffeur, in the Buick. She took her lunch to school. The children were issued with small wooden pegs and wedges and, using these, they converted their sloping desks into level tabletops and ate in the classroom. Elizabeth's first class was 'Lower Transition' and she would have remained long enough to pass into 'Lower Preparatory', big names for such activities as finger painting, weaving and watching beans sprout behind blotting paper in jam-jars. Few recall Elizabeth at school, and even those who do cannot remember her with precision – which suggests that her natural high spirits were quieted by other children's company and the good management of a well-run school. She was commended for careful writing and for eurhythmics: Miss Terry, the headmistress, found her to be communicative and friendly. In view of her later spectacular record of bad health, it is interesting that she appears not to have had a day's absence. A class photograph survives: it shows a markedly smaller, almost diminutive child compared with her sturdier classmates, though this impression is exaggerated by the pale cardigan she is wearing. But her oval face and shoulder-length hair anticipate the way in which this unfledged version will develop.

Snapshots that must have been taken around the same time in someone's back garden reveal a merrier disposition. Some mother's Box Brownie has caught one of the most informal and happy-looking pictures ever taken of Elizabeth Taylor. The face still has a childhood chubbiness, but the thick eyelashes are there. The amusing thing, however, is the sheer ordinariness of the rest of her appearance. In no detail does Elizabeth look any different from the thousands of other London schoolchildren in their gym-slips and tight-buttoned blazers and snake-clasp belts who were soon to be evacuated in the great diaspora of tearful leave-takings less than two years later. This is our last glimpse of Elizabeth the 'English' schoolchild.

Her childhood was comfortable in a very English way: not unduly privileged considering the class she belonged to and the way her parents had been taken up by the society of influential and rich people on whom they had modelled their own day-to-day routine. She was raised to be obedient, which she sometimes resisted, but never for long. Politeness, punctuality, proper speaking: these were what Sara called 'the three P's'. (One would love to hear how Elizabeth spoke at that age.) As mentioned, the *very* worst punishment for naughtiness was to be denied her mother's love by being temporarily 'sent to Coventry'. How you view yourself, Sara told her, is linked with how you esteem yourself: and it has nothing to do with beauty. Beauty is merely vanity. What's needed is to have a good opinion of yourself in the plain, old-fashioned sense of the word. Throughout her life, a compliment anyone paid to Elizabeth on her beauty evoked little thanks; sometimes it even brought a cold put-down. Beauty was something to mistrust, something that limited the perception of her other qualities: or so she had been taught by her mother. The fact that her employers in the film industry held a totally opposite view, and believed that Elizabeth Taylor's looks were her greatest asset and a large part of their profit, did not endear them to her, either.

A stranger running across little Elizabeth in the years just before the war would probably have found it hard to believe she was the child of American parents, so successfully had she been made over into a pattern-plate English girl.

There is a revealing story about how each of her parents viewed this transformation, which suggests that they didn't always see eye to eye. It also shows the pain that such cross-cultural confusion could cause a shy child.

Illness in Francis Taylor's family took them all over to Arkansas City at short notice, probably in the late winter of 1937 or early spring of 1938. The children were sent to a local school for the two months they stayed there. Mrs Taylor proudly recalls that Elizabeth's 'decided' English accent impressed the local kids and established her in class – probably as a good example to the other girls. This degree of parental insensitivity would be hard to credit were it not for the fact that Howard had been sent to the same school – in a higher class – wearing his English uniform of red blazer and grey flannel shorts. He had an understandably tougher reception and came home with a tousled and indignant look, demanding to be re-equipped immediately with long pants, a lumber jacket and a plaid shirt. Mr Taylor took him directly to the outfitter's and the boy returned to school suitably Americanized. It is not recorded if Elizabeth needed to make similar concessions. Mrs Taylor's silence suggests she didn't – not yet, anyhow.

The family decided to spend Easter 1939 down at Little Swallows in 'a wholesome, unhurried, relaxing and free way', just as the English did, or at least those of the English who owned a second home in the country. It was rainy weather – but raincoats and Wellington boots made them proof against that. Mother and children tramped through the damp woods, 'breathing in the clean, fresh air, gathering primroses in the rain'. They hadn't the slightest warning that this quintessentially English outing would be the last of its kind they would ever enjoy together. When they got back they found a deeply worried Victor Cazalet at the cottage. He had been to tea with Winston Churchill at Chartwell, the latter's nearby country house. He brought the worst possible news. War was on the way, he warned Francis Taylor – he had Churchill's authority for saying so. The war scare of the year before, which had seen gas masks issued, trenches dug in Hyde Park and air-raid precautions instituted, was about to become reality. He advised Francis to send his wife and children back to America without delay, on the first available boat. 'It was a bombshell to all of us,' Mrs Taylor recorded; but there was no appeal against it.

Exactly two weeks later, tearful goodbyes to Uncle Victor and Auntie Molly were said on a last visit to the Cazalets' beautiful Belgrave Square home (soon to be bombed into rubble). Then the Buick, with Mr Taylor at the wheel, pulled out of Wildwood Road bearing Elizabeth, Howard and Sara Taylor down the hill, past a sandbagged Buckingham Palace to Victoria Station, to catch the boat-train to Southampton.

Francis was staying behind to close down his gallery and see the pictures crated up for transport to California, where Howard Young had decided they would open a branch of his New York business. He hoped to rejoin his family in Los Angeles in time for Christmas.

The Taylors found themselves almost the only English-speaking refugees aboard the liner *Manhattan*. French and Germans, fleeing from a nervous Continent, made up the bulk of the passenger list. True to her character, Sara did her best to rise above it all. With luck, she thought, they'd only be staying temporarily in America. The war panic might well die down before they reached the West Coast and then Francis would send for them to come back and resume their old style of life. She organized games of shuffleboard and deck quoits; she read to the children; and one afternoon her eye was caught by a name both familiar and dear to her affections on a poster for the ship's entertainments. It was a film. *The Little Princess*, starring Shirley Temple, had opened in New York in March, and it was now being shown in the ship's cinema. But the infant star wasn't the attraction for Mrs Taylor. The movie was adapted from a book by Frances Hodgson Burnett.

The coincidence was rather more apt than Sara Taylor could have appreciated. For Shirley Temple played a stout-hearted little heroine also called Sara. Bosley Crowther, in his *New York Times* review, had referred to Mrs Burnett as 'a lady with coronets on the brain', a description it would have been cruel to apply to Sara Taylor, though she had certainly been infected by Anglophilia.

Understandably, Mrs Taylor was tempted: a film about 'a baby Bernhardt'; a setting in the England of 1899. Surely there was nothing offensive in this tale, nothing too vulgar for the children to see. And so, for the very first time in her life – a momentous juncture – Elizabeth Taylor was taken to the pictures.

The family's destination was dictated for them by the presence of Mrs Taylor's widower father in California, where he had started a chicken farm near Pasadena a few years earlier. The family arrived there on 1 May. Years later, Elizabeth Taylor used to take the train, if time allowed, and get out at the same railroad depot in Pasadena en route to Hollywood – as if recalling that first experience. In 1939, many movie stars still used to alight there from the train called the *Twentieth Century* and switch to their waiting automobiles in order to enter Beverly Hills in unhurried style, rather than have to tussle with the mob at Los Angeles's downtown railroad terminal. The Taylors arrived tired and rather anxious. The heat of an American summer struck them stickily and unpleasantly. And for the first time, Mrs Taylor began to realize the full extent of what she had been forced to abandon. Where were the temperate English summer weather, the herbaceous borders and roses of Heathwood, the farm animals and weekend rambles around Little Swallows? This land was dry and dusty. The flowers were positively lurid beside the gentler English varieties. The semi-rural house where they unpacked their belongings felt cramped and looked shabby compared with the solid brick Hampstead mansion. They'd been unable to take much money with them; the new exchange control regulations governing precious dollar reserves had made that impossible. Not that they were ever in need: Uncle Howard came up with a loan. But the culture shock was severer than the financial squeeze. Mrs Taylor soon found she couldn't get anywhere without a car. The trouble was, she couldn't drive. Many middle-class women in England in those days left the family car to the man of the house; it was his prerogative. The Taylors had had their own chauffeur, in any case. Still, they had enough money to buy a second-hand Chevrolet and, with back-seat encouragement from Elizabeth and Howard, Mrs Taylor learned the American way – by doing.

She enrolled the children at Willard Elementary School, not lingering sentimentally in the classroom, as an English mother might have done, but delivering them in a business-like, trustful style to the care of the supervisor while she went house-hunting. By all accounts, the school supervisor was shrewd. Instead of exposing Elizabeth and Howard to the jibes of classmates curious about their stiff manners and clipped English vowels, he introduced them at assembly as legitimate objects of comment, newcomers who must be helped to fit in.

'The children very quickly lost their [English] accents,' Mrs Taylor noted later, perhaps with a twinge of regret. Not strictly true. In childhood, anyhow, Elizabeth retained the ability to switch back to the accent acquired in her birthplace whenever the film role demanded it. In other ways, too, her voice didn't make the full Atlantic crossing. What emerged at this decisive stage of her life was a curious compromise between flat populist American vowels and a lingering upper-class English imperiousness. It was to be her distinctive voice. In some cases, in the right role on and off screen, it suited her. Its emphasis was the very sound of the will-power her mother's training had fostered. It was to make her respected, sometimes even feared. It was good, too, for relaying the snap decisions of temperament. And, most effectively, it could swell to the edgy pitch of alarm and crest in hysteria. On the other hand, it remained an untrained voice; she never took speech lessons. It lacked the modulation to convey the warmer inflections of humour or love, in which Elizabeth herself certainly wasn't deficient.

Mrs Taylor's dating is right. The voice we know as Elizabeth Taylor's was formed in these months and signified a status that was still beyond the understanding of its tiny owner. It was the voice of a displaced person.

4

'SING FOR MISS HOPPER'

Francis Taylor rejoined his family in December 1939. Mrs Taylor was keeping up, as best she could, a lingering sense of their English life-style. That Christmas, in her father's Pasadena home, was memorable for the baking of fruit cakes and cooking of plum puddings: fare infrequently to be found in sunny California. Elizabeth also let her English nostalgia colour the plainer day-to-day existence. She'd asked for a ballet dress: two dresses, in fact, one for her (in pink) and one (in white) for a neighbour's child who'd made friends with her. Then, they said, they could put on a concert together. Mrs Taylor made a gallant effort to run up tutus, but fell back on an obliging dressmaker who worked in one of the film studios.

As Francis hadn't been allowed to export much of his financial capital in Britain, he had taken his investment out of the country in the form of paintings and drawings. Augustus John was a fashionable if personally erratic artist, often unreliable and irascible, and sometimes drunk. The dealer had seen him crumple up preliminary sketches he considered hadn't succeeded – and these he often rescued from the wastepaper basket in John's studio. Now they were to be the seed corn of the new gallery that he opened, early in 1940, at the Château Elysée Hotel, Hollywood. He soon moved to the more prestigious Beverly Hills Hotel. One elderly employee there recalls young Elizabeth helping her father dress the gallery's window display. Old Bond Street it was not: but Hollywood money was beginning to be put into good pictures – of the kind that hung on walls. Collectors like Edward G. Robinson, George Cukor and Billy Wilder visited Francis, and supplying the taste of these discerning men turned the dealer towards the modern European artists whose works could often be bought at bargain prices from hard-up wartime refugees in America. As it had done in London, Francis's gallery opened many doors for the Taylors, leading them directly into the society of money and prestige: this time not the county families and the aristocracy of pre-war England, but the movie colony in a Hollywood that in the golden year of 1939 had never been busier or richer.

The Wizard of Oz and *Gone With the Wind* appeared that year. The latter was still shooting when Mrs Taylor and the children arrived. She quickly discovered that Hollywood was a place where people habitually saw a movie future for every pretty face. David Selznick, the producer of *Gone With the Wind*, still hadn't filled a few minor roles in his epic. (He had actually begun shooting it the previous December with the Scarlett O'Hara role uncast, trusting to luck and his gambler's hunch that the right player would turn up: she did, Vivien Leigh.) In a society where social life and gossip revolved around the movies, Mrs Taylor found acquaintances, even strangers in the street, urging her to have her beautiful little girl screen-tested for the role of Bonnie Blue, Scarlett's child by Rhett Butler. She always said no. A mother without a stage background might have been tempted. A mother like Sara, with a stage reputation, albeit in the past, still looked a little disdainfully on the movie industry that had killed off the beloved touring companies of her youth. The idea of being a child in films was alien to Elizabeth's upbringing; and, anyhow, they were all going back 'home' one day, weren't they?

With the outbreak of war in Europe, the date for repatriation faded – and with it, Sara's memory of England and all things English.

She was, indeed, the member of the family most deserving of sympathy. Her husband was busy rebuilding his gallery clientele. Her children were experiencing the daily excitements of adapting to life in California. But for this woman of sensibility and intelligence, a whole world had suddenly disappeared from her experience. She had successfully constructed a way of life in England that resembled the idealized world of her own imagining. Gardens; the outdoors; country cottages; Royal parades; important friends in politics and society; prep schools; a suburban mansion; a cook, maids, a chauffeur; high hopes for Howard becoming a little Englishman; even higher expectations for Elizabeth; a good boarding school; then a 'coming out' round of balls and receptions and social engagements for the season; maybe marriage into one of the great families. It was suddenly not to be. Now she had to face America: the very contradiction of all the things she held dear. Sara Taylor had left more than her heart behind in England: she had left her dream world. She did the only thing possible – the only thing thinkable for a woman of her resources and strength of will. She set about rebuilding her world in the American style, or, rather, in the Hollywood style. She re-invented herself – and Elizabeth.

From 1940 onwards, all Sara's frustrated energies were diverted into a different channel of endeavour. As one fantasy receded, its place was gradually, and at first imperceptibly, filled by another that was all the more potent for being on their doorstep: the movies. In place of the English upper classes, there was now the stratified power structure of 'the industry'. In place of statesmen and politicians and clubmen and Royal patrons, there was now a society of stars and producers and directors. In place of the shopping and gossip and social events of London and Mayfair and the Royal Court, there were now the shopping and gossip and social events of Beverly Hills and Hollywood and the studios. It was a very different class of people from those Mrs Taylor had prided herself on being able to call her friends in England. But adaptation was her strong point; after all, she had been an actress herself. She could play any role, she had said, 'once I set my mind to it'. Now, gradually, by accident probably more than forethought, she proceeded to do so; and, in the act of reconstructing her world, she found a role in it for Elizabeth.

There was already one link between the two worlds: an ominous one in retrospect, but at the time simply a useful connection.

Before Mrs Taylor left London, Thelma Cazalet, Victor's sister, had given her a letter of introduction to Hedda Hopper. The Hearst gossip columnist might seem to have been an unlikely acquaintance for the British Member of Parliament, but in fact the women had taken to each other – both, after all, were achievers for their own sex and in their own ways. Thelma had met Hedda in London in 1937 and shown her around Parliament. 'Better than a prizefight,' Hopper called it. Now she responded to the note Mrs Taylor dropped her in the most practical possible way. She came along to the opening of Francis Taylor's art gallery at the Beverly Hills Hotel and, for $150, bought a small Augustus John sketch, one of dozens that had arrived on the West Coast in crates stamped 'Convoyed by the Royal Navy' – evidence, perhaps, of how useful Francis Taylor's political connections had been to him as he prepared to leave England. 'That's what the family lived on then,' said Hopper later, referring to the works of art. She duly mentioned the opening in her syndicated column, recalling Sara's early overnight fame in *The Fool* and alluding to her 'beautiful' child, eight-year-old Elizabeth. It was probably the first appearance of Elizabeth's name in a Hollywood gossip column.

Hopper's good turn had an immediately beneficial effect on the gallery's fortunes. It brought in clients. One of them was a young woman, Andrea Berens, who was engaged to Cheever Cowden, chairman of Universal Pictures. Miss Berens had been painted by Augustus John in London some years earlier and her appreciation of his work hadn't diminished. She proceeded to buy other Johns in generous helpings – $21,000 worth of sketches and paintings in one afternoon's visit to the gallery where Elizabeth and her mother (Francis was in New York) displayed them on the floor. 'When we said goodbye,' Mrs Taylor recalled, 'Andrea remarked, "I would like Cheever to see Elizabeth."' An invitation was issued for the following Sunday, at the Taylors' home, where there happened to be even more Augustus Johns on the walls.

By this time, it appears, the family had moved from their temporary accommodation in Pasadena to the more fashionable community of Pacific Palisades. Their neighbours were movie people: Darryl F. Zanuck, for instance, head of Twentieth Century–Fox; and Norma Shearer, the actress who had been married until his death three years earlier to Irving Thalberg, MGM's brilliant production chief. Elizabeth played with the Thalberg son and daughter, and she made other friends at the dancing classes she now attended on La Cienega Boulevard. They included the late John Gilbert's daughter Susan; Louis B. Mayer's grandchildren Judy and Barbara Goetz; and Evin Considine, whose father Johnny was a producer with a reputation for quality films, as well as box-office success. With families like these in the vicinity, the Taylors' familiarity with the movie world followed as naturally as their hospitality. In retrospect, anyhow, one could almost say that Elizabeth's future career was preordained.

Cheever Cowden and his fiancée came out to Pacific Palisades, took tea and set eyes on Elizabeth as well as the Augustus Johns. Sara had put her child on her best behaviour – in order, though, to help sell her father's pictures, not Elizabeth herself. But it was Elizabeth that Cowden bought, perhaps assisted in his choice by his fiancée's approval. Would his hosts let their child do a screen test at Universal?

By now, it seems, even Mrs Taylor was beginning to convince herself that 'this motion picture thing' was meant to be. If faith could heal the lame, like the little cripple in *The Fool*, might it not also distinguish the humble? Elizabeth's mother was learning to live for the dream that had enraptured – and all too often subsequently afflicted – the many who had come to Hollywood in search of fame and fortune. She already possessed the zeal to see it fulfilled: only now she made a fateful mistake.

Elizabeth had developed an untrained but lively singing voice. Her proud mother used to ask her to display this accomplishment when guests called. One of them, Carmen Considine, was so taken by it that she telephoned her husband Johnny, at the time an MGM producer, and recommended that he hear Elizabeth, too. Mrs Considine had perhaps more of a vested interest than Cheever Cowden. MGM had earlier let one of their child singing stars, Deanna Durbin, out of her contract, preferring to retain Judy Garland instead. Durbin had been instantly snapped up by Universal for whom she was turning out hit after hit. Another beautiful child who could sing might well have the potential to restock MGM's cage of singing talents. John Considine thought so, too, when he had little Elizabeth over to his office and heard her perform. There can be little doubt that what swayed him was her beauty, not her voice. But filmmaking is a gamble, and star-making is a big gamble: he took the risk. 'Sign her up, sign her up,' Louis B. Mayer reportedly barked, 'what are you waiting for?' Perhaps he did: the MGM archives have no record of it, however, and this in a studio that put every kind of commitment and opinion into writing with bureaucratic punctiliousness.

Anyhow, Mrs Taylor now had two offers for the talents her daughter might, or might not, possess. She may have felt she was in a good bargaining position.

A more cynical and disinterested party like Hedda Hopper could have told her otherwise. In fact, Hopper's records show that she had already evaluated Elizabeth's chances as a second Deanna Durbin and decided they were practically zero. 'Now sing for Miss Hopper,' Sara instructed Elizabeth some time previously, and 'in a quivering voice, half swooning with fright, this lovely, shy creature with enormous violet eyes piped her way through her song. It was one of the most painful ordeals I've ever witnessed,' wrote Hopper. A judgement confirming what one suspects: that what the film people were interested in was looks, not pitch.

However, Universal was now informed of MGM's interest, and told that if they didn't hurry they might lose Elizabeth to their rival. Cheever Cowden, then in New York, was telephoned: sign her up, he ordered, don't even wait for a screen test. Cheever Cowden owned 17 per cent of Universal's stock: a nod from him was as good as a command.

What ensued, and why Elizabeth Taylor was fired by Universal after less than a year under contract, can only be guessed. It didn't entirely have to do with her inadequacy on the screen. Her original contract exists and with it are a number of memos on the studio's new acquisition. Unlike those at MGM, which can be amazingly frank, the Universal memos are more guarded, signifying perhaps a desire not to offend someone important, and conveying decisions, rather than reasons for dismissal. That someone was most likely Cheever Cowden. One feels that the pressure from the company chairman to sign up an unknown child of doubtful talent principally because she appealed to him and his fiancée was accepted with bad grace, if not actively resisted, by those who had to make the deal – and then make it work.

The contract itself wasn't out of the ordinary: a standard seven-year term with two options at six-month intervals for the first year, remuneration of $100 a week (minimum twenty weeks) 'payable each Wednesday', with $10 to Mrs Taylor for each day she accompanied Elizabeth to work on the set. Universal agreed to pay for 'a competent music teacher ... all dental work ... period clothing if necessary except for stockings and underwear'. Elizabeth was represented by the top Hollywood agent Myron Selznick, who had recently negotiated Vivien Leigh's contract with his brother David. It was a good beginning. Elizabeth's contract is dated 21 April 1941, when she was just over nine years old. If all went well, she would be earning $2000 a week (with a forty-week minimum per year) by 1948, with $100 a week going to Sara. All did not go well – from the start.

It wasn't just Elizabeth's sharp intuition that told her she wasn't really welcome at Universal. The studio casting director, Dan Kelly, growled, 'The kid has nothing' after she had done a test. Even what was to be her most striking feature left him unimpressed. 'Her eyes are too old, she doesn't have the face of a child.'

This was not so far off the mark as it may appear now. There *was* something slightly odd about Elizabeth's looks, even at this age – an expression that sometimes made people think she was older than she was. She already had her mother's air of concentration. Later on, it would prove an invaluable asset. At the time, it disconcerted people who compared her unfavourably with Shirley Temple's cute bubbling innocence or Judy Garland's plainer and more vulnerable juvenile appeal.

As they came away from Universal, Mrs Taylor noticed how morose Elizabeth looked.

'What's the matter, honey?' she asked. 'You're the one who wanted to be in pictures.'

The switch from her former endearment of 'darling' to the more homey American 'honey' suggests the adjustment that Sara was making as she observed what her daughter's future was going to be in America.

Elizabeth wasn't happy. She wanted to make those pictures over at MGM. Its studio was nearer home, for one thing. For another, she said, people there had been nicer to her when she went to audition. A man called Benny Thau had offered her gum. (Sara had declined – she was not *that* American yet.) Thau had succeeded Thalberg at the studio as production chief: he was to remain the only MGM executive Elizabeth really trusted in the years ahead since he had, out of kindly habit, made the gesture that showed her she was loved. Moreover, MGM was a glamorous studio. Universal's fortunes, founded on a cycle of horror films at the start of the 1930s, had dipped into near-bankruptcy, from which Deanna Durbin had only recently rescued them. MGM, by contrast, was flourishing – and showed it. It boasted that it had, in the phrase of Howard Dietz, its East Coast publicity chief, 'more stars than there are in heaven'. Elizabeth and her mother may well have verified that, if they lunched in the commissary or tiptoed on to the sound stages during their visit: Gable, Crawford, Shearer, Tracy and Robert Taylor were all at work, the men who had not yet left for the war. Garbo was about to enter life-long retirement – unplanned, though not unwillingly embraced by the reclusive star – but MGM jealously preserved her mystique. Small wonder if Elizabeth wanted to be part of this.

But her mother opted for Universal, perhaps out of indebtedness to Andrea and Cheever Cowdin: or perhaps for the simpler, more brutal reason that she really didn't have a choice. MGM was a hard-headed outfit. If Sara had hoped to panic MGM into bidding for Elizabeth by hinting at the other studio's interest, she miscalculated again: as far as MGM was concerned, Universal could have her.

Victor Cazalet, back in England, wrote in his diary entry for 16 April 1941: 'Imagine excitement of Taylors. Elizabeth has a contract for seven years with a big cinema group.'

It barely lasted out the year, never mind seven. The only work Universal found for Elizabeth Taylor was a few days on a movie entitled *Man or Mouse*, later retitled, no less ominously, *There's One Born Every Minute*. She played opposite a fifteen-year-old veteran, an ex-*Our Gang* performer called Carl ('Alfalfa') Switzer, a curly-headed, freckle-faced kid whose speciality number was singing atrociously off-key. Elizabeth wasn't asked to sing at all – though she had been taking daily lessons. In fact, she wasn't asked to do anything very much except, as she recalled, 'run around firing elastic bands at fat ladies' bottoms'.

Nearly eighteen years later, Alfalfa Switzer was shot dead in a drinking brawl. He thus became the first of a growing number of Elizabeth Taylor's co-stars to die tragic and premature deaths.

Hedda Hopper had broken the story of Elizabeth's contract in her column and fulsomely complimented her ex-actress mother by forecasting, 'If there's anything in heredity, Elizabeth should be a hit.' Heredity, however, mattered less than a good picture or an interested studio: Elizabeth had neither. Universal fired her with a finality that suggests they had done as much as they needed to do for their chairman's little 'discovery' – and perhaps that would teach him to look after the money and leave the art to them. The studio picked up Elizabeth's first six-month option (at $100 a week) on 18 September 1941; but less than a fortnight later, in a memo dated 30 September 1941, production chief Edward Muhl wrote: 'The above artist [Elizabeth Taylor] is to be laid off without pay for an indefinite period commencing September 29, 1941.' On 24 February 1942, three days before her tenth birthday, Universal refused to pick up the second option (for $250 a week) and '[the contract] will therefore terminate on March 23, 1942.'

For the moment, however, any disappointment the Taylors felt was dispersed by the excitement of moving house again. Their new home at

307 North Elm Drive, Beverly Hills, was a total contrast with the old one on Wildwood Road, Hampstead. A low building in the Spanish style, with pink stucco walls and red roof tiles, it had a huge round-arched window facing the road and a dusty front 'yard' with an olive tree in it. The sunlight was harsh, but the rooms remained dark. The seasonal changes that the Taylors had loved in England were barely perceptible here. But they had now committed themselves to the new life. Francis's gallery in the Beverly Hills Hotel was almost within walking distance – not that anyone ever walked much, even in those days. Elizabeth and Howard were enrolled at the nearby Hawthorne School and, for a few months, it looked as if a normal American childhood had begun for Elizabeth. Actually, after the false start she had made, she was about to be forced into a Hollywood childhood.

'Forced' is perhaps too strong a word. Indeed, Sara used to insist – later – that they had never really wanted Elizabeth to be a film star. If so, they certainly didn't make very strenuous efforts to turn fate away when it came calling a second time. That must be the test of the Taylors' protestations. The family had already seen how cruel a movie studio could be to a child's ambitions, and Elizabeth had been long enough at Universal for them to have sensed the driving pressures applied to a child player, never mind a star-in-embryo.

Back in England, if there had been no war, Elizabeth's mother might have been grooming her for the goal of many an upper-class English mother: a good marriage. Here in Hollywood, she simply aimed at the target which this other highly self-conscious society took to heart. In England, it had been class: in Hollywood, it was status. In the world the Taylors had lost, money or a title were evidence that a girl had succeeded in life (or at least that she had fulfilled her mother's ambitions). In a company town where movies were made, lived and endlessly gossiped about, money and stardom distinguished those who had made it to the top. Sara simply realized her child's ambition, and her own, to become what the society around her clearly conceived of as the paramount object of desire.

Accident played less part in this than connections, despite the accounts of various biographers.

It's true that Benny Thau remembered the little dark-haired beauty whose puppy fat had now melted away to disclose slim limbs, if a still slightly undersized physique – and especially those strange and lovely eyes that gave the face its central focus, oddly powerful in someone so young. When Thau heard that Universal had dropped her, he had MGM make an offer.

This was probably in September or October 1942. But it wouldn't be at all correct to say that MGM now recognized its earlier error in passing over Elizabeth Taylor and wished to rectify it and thereby enrich itself. The studio wasn't sure it wanted Elizabeth for anything bigger than a minor supporting part in a film with a much more important star – a collie dog.

Pre-production on what was to be *Lassie Come Home* had begun much earlier. 'Please photocable close-up of dog's face,' one Ted Butcher, a production manager at MGM, had cabled a canine talent scout at the studio's New York parent company, Loew's Inc., on 19 March 1942. By May, he thought he had found a star among a litter of hopefuls. 'Would like to see animals looking pensive, happy, and other possible expressions you can secure,' he cabled. Shooting began at the end of the summer, with several dogs (presumably chosen for possessing a variety of expressions, but a similarity in everything else) playing Lassie.

The rushes soon disclosed a slight problem that would have been visible only to the camera. A child actress called Maria Flynn had been picked to play the English grand-daughter of the old Duke, played by Nigel Bruce, to whom Lassie is sold – and from whom she escapes to get back to her young master, played by Roddy McDowall, the fourteen-year-old evacuee from England who had just made a name for himself in *How Green Was My Valley*. Maria Flynn had done well in *Intermezzo*, playing the kind of adorable child common in 1930s' films, opposite Ingrid Bergman. But *Lassie Come Home* was being shot in Technicolor: it required very strong lighting and the rushes showed Maria's eyes watering. Sadly, but firmly, MGM let her go. Who could replace her at short notice?

There are two versions of what happened next: one of them disseminated in years to come by studio publicists.

In this account, the film's producer Sam Marx is doing his wartime duty as an air-raid warden in Beverly Hills, patrolling the leafy drives and avenues with his neighbour, Francis Taylor, in the nervous period when rumours were rife of a possible Japanese attack on the coast of California. He mentions that he needs to find another child with an English accent – quickly. The rest we know. However, Sam Marx himself says that Francis Taylor had told him plenty of times before about his beautiful little girl who'd been so badly treated by Universal. In suggesting a third way of accounting for Elizabeth and her mother being so suddenly summoned to an audition at MGM, one need not deny that there may be some truth in either of these versions.

Lassie Come Home was being made by Fred Wilcox, who had been promoted from MGM's B-picture unit to direct his first feature; Wilcox's sister was married to the playwright turned film producer Edgar Selwyn; and Selwyn was the Broadway impresario who, with his brother Archie, had staged Sara Sothern's one great hit *The Fool* twenty years earlier. With Elizabeth 'at liberty', and with connections like these, it would have been odd indeed if news of the sudden vacancy in the cast of *Lassie* hadn't reached 307 North Elm Drive early in the day. Sara and Fred Wilcox were certainly very much on the same wave length; six years later the director was to film her favourite childhood classic, *The Secret Garden*.

5

NATIONAL IDOL

As the screenwriter Sam Marx recalls it, when the idea of using Elizabeth as a last-minute replacement for Maria Flynn was suggested – or occurred – to him, he telephoned the Taylor art gallery. Sara and her daughter, who were visiting grandfather in Pasadena, drove quickly back to MGM's Culver City studios, reaching there by 5.45 p.m. on a Saturday afternoon. California law prohibited minors from working after 6 p.m. Six little girls, the story goes, were already waiting to audition. But immediately Elizabeth was brought in, Fred Wilcox packed them off home – which suggests Wilcox was expecting the result he got. Mrs Taylor quickly coached Elizabeth in the specimen dialogue supplied and the child played the scene in a crisp-edged English accent to a floor mop representing Lassie, with Wilcox standing in for the Duke. She appeared totally without nerves. Her concentration gave the little scene a conviction which was confirmed a few days later by the rushes. She was awarded the part then and there.

Yet the MGM executives didn't rush their find into a long-term contract. The studio's archives hint at a reticent approach. Instead of a seven-year contract, a simple 'test option' was drawn up, dated 15 October 1942, to cast Elizabeth 'on a freelance basis for $100 a week for three months (with a ten-week term guaranteed)'. A memo of the same date to Floyd Hendrickson's legal department adds that 'her last salary at Universal was $100,' but due to the wage freeze then enforced as a wartime economy measure, she could not be paid the $150 a week demanded by her agent. 'She is to be paid this if and when it is possible,' the memo ended; MGM was a *very* cautious outfit.

It's worth noting that MGM attached more immediate importance to the remuneration of Lassie (real name Pal), who started out at $90 a week, but, after the first few days' rushes were viewed, was upped to $250. Even

Lassie's stand-in commanded $100 weekly. It was better to be an unknown canine discovery than a human hopeful with a poor track record like Elizabeth Taylor.

As her part was small, mention of Elizabeth in contemporary reviews was brief, too. Not many named her; the few that did, though, were positive: 'a pretty moppet,' said *Variety*, while the *Hollywood Reporter* declared, 'Elizabeth Taylor looks like a comer.' Hedda Hopper gushed, 'Little Elizabeth Taylor is lovely.'

Lovely she is, but her performance is already remarkable for its total self-assurance. Remember, however, that Sara had brought her up on childhood stories not too far removed in tone and period from Major Eric Knight's sentimental odyssey of a boy and his dog. Nigel Bruce's old duke was exactly the sort of godfather-figure Elizabeth had fixed in her imagination already: he was a more venerable version of Victor Cazalet. 'She was the least troublesome player I have ever had to deal with,' Fred Wilcox said. Mrs Taylor had been present throughout the shooting and it was remarked that the little girl seemed to want to do nothing except please her mother. Elizabeth's fellow juvenile Roddy McDowall thought she was 'perfect, an exquisite little doll . . . totally unaware of her beauty', and saw her compliance as a kind of composure that gave her a gravity beyond her years. Her unselfconsciousness amused McDowall; and even then, being treated for what she was rather than for how she looked appears to have pleased Elizabeth. It was the basis of a life-long bond of friendship, even complicity, between the two evacuees from England. Both she and McDowall were to be marked by the same experiences of foreshortened childhoods and a public image that they had to live up to, whether they liked it or not. McDowall became one of the very few intimate friends, outside her immediate family, whom Elizabeth knew she could rely on throughout life.

As regards filming, she found she liked being the centre of attention. She enjoyed the surprise she gave the cameraman who had said she was wearing too much mascara for a child and told her to go back and have it removed. It was simply her own natural double line of black eyelashes.

Elizabeth didn't receive a long-term MGM contract until the beginning of 1943. On the eve of the day on which it was to be signed, Mrs Taylor sat down with her child in their living-room. She wanted a final sign of revelation. Had Elizabeth a God-given talent? Was there a divine plan for her? Mrs Taylor took her old script for *The Fool*, in which she had played the scene of the girl whose faith is answered by a miracle cure. Now she asked Elizabeth to read her own part, while she read the lines of the leading man. She confessed to weeping openly. She said: 'There sat my daughter playing perfectly the part of the child as I, a grown woman, had tried to do it. It seemed that she must have been in my head all those years I was acting.'

Before the contract could be signed, however, Elizabeth's birthdate had to be altered: it was set down, erroneously, as 17 February 1933, one year out. The contract and guardianship agreement came into force on 5 January 1943. Beginning at $100 a week, Elizabeth would rise to $750 a week at the end of seven years. Forty weeks of work were guaranteed annually; for the rest of the year, constituting lay-off time, she wasn't paid anything. The yearly option clause – standard at the time – gave the studio the whip hand, by enabling it to drop her without penalty at any time and for any reason it thought fit. For an eleven-year-old child of promise, the money was good if unsensational. In no way did it enrich the Taylor family. Minors like Elizabeth were well protected from parental exploitation by the Coogan Law, named after Jackie Coogan, who made the belated discovery on reaching manhood that his step-father and mother were unable to account satisfactorily for the fees he had earned as a child star and had thought were due him. A child star's earnings now had to be invested on his or her behalf with a judge's approval. Thus, 10 per cent of Elizabeth's gross compensation was immediately put into war bonds. Later on, this sum would be a handy means of defiantly asserting her own independence; at the time, it was simply a child's savings.

Contrary to what is often asserted, Mrs Taylor did not go on the MGM payroll immediately; and when she did, on 31 July 1944, she did not receive anything like 10 per cent of her daughter's salary and bonuses. Her fee was only $100 weekly as coach and chaperone. She had neither chance, temptation nor inclination to exploit Elizabeth.

All the same, the child was obediently following all her mother's aspirations: and many times in succeeding years, Elizabeth was to say with pride, tempered by a certain sense of what it had cost her in terms of a lost childhood, that she had been a breadwinner since she was ten years old.

For the moment, anyhow, financial reward bypassed her. Her pocket money was twenty-five cents a week, only reluctantly increased to fifty cents when she was signed by MGM. The Taylors didn't want to spoil her, but this prudence may only have prompted a characteristic she was to exploit to the full in later years when the power had passed to her: she made sure she got her money's worth. There were already some early signs of this. On one occasion, she and a playmate, Anne Westmore – daughter of one of the famous Westmore make-up brothers who lived across the street – dressed up as gypsies selling paste trinkets off genuine (borrowed) silver trays at the doors of the Beverly Hills mansions. On another, she put the Lux soap endorsement, to which MGM had signed her, to domestic use by selling off the cakes of free soap sent her by the manufacturers. Mrs Taylor recalls her saying, 'It'll be good business training for me.'

Somewhat more quickly absorbed, perhaps, was the lesson she was soon taught at MGM – that contract artists are in the business of making money, and generally more of it for their employers than for themselves.

Her next screen role consisted of a very small part in *Jane Eyre*, for which she was sent on 'loan out' to Twentieth Century–Fox at $150 a week – a clear profit of $50 to MGM. So tiny was her part, as one of the classmates of young Jane (Peggy Ann Garner), that she got no billing on the credits; and years later, when she wanted her own children to see the film on television, she discovered she had been entirely cut out of the version re-edited for commercials. By then, though, the omission could be treated as a joke on the TV people. In 1944, it was a cause of grief and mistrust – was the Universal experience going to repeat itself? – when the *Hollywood Reporter* noted that 'the little girl Jane befriends in school wins a credit which is regrettably omitted.' Even Hedda Hopper failed to find her in the cast this time.

Another small role followed in *The White Cliffs of Dover* – but at least she was back home at MGM for this sentimental weepie, a hymn to the Anglo-American alliance, about an American girl marrying (and losing) a titled Englishman in World War One, then rearing (and losing) his son in World War Two. Elizabeth liked it: for although all she did was provide the puppy-love of a local girl for Roddy McDowall, playing the little milord (replaced as an adult by Peter Lawford), she was reunited with one of the few friends who shared her confidences. Despite the war, MGM retained great faith in 'British subjects': at least the box-office in Britain wasn't in enemy hands though the British Treasury, which froze its earnings, was sometimes regarded by Hollywood as if it was the enemy. MGM owned a large London distribution office as well as a recently built studio at Borehamwood, just outside London.

Elizabeth's familiarity with English manners and speech were definite assets in casting her in patriotic Anglo-American features. And in the film in which she was about to become a star, they were absolutely essential attributes.

National Velvet is thought by many people, including one of Elizabeth's later lovers, to be the first film she ever made. There can be no surer evidence of one's arrival than to efface the memory of all that has gone before. People fell in love with Elizabeth Taylor when they saw her in it. Not sentimentalists, either, but hard-headed critics like James Agee, then in his early forties, who unblushingly declared that, 'she strikes me ... if I may resort to a conservative statement, as being rapturously beautiful.' Indeed, Agee went on to confess that ever since seeing her on the screen –

he didn't name *Lassie Come Home*, but he probably had it in mind – he had been 'choked with a peculiar sort of adoration I might have felt if we were both in the same grade of primary school'. This carries a hint that the film released in Elizabeth something even more potent than rapturous beauty: in short, sex appeal. It was not the seductive innocence of the nymphet, but, rather, the peculiarly androgynous English innocence of the girl who loves ponies with a boyish passion and sets racing the hearts of men who can see themselves teaching her to transfer her affections to them. But there is more to the film than just sublimated sex. Its enormous popularity rubs off on to its heroine because she expresses, with the strength of an obsession, the aspirations of people – people who have never seen a girl on horseback, or maybe even a horse race for that matter – who believe that anything is possible, including winning the Grand National, if only they set their minds to it. A philosophy of life, in other words: surely not too inflated a description for a film which, nearly fifty years old and simple-hearted if rather more psychologically complex than the first sight of it suggests, has acquired the status of a generational classic that parents and children alike still regard as the memory-mark of their coming of age. A philosophy, too, that was closely akin to the practice of the mother and the daughter it made into a star.

Enid Bagnold's story of a girl who wins a classic English steeplechase disguised as a boy jockey, riding a horse called 'The Py' that's been won in a lottery, had been bought for filming by Paramount soon after the book's appearance in 1933.

But a tale of simple faith and family love with an English background was not to the worldly tastes of a studio then in thrall to von Sternberg and Dietrich. It was sold on to MGM in 1937 and thought of, first and foremost, as a Mickey Rooney vehicle. Rooney, then just past his mid-teens, was Louis B. Mayer's 'favourite son' due to his success in exemplifying that all-American boy, Andy Hardy. He was to play the ex-jockey who is in league with Velvet Brown, the girl who believes that if she has enough faith she can sail over the Aintree jumps and fulfil her dream. But who was to play Velvet? Katharine Hepburn and Margaret Sullavan, then thirty-six and twenty-five respectively, are reported to have been tested; if so, nothing came of it. No one who was on MGM's payroll was suitable. Having already got a popular star in Rooney, the studio could afford to go for a complete or relative unknown to play Velvet Brown. But it wished to shoot the film in England and kept putting off pre-production until its new studio there was open. Then came the war.

It says something about California's remoteness from the war front, or perhaps MGM's determination, that even with hostilities at their height in 1943 the studio still pushed ahead with its plan to make the movie in

England with a re-staged Grand National. Possibly MGM's reserves of blocked box-office currency were an incentive; they would pay for the production. On 17 January 1943, Sydney Wright, a casting agent in London, received a cable from Hollywood. Ben Goetz, a studio production executive, ordered him to 'please have Harold Huth [a British MGM executive] read book with idea of finding ideal English girl between 11 and 14 to play part of Velvet . . . Have Huth make tests of any youngsters with suitable personality . . . and ship to us as soon as possible. Please get usual options for seven years term when tests are made.'

Just in case the ideal English girl might have been evacuated to a place of greater safety than wartime England, another cable went out on the same date to an MGM field executive, instructing him to 'get what info you can about English children in Canada'. However, MGM soon learned that the English law was not a good ally in such a talent search. Goetz was informed by London that 'by section 25 of Children and Young Persons Act, 1933, no person under 18 "shall be allowed, caused or procured to go abroad for the purpose of performing for profit unless he (or she) has attained the age of 14 years and a licence has been granted by a public magistrate." No such licence can be granted in regard to a child under 14, however.' Ben Goetz must have protested hotly at the unfairness of legislation that would deprive such a child of MGM fame and a contract in the movies, for Wright replied on 1 February 1943: 'Kindly appreciate neither a magistrate nor the Government itself can set aside Act of Parliament save by an amending Act.' Goetz persisted: 'We understand situation re. permit, but feel girl may be found who is over 14, but looks younger, or a girl of 13 may be found who would be 14 before picture is produced.'

All this time a girl who was eleven but easily looked fourteen was in MGM's own studio in Culver City, being signed to a long-term contract in the very month the studio decided to go ahead with *National Velvet*.

The search for Velvet Brown, while not as exhaustive as that for Scarlett O'Hara, has spun off a small myth of its own. For many years, people in Britain have believed that another English girl ran Elizabeth close for the role. That girl was Shirley Catlin, daughter of the novelist Vera Brittain, and today the politician Shirley Williams. Had she indeed won the role, it might have altered the course of British politics – but not as much as it would have changed Elizabeth's life had she lost it to this wartime evacuee. Unfortunately (or fortunately, depending on one's own attachment to politics or movie apocrypha), Mrs Williams denies she was ever in the running. 'I was ten or eleven when I was evacuated to St Paul, Minnesota, in July 1940, and I remained there until 1943. I believe there was a nationwide search for a suitable girl to play [Velvet Brown] and the specifications were that the child had to be a good rider, speak English and be of a suitable age ... The film critics in each region were asked to suggest a name and my name was suggested by one in Twin Cities. We were then interviewed locally, but not taken to California for a screen test, at least not in my case.'

Several hopefuls were tested until Clarence Brown asked what now seems obvious. 'Why not Elizabeth Taylor?' He had directed her in *The White Cliffs of Dover* and liked working with children and animals. He had been the first choice for this film. The approval of Pandro Berman made Elizabeth's selection a near certainty, for this producer was one of the very few whom MGM's front office trusted with the delegated power to seal a deal. But there was one thing Elizabeth lacked in Berman's eyes: the requisite inches. Even though she would be impersonating a jockey, she was still too small a child to look convincing in racing silks. Out of this commonplace fact has grown one of the hardiest legends of filmland, all the more believable because it can accommodate the atmosphere of positive thinking and even religious faith with which Mrs Taylor surrounded her daughter. It is that Elizabeth actually willed herself to grow the extra inches and qualify for the part. No one scoffs more loudly at this 'miracle' when it's mentioned to him today than Berman himself: 'It had more to do with a growing girl's appetite than her religious will-power.' Berman cancelled the starting date of 11 September 1943, and pencilled in 4 January 1944 in order to give Elizabeth the time to grow.

Elizabeth meanwhile was sent, in Sara's safekeeping, to the Riviera Country Club to take riding lessons – and stuff herself. Every day, at a diner called Tips, she ate two 'Farm Breakfasts' consisting of four hamburger patties, four fried eggs, two mounds of hash browns and a stack of dollar pancakes with maple syrup. For lunch, she had steaks and salads. She swam a lot and exercised twice daily. 'I measured her progress with pencil marks on my office wall when she presented herself each Friday, until she'd put on three inches. Then I told her the part was hers. She might have got down on her knees to thank God, but she didn't need to talk to God to grow. This was MGM, not Lourdes,' says Berman. Elizabeth herself, while admitting that 'I ate a lot, slept a lot and left the rest to God,' added, in words that echoed her mother's prayer for guidance on the MGM contract, 'I knew if it was right for me to be Velvet, God would make me grow, and He did.' Miracles aside, what is significant about the episode is that gluttony for Elizabeth Taylor was associated with success, not self-indulgence. Not at first, anyhow.

She alternated between riding lessons at the Dupee stables in Hollywood, which many stars used, and jumping instruction at the country club from an Australian polo player called Sonny Baker. It was during one of these jumping sessions that an accident occurred, the consequences of which Elizabeth Taylor has had to live with, often in pain, to this day. She fell off her horse two or three times when neither Sara nor a studio representative was present. A spinal X-ray taken some years later, following an accident on another film, showed two of her vertebrae jammed into each other by the force of the earlier impact when, she confessed to her mother, she 'landed very hard'. A spinal weakness may have run in the family; Sara suffered periodic back trouble, too. But Elizabeth wasn't treated immediately, and if will-power healed some of her minor upsets, it did nothing to correct a spinal deformity of increasing seriousness. At this time, too, she had to submit to having braces put on her front teeth. As two of her baby teeth were ready to fall out, temporary teeth were painfully rooted in the sockets from which the studio dentist had pulled the baby molars. It was the beginning of Elizabeth's experience of the hundreds of ways in which a star could be treated by the studio as a chattel or object. Young though she was, she felt her childhood independence being filched from her little by little.

It was her father who refused permission when MGM ordered her hair to be cut in a more masculine style so as to make her imposture more plausible. Sidney Guilaroff, the studio's top hair stylist, was secretly appealed to and he deftly created a wig in the same raven tones as her own hair, fitted it to her head, then gave it a boyish crop successful enough to take in Clarence Brown. For this reprieve, she remained ever grateful to Guilaroff. Elizabeth seldom wavered from friendships and loyalties formed early on. These were the people she could trust.

This is one of the few instances of Francis Taylor getting his way in the matter of his daughter's career and happiness. Otherwise, Sara made all the decisions. 'Elizabeth and I are so close,' she said, 'we practically think as one person ... When she does make a decision [for herself], I always find it's the same thing I would have done ... We always seem to agree on everything.'

The filming had already created a split in the Taylor family by taking mother and daughter away for most of the week while Elizabeth was trained in riding and jumping. During the shooting, Francis and young Howard went off to Howard Young's Wisconsin estate, Cedar Gates, overlooking Lake Minocqua, one of whose islands Sara had renamed 'Elizabeth's Island'.

Ever a sentimental romantic, she said it reminded her of J. M. Barrie's enchanted island in his play *Mary Rose*, the magical Hebridean spot where the eponymous heroine vanished so inexplicably, only to turn up many years later, not looking a day older. Sara wanted Elizabeth to play Mary Rose sometime. The day would come when Elizabeth showed an almost neurotic desire for grown-up roles: a notion at odds with Sara's pre-dilection for characters like Mary Rose and Peter Pan, who were famous for not growing up.

The horses in *National Velvet* supplied Elizabeth with the companionship that boys, or indeed other girls, would have provided had she been living a normal childhood existence. Miss Charles, who owned the Riviera Club, stabled a string of thoroughbred horses and was astonished one day to see that Elizabeth had climbed down from the hay loft and was petting and pampering a notoriously unpredictable gelding called King Charles. Very soon afterwards, interviewers began writing about Elizabeth's power to cast a spell over the birds and beasts and 'hold familiar conversations with them, like the troubadour saint of Assisi'. The sentimental fallacy enshrined in the Victorian books her mother had read to her was being converted into a star image by the Hollywood myth-making machine.

Elizabeth didn't dance, didn't sing and, at that age, at that period, certainly couldn't be publicized as taking a sexual interest in boys. Associating her with animals was appealing and safe.

All the same, the remarks of hers quoted in contemporary interviews about her passion for horses come close to implying the same sort of idealized attachment to men that she frequently and profusely expressed in later years. The basis for both was love. 'The [studio] was afraid for me to ride him,' she said, referring to the front office's alarm at the news she was doing up to forty jumps a day on the temperamental King Charles, who was to double as The Py in the film. 'But he loves me,' she protested. 'He wouldn't hurt me. You don't have to worry about King when you get on his back. You just leave everything up to him. I think that he likes to know that I leave it to him – that he's the boss, and I trust him.' She expressed much the same sentiment about every one of her later husbands – at the start of the marriage, anyhow.

The closeness of mother and daughter in the film of *National Velvet* reflects the symbiotic relationship that existed between Sara and Elizabeth. A coincidence certainly, in this case; though later on, when Elizabeth was established enough to seek, or sometimes still compelled to accept, film roles that reflected her own self-image or the image that had been created in the public imagination, the interplay of fiction and autobiography becomes a strange and potent aspect of Elizabeth Taylor's life. *National Velvet* is its earliest manifestation. The gelding that Velvet sees cantering majestically over a meadow captures the child's heart and makes her determined to own and train him – and eventually to win the grandest race in England on his back. But Velvet's mother is also an obsessed woman, who has had an hour of glory in her own youth when she tried to break the record for swimming the English Channel. She it is who gives her child the faith to win – as well as the fee to enter – the race. 'Everyone should have the chance of a breathtaking piece of folly at least once in their life,' says Anne Revere, the screen mother. Mrs Taylor had had her own chance of a piece of folly when, as Sara Sothern, she had been applauded for her role in *The Fool*. Marriage had claimed her and put an end to her ambitions, just like Velvet's mother. Now she was passing her faith on to her precocious child. Elizabeth's childhood had familiarized her with the film's theme even before she went in front of the camera. The pressures of her upbringing at the hands of this remarkable but driven woman formed in Elizabeth an intuitive nature that could connect with movie acting – when the connection was worth making – more powerfully than any technical accomplishment.

National Velvet isn't just a study in wish fulfilment, though that is certainly part of its durable appeal. As *Time* magazine's unnamed critic put it, 'It is ... an interesting psychological study of hysterical obsession, conversion mania, pre-adolescent sexuality.' Phew! one is tempted to gasp, until one sees how Elizabeth's 'two or three speeds of hysterical or semi-hysterical emotion', as James Agee called it, keep the story in a state of tension more gripping than the conventional suspense of seeing her win the race. Mrs Taylor attended the shooting of her daughter's scenes and was observed giving her pre-arranged hand signals – sometimes to Clarence Brown's irritation – to convey the degree of feeling she thought Elizabeth should be showing. The bond between mother and child was, throughout the shooting, taut with empathy: as *National Velvet* shows. It is as if Elizabeth in the film is undergoing a variety of religious experience. Her face in close-up, gazing at The Py, possesses a celestial radiance, not altogether reducible to the tricks of lighting and photography. Perhaps Anne Revere's presence helped a little. Barely two years earlier, she had played another mother in *The Song of Bernadette*, which had made a star of Jennifer Jones. Campbell Dixon, film critic on the London *Daily Telegraph*, echoed critical sentiment when he called Elizabeth's highly charged state 'a mania', and continued: 'Whenever she speaks or thinks about horses – and this is all the time: she even practises horsemanship in bed – her strange azure eyes gleam and her whole frame trembles with the intensity of her passion.' Whether healthy or not, Elizabeth certainly exhibits a flair for ecstasy worthy of St Bernadette: and the concentrated intensity of her emotion is, at times, eerily reminiscent of the photographs of her mother playing the little cripple in *The Fool*.

A sure sign that MGM now realized the huge potential of their child actress came not only with the film's enormous success everywhere from the day it opened at Radio City Music Hall at Christmas, 1944. It was also apparent in a much rarer event than a box-office hit: namely, a Hollywood studio's desire to show its gratitude. For MGM decided to make Elizabeth a present of the horse she rode in the film. Biographers have blamed her for pestering Benny Thau to give her the horse, even though her parents were prepared to buy it for her. Not so: the initiative came from MGM. But ever mindful of the risks attendant on generosity to its stars, even this impulse was monitored by the legal department. A memo dated 15 February 1945 says: 'Mr Thau stated that we purchased the horse for $800 and that the present re-sale price would be between $500–$600. Would this be considered income on which [Elizabeth Taylor] would pay tax?' Apparently not, a lawyer ventured. So Elizabeth was told the horse was hers. Whether or not she was also told he was now lame isn't recorded.

Some of Elizabeth's interviews at the time convey the impression that God had willed MGM to give her the horse. But as the above memo confirms, a corporation is not usually moved by acts of divine will. In any case, whether or not God brought His pressure to bear on MGM, there were more uncomfortable portents at hand. The Taylors or their agents, it seemed, were learning to apply pressure of their own.

6

LOVE AND THE LONELY CHILD

In later years, Elizabeth often mentioned a very stormy meeting between her mother and Louis B. Mayer, at which she was present. Mayer was exceptionally angry over something – but the cause of his displeasure has never been disclosed. It is very likely it had to do with what the studio mogul regarded as a maladroit attempt to force a renegotiation of Elizabeth's contract following her triumph in *National Velvet*.

At the beginning of 1945, the studio notified MCA, the agency which it thought was representing Elizabeth, of its intention to pick up its option on her services. Any other decision would have been unthinkable, considering how well *National Velvet* was doing at the box office. MCA replied that it no longer had any relationship with Elizabeth or her legal guardians. A copy of the letter had gone to Mrs Taylor, but no reply had been received. A somewhat anxious MGM now called Francis Taylor at his art gallery, only to be told by him that his wife had spoken to him and he had advised her not to sign the new option agreement so that – as the suspicious studio memo put it – '[we] would give her a new contract and tear up the present one'. Mr Taylor now alleged that MGM had not renewed the option 'in time'. The studio replied hotly that if there was a fault, it lay with the Taylors for not notifying them of the change of agency.

Louis B. Mayer regarded himself as a stern but caring family man. He demanded obedience and gratitude from his own daughters and, in turn, from his extended family of studio stars. To have a mother and daughter who owed him everything – or so he would have seen it – now apparently demanding more money might well have provoked the outburst that drew the robust rebuke from little Elizabeth, 'Don't you dare talk to my Mummy like that.' Ever afterwards, Elizabeth loathed and mistrusted Mayer. She found him a 'gross, thick' person ...'He alarmed me terribly

... to know him was to be terrified of him.' She followed up her spirited defence of her mother with a rebuke to this man: 'You and your studio can both go to hell.' Mayer ordered Benny Thau to tell her to apologize. She refused. She later made the shrewd comment that Mayer was good at giving orders, but not at holding discussions – or forgetting insults, she might have added. In the years ahead, he and his successors were to teach her the nature of 'the MGM family'. 'She had an artificial patriarchy imposed on her – the studio,' said George Stevens, one of her directors, though not an MGM man. 'It took the place of her retiring father. The studio, like a domineering parent, was alternately stern and adoring.' What made it easier for Elizabeth to resist Mayer's tyranny is the fact that she was never consumed by ambition for herself, only by an overwhelming desire to please her mother.

Sara Taylor has related that around this time, in her early teens, Elizabeth made some kind of slighting remark about her film career – the context is vague, but it seems that she set small store by it, and this deeply distressed Sara. This time, though, there *was* an apology, which Sara quoted proudly: 'I realize that my whole life is being in motion pictures,' Elizabeth wrote in a note to her mother. 'For me to quit would be like cutting away the roots of a tree ... I've made up my mind for *myself* and I'll take all the hardship and everything else that comes along.'

This 'hardship' included the kind of education she was now receiving. The obligation of filming interfered with normal school hours, as well as singling her out for the sort of attention that her head teacher thought undesirable for a child of her age. (Clarence Brown had probably had the same thought during the shooting of *National Velvet* when he ordered the gold star that someone had fixed to her dressing-room door to be removed.) As a result, Elizabeth gained nearly all her education from the age of twelve, or thereabouts, on the MGM studio lot in the privileged but isolated building, formerly Irving Thalberg's bungalow, now known as 'The Little Red Schoolhouse'. At a time when most girls her age were sorting out life in the competitive rough-and-tumble of junior high school, Elizabeth was part of an elite in a school run for children who were already breadwinners. Her classmates were other child stars or the children of stars or studio executives. Instruction was given by a strict, kindly and well-intentioned pair of teachers. Mary MacDonald was the resident teacher and her assistant was Dorothy Mullen. The curriculum was approved by the Los Angeles education board; but the teachers were as subject to MGM work schedules as their wards. Miss Mullen got to know Elizabeth when she was about ten years of age. 'She was a fair student then,' she says. 'As she grew older, she showed me what a good student she was. She always had top grades in the subjects that interested her.'

Elizabeth and the others had to be taught for at least three hours daily, between 8 a.m. and 4 p.m., but the time was broken up irregularly by the demands made on them to close their books and present themselves in costume and make-up. Teaching became a series of anticipated interruptions and scheduled dislocations. This inevitably produced a special kind of mind: one that could switch, on demand, from arithmetic, geography or English to pouring out emotion in front of the camera as another person. As Elizabeth began playing roles that were more 'adult' than her personal experience, it grew more and more unsettling to try to conform to her teacher's expectations of what a child her age should know.

She had no freedom outside the studio gates; or even inside them. The 'star children', as they were known, being company assets, were supervised very strictly. They were even accompanied to the lavatory; they were never left alone lest some intruder, attracted by their celebrity, might attack them. As well as school homework, Elizabeth had to study her scenes for the next day – though sometimes she memorized these in the car taking her to work. Directors would compliment her later for being a quick study: but she had started early. Classes ended at four o'clock, and if she wasn't required on the set, she took singing and dancing lessons until six. Morning, noon and night, she had hardly any life to call her own.

A few years later, when she was making *A Place in the Sun* and still receiving tuition on location, Paramount's publicity department issued a release intended to promote the picture. But it made sad – and, for MGM, probably embarrassing – reading. Though concocted in a publicist's usual upbeat style, its opinions are identifiably Elizabeth's. They are a lament for all she felt she had lost by not attending a regular school. She had missed 'the real fun'. 'Those in regular schools have an opportunity to work on school papers, to take part in debates, to join clubs, to go to dances ... Now I've reached college age, other girls of my age are ... dreaming of proms and football games, campus groups and late coffee sessions where they talk over all the problems of the world. These things aren't listed in our curriculum.'

Very soon she would be put into movies where she had to play girls like these, ones who had all the advantages of 'normality'. She got as good an education, scholastically speaking, as many American children; but she never participated in the growing-up rites and revelations of ordinary children her own age. What she learned of the wide, exciting and dangerous world of girls and boys, she learned from the films in which she starred.

It is perhaps not true to say that at the age of thirteen she took no interest in boys; but truer to suppose that Sara did not make it easy for her to do so. A fan magazine interviewer around this time reported seeing 'two big boys and a little fellow' patrolling the sidewalk outside the Taylor home like a picket line, carrying a placard which read: 'Elizabeth Taylor Unfair to Boys'. They took to their heels when Mrs Taylor came out. Elizabeth's response to the inevitable question was usually, 'Boys ... they are silly.' On a Louella Parsons radio interview, she said she spurned them: but this opinion was considered a mite too strong, and before the interview was recorded the word was struck out of the script and a more placid expression substituted. One fan writer said to her: 'You do not like boys? ... You will be lonely in your old age.' She squirmed, but did not look up. 'Will you ever marry?' he asked.

'I plan to have many children,' she mused, 'so I suppose so.'

Her interviewer replied, 'It might be as well.'

Animals took the place of boys in Elizabeth's interests outside her family. The image of her as a child who had a special relationship with them had proved immensely profitable in two movies – to the extent that Louis B. Mayer, despite his row with the Taylors, authorized a $7,500 bonus payment to her for her work in *National Velvet* and raised her salary to $300 a week. MGM swiftly repeated the girl-loves-dog formula in *Courage of Lassie*, a film set in wartime which showed the famous collie as an Allied combatant continually outsmarting the Germans. Elizabeth's role was very small, but this, her third Technicolor film at MGM, showed her growing more and more beautiful, yet in a natural and tomboyish fashion.

The outdoor-girl image wasn't entirely fictitious, but the way it was exploited reached into what little private life the child could still call her own. With her mother's compliance, MGM even redesigned her bedroom as a shrine to *National Velvet* with a wooden horse, saddle, curry combs and bridles keeping company with white tufted organdy curtains and a dressing table with a seat of quilted white silk. 'A mistake,' Mrs Taylor later conceded; 'it was more her room the way *I* liked it.' It was also, of course, the way that her growing public now liked to see Elizabeth.

In 1946, an event occurred that would be easy to pass over. Yet examined judiciously, it reveals much about the way in which the adult Elizabeth Taylor's sexual nature was set within the expectations of the child and her mother's influence on her. Around the age of fourteen, Elizabeth became an author as well as an actress.

Nibbles and Me was the book on which her name appeared. A mere seventy-seven pages, comprising sixteen short chapters and thirty-four decorations in the text or margins (also attributed to Elizabeth's hand), it was meant to be a book for children by a child. But as almost all of it is autobiographical, this is a very special child. And the writer's unconscious revelations about herself are far more interesting than its simple tale of a chipmunk named 'Nibbles' might suggest.

The full story of how it came to be written and published is still somewhat imprecise. It began as a class essay, no doubt written by Elizabeth. There are signs that Mrs Taylor may then have helped her child to elaborate the story. A studio publicist no doubt saw the possibilities of using it to promote the MGM films that Elizabeth had appeared in. For although the book appeared under the imprint of Duell, Sloan and Pearce, a respectable Madison Avenue publishing house, it was timed to catch the interest of people who were going back to see *National Velvet* a second time and already looking forward to *Courage of Lassie*: stills from both movies appeared in the book. According to D. Halliwell Duell, president of the publishing house, the manuscript arrived in the form of a school copybook in the pencilled handwriting of its thirteen-year-old author. 'There is a quality of unself-conscious simplicity ... which immediately pleases the adult reader,' Mr Duell wrote to MGM on 31 October 1945, when accepting it for publication, and he added: '[it] makes the tone of the book exactly right for a children's book. [It] has an introduction, a point of climax – incidentally not the chapter called The Climax – and a delightful ending ... The fact that the book has form cannot be under-estimated.'

However, it's this very finished form that makes a sceptical reader suspect, as one American reviewer put it, 'the toothmarks of an editor' – but perhaps reflects no more than a mother's influence upon her daughter's imagination. For in spite of Elizabeth's first-person comments on life in a movie studio, *Nibbles and Me* has the tone of the late-Victorian children's books that were Mrs Taylor's favourite manuals of worldly improvement. The sensation of being isolated by her daydreams, of living in the world and yet cut off from it, of coping with love and death in ways that turn the experience into a moral lesson: these things and others that Elizabeth describes are also present in *The Secret Garden*. Elizabeth, for example, recalls that the name of the country cottage on the Cazalet estate, Little Swallows, came from the nest of birds just outside her bedroom window; but she never mentions the Cazalets' mansion already known as Great Swifts. She writes: 'It seemed as if I was right up there with the birds ... They would fly down so low all around me and sing and chatter away – just as if they were trying to attract my attention.' Mary, the lonely little heroine of *The Secret Garden*, also forms an attachment to a bird, a robin, which 'flew down from his tree top or hopped about or flew after her from one bush to another. He chirped a good deal and had a very busy air, as if he were showing her things.'

To both Elizabeth and Mary, the chipmunk and the robin which they make their respective pets are more than simply nature's companions. They represent human beings. They are described in terms of people who love their little mistresses. To these girls, love is the most important thing in the world – so important that the passion for requited love permeates the whole of their anthropomorphic playtime. Mary talks to her robin redbreast in terms of pubescent esctasy: 'Oh! to think that he should actually let her come as near to him as that! He knew nothing in the world would make her put out her hand towards him or startle him in the least tiniest way. He knew it because he was a real person – only nicer than any other person in the world. She was so happy that she scarcely dared breathe.' Elizabeth Taylor, in her tale, writes: 'I held Nibbles to my face and kissed and kissed him. I couldn't see – my eyes were so blinded with tears – but the feel of his dear little body I'll never forget.'

Their relationship becomes quite eroticized at times, so much so that it is disquieting to remember this is a thirteen-year-old girl speaking. '[Nibbles] stretches himself so that he can reach my mouth . . . He is happy with me. He keeps showing me that he is – and can you wonder that I love him so much?'

Nibbles had a featured role in *The Courage of Lassie*, but like many another film hopeful he wound up on the cutting-room floor. 'He was too good. It didn't look real,' Elizabeth wrote. There may be a precocious hint in such an opinion of the lack of interest, verging on contempt, with which Elizabeth would later come to view most of the films she made.

Nibbles also serves as a surrogate Elizabeth Taylor. He gets introduced to the MGM power hierarchy, including 'Mr Louis B. Mayer (with whom he knew to mind his manners)'. When the book was serialized in *Photoplay* in August 1946, the crack about minding his manners when he looked at Mayer was dropped.

It gradually emerges that the pet name 'Nibbles' is a generic one: there are several Nibbleses in the book, just as there were several Lassies on the screen. When one Nibbles dies, Elizabeth demonstrates how completely she has assimilated her mother's concept of death, drawing strength from the Christian Science tenet that the loved one does not die, but simply passes out of sight. Otherwise, how can life be said to die? This point has an especially painful relevance. Victor Cazalet had managed to visit the Taylors early in 1943 – Hedda Hopper helped him overcome currency problems by arranging lecture fees. A few months later, on returning to England and wartime service as Churchill's liaison officer with General Sikorski, the Polish leader-in-exile, Elizabeth's honorary godfather was killed with the general in an aircraft crash. A talk with her mother persuaded the sorrowing child that there was no such thing as death, so long as memory held the key to life. Many years later, after the unexpected death of her ex-husband Richard Burton, Elizabeth appeared in an interview on British television and made exactly that point. Nibbles had indeed many lives.

Even if *Nibbles and Me* is not all her own unaided work, its attitudes to love and death are those which the child was taught to accept and expect. Furry animals are not usually good guides to life's complexities; but at this formative stage in growing up, they were the only guides, besides her mother, that Elizabeth had. Brenda Maddox's monograph on the star, *Who's Afraid of Elizabeth Taylor?*, shrewdly teases another clue to the mature woman's attitude to love out of this small childhood book. For even though the dear departed chipmunk would always live in her heart, his destiny was always to be replaced: a new one 'would come to me – not to take his place, but to bring the same sense of love to me, and he did – and I knew him immediately, and I named him Nibbles – not Nibbles the second, but just Nibbles – my favorite chipmunk'. Husbands, suggests Maddox, came serially too, like chipmunks, each replacing the last, yet treasured for himself alone. Husbands can of course be more trouble than small rodents. Perhaps Uncle Howard Young had this in mind when he said to the young star: 'As long as you love horses and chipmunks, you're safe.'

To this little girl, love is already the most important thing in the world – but it is absolutely vital that she be loved for herself alone. She has to be completely sure of that. This means putting a candidate for her affections, a Nibbles, for instance, through a series of tests until the ultimate one is reached: if given the chance, would he desert her? This is probably what the book's publisher was referring to when he spoke of the climax not being the obvious one: that's to say, not the episode of Nibbles getting lost in a Chicago hotel and being almost killed by the staff, but the one in which his little owner leans down and sets him free on the ground. Will he stay with her or go back into the woods? 'He ran to the edge of the wood ... My heart cried out to him. Goodbye, Nibbles! – and then – the next thing I knew – he ran to me and jumped on my shirt and *into my hand*. Oh, I can't describe what I felt ... There was no more doubt. He was *mine* – by his own choice.'

Nibbles grew to tribal proportions: for Elizabeth caught twenty-five chipmunks during the three months' location work on *Courage of Lassie*. She let them all go, but the one presented to her by Curly Twyford, one of the film crew, became the 'literary' Nibbles and stayed with her. Nibbles was thus a test of how strongly, how devotedly, Elizabeth felt she was loved; and she was to repeat this test over and over again in years to come, and gain a reinforced sense of security when the lover who was being tested responded with a gift that was worthy of his passion and her need. The price tag on the gift, or even its uniqueness, didn't satisfy simply her acquisitive instinct, though it may have looked that way to some of those who paid the price. It also proved her own worthiness to be loved. But to be abandoned by Nibbles – why, that was the worst of all judgements on her. Later on, Elizabeth would insist, despite apparent evidence to the contrary in wrecked marriages and serial divorces, that she always lived by her principles. This kind of statement seems inexplicable to many – and even hypocritical to some of those who have rebuked her for her 'promiscuous' life-style. But to the little girl who, as she wrote to Mr Duell, found the words 'tumbling out so fast I can't keep up with them', there was never any contradiction between principle and practice. *Nibbles and Me* may have been an unlikely catechism for life, love and marriage, but Elizabeth Taylor never departed from its beliefs and convictions.

7

'WHY, SHE IS A WOMAN!'

Time magazine's issue of 22 August 1949 considered the current crisis in Hollywood. There was a dearth of new stars. The established ones were no longer drawing big audiences. Joan Crawford's 'sophisticated fortyishness' had outlived its shelf-life: the public weren't clamouring to buy it. Nor did they rush to sample the 'well-preserved charm' of Claudette Colbert, Barbara Stanwyck, Bette Davis or Marlene Dietrich. 'One studio,' the magazine's sardonic commentator conceded, 'is less desperate than most. MGM. That is probably because MGM has turned up a jewel of greater price, a true star sapphire. She's Elizabeth Taylor.' And there she was, just turned seventeen and on *Time*'s cover.

The magazine made a forecast that was all the more interesting for being so far-sighted. It quoted MGM's casting director on Elizabeth. 'Billy Grady thinks she has the temperament as well as the talent to become a great star – "And when she begins to show it, oh brother!"'

The studio, however, didn't find it easy to match its sapphire to the right setting. Until her fifteenth birthday, in 1947, Elizabeth was still being promoted as a nature girl and publicity releases about her possessed a fairy-tale quality. When she wasn't being Velvet Brown, in thrall to horses, she was Snow White, beloved by all the birds of the air and beasts of the field, at least the cuddlier ones. Occasionally this hype went over the top. 'She whinnies just like a horse,' a studio publicist told a visiting journalist. 'Most unearthly sound you ever heard ... She also chirps like a squirrel and makes bird noises.' The visitor, a cool customer, said to Elizabeth, 'Let's hear you whinny.' Before she could oblige, the publicist intervened. 'The studio doesn't want her to whinny any more. It's too rough on her throat.'

Obviously, there was a point where pantheism, if overdone, could make a potential star seem no longer sweet and fanciful, but definitely odd and even stupid. A new image had to be developed for Elizabeth. But what should it be?

The studio had purchased the rights to W. H. Hudson's novel *Green Mansions*. The heroine was admittedly another nature girl, a wild child called Rima, who lived in the woods and talked to the animals. But she also talked the language of the romantic young man who falls in love with her. Elizabeth was all for doing more mature roles, but it seems Mrs Taylor didn't think the time was yet quite ripe. The project was quietly shelved, even though Warner Bros. offered to take it over if MGM would loan out Elizabeth. A studio fears nothing as much as a rival making a box-office hit out of a project on which it has blown cold. Next MGM tried to find a role that would suit Elizabeth's English background, and *Introduction to Sally* was purchased. It was described as 'a touching story of a little English cockney girl' – and it got nowhere, either. Life in London's East End being out of favour, MGM then had a brainwave; Elizabeth would play the other Elizabeth, the Tudor queen, during her childhood years. But scripting *Young Bess* presented problems, principally because one MGM producer wanted Elizabeth in the role while another saw it as a part for Deborah Kerr. So Bess's 'youth', which spanned the years from eleven to sixteen when Elizabeth was in the script, kept being altered to encompass the twenty-two to thirty-six age group when Deborah Kerr was the star. Elizabeth had grown into the saddle for *National Velvet*; it was asking a bit much of even her at fifteen to will herself on to the throne as a plausible monarch of thirty-something.

Paradoxically, MGM's casting problems weren't rendered any easier by the precocious physical maturity that Elizabeth was demonstrating with every week that went by. Between her fourteenth and fifteenth birthdays, she developed the bust and some of the other physical attributes of a ripening girl in her late teens or early twenties. Before she was sixteen, she was displaying a thirty-five-inch bosom, thirty-four-inch hips and a twenty-two-inch waist that she used to cinch even more tightly into the dirndl peasant skirts then fashionable. 'Why, she is a woman!' Mickey Rooney exclaimed to Hedda Hopper, who immediately warned him off, though she herself hastened into print to identify the new dimension to Elizabeth's appeal – sex. 'The eyes still have it, but the fellows in her youthful set today describe her with a whistle that is sweet and low and soft.' This 'ravishing young lady', to Hopper's mind, was now 'a potential young Bergman'.

The effect was inflammatory even inside MGM, where the studio staff were well used to seeing myths made flesh lunching daily in the commissary. One employee candidly described Elizabeth as 'jail bait', which is said to have amused her – later on, anyhow. To observe this full-bosomed child still chaperoned by her watchful mother and feeding the latest version of Nibbles, which she was permitted to take to lunch, was a freakish sight. Her physical maturity set her apart from all the other child stars. It was as if she were thrusting herself, literally, out of all those wholesome outdoor roles, whose sexuality was sublimated into the affectionate bonds between little girls and their animals, in order to assume the attributes of a more blatant world of gyrating cheerleaders and flamboyantly provocative cover-girls. Somewhere between the extremes of carnality and rectitude, there had to be a role for Elizabeth Taylor – but where?

Part of the difficulty lay in deciding where Elizabeth fitted into the times. America's young people were – like Elizabeth herself – developing fast. A child, such as she still was officially within the confines of studio and family, had given way to the teenager with his or her subculture of popular music, pop idols, fan magazines, teen fashions and a curiosity about sex only exceeded by sheer ignorance – and that would soon be corrected. The rate and nature of teenage change were apparent everywhere. There were even instructional shorts aimed at teenagers. But they were often accompanied in the cinemas which showed them by sarcastic whistles and wolf-calls of incipient rebellion. These short films offered advice on how to date a girl and what to do – as well as what not to do, which was possibly thought more important by the sponsors – when out on a date with her. In short, the kids who were the biggest fans of Elizabeth Taylor's were far more sexually adventurous than MGM's well-protected young star.

Elizabeth felt so left out of things that she was overjoyed when one of her few friends of her own age presented her with a couple of trendy items – a short skirt and bobby-sox – from her own over-stocked wardrobe. There was not much chance to wear them, though. Sara still did the shopping for her child; and the clothes she picked were more in line with her own idea of a talented child whose charms had been turned to profit and had to be made to last as long as possible.

For signing Elizabeth's new contract, dated 18 January 1946, which put the star on $750 a week (forty weeks guaranteed), Mrs Taylor received a bonus of $1500. She was also to receive $250 a week during Elizabeth's guaranteed employment. Throughout her daughter's seventeen and a half years with MGM, Sara and the studio never got round to signing any written agreement between them; but MGM was realistic enough to know that if mothers were kept happy, then their talented offspring were happy, too, or at least not allowed to complain too loudly. Mrs Taylor was treated with a considerateness bordering at times on obsequiousness. She shared in all the product tie-ins arranged for Elizabeth subject to MGM's permission: Lux soap, Max Factor cosmetics, paper dolls, painting and crayoning books, and the radio appearances she made. No one suggests that she ever abused her position or exploited her child. But she made sure Elizabeth's breadwinning abilities didn't lie fallow. She had less luck with her son, who went to a barber and had his hair cropped to the scalp so as to sabotage a screen test that his mother had helped set up at Universal. Elizabeth said, years later, how much she admired Howard's disregard for the superficiality of the movies.

There was another side to Elizabeth's early earning capacity. It is revealed in MGM's meticulous bookkeeping, which listed the charges that had to be met by Elizabeth herself, or at least legitimately laid off against taxes. In her first full year, these broke down as follows: food (lunch for two, presumably mother and daughter, and tea), $65.00; clothing, $60.00; insurance (life and car), $8.96; transportation (gas and parking), $17.20; medical expenses, $25.00; dental expenses, $6.00; entertainment, $50.00; make-up, none; lessons, $100; War Bond purchases, $93.75; laundry, $33.50; cleaning, $15.00; car expenses (repairs, auto club dues), $12.00; charity donations, $5.00; miscellaneous (end-of-picture gifts, Christmas presents, publicity photos, fan mail), $56.00. Such figures, like a child's piggybank, retain the nostalgia of a simpler era.

Evidence of how much MGM's own valuation of Elizabeth's services exceeded what the studio currently paid her is revealed by the remuneration it earned from loaning her out to Warner Bros. for *Life With Father* between 20 April and 21 July 1946. The rate was $3,500 a week, five times her MGM salary.

A period comedy like this, with Elizabeth playing a girl who wins the love of the household's eldest son, was obviously one way of promoting her to an outright romantic role while postponing the day when she would have to grapple with the conventions of modern girls. She liked making it. She got her first taste of working in a studio noted for its relaxed, even raffish ways, compared with MGM's strait-laced autocracy. And the part comfortingly confirmed what her mother had taught her – that well-brought-up girls get the man they deserve.

For Mrs Taylor, the filming seems also to have confirmed something else – that romance need not be extinguished for the married woman. During its five-month schedule, this fifty-year-old woman struck up a relationship with the movie's director Michael Curtiz, which was subsequently blamed for the temporary separation that took place between Sara and her husband. Such incidents were not uncommon in Hollywood and were usually discreetly conducted. Curtiz, however, was not a man to be reticent about his affairs, no matter how fleeting, as proved to be the case here. Perhaps the film's unusually long shooting schedule liberated Sara Sothern Taylor's old yearning for the star role which she had forfeited on marriage. Francis and young Howard went off again to Howard Young's Wisconsin estate. The Youngs were shocked by the rupture in a perfect marriage. They were strict Episcopalians. There had never been a divorce in the family. Soon, persuasion and pressure were at work.

Elizabeth has been quoted as saying of her father's moving out: 'It was no special loss.' She is most unlikely ever to have voiced such a thought. She loved her father to the end of his life. On the other hand, she. is on record as making a comment about her parents' separation that sounds as if she is referring obliquely to her own lonesome status: 'Maybe they loved me too much. They had no life of their own, especially my mother. I was too much a part of their lives.'

The studio was even more disturbed than the Howard Youngs, though not on religious grounds. To have a scandal involving the mother of an impeccably pure, not to say spiritual child star with a hefty box-office to make her a solid asset – this would be worse than a moral embarrassment. It would be a financial calamity. MGM must have acted fast. A speculative item about the Taylors' problems that appeared in a film trade paper remained just that – an item. And the old strategy of separating promiscuous parties was put into effect, in the hope that distance would encourage disenchantment.

So Elizabeth and Sara left for England. Ostensibly, it was a publicity trip; an MGM photographer sailed with them on the *Queen Mary*, and so did a full wardrobe of sports clothes and afternoon and evening wear provided by the studio. It was meant to be a floating photo-opportunity – and thus tax-deductible – but food poisoning forced both Elizabeth and Sara to remain below deck.

At the Dorchester, in London, illness continued to afflict Elizabeth. Her temperature soared to 104 from a virus infection. In the first three-year term of her MGM contract, she had had eight weeks and six days off through sickness. No doubt the illnesses were genuine enough; but some seemed to coincide – not surprisingly – with periods of strain and stress like the present one. However, as the news from Hollywood improved and a reconciliation between her parents was engineered, Elizabeth's condition improved, too. Soon she was establishing the pattern of another life-long habit: purchasing pets, in this case two terriers named Pee-Wee and Colonel Blimp. Mother and child paid their sad respects to Victor Cazalet, visiting his estate where they discovered Little Swallows looking 'rather the worse for neglect', though Mrs Taylor was gratified to learn that it had given wartime shelter to none other than the ex-queen of Yugoslavia: a fit ending for a fairy-tale habitation. Their old Hampstead home had been commandeered by the Women's Voluntary Service, and, lacking even the aura of resident Royalty, looked simply shabby. It was fortunate, Mrs Taylor may have reflected, that the new dreamtime of Hollywood had replaced the one that now existed only in Elizabeth's memory.

The spirits of Elizabeth and her mother picked up on the return voyage. 'We wore some of the pretty clothes we had missed wearing on the trip over,' Sara recalled. Pretty clothes were always capable of giving Elizabeth's spirits a lift. Later on, producers who knew this would design a wardrobe for her to get her interested in the film they wanted her to make. 'The way to this woman's art is through her clothes,' said one.

The trip was expensive: $1,500 for their transportation and another $1,000 for the Dorchester bill. What made it a happy homecoming was the reunion that took place between Mr and Mrs Taylor: yes, MGM was *very* happy about that, and happier still when Mr Taylor paid Sara's share of the trip.

Elizabeth's mother and the studio now got to work on giving the young star a more mature image, in keeping with her well-developed appearance and anticipated film roles. Out went the pony-club decor in her bedroom, in came a 'junior miss' interior: a dark red carpet and white, pink and red tones in the bedspread, sheets, curtains and upholstery. The equine pictures were put out to pasture; roses took their place. Roses were Mrs Taylor's favourite flower. The new decor was what a film studio would have designed. It bore precious little resemblance to the bedrooms of most of the nation's teenagers, adorned with sentimental tat, bobby-soxers' pin-ups, high-school and campus iconography and such like. It was harder still to fit Elizabeth into the rites and pleasures of the world outside her family home or her place of work. Her brother urged her to start calling guys – maybe get invited over. But all the guys Howard had made friends with were at Beverly Hills High; they knew Elizabeth only through her screen roles. Either they were in awe of her, or they dismissed her as 'Howard Taylor's movie-star sister'. It was hard for her to start calling, for the only experience she had had of forming relationships was within the MGM family.

However, with MGM's help, a parallel life resembling that of the teenage world, but separate from it, was fabricated for her. In this she participated – though the feeling is that of a visitor who is being initiated into other people's ways, rather than sharing in them as an unselfconscious participant.

She was bought a silver choker and a pair of flower earrings, just like the ones every high-school senior was wearing that year. The studio bought her a brand new Ford – the kind that had the twin exhaust pipes which rebellious adolescents were even then adding as an optional extra to the jalopies they owned, so as to let parents hear the 'vroom' of their offspring's independence behind the wheel. Not that the Taylors had to fear the dreaded back-seat romancing that went with such vehicles. The car remained a maturity symbol for Elizabeth, not an invitation to sin. She never drove it outside the studio parking lot, where she showed it off to studio employees and asked, 'Do you want to hear my pipes?' – whereupon she would step on the gas and make the stationary vehicle reverberate. One producer, hearing the yearning roar of independence, said, 'Wait till that "lassie" leaves home.'

Other whims and fancies that expressed an urge to be like her peers were discouraged, or else fulfilled for her in ways the studio and her parents thought best. She wanted to sprinkle silver stardust through her black hair, having heard of its vaunted power to fascinate the opposite sex on campus. The notion was vetoed; she was told she, of all people, didn't need to sparkle. The clothes she bought with her monthly dress allowance had to pass studio inspection – and they reflected Louis B. Mayer's patriarchal idea of what suited well-bred girls. Such campus gear as pedal-pushers were out. Rather pitifully, Elizabeth begged her parents to give her a lump sum and let her splurge on whatever she fancied. They agreed, until her fancy turned to a seventy-three-dollar hat designed by the 'in' milliner, John Frederick, trimmed with black velvet ribbon and a big pink rose. 'But Elizabeth, you never wear a hat,' Mrs Taylor said. 'If you want one, I have plenty that will do.' And then and there her mother dusted off a black hat belonging to her own earlier days, put a ribbon on it and shopped at Sears Roebuck for a $2.50 pink chiffon rose. Elizabeth never wore that hat, either.

But the big question remained, how could Elizabeth meet boys safely? Howard was prevailed on to get one of his classmates, Danny Buckley, to invite her to the senior prom. The studio vetted Master Buckley first. Their star mustn't be paired with a complete nondescript. One imagines their relief on discovering that young Buckley's nickname in the class yearbook was 'Best-Looking Boy'. The MGM wardrobe department fitted Elizabeth out with a prom dress of blue and silver chiffon. She was collected from her parents' home and returned there safely and early from the dance. Sara and Francis had been waiting up. She gave them a starry-eyed account of the evening that sounded like a visit to a foreign country. 'They talked to me about all the other kids at school ... just as if I were one of them. Just as if I knew all of them. And I pretended I did.' Obligingly, they had 'forgotten' she was an MGM movie star.

'What did they call you?' Mrs Taylor asked.

'Howard Taylor's sister,' came the reply. What else would they call her?

Seventeen years later, in a more candid mood, Elizabeth remembered the evening as 'perfectly miserable'.

Occasionally, a more sophisticated atmosphere had to be created for Elizabeth than a school prom. Then she was taken dancing, often at the Coconut Grove. Her escort was usually some hand-picked MGM publicity man, a surrogate father rather than any true boyfriend. Keeping company with older people made Elizabeth seem even older than she was; she played the scene, as it were, in the manner expected of her had it been a film script, so that when she was in the company of boys and girls her own age, they sensed that she had acquired a range of experience as yet beyond their own years. She hadn't actually; but her composure was enough to make them shy away, or else treat her with the last thing she needed, or maybe wanted – respect.

As there were no dates clamouring for her company, the Taylors took the initiative. To promote the high-school image of a fun-loving Elizabeth, they threw a beach party at the summer house they rented at Malibu. Francis was despatched in the car to buy out the shelves of the local grocery store; Sara rolled up her sleeves, the way she had done at Little Swallows or for the English picnics she'd once organized down to the last crustless sandwich, and produced turkeys, sweet hams, corn-on-the-cob, peanut-butter sandwiches, mountains of potato salad, enough for several dozen. A barbecue was built on the beach. They planned games and charades, with banjos and bonfires and marshmallows ready for toasting, just like an MGM production full of harmless fun and aseptic togetherness. Unfortunately, Elizabeth's parents' idea of such an event derived from Hollywood's own morally sanitized idea of how the teens would behave, rather than how many of them were beginning to do. The kids stuffed themselves with the food, then took advantage of the sunset to slip away in suspicious couples and start smooching behind the rocks or above the tide-line – things the Motion Picture Production Code administrators were not yet keen on allowing in the finished movie. The Taylors, mindful of their parental status, patrolled the beach with flashlights. Elizabeth was left at the barbecue pit, keeping company with the 'drips' and the 'dogs', as campus slang classified the least favoured, or, at any rate, least venturesome teenagers.

The difficulty of trying to get a romance going with the most beautiful and desirable young girl in the movies is illustrated by the fate of Marshall Thompson, a young actor who had caught Elizabeth's eye in the MGM commissary. Mrs Taylor proposed he take her daughter to the premiere of *The Yearling*. Thompson would probably have jumped at the chance, if left to himself; but he knew enough about studio politics to realize that even an innocent outing with Elizabeth Taylor had to be vetted by MGM, which paired such couples in strict accordance with their current screen status and potential investment value. A small-part player did not go out with a budding star. Thompson apparently played safe, suggesting Elizabeth was maybe still too young to go out on a date unchaperoned – why didn't Mrs Taylor come along? Mrs Taylor trumped Marshall's offer. Why didn't they get another ticket and take his mother, too? It was scarcely a foursome to incite unchaste thoughts.

However, Thompson knew the rites associated with coming of age in the movies – and, for the moment, that had to do for real life. 'Oh, mother, he kissed me!' Elizabeth cried, running into the house after Thompson, on seeing her to the doorstep, had done what was expected of him in the script. Given the constraints of parental proximity, his kiss was a social compliment that in no way suggested a sexual act. But it was enough, for the time being, anyhow. 'Another milestone had been passed,' Mrs Taylor recorded.

8

. . .AND A 'DANGEROUS' WOMAN

The illusory teenage world created around Elizabeth by the studio was far more manageable than the real one she was admitted to only occasionally, and then in the safe company of her mother or a chaperone. Make-believe became the alternative reality to the world outside her direct experience. The interviews and photo-spreads in the newspapers and national fan magazines not only provided readers with the illusion that they knew what Elizabeth was *really* like: they gave Elizabeth herself a vicarious experience of the sort it was difficult for her to find among her own age group outside her home and workplace.

The October 1948 issue of *Photoplay*, for instance, contained a well-illustrated article entitled 'Elizabeth Taylor's First Formal Party'.

'The boys were smooth,' ran the text, 'the girls were SDB ['strictly dream bait', in the teenage slang of the time] – even the moon came out.' The pictures showed Elizabeth in a pink and silver formal dress with the obligatory orchid corsage, apparently the centre of the fun at what might have been taken to be her parents' home. She presided over the chafing-dish buffet – 'her family disappeared as they had promised to do' – and played 'the large collection of records she's so proud of . . . [first] a waltz to get the gang in a groove'. Then, later, she was pictured 'cutting a rug with some fast jitterbug steps' until midnight came and the guests dutifully departed. 'But for Liz, a weary Cinderella, there still remains the eternal battle of the dishcloth.' The last photo showed a happily tired star contemplating the stack of washing-up. Since the affair had been catered on a studio set, dressed to resemble a cosy domestic interior, it is unlikely that she had to dip her hands into the suds.

Moreover, none of the guests were lowly seniors from the high school over the hill; they were junior film stars like herself, the very same people she worked with in movies, now playing the roles of 'normal' kids and doing the things that the newly launched magazine *Modern Screen* advised beaux and bobby-soxers to do: 'Dress with real care, apply your party face with skill: be lavish with the mouthwash and non-perspirant. Be convinced, when you meet your fella, that you couldn't possibly look better.'

Thus young Marshall Thompson, Elizabeth's studio-designated date at the photo set-up, bowed to her on the staircase; Roddy McDowall shared a pensive tête-à-tête with her on the terrace; and Anne Westmore and Lon McCallister joined in the after-dinner charades. Jane Powell and Larry Breen both happened to be out of town, it was stated, lest fans imagined they hadn't been invited. If the purpose was to show the fans that junior stars were like themselves, just normal people, only that little bit more special, the feature succeeded brilliantly.

It wasn't simply easier for Elizabeth to surrender to this sort of fantasy; it was inescapable. It was a part of the job that was now the whole of her life. The first role she played as a modern teenager might have been devised by screenwriters inspired by her own dilemma – a girl who wants to go to the school prom, but has to shake herself free of the domination of her loving, but overly concerned parents.

Cynthia, which began production in October 1946, was, in fact, based on a stage play entitled *The Rich Full Life*. It didn't enjoy a rich or even a long life on Broadway, but lent itself well to the expansion and greater realism of the screen. Elizabeth played the beautiful but sickly daughter of George Murphy and Mary Astor, apparently doomed to a life of semi-convalescence by her own insecurity and her parents' fear for her health, until a boy, played by Jimmy Lydon, does what the boys were significantly *not* doing to the real Elizabeth: he asks her to the school dance. Will weak-lunged Cynthia risk cold and rain to be with her date and collect what the advertising called 'Her First Kiss'? Howard Strickling, the studio publicity chief, compressed this momentous adolescent rite of passage into a pithy synopsis when he cabled news of it to his boss Howard Dietz, at Loew's Inc., in New York: 'Elizabeth Taylor will portray a modern teenage Camille.'

Cynthia recalls Elizabeth's comment about her own parents loving her too well. Her screen parents subject her to the rule of life, which is 'You can't, Cynthia.' Her triumph is to prove she *can*. And she does so in an entirely winning way. This film is one of Elizabeth Taylor's unjustly forgotten triumphs of tact, sympathy, pathos and insistent self-assertion; and the identification with Cynthia by the bobby-soxers who saw it must have been total. It is one of the most likeable movies of adolescent independence – not yet rebellion, which was still a few years away, waiting for James Dean and Natalie Wood – that Hollywood produced in the mid-1940s. 'You're so young, girl,' sighs Mary Astor. 'You were young, too,' says Cynthia; and, of course, mother realizes, as Velvet Brown's mother did in *National Velvet*, that everyone should have the chance of 'a breathtaking piece of folly' at least once in their life. In this case, letting delicate Cynthia brave the elements in the sort of strapless chiffon evening gown that college girls across America would have killed for. The gangling young Jimmy Lydon brings her home from the dance in his beat-up jalopy, carries her across a rain puddle and gives her a goodnight kiss on the porch. She has lost her galoshes, and her feet are wringing wet, but 'Oh, it was wonderful, mother. He kissed me good night.' The line echoes Elizabeth's own report on her own invitation to a school prom, but this time it's not belied by Cynthia's subsequent memory of it. Elizabeth, characteristically, later dismissed the romanticized image of her screen self with the sniffy comment, 'That buss was more like a handshake.'

Maybe so, in retrospect, but the evidence on the screen under Robert Z. Leonard's light, witty but involving touch as director, shows that Elizabeth could project a vulnerable sense of conviction about the character she was playing that made one anxious to see Cynthia win the happiness she deserves. It is a performance like Claire Bloom's in *Limelight* or Audrey Hepburn's in *Roman Holiday*; it sings with youth, beauty and innocence. No wonder it won the permanent adoration, as he later confessed, of one young moviegoer, the future film director Mike Nichols, who guided Elizabeth through the darker ages of the emotions in *Who's Afraid of Virginia Woolf?* twenty years later.

What her performance in *Cynthia* also contains, though at a lower pitch, is the same note of unrepressed desperation – she *must* go to the prom dance, just as, a year or so earlier in *National Velvet*, she *had* to win the Grand National. Cynthia's yearning is close to a neurotic need, though it is not sublimated sex that urges her on this time to take the jumps in life, but a self-assertive fever to prove that the answer to 'You can't, Cynthia', is 'I can, mother.' The impatience Elizabeth was feeling with the restraints that her own life placed on her independence is the mainspring of her performance; it drives it.

Realizing, perhaps, that the film was acquiring a deeper emotional tone than its campus and family situation-comedy suggested, MGM reshaped it in the editing stages to put it more clearly into the class of a romantic story. The editor, Frank Whitbeck, was ordered to concentrate on Elizabeth's close-ups, which held the emotional weight of the story, though he was told to remove at least one shot where her well-rounded breasts pressed too invitingly against her blouse. The trailers for *Cynthia* also eliminated most of the jitterbugging at the school prom in order not to convey the impression that this was just another high-school musical.

Mary Astor has left evidence of the effect that such role-playing was having on Elizabeth at this impressionable time in her life. 'I had seen [her] during the making of *National Velvet*,' Astor wrote in one of her volumes of autobiography, 'and she had at that time a serious, dedicated look. That was gone, she was no longer quite as shy, and she was beginning to be conscious in a very normal, teenage way of her own beauty. She was also bright. Very bright. Head-of-the-class type of brightness. For a kid, she concentrated very well on the work – and I liked her. But I liked another "daughter" better – Judy Garland [in *Meet Me in St Louis*]. Judy was warm and affectionate and exuberant. Elizabeth was cool and slightly superior. More than slightly. There was a look in those violet eyes that was somewhat calculating . . . as though she knew exactly what she wanted and was quite sure of getting it.'

Louella Parsons was also a willing accomplice in helping to project the image of a more poised and provocative Elizabeth. They did one of Parsons's apparently live, but actually carefully scripted radio interviews on 13 July 1947, just before *Cynthia* was released. The theme shows that the innocence of the waifish Cynthia is already being overtaken by an impatient quest for experience such as the fan magazines were increasingly serving up to their youthful readers. Elizabeth discounted that kiss on the porch as 'just a little ole peek' and added, 'Why, I tell you if a boy kissed me like that in private life, I think I'd slap him.'

What was this, Parsons asked, about Elizabeth going steady at the age of fifteen? 'How long did it go on?'

The answer was a calculated balance of desire and ingenuousness: 'Two weeks. Gee, it was awful! A girl misses so many dates that way, and as for your clothes allowance . . . Oh, it just simply eats it up.'

Parsons said she thought Elizabeth was a flirt. What was her ideal? 'To do crazy, silly things with men of nineteen or twenty,' came the pat reply; 'boys my own age are so young.' She followed that by saying she was dieting to get her waist down from twenty-two inches to twenty inches, but 'a candy shop with peppermint malts' was a terrible temptation. What did she want most? her interviewer asked. To be a great actress, Elizabeth said, but lest that sound too far removed from the possibilities of other fifteen-year-olds listening to the broadcast, she added a homelier confession. 'Most of all, I want to snare a husband.'

Louella Parsons ended the interview with an observation that was to prove an understatement, if anything. 'I think you can relax, Elizabeth. I doubt that you'll have any difficulty in that line.'

'Thank you, Miss Parsons,' said Elizabeth. 'It's been positively dreamy.' In the text as broadcast, 'positively dreamy' was replaced by 'wonderful'. No need to overdo it.

Cynthia and *Life With Father* were both released, back-to-back, so to speak, in August–September 1947. The double event caused *Life* magazine to proclaim: 'Elizabeth Taylor has suddenly become Hollywood's most accomplished junior actress.'

MGM rushed her into another picture without delay, her first fully-fledged musical. *A Date With Judy* began shooting in October 1947, and finished in early January 1948, ready for a summer holiday release.

A Date With Judy revealed a different Elizabeth: no longer the frail orphan crossing her fingers behind her back in desperate hope of getting invited to the prom, but a cool, even calculating, spoiled rich brat who's the menace of her high-school year and steals another girl's fella from under her nose. It was based on a popular radio series and had the unusual distinction of a screenplay written by two women, Dorothy Cooper and Dorothy Kingsley. It's tempting to say this is why it is an unusually tart examination of women in the 'junior miss' sizes of the sex trying to twist men around their fingers. That certainly is what makes Elizabeth's role such fun, from the minute she sidles into the rehearsal for the school prom, where Jane Powell (as the eponymous Judy) is belting out 'It's a Most Unusual Day', and shoots a quizzical, sideways look at this essentially 'nice' girl – the Melanie to her own Scarlett O'Hara. It is Elizabeth's first screen appearance as a manipulative modern flirt who thinks of the school campus as simply the best place to go husband-hunting. She speaks in epigrams of precocious cynicism: 'If you know one man, you know them all'; 'Once a person is a man, there's nothing anyone can do about it.' And when Elizabeth reprises Jane's jaunty version of her opening song, she does so in a slow-tempo, self-absorbed way designed to attract the boys rather than simply accompany the band. Her home background – significantly minus mother – reinforces the impression of her as a WASP princess. In the evenings, she stretches out on the sofa in a blue chiffon gown and is handed the telephone by the butler – no hunched girl-talk down the line for this elegant young beauty whose make-up is enhanced by the saturated tones of the Technicolor system then in use at MGM.

Elizabeth's character has absorbed the lesson being delivered in the weekly fan magazines: 'Marry early', ('Marry often' was still beyond the bounds of permissiveness.) She confidently gives an older man the eye – older indeed, since Robert Stack, who plays this ex-GI who's working at the soda fountain in order to finance his way through medical school, was then twenty-nine, nearly twice Elizabeth's age. The romance puts her into rivalry with Jane Powell, her sometime classmate in the Little Red Schoolhouse at MGM. Although Jane has perfect command of the singing notes with her coloratura soprano, it is Elizabeth who vocalizes her desires, and does so with the shameless confidence of a society that sanctions the wiles that women use to catch their men.

Jane Powell's adolescent image would stick with her well into mid-career, and ultimately disqualify her from a range of more dramatic roles that might have prolonged her screen popularity. In contrast, Elizabeth, just coming up to sixteen, is displaying the signs of striking womanhood that would soon enable the studio to transfer her, without a break in her career, from playing adolescent girls to portraying romantic and sexy young women. 'That was the beginning of the glamour build-up,' her mother wrote.

Stack ends up handing Jane Powell over to the beau she wanted in the first place – Elizabeth's nice but slightly dim kid brother, played by Scotty Beckett – but then joins Elizabeth at her family's table and promises to wed her in a few years. An unlikely event, one reflects, given the impatience of the girl to make an instant catch, even though she has not yet finished high school. Don't dare wait, lest you turn into a spinster, go after your man, lest you get stuck at home; and, as *Modern Screen* advised its readers, 'There's nothing wrong with scattering a few come-ons where they'll do most good, either.' Elizabeth's screen image had begun to send out the signals that social pressures for early marriage were already alerting her fans to put into practice. Soon her own off-screen life would follow the example she herself set.

Elizabeth was willing to be moulded into the new image. She celebrated her sixteenth birthday on the set of her next film, *Julia Misbehaves*, a mistaken attempt to make a comedienne out of Greer Garson. Garson played Julia, who deserts her husband and infant for a stage career, then comes back, when her daughter is about to be married, to upset the wedding arrangements. The movie shows MGM faltering over the problem of what to do with ageing stars – Garson's reviews would have driven another actress into retirement – but as far as Elizabeth was concerned, it brought her a step closer to the state of millions of girls who, for the first time in American history, were about to form a numerical majority of the population and were increasingly feeling the pressures building up on them to find a man and marry him.

Elizabeth's man in *Julia Misbehaves* was Peter Lawford, then twenty-four, still with a bearing and an accent that incorporated gentlemanly echoes of her own English childhood.

'Oh, Ritchie, what are we going to do?' she had to say to him while in his arms. Instead, she fumbled the dialogue and it came out as 'Oh, Peter ...' The set roared with sympathetic laughter. And the publicists bustled off to cable news of the *faux pas*, whether real or pre-arranged, to the wire services. There is no doubt that Elizabeth's private life was now being shared, almost indecently, with the world: the scene was being refurbished, with due deliberateness, for her to move on to a more adult plane of romance. She spent the night of her birthday dancing at the Coconut Grove, arriving in a white mink, part of the wardrobe that was MGM's anniversary gift.

Her parents' gift was a powder-blue Cadillac with a gold-plated ignition key. Once the photos had been taken, she considerately handed it back to them. She would stick with the old open-top Ford she had been given a couple of years ago. Rich but unspoilt was the message, though a remark she made might have had a few people wondering if there wasn't an edgy resentfulness beneath all this well-drilled ecstasy and obedience. Driving the old Ford convertible back and forth to the studio, she said, was the only time she could count on getting fresh air.

Critics were generally dismissive or censorious about *A Date With Judy* and *Julia Misbehaves* when they were released only a week apart, calling them 'silly', 'vacuous', 'trivial' or 'vulgar'. This reflected a national concern over the restlessness of teenage youth, or, in poor Greer Garson's case, a disbelief in the agelessness of actresses. But Elizabeth herself came in for the kind of praise that signified her independence of the quality of whatever picture she is in – the surest sign of incipient stardom. Archer Winston, in the *New York Post*, wrote: 'The time, the clichés and the silly chatter [of *A Date With Judy*] pass quickly when you begin to realize the roles she could now enact with enchantment.' The fan magazines agreed.

Photoplay featured Elizabeth in a two-page spread along with other actresses. All of them were her seniors by several years or more, though it would have been difficult to tell. Elizabeth Taylor, just turned sixteen, looked every well-groomed inch the equal of Jean Peters (twenty-one), Diana Lynn (twenty-one), Jane Powell (nineteen), Coleen Gray (twenty-five) and Barbara Bel Geddes (twenty-six). Sheilah Graham, the gossipy rival of Hedda and Louella, included Elizabeth in a gallery of 'Hollywood's Dangerous Women'. Other candidates were Ava Gardner, Jane Wyman, Rita Hayworth, Joan Crawford and Lana Turner. Tactfully, Mrs Graham didn't define 'dangerous' in any sense that would threaten the conventional stability of married life in Hollywood. It was simply meant to denote those whose 'wits, courage, determination and sex appeal give them the highest potential for succeeding in whatever they have made up their minds to do'. Well, maybe ... but the writer herself later admitted, 'Some eyebrows were raised at *Photoplay* when I included Liz and I was asked to make it clear that she was still a child. It was obvious to me that when you saw her in the studio commissary she was, in heart and mind, anything but child-like. It was her mother who still treated her, in public anyhow, like a child, but it was amusing to see how Liz over lunch would cease to "sit up straight" and "pay attention" and instead start to show off the amazing part of her above the table level and, until she was snapped back to reality by a slap on the wrist, begin to pose like the fully-fledged female stars at the adjacent tables. I sometimes thought it very provocative. There was an argument one day when she took out a lipstick and began applying it – but whether Sara Taylor thought it was a breach of social manners or a seductress's trick she'd picked up from some film she'd watched, I'm not sure. Elizabeth is suddenly getting a thrill out of the blatantly masculine admiration she meets. But she still has the crucifying candor of a child.'

But if Sheilah Graham was constrained by professional etiquette to give Elizabeth the benefit of the doubt, others weighed in with the crucifying candor of their own age group. 'Why doesn't someone wise Elizabeth Taylor up?' wrote Sally Winters, of Trenton, New Jersey, to her fan magazine. 'After all, she's only 16 years old, but she dresses or acts like she's 20 or so.' The gulf between the ages of sixteen and twenty is, to the teenage sensibility, a wide and profound one.

The studio itself was guilty of giving out confusing signals: perhaps it, too, was confused. Elizabeth, in a photo spread taken by the fashionable photographer Valezka, could pass for thirty with her hair drawn back close to her skull. And one picture of her, bosom thrust forward and stretching a tight, off-the-shoulder blouse, while she tilts her head back in a look of unashamed enjoyment of her own sexuality, must rank among the frankest erotic poses MGM permitted an up-and-coming star – and a legal minor, too – to be pictured in at this time.

Yet immediately after *Julia Misbehaves*, Elizabeth was assigned a role in a children's classic, *Little Women*, that confined her ripening womanhood to a period wardrobe and had no 'dangerous' features in the story. Even her raven hair was hidden beneath a blonde wig.

Now turning the clock back, so to speak, and reverting from the sophisticated modern miss who had caught teenagers' fancy to the mis-chievous tomboy Amy of Louisa M. Alcott's story, who enthuses over apple pie and goes to sleep wearing a clothes peg to straighten her nose, might not seem wise policy, until one appreciates that almost no Hollywood studio had a blueprint for star-making. Stars were working employees. Elizabeth was currently 'hot' and putting her into a new picture, whatever the story or period, was box-office insurance. It was really June Allyson's picture – she played Jo, at thirty-one! – but Eliz-abeth's recent contemporary roles might bring a dash of modernism into the period picture as a carry-over bonus. Moreover, she and Peter Lawford had made an attractive duo in *Julia Misbehaves*, and they repeated their romance in *Little Women*, with Elizabeth, ably embodying Amy's brattish determination to get her man, virtually stealing her sister's beau for herself.

Yes, even in nineteenth-century costume, Elizabeth proved that the role of a predatory minx was a becoming one.

Little Women began shooting in June 1948, and didn't finish until September. Sometime between those dates, Elizabeth acquired a beau of her own. His name was Glenn Davis.

Like almost everything else about her life on and off screen Elizabeth's boyfriend was a studio-made date. So it looks, in retrospect, anyhow, although it's probable that the arrangement didn't allow for the genuine degree of attachment that formed between Elizabeth and the young man of twenty-four. Davis was an army lieutenant, and a star in his own right and in his own world – the sports pages, not the movie columns. He had captained West Point's victorious baseball and football teams. He was not exactly a stranger to the movie world; the year before, he had starred with 'Doc' Blanchard, the co-captain of the academy football team, in a low-budget film about army life and athletics whose best asset was the pair's brilliant reputations. Elizabeth was playing touch football on the beach at Malibu when she first saw Davis coming towards her, accompanied by the ever-present MGM publicist.

The studio probably believed it was little more than a short-term made-to-measure romance that would yield both parties good press coverage – Davis was in Los Angeles for an exhibition game before shipping out for service in Korea. In retrospect, it looks as if young Davis had been written into Elizabeth's story, the way a character might have been written into the script for a heroine who hadn't yet met *the* man in her life, but needed ways of proving that, when she did, she would know what it was all about. Remember, up to now, Elizabeth had not spent a night by herself away from the family home, and scarcely a day that wasn't supervised by her mother or her employer.

Sara Taylor, though, later professed to take a more romantic view of that encounter on the sands. 'When I saw that frank, wonderful face, I thought, "This is the boy." I felt such a sense of relief. My [*sic*] worries were over.'

They had over half a dozen dates that summer, most of them officially arranged, some providing Elizabeth with valuable cross-over publicity, since Davis's athletic prowess pushed her into prominence on the sports pages where she would be seen by the kind of people who might never have paid to see her in films. She was very happy. Davis had a frank, open, unspoiled attitude and could be quite funny. Having a boyfriend after work while *Little Women*, her current film, provided her with a lover in the storyline, seemed to give her the best of both worlds. Davis presented her with a tiny gold football charm. She vowed to wear it around her neck, like the locket she had worn in *Cynthia*, and wait loyally for him to come back from Korea – that was what girls did in movies, wasn't it? There are some accounts suggesting an infatuation so torrid that Elizabeth tried to get Glenn Davis's foreign service postponed, or even cancelled, by persuading Uncle Howard Young to have a word with his close Republican crony President Eisenhower. Glenn Davis today emphatically denies any knowledge of this. 'I have no idea how that story arose. Elizabeth and I were very fond of each other, though of course it was all completely innocent. It wasn't quite the "great romance" that the newspapers made it out to be. We were simply young people and we wanted to have fun and we'd nothing else to do that summer.' Of course the press *did* see things differently; and as the stories and accompanying photos transformed the 'steady date' into a 'likely husband' and the 'accomplished actress' into a 'future wife', the two of them began to discover that marriages can be made in the media as well as in heaven, and sometimes faster. As the more impressionable partner, Elizabeth had it brought home to her, for the first time in her life, that the public's expectations were not to be easily denied. Moreover, the phenomenon of celebrities forced to play the public roles assigned to them – even when the roles are at variance with what they know to be the truth of the matter – begins to exert its own subtle influence. It may be difficult and unwelcome to have to break the illusion that has been fostered. And if one has begun to enjoy it, it may even be very attractive to play along with the fiction – and find it becoming fact.

Pushed by reporters to answer the one question they all thought they had a right to know, Elizabeth would fall back on the teasing half-truth: 'We're engaged to be engaged.' After that was printed, she would indeed have found it difficult to back out of an affair that had become public property. But then she was enjoying it. She gave no sign of wishing to break it off. After all, hadn't she been brought up to believe that if love is true enough and constant enough, it always leads to marriage?

9

CONSPIRACIES AND SUITORS

Few things alarmed a Hollywood studio of that era more than an approaching marriage commitment by one of its stars.

Elizabeth had just turned sixteen and, in all likelihood, would grow out of her infatuation before she was much older. But however remote the prospect of her marrying Glenn Davis, it was a distraction from the star build-up being contrived for her. It might even be a fatal interruption. What if she did marry him? Would she have the same appeal to her fans as Mrs Glenn Davis that she had as the campus flirt who made the boys' heads whirl and had girls copying the manipulative wiles they had seen her practise in *A Date With Judy*? At this time she was receiving more than nine hundred fan letters weekly, and scores of requests for personal appearances on campuses around the nation. Harvard University's freshman intake had just voted her 'The Girl We Would Never Lampoon' – a verdict that was to be reversed in years to come.

The studio could certainly manage the publicity such a wedding would reap, and make sure it enhanced their star. But what then? Suppose Elizabeth wanted to retire from the screen: could she be held to her contract? Very likely; but suppose she wanted to start a family? Children on the way were the greatest single hazard to an actress's career, for the Hollywood production machine was still running at full blast and stars were required to turn out just as many pictures as the studio thought them capable of fitting into the customary forty weeks of the year they were employed. Matrimony meant going off pay – and also, possibly, losing momentum, or, worse, the beauty and glamour that had gone with the premarital persona. The studio again acted quickly to safeguard its investment. It wasn't enough that Glenn Davis was thousands of miles away in Korea; Elizabeth was to be sent thousands of miles in the other direction.

In the event, it was ironic that the role which took Elizabeth Taylor to England in 1948 and away from a possibly unsuitable marriage should have been that of a wife whose husband is a Communist spy and, as if that were not enough, is attempting to murder her as well.

It has always been something of a mystery why Elizabeth should have been so calamitously miscast in *The Conspirator*. One explanation may be that MGM needed a film that could be shot abroad, thus making it difficult for Elizabeth and Glenn Davis to meet for several months. But Hedda Hopper has put forward another reason that makes a kind of sense, given Hollywood's predilection for remaking established hits. In her column a few months before, Hopper had called Elizabeth 'a potential younger Bergman'. Ingrid Bergman had won an Oscar four years earlier in the thriller *Gaslight*, itself a remake of Thorold Dickinson's British film of the same name that had been made in 1940. Bergman played a newly married wife who discovers that her husband (Charles Boyer) is conspiring to kill her. 'They thought Elizabeth and Robert Taylor would fit the same sort of roles in *The Conspirator*,' Hopper said to the director Victor Saville some time afterwards. They were to be proved very wrong. But that wasn't apparent then in the rush to get Elizabeth over to England.

Sending a minor to work abroad – the first time it had happened at MGM – raised problems with the Los Angeles Board of Education. There was also a flurry of concern over which passport the child should travel on. The studio at first favoured her using the British passport she legally possessed by reason of being born in England; this would mean that the American company wouldn't have to seek a work permit for her, with possible opposition from Equity, then a militant part of the film business in Britain. But the MGM legal department advised against this; it might make for difficulties later on, if Elizabeth wished to make a declaration of American citizenship when she was twenty-one. In any case, as she still had dual nationality, the question of a work permit needn't arise.

So she and her mother sailed for England aboard the *Queen Mary* in October 1948; and along with them sailed a white-haired schoolmarm called Miss Birtina Anderson, who had been appointed Elizabeth's tutor by the Los Angeles education authority. The child had thus to bear the burden of two strict duennas: her mother to look after her good behaviour and material welfare, and Miss Anderson to look after her English, algebra and history (in which she was lagging far behind). Study periods would be fitted in between the clinches with the duplicitous but of course desirable Robert Taylor.

Though officially still a schoolgirl, Elizabeth rated star treatment whenever she was not sitting in front of an exercise book. Orchids awaited her in her Claridge's suite, and a bouquet of red roses had been cabled in

Glenn Davis's name – so long as the romantic connection could be kept at a safe distance, it had its publicity value. She had brought twenty-four pieces of luggage with her. The film-star wardrobe was beginning to take shape, too: an Indian lamb top-coat in the fashionable ankle-length 'New Look' and a couple of evening dresses described as being 'of the will-power type' – i.e., strapless. Mother and daughter paid an early visit to Westminster Food Office to draw their ration books for the stay in England; Claridge's, one can safely assume, was able to supplement the austerity diet of post-war Britain.

Almost every despatch filed by reporters visiting the set of *The Conspirator* describes the odd contradiction of an apparently mature and beautiful young woman being held in Robert Taylor's arms one minute and the next – with the cry of 'Cut ... Print it' from Victor Saville – being reluctantly reclaimed by her lessons and turning into a schoolgirl again. Even the physical setting of her education reflected the schizoid world that Elizabeth was compelled to inhabit. 'You are looking through the fourth wall of a gentleman's house in Belgrave Square,' wrote a *Picture Post* reporter in an account that catches the sound of Elizabeth's emotional gears being crashed. 'A pretty dark girl in a long evening dress runs from the drawing room into the hall to take a telegram. She looks very young, but sophisticated – about eighteen perhaps.

'"Break for tea," shouts the director. Elizabeth Taylor puts down the telegram and walks through the fourth wall of the house in Belgravia, across the coils of rubber flex in front, to a prefabricated two-room shack. There her governess ... is waiting to take her on with her history lesson.' Her mother, meanwhile, 'rested vigilantly' in the outer room.

Yet there are signs that Sara's control was no longer absolute. 'Elizabeth gave me the feeling that she was tired of being watched,' said Victor Saville. And a magazine photographer, posing mother and child against a background of the Changing of the Guard, had to remind Elizabeth that what was wanted was a family twosome, not a pin-up – could she look just a little less provocative? On the set, however, according to Robert Taylor, 'she did as she was told. No trouble at all. When they told her to kiss me, she kissed me. All I had to teach her was to powder down her lips.' But it wasn't Elizabeth's lips that gave MGM cause for concern when the first rushes were flown over to Hollywood from the studios at Elstree: her bath-robe had dropped open during a struggle with Robert Taylor, revealing more than the censors might think fit for any woman to show, never mind a precociously mature child.

A cable to Victor Saville ordered him to retake the scene without delay – and to have the original negative destroyed. Elizabeth laughed at the fuss that her brief exposure had caused. Although she was 'no trouble at all' for the moment, the signs were growing that she was beginning to savour the power of her beauty and her bountiful endowment. Precisely what kind of power it might be, and how she could make it serve her, were still matters beyond her complete understanding. But it wouldn't be long before experience, and experiment, began supplying her with the answers.

Hopes were high for *The Conspirator* when shooting began on 9 November 1948. After a week or two, Ben Goetz cabled Hollywood enthusiastically: 'Both Taylors a sensational team and Elizabeth Taylor so beautiful and so capable there's no doubt she will develop into one of the greatest stars the screen has known.'

Soon, however, there was unease about the way the film was turning out. Elizabeth's voice hadn't the power or character she needed for her first dramatic role. What fitted campus musicals and family comedies didn't convincingly match the emotions released by discovering that her husband is under Communist Party orders to kill her, which he first tries to do during a duck shoot and then, on learning she is about to denounce him, by an attack on her at home. The dialogue is risibly unsubtle (Elizabeth: 'You're a traitor and a spy.' – Robert Taylor: 'Just remember you're my wife.') and the message that Party membership breaks up your marriage falls somewhat short of the threat to world peace that Communism posed in 1948. There is one tiny but freakish coincidence in the movie: Elizabeth's character is called Melinda. Donald MacLean, the British traitor who fled to Russia with Guy Burgess three years after *The Conspirator*, had a wife of the same name.

MGM didn't release the film for over a year. This wasn't due simply to its dramatic deficiencies. The studio found itself running into trouble on the wider scene of diplomatic relations. Was it an anti-Russian film? The State Department was concerned, despite a soothing interview that the producer Arthur Hornblow had given prior to shooting. '[It] is only a study in treachery by an Englishman ... The Russians with whom he works in England are not traitors.' But the British censors weren't mollified. 'The diplomatic situation is such,' said an MGM internal memo, 'that the depiction of Russia in an unfavourable light may be banned [by the censors in England].' There was also concern over references to actual British traitors – the Anglo-Irish William Joyce (also known as 'Lord Haw Haw' for his broadcasts from Nazi Germany), John Amory, the treasonous son of a British Cabinet minister, and Norman Baillie-Stewart, a Guardsman (like the Taylor character), imprisoned in the Tower of London for five years in the 1930s. The MGM memo continued: 'While these people may fairly be referred to as traitors, a small but powerful minority might create difficulties if it is *suggested* that they sold out their countries [*sic*] for money. It must not be overlooked that the Baillie-

Stewarts are a respected family and that Amory's father is a public man of good reputation and a leader of the Conservative Party and may again be a Cabinet minister. A reference to Amory might be considered as a reference to the father ... [it is suggested] you confine your references to Lord Haw Haw.' Most of these specific risks had been eliminated from the film by the time shooting began, but the memory of the famous libel case in the 1930s, when an MGM production had inadvertently libelled a living member of the former Russian aristocracy by suggesting she had been raped by Rasputin, still haunted the studio. It didn't want a repetition of that costly episode by rubbing the sensibilities of some powerful British families the wrong way.

All this, quite as much as the lacklustre production, accounts for MGM's lengthy delay in releasing 'Elizabeth Taylor's First Adult Love Story'. The studio, quite simply, fell out of love with it.

Whatever its failings as a film, making *The Conspirator* had a considerable influence on Elizabeth at this impressionable stage of her life. For the first time, she was playing a grown-up woman. Though she was considerably less mature than her appearance suggested, the film gave her the vicarious sense that she could cope with the vicissitudes of married life – even life married to a traitor – and survive to tell the tale and begin all over again. She admitted later that, once in the role, she felt she could handle anything. A fusion of this kind between an actor and the role that he or she is performing isn't that uncommon on stage or screen. Nor is it necessarily ominous: most performers soon shake it off and resume life as it has to be lived between jobs. However, some don't find it easy to dissociate themselves from the feelings they simulate, and the role may add its own consciously felt or unconscious layers of vicarious living to their off-screen life. Sometimes it enhances it: occasionally, it can create trauma and even tragedy. The case of Vivien Leigh is frequently quoted. She always maintained that playing Blanche DuBois in *A Streetcar Named Desire* on stage and screen 'tipped me into madness'. She was already a manic-depressive, piteously fighting the tightening hold that such uncontrollable moods had on her life and personality, and feeling the pressures upon a dedicated actress to connect with emotions in Blanche that lay too close for comfort to her own state of periodic insanity. It undoubtedly contributed to Vivien's unhappiness and instability.

Hers is an extreme case, fortunately. But even with an actress like Elizabeth Taylor, who was so often to express a detached and sceptical view of her own work, the screen supplied a range of experience of life – or, at any rate, life as the movies and the moviegoers viewed it – that seemed to fuse with her own character and temperament. Her later life often produced astonishingly close parallels to the films she made, and some of the films, in turn, reflect the kind of crisis she has herself been through. There are various ways of explaining this phenomenon, some as banal as the desire of potential producers to secure her services for a film by offering her an opportunity to relive in fantasy the experience she had already been through in reality. Viewed overall, however, accepting or seeking autobiography in the make-believe – which accounts for a great deal of her celebrity, if not her notoriety – is a strong, recurring feature of Elizabeth's life on and off screen; it is one we shall have to reckon with frequently.

Here she was, not long past sixteen, playing Robert Taylor's wife, an experience she was later reported to have commented upon – crudely maybe, but tellingly – with the remark, 'How can I concentrate on my education when [he] keeps sticking his tongue down my throat?'

Taylor himself innocently contributed to accelerating her feelings of maturity. Between camera set-ups, he used to return to his dressing room and, while Elizabeth was doing lessons with her governess next door, he would put in the time writing long letters to his wife, the actress Barbara Stanwyck. He later read parts of them to Elizabeth, praising Barbara for her love, steadfastness and professionalism. Elizabeth had never met Stanwyck, but she digested this almost daily diet of husbandly praise and was impressed by the bond between the couple: it was exactly the romantic match she'd been taught to expect, and it touched strongly on the feelings she still cherished for the faraway Glenn Davis. To have this paragon of husbands simulating love for her in *The Conspirator* had a stimulating effect that outlasted the role and indeed dimmed what a clearer perception of Robert Taylor's part should have made obvious – that love can turn destructive, in life as on screen. Ironically, Taylor and Stanwyck separated very soon afterwards.

Writing of this period of her life forty years later, Elizabeth admitted that she thought she knew all the tricks. 'But ... the tricks,' she added, as if making a belated discovery, 'could not be applied in real life.'

Elizabeth finished the film in great pain as a result of the injury she suffered during shooting. It was being slammed up against a landing wall on the set in a scene with Robert Taylor that worsened Elizabeth's already serious spinal injury. A technician recalls entering her dressing room and finding her stretched out full-length on the floor. He immediately thought she'd fainted; then he saw she had placed a couple of schoolbooks in the small of her back, trying to relieve the pressure on her bruised spine.

Her fortitude was rewarded with a trip across the Channel to Paris after *The Conspirator* finished shooting in February 1949. At first MGM refused to let her risk the influenza infection then raging in the French capital. So she went around the studio with a petition collecting signatures from high and low, eked out with a few other notably independent-minded celebrities like 'Scarlett O'Hara' and 'Lord Byron', and promising a) to be a good girl, b) to shun all germs and c) not to contract even a runny nose. She and Sara were shopping in the Rue Royale, buying a few of the 'hand-made pink unmentionables' that she'd coyly mentioned in the petition, when she noticed a crowd outside spilling into the road and causing traffic congestion. At first she thought someone had been injured. Then she saw the people were facing her way. They were squinting into the shop. They were trying to catch a glimpse of her. 'It feels so strange to be stared at in French,' she said to Sara. As *bons mots* go, a modest one maybe; but it marks Elizabeth Taylor's first face-to-face encounter with the unsettling and even dangerous implications of international stardom.

Her burgeoning sexuality was literally thrust in front of her around this time by the experience of sitting for the photographer Philippe Halsman, who had been commissioned to take a seventeenth birthday picture of her for *Life* magazine. 'You have bosoms,' he barked at her, 'so stick them out.' He also told her that one side of her face – the one he preferred – had a much younger look to it than the other. Predictably, perhaps, Elizabeth liked the other better. The *Life* photo is a frank preview of a sex goddess, sensually inviting, yet protectively distanced, her half-bared breasts like well-filled moneybags beneath her satin gown. Its mammary emphasis was characteristic of the post-war era of fashion marketing and mass-market magazine publishing, which had shifted the erogenous interest upwards from the legs. And it wasn't surprising that Halsman's photo should catch the eye of a man who had pioneered the shift by developing a cantilevered bra for Jane Russell to wear in his erotic Western *The Outlaw*.

Howard Hughes was already a man with a mania for secrecy, but not yet the hypochondriac recluse he became. He had dated Ginger Rogers, Lana Turner and Ava Gardner, among other screen stars. But since the appalling injuries received in a test-flight crash in 1946, he preferred to begin his courtships through intermediaries and then let his vast fortune speak for him more eloquently than his own tongue-tied nature could manage. As soon as he saw Elizabeth's picture in *Life*, Hughes was smitten; but, typically, he began to stalk her indirectly, by having a couple of paintings bought in his name from Francis Taylor's gallery, and then intimating that he hoped the Taylors would meet him socially. A client as rich and famous as Hughes couldn't be denied. The Taylor family spent a weekend as his guests at a hotel in Reno. Hughes reportedly asked for Elizabeth's hand in marriage, promising a six-figure dowry. 'But he left her cold,' says Richard Brooks, one of the directors who came to know Elizabeth best. 'She simply couldn't envision him as a romantic suitor.'

Despite his wealth, Hughes was shabby-looking and a dour table companion. He didn't even ask Elizabeth to dance. Mostly, he talked money. While her parents may have been interested to hear the figure he put on her dowry, Elizabeth was reminded of those other 'old men' – Hughes at this time was forty-four – who sat in the front office at MGM and judged people by the money they made for the studio. Moreover, Hughes had paid nine million dollars in 1945 for the ailing RKO film studio, and Elizabeth may well have suspected a business motive in this anti-romantic individual who brought her none of the little gifts that a young man would, but preferred to open his chequebook to her father. Her bride-price was not for barter; she gave Howard Hughes the brush-off.

In any case, a much more glamorous suitor had emerged – one she could see in terms of a romantic movie hero – during her birthday celebrations in February at Uncle Howard Young's estate in Florida.

William Pawley, Jr was twenty-eight and handsome in the manner of Robert Stack, the square-jawed actor who had been Elizabeth's catch in *A Date With Judy*. His family's wealth came from a bus transit company, but was solid enough to hold its own against the old money in Florida (and nowadays, of course, would probably be regarded as old money itself). He was an ex-serviceman – he had flown wartime escort patrols – and he showed a flair for business. The Pawleys were soundly Republican – Pawley Sr had been US ambassador to Brazil – hence their friendship with the Howard Youngs.

Pawley Jr would have made a very attractive son-in-law for the Taylors. In Elizabeth's eyes, too, he was Hollywood's ideal of an eligible bachelor. The only trouble was the rest of America. In *its* eyes, she was already spoken for by Glenn Davis.

Rich man versus (relatively) poor man: the story line was a cliché, but none the less real for that. And it played well, too, when Glenn Davis suddenly turned up in Miami, on leave from Korea, and caused much commotion among the photographers eager to record Elizabeth giving her wartime beau his first landfall kiss. For some reason, Mrs Taylor wasn't all that anxious to have a public record of the event. But her plea for the couple's privacy was ignored in the mêlée. Even Elizabeth was irritated by the invasive hubbub – one of the earliest of many future occasions when unwelcome publicity was, well, unwelcomed. 'Maybe I should have fallen for a busboy, or something, then the whole thing wouldn't cause so much attention,' she said. A naive sentiment if ever there was one – as if it was her boyfriend's status alone that caused the flashbulbs to pop.

The Pawleys threw a party for Elizabeth and Glenn. Maybe this was generous of them; but maybe it was a shrewd move, too. The young West Pointer in his simple suit of army khaki, with a modest bank account – his service pay had been supplemented by a starring role in a minor movie, *The Spirit of West Point*, that enshrined the academy's ethos of honour and athletics – was brought face to face with the material affluence of the Pawley clan. Nice guy though he undoubtedly was, young Glenn was outclassed. Moreover, he found Elizabeth had changed – no longer the breathy campus girl out of the movies, but a poised young debutante. She accepted his present of a string of Japanese cultured pearls, but he never got to present the engagement ring he had carried all the way from Seoul. He left a week later for Los Angeles and in the last few months of their relationship, he acted as a West Coast escort for Elizabeth, taking Pawley's place when business held the latter in Miami, and squiring Elizabeth to the Academy Awards in March 1949. They still made a handsome couple; but as *Time* magazine said in its issue with Elizabeth on the cover, 'Suddenly, it was all over and Glenn was gone ... It seemed to friends of the family that Elizabeth's mother felt no pain.' Sara endorsed this: 'Like any young girl, [Elizabeth] wore his gold football. But she was never engaged to him.' Davis finally left to finish serving his country in Korea. Later he married (and divorced) the starlet Terry Moore, then turned businessman, and later worked for the *Los Angeles Times* promotions department where he put his sports star past to good use. Today he lives quietly in California with a new wife and family, oddly enough in almost the same wealthy desert community that houses Sara Sothern Taylor. He had served America dutifully. But the service for which some remember him best was helping Elizabeth Taylor grow up in the eyes of America.

10

THE FIRST DENT

This time there *was* an engagement. On 5 June 1949 Sara announced that her daughter would marry William Pawley, Jr. No date was set for the wedding, though, and her fiancé's age – at twenty-eight he was eleven years older than Elizabeth – was discreetly omitted, too. Sara said that Elizabeth's education came first; in other words, she must have a diploma as well as a ring. Quite clearly, the normal order of a young girl's progress into life was becoming unusually disordered in Elizabeth's case. She had had no experience of reconciling the different demands now being made on her – not least by MGM, which kept her working at full stretch – and all too soon she was being asked which came first, career or marriage? The future she envisaged for herself was found to lie somewhat in the realms of fantasy.

Where would she and her husband make their home? She replied: in Beverly Hills, when she was working; in Miami, when she wasn't. She assumed Pawley would fall in with this. Oh, yes, and she looked forward to being known as 'Elizabeth Pawley'. But by all the rules of stardom, that certainly is not the name she would have been known by, wherever domiciled. Whether it ever crossed her fiancé's mind that he might be known in Hollywood as 'Mr Elizabeth Taylor' needs no answer. Bill Pawley might have resembled film-star material, but movie stardom never dazzled him. He looked to a wife to provide him with home and children, a supportive community life and a well-run household. In other words, a man and his career came first. His desire to settle down with a wife coincided with Elizabeth's impatience to assert her independence of her family – and, indeed, of her studio. 'What I'd *really* like to play,' she told a magazine at this time, 'is a monster – a hellion.' It didn't sound a good omen for a marriage in which the man made the rules.

They had made mutual promises to have no dates with anyone else when work kept them apart. Elizabeth was the first to break her promise. She felt such a wallflower, she said, sitting out the dances at parties in Beverly Hills. It is probable that she also discovered that her fiancé could be very possessive. Hedda Hopper is the source for a story that has Elizabeth on a visit to Pawley's Florida home in early September. She went off on some errand with a male friend of his and got back later than he or they expected. Hopper reported: 'He hustled [Elizabeth] into his car and roared away . . .' Taking out his anger on the gas pedal, said Hopper, showed a side to her fiancé she had never suspected: a high temper and a dogmatic disposition. Whether or not this is so, Elizabeth could now show her own temper to someone outside her immediate family without the necessity of writing a 'sorry' note. A strong-willed man encourages a similar response in a woman, if she has a disposition for it. Elizabeth needed an outlet for all the pressure she was under. An engagement mightn't be considered a conventional opportunity for exploring your differences with your suitor, but now that she was being forced to define herself in a role she so far had no experience of, Elizabeth's will-power was starting to shape her own decisions.

Yet there was a more powerful if intangible presence laying prior claim to her: her movie career. MGM had announced that marriage prospects wouldn't change Elizabeth's contract commitments. She hadn't been allowed to join Pawley in Florida that summer until it was decided whether she was needed for retakes on *The Conspirator*, though the studio pretty much despaired of the film. Then it attempted to send her abroad again for a rematch with Robert Taylor, who was making *Quo Vadis* in Rome; it was almost as if obstacles were being put in the way of an early marriage. But the Los Angeles education board refused to sanction another lengthy foreign trip for the girl who had everything – except a graduation parchment. So she was put into a potboiler called, appropriately enough, *The Big Hangover*, which began shooting on 8 August 1949, and must have made for a weary summer. A cross between *Harvey* and *The Lost Weekend*, it starred Van Johnson as a junior lawyer in Elizabeth's father's firm. He is also an alcoholic and hears his dog talking to him. She turns amateur analyst, sobers him up – though first she has to join in a duet with Van Johnson and his dog – and substitutes an addiction to public service for one to alcohol. It is essentially a stooge role and she plays it dutifully – cool and managerial in lace-fronted blouse and cuffs which are replaced, once the cure gets under way, by a professional-looking shirt and tie. Only an occasional line hints at the more complex nature of a girl who always goes for social misfits and feels concern when they turn out to be a little too noble for her liking.

Even before she began work on *The Big Hangover*, MGM informed her that she was to be loaned out to Paramount for a version of Theodore Dreiser's novel *An American Tragedy*, to be directed by George Stevens. For once, MGM wouldn't earn a cent from the deal. In exchange for Elizabeth, it was to get John Lund from Paramount to star in *The Duchess of Idaho*. This would turn out to be one of the most one-sided exchanges of talent in film history.

And then she could get married, perhaps? No, after the Paramount film, which was to begin shooting on 21 September 1949, she was to step smartly back on to MGM's lot for a film called, not entirely coincidentally, *Father of the Bride*. But when would they find the time to fix the date for her own wedding? As each film assignment rolled up like endless screen credits, Pawley found his wedding prospects receding. Marriage, to his way of thinking, was inseparable from settling down. It had become clear to him that a housewife's role for Elizabeth didn't look like natural casting. Like it or not, the world that had claimed her at the age of ten was not going to be easily parted from her future. He flew to Los Angeles in September and, ironically, escorted Elizabeth to the wedding of one of her few intimate friends, Jane Powell, at which she was a bridesmaid; then, while Elizabeth went on with the wedding party to the Mocambo, Pawley left for his father's estate in Virginia. He was on the farm when Hedda Hopper announced his engagement was over – in such crucial matters, Hedda took precedence over even the would-be bride's mother. Pawley confirmed it: 'We talked it over last night [September 19 or 20] by telephone and decided, because of circumstances over which neither of us has any control, to end [it].' He still had a faint hope, he said, that 'the thing between Elizabeth and me might eventually work itself out'.

Hardly was the hope expressed, than it expired. The day after the engagement had been annulled – in some cases in the same edition that had carried the news – a photograph appeared of Elizabeth at the Mocambo. She had made no secret of her distress and had even burst into tears. The singer Vic Damone, who was topping the bill, sat down beside her between numbers in an effort to cheer her up. The photographers got their picture. People who had read the understandably rueful statement from Elizabeth's ex-fiancé now saw what seemed like a picture of Elizabeth Taylor making merry at a night club with a crooner. They drew from it the moral of a jilted man and a fickle woman. Two broken engagements – to Glenn Davis and now Bill Pawley – within months of each other. And the girl in question apparently not giving a damn! Elizabeth's image as the ideal American girl received its first dent.

The powerful magazine *Photoplay* was particularly embarrassed by the broken engagement. It had a three-month lead time – the gap between going to press and appearing on the newsstands – and it was most displeased to have to come out in October 1949, with an article by Ruth Brigham headed 'That Young Magic', which designated 1949 as Elizabeth's jackpot year and quoted her as saying, 'it brought me my first adult role in *The Conspirator*. And it brought me Bill.' Fan magazines take such embarrassments personally and ill-temperedly, as if the star had committed a breach of trust. This is understandable. They are exposed to the ridicule of readers with whom it is all-important to have credibility – to know what's going to happen before it does, not to have to apologize for what hasn't happened when they said it would. An erring movie star is not forgiven – or, at least, not for an issue or two.

Thus Elizabeth incurred a backlash that deeply upset her and her mother. 'If I'd known it would turn out like this, I would not have allowed Elizabeth to go into pictures,' said Sara. 'If I were the kind of person they write me up to be, I'd hate myself,' said Elizabeth. The public view of her as a woman who goes from man to man, discarding each one after she has taken her pleasure, owes its origins to this coincidence of circumstances.

There were international repercussions. Over in London, the chorus of disapproval was led by the *Sunday Pictorial*, in an article that proposed, 'somebody should administer a series of resounding smacks behind the bustle of her latest Paris creation.' (This was a sneaky attempt to wing two birds with one stone, by linking Elizabeth to the still much derided New Look being imported into Britain from Dior's cutting rooms.) The writer went on sanctimoniously: '[Elizabeth Taylor] is a living argument against the employment of children in the studios.'

For the first time in her life, Elizabeth was experiencing the novel and unpleasant sensation of her public image coming under attack for reasons that she couldn't associate with her private self. She felt violated in a way she couldn't understand. Why so much hatred? What had she done? Who were these assailants? How could they really know the truth? It was worse than being 'sent to Coventry' as a child – and that denial of love had been bad enough. Now the rejection was accompanied by a clamour for punishment. The media's intrusiveness had hitherto been tempered by their collusive understanding with the studios which threatened to deny them access to the stars if ever they 'dished the dirt' – or at least if they dished it before the studios had extracted the payload from it. But the fiasco of Elizabeth's engagement had been a public event. It had left her feeling unshielded and sullied. For once she was glad to return to the security of MGM and the shelter of life as it was lived in the movies.

PART TWO

· · ·

A Star Is Made

11

THE SUN AND THE STARS

Fortunately for Elizabeth's smarting sensibilities, powerful balm was to hand. *A Place in the Sun* was the film that made her an international star.

Theodore Dreiser's original novel, published in 1916 and already adapted for the stage and filmed once before, in 1931, was the story of a poor boy who murders the factory girl he's made pregnant so that there'll be no bar to his marrying a rich and attractive upper-class girl. He pays for the crime by going to the electric chair. Dreiser had portrayed American capitalism as a social villain, making the youth indifferent to human life and love in his envious reach for material comfort and success. But Hollywood was under attack in 1949. The House Un-American Activities Committee was accusing the film industry, or left-wing members of it, of Communist sympathies. No studio wanted its trademark on a film attacking American conservatism, especially as the capitalist values were Hollywood's own. So Dreiser's original title, *An American Tragedy*, was changed to a new one that emphasized opportunity, not tragedy – *A Place in the Sun*. The blame was shifted from the dehumanizing effect of big business on to the more pardonable weakness of the flesh in a single individual. Clyde Griffith – his name in the film was changed to George Eastman – could have been any American boy engaged in the commendable pursuit of life, liberty, happiness and profit. The story was updated and rendered even more palatable by turning the murder into a plausible accident by drowning – and placing the accent of interest less on the tiresome factory girl and more on the seductive society girl who represents the American dream. The factory itself, by the way, ceased to be a dreary place that made shirts and collars; now it turned out bathing suits whose all-American contours were emblematic of sex, wealth and leisure in the consumer society of the 1950s.

George Stevens has said that he selected Elizabeth Taylor without ever having seen a foot of any film she had made. Maybe so; but he knew so well what he wanted in whoever played the part that the casting search would have led him almost straight to her. He wanted: 'Not so much a real girl as the girl on the candy-box cover, the beautiful girl in the yellow Cadillac convertible that every American boy sometime or other thinks he can marry.'

Judged by these standards, Elizabeth was a dream come true. The roles in her MGM films released up to then – the studio was still brooding on *The Conspirator* and *The Big Hangover* – all exhibited her beauty, privilege, self-confidence and, most important for Stevens's film, her virginity. If Angela Vickers, as her character was called, had one tantalizing, intangible quality among her other worldly attributes, it was the sense she radiated that she was saving herself for the right man. In this, too, Elizabeth was a perfect choice. Her two broken romances amply testified to her desirability and elusiveness. If Angela tempted men, it wasn't by her behaviour, but simply because she personified sex in its most glamorous form, waiting for the right man to unwrap it. That, too, was Elizabeth's current status.

Indeed her first appearance in the film is as unreal as a vision, standing in the drawing-room of the rich Eastmans, wearing a white mink stole over a low-cut cocktail dress with a single string of pearls – and totally ignoring Montgomery Clift, as the poor but handsome side of the Eastman family, cringing in his thirty-five-dollar suit. Just coming up to eighteen, Elizabeth had a peerless young beauty. She also, for the first time, had a director who knew how to use it.

When George Stevens had sent Montgomery Clift the screenplay and told him who his leading lady was, the actor had asked sarcastically, 'Who the hell is Elizabeth Taylor?'

Clift's self-absorption was perhaps pardonable. At twenty-nine, he had established himself swiftly and effortlessly as a star, with Howard Hawks's *Red River* and Fred Zinnemann's *The Search* already on release, *The Big Lift* (a docudrama on the Berlin airlift) about to open and William Wyler's *The Heiress* just completed. He was a practitioner of the Method style that Hollywood reluctantly accepted – its emphasis on the actor's ego threw grit into the well-oiled studio production machine – in the hope it would bring a transfusion of new blood to the ranks of ageing stars. He had immediately appealed to the hurts, anxieties, confusions and romantic agony of the post-war generation. Fan clubs sprang up spontaneously across the country. Despite his neurotically shy nature, Clift was profiled, interviewed and physically pursued. At the time, he was rated a much bigger talent than Elizabeth Taylor. Yet he was far more insecure, already on the milder tranquillizers. In short: nervous company.

What he and his co-star found they had in common was the wish to escape from their parents. In spite of his age, Clift had only recently set himself up in an apartment of his own – Elizabeth hadn't even managed that – and almost at once, as if in need of a mother-figure, he had put himself in the hands of his drama coach, Mira Rostova, who rehearsed him in exhaustive detail, aiding and abetting his compulsive research into all aspects of the role he was to play. To some, it seemed as if he was seeking sanctuary rather than enlightenment, and feared the painful self-exposure of the actual filming – something that held no terrors at all for Elizabeth, who *never* researched any role she was assigned but trusted to pure instinct. Sara had long since abandoned the hand signals she used to give her daughter on the set.

Elizabeth had a barely containable need to free herself from Sara's continuing constraints. 'My goddamn mother,' some recalled hearing her say. Her increasingly free and forceful use of expletives also testified to her impatience to be free of the disciplining conventions imposed by home and studio. She admired Monty Clift for being an 'independent', for turning down the same kind of seven-year 'slave' contract she had had to sign, and for making Louis B. Mayer angry at his insolence.

Both stars were somewhat on the small side physically – but it was the sort of stature that a movie camera magnifies benignly into a larger-than-life image. Their strongly arched eyebrows and riveting eyes might have made some people take them for brother and sister. Clift even suffered from the same affliction of excess body hair that had given Elizabeth some embarrassment in her adolescent years.

She did not know he was a homosexual. He didn't make amorous advances to her, but it would have been hard for him to have done so with her mother present. From the moment they met, however, they established an unspoken understanding regarding everything they'd missed in life and could make up for by a friendship that was all the stronger for being sexless. Clift showed her a cuddly affection and she wrote him a few love notes expressing a girlish crush. He showed them to his male lover of the time, not in mockery, but with a childish delight at the 'normal' tenderness expressed in Elizabeth's plain round handwriting.

It was Paramount's idea to pair them off in public at the Los Angeles premiere of *The Heiress*, figuring the synergy would help both it and *A Place in the Sun*. Mira Rostova rode with them in the studio limousine and recalled Elizabeth's swear-words and unflattering references to her mother.

Inside Grauman's Chinese Theater, Elizabeth got the first shock in her relationship with this complex young star. As he viewed his performance,

Clift cowered lower and lower in his seat. This was strange to her. She viewed her own performances as simply a job she had done. To discover that someone could be painfully, physically involved with his acting, unavailingly willing it to become better as each sequence came and went – such a degree of commitment intrigued her. Afterwards, Clift kept repeating 'I'm so awful, Bessie Mae. I'm so awful.' 'Bessie Mae' was a nickname for her that Clift coined on the spot, the device of an insecure individual who liked linking people to him by such intimate little knots of childish possessiveness. Clift's nature appealed to the child in Elizabeth; she took him on trust and felt safe to let her guard drop.

George Stevens took the film unit to Lake Tahoe, in northern California, around the middle of October 1949, so that he could shoot location scenes before the weather worsened. Even so, it was so cold that newly fallen snow had to be hosed off the ground to restore the look of high summer. Stevens never let the discomfort of his players worry him unduly. He believed in keeping them on their creative edge. Early on, he ordered a set-up in which Elizabeth and Clift would strip off down to their swimwear and run frolicking into the lake. Clift refused to disrobe, perhaps embarrassed by his body hair. So Elizabeth alone appeared in a swimsuit, scampered playfully into the water, ran back and splashed her reluctant companion. Mrs Taylor threw a fit. Her daughter was menstruating, she told Stevens crossly. After a few more takes of the scene were ordered, she rushed Elizabeth back to their hotel and kept her confined to her room for three days. 'She'll never be able to have babies if this goes on,' she rebuked Stevens.

Shelley Winters, who played the poor factory girl, sympathized with Elizabeth, though reluctantly, being envious of her beauty and smart wardrobe for the part. But she saw the girl's independence strengthening, perhaps because she now had an affinity with a loner like Monty Clift. 'She was longing to have her own home and get away from her parents,' Shelley Winters later wrote. She also noticed, with some surprise, that Elizabeth was so much in thrall to her family that it had never occurred to her that, with the money she was making, she could well afford her own home or apartment as soon as she was eighteen. 'Instead, she thought she had to have a husband and a huge wedding.' She was in thrall to romantic convention as well.

The twenty-seven-year-old Winters picked up at least one tip from this girl, which showed how well she tended to her own effects. Elizabeth taught her to use the little steel eyelash-curler she herself applied so deftly. 'It'll open your eyes wider, Shelley,' she said.

How is it that Elizabeth came to discover how much more there was to her talents than any earlier film had managed to reach? Certainly by emulating Monty Clift: but also by trusting George Stevens. These two were her mental and emotional tutors.

Stevens rehearsed his stars with unbroken concentration, usually on a set cleared of any unwanted crew. His method resembled the shooting of a silent film. In important scenes, like the grand party where Clift first talks to Elizabeth, he obliged his players to express what the characters might be feeling without any dialogue at all – just by 'thinking' the emotions. It was a technique that Clift often practised, but it was alien to Elizabeth. Her previous directors, working tightly within studio schedules, had simply shot the script, unable to allow stars the indulgence to research their emotions. Now she had to make the effort to 'edit' what she was feeling, and bring herself up to pitch. Music helped. Stevens played the pre-recorded Franz Waxman score – another silent film technique that assisted the emotions to show themselves in performance. Sara's old set of hand signals was replaced by something more organic in feeling. Though Stevens had banned Clift's teacher Mira Rostova from the set, she still took him through his part in his dressing room. Elizabeth was sometimes present as an absorbed spectator; sometimes, too, as a participant in their scenes. Clift would even mime her role, displaying with bisexual finesse the feelings he was otherwise wary of allowing to show in public.

Elizabeth was thus awakened to what acting could create, when a worth beyond the production process was the aim. It was like being in love, she has said; it was contagious. 'When [Monty Clift] would start to shake, I would start to shake ... Only two actors I know ... give to the degree that it's almost a physical thing, like an umbilical cord, an electricity that goes back and forth.' One was Clift, the other would be Richard Burton.

Off the set, though, Elizabeth was the stronger partner, despite the ten-year age gap between them. She was as sure now of her sex appeal as Clift was insecure about his. When he was unresponsive to that side of her, she didn't feel rejected; she treated him with a protective sympathy. Stevens didn't miss any of this. Often rewriting the dialogue the night before he shot the scenes, he came to recruit something of his stars' own relationship into his direction. It isn't just the Gatsby-like aura of a rich girl surrounding Elizabeth that makes her the dominant partner in the film, the girl who leads, manipulates and, with her own sexual interest aroused by her hesitant lover, captures and at the same time comforts him. The different world that Clift's character is introduced into is the one in which a girl sizes him up sexually and then bestows an almost maternal affection on him, alternately arousing and lulling him. This was all part of both players' natures, even before it emerged in their performances.

Elizabeth in the film grows more possessive as she becomes more enamoured of Clift. This was the schooling for many of her later romances. First, there is the initial shy seductive glance up from under those enormous lashes; then she mutates into the choosy sort of girl, signifying her nature by picking through the cocktail canapés and rejecting the ones that don't please her, exploding a champagne cork like a starter's pistol and slyly mocking Clift's awkwardness: 'Did you promise to be a good boy – not to waste your time on girls?' A line spoken like a 'little mother'.

George Stevens had been a photographer before graduating to direction; it was one of Clift's complaints that his director tended to see everything through a viewfinder. But Stevens made his technique serve his instinct about his players. Without telling them what he was doing, he 'edited' them in the camera while shooting, letting an expression, a feature, the angle of a head, represent the fuller scene they thought he was recording. Elizabeth had more close-ups in *A Place in the Sun* than in any previous film or many subsequent ones. Her full beauty swims into sensuous close-up as she dances with Clift, the mole on her right cheek, a natural beauty mark, throwing the delicacy of the flesh into luminous relief by its deliberate blemish.

When she saw the rushes – as Stevens insisted his stars did – she picked up the emotional clue right away. She began responding as he wished her to: tenderly, but managerially, maternally. Clift becomes a child-lover with whom, her head on his shoulder, she can half-joke: 'I'll make your breakfast for you every morning, so that you can sleep late.'

For later scenes, Stevens advised her to change her vocal tones, to move into a huskier register to show concern mingled with desire.

If Monty Clift hadn't been her co-star, it's possible her concentration would have flagged. His dedication made a deep impression on her. She was used to other stars hanging the character they were playing in the closet when they knocked off work. Clift kept his on like a second skin, even going to spend a night on Death Row at San Quentin prison to work himself into the mood for George Eastman's long walk to the electric chair at the end of the film. 'It was the first time I ever considered *acting*,' she was to write. Occasionally, however, the leap into a sophistication of character and motive gave her quite a jolt.

Stevens confessed himself 'a tremendous believer in the hazard that goes with not knowing quite what you're going to do'. That feeling overwhelmed Elizabeth one morning when he handed her a freshly written page of dialogue for her and Clift to whisper to each other during one romantically charged scene on a balcony. Stevens reported: 'The little lady said, "Forgive me, what the hell is that?"' Elizabeth was startled and indignant at the lines she had to speak.

It was the moment in the film when George Eastman, guilt-ridden by the knowledge his working-class girlfriend is pregnant by him, still clings to Angela and her dream world. 'Oh, Angela,' he murmurs, dry-lipped, 'if only I could tell you how much I love you ... if only I could tell you all.' Angela pulls him gently but strongly towards her. 'Tell mama ... tell mama all,' she coaxes, as if he were a child unburdening himself on her bosom. That 'mama' was what threw Elizabeth; it was as if she was stepping into her mother's shoes. Stevens patiently explained that what he wanted 'wasn't just some meeting and hand-holding and "a nice weekend to be in the woods" relationship'. He wanted the feeling of a relationship that had begun in the womb, so to speak, something pre-ordained. 'I explained that I'd like [them] to get it in their heads and then rehearse it off-screen,' said Stevens later, '[and then] get them in there and throw them at one another and move twice as fast as fact, compulsively, one talk on top of another ... the girl's not guarded by her parents. It's an instinctive thing [with them] that they've got to join together.' So they did it his way, both of them rendering it perfectly, intuitively, in the first take.

Stevens took the better part of a year in the cutting room to edit his 400,000 feet of film. Here again, his technique of selecting and combining created a romantic dimension that Elizabeth had never before inhabited. Using two projectors, Stevens screened the scenes between Elizabeth and Clift, the takes where the camera had been on Elizabeth side by side with those where it had been on Clift, and spliced them into each other's romantic world. 'I tried to thrust them together with something that would last. And it did, it had that effect.' It was disconcerting, he confessed, to see how well he had taught Elizabeth to play to an audience of one – the camera. He felt her power to enlist conviction – to make voyeurs of an audience, intensely preoccupied with the way she could signal her needs and enforce her desires. The Elizabeth Taylor that the world thinks of came of age with *A Place in the Sun*.

It was to bring her the best set of reviews since *National Velvet*. What impressed almost all the critics was the sense of 'experienced truth' she imparted to the role of a pampered rich girl finding passion and a purpose in life just as fate is set to deny her the fulfilment of both. Her beauty this time makes it seem all the more tragic. 'Always beautiful,' said *Look* magazine, 'Miss Taylor here reveals an understanding of passion and suffering that is electrifying.' 'A shaded, tender performance,' wrote A. H. Weiler in *The New York Times*, 'and one in which her passionate and genuine romance avoids the bathos common to young love as it sometimes comes to the screen.' *Variety* recognized that '[George] Stevens's skilled hands on the reins must be credited with a minor miracle.'

Stevens's hands, in fact, had wrought a more ironic event. If Elizabeth had felt sexually attracted to Montgomery Clift, the experience of acting with him in a way that played on his innate weakness and brought out her latent strength had convinced her that they were destined to be friends and confidants, but never husband and wife. Clift's biographer Robert LaGuardia quotes her as saying, 'Look, Monty, I'm always here for you – for whatever you want.' ('Tell mama', indeed!) For Clift, love was always to be a matter of passing intensity – passed, in the main, with his own sex and limited to the promiscuous thrills of a constantly changing partnership. But if he wasn't a prize Elizabeth could possess, neither was he a threat; she felt safe in giving, knowing that this deeply insecure and dependent companion would never be demanding enough to take. Monty Clift had become family to her.

The Paramount publicists, of course, had played up the screen romance between the two stars so as to keep public interest at a high pitch during the long months the film was in George Stevens's editing room. Inevitably, this created renewed speculation about Elizabeth's marriage intentions. 'I never saw a girl more ripe for love and marriage than Elizabeth,' Hedda Hopper reported. That understated Elizabeth's impatience – and also her frustration. 'Love and marriage', as Shelley Winters had noted, were seen by Elizabeth as the only sanctioned escape route to independence. Patiently she repeated, 'When somebody comes along and we're in love, we'll be married.' What she didn't add was that this somebody had already come along. And with the timeliness of their encounter matched by the strength of her desire, she fell in love with Nick Hilton with the same impulsive and total commitment as Angela Vickers had fallen in love with George Eastman in *A Place in the Sun*.

12

A MOVIE ROMANCE

Nick Hilton shared with George Eastman, the character Clift played in *A Place in the Sun*, the surname of a commercially powerful American dynasty. Otherwise, there was nothing in common between fiction and fact. He was the eldest son of the hotel tycoon Conrad Hilton and, at twenty-three, already a vice-president and manager of the Bel Air Hotel, a comfortable training school which would qualify him to oversee the building of the family's newest link in their chain, the Beverly Hilton. Like Elizabeth, he made up in good looks what he lacked in maturity. Like her, he had been at work from an age when other children would still have been at play. At fourteen, he had been 'in hotels' as she, at ten, had been 'in films'. Like her, his life-style had been formed by work in California. But it is safe to say that Conrad Hilton hadn't reared his son and heir on the sort of romantic expectations imparted to Elizabeth by her mother and the movies. Nick Hilton's fantasies were solidly commercial and healthily carnal. Already he had a reputation as a sometimes wild playboy around the Hollywood nightspots and in the gambling casinos of the newly booming Las Vegas. He had first spotted Elizabeth in the flesh at the Mocambo, on the night that Vic Damone tried to lift her spirits after her broken engagement. He later said that his determination to woo and win her began there and then.

His father, whose wealth was then estimated to be over $120 million, had recently had his marriage to Zsa Zsa Gabor annulled – the Hiltons were Roman Catholics and prominent laymen in their church's affairs. At the same time as he shed his wife, Hilton Sr had acquired a huge estate on Bellagio Road, Bel Air, a sixty-four-room mansion with sixteen bedroom suites, twenty-six bathrooms, five kitchens and as many wet bars, a poolroom, a rose garden, two swimming pools, and badminton and tennis courts. A father on the lookout for a new wife to go with all this was also minded to see his son acquire a wife of his own, to burnish the family name further and protect the succession.

Through his friend Pete Freeman, the son of Y. Frank Freeman, head of Paramount, Nick Hilton's way was smoothed towards a meeting with Elizabeth on her own territory, the day after the film unit had returned to the studio from upstate locations – which must have been about the beginning of November 1949. Clift always ate lunch alone in his dressing room – he was an early devotee of health foods and meditative yoga. Elizabeth hated the Paramount commissary, where every table had its little square of corn-bread named 'Mr Freeman's Favorite' after the studio patriarch. It was almost as bad, in her opinion, as 'Mr Mayer's Chicken Soup' over at MGM. She showed her indifference by eating at Lucy's, a café across the road. On this particular day she was still in her film wardrobe – the dark suit and cloche hat that Angela Vickers was to wear for her last encounter with her lover: as he awaits execution in jail, she offers him the reason for hope that Elizabeth herself had made part of her faith – that one day in the hereafter they would meet again and continue their love. Clift had become oppressively fatalistic about 'his' approaching death scenes in the electric chair and Elizabeth's mood retained the tenseness of the encounter that Stevens had just guided her through. Discovering a handsome young table companion was a welcome relief – the lunch had been set up earlier by a phone call from Pete Freeman. 'Liz, Nick Hilton's a friend of mine, he'd love to meet you.' – 'Love it.' As simple as that.

She thought him 'nice' and 'attractive', but her thoughts were still with the doom-stricken Monty. When she got back home, a long transparent case of three dozen yellow roses greeted her. 'To bring back the Sun – Nick.'

Monty Clift as best friend, Nick Hilton as new boyfriend: there was room for both sets of feelings. By now, too, Elizabeth's parents had begun to feel uneasy. There was a risk that unless their child's growing fame and glamour were matched by a settled relationship with someone suitable, she would 'run wild', as Hedda Hopper had expressed it to Sara.

The romance that followed over the next few months was kept well under wraps. The Taylors wished to take stock of the Hiltons, and of course vice versa, but Elizabeth was wary of falling again into the bitchy clutches of columnists who, after two aborted affairs, had nicknamed her 'Liz the Jilt'. Filming, in any case, compelled an early-to-bed routine. So Nick Hilton's courtship took the form of intimate family dinners on Elm Drive, or more impressive affairs at the Hilton residence. Weekends were spent riding quietly on the Bel Air bridle paths, and the Freemans drove Nick and Elizabeth up to Arrowhead Springs for a well-chaperoned New

Year's vacation, immediately after she completed her role in the film on 29 December. The start of 1950 was ushered in with a party that resembled the one in the Eastman home in the film. Nick handed Elizabeth a jewel box: diamond earrings set in pearl clusters. He then asked Mr Taylor for his daughter's hand. It was like *A Place in the Sun* with a happy ending. Sara was overjoyed; the Taylors could scarcely have made a more resplendent match. Only Monty Clift was less than raptuous: 'Are you sure he's the right guy, Bessie Mae?' To him, Hilton was merely a spoilt rich California playboy with a glamour that wouldn't necessarily outlast the first experience of housekeeping for him. But by this time Elizabeth was determined on marriage: exchanging rings and vows was an essential preliminary to exchanging her chaperoned existence for a wifely status, and she was not going to risk the chance of losing it a third time and catching the backlash of smirking publicity.

She had the sense that she was coming of age in other ways, too. In February 1950, she would be eighteen, legally an adult. And even earlier, on 26 January, her protracted 'education' at last reached its apogee. As high-school diplomas of competence weren't presented at the MGM schoolhouse, the studio used to whip its famous pupils across town to University High to receive their scroll there. So just as Linda Darnell, Judy Garland and Deanna Durbin had all done before her, Elizabeth, in cap and gown, suddenly surfaced among the surprised 206 other graduating students. She left immediately afterwards for the Mocambo, clutching her parchment, and deflecting a sneaky question by a reporter who asked if her life was going to change. Presumably, he had marriage in mind, not scholarship. She refused to reveal the still secret match with Nick Hilton. 'Being eighteen won't make much difference. I don't get control of my trust fund until I'm twenty-one and I drive my own car and have had grown-up roles for a year now ...' The reporter persisted. Was there nothing she wanted that she hadn't had before? Elizabeth wrinkled her nose like one of her chipmunks. 'I'd like something besides rich-girl parts. Something dramatic. A half-breed, maybe.' The note of sarcasm showed her defences strengthening.

It was Conrad Hilton who couldn't keep the secret when asked by a reporter in New York if the rumours were serious. 'Serious? Of course they're serious. They're going to get married on 6 May.'

Later on, Nick Hilton's friends would feel that he was as much in love with Elizabeth's film-star image as she was with the picture she was constructing in her mind of herself as a wife and mother. Sometimes the two had met secretly at the home of Nick's younger brother, Baron Hilton, already a married man with two children. 'Elizabeth would be motored straight from MGM up to the Baron Hilton home and there would be this idyllic-looking young couple with their kids,' said a friend. It was as if she was looking at a scene on the screen with stand-ins for herself and Nick. Baron recommended early matrimony. It was the best game in town: a gambling metaphor that fitted the successful operation of the hotel chain's casinos.

But if these scenes of family happiness encouraged Elizabeth in her belief that she, too, could step straight into domestic felicity, their effect on Nick Hilton was to make him jealous of his younger brother's settled life and greater maturity. He saw marriage to Elizabeth as a way of closing the sibling gap. 'Naturally we don't want to wait too long for children,' he said. 'My brother's a year and a half younger. He has two children with another on the way. I can't let him get too far ahead.'

But Elizabeth had other ideas. She didn't want to have children until there was a stable married basis for family life. 'We don't want children for two years yet,' she said, adding, 'Nick and I want to have fun.' From the beginning, therefore, there were differences in the making, though unrecognized.

Mrs Taylor might well have suspected, as she watched her daughter floating to the telephone after work to take a call from Nick and then apparently sinking into a trance, that she looked like an actress playing the part of a young girl in love.

Fantasy, as it happened, was again keeping step with reality. For Elizabeth had begun her new film, *Father of the Bride*, so soon after finishing her role in the last one that she'd had to give her weekend time to trying on the costumes that Edith Head was designing for this MGM comedy. It was about a young bride and the devastating effect of her marriage preparations on her loving but bewildered parents, played in the film by Spencer Tracy and Joan Bennett.

Elizabeth behaved in the film exactly as she was doing in real life – blissfully in thrall to her fiancé and touchingly grateful to her parents for bringing her up and providing for her. There was one major divergence, though. In the film Tracy and Bennett are fearful at one point that the wedding will be called off and their daughter will be thrown back into the family nest. In real life, that was Elizabeth's nightmare. On screen, her fiancé's wealth doesn't begin to match the Hilton boy's fortune; but then, if it had, MGM wouldn't have had the comedy of Tracy's wrestling with the expenses and deciding that the sum total of his daughter's happiness was worth the figure on the bottom line of the bills to come. The MGM publicists ensured that Elizabeth's quoted comments still radiated an 'ordinary girl's' delight in marrying Hilton, lest audiences for the film, whose release was scheduled to coincide with the wedding, felt that 'their' Elizabeth was abandoning them for wealth beyond belief, or, at any rate, beyond their own modest budgets. 'We both love hamburgers with onions, outsize sweaters and Pinza,' said Elizabeth. Ezio Pinza, the *basso profundo* from the Milanese opera house La Scala, was then currently appearing in two MGM musicals.

Mr Taylor himself was beginning to feel that life was an MGM comedy, except for the fact that he was paying to be in it.

'I keep thinking of Spencer Tracy,' said this usually urbane man, somewhat enviously now. 'All he has to do is stand up there and act the part I'm living.' Another scene that might have come out of the film, or been written into it for Vincente Minnelli to direct, occurred when Hedda Hopper and Esther Williams sat between Elizabeth and Nick Hilton at a post-engagement party and began ribbing the young couple about 'the things you ought to know'. As predictions, their words are interesting. 'First,' Esther Williams told Elizabeth, 'you'll make two pictures, then it will be time for the first baby . . . Then two more and time for the second.' She continued in this vein, alternating career moves with maternity gowns, until Elizabeth, feeling the air hissing out of her romance like a deflating balloon, interjected: 'Esther, that's enough . . . I've never been talked to like this in my life.'

'Bet you never learned so much, either,' the senior star cracked back.

Nick Hilton showed an early grasp of the obligation that kept Elizabeth happy by dropping in on George Headley's, the Beverly Hills jeweller, and demanding to see 'something nice'.

'Blonde or brunette?' Mr Headley asked.

'Platinum and diamonds,' answered the Hilton boy.

In her way, Elizabeth tried to repay some of these expensive attentions. When she and her mother went off to New York to shop, leaving Mr Taylor (like Mr Tracy) wrestling with the myriad chores of the wedding, she discovered that her agent, Jules Goldstone, was in town, but staying at the Sherry Netherland. 'Jules,' she cried over the phone, 'that's not a Hilton hotel. Why aren't you staying here, at the Waldorf? That's *our* hotel.'

From Nick, Elizabeth had received a four-carat diamond engagement ring (insured for $10,000): a useful starter for her collection. A few months earlier the Jewellery Industry Council of America had celebrated its diamond jubilee by placing a $22,000 diamond diadem on her head. 'May I keep it?' she asked. Mrs Taylor might have been pleased to see that Elizabeth had apparently no difficulty now telling the difference between 'may' and 'can'. She might also have noted her daughter was acquiring expensive tastes.

Elizabeth rushed off to flash her engagement band around the SLOB club. This was a coterie of girlfriends – all connected with movies or the media – that she and Ed Sullivan's daughter Betty had formed after both of them had simultaneously caught the bridal bouquet Jane Powell had tossed to her bridesmaids after her recent wedding. 'SLOB' stood for 'Single Lonely Obliging Babes'. Elizabeth was president; other members included Betty Sullivan, Terry Moore, Barbara Long Thompson and Marjorie Dillon, who was Elizabeth's official movie stand-in, as she possessed the same colouring and figure. Strictly speaking, a girl left the other SLOBS after marriage, but could return to the club as a technical adviser – i.e., she advised the rest on how to snare a husband. After a club tea party at Jane Powell's to celebrate the engagement, Elizabeth volunteered to wash up. By the time she'd finished, Jane was minus two plates, a saucer and a cup. Surveying the breakage, Jane commented: 'Liz, you'd better marry someone who owns a hotel. You'll never make a good housewife.'

Nick Hilton had that qualification, but in retrospect he can be seen to have possessed few of the other domestic virtues that make for a stable marriage. Stories that suggested he had a violent temper and an arrogant nature had come into the open with the marriage announcement. But it would have been hard to stop the arrangements. Once set rolling, the wedding was like a film production – which indeed it became. It developed its own costly momentum. Elizabeth, besides, viewed her future spouse with the adoring deference of the girl she was playing in *Father of the Bride*, who prefaces every dinner-table opinion that drops from her lips with the sanctioning recitative of 'Bradley says' this or 'Bradley says' that. 'It was "Nick this . . ." and "Nick that . . ."' said a friend. 'Liz would have had a nervous breakdown if she hadn't become a married woman.'

Only one or two features of the engagement period brought Elizabeth up against a reality that she would not have found in any Hollywood movie of the time. She discovered that the children she hoped to have must be reared in her husband's Roman Catholic faith. At first she demurred. To sign an undertaking saying what religion one's children would be before one had had any, or had even created the home life in which she wanted to raise them, seemed to her the wrong order of events. Such peremptory requirements resembled the clauses in her MGM contract binding her to commitments that took no account of what her wishes might be in the foreseeable future. But she was won over by the convention of those days, which made a bride subservient to her future husband's wishes. She even took instruction in the Catholic faith – it was like a rehearsal for a new role – though she never converted to it. Sara was pleased. She had seen her daughter pen those 'sorry' notes as a child and promise to work hard at her movie career; now Elizabeth was preparing herself to work as hard at her marriage. Gladys Culverson, her nanny back in the days when the family had lived in London and now their housekeeper on Elm Drive, reflected the certainty of mother and daughter when she told reporters: 'Elizabeth loves and respects Mr Hilton. He feels the same about her. That's why this will be the first and last marriage for both of them.'

13

'WEDDING OF WEDDINGS'

Elizabeth and her mother had spent three whole days in Chicago, en route to New York, going on a shopping spree at Marshall Field, a large department store: Wallace sterling silver flatware in a 'Grand Baroque' pattern, powder-blue Wedgwood china, initialled Italian linens, Swedish crystal ... In New York, it continued: they shopped round the clock for her bridal trousseau. Conrad Hilton had said to her, 'Elizabeth, when you walk through the doors of the Waldorf, I want you to feel perfectly at home.' When she went to register, the desk clerk handed her an envelope. Inside was a block of Waldorf-Astoria shares, making her a part-owner of the place right away. She felt perfectly at home.

She settled for the pick of the couturier Ceil Chapman's collection for her honeymoon wear: a honey and amber banded dress in Italian shantung, a shimmering cocktail dress of blue cotton Jacquard, a yellow and blue checked evening gown in silk organdy, a silk letter-print afternoon outfit, and a bouffant white dress in imported Swiss organdy – the blue embroidery on it was redone to match her eyes. MGM paid for all of this wardrobe, a publicist instructing the press not to call some of them 'cocktail dresses ... because Liz is too young at eighteen to drink alcohol'.

The studio had a problem of its own: who should design the wedding gown? Helen Rose, who was MGM's in-house designer, or Edith Head, over at Paramount, who had done the party dresses for *A Place in the Sun*? A compromise was reached: Helen for the wedding dress, Edith for the going-away outfit. A collection was taken up among MGM office employees to defray the cost of the bridesmaids' dresses.

The wedding dress, a spy in the MGM publicity department reported to the newspapers, would be a billowing creation in white satin embroidered with bugle beads and seed pearls, 'about twenty yards of it', and would be tightly cinched to emphasize Elizabeth's waist (and bust). The chiffon at the neckline, the same undercover agent whispered, 'doesn't even count, the flesh shows through it!' She would wear a 'crown-like halo' of seed pearls. Her veil would be 'misty'. She would carry a bouquet of white orchids. Helen Rose confirmed all this and said of the dress, 'It's about as plunging as anything could be.' She was probably delighted not to have to worry, for once, about the Ratings Code rules restricting the amount of cleavage a film actress could decently display on screen. But in case there was anyone who imagined that Hollywood didn't know what good taste was, she added, 'It's not half as revealing as Princess Elizabeth's wedding dress.' The nuptial nightgown to be worn by MGM's Elizabeth was described by a friend who had been admitted to a private view of it as 'very ladylike'.

MGM had dressed many a wedding on its film sets. This one was no different. The studio knew how it should be done down to the last stitch and swag, so that the illusion of screenland would not fade in the common light of day.

The members of the SLOB club gave their retiring president a shower party at Jane Powell's home, co-hosted by her and Barbara Thompson. The cake featured figurines of the bride in vanilla ice-cream (Elizabeth's favourite) and the groom in chocolate (Nick's) surrounded by bridal-party dolls with the matron of honour in pale green crepe paper and the bridesmaids in yellow – the key colours of the wedding on the MGM artists' sketchboards. The SLOBS gave Elizabeth a musical cigarette box and a penny to put in her white satin wedding slipper for luck. Not that anyone thought she'd need it.

The Taylor home began filling up early with presents, which arrived every hour of the day, and even some at night so that they could be kept secret from Elizabeth. The presents stacked in the spare bedrooms soon overflowed into the living room. Her father gave her a painting by Frans Hals and a 'Breath of Spring' mink coat. Sara's present was a mink stole in white – distinguished from the brown tone of Francis's pelt. Uncle Howard Young gave her a $65,000 platinum and diamond ring. From Conrad Hilton came a plainer present, but none the less acceptable: a block of one hundred shares in Hilton hotel stock. A three-month holiday in Europe had already been ticked off on the suggestion list.

Mr Taylor, feeling more and more like Spencer Tracy by the minute, coped with an event that had now taken on the scale (and cost) of a major motion picture. He discovered in the nick of time that the Beverly Hills Hotel, where the reception was planned to take place, had been double-booked: the reception was transferred to the Bel Air Country Club. As he collapsed into an armchair after sorting out the Napoleonic seating plan for five hundred guests that had to reflect the vanity, power and politics of Hollywood, Mr Taylor was presented with the kind of decision that would set the tone: the choice between cold *hors d'oeuvres* (smoked salmon) or hot (*vol au vent*). This usually diffident and quiet man bellowed, 'I won't have cold fish at *my* daughter's wedding.'

MGM was planning to release some cold fare of its own, two 'turkeys', *The Conspirator* and *The Big Hangover*, in confident expectation that the wedding publicity would deflect attention from them and that *Father of the Bride* would be formidable compensation. Hollywood was itself, in a very real sense, the father of the bride. Its patriarchal rule was being converted into the fond patrimony of a proud parent who lavished presents on his star daughter – a daughter whose value to any MGM picture she was in would soon be calculated as worth a million dollars at the box office even before it had opened. Nor was Elizabeth's mother forgotten as the corporate cornucopia spilled its gifts on her child. Some insensitive studio bureaucrat chose this very moment to observe that Elizabeth was no longer legally under Mrs Taylor's control and custody: was there any need to continue paying her mother the $250 a week she had been drawing for the last five years? The memo to that effect produced a pencilled (and unsigned) note in the margin: 'Keep her on salary,' at least until Benny Thau returned from New York. Mr Thau returned, presumably saw the danger in such economies and blew up. Result: a further memo was added to Mrs Taylor's file: 'Keep her on salary until further notice.'

There were a few snags of the kind that shows how perilously close life is to a Hollywood comedy – if, that is, it is Hollywood life. Nick Hilton went along to get the marriage licence and was refused it until he could prove his age. He managed to do so with his driving licence.

He and Elizabeth had a rehearsal on 5 May; but during it, Elizabeth began running a fever, a reaction that was to recur at other turning points and crises in her life. No cause for alarm, said the doctor; but just to be sure, he gave her penicillin injections and packed her off to bed. By this time, most of the moveable furnishings in the Taylor home had been packed tightly together to make space for the continuing arrival of wedding presents; they now overflowed into the housekeeper's bedroom. Delivery vans arrived in relays, disgorging presents from last-minute hopefuls who hadn't yet got their invitation. On the eve of the event, Mrs Taylor took in six coffee services, three sets of silverware, and fourteen sets of glasses, bringing the total amount of crystal given to Elizabeth up to almost five hundred pieces, enough to stock a Hilton hotel.

Soon after sunrise, fans began settling down with their bagels and coffee-flasks around the Church of the Good Shepherd, Beverly Hills. Some brought folding chairs to stand on, others periscopes. Police barriers had been erected the night before. Supplementary security came from

MGM in the burly shape of Whitney Hendry, mustering his musclemen with the nonchalance of a veteran who had protected many a star's wedding. The first fans appeared outside the Taylor home around noon. The roadway had to be closed off. 'I'd prefer a gang war to another Hilton–Taylor wedding,' said the Beverly Hills police chief later. Expectancy rose in volume as the bridesmaids arrived to change into their saffron-yellow dresses at Anne Westmore's parents' home opposite. Besides Anne herself, there were Jane Powell, Marjorie Dillon, Marilyn Hilton (Nick's sister), Barbara Thompson and Mara Regan, who was shortly to marry young Howard Taylor.

Yet the drama most people missed occurred when a lithe young man walked briskly up the Taylor driveway, past the police cordon, as if expected: Bill Pawley Jr, Elizabeth's ex-fiancé. There appeared to be a delay at the door, until Gladys Culverson, who'd opened it to him, called Mrs Taylor and he was admitted. Why he came at that eleventh hour, none of the parties to the meeting in Elizabeth's bedroom, where she was still in her night attire, ever disclosed. It was believed afterwards that he reproached her for not living up to her promises to him; but others, in the light of the subsequent marriage, held that his intention had been to give Elizabeth a last-minute warning about the intemperate nature of the man who was about to make her his wife. Bill Pawley had a very cut-and-dried view of right and wrong. He later became a power in the Moral Rearmament movement: and a sense of religious responsibility for a marriage which must have hurt him personally and which filled him with misgivings for Elizabeth's future happiness may well have impelled him to make that extraordinary visit. He stayed for about fifteen minutes, then left as tight-lipped as he'd arrived. There were reports of him being seen in the crowds around the church, grim and silent. It was twenty-five years before he himself got married: by then, Elizabeth had been through five husbands.

Sidney Guilaroff arrived at 3.00 p.m. to do the bride's hair, followed by the studio's head fitter, Mrs Ryan, detailed to help Elizabeth into the fantasy wedding gown, on which fifteen seamstresses had worked for two months, along with the ten yards of veiling, the pearl-encrusted cap and the tiara. It was noticed that Elizabeth had got slightly, if imperceptibly, thicker in the waist. She gasped when the dress was cinched in. Eccentrically, she refused to wear stockings.

Then it was the turn of the crowds to gasp when, around 4.45 p.m., in Technicolor sunshine, Elizabeth appeared at the front door and stepped carefully out to the waiting limousine – a dream bride, indeed! MGM had stage-managed it down to the last detail.

Among the virile-looking motorcycle cops assigned to pilot the car smoothly through the crowd-lined streets to the church was one called Ed. She had got to know him well when he'd done guard duty at her parents' home after threats had been made against their daughter for jilting her two suitors – Elizabeth's earliest brush with the physical risks that accompany notoriety. Now she stepped up to him, pecked his cheek playfully and said, 'Let's hear it for the bride. Turn on your siren, Ed, and let them know I'm coming.'

Ed hesitated. It was against police department rules to sound his bike's siren when out on hire for an unofficial event. Then he softened. 'Seeing it's you, Miss Taylor, the department'll make you a present of it.'

So, with her bridesmaids in the preceding car and her father by her side, she glided down the drive for the last time as Elizabeth Rosemond Taylor, and out into Beverly Hills behind the motorcycle cops, their sirens screaming.

It was one of the only occasions when she arrived, if not precisely on time, then near enough – only five minutes late. Just as well, perhaps, as the church organ had been giving trouble and for a time it looked as if a gramophone record might have to be played. Then someone switched on the power that, in everyone's nervousness to make sure all was in perfect order, had been completely overlooked.

All the MGM executives had been invited: likewise, every manager of a Hilton hotel. The faces of Big Business looked at each other across the aisle, for naturally the MGM crowd were 'bride's family'. The wedding guests numbered stars from every major studio except Disney, which was regarded as something of an outsider in the tight-knit community of Jewish Hollywood. Prominent pews had been assigned to the William Powells, the Phil Harrises (wife, Alice Faye), the Gene Kellys and Fred Astaires, the Walter Pidgeons, the Dick Powells (wife, June Allyson), the Red Skeltons, the Van Johnsons, as well as Peter Lawford, Margaret O'Brien, Ricardo Montalban, Ginger Rogers, Ann Miller, Janet Leigh, Mickey Rooney, Roddy McDowall and, of course, Spencer Tracy and Joan Bennett, the bride's screen father and mother. The extent to which MGM had consulted its own interest in arranging the guest list was evident in the pairing of other 'couples' who had played Elizabeth's parents in their productions: Donald Crisp and Anne Revere (*National Velvet*), George Murphy and Mary Astor (*Cynthia*), Greer Garson and Walter Pidgeon (*Julia Misbehaves*), Leon Ames and (again) Mary Astor (*Little Women*). Unfortunately, no mother had been visible in *A Date With Judy*.

As sacred music flooded the church with the restoration of organ power, Mary Jane Smith, an MGM contract artist, opened up with 'Ave Maria'.

Outside, a slight hitch had developed: more a snag, really. The hem of

Elizabeth's dress caught on the door of the limousine as she was assisted out of it, and began tearing. Her matron of honour rushed forward and tugged it loose.

Elizabeth had stowed away on her person some amulets against just such an ill omen. In her palm she crushed the white lace handkerchief, 'something old', that her mother had carried at her own wedding; inside her satin slipper, her toes were curled tightly round the penny, 'something new', that the SLOBS had given her; a lucky charm belonging to her brother, 'something borrowed', was tucked into her bridal cap; and in a fold of her voluminous dress was pinned an artificial posy of forget-me-nots − 'something blue'.

As the music changed to 'The Wedding March', she began the first of what, over the years, would be half-a-dozen other advances, more or less formal, more or less premeditated, towards the man who would become her husband.

She later told Elsa Maxwell that when she was secretly engaged to Nick Hilton and just finishing *Father of the Bride*, 'every time we did the shot of me walking up the aisle to the altar, I was living it'. Did life come up to the thrill of artifice, one wonders. For Hedda Hopper, there could be no question of leaving her readers in doubt. 'No scene that Elizabeth will ever play can have this glow,' wrote this incorrigible woman, a veteran scrutineer of visionary Hollywood brides from the days of Vilma Banky and Norma Shearer to Shirley Temple, Deanna Durbin and now Elizabeth Taylor. 'Not if she turns into a second Bernhardt can she recapture the reality of these emotions. This is the Hollywood wedding of weddings.'

MGM's set decorators had taken over the church the day before and laid a white runner down the centre aisle, filled every alcove with huge bouquets of white carnations and lilies, and tied white silk bows to the top of every pillar.

Elizabeth's measured pace slackened as she and her father neared the pew where Sara sat. She halted beside her mother, leaned slightly towards her, and blew her a kiss before resuming her walk to the altar. Pure Hollywood, but none the less sincere. For she was acting on the impulse that had been drilled into her by everything in her working life. She made no obeisance to Louis B. Mayer, however, as she passed the pew where the movie mogul sat dabbing at his eyes with a silk handkerchief − a technique he used on less sentimental occasions against stars who were hard-hearted enough to place a value on their worth in terms of contract figures and not their boss's finer feelings.

Nick Hilton joined her at the altar, lily-of-the-valley in the lapel of his cut-away coat. The ceremony conducted by Monsignor Patrick J. Concannon lasted twenty minutes. As they were pronounced man and wife, Nick drew the new Mrs Hilton into his arms and pressed his lips to hers in an embrace that, in the view of those close to them, was more in the style of a Hollywood fade-out than the start of a sacred relationship.

The pencils of Hopper, Parsons and Sheilah Graham, seated up front but at a diplomatic distance from each other, worked overtime. They noted the perspiration standing out in bubbles on Nick Hilton's brow; nervousness was not entirely to blame, it was 104 degrees outside. They noted how the couple kept on kissing, until a discreet cough from the priest had the same effect as the cry of 'Cut!' from a movie director. They broke, then turned and walked up the aisle – Elizabeth stopping to hug her parents this time – and out into the early evening sun. On the steps, they embraced again, even more demonstratively than before, while Whitney Hendry's two hundred studio police strained against the pressing, cheering crowds. Then it was into the limousine, still locked in an embrace, and off to the reception for five hundred at the Spanish-style Bel Air Country Club. It took over an hour for the last guest to file past with 'Bless you's' and then the five-tier cake, whose surrounding ice sculpture looked as wilted as many of those present, was cut, distributed, wrapped up for future anniversaries. Then Elizabeth tossed her bouquet to the kids at the foot of the staircase – history doesn't record the catcher – and vanished into her suite to change into Edith Head's going-away outfit: a blue silk suit with dyed-to-match linen shoes and bag, worn with a white-on-white embroidered blouse and gloves.

Already stowed away in the trunk of their waiting convertible was a travelling case with her nuptial nightgown of white satin and a negligé of sheerest marquisette with two huge pockets of rose-point lace at the bosom.

Clutching a blue-grey mink stole – it was too hot to wear it, but crowds expected mink to be among a star's appurtenances – and giving her mother a last hug, she and Nick ducked through the crowds of confetti and rice and into the car. It halted for a moment at the gates to allow the pursuers to fling their last gritty handfuls of good wishes at the newlyweds. Then it slipped out into the evening traffic, bound for Carmel, the traditional first-night stop for honeymooners on the coast of California. Elizabeth rested her head on Nick's shoulder – after the 'wedding of weddings', she remained magnificently unprepared for the reality of married life.

14

A CLASH OF DYNASTIES

The couple spent most of their first week as newlyweds at an exclusive golf club on the outskirts of Carmel. Neither played golf. Elizabeth was on the phone constantly, calling her mother. It was the first time in her life that she had been without her family. Maybe winning independence before she was sexually prepared for it was a lesson that sank in quickly, and disquieted her. Hilton was far from inexperienced where women were concerned, but he soon showed himself temperamentally incapable of acquiring any husbandly virtues. In short, the two had plenty of time on their hands to discover how little they had in common. Each had reasons for marrying the other that ceased to be compelling once they were married: Elizabeth to escape from being a perpetual daughter, Hilton to conquer a young woman universally celebrated for her beauty. But new-found liberty didn't fit well with the married state, especially as the chauvinist conventions of the time defined the respective roles of husband and wife, and the roles of these two in particular. Both were spoiled children. One was heir to a fortune: the other, a symbol of glamour. But these very inheritances were so vested in their separate worlds that they dominated the marriage from the start.

Young Hilton, though proud of his conquest, wasn't awed by movie celebrity. And though Elizabeth loved the material luxuries with which he'd surrounded her, she wasn't interested in a business empire like the Hiltons'. When asked before the wedding if she were prepared to give up her career and settle into a wife's role, she had replied that she was. Her career had been masterminded by others: her mother and her studio. Marriage, on the other hand, had seemed like a life she could make her own. But not this marriage, she soon realized; it quickly ceased to exist, except in name and formal relationship. And if she couldn't be a good wife, then what could she be? She had no identity of her own, other than

'Elizabeth Taylor, film star'. Hilton, for his part, soon resented his wife's celebrity impinging on his own ego. A couple of the club employees had even called him 'Mr Taylor' – no insult intended, but all the more irritating because of it. He wasn't going to be seen as *that*! It reinforced all his own chauvinist traits.

Elizabeth's total lack of sexual experience may at first have gratified, even touched him, as it would any young man with a beautiful bride. 'But Nick ran with a faster crowd than Elizabeth's set,' a friend said, 'and he didn't waste time letting girls know what he wanted, and how.' He'd already been involved in one unpleasant episode with the daughter of a family friend, which had been hushed up. Some of the honeymoon must have been a brutal shock to a nice girl like Elizabeth. In most of her films, she'd played *ingénues*, or girls in love with men considerably older than she was, or sweetheart types with a crush, or, in *The Conspirator*, a young wife whose disenchantment with her husband doesn't come from sexual incompatibility, but simply from discovering his political affiliation with the Communists. Even in *A Place in the Sun*, it was a romance between a girl who's the epitome of her world and a boy who's outside his class. 'Sara hadn't prepared her for marriage to a rich brat who was used to getting his way – that wasn't in the script,' says a contemporary acquaintance.

Friends believe that the love affair died in that first week. The marriage took a little longer to be declared defunct.

Elizabeth was back home on Elm Drive within ten days of setting out from that address with the sirens sounding. But it was Mother's Day that, appropriately, recalled her from her husband's side. 'Elizabeth and I have never been apart on Mother's Day,' Sara told a newsman somewhat ingenuously, after he had queried her new son-in-law's absence.

On 20 May Mr and Mrs Hilton appeared together at Los Angeles airport to fly east and board the _Queen Mary_ on 23 May bound from New York to Europe and the first leg of their honeymoon in France, Italy and England. As this part of the marriage was being paid for by Conrad Hilton, MGM had less say in what Elizabeth did. But it had persuaded her and Nick to attend the London premiere of *Father of the Bride* on 12 June. A huge amount of luggage accompanied them to the airport. Only four of the bags were Nick Hilton's. The other fourteen, and two steamer trunks, were Elizabeth's. One trunk held nothing but shoes and purses for day and evening wear; another held some of the sixteen hats made for her by Rex, the 'in' milliner. One bag contained only cosmetics, bath lotions, soaps and toilet waters. Every item bore a label itemizing its contents: 'Bathing Suits and Play Clothes'; 'Evening Dresses'; 'Suits'; 'Furs'. All the labels were in Sara's handwriting. When asked by a fashion-conscious reporter what exactly such and such a bag held, Elizabeth's face betrayed not the slightest interest. 'My mother packed them,' was all she said.

Sara knew the extent of her daughter's marriage troubles, but, for once, was unable to give Elizabeth any hand signals beyond a mother's conventional advice to her child in such circumstances – to look the part and persevere. Nick Hilton made a sarcastic quip to the reporters about 'travelling with a film star' – and paid an overweight surcharge.

They had not been able to secure the bridal suite on the Cunard liner, but there was compensation on board in the form of the Duke and Duchess of Windsor, themselves frequent recipients of hospitality (and discounts) at the Hiltons' hotels. They promised the young couple a supper party in their honour in Paris.

When Elizabeth appeared on deck, she was often alone, and looked listless. When she went to take the sun in a playsuit on the games deck, a bystander noticed the shadow of fine black hairs on her upper arms – the hypertrichosis of childhood, it appears, was still returning periodically. Hilton was heard shouting 'Hey, monkey' at her once or twice. He looked the way that conventional American tourists of those times were pictured, or caricatured: crew-cut and gum-chewing, with a taste in neckties that ran to patterns featuring Eskimos and igloos. 'You would never have imagined him as Elizabeth Taylor's husband,' said a crew member. 'He was always calling her to come and do things he wanted done, but which she made pretty plain were a bore to her. Like "Elizabeth, come and put a call through to dad", or "Hey, hon, come and see a movie." She often just walked away. That really enraged him. One time he pushed her roughly up against the bulkhead and wagged his finger in her face and said, "Don't you ever do that to me – *I'm talking to you!*"'

The card game canasta was all the rage then and Elizabeth took to it at once. She and the Duchess of Windsor turned out to be good players. The Duke preferred bridge in the ship's card-room. Nick Hilton clearly didn't fancy, or excel, at games of skill and would sit by Elizabeth, a bored spectator, or, occasionally, when he had had enough, take her and pull her towards him in a way that some people interpreted as husbandly companionship and others as childish possessiveness. 'You'd have thought at times they were a couple reaching the end of their marriage, rather than beginning one,' the Duchess of Windsor confided some time later to her friend, the socialite and professional party-giver Elsa Maxwell. But the Duchess herself was well resigned to the necessity of keeping up appearances. She invited 'Mr and Mrs Nicholas Hilton' to supper a day or two after their arrival in Paris.

Elsa Maxwell, one of the guests on 31 May, noticed that Elizabeth had lost weight. But as she was taken by the hand and introduced by the

Duchess to each guest in turn, Elizabeth became more animated than Maxwell could remember. Usually, she was shy in the company of strangers. Maxwell recalled that whenever Elizabeth became excited, she actually stuttered.

'Now you have the whole world before you,' Maxwell said fulsomely.

'I am married to a wonderful man,' Elizabeth answered tonelessly, 'and' – turning to Nick – 'he is the only world I want.'

A few days later, they drove on impulse to Deauville. The 'wonderful man' had taken a sudden urge to play blackjack at the casino. They showed their passports and Mr Hilton was waved through. His wife was not. Being only eighteen, she was under age. Tempers rose. The burly men in black ties and tight shirt-fronts began to close in. Elizabeth stood there looking humiliated, according to one witness. But the Hilton name was a power in the hotel world, even though the Hilton hotels hadn't yet made it as prominent in Europe then as it is now. A compromise: Elizabeth could enter the *salle des jeux* with her husband – who had insisted on his wish to gamble – provided she promised on her honour not to place a single bet. Hilton played a sulky and losing game and returned to Paris in a bad temper.

They had made no firm plans for their stay on the Continent and Elsa Maxwell tried to shape an itinerary for them. They seemed interested only in shopping and eating. She gave a party in their honour at Maxim's. Who would Elizabeth like invited? The only name the star could suggest was that of another star – Maurice Chevalier. Hilton, looking profoundly bored, merely indicated that any of Elsa Maxwell's friends were 'okay by me'. In the event, allowing for the absence of her usual 'okay' people from the capital at this time of the year, she netted Chevalier and Orson Welles, the Maharajah of Kapurthala – who instantly invited them to visit his princely state – a couple of French barons and baronesses, an English earl and countess, an unattached marquise, Jimmy Donahue, who was Barbara Hutton's ne'er-do-well playboy nephew, and several others who answered the description, familiar to readers of the Elsa Maxwell social column, of 'my great friends'. The Hiltons greeted them at the entrance to the *salle privée*. Nick Hilton, who found virtually all of them strangers, said little – but then his mouth was full of chewing gum. Before they sat down to eat, he removed the gum, placed it carefully in a piece of paper and put the paper in his trouser pocket. He was either going to dispose of it or, as one observer thought more likely, resume chewing it after Maxim's dishes had been consumed. Their hostess chose her words with care – more care, anyhow, than, according to her friends, she felt – when she came to write up her own party. After all, she spent a lot of her life in Hilton hotels. She praised Nick for his 'manliness'.

After the London premiere of *Father of the Bride*, the Hiltons were interviewed in their Savoy Hotel suite. How did he feel being the husband of a famous film actress? Hilton scowled and said, 'Let's leave that one alone, will we?' Savoy staff found them demanding guests. Gambling wasn't then legal in Britain, the licensing hours were inconvenient for entertaining friends. Hilton laid in the contents of a small liquor store. Room service caught him frequently in a belligerent mood, charitably attributed to 'boredom and booze'.

There was general wonder that a star like Elizabeth should have to put up with such a boor. When they arrived, their sitting room was filled with flowers – bouquets of roses, orchids, sweet peas. In many cases the cards bearing the senders' greetings remained unopened. The couple slept late, often until 11.00 a.m., then lunched on breakfast orders. At other meals, they showed no interest in looking at the menu; it was left to the headwaiter to order for them. Arguments were overheard, usually about money and the amount of it Elizabeth was spending. Nick's sartorial demands were simpler than hers, and cruder. Somewhere in Bond Street, he located a haberdasher's who came up with the flamboyant ties that were his trademark and always excited derisive press comment. The Savoy was treated to a preview of one he had bought 'to wear around home' – a broad black number with a white skull-and-crossbones motif.

They managed to rise early on the morning of the Ascot Gold Cup, to be in place for a good view of the King and Queen's open landau driving down the course. Elizabeth wore a suit of pale blue gabardine, a brocade-trimmed cream blouse and a straw hat with a daisy motif. She passed the gratified inspection of the gentlemen at the entrance to the Royal enclosure; this time, it was Nick Hilton who didn't pass muster. Disdaining formal Ascot wear, he went hatless and in a grey flannel business suit. More humiliation.

They didn't go out much in the evening, preferring to eat in their suite, or downstairs in the Savoy Grill. One night when Hildegarde was performing, the singer offered Elizabeth a rose and was later invited to join their table. Elizabeth looked tense and bored, and merely toyed with a half-glass of champagne. Nick Hilton was less abstemious. He was very drunk. Finding the Savoy's way of mixing his drinks unsatisfactory, he had ordered bottles of whisky, gin, vodka and vermouth and turned his corner of the table into a bar at which he mixed his own and his guests' refreshments.

They went back to France in July and down to the Côte d'Azur. By now, theirs was clearly a marriage in trouble. Nick spent nights at the Cannes casino, turning a deaf ear to Elizabeth's pleas to come home, sometimes leaving her to finish supper alone in his haste to get to the tables. Not surprisingly, the Hilton heir was a magnet for some of the unattached women who found a good living to be made in and around the white stucco, Moorish-style *casino d'été* at Cannes. The night staff at their hotel sometimes saw him return with one of the *poules de luxe* whom they knew well. Elizabeth had usually gone to bed by this time. Again, there was general wonderment that the star should put up with this treatment. She was observed crying, or near to tears. What sounded like blows or slaps were heard from the vicinity of their suite.

They went on to Rome, Florence, Verona and Venice, then back to the capital where the Pope favoured them with an audience.

There was tenseness back in Hollywood, too. The MGM chiefs were frantically working on Jules Goldstone, Elizabeth's agent, to reassure themselves that their star would sign a new contract with them when her old one expired at the end of the year. *Father of the Bride* was proving one of MGM's most profitable films ever, and a sequel was in hand, *Father's Little Dividend*, which could only be made with Elizabeth. A studio publicist, mindful perhaps that it was never too early to start beating the drum, had already placed an item about which dividend would come first, Elizabeth's screen baby or the new Mrs Hilton's. To MGM's surprise, this innocently intended plug evoked a howl of anger from Europe. Over the phone, an outraged Elizabeth denied the interpretation being placed on the studio release by columnists who should have known better. The columnists were bewildered in turn. Wasn't starting a family supposed to be what marriage was all about? A different sort of story about the Hiltons began to spread.

When Elsa Maxwell saw Elizabeth again on the homeward stretch of a honeymoon that had gone on far, far too long and, by its very duration, had denied both parties the chance to try and settle down, establish a routine and maybe find a compromise between their conflicting interests, she was astonished to see Elizabeth had lost a lot more weight. She looked about twenty pounds lighter, but appeared haggard, not healthy. And she had taken up smoking.

The Taylors, back home in Beverly Hills, were beside themselves with concern. Both parents would be waiting in the den for Elizabeth's call to come through – an almost daily event – over a crackling line from Europe. Sara's advice was inevitably met with reproaches. 'All her life, people have done things [for Elizabeth] and told her what to do,' said her former co-star Shelley Winters. No longer, though. Nothing had prepared her for this misery and humiliation. Looking back, Elizabeth was to say, 'I really did think that being married would be like living in a little white cottage – with me in an organdy apron.' For the Paris ball they attended before sailing home, Elizabeth wore a $15,000 Balmain gown – and it still didn't feel like marriage.

Nick Hilton, too, had made some disagreeable discoveries. One was that he hadn't simply wed Elizabeth Taylor; he had married into MGM. The studio was not going to surrender her to matrimony without a fight to preserve its investment. And indeed, the less Elizabeth pictured herself in that organdy apron, the stronger her conviction grew that the other image of herself, Elizabeth Taylor the film star, might offer a preferable alternative. At least she could take its measure with the same well-practised precision that the focus-puller on the film set displayed when he laid down the mark for her to 'hit' for the camera. She knew who Elizabeth Taylor was – or thought she did. Who Mrs Nick Hilton was, or might be, was something as yet unanswered. It was better to put it behind her, blot it out of memory, avoid dwelling on it. All the shibboleths of her Christian Science upbringing seemed to her a truer guide than the marriage coun-selling she would soon be urged to seek. That romantic will of Elizabeth Taylor's didn't prove unstable when stress put it to the test. On the contrary: under pressure, it was annealed. It was a harder, tougher Eliza-beth who eventually emerged.

If Conrad Hilton was appealed to in the crisis, no doubt he took his son's side. Apart from the filial bias, there was another good reason for the hotel magnate to lean this way. The Hilton empire was like the MGM empire: both were vast business operations, worldwide in reach, selling a view of life and living that some could dream about or aspire to. Both were run autocratically. Their respective rulers, Louis B. Mayer and Conrad Hilton, identified with their businesses in the way that patriarchs identify with their families. Any threat to family unity, any exogamous intrusion, was repulsed with heartless self-interest. Conrad Hilton was later heard to say: 'To stay married to a Hollywood star, just take no notice of Hollywood.' In turn, the MGM spokesman, or 'one of the top MGM management' whom the powerful columnists quoted anonymously but authoritatively in the post-honeymoon period, did nothing to mollify any hurt feelings among the Hilton clan. In the MGM statements, the emphasis is put on the notion that Elizabeth was still theirs and they meant to keep her: a human investment, admittedly, but every bit as valuable to them as any prime piece of real estate targeted by the Hilton dynasty for another of their luxury hotels. The studio stood by Elizabeth; the Hiltons by their son and heir. The coming divorce, though it would be muted by self-interest, was nothing less than a clash of dynasties.

15

DIVORCE — HOLLYWOOD STYLE

'His name is Bianco,' Elizabeth said, holding aloft a tiny white French poodle, rather overawed by the crush of press men aboard the trans-Atlantic liner at the Cherbourg dockside. 'And I bought him in Paris,' she added, shooting an emphatic look at her husband, 'with – my – own – money.'

By the time they returned to New York, the Hiltons' luggage had swollen to thirty-seven pieces, and their marriage had collapsed in on itself. None of their families met the ship on arrival, though of course Hilton and MGM functionaries danced attendance on them. It was a crushing homecoming for Elizabeth. Somehow, the magic of a Hollywood princess had failed to protect her.

According to Louella Parsons, Elizabeth was on the telephone from New York to MGM within two hours of getting back from her three-month honeymoon. 'Send someone to bring me home,' she sobbed over the line, 'I can't take any more of this.' An hour later, she checked out of the Plaza Hotel and flew alone to Chicago to await the studio agent. But Nick Hilton was having none of this. He caught up with her there, a reconciliation took place, and they proceeded by car to Los Angeles.

Once in Los Angeles, they moved into the two-bedroomed suite at the Bel Air Hotel which was to be their home. (As well as helping to manage the hotel, Nick had bought a 41 per cent interest in the place.) Elizabeth didn't even try to settle in. She showed little animation. If she called her girlfriends, it was from the studio, not the hotel – as if she had fears that she was being spied on. Hilton had his suspicions, too. Shortly after they returned to Los Angeles, Elizabeth's friend Barbara Thompson was lunching with her in the living-room when Nick walked in. Seeing them with their heads together, he apparently decided that Mrs Thompson was hearing nothing to his credit. 'What the hell's going on here?' he barked.

An argument broke out. Barbara Thompson, embarrassed and a little apprehensive, made to leave, taking with her the gifts Elizabeth had brought her from Europe. 'Would you please carry the bag down to the car?' Elizabeth asked Hilton with a show of dignity. 'Get the bellboy to take them,' he snapped.

As it happened, Sara Taylor then walked in unexpectedly. A grudging peace was made and Hilton gracelessly carried the gifts to the car. 'Very tired and very moody,' was how the divorce court evidence would later characterize Elizabeth at the time. Even 'friendly' columnists, fearing they were losing a good story, turned interrogators, anticipating the worst. 'I understand he threw poker chips in your face?' Hedda Hopper alleged.

'False,' Elizabeth said, flustered, 'they don't play poker in France.'

But she was quibbling over details. The reality of the situation, however, couldn't be denied. Celebrity was a handicap now. 'Other young people can quarrel,' said Elizabeth, 'but before we have time to kiss and make up, it's in the newspapers.'

What kept her going throughout these months of September and October 1950 was work. *Father's Little Dividend* cast her, with oppressive irony, as a newlywed whose post-honeymoon problems were all happy ones. Now it was almost as if the role she played was punishing her, not burnishing her. Elizabeth was being denied or was denying herself – there is no telling for sure – the very thing that made the girl she played in the film rejoice: the news that she was having a baby. As there was plainly no happy household in which to rear a child, she probably didn't want to bring one into the world. Not to see his son's marriage consummated with an heir – which he would have hoped for – was the bitterest blow of all to Conrad Hilton.

In the film, Elizabeth was also compelled to play scenes closely resembling the trauma she herself was undergoing: like the night she leaves her husband after a spat and comes tearfully home to her parents. But there was a happy ending already written and waiting in the Hollywood scenario. She knew the ending her own story was likely to have, and dreaded it.

Soon after shooting finished, on 1 November 1950, the Hiltons made a lame reconciliation attempt by flying to New York for a spending spree. In fact, fate was almost more decisive at the start of their journey than extravagance might have been persuasive at the end of it. Their aircraft suddenly lost height soon after take-off. It managed to return to the runway safely, but only on one engine. According to some of her intimates, Elizabeth had prayed that, if spared, she and Nick would have the baby they both had hoped would by now be on the way. But like the moment of danger, the moment of penitence passed, too.

They had moved into a rented house in Pacific Palisades that December, when a bitter row broke out over Hilton's drinking. Elizabeth moved out and took refuge with her studio stand-in, Marjorie Dillon. She spent several weeks in virtual seclusion, sobbing and unwilling to see her parents. This was probably the time she set her mind on what had been hitherto unthinkable – a divorce.

Her misery must have seemed to her complete. Even her parents, during their short-lived separation, had avoided what was then considered a cause of public shame and embarrassment. Now she, their daughter, was to inflict both on the family. And she, the sex goddess, the dream bride, the dutiful daughter – it was ruin!

To her studio, of course, it was nothing of the sort. The break-up of a star's marriage doesn't necessarily hurt her career so much as add a fresh dimension of public interest to her image. In Elizabeth's case, as MGM was well aware, this image had served its turn. Other pictures, other roles, could incorporate whatever novelty the new image of Elizabeth held for the public. People at MGM were not unsympathetic. But a film studio – an autocratic community that no longer exists in today's Hollywood, which is ruled by a loose confederacy of agents – has been through it all before with the ones it loves, hates and employs: its stars. Stardom is a damaged state, anyhow, an imbalance in the human personality that catches the public interest and imagination, then is standardized so as to be repeatable and rotated through role after role so as to offer a variety of changeless appeal. Such was the *modus operandi* that made Hollywood function in those days. It knew no other. Almost no star, however great, was successfully built to a preconceived plan. The accidents of public taste, as reflected in the box office, had more to do with fame and fortune than all the skilful blueprints of producers. The stars themselves were frequently the ones who changed the ways they were perceived – ways that often caused them pain, shame or even disrepute through divorce, promiscuity or adultery.

Social scandals like these had once proved fatal: but America in the 1950s was a very changed place from Hollywood in the 1940s. Kids were undergoing excruciating yearnings to become adults. James Dean and Natalie Wood, to name only two talents among that charismatic and now mostly posthumous band of 1950s icons, projected in their performances the romantic agony of being young. They focused and vocalized the needs and desires of America's youth.

Elizabeth had been seen as a young newlywed in *Father of the Bride,* released in May 1950; and she would be a divorced woman before her tremulously fresh and virginal girl, succouring her man, was seen in *A Place in the Sun*: it was due for its premiere in August 1951. The contradiction between image and reality would only be to her advantage –

however painful the reality was. The headlines would increase the public's fascination with her by provoking endless, media-fed speculation about 'the *real* Elizabeth Taylor'. It is in the space this creates, between the visible image and the public's perception of the real person, that a star takes shape and renews herself.

So MGM kept fairly quiet in these weeks, letting events determine Elizabeth's life. For the moment anyhow, it was beyond a studio's protection or mediation.

Elizabeth moved into the home of her agent Jules Goldstone and his wife. Goldstone, a lawyer, cemented her resolve to get a divorce – and even repulsed a furious Nick Hilton who came barging in, screaming abuse and smarting at the implication that his wife's running out on him somehow impugned his manhood.

The first that Sara Taylor heard of her daughter's formal separation was when she read it, courtesy of Louella Parsons, in the papers on 7 December 1950. Like any mother, she put on her best face: 'If they are left alone, we feel they will work it out.'

Much more remarkable was the unwonted candour of MGM's reaction: 'There is no denying that they have been living apart ... They have had a quarrel ... It's doubtful they'll get together again. This isn't the first time they've been separated. They always fight about the same thing, his gambling and playing around and ignoring her as a wife.' The unnamed author of this statement added, perhaps feelingly, 'They both have a temper.'

Part of this candour may be attributed to Louis B. Mayer's waning influence at the studio he once ruled. The studio personnel sensed things were in transition under their recently appointed new production chief, Dore Schary. But it was also MGM's signal to Elizabeth that it was on her side.

And on 17 December 1950, it was MGM that made the formal statement on her behalf: 'Nick and I ... have come to a final parting of the ways ... there is no possibility of a reconciliation.'

Nick Hilton, the statement added, was out of town – on a hunting trip. In a nervous, exhausted condition, determined not to suffer the further public humiliation of going back to mother, yet without a permanent home beyond what temporary shelter she was afforded under the roof of her stand-in and her agent, Elizabeth was thrown back on the practical sympathy of the studio. It assigned her immediately to a new film. The title was *Love Is Better Than Ever*.

By the time she reported for work, it was all over bar the divorce. She filed before December was out, and a hearing was set for the end of January 1951. She found the director of her new film, Stanley Donen, more than usually understanding. Donen's own marriage to Jean Coyne, a dancer, had broken down around the time of the Hiltons' wedding. Then twenty-seven, this brilliant choreographer had made his debut as co-director with Gene Kelly in *On the Town* and had just finished *Singin' in the Rain* for MGM. Donen was now separated from his wife and as much in need of company and consolation as Elizabeth. Why either of them needed to make a B-picture like *Love Is Better Than Ever* is a mystery: except that, despite their celebrity, both were employees, there was a project ready to go and they were available. There may also have been a slight element of corporate disciplining in making them do a film that wouldn't enhance, but couldn't hurt, their reputations: the logic being that they shouldn't be allowed to get above themselves.

The plot can be summed up (or dismissed) as 'small-town girl makes up her mind to live'. But there is an element of autobiography in the script and direction that cannot have been entirely co-incidental, and at times produces an eerie sensation. For instance, the photos of his daughter as a child that Elizabeth's screen father shows her brash, street-wise lover, played by Larry Parks, all come from her own family's snapshot album. Nothing startling about that, perhaps, as actresses in other films have made use of childhood memorabilia, except that *Love Is Better Than Ever* makes an almost neurotic point of emphasizing the struggle that Elizabeth, as a dance-school teacher, has to wage in order to cut loose from her mother's apron-strings. Endless notes under the door read 'Your mother called,' while the mother is forever ordering her about ('Wear your pink') or taxing her with reproachful guilt ('Sure, I'm not supposed to say anything: I'm only your mother'). The plot, too, echoes episodes all too painfully recent in Elizabeth's off-screen life: like an engagement 'arranged' so as to stop gossip about being a flirt, and then broken off when it has served its purpose.

She plays a tougher role than usual, that of a girl who learns to look after herself, thanks in part to Larry Parks as a grasping talent agent. Her performance also has the bite of an unexpected comedienne. One can see she has lost weight – much of the time, she wears leotards and dance outfits. The disquieting surprise is just how taut and tense she sometimes looks: the strain of impending divorce shows up in this film that Donen shot in seven weeks, perhaps realizing that he had a sick woman on his hands.

'Stanley is a little boy at heart,' says an acquaintance. 'Elizabeth mothered him: they were both in the same "semi-hitched" state. He nursed her. Her mother seldom showed up during the film as it was such a tense time for the family. I think Elizabeth was afraid to go home to her parents in case they put pressure on her to go back to Nick Hilton. An awful lot of money, never mind family pride, was at stake.' Donen ordered all Elizabeth's meals. She was suffering from colitis and the doctor had diagnosed what looked like an ulcer. All she could eat was strained vegetables — baby food. Donen used to spoon-feed her pabulum. He was really considerate, something she'd never had from the Hilton boy. But it wasn't all one-way. She listened to his marital sorrows. She was gradually getting a new slant on what love was all about. It's doubtful if she finished the picture thinking love was better than ever.

In fact, she finished it in an isolated room at the Cedars of Lebanon Hospital. Admitted under the name of 'Rebecca Jones' (or 'James'), she remained there from 9–16 January 1951, being treated officially for flu, though the hospital bill of $500 and sizeable doctors' bills suggest a more serious illness. The pattern of collapse, retreat, recuperation and recovery whenever she could no longer fight stress on her feet repeats itself over and over again in Elizabeth Taylor's life. It was often to be the salvation of a woman harried by illnesses and accidents well above any individual's average: a triumph of mind over body.

Even after Elizabeth had checked into hospital, the studio limousine whisked her to the film set each day, then returned her in the evening to her hospital bed. This went on until the doctors forbade it and the film had to close down temporarily.

Elizabeth still looked under strain, and trembled visibly, when she entered the Santa Monica divorce court on 29 January 1951, to shed her husband. Barbara Thompson buoyed her up; her agent and another lawyer also lent support. Her parents were nowhere to be seen. She had managed to 'kick myself out of the nest' without doubt: but it was a hard landing.

In hesitant, barely audible tones — the court stenographer, a few feet away, asked her to speak up — she testified that her husband 'was indifferent to me and used abusive language'. To spare her as much humiliation as possible, the evidence she would have given in her own words was encapsulated in the form of 'leading questions' by her lawyer-agent Jules Goldstone.

Mr Goldstone: 'Mrs Hilton, starting almost from the beginning of your marriage ... your husband was very argumentative ... for no apparent reason [and] would become very violent ... That recurred repeatedly during your marriage. In addition, he spent most of his time away from you ... This continued after [you] returned from Los Angeles.'

Judge: 'Mrs Hilton, is all that true and correct?'

Answer: 'Yes.'

Mr Goldstone: 'You have a substantial income from your work as a motion-picture actress and I understand you wish to waive any alimony.'

Answer: 'Yes.'

Mr Goldstone: 'And you seek the return of your maiden name.'
Answer (in a very low voice): 'Yes.'
Judge: 'The divorce will be granted.'

Elizabeth clasped her white-gloved hands to her face and started sobbing. The judge, having exercised his discretion on her behalf, no doubt felt entitled to exercise tenderness: he took her into his office for a cigarette. She was well enough on her return to pose for photographers.

Although she had waived alimony, her attorneys fought the Hiltons for a private-property settlement. The battle lasted months and was robustly contested by the hotel heir and his family, with the block of stock Elizabeth had received from Conrad Hilton a hotly disputed prize. Most of her wedding presents had been put into storage. Elizabeth never looked at them again. Possessions didn't greatly matter to her, except the ones that came with love. Even the price tags on lovers' gifts were translated as the strength of passion, rather than the gift's intrinsic worth in carats or precious metal. Elizabeth consumed experience; but she didn't ever hoard its material compensations.

Once divorced, she faced the question that was a continuous source of harassment throughout the rest of her life: who would her next husband be? Marriage is the matrix of the myth that began surrounding Elizabeth Taylor from this early date. Whether it pleased her or not, she began to discover the public's craving to participate vicariously in her love life. There was nothing new in this phenomenon; it was as old as the movies themselves. The most common technique for promoting a film was the arranged affair. Stars were publicized as being in love with other stars; romancing couples starred together in films. The underlying premise was the public's assumption that the stars had the same irresistible sexuality as the creatures they played in their films. The ferment of curiosity would thus boost the box office receipts. Sometimes, it also hoisted up the fees of stars with agents unromantic enough to put a price on their clients' love affairs. The same ferment was to be produced cyclically in Elizabeth's case through her successive marriages, divorces and remarriages. And the periodic fits of outraged morality which such serial monogamy provoked, far from hurting her at the box office, actually enhanced the worldwide interest in her 'nature', her 'power', her 'mystery', her 'sexuality'. It also, of course, enhanced her fee.

The Hilton divorce, and her previous engagements, marked the beginning of this syndrome in Elizabeth's life. Conditioned by the publicity, people quickly absolved her of any sense of guilt or failure she felt about herself; they perceived her as a woman of instinct, likely to follow where the heart led, not worrying overmuch about messes that had to be cleared up as she went along. Later still, when so-called 'illicit love' became married life in the course of time and the decree nisi, the suggestion of enjoyable sex would still be central in the life she was pictured leading with her latest husband.

By February 1951, as gossip columnists began hinting that she might be the next Mrs Stanley Donen, Howard Hughes, hope rekindled by her divorce, as well as by the approaching expiry of her MGM contract, re-appeared out of the shadows — though, naturally, not too far out — with proposals to set up an independent production company for her. He offered to finance six films. She was then making about $2,000 a week. If she had accepted Hughes's offer, she would have had several years' head start on such stars as Burt Lancaster and Kirk Douglas, who were among the first stars to become their own producers in the new decade. Of course, with Howard Hughes as a backer, she would hardly have been a free agent. And fear of that unromantic entanglement, as much as anything, made her reject Hughes's seductive proposals a second time.

She continued to see Stanley Donen. To the inquisitive press, he denied all talk of a romance. 'I can't talk about the future. Liz won't be free [of her MGM contract] until January, 1952 ... Besides, I'm still married, at least technically.'

Still wary of her parents, and fearing that they would pressure her to change her mind and return to Nick Hilton even this late in the day, Elizabeth moved into a five-room apartment at 1060 Wilshire Boulevard with Margaret (Peggy) Rutledge, a secretary-companion who had once worked for Bob Hope.

Hedda Hopper visited Elizabeth in her 'bachelor girl' apartment on Wilshire Boulevard. She found her in a nightgown that had been part of her wedding trousseau. 'The main thing is — are you happy?' Hopper asked. Though the answer was plain to see, Elizabeth defiantly refused to admit she was not.

'Yes,' she said.

'"This is your Aunt Hedda asking," I reminded her.

'"Well," she backtracked in a sad little voice, "I am happy. But I am not nineteen happy."'

She confessed to Hopper that her savings had been badly depleted by the layoff caused when she had had a nervous collapse during the making of Love Is Better Than Ever. 'I had to spend thousands of dollars on doctors' bills to be able to finish the picture. I even had to have a nurse with me on the set.' Hopper asked her about the block of shares that her father-in-law had given her upon marriage, but she hadn't thought about that. She looked very disorganized. Her visitor opened a refrigerator and found inside only a jar of peanut butter and some soft-drink bottles. Belongings were strewn over the room. No books were to be seen, only fan magazines.

'I am trying to re-organize myself,' Elizabeth admitted. 'I was certainly a mixed-up eighteen. Eighteen seemed to last forever. It got me in such a tension that even now I can't relax. For the last year, I've been like a person trying to catch a train.'

One day she brought Donen round to her parents' home. It was an unrewarding visit. Donen was no substitute in Mrs Taylor's eyes for the Hilton boy. He had no fortune, and he was still 'technically' married. In time, Elizabeth and her parents would be reconciled and she would find them, as she put it, 'a fountain to be tapped' in adversity. But the current estrangement left her trembling and indignant. It also left Sara Taylor in no doubt that the little girl who used to pen apologies for any insubordination had disappeared for good into a headstrong and very direct young woman.

Elizabeth tried consoling herself with the reflection that divorcing Nick Hilton was the first adult thing she had done. Henceforth, she was going to do what seemed right to her: she would pursue an independence based on instinct. Such thoughts hardened her against the attentions that she and Donen attracted wherever they went together – dancing at the Mocambo, dining at the Brown Derby, or night-clubbing in Palm Springs at The Doll's House. On 5 April 1951, Donen escorted her to the Hollywood premiere of *Father's Little Dividend* and both were extensively photographed. Donen's wife had flown to California soon after Elizabeth's divorce – to discuss her own, said the columnists. Within days of the film premiere, she filed the divorce papers.

16

'GIVE THE GIRL ANYTHING SHE WANTS!'

In retrospect, it looks as if Elizabeth was sent to England in June 1951, to make *Ivanhoe*, in order to spare her any undeserved publicity from Stanley Donen's marital troubles. But if so, this was not the only reason. MGM was a business first, not a moral welfare society. Moreover, with Louis B. Mayer's power passing to Dore Schary, the studio was noticeably more relaxed about the moral standards it expected its stars to observe (or, at least, not to infringe openly). Time was running out on Elizabeth's contract. Negotiations for a renewal were already under way, but not making much progress. The studio wanted all the value it could squeeze out of the expiring agreement. *Ivanhoe* would serve.

Besides, MGM had good reason for casting one of its available top stars. It had already sunk $100,000 in the costume epic, mainly to acquire the various scripts of Scott's novel that RKO had prepared as long ago as 1939 without getting into production.

Robert Taylor was Ivanhoe; Joan Fontaine, the heroine Rowena; and Elizabeth was to play Rebecca the Jewess. She protested; it was the inferior role. No avail: MGM assigned her to it on 7 May 1951, and ordered her to report for costume and make-up tests on 7 June. On the same day, she applied for a new passport. Her current one was in her married name; she wanted to make it clear to the world that she was consigning that episode to oblivion. But the prudent passport office in Washington DC required an affidavit from her and the studio head of contracts, Floyd Hendrickson, that she had abandoned all intention of ever again using the name 'Hilton'. The assurance was promptly given. Interestingly, the application for the new travel document listed a scar (or mole) on the right side of her neck as one of her distinguishing characteristics. Typically, MGM had tried to persuade the eleven-year-old child to have it removed when it signed her up in 1943; perfection was the end in those days. Her father had refused.

Peggy Rutledge, her secretary-companion, was put on the MGM payroll from 16 June: this required her to report to the studio on Elizabeth's activities and welfare when she accompanied her to England. Mrs Taylor, though technically still employed by MGM to do that, was to stay behind – a sign of the changed balance of power between mother and daughter.

Though she was still subject to what was called a 'slave contract', Elizabeth enjoyed all the privileges of stardom. She had a night's stopover in New York en route to London. A top official from the British airline carrying her actually sat all night in her uncle's New York apartment, where she was sleeping, so that there would be no risk of her missing the flight in the morning. No sooner had she arrived in England than Lord and Lady Mountbatten invited her to a ball they were giving. She was treated with awestruck curiosity by guests who usually merely condescended to Hollywood celebrities. It was a new kind of power that she began to experience. She danced with Prince Philip. Stanley Donen was being forgotten.

Elizabeth's daily schedule was taxing, considering she was still on her diet of baby food and was suffering from migraines. She had to leave her Savoy Hotel suite by 5.15 a.m., get to the 120-acre MGM studio at Borehamwood by 6.00 a.m., then endure a lengthy session in wardrobe and make-up to costume her in medieval robes and turn her own raven hair into glossy plaits interlaced with gold thread. A wig was eventually made to spare her some of this daily ordeal – but the wig itself proved a burden. 'It weighs two pounds,' she complained. 'It's full of pins that stick into me all day long. By night, I have a neck-ache to add to my headache.'

Even the film's historical authenticity was a cause for complaint. 'We wear long dresses of wool jersey and heavy capes, and it sometimes seems to take an hour to lace [me] up.' She didn't usually get back to London until after 6.00 p.m. And what did she do then? 'Stay home and improve my mind reading mystery stories – ha-ha.'

Elizabeth had a poor opinion of the film, though it was to prove one of MGM's most consistent money-earners, a true 'annuity' film, bringing in profit every time it was re-released. 'A piece of cachou,' remained her unrevised opinion of it. Her role was a 'nothing' one – or might have been, had her beauty and composure not endowed it with that passive gravity that lighting photographers love. What probably upset her most was the perception that it was a victim's role – Rebecca the Jewess loses Ivanhoe to the gentile Rowena. Playing the loser in a romantic tale seemed too close for comfort to someone whose feelings were still raw from her failed marriage. Then again, there was no big love scene of the kind that had transfigured her in *A Place in the Sun* – not that the director, Richard

Thorpe, was a George Stevens. Instead, the interest was fixed on a rape scene, in which she saves herself from the advances of George Sanders, as the Templar knight Sir Brian de Bois-Guilbert, by means of a timely faint. 'Rebecca, you mistake the nature of our bargain,' Sanders chides her. 'I want you alive, not dead.' Later, Elizabeth almost became a witness in a French lawsuit that a descendant of the real de Bois-Guilbert attempted to bring against MGM after the film's release, claiming that his ancestor's rapacious approach defamed the contemporary branch of the family. The ever resourceful Maître Blum, who was also the Duke and Duchess of Windsor's lawyer, cleverly deflected the charge by arguing that since the Knights Templar took a vow of chastity, the de Bois-Guilbert line must sometime, somehow, have strayed from celibate grace in order to produce heirs who could sue for their reputation.

Elizabeth betrayed her lack of interest in the role by the flat and listless way she spoke the dialogue – her voice remained her greatest deficiency, except when the edge of hysteria or the lash of anger was required. It required dubbing afterwards in Hollywood. Thorpe appealed to the producer Pandro Berman, whose relationship with Elizabeth went back to *National Velvet* and included her most recent MGM success, *Father of the Bride*. Thorpe said that Elizabeth's nerves made him reluctant to risk upsetting her with retakes of her lines. Berman, more pragmatist than diplomat, said, 'I told him to get what he could out of her, then do every damn line over again when they got back to Hollywood. The lady was always good at improving a performance in the dubbing stages. She'd do it professionally, even if she disdained what she was doing.' Berman was again to gamble on this approach when 'the lady' rejected one of his later films with a monumental show of temper.

While making *Ivanhoe*, Elizabeth paid yet another visit to her old home in Wildwood Road. She found it was now a day nursery and she stayed for an hour or two, happily looking after other mothers' children. That visit may well have strengthened her own wish to get married again and have children.

Back in 1949, when she was making *The Conspirator* at MGM's British studios, Elizabeth had invited an actor over from the neighbouring set of a film called *Derby Day*. A school chum of hers, Sheran Cazalet, the grand-niece of Victor, had wanted to meet Michael Wilding. Wilding was then the most popular leading man in the romantic comedies that teamed him with Anna Neagle. Their films served as an antidote to the austerity of post-war socialist Britain. *The Courtneys of Curzon Street*, *Spring in Park Lane*, *Maytime in Mayfair* and other light-hearted fantasies of West End postal districts had given this team an enormous box-office success. Wilding dropped in on *The Conspirator* production and made Sheran

Cazalet's day. The next year, in Hollywood, he dropped in on Mrs Taylor, and made an even profounder impression. So much so that when the Hilton marriage broke up, Sara found herself reflecting, 'There is only one man I can think of who could make [Elizabeth] happy again ... and that is Michael Wilding.'

It is not surprising that the mother should have fallen for this urbane Englishman. He was everything she admired in the upper classes, which a negligent eye might have assumed Wilding had been born into. He had an air of gentlemanly good breeding, a lazily diffident manner, and a man-about-town charm that went back to the well-mannered days of the musical star Jack Buchanan, which was just about contemporaneous with Sara's own success in the West End theatre and London nightclub society. He had also an eye for well-developed little girls like Elizabeth, whom he had noticed wiggling her hips at him in the MGM commissary – no doubt during one of those rare moments when, as Sheilah Graham had observed, she was asserting her sexuality under her mother's nose.

Wilding had been in Hollywood to make *The Law and the Lady* with Greer Garson. This may seem unlikely casting. In his films with Anna Neagle, Wilding's sense of humour set the tone for both himself and his co-star, who looked, and was, a lady, but who needed guiding on the comedy side. Hollywood borrowed him in 1950 – he was under contract to Anna Neagle and her husband, the producer Herbert Wilcox – to fulfil much the same function with Greer Garson, also a lady, but no madcap. His MGM contract was worth £18,000 for the 13-week schedule, plus £2,250 in overage (further fees incurred if the film overran its schedule): quite good for the time, but not likely to be repeated in Hollywood, as the movie was a disaster.

Wilding, however, was not a man to succumb to despondency. He had the consolation of the friendship he had struck up with Marlene Dietrich, with whom he had made Hitchcock's *Stage Fright* in England. Dietrich is credited with the change that came over Michael Wilding's appearance after he had made the rounds of London tailors, shirt-makers and barbers. He was now a flattering escort to any woman: he had a charm of the sort that didn't put a question mark on his virility. He was thirty-eight when he ran into Elizabeth Taylor again. They were soon in love.

In many ways, it was the attraction of opposites. The opposites in this case, though, are Michael Wilding and Nick Hilton. Wilding looked and sounded like the antithesis of the man who had driven Elizabeth into a breakdown after barely half a year of marriage. He was over six feet tall and elegant, with a line in chatty self-deprecation that concealed his nervousness. Hilton had been crude and assertively chauvinist, with no small-talk. Wilding had a throwaway sophistication that made Elizabeth's ex-husband look like a hick. Thanks to Dietrich's grooming, he made a well-tailored, flatteringly masculine and uncompetitive foil for any woman he was going out with: in short, a ladies' man, not a womanizer.

All these attentive qualities were particularly appealing to a girl like Elizabeth, whose self-esteem had suffered a devastating blow. The age gap between them – nineteen years – stimulated her enjoyment of his company. He was like a young father. Moreover, he didn't take his career that seriously – just like herself, or so she told herself when MGM assigned her to 'cachous' like *Ivanhoe*.

He was soon dating Elizabeth and taking her out on the town, to the Savoy Grill, the Mirabelle, the Ivy or the Caprice. Quizzed about their relationship, he said he admired her courage – the fact that she was 'undismayed by disaster' – a politely English way of referring to her divorce. He liked her strength of character, he said. Elizabeth was positively melting. Wilding had yet to feel her strength of will.

Wilding had another flattering, if negative characteristic. He was exceptionally vulnerable to women giving him advice. He used to tell the story that in his youth as a jobbing film actor – he had carried a spear in the epic British folly *Caesar and Cleopatra* – a woman with whom he struck up a conversation in a theatre bar told him he was wasting his time in films. 'Get experience. Join a [theatre] repertory company.'

'Anything in mind?' he asked genially.

'Try Watford.'

The next day he took the train to that dismal rail junction to look for work. Chance had made up his mind for him – and if chance this time meant Elizabeth Taylor, well, what luck!

Wilding had also tried to be a serious painter, but had drifted into commercial art. In Elizabeth's starry eyes, that gave him an immediate link with her art-dealer father. On one of his CVs, in the box for 'Ambition', he entered: 'To be rich and not have to work.'

But he had other desires that were not so manifest. Under his slightly dithering charm, there was a strong sex drive. He gave tireless satisfaction in bed. Anna Neagle said of him later: 'Michael always kept that side of him to himself when we were together. But Herbert [Wilcox] used to warn him that any scandal, like the life Errol Flynn was leading at the time, would be absolutely disastrous to his career. With me, he was a romantic actor – never anything more. He owed his British stardom to Herbert and I don't think he ever contemplated doing anything that would harm him. But from time to time, we used to hear of Michael having an affair with someone, perhaps someone who was married, and then Herbert would have to have him up "for a talk".'

Wilding's first marriage had broken down because of his admitted promiscuousness. Whether or not he put it to conscious use, his charm eased his way into many a physical relationship. Other actors have that facility, of course. But with Wilding, it was an attempt to regain a pleasurable discovery he had made in his childhood days in pre-revolutionary Russia where his father, who had been born in St Petersburg, had briefly served in military intelligence. Young Michael had been swimming at a fashionable resort and surfaced among the large-bosomed women who were taking the waters. To his excited astonishment, he made the Fellini-esque find that women had bumps where men had flat chests. He later asked the family housekeeper to show him her bumps, and the amused woman obligingly opened her blouse to the small, solemn boy.

It wasn't always the big-breasted woman to whom Wilding was drawn, or Dietrich would scarcely have qualified. The 'little boy' that peeped out of him, giving him an inviting air of innocence on and off screen, was also attracted by the woman who could be a stern but motherly type, taking the decisions, telling him what to do, asking to be pleased. He found Elizabeth at just this stage of development, as his attentions helped her regain her sense of self-worth and direction.

But according to Anna Neagle, 'What made the biggest impact on Michael was Elizabeth's physical maturity.' And he himself was even more candid. 'I had never seen a more shattering sashay,' he confided in his posthumously published memoirs, after he witnessed her walk through the commissary at MGM.

She finished her role in *Ivanhoe* on 14 September 1951, and didn't hurry home to Hollywood. She stayed on in London, revelling in the unaccustomed feeling of independence – and in Wilding's company. Baby food was replaced by hearty meals. Soon, she confessed, 'I was cured of all my ailments.' It was in fact a full-blown crush she was nurturing.

Before she took off for Los Angeles on 7 October, she had resolved to marry Michael Wilding. It's been said that this took him totally by surprise. That was not how it appeared to Anna Neagle nearly forty years later. 'Michael was nearly forty at the time. He had been friends with Dietrich, but she was a married woman, though she didn't advertise the fact. He said Elizabeth made him feel young again, which made Herbert and me smile. But then he told us that, as Elizabeth's husband, he would have a bigger career in Hollywood than Herbert could give him here. He wanted to be a truly international star. He'd made films with Marlene and with Ingrid Bergman [including *Under Capricorn*] and he saw himself starring with this girl who had just had the most wonderful success in *A Place in the Sun*. Michael wasn't the strongest-willed man where women were concerned – and this one seemed to have everything on offer.'

What held Wilding back from making Elizabeth a formal proposal was

the doubt that her parents would consent to her marrying a man twice
her age – she was still under twenty-one and needed their permission. But
the notion of returning home with an engagement ring on her finger –
compensation and sweet revenge – made Elizabeth step up the pace. He
noted, with wry amusement, that she started plastering on more make-up
in an effort to close the age gap between them. She had played this sort
of scene in *A Date With Judy*, successfully setting her cap at Robert Stack
as the older man. She teased Wilding: 'If only I was older, you would ask
me to marry you.'

One reason why Wilding didn't is that he was still in the process of
getting his divorce from the actress Kay Young, though they'd been living
apart since 1945 – his little publicized marriage helped him, like Dietrich,
to wear an air of intriguing eligibility. He would telephone Anna Neagle
after a date with Elizabeth: 'I'm running after this dear girl, Anna, and
she's desperate to catch me.' She was not so desperate, though, that she
had forgotten a trick or two from her days with *Judy*. She started going
out with another man, Tab Hunter, the blond and bland idol of American
teenagers, who was in London making *Island of Desire*. Wilding guessed
what she was up to. It didn't make him jealous, but simply amused at her
deviousness. It flattered him. When he told her he'd never seen her in a
film – *A Place in the Sun* hadn't yet opened abroad – she had *National
Velvet* run for him; he came out of it impressed by her strength of will. 'I
do believe she's going to get me,' he told Anna. Elizabeth had the United
Press International man in for an interview at her hotel, and roundly
declared herself mentally equipped for remarriage. 'But I have not picked
the time nor the person,' she added, while 'demurely pouring tea'.

Michael Wilding and Tab Hunter both saw Elizabeth aboard the New
York-bound flight in October. She kissed Wilding twice before take-off.
'Good-bye, Mr Shilly-Shally,' she said, 'let's forget we ever met.'

She installed herself at the Plaza Hotel, New York, as a guest of the
management, or so she believed. One person who visited her was her ex-
husband, Nick Hilton. They sat on a sofa four feet apart. A photographer
asked them to move closer. 'Well, not *too* close,' said Elizabeth, 'after all
...' Behind the scenes, the parents and relations of both parties were trying
to promote a more permanent closeness. It was proving difficult to
disentangle the property settlement. Moreover, it is believed that, failing
a reconciliation, the Hiltons were anxious that no obstacle should be
placed in the way of Nick Hilton's future remarriage in a Roman Catholic
church. Elizabeth's agreement to an annulment was vital. A summit
meeting was held at Howard Young's estate at Ridgefield, Connecticut,
on 18 October 1951; but as Elizabeth was telephoning Michael Wilding
several times daily, auspices for a rematch were poor.

Wilding, meanwhile, was in a dither. 'This is one occasion Anna and I can't make up your mind for you,' Herbert Wilcox told him. Friends tried to dissuade him. John Clements told him, 'Michael, it'll be the end of you. Your kind of talent simply doesn't have a future in Hollywood.' Anna Neagle says: 'We were all concerned to see what was happening to David Niven at the time. He and Michael had the same sort of gentlemanly manner and his Hollywood career was collapsing. The children didn't want to know about stars like David with all those young Method actors around. But Michael thought Elizabeth's stardom would rub off on him somehow. And of course, with her sex appeal and the possibility of starting a family at his age . . .'

Then MGM ordered Elizabeth back to Hollywood for retakes and post-synchronization of her *Ivanhoe* dialogue.

She got an unpleasant surprise when she asked the Plaza's front desk to send up her bill. She wasn't the management's guest that she thought she was: only the first few days had been a courtesy stay. The rest of her visit had been at the full daily rate: the bill came to more than $2,600. Incredulity was followed by indignation, then by impetuosity. The leading reins of a mother's life-long discipline were kicked over in the rampage that followed, when her friends Monty Clift and Roddy McDowall, who had been summoned to her suite to help her pack her things, turned the occasion into a madcap spree fuelled by a pitcher of martinis. The boys seized the long-stemmed chrysanthemums out of their vases and put on an impromptu bit of swordsmanship while Elizabeth stuffed her clothes into a dozen valises in the bedroom. When she returned, the suite was splattered with flower petals and foliage, pictures had been rehung upside down and Clift had had to go to the bathroom to be sick – or so they thought. When she unpacked in a temporary (complimentary) suite at the St Regis Hotel, out fell every moveable fixture from the Plaza bathroom that the inebriated Monty Clift had managed to detach or unscrew – tap tops, bath towels, cabinet handles – and even the empty martini pitcher. Elizabeth got down to writing one of those sorry notes . . . this time to the management, not mother.

Clift didn't warm to the idea of her and Wilding getting married. The English actor's style wasn't his; it belonged to a dated romanticism, not the Method's soul-searching. On the other hand, he knew Elizabeth's passion for motherhood; and since he couldn't, or wouldn't, satisfy it, the next best thing was to be a wife's best friend.

Wilding came to California in December 1951, ostensibly to help Anna Neagle and Herbert Wilcox publicize their Florence Nightingale biopic, *The Lady with the Lamp*, in which he had a token part. He stayed with Stewart Granger, whose best man he had been when he married Jean

Simmons the year before in Texas. He relaxed in the sun with the Grangers – his host was under contract to MGM and Jean Simmons was at Fox, after freeing herself from the bonds of a Howard Hughes contract of the kind that the millionaire had hoped to wrap around Elizabeth. Looking at the Grangers, Wilding perhaps had a vision of himself and Elizabeth, husband and wife like these other two English film stars, residents of Beverly Hills, driving to the studios, making films together, *real* films, films sold and seen the world over, not the 'little British pictures' which the Anna Neagle–Herbert Wilcox productions became when viewed from this perspective.

'I was twenty years younger than [Michael Wilding], so in a way my personal life was again falling in line with my image on the screen, where I'd so often been cast opposite an older man.' So wrote Elizabeth years later, looking back on this decisive time. She knew very well what she wanted – and now she knew how to get it.

In London some months before, Wilding had gazed across a dinner table at the pendant round her neck and told her, with the teasing condescension of that twenty-year difference, that she was too young for such a sophisticated bit of jewellery – and hers was too beautiful a neck to need it. She returned it to the shop. He told her, flippantly, that she should wear sapphires to match her eyes.

Now in California, he was awakened by an early call from her. She needed his advice again. She was having trouble choosing between two sapphire rings. Wilding hadn't more than twenty dollars on him; his recently completed divorce had cost him dear and the currency restrictions in England meant he could hardly have bought Elizabeth a square meal, never mind a fine sapphire. Still, he gave his opinion; that, at least, cost nothing. Then, maybe with relief, he watched her pay for the ring. Gallantly, he offered to slip it on her finger, but she demurred. 'I think that's the finger it should go on, Michael, the engagement ring one.'

Losing neither time nor momentum, she had their engagement announced as the New Year dawned: 'That makes it official, doesn't it?' Then a press conference was called; in Hollywood, that made things even more official. 'It's leap year, isn't it? Well, I leaped,' she told the newsmen.

'He's gone and done it. God help him!' said Herbert Wilcox.

'But of course we put on the best face we could,' said Anna Neagle. 'Herbert agreed to release Michael from the contract he'd signed just a few months before. He told the newspaper people, "Let's just say he's had a better offer, a lifer." People expected Herbert to make that kind of joke. But he was very bitter – *very*! Not that there was any use suing Michael – he was almost broke.'

Wilding explained it in his usual laconic way: 'I had thought we would wait a few weeks. Elizabeth didn't.'

One reason why Elizabeth was in a hurry was her new film. She had to report to MGM on 25 March 1952, to begin *The Girl Who Had Everything*. Her whole mood was one of making up for lost time. When someone asked her why she had paid overweight air charges on the twenty-two pieces of luggage with her when she checked into the Plaza – why not ship them as freight? – she had looked horrified. 'I couldn't. I had to have everything right away.' Now she had to have a husband right away.

When Wilding returned to London on 17 February, Elizabeth accompanied him. Her picture of the perfect husband had now taken on a distinctly English coloration. No nightclubs, no barbecues, no pool parties. 'I just want to be with Michael and be his wife. He enjoys sitting home, smoking his pipe, reading, painting. And that's what I intend doing – all except smoking a pipe.' She was already demonstrating what was to become one of her strongest and most constant traits, projecting herself in imagination into the marriage she had yet to contract, taking on her husband-to-be's characteristics as if they were her own, evincing the most wifely kind of loyalty by adopting the most husbandly virtues she perceived in her man. To her, Wilding represented peace of mind, domesticity, security, maturity – and a family. She was looking to someone else for the things she hoped to find in herself.

Another characteristic was revealed almost the moment the aircraft touched down. A representative of the Westminster registrar of marriages was waiting for them at the Wilcoxes' home. But Elizabeth had forgotten to bring her divorce decree. Organization was something that, throughout her life, she never considered a virtue, but a forced duty. Mrs Taylor had good cause in the years ahead to regret trying to instil discipline in her child. 'To the day she left it, [her room looked] as though it had been stirred, vigorously, with a giant teaspoon.' She might have been commenting on the wider disorder of her daughter's later life. Elizabeth, people were to notice, could sit in the middle of chaos as if she had somehow found the still centre that was untroubled by the storm, whether whipped up by a teaspoon or some larger instrument of fate.

Fortunately, the missing proof of her divorce was telegraphed to her and the registrar's assistant drove back to Caxton Hall, awoke the porters and, at twenty minutes to midnight, posted notice of the wedding for three clear days later, 21 February. She had hoped to be married on, or near, the late Victor Cazalet's estate by a Church of England minister. Wilding, more realistically, spoke of a 'service of blessing', the acceptable rite for a couple who were both divorced. But time didn't allow for even this.

As before, Helen Rose made the bridal outfit, but this time adapted it to the rigours of the English climate: an anthracite grey wool suit, with a three-tiered organdy collar and cuffs, a full skirt, grey accessories and a hat of tiny white flowers. Anna Neagle helped dress her in her suite at the Connaught Hotel. Her parents had stayed in California. It was to be an economy wedding, compared with the huge production less than two years earlier. The ceremony lasted a mere ten minutes. Only the crowds deserved the description 'spectacular' – some three thousand people milled around Caxton Hall, blocking the road, reaching out, trying to touch Elizabeth or, worse, grab at her – she lost her bridal hat and might have suffered worse injury had a policeman not carried her bodily through a passage cleared in the mob by fellow officers and into an immobilized but secure limousine. Photographers besieged it, begging, imploring, commanding a kiss from the newlyweds – this time in a modest English embrace, not the voluptuous Hollywood clinch. Elizabeth excused herself: she was too shy, she said.

The reception was at Claridge's; a more intimate one took place in Wilding's maisonette at 2 Bruton Street, Mayfair. Then the couple drove a few hundred yards to the Berkeley Hotel, said they were exhausted and had room service bring them bowls of soup, bacon and eggs and champagne: the sort of meal two giggly kids would have pitched into – and to hell with etiquette.

They snatched a week's honeymoon in France and Switzerland, and then it was back to Bruton Street on 2 March. Wilding reported for work on his final film for Herbert Wilcox, *Trent's Last Case*. Elizabeth had a couple of weeks' grace. She gave an interview to David Lewin of the *Daily Express*. 'I never put my career first,' she said. 'A career is not all that important, anyway.' When this was cabled to Hollywood, it caused panic and despondency at MGM. Elizabeth had not yet signed a new contract and her old one had less than a year to run. The studio was desperate. She was now unquestionably the biggest female star it possessed. Other studios would hold off for only a 'polite' length of time; there was an unwritten agreement among the moguls not to chase another company's star until her employers had quit their own pursuit. But what if Elizabeth turned 'independent'? What on earth would keep her with MGM? The year before, the writer Lillian Ross had been with Dore Schary in the Sherry-Netherland Hotel, New York, when Elizabeth, just back from making *Ivanhoe* in England, had called on the MGM production chief with Jules Goldstone. Ross caught – and reported in her book *Picture* – the over-anxious desire to please:

Schary asked Miss Taylor if she wanted a drink. She asked for a gin-and-tonic.

'Take sherry,' said Goldstone.

'Gin-and-tonic,' said Miss Taylor.

'Give the girl anything she wants!' Schary said exuberantly.

But what *did* she want? More money – obviously. No problem. The promise of first-rate parts? Well, that could be arranged, and promises were renegotiable later. But the marriage had suddenly introduced a new element into the equation of star and studio: namely, the star's husband. Maybe if *he* could be given what *she* wanted, then Elizabeth would be MGM's for the full seven-year term of a new contract. And that might be longer than her marriage.

Thus Michael Wilding found himself employed by a studio that had never dreamed of hiring such an actor, for so long a term, and at so high a price.

17

BIG MAMA

Money was the first need of the newlyweds. Wilding had alimony to pay to his ex-wife. And when he announced he was leaving Britain to work in America, the tax man flourished a £35,000 bill for unpaid taxes. Wilcox lent him the money, otherwise Elizabeth's husband might have been a long time rejoining her in California.

The main source for ready cash in the quantity they needed to reflect their status was MGM. Jules Goldstone had done a good deal for both of them. Wilding was offered – and instantly accepted – a three-year deal at $3,000 a week (forty weeks guaranteed) with an option for two years at $4,000 a week. (The option was later changed to $5,000 a week.) Princely compensation for a man who was a pauper, it reflected a consort's fee, rather than a star's value.

The MGM offer to Elizabeth was more munificent still: $4,700 a week for five years (forty weeks guaranteed). Sara Taylor, too, got a new deal: $300 a week, when Elizabeth was working. Wilding's contract was to come into effect with his arrival in Hollywood, but not later than December 1952. He entered the country on 5 July 1952.

However, it wasn't simply the enhanced value that MGM put on her husband's talents that decided Elizabeth to stay with the company. She knew by now that sentiment was a commodity in short supply all over Hollywood. Her MGM upbringing – strict though it had been, and sometimes punitive – decided the day. It was a family she could not leave, for she knew no other life.

Even so, she didn't come docilely to the tethering post. Getting her to sign the contract was a protracted affair: MGM feared she would never pick up the pen. It still wasn't signed by July, and Benny Thau was compelled to write to Nicholas Schenck, head of the parent company, Loew's Inc., warning him of 'great difficulties' and 'new demands'. Among the latter was a limit of two films a year, another concerned the TV rights in films starring Elizabeth. Thau said, 'If they stand pat, of course, in not signing the contract, we will follow through with the procedure as discussed, namely that we claim a definite agreement with these people and we will notify all studios to that effect and go to court if necessary to make them live up to it. In the absence of a signed contract, there is a good chance of it being decided against us [by the court]. Nevertheless, we feel it is the proper procedure ... I believe only independent [companies] might deal with them until a court decision is handed down.'

What was the reason behind Elizabeth's reluctance to complete the deal? It came down again to ready cash – or, rather, the lack of it. Undeterred by a very low bank balance, she had set her heart on moving out of the Wilshire Boulevard apartment, which carried memories of being a refuge from home and husband and reminded her of life with a mother substitute like Peggy Rutledge. She wanted a home of her own – a star's home. This was costly. Would MGM come through with more money?

She had announced on 21 June that she was pregnant and expected the baby in January 1953. So a house with a nursery was essential. Benny Thau's letter to Schenck stressed the comparative penury of the newlyweds. In talks the Wildings had had with Schenck, the sum of $75,000 had been mentioned for financing the purchase of a house, the loan being repaid over five years. Thau wasn't in favour of that – or, indeed, any loan at all. But he realized the dilemma that MGM was in. 'I am one hundred percent in accord with the policy of no loans, except in very rare and unusual cases, but in this particular case it gets down to a basis of a contract being finalized or not finalized.'

So MGM agreed to lend the Wildings $50,000, repayment to be set at $16,666.67 per year, over three years. Elizabeth jubilantly signed her new contract, announcing, 'I re-signed because I got cornball sentimental about Benny Thau and all the other nice people at the studio and because Michael and I would be working there and we could have lunch together.'

This must be taken with a pinch of sarcasm. Then she spoke of what really concerned her: 'But mainly it was because I was pregnant. We needed money to get a home of our own – a nest in which to hatch the egg.'

Though Elizabeth intended her marriage to signify her new-found independence, the effect of the commitment she had chosen to make to MGM brought about the very opposite. It put her more completely into the studio's power. That discovery lay ahead, however; for the moment, she felt sublimely happy and fulfilled.

She had made herself up to look older when she started going out with Wilding. Now she was going to be a mother before she was twenty-one.

he Taylor family in their London period: Sara, now the smart 'English' mother (one string of pearls); Elizabeth, out two years old, in her party frock; Howard in his sailor jacket. He had the looks at this time, circa 1934.

lizabeth's mother, Sara Sothern (the girl on crutches), in the London stage production of The Fool *in 1924, with enry Ainley (centre). Faith heals and will-power gets one what one wants. The lesson was passed on.*

(Above) *Heathwood, the Hampstead house (as it is today) where Elizabeth was born in February 1932.*

(Above right) *School days at Byron House, Highgate: Elizabeth (in pale jumper) sits for a formal class photo in 1937.*

(Below right) *An informal snap in a Hampstead back garden, circa 1938: Elizabeth (the girl on the right) spends her last summer in England at play with friends. Hollywood would soon be picking her friends for her.*

(Left) *Elizabeth, aged about five, with her pony Betty. Behind her is Little Swallow, the cottage on the Cazalet estate where the Taylors spent their pre-war weekends.*

(Above) *At home in Beverly Hills, circa 19*
Her face already has a maturity that fits in
uneasily with childish things.

(Left) 'I held Nibbles to my face and kissed h
... The feel of his dear little body I'll never
forget.' *Her pet chipmunk received the love sh*
was later to seek when men entered her life.

(Below) *Graduation at last. Elizabeth ends her formal education with a B-plus smile in a 1950 photo with her mother on the porch of their Beverly Hills home. Then it was off with the mortarboard and on to the Mocambo.*

bove) *Howard shows his sister the latest steps, but friends were hard to find. The cinched-in waist of her ndl skirt shows she was already conscious of her charms.*

elow) *A daughter impatient to take the driving wheel m mother and decide for herself where she'll go.*

(Above) *Lassie was being paid more money, but her self-assured performance already marked Elizabeth as a 'comer'.*

(Left) *With King Charles, her horse in* National Velvet. *Critics noted the obsessional nature of her performance and MGM publicized her power over animals.*

en, boys were in short supply, but in
a, Jimmy Lydon carried her home from
ol prom . . .

. . . and gave her her first screen kiss on the porch. Later, with more experience, she was to describe 'that buss' as more like a handshake.

With Jane Powell in A Date With Judy. *The sophisticated 'man-stealer' prepares to put the 'nice girl' in the shade. Though Elizabeth was only fifteen at the time, the gossip columnists were already calling her 'dangerous'.*

A star who still has homework to do. Elizabeth made up to play a married woman in The Conspirator, *in 1949, is given a history lesson between takes by her tutor Miss Birtina Anderson.*

(Right) *May, 1950: Elizabeth and Nick Hilton cut the cake at the 'Wedding of Weddings'. Eight months later, it was all over.*

(Below) *Summer, 1951. The romance with Michael Wilding begins to sizzle. Relaxing on the set of* Ivanhoe *while in costume (with un-historical cigarette), Elizabeth is fascinated by the charm of the English leading man. The next year, she became his wife.*

(above) *Art anticipates life. While
Elizabeth prepared for her marriage to Nick
Hilton, MGM starred her with Spencer Tracy
in* Father of the Bride. *'Every time we did
a shot of me walking up the aisle to the
altar, I was living it,' she said. Life did not
end as happily, though.*

(above left) *That 'Tell mama . . . tell mama
everything' look. Elizabeth and Montgomery
Clift in* A Place in the Sun.

(below left) *A lighter moment on location for*
A Place in the Sun. *Elizabeth, at the wheel
of the speedboat, laughs as Shelley Winters is
tipped overboard.*

(right) *On the receiving end: Fernando Lamas
handled her roughly in* The Girl Who Had
Everything *— and the spoilt rich girl she
played found she liked it that way. Eroticism
made its appearance in Elizabeth's screen
image — as far as Hollywood's morality code
let, anyhow.*

A Place in the Sun, *in 1951, earned her a place among the stars as the rich girl who is touched by tragedy: an omen, too.*

(Left) *Thinner with anxiety over a collapsing marriage, her role as a dance teacher in* Love Is Better Than Ever *was interrupted by a nervous collapse.*

(Below) *Francis and Sara Taylor, Elizabeth's father and mother, make a rare visit to the set of* Love Is Better Than Ever *during their daughter's marriage troubles. Everyone puts on a brave face for the camera.*

(Above) *With Rock Hudson in* Giant. *The good turn he did her at the time played a part in her* AIDS *campaigning after his death thirty years later.*

(Right) *James Dean was cool to her, and his habit of calling 'Cut' when dissatisfied with his own acting in* Giant *irritated an instinctual player like Elizabeth.*

(Above) *February, 1957: With Mike Todd, her third husband, at their wedding in Acapulco. Elizabeth's mother and father are at the left of the picture.*

(Left) *A new kind of man, a new kind of world: Elizabeth, Mike Todd and the look that says it all.*

(Above) *June, 1957: All good friends at Ascot. Mike Todd and Elizabeth go racing with Eddie Fisher and his wife Debbie Reynolds.*

(Right) *May, 1959: Widowed and a Jewish convert, Elizabeth marries Eddie Fisher in Las Vegas. They soon discovered that all they had in common was Mike Todd.*

No wonder she felt she was rushing towards maturity. What did it matter if it was incompatible with her career? In her eyes, producing a baby was an infinitely more creative act than being produced in a picture. It was a fine sentiment – but a dangerous one, too, when one was in debt to the picture producers. Elizabeth was about to suffer a traumatic humiliation; her response to it would simply make her more stubborn and, even more importantly, perhaps, less concerned for the consequences of her acts, as long as she felt she had acted justifiably and with integrity.

When she said later, 'I vowed then and there that I would never have to ask anybody for anything again,' she was unconsciously – perhaps consciously? – echoing Scarlett O'Hara's oath after the burning of Atlanta, as she scrabbles in the earth of Tara for raw vegetables to kill the ache in her stomach and swears she would never go hungry again. This romantic novel must be credited with an enormous influence on the generation of women who read it in print or saw it on the screen – and indeed on all later generations. Elizabeth Taylor was one of those who found Scarlett's total self-absorption readily pardonable in terms of survival and sincerity. The qualifying condition, of course, was that they were her *own* terms. Very shortly Elizabeth was going to have to step into the shoes of an ailing Vivien Leigh – and Leigh's fate, too, would only reinforce Elizabeth's determination not to let the world grind her down, but always to 'cry tomorrow' and at the same time try to get what one wanted today.

While house-hunting, the Wildings had moved into Elizabeth's parents' home on Elm Drive – the Taylors taking themselves off to Howard Young's Connecticut estate. She looked at many Beverly Hills homes and rejected most of them on a walk-through. She was looking for something to suit her mood of romantic expectancy. She wanted to rediscover that feeling of an enchanted garden which had surrounded her childhood. She found it at 1771 Summitridge Drive, Beverly Hills, a house perched high above Los Angeles – and therefore agreeably remote from the movie business. On her first visit, Elizabeth furnished it from her imagination. 'We will have the outside painted yellow, with white shutters, the living room will be in grey with periwinkle blue – my favourite colour.' Wilding, on hearing this, used to wrinkle up his nose mockingly and disparagingly call it 'mauve'.

He had proposed having some of his antiques freighted out from London. Elizabeth vetoed this. They must have everything new and modern. Right now, their furnishings amounted to four paintings and three lamps. The MGM house-buying fund had to be drawn on quickly, if the house was to be ready for the baby's arrival in January. Its price was steep, $75,000, and Elizabeth reckoned another $40,000 would be needed for furnishings.

Elizabeth freely admitted she was 'the world's worst housekeeper', and her mother backed this up. The only 'wifely' talent Elizabeth had, she said, was sewing. 'She is very clever at sewing, at changing a neckline, fitting a dress in around the waist ... Apart from that, [what] Elizabeth can't do around the house includes almost anything you could mention ... The dustpan and brush, the skillet and the stove are mysteries with which she never coped – or almost never. She used to make popcorn and fudge. And one time she made icebox cookies which didn't, unfortunately, "ice". And she had one favourite dish which she loved to make at home – sliced tomatoes and capers fried in fresh bacon grease. That was her one and only "dish".' However, by the time she and Wilding were married, her repertoire had extended to breakfast: coffee and toast. Bacon and eggs, she had mastered, too; they had it for supper almost all the time. Luckily, it was Michael's favourite dish.

None of these domestic deficiencies worried the mother-to-be. She had more important things on her mind, like naming the baby. If it was a son (which she wanted), it would be 'Michael', if a girl (which he wanted), 'Michelle'. She was filled with good intentions, chief of which was a compulsive resolve to please her husband. This was to be the pattern of every one of her subsequent marriages.

Ominously, the circle of friends she and Michael had made wasn't growing much wider. Making friends in a place like Hollywood meant getting acquainted with people of your own status in the industry. True friendship was probably best made early on; afterwards, it was hard to trust people not to have ulterior motives. What tended to happen was for the entourage of paid assistants and advisers, secretaries, lawyers, agents, nursemaids, cooks, chauffeurs and bodyguards to replace friends. The Wildings were still within the average number of Hollywood servants but it was sometimes easier to add an adviser than to solve a problem by oneself. Problems ended up being shunted on to advisers, which was not always wise and added an insulating layer to the unreal existence of stardom.

Their financial situation typified this pattern. What may have seemed affluence when contract figures were being tossed around publicly was in fact near the overdraft line when their liabilities were subtracted from their joint income.

Elizabeth's gross income would have been about $190,000 in a working year; Wilding's was $120,000. Their business expenses – agent, secretaries, etc. – probably accounted for $60,000. That left them with $250,000 gross between them. Tax on that at the then current rate would have been roughly $185,400, leaving them a net income of only $64,000, out of which they had to repay the MGM loan. Their living costs were probably in the region of $35,000. That left them a net spending amount of about $11,150. The truth was, they were almost broke even before they began earning their keep at MGM. An ironic fate for the star of a film called *The Girl Who Had Everything.*

MGM had to put production into overdrive to get the film finished before Elizabeth's pregnancy became visible. The movie was a remake of the 1931 drama *A Free Soul,* with Norma Shearer and Clark Gable, about a society girl who becomes a gangster's mistress. The film had made Gable a star and given him his reputation for manhandling women in a tough but sexy way that they were supposed to like – and at least in his case, did. The rough male decisiveness that Shearer felt when Gable slammed her into a chair and told her to listen gave the character a sexual jolt: 'A new kind of world, a new kind of man,' was her reaction. The linked eroticism of crime and class; the woman's pleasure in degradation; the man's stimulation in encountering a girl who looked the lady but had the soul of a tramp: these elements were also present in the remake, in which Fernando Lamas was the racketeer and William Powell played Elizabeth's father, a big-time lawyer who fronts for crooks. The film still had to conform to Hollywood morality, but the tension between what it would like to say and what it may only hint at gives it a peculiar eroticism that is startlingly suggestive of perversion and even incest. It was this film that began the build-up of Elizabeth's image as a wilful free spirit – one who is prepared to make her own mistakes and pay for them.

A compulsive pursuit of love and risk is established as the central part of her nature the very minute the film opens, with father and daughter watching a telecast of a Capitol Hill crime commission investigating Lamas's rackets. 'What's he like?' she asks her father, and then, 'Is he married?'

'An animal,' Powell tells her. Her interest sharpens even more.

The pair of them meet at a horse auction, where Lamas bids up the price of a colt to get what he wants – just as he will raise the social stakes to secure Elizabeth. She agrees with his axiom: 'Nothing is too much if you want a thing, and don't mind paying for it.' Later on in life, that could have been her motto.

Dressed in cool, creamy, close-fitting clothes, she conveys a sharp sense of a society girl waiting, yearning almost, to be sullied. Lamas's directness – 'Nobody has any time to waste anymore' – is a substitute for sexual scenes that would assuredly be included in a present-day film, but had to be left out of a 1950s' one. This movie is unusually short, only seventy minutes, betraying, perhaps, the possibility that MGM put rather too much in and then had to have second thoughts. Acting on his conviction, Lamas seizes Elizabeth and kisses her. She responds in the time-dishonoured way; 'You're no gentleman.' But in her protests, there is a feeling of sexual liberation.

Powell treats his daughter more like a girlfriend. His jealousy when Lamas literally carries her away has an incestuous force unprecedented in any film from MGM up to then. No doubt the competition of television was provoking a bolder approach than Louis B. Mayer – now retired – would ever have countenanced.

Despite its brevity, or because of it, the movie is concentrated into a series of vivid highlights – showing aspects of Elizabeth Taylor that other screenplays had not reached so directly. Still not twenty-one, she possesses a physical eroticism that, for once, is enhanced by a voice, less mature than her looks, which hints at the wantonness of the child that she still is inside. *The Girl Who Had Everything* is one of those films that, when viewed retrospectively, seem to have prophetic power.

In fact, the actual child inside her, in its fourth or fifth month of life – a fact very well concealed in her scenes – was indirectly responsible for a decisive change in Elizabeth's attitude to MGM. She finished the film on 4 August 1952. The next day, the studio notified her that she was being put on immediate suspension for six months at least. She took this like a slap of callous ingratitude, even though MGM had every legal right to act as it did. She made no attempt to conceal her resentment in interviews in later years. In these, her version of her treatment by MGM is more dramatic than any that the company's archives record. She describes how she had to go down on her knees to an (unnamed) MGM executive, begging for a loan to tide her over. The man humiliates her by pulling out his wallet, 'choked with hundreds of thousands [of dollars]', gloatingly gives her a severe dressing-down, then makes it a condition of the loan that she do a personal appearance tour for one of her pictures – while pregnant. Cash, despotism and a corporate priority that considers a baby less precious than a motion picture: all the pride, passion and hatred felt by protective motherhood is present in this anecdote.

The studio's attitude to her pregnancy is on record, however; and much more merciful it appears to have been than Elizabeth remembers it. It didn't totally suspend her remuneration for six months – which would have cost her $130,000 – but placed her on a reduced salary of $2,000 a week (down from $4,750), which would continue for a full four weeks after the termination of her pregnancy. Hard terms, but not harsh for the time – or the place.

Having a baby did a lot for Elizabeth's self-respect in the wake of her divorce. She felt cleansed, important again and serving some *real* use, not a screenwriter's fantasy. Motherhood was a licence to do everything she had had to deny herself while filming. Though on half-pay, she had the whole day free to indulge her casual, untidy, unpunctual nature without costing anyone money in lost shooting time. She could gorge herself. Her swelling waistline – she ballooned to 150 pounds – was a defiance of every taboo imposed by stardom. Hitherto, every bit of her that screen censorship permitted to be seen had been marketed to the profit of MGM; now she was experiencing the primal joy of the great mass of undifferentiated womankind. No wonder child-bearing became, for Elizabeth Taylor, the first and last assertion of self. No wonder that, when nature took its cruel way and it was no longer possible for her to have children of her own, she turned to adoption with such tenacity and zeal. Now she waddled around, sticking out her belly the way a disobedient child might put its tongue out at adult authority.

Fatherhood suited Wilding, too, though he saw it from the self-flattering angle of his sex's potency. 'The happiest days of our marriage were when Liz was totally dependent on me.' He lazed around with her – for he was naturally an idler – in rumpled clothes and a yachting cap that now replaced the trilby he kept to hand in Britain when he hadn't fixed the toupée that hid his receding hairline.

He tried to learn to work the camera she bought him – 'for when little Michael comes' – but he was notoriously not mechanically minded. Once, when he had fixed up floodlights for their garden, he left them on all night rather than hazard the chance that they wouldn't come on again if he turned them off. He saw their home fill up with pets – cats and dogs, the gifts of their friends, or strays Elizabeth had rescued from animal pounds. He also smelled the constant stench of cat urine and viewed the mess the dogs made. It did not seem to matter at all to Elizabeth. She had turned into an extrovert Earth Mother – anything that lived, she embraced, whatever its habits. Later, when Sara reprimanded her for allowing a dog to lick the baby's face, she would defiantly say that an animal's saliva was the best antiseptic. All the publicity about her as a child, talking to the animals in virtually their own language, now assumed the look of daily reality.

Then the wicked studio struck again, as ogres do when things are going far too happily for the enchanted heroine. One day a script was delivered to Wilding: his first MGM film assignment. He read it – and felt humiliated. It could not have been more cruelly chosen to remind him of his 'kept' status rather than his star value. 'Michael Wilding joins Lana Turner in *Latin Lover*,' went the MGM cable to New York on 25 September 1952, 'in the role of a wealthy suitor who loses out to Fernando Lamas.'

It didn't matter that, by the time shooting was due to start, Lamas had fallen out with Turner and been replaced by Ricardo Montalban. Wilding wasn't mollified. The script was 'terrible', his role an insult. Benny Thau ordered him to report to wardrobe. He refused. He would be suspended, they threatened. Suspend me, he said. They did. He was promptly replaced by John Lund and informed he would be kept suspended, minus his $3,000 a week salary, until his substitute completed the role – until, that is, 23 January 1953. The baby was six weeks away at this time. The payment on the MGM mortgage was almost due. Elizabeth had every reason to be anxious about paying the bills – then and in the future. But she was not.

When the crunch came, not only did she show no disposition to buckle under, but she demonstrated solidarity with her husband.

Down she went, very publicly, on 20 November, to the Los Angeles Hall of Records and claimed the backlog of fees, amounting with interest to $47,000, that represented the 15 per cent of her childhood earnings which her parents had been required to put into savings bonds on her behalf.

Waving the certified cheque at photographers, for all the world like a rebel flag in MGM's face, she was then driven to Jean Negulesco's house for lunch and a game of croquet – though she could hardly see the ball because of her advanced pregnancy.

She had her baby in the same hospital room at Santa Monica where Shirley Temple had been born – a good omen, some thought. She was terrified of the Caesarean the doctors advised. Afterwards, still half-sedated, she cried 'Michael, Michael, Michael,' as they wheeled her back to her bed. It was presumed she meant her waiting husband, although her wish for a boy had been granted by the arrival, on 6 January 1953, of Michael Howard Wilding.

She was overjoyed. But with another mouth to feed, Wilding still on suspension and herself on half-pay, she wanted to return to work as soon as possible. That proved more difficult than she expected. She weighed 132 pounds on leaving hospital; a month later she was still well above her usual 110 pounds, too noticeably overweight to photograph well. She was unable to do the movie, *All the Brothers Were Valiant*, that the studio had prepared for her, Robert Taylor and Stewart Granger. Her weight became the subject of inter-office memoranda. Floyd Hendrickson noted on 27 February 1953: 'She is to come to the studio to see Mr Thau who will look at her, and then decide, at that time, whether or not her physical appearance is such that her contract should be renewed at full compensation.' Thau decided that a few more weeks were needed.

Then an event happened in Ceylon that decided otherwise. Vivien Leigh had a manic-depressive breakdown during location shooting on *Elephant*

Walk. Heavily tranquillized, she was flown back to Hollywood early in March for interior scenes, but her mental state was deteriorating. Either the film would have to be abandoned, or a replacement for Vivien found quickly. Suddenly, MGM discovered that Elizabeth had regained her former physical allure. Back she went on full pay, and on 19 March 1953, the same day as Vivien Leigh was carried aboard an aircraft for home, Elizabeth was assigned her role in *Elephant Walk*. Paramount paid MGM $150,000 for the loan-out – ten times the full salary Elizabeth was now receiving.

18

FAME AND FRUSTRATION

By the time it finished shooting, *Elephant Walk* had accumulated enough costs through over-run schedules, retakes and the replacement of Vivien Leigh by Elizabeth Taylor to make it the most expensive Paramount production of its time – $3 million in all. Even while shooting was going on in Ceylon with the emotionally disturbed Vivien, William Dieterle had been doing 'covering' shots. These were scenes where Vivien was either present, but unrecognizable as a distant figure, or she had her back to the camera. Elizabeth slipped into these set-ups with practised ease. It is impossible to detect the substitution.

The film was an exotic variation on the *Rebecca* theme, relocated to the tea plantations. The planter's new wife finds herself virtually ostracized by the servants, the guardian spirits of the palatial mansion, and excluded from the all-male club of her husband's friends who pass the night carousing, drinking and playing bicycle polo in the hallways. Vivien had the pathos to play a woman abandoned by her husband at bedtime for the chauvinist company of expatriate buddies. Not so Elizabeth: she was fatally miscast. Her sexuality was now so apparent and inviting that audiences were left bewildered at why on earth Peter Finch, as her husband, didn't sprint up the grand staircase and into bed with her. Had *he* a problem?

Finch, then thirty-six, married but compulsively unfaithful, a notorious hell-raiser and womanizer and, in spite of that, an actor of great discipline, classical ability and range, was for Elizabeth a foretaste of the man whose fortunes (and misfortunes) were to be linked with her own some ten years later: Richard Burton. In a very practical way, he prepared Elizabeth for that other fatal liaison. Like Burton, Finch often showed Elizabeth his contempt for filmmaking, as simply a way of generating a disproportionate fee for what it involved. Like him, he drank to excess off the set, but was the total professional on it. To kill his unease at accepting Hollywood's blandishments and having to go along with its hypocrisies, he sought to maintain his self-respect by adopting an elaborately rebellious life-style. Elizabeth loved all of this: it was what she felt, but didn't dare act out, as yet. Finch gave her a taste for obstreperous camaraderie. Together with Dana Andrews, who was playing the sensitive, cultured 'other man' in the film, they formed the 'Fuck You Club' which ate a noisy daily lunch at Lucy's El Adobe, the diner across the street from Paramount where Elizabeth had met Nick Hilton.

It may have been because of Finch's powerful sexuality that Michael Wilding's nonchalantly good-natured English appeal, so reassuring at one time in her life, began to lose its initial attractiveness. If Finch had stayed on in Hollywood – where he had a reputation as an actor in demand – it is intriguing to wonder what effect he might have had on the Taylor–Wilding marriage. But when Finch discovered that the next picture Paramount was offering cast him as a Spanish gigolo on an ocean liner in a story starring Jane Russell, he gave the rude gesture that was the membership emblem of the FYC and left for home.

While doing a publicity shot for *Elephant Walk*, Elizabeth suffered the first of those freakish accidents that were to give her career its almost jinxed reputation. A tiny sliver of metal was blown into her eye by a wind machine. 'A foreign body,' the doctor called it. 'Anybody I know?' she joked.

Bravely, she underwent surgery without an anaesthetic, since she had to respond to the surgeon's instructions as he cut the object out with a sound she later said was like 'eating a watermelon on a minor scale'. Her fixation with recalling grisly surgery later became a source of wary wonder to her friends. Teitelbaum, the Hollywood furrier, sent her an ermine eyepatch: she couldn't wear it in case it infected the eye, but she thought the idea 'rich'.

Then things took a serious turn when baby Michael thumped her on the injured eye, and for a time it looked as if she would lose the sight in it. As she lay blindfolded in hospital for several weeks, in total darkness, her mother gave her daily readings from the childhood books that had had such a formative influence on her – including *The Secret Garden*, with its emphasis on the power of positive thinking. 'Thoughts – just mere thoughts – are as powerful as electric batteries.' Strangely, this crisis calmed Elizabeth. 'She is incapable of worry,' said Michael Wilding, who was then, by horrible irony, playing the role of a blind pianist in Joan Crawford's *Torch Song*. Most film stars – or anyone else, for that matter – would have been in crisis over the possibility of even partial blindness: not Elizabeth. 'I didn't think I wouldn't see again ... I had enough faith.

I believed it would [work out all right]. If it hadn't, it would have been the end of my career, but not of my life.'

It ended happily: the 'batteries' worked for her and within the month, stronger than ever, she was reporting to MGM for her next film, *Rhapsody*, with Vittorio Gassman.

Had her injury not delayed the start of the film, her co-star would have been Richard Burton. Instead, he went into *The Robe*, and CinemaScope. They had already met, in a manner of speaking. Burton had come to Hollywood in 1952 to make three films for Fox: he coveted the 'easy' rewards of filmmaking, but despised himself for doing so. Years later, he entered his impressions of Hollywood in his personal journal. He recalled one Sunday brunch around the pool at a luxurious Bel Air home, where he had been immediately lionized, fed a generous selection of alcoholic liveners and, as was his wont when drunk but articulate, done his 'poor miner's son among the sybarites' act. And then: 'a girl sitting on the other side of the pool lowered her book, took off her sunglasses and looked at me. She was so extraordinarily beautiful that I nearly laughed out loud ... She sipped some beer and went back to her book ... She was unquestionably gorgeous ... She was lavish. She was, in short, too bloody much, and not only that, she was ignoring me.' According to Melvyn Bragg, Burton's biographer, Elizabeth had also thought the star too bloody much: he'd never stopped talking, so she had pointedly ignored him – hence, perhaps, her book. She was reported as finding him 'coarse and self-important'. A Hollywood scenario could hardly have devised a better example of one of those unpropitious 'meetings cute' in which opposites inevitably attract each other. But it was not yet time for the parties to feel that fatalistic pull.

Elizabeth, once shy even in a crowd of her peers, had developed a noticeably more self-confident manner in public. At the start of their marriage, she had deferred to Michael – a much more social animal: 'I used to watch, observe, overhear conversations and make my own comments to myself, some cynical. I was never bored, but neither did I mix.' Then one day Humphrey Bogart fixed her with his stern eye: 'Let me talk to you, kid ... It's damn stupid for you to keep following your husband around. You should be asserting yourself. Be something in your own right. Stop being a shadow.' She took this to heart, and began moving more confidently among groups of people she didn't know, or knew only by celebrity kinship, stopping, talking, table-hopping – but this didn't feel right, either. Then Monty Clift gave her the clue which would shape all her future behaviour. 'Don't make yourself too available. When you're at a party, don't put yourself around. *Sit down ... wait ... let them come to you.*' It was the same technique she practised before the camera: now she took it into social life.

Clift had become like an extra child in the Wilding household – always hanging around, quick to sulk when Elizabeth didn't give him the attention he claimed. He had a deepening dependency on drugs and alcohol. But his intuitive powers were acute; he offered sympathy and support when she, in turn, needed him – massaging her back, feeding her soup like a mother and child. Their shared vulnerability coupled them together, as did their desire to remain outsiders in a milieu where people packed self-protectively together in status groups.

Rhapsody, which opened in March 1954, was a foolish picture. But it was immediately evident how motherhood had brought Elizabeth's beauty to full bloom. Supplementing it was a Helen Rose wardrobe – one of the consolations she had for making the film – which was indeed fit for the heiress she played, whose infatuation for the musician she pursues across two continents and through several seasons leads to her suicide attempt when he puts music before marriage. Whatever she does, her power to carry the audience's interest is now total. Moreover, MGM understood audience psychology well enough to know that there is no dramatic interest unless someone, or something, eludes the girl who has everything. 'She wins [her men's] reluctant hearts by means of sheer grit rather than through her natural charms,' said a *Look* critic, commenting on the lovers in *Rhapsody* and *Elephant Walk* (released ten days later) who had rejected her. Audiences perceived her not simply as a beautiful heiress, but as a determined huntress. Again, as in her last MGM film, she is provided with a playboy father (Louis Calhern this time) whose worldly advice sounds like a comment on the emerging persona of Elizabeth Taylor. 'You have a neurotic need to be needed,' he tells her, and asks, 'Have I ever stopped you from doing anything?' To which she replies, 'No – unfortunately.' There is a life story in such dialogue.

In the summer of 1953, Elizabeth was told her next film would be *Beau Brummell*, a Regency period romance to be shot in England. Her dislike of historical costumes – and all that this meant in make-up sessions at dawn – was tempered by the economies of a trip to Europe (and a second honeymoon) at MGM's expense. The Wildings had tried living to a budget in Beverly Hills. All this really meant was that they cut down the gardener's visits from three days a week to two. *Beau Brummell* looked to be a bargain.

Ready money was in short supply, however. On a stopover in New York, Elizabeth was robbed of $17,000 worth of jewellery. Like anyone, she put an insurance claim in and then – perhaps not quite like anyone – went straight out to Bulgari for replacements. As the compensation might take time to filter through, she was obliged to cable Benny Thau urgently at MGM: 'Please be sweet enough to wire permission to New York allowing me $1,600 extra ... for jewellery I have with me. I would just die of embarrassment if jewellers come ... to reclaim it ... Fondest love, Elizabeth.' Benny Thau obliged, no doubt feeling 'cornball sentimental'.

The wardrobe from *Rhapsody* also came in handy when she and Michael left for Copenhagen – leaving seven-month-old Michael Jr with Wilding's parents – to do some personal appearances for *The Girl Who Had Everything*. The weather suddenly turned chilly. Another 'Dearest Benny' cable was despatched: Elizabeth needed warmer clothes and clearly remembered how fashionably the MGM wardrobe department had kitted her out for the winter sequences in *Rhapsody*. Soon the Helen Rose creations were on their way to Denmark.

More alarming than cold weather, however, was the influenza virus she caught, along with an apparent attack of tachycardia, a novel ailment for a girl of twenty-one with no history of heart trouble. She recuperated in North Zeeland, sent for baby Michael and regained her spirits on discovering he had cut his first tooth. After Madrid (where she walked out of a bullfight) and Capri (where she created instant fashion by slipping on the new wide-cut coat which became known as a 'Capri jacket'), filming began on *Beau Brummell* with Stewart Granger as the eponymous fashion-setter. A dreadful film, which even managed to offend the Queen of England by presenting Her Majesty, at the following year's Royal Command Performance, with a picture of her ancestor King George III as a mental defective.

'I never saw [it] until after Richard and I were married,' Elizabeth said. 'It was on television. Richard turned it on. I had to change stations after about five minutes – I mean, I was so embarrassing in it.' She played a courtier or a courtesan – it is never quite clear which – called Lady Patricia Bellamy to whom Granger pays one of the most asinine compliments that any woman in a movie has ever received. 'Never embellish what's already perfect,' decrees the Beau, removing her diamond earrings, 'the wind gives your ears all the colour they need.' She often used to hoot with laughter at the memory of that when paying a visit to a jeweller's shop. Her eyes also come in for attention when Brummell decides to have 'the contemplation room' of his townhouse done over to match Elizabeth's periwinkle irises. Considering everything, she got off lightly when Bosley Crowther, in the *New York Times*, described her part as that of 'a foggy and vacillating creature', at the film's New York opening in October 1954. But she didn't even have the consolation of being able to borrow the wardrobe; there are not many places where one can wear a Regency fashion. Her next film, Richard Brooks's *The Last Time I Saw Paris*, sounded much more promising in this respect.

Unfortunately, the Wildings' finances hadn't been topped up in the way they'd hoped. Michael had again opted for suspension rather than play the role of a Pharaoh in *The Egyptian*, which he described as 'a nightshirt part'. Only threats of a lawsuit and the household bills drove him back to work. His career, which had got off to a faltering start, was in trouble.

Elizabeth's ambitions were being thwarted, too. The best films being made in America at this period were frequently ones originating with writers and/or directors. But MGM was still a producers' studio. One lost opportunity in particular embittered her.

'She met me in Rome when she and Mike [Wilding] were on their second honeymoon,' the writer and director Joseph L. Mankiewicz said later, referring to the period just before *Beau Brummell* started shooting. 'She knew I was preparing *The Barefoot Contessa* and asked to read the script. She was desperate for the part.' Elizabeth cabled Benny Thau: 'Help me with this as you know it would do me more good than anything I have ever done.' But Thau knew that Ava Gardner, for whom the script was intended, was having an affair with Joseph Schenck, head of United Artists, which was financing the film; and he thought it risky to disturb things. So Elizabeth had to go into the pantomime of *Beau Brummell*, knowing that Ava Gardner was working with an Oscar-winning writer-director in a film that would have brought her even greater stardom had she been in it instead of Ava.

As for *The Last Time I Saw Paris*, she said later, 'I did enjoy doing [it], even though it wasn't supposed to be a good film.'

It wasn't. It had every cliché associated with Americans in Paris, including the one that Paris is a distinctly unhealthy place for most of them to be. Based on F. Scott Fitzgerald's story *Babylon Revisited*, it follows an American married couple (played by Elizabeth and Van Johnson), neither of them ageing visibly during a decade or more of traumas involving love, family, infidelity and his labours on the Great American Novel. Elizabeth's character changes without really evolving: she is in quick succession the good mother, the patient wife, the devoted muse, the bruised spirit, the accusing woman and the tragic victim. (Helen Rose designed a stunning creation for each change of mood.) In brief, she exemplifies a sort of 'Life Force', with lightly touched-in manic-depressive shadows for interest. There is no way at all that this chronicle of a crack-up can hang together, and some lines would have defeated even Garbo. 'Is it really over, the war? Then I want to buy you silk shirts, silk socks and silk shorts' sounds more like a tongue-twister than a lover's sentiment.

Yet Elizabeth has a way, in this particular film, of asserting romantic values as if they were moral imperatives. When Roger Moore shows up as a gigolo in white tie and tails and proposes she take him as her lover while keeping quiet about him to her husband, he has picked on a sure way of losing her. Confess, and you can live with your man; conceal, and you can never live with yourself. Elizabeth took this to heart in her later affairs. Borrowing such movie-made morality and applying it to life naturally invited charges of hypocrisy. Yet her behaviour over the years ahead exhibited all the conviction of someone who has been coached to apply the first rule of such movies: 'Make your mistakes in the name of romance.'

She pays for her mistakes in *The Last Time I Saw Paris* with her life. It is the first time Elizabeth is allowed the self-indulgence of dying on screen. Stars, and performers generally, love such moments. A good death, even a merely well-timed one, can transfigure a dud part. Audiences usually find it deeply satisfying, too. A star who dies in a movie – to live again and be loved in her next one – closes the gap with filmgoers' sympathies in the most secure manner possible. Like a dear departed friend, she 'lives' through other people's memories in a more intense degree than even the happiest of happy endings could provide for. Typically, Elizabeth's will is strongest as her body is weakest. Her death in the film has a suicidal strength, a self-willed intensity that turns it into affirmation rather than defeat. Locked out of her Paris apartment by her alcoholic husband, she chooses to walk through the snow to her death from pneumonia. Helen Rose created a striking gown for this sequence, but it was Elizabeth who suggested the most effective stroke.

'What's pneumonia?' she suddenly asked Richard Brooks, as he was discussing the story.

'A kind of congestion ... blood in the lung often causes it.'

'I see ... [pause] ... and what shall I be wearing?'

'A long gown: you've just got back from a ball.'

'And how will you be showing me walking through the snow – close-up or long shot?'

'Close-up.'

There and then she decided she must wear a scarlet gown – 'like a bloodstain in the snow'.

Her absorption in constructing such a scene matches her objectivity in recalling the gruesome operations she has had to undergo in her life. But people who attribute it to a morbid fixation may be missing the point. It has more to do with a histrionic heightening of her own will to live whenever she has been near death. She certainly plucked affirmative artistry out of mortal illness in this film.

Richard Brooks became one of her closest friends, trusted for his no-nonsense directness. He is among the earliest commentators on her accident-proneness – or, as Burton was to call it, 'incident-proneness'. 'If she opens a beer can, she cuts herself,' Brooks said to an interviewer in

1956. 'If there is a chair in the middle of the set, she falls over it while talking over her shoulder to someone.'

It was probably not by accident, though, that half-way through the film Elizabeth had to announce to MGM that she was pregnant again. 'She was a ravenous mother,' Wilding said. 'I don't mean she stuffed herself. Just that she couldn't seem to get enough of maternity.'

Even morning sickness, Wilding noted, seemed to make her ecstatic. Child-bearing was the most serious thing in life for her. Once, when she was making *The Conspirator* with Robert Taylor, he had jokingly proposed that they get married. They were sure to have 'fabulous-looking kids' that they'd be able to sell. For what? Elizabeth had asked. 'For a fabulous profit,' her co-star said, eyes agleam with mock avarice. She did not think it remotely funny.

This time she was more prudent. Taking weight off after her last pregnancy had not been easy or pleasant. She went on a diet until the low-calorie pink grapefruit ran out of her ears.

But MGM was again far from pleased by the prospect of maternity keeping her off screen, especially when Brooks's film got her good notices on its release in November 1954. The Wildings' finances were still shaky. The studio was taking $300 a week each out of their weekly pay. Repayment on the house mortgage was $2,200 a month, more than they could comfortably carry. Doctors' bills would run into hundreds of dollars, if not a thousand or so. When they had had their first child, the spendthrift Wildings had gone in celebration to I. Magnin, in Beverly Hills, and bought the largest teddy-bear in the store. This time round, they paid a visit to a store without frills and did some thrifty shopping for maternity necessities.

And finding she couldn't face suspension without pay again, Elizabeth agreed to have another year added to the term of her MGM contract. This decision was to be the most frustrating one she ever made.

19

THE CRACK-UP

While Elizabeth was trying to make her own household economies, Hollywood was making a more thorough and painful cutback. The mid-1950s saw the ending of the long-term contract system. Henceforth stars went to work on one- or two-picture deals; they were no longer carried on the payroll by the studio between films. Misbehaviour that cost time, and therefore money, was likely now to lead to firing, not suspension. By the end of 1955, MGM retained barely half a dozen stars on long-term contracts: Elizabeth Taylor, Robert Taylor, Ava Gardner, Leslie Caron, Debbie Reynolds, Grace Kelly (about to quit because of her engagement to marry Prince Rainier) and Cyd Charisse.

Yet these economies, caused by television's rivalry for audiences, brought Elizabeth a bonus. Because the routine picture was disappearing, killed off by audience indifference and cheaper imitations on TV, the studios lavished more money on fewer, bigger and (they hoped) better quality productions. From now until she left MGM, Elizabeth would appear only in front-rank movies.

But for the moment, she was appearing in no movies at all while awaiting motherhood for the second time. Despite financial commitments, described as 'rather desperate' by a studio executive, she began looking for a larger house. 'Write me a cheque and I'll pay it back tomorrow' had been her attitude to money when she was a juvenile star chaperoned by an MGM publicity girl with a purse. (She once reputedly told the girl to write one out for a $5,500 Cadillac for her mother's birthday present, and had to be informed that although the girl's account could run to a Hermes scarf, it would be overdrawn for a Cadillac.) Money was for impulsive spending; that's what money was for – though, on scenting a bargain, Elizabeth's face would set hard, her eyes narrow suspiciously and 'then she became a pirate, proud of her high art as a chiseller.'

She found what she wanted at the end of a high, twisting road in Benedict Canyon, a ruthlessly modern American home designed by the Los Angeles architect George McLean in glass, steel and adobe (baked earth). Its living room was the most dramatic feature. One wall of sheer glass overlooked the valley far below, at that time relatively undefiled by development. Through another glass wall, the swimming pool was visible. The third wall was faced with natural tree bark, tufted with clumps of ferns and orchids: a many-branched driftwood tree appeared to support the ceiling. The fourth wall, forty-five feet long, was built of fieldstone curving into a bar with a huge open fireplace. The price was $150,000. The house the Wildings were living in was put on the market and a second mortgage arranged: MGM spread its loan over a few more years and reduced its weekly take from the Wildings' pay packets to $150 each. Asked what she wanted for a house-warming present, Elizabeth would answer briskly, 'Just money.'

The new home, at 1375 Beverly Estate Drive, represented a subtle change of emphasis in the marriage. One visitor noted that not only was it 'in sharp contrast to the [Anglo-Saxon character] of their first home', but 'there is nothing of Michael in it.' It was an aggressively 'Hollywood' house. Its rooms were wired for music: an intercom system enabled the occupants to keep in touch with each other, which generally meant Elizabeth's voice crackling out of the air with some order or other to Michael; the doors were automated; push buttons dimmed the illumination, opened and closed the curtains, lowered the inevitable cinema screen; guests announced themselves by entryphone before being admitted. It was a true film-star house, with no degree of cosiness, but a great deal of casualness that reflected not Michael Wilding's easy-going nature, but Elizabeth's self-confessedly neglectful approach to domestic chores.

'Our home is like an animal shelter,' Wilding said. Eleanor Harris, writing a *Look* magazine series on Elizabeth, counted three cats, as many dogs, and a pet duck that was given the run of the house and naturally made no distinction between a rug and a lawn when it defecated. Cats' claws had ripped the wallpaper and the sheets of the seven-foot-eight-inch bed in the master suite. Guests were served off plates that were mismatched or cracked. They found themselves using long-handled spoons, meant for stirring iced tea, to pry sections out of grapefruit. Peggy Rutledge now doubled as general factotum, replacing clothes-hooks that had collapsed from the weight of garments on them, or swabbing up after incontinent pets. Household budgeting was, well, spasmodic. Meals were decided at the last minute, with Peggy being despatched down the hill to bring home dinner just before the shops closed.

Amidst it all, Elizabeth was perfectly happy. Though her housekeeping might be unpunctual, sloppy, eccentric and even unsanitary, she was the mistress. What she said, went. The balance of the marriage had been irreversibly altered.

This was reflected in other ways, too. When the Wildings went to parties, it was noted that they separated as soon as they had greeted their hosts, seemingly indifferent to each other until it was time to go. Humphrey Bogart, though hardly cut out to be the Mr Manners of the movie colony, rebuked Wilding: 'You're always surrounded by the most beautiful babes at one end of the room, while Liz holds court with the most attractive males at the other ... Married folk didn't ought to act that way.'

Louella Parsons scolded them in print. And even Wilding's half-jokes about his wife's unpunctuality took on a snide, carping tone when repeated by the gossips. Generally, he estimated, it took Elizabeth two hours to dress for an outing. Much of that time she spent in the bathroom, at the long marble console basin, seated on a cushioned stool facing a huge wall mirror framed in theatrical lightbulbs, painting her toenails and fingernails, plucking her eyebrows, brushing and re-brushing her hair – not beautifying herself, though, so much as delaying entry into the outside world. She also did a lot of what she called 'Walter Mitty-ing' – daydreaming, refusing to meet reality until necessary.

Her makeup tricks, on the other hand, showed her cool, professional understanding of how 'Elizabeth Taylor' should look. She never applied a makeup base to her face, or rouge. The flawlessness of her skin was emphasized by the mole on the right cheek. She wore three different shades of lipstick simultaneously: one for the corners, a lighter one in the centre, and lip gloss. She mixed her own eye shadow. Dark grey combined with blue was painted on to her lids using an artist's brush. For her heavy eyebrows, a drawing pencil was used.

At this time, she owned over one hundred dresses, some eighty belts, forty cardigans and sweaters, and five furs (mink, ermine and fox stoles, a crystal mink stole and a full-length mink coat).

The age difference between Elizabeth and Michael was beginning to tell. She had once valued the 'older man's' air of calm, quiet and security. Now, as she shaped her own world, messy though it was, his playful admonitions about lateness and untidiness sounded like paternal rebukes. 'I'm your wife, not your daughter,' she would snap back.

She became a mother for the second time on 27 February 1955, her own twenty-third birthday, with the birth, again by Caesarean section, of Christopher Edward Wilding.

Immediately, she began a crash diet. She knew that George Stevens was planning an epic production called *Giant* for Warner Bros., starring Hollywood's newest sensation, James Dean. She was determined to be in it. It was touch and go. The role, as a girl from the bluegrass country who goes as a bride to oil-rich Texas and founds a family dynasty, had been pencilled in for Grace Kelly. But as soon as Kelly's wedding to the Prince of Monaco was announced, MGM put her to work on two films, *The Swan* and *High Society*, so as to get the last ounce of value out of the royal liaison and her MGM contract. This gave Elizabeth an unexpected opportunity.

MGM also wanted a chance to use Dean, already cast in *Giant* as the Texas dirt farmer who strikes it rich in the oil fields and turns into an autocratic millionaire like Howard Hughes. In an agreement prepared in mid-May 1955, Warners undertook to pay MGM $175,000 for Elizabeth and to do 'the best they can' to deliver Dean for an MGM picture, though they warned there was a risk of his being drafted into the army and becoming unavailable. So MGM still hesitated to complete the agreement. It was Rock Hudson who decided things. Stevens had surprised everyone by casting this handsome but otherwise limited he-man for his hero. To boost Hudson's self-confidence, the director would ask his opinion on many aspects of the movie. Who did he want as his leading lady? 'Elizabeth Taylor,' said Hudson.

Her gratitude to Rock Hudson lasted all his life and continued even after his death from AIDS, when Elizabeth chaired one of the principal fund-raising organizations that the tragedy gave rise to.

But her delight in getting the choicest female role then going evaporated quickly when Stevens took the unit on location in August. She realized then how well-protected she had been when making *A Place in the Sun* for him. No longer a minor, and without chaperones, she was exposed to her director's professional ruthlessness. He showed her no tender mercies in getting what he wanted, beginning by unsettling her in order to break her will and make her more malleable. He attacked her on a point on which, in other circumstances, she might have agreed with him. She was too beautiful, he said; she didn't look touched by living. He threw her a public challenge – look dowdy. He assigned her a grotesquely unkempt wardrobe for the scene where her husband has left her and she is feeling miserable: thick-soled brogues, heavy woollen stockings, a burdensomely long skirt and a man's slouch hat. Elizabeth couldn't credit that the trimly turned-out woman she played in earlier scenes would let misery drag her down to the point where she looked, as she put it, 'like a lesbian in drag'. A fight ensued with Stevens in front of the unit. It ended with her wiping her make-up off, shaking her hair out of the tight bun in which the director had ordered it to be confined, and stalking off, to return, minus the hated hat, defiant and friendless, but the total professional. Stevens got the effect he wanted.

'He wanted to create a state of total dependency,' Rock Hudson said. 'If he'd gone about it with love and tenderness, Elizabeth could have accepted it easily. But George was a tyrant and she could be a termagant. Whenever they clashed, I stood well back.'

Elizabeth and Hudson, in contrast, got on, as he put it, 'like brother and sister playing husband and wife'. 'Beautiful?' said Elizabeth, after he'd paid her the usual tedious compliment. 'Beautiful? I'm Minnie Mouse.' Off she flounced into her dressing room, re-appearing more quickly than her husband could ever remember, her hair pinned back, and wearing a red miniskirt and oversize black pumps. 'It was true,' said Hudson. 'There stood Minnie Mouse.'

The two of them horsed around, joked, played pranks on location. They induced jumbo-sized hangovers by inventing the chocolate martini (vodka and Kahlua chocolate liqueur). Fortunately their reflective-mood the morning after suited the homesickness of the scene, though Stevens thought that rushing out to the 'honey wagon' to throw up between takes was overdoing it.

One day, the folk in their location township looked out to see Elizabeth Taylor and Rock Hudson rushing to and fro down the main street, holding aloft zinc buckets to catch the outsize hailstones that were falling, so as to use them as ice in their Bloody Marys.

James Dean proved just the opposite of Hudson: he was cold, indifferent and rude to Elizabeth. A shy, intensely insecure actor, he was a selfish co-star. She particularly resented his imperious habit of calling, in the middle of a take, 'Cut – I fucked it up.' Stevens resented it even more. But Dean's *East of Eden* had opened a few months earlier, in March 1955, and he had become an instant icon to the teenagers, the new audience Stevens had to learn to 'talk' to. Dean knew the body language of the inarticulate kids. So although Stevens despised him, he deferred to him. Elizabeth, on the receiving end of Dean's egoism, found it demeaning – and physically exhausting – to have to do and redo the scenes while he explored his Method rapport with the character.

Her health nearly broke down. She had had little time to rest after giving birth. Her postpartum mood had to be jolted back on to a professional overdrive. Her dieting had been compulsive; someone saw her spitting out a chocolate that she had only licked, so that she absorbed just the flavour, not the calories. Now her constitution hit back. Though she looked in the bloom of youth, her body developed the symptoms of a person approaching middle age. Sciatica had her calling out in pain, taking to a wheelchair, unable to perform for a bullying director who refused to believe she was as bad as she made out. It later crossed her mind to send him her X-rays of a pinched sacroiliac nerve as a Christmas card. She was hospitalized after her tight riding breeches had cut off the circulation in her legs and ankles and caused a thrombosis. 'She would cry when she tried to walk,' said one eyewitness.

Wilding showed up, but not just to take care of her. 'You'd better know right away, Mike, I've fallen in love with your wife,' Dean greeted him maliciously. But what concerned Wilding more was Hollywood gossip about a relationship between Elizabeth and Rock Hudson. The twenty-nine-year-old Rock was being urged by the fan magazines to get married. That he was gay was not widely known – perhaps not even by Elizabeth at this time. Eventually a marriage would be arranged for him with his secretary, so as to protect his orthodox image. Elizabeth reassured her husband; yet she was shrewdly intuitive about this aspect of her own performances. 'I can't help it, but I always seem to fall a little in love with my leading man,' she told Wilding. 'And I guess I always will.' But it didn't mean anything, she added. 'I have never two-timed any man, and I never will.'

Only a few scenes were left to shoot back at Warners and, as was his rule, Stevens brought the stars and the leading crew members together in a screening room to view the rushes. This was part of his method of asserting authority. Elizabeth had to endure his continuous commentary on why she was no good in that take, a little better in this one, had 'something' in the other, would be 'usable' in the next, and so on.

In the middle of the screening, Stevens took a call, grunted a few times, hung up, then ordered the lights turned up. He announced that James Dean, who had finished his role, had been killed that afternoon in a car collision.

Feeling small and crushed by someone else's catastrophe, Elizabeth was still visibly shocked when she ran across Stevens in the studio parking lot.

'I can't believe it, George.'

'I can,' he answered, in the tone of a man who had just seen the last act of a play of which he had not been over-fond.

That night, the assistant director called. George expected Elizabeth on time in the morning to pick up the reaction shots of a scene she had done with Dean a few days before. She realized, with anguish, that she would now be 'reacting' to a man who lay in a funeral home at Paso Robles. On the last day of work on the film, she collapsed with stomach cramps and was rushed to hospital. *Giant* had been a gruelling experience. It was not over yet. After treatment for a twisted colon, she had to go back to the studio and finish the scene.

Yet film can be a strangely forgiving thing. *Giant* contains almost no signs of her suffering, and many indications of how she had matured.

Though required to end the film as the mother of a teenage daughter – played by Carroll Baker – with no help from any agency except the blue hair-dye that passes for signs of ageing in Hollywood movies, Elizabeth in her early scenes shows a girl toughening before our eyes into a potential matriarch. And the scene where Dean entertains her to tea in his shack demonstrated, through her skill at hanging on to another actor's words (and pauses), that the quality of 'presence' can more than hold its own against the Method actor's mannered mumble.

Meantime, her husband was having his own troubles. The unravelling of Michael Wilding's career matches so exactly the dissolution of his marriage that it almost looks as if a conspirator's hand has been at work. He had been ordered into a musical version of *Cinderella*, retitled *The Glass Slipper*, in which, at forty-three, unable to do a single step of classical ballet, he was compelled to don white tights and play Prince Charming. This was indeed dancing to the studio's tune!

Then he was caught in an even more undignified posture. *Confidential* was the most flagrant of a new breed of scandal-raking magazines that appeared in the mid-1950s. By pushing their prurient noses into the private lives of the stars, they helped change the public perception of celebrity. Tired of the fan magazines' bland pap, a fresh generation of young readers lapped up the lubricious revelations, usually invented, but sometimes true (or true enough) about the stars. Hitherto only prone to watered-down human failings that invited readership sympathy, stars were now depicted with base appetites and even unnatural desires. Not all of this was unwelcome to the studios. It whipped up a voyeuristic interest that translated into ticket sales. But on the stars themselves, the effects were more mixed. Even if a *Confidential* story of infidelity (or worse) had no basis in fact, its very appearance, with plausible detail, could start a chain reaction that sometimes brought about a fulfilment of the curse.

'When Liz Taylor's Away, Mike Will Play' was the runic innuendo cast by *Confidential*'s cover slogan. While Elizabeth was making *Giant*, it reported, her mate was entertaining two strippers at the Beverly Hills house. After performing their act by the pool, the girls had gone indoors. Wilding found one of them, bra-less, in the master bedroom and ordered her out. That was about the extent of it: more a matter of etiquette, really, than anything more aphrodisiac. Elizabeth thought so, too. 'Whether it's true or not, you can't let an article like that break up your marriage,' she said. But in the long term, the threat was scarcely necessary. The marriage was drifting apart, breaking up in a way that is often imperceptible to the partners. Elizabeth had changed, Wilding had not – it was as simple as that. She had now acquired an identity that was completely separate from her mother – as a mother herself. She had a home that represented

Hollywood stardom, not English tradition. Her experience of *Giant* had buttressed her intuition that her future in a changing Hollywood was going to be as big as the movies for which she was now in line.

Michael, however, had stayed the same lazy, unambitious individual. Once upon a time, that had had its charm, but the fairy-tale days were over. Now she saw him as a loser, who got on her nerves and who provoked her resentment by his idleness. Open quarrels broke out. Where previously they had defused these by each of them counting up to ten, now they didn't even bother to count. If she reproached him now, it was not for infidelity – but for being 'such a goddamn Englishman'. Every week that passed this way made her feel, more and more, that she was 'Elizabeth Taylor: American'.

They went to a private preview of *A Star Is Born*. Elizabeth felt the truth of every scene in which Judy Garland struggled to retain her identity and sanity in the same kind of film studio that Elizabeth herself had characterized as 'The Iron Lung', where 'they won't let you breathe by yourself'. Wilding felt the truth of it, too. But he identified with his compatriot James Mason, as Norman Maine, the star's redundant husband – 'a displaced person, strictly not wanted on voyage'.

20

'A NEW KIND OF MAN, A NEW KIND OF WORLD'

The studio heads were not surprised by the break-up of Elizabeth's marriage. They scarcely needed to say, 'We told you so.' They had witnessed such break-ups often enough, when the careers of stars who are married to each other begin to go their separate and unequal ways. There is no disguising the fact that it suited the unsentimental executives very well not to have to court Elizabeth through her husband. This is not the same as saying that they engineered Wilding's eclipse. They knew his value to them, and it was not great. He was an actor out of his time and his place: too English to fit into available roles or appeal to young moviegoers now seeking a more emphatically American cinema than the international one of their parents' generation. Even the careers of Mason and Granger were faltering on their imported 'Englishness'.

Wilding was assigned one more MGM film, *The Scarlet Coat*, a military drama set during the American Revolution. When his contract expired early in 1956, the option on his services was not renewed.

Elizabeth felt pity for him, despite his shortcomings: all such hard cases brought out her compassionate side. She got MGM's permission to accompany him to Spain and Morocco, where he was to make *Zarak Khan* for Columbia, with two other falling stars, Victor Mature and Anita Ekberg. It was by no means just a sentimental journey for her: in the Arab state she acquired her life-long taste for costume jewellery and the loose robes that were so flattering to the fuller figure – though the day when they would fulfil that function for her was still far off.

Her next film, scheduled to begin shooting in April 1956, was *Raintree County*, a $5.3 million companion piece to *Gone With the Wind*, showing the War Between the States from the viewpoint of the North. Her co-star was Montgomery Clift, fresh from his triumph in *From Here to Eternity*, at the top of his box-office power, in the prime of his reputation as an actor – and in an increasingly debilitated state due to drugs and alcohol.

As his condition deteriorated, he spent more time with the Wildings than in his own nearby home, spooning baby food into young Christopher (and sometimes into himself, too), and hearing from each side why their marriage had failed. As Michael Wilding was later to say, '[Monty] acted as interpreter for two people who no longer spoke the same language.'

Elizabeth and Monty rehearsed their scenes together in the evenings, and they soon realized the script was inferior stuff: verbose, tediously explanatory, not so much tragic as simply depressing. Elizabeth saw she would have to rely on what was becoming her own 'don't give a damn' nature, to make a flat character appear a rounded one; she played a Southern belle in continuous pursuit of her man. She had already doubled for Vivien Leigh in *Elephant Walk*; now she was to step into Vivien's fiddle-dee-dee persona as a more neurotic Scarlett O'Hara type. The affinity she already felt with the tragic and stubborn-willed English actress was sharpened. Clift was unfortunately not cut out to portray a poetic Rhett Butler. 'I had an interesting part as a schizophrenic bride,' Elizabeth recalls, 'but the picture was bad.'

It was worse: it was dull, notable only for Elizabeth's descent into madness and her final suicide in a swamp, driven mad because of the fear that she was the daughter of a black slave. It is a role that has to be based on mood, not plausibility, and she handles the mood well enough to save the character from seeming ridiculous or monstrous. As with *The Conspirator*, MGM's initial euphoria was overtaken by censorship anxieties, some of them again to do with the extent of Elizabeth's exposure – 'One breast is clearly uncovered,' said Robert Vogel, the producer, in a memo to the studio's celebrated editor, Margaret Booth. 'There is no possibility of this scene [where Elizabeth is hysterical and implores Clift to beat her] being used ... We ... warned [Edward Dmytryk, the director] as soon as we saw the dailies.' Having MGM breathing hotly down his neck did not improve the confidence of a filmmaker unsure of his footing in historical epics.

A few weeks after filming had begun at the studio, and just before the cast and crew were due to leave for location in Kentucky, tragedy again overwhelmed a co-star and intimate friend of Elizabeth's.

Clift had been invited to dinner at the Wildings' on Saturday 13 May, along with Rock Hudson and Hudson's new wife, his ex-secretary Phyllis Gates, and the actor Kevin McCarthy. Clift drove himself up the high winding canyon road, having given his driver the night off. He was dozy all through dinner – from having taken barbiturates – and two glasses of *vin rosé* compelled him to lie down on the floor. He still looked so woozy when the time came to go that McCarthy volunteered to pilot Clift's car home by driving his own in front of it.

As the others were preparing to leave, a pounding and shouting was heard at the front gate. 'There's been a terrible accident,' McCarthy shouted, 'I think Monty's dead.' Barely a quarter of a mile from the house, Clift's car had veered into a telegraph pole. 'We all ran down the hill,' Elizabeth recalled. She could make out Clift slumped beneath the steering column. It had cleaved into his face like an axe blow, making a vertical dent from chin to temple. By the light of other cars' headlamps, the jammed door was forced open and he was extricated, 'suffering terribly from shock, but ... absolutely lucid,' Elizabeth said. A tooth was hanging by the end of a scarlet blood thread. He asked her to pull it off, but to save it – 'I may need it later.' The newsmen arrived before the ambulance, which got lost and took forty-five minutes to locate the crash. All that time, Elizabeth cradled Clift's head on her lap with maternal tenderness. She had placed her own light silk scarf over his famous face, now so terribly mutilated, to ensure him a measure of privacy. People were struck by her deadly calm. 'I'd never seen her so calm,' Hudson said. 'It was like she was being "directed" – in a film. I mean. Her dedication to poor Monty was total. If we'd spoken to her, I doubt she'd have heard.'

The other party guests clustered tightly around to discourage photographers. But it was Elizabeth who effectively ensured that no photographs were taken. In a completely level tone, she said to the newspaper men, 'If you take as much as one picture of him, I'll make sure every damn one of you is banned from every studio in town.'

'That shook them,' said Hudson. 'It was like the mother snarling over her cub. Even when the ambulance got to us, she didn't want to let go of Monty.'

She travelled with him, still holding his hand. Her dispassionate description makes chilling reading: 'By the time we reached the hospital, his head was so swollen that it was almost as wide as his shoulders. His eyes by then had disappeared. His cheeks were level with his nose. It was like a gigantic red soccer ball.'

Considering the extent of his injuries – his jaw (broken in four places) and his nose (in two) needed resetting – Clift spent a surprisingly brief time in convalescence, though *Raintree County* had to be shut down for six weeks. Fortunately for MGM, Dore Schary, who knew of Clift's drink and drugs problem, had insured him for $500,000, and nearly $450,000 was paid out in compensation to the studio.

It was during these idle weeks that Elizabeth and Michael Wilding gave up hoping that their marriage could be put together again, like poor Monty Clift's face.

Coming so soon after James Dean's death, Clift's near-fatal crash concentrated Elizabeth's thoughts on the futility of trying to lead one's life as if there was purpose and direction to it. Better to experience it one day at a time: to put everything you had into living for the moment and be surprised by happiness when it arrives. Hedda Hopper visited her and noted this withdrawn seriousness: '[Elizabeth] seemed moody and quiet to me – her mind removed from things at hand.'

Then, as if the sun had come out, she was suddenly restored to the sparkling young wife that Wilding remembered from their early days together. He put this down to Clift's unexpectedly quick recuperation. Only later did it strike him that her animation might owe more to a restless, stocky forty-seven-year-old man with deep-set eyes and a chin that seemed permanently thrust forward as if the owner were asking himself, 'Is the world ready to face me?'

The Wildings had accepted Mike Todd's invitation to go cruising with him and other guests aboard a rented yacht in Catalina Sound over the weekend of 30 June. Elizabeth had met Todd off and on over the previous months, but always in the company of others, and rarely for more than an hour or two. He had tried to get MGM to loan her out for a cameo role in *Around the World in Eighty Days*, his star-packed spectacular which was then in post-production. MGM didn't like one of its leading stars appearing so briefly, especially as Todd's fee was offered to Elizabeth in kind (a new limousine), not in cash. Moreover, Hollywood still tended to see Todd as a Broadway carpetbagger, not an indigenous movieman.

The weekend at sea had been an odd, disquieting experience for Elizabeth. Todd, she felt, was pointedly ignoring her – the way people do when they are unwilling to reveal the extent of their interest. A series of invitations followed; now his attitude was just the reverse. He lavished his attentions on her. Todd had been close to Evelyn Keyes – an actress best known as Scarlett O'Hara's younger sister in *Gone With the Wind*. It was obvious he had broken with her. Every time Elizabeth's shoulders and Todd's touched – on one occasion when they were seated practically back-to-back on his living-room 'love seat' – she felt a tenseness between them more potent even than eye-contact. Eventually she moved to another part of the room. At the same time, Todd made a show of his sexual chauvinism, telling Wilding, who had accepted the blame for the breakdown of his marriage to Elizabeth, not to worry too much – 'All actresses are more temperamental than burglar alarms. They go off for no goddamn reason. They need a good thumping to stop.' Wilding said Noël Coward would have agreed with that, quoting the Master to the effect that women were like gongs and should be struck regularly. That set Todd veering off on a new tack – would Wilding star with Elizabeth in Coward's *Private*

Lives if he produced it on Broadway? It was a proposition Elizabeth did take up – but not until twenty-five years later, and then with an ex-husband.

Early in July 1956, the Wildings were over at Todd's home again – this time at Elizabeth's request. They and their children helped Todd at the barbecue pit, swam in his pool and drove home tanned and happy. It was one of the last perfect days they spent together. On the way back, Elizabeth said dreamily that Todd was like something out of the *Arabian Nights* and that 'she admired men who could get anything they wanted so long as they set their hearts on it' – one of her own mother's rules of life. This stung Michael, as he had just turned down the role of Professor Higgins in a nationwide tour of *My Fair Lady* and had been taunted by Elizabeth for cowardice.

He was at his agent's next morning when he took a call from Elizabeth. She wanted to read him something before he saw it in the papers. The 'something' turned out to be an announcement of their legal separation – which followed from an MGM spokesman on 19 July. 'Thanks,' said Wilding, more calmly than it later seemed possible to him, 'but I'd rather have read it in the papers. Then I can believe it's about two other people.'

In the gossip columns, Wilding tended to be blamed for being 'too bossy ... making all the decisions'. The truth was the very opposite.

If evidence were sought to show how much Elizabeth relished a strong man who made decisions for her, then the scene that took place at MGM the day after the statement had been issued could have provided it.

'Come with me,' Todd barked at her when they met in Benny Thau's office. He pulled her by the arm out of the suite, along the corridor, into an elevator and down to a first-floor office he sometimes used in the Thalberg Building. He rammed her down into a chair, sat himself opposite like the chairman of the board, and proposed marriage. 'I see you have decided to shed that guy. Now understand one thing and hear me good, kid. Don't start looking around for someone to latch on to. You are going to marry only one guy, see, and his name is me.'

'He didn't ask me,' she said later, 'he told me. He was irresistible.'

Once more, it seemed, life was repeating art. Fernando Lamas, the socially ambitious gangster in *The Girl Who Had Everything*, had treated her with the same rough but stimulating curtness – not as a free soul, but as a captive conquest. And Rock Hudson, the Texas millionaire in *Giant*, had boldly stolen his new bride away from her lush kingdom of Maryland and borne her south to be his consort in the near feudal kingdom he ruled in Texas. In both films, Elizabeth had joined her fate to that of men who were a little bit crazy, who had the nerve to act on impulse – as she herself was moved to do. They were men who looked neither before nor after, but seized their chance and endowed it (and her) with a powerful sense of the inevitable.

Todd's proposal had the dramatic brutality of a film scenario – the sort of scene she knew instinctively how to play. Todd recalled that she looked at him with a stare that said, 'Are you mad?' followed by a half-smile that he interpreted as implying, 'Perhaps you are, but ...'

In later months, when announcing his plans for someone who probably hadn't yet been acquainted with them, and was very unlikely to assent to them, Todd used to quip, 'He [or she] hasn't said no.' On this occasion, Elizabeth didn't say no, either. Nor did she say yes. But they gave each other a kiss before she drove herself home, scarcely believing what had happened. Todd's proposal had the boldness of an entrepreneur, not a suitor. He took what he wanted in business, and now he did so in courtship, in the conviction that all parties to the transaction would benefit if no time were given them to think over the deal. The flair he had already shown for grandiose plans backed by his own money or credit – 'I'm the shrewdest spendthrift in the business,' he boasted – could be made to yield the same high returns when applied to other people's lives, or so he was convinced. Forget the consequences; they can be changed later. He and Elizabeth were, in many ways, two of a kind.

Elizabeth's life was now becoming more newsworthy than her film career. Her future was speculated about even outside the fan magazines. Columnists and profile writers, generally speaking, were still uncertain about her character or desires. Most reflected what they felt their readership wanted: pity or censure, disapproval or intrigued perplexity. She was analysed exhaustively, with the new candour that *Confidential* and its imitators were making commonplace even in orthodox publications. She was one of the earliest victims – or beneficiaries, depending on where one's interest lay – of this change in the nature of media exposure. Once her name was linked with Mike Todd's, the columnists explored her 'crushes' on 'the older man' – conveniently ignoring her still quite recent episode with the immature man in the person of Nick Hilton. A father complex was attributed to her. This, it was confidently asserted, would 'set the pattern of her relationships for the rest of her life'. Such tendencies weren't seen as evidence of her emotional maturity; rather the reverse. '[It] points to the fact that the troubled star is still a child struggling to grow up and find peace of mind, torn between the demands of the woman and the child.'

Since direct testimony from the child-woman herself was not forthcoming, the statements that Michael Wilding had innocently made during his years of romance and marriage were sifted for the corroborative detail:

her unpunctuality, her inability to cook or run a home, her passion for the sort of junk food that children unerringly went for instead of wholesome diets and, especially, her enthusiasm for being given presents and squealing with delight over them. She was a grown woman with a child's stubbornness, it was said. The phrase 'whim of iron' hadn't then appeared in print, but it would have suited the columnists' warnings. Wilding's misfortunes were trotted out again and again to serve as a warning to the next man to marry Elizabeth Taylor, whoever he might be.

A day after the announcement of their separation, wearing a red sweater and matching matador pants, she saw the 'last man' off from Los Angeles airport aboard a flight to Europe, where he was to start location work on a low-budget thriller entitled *Breakout*. Wilding dropped an arm round her shoulders; she kept her own arms folded; the inevitable paparazzi took their pictures and, for once, she didn't protest or resist – to those watching, she simply seemed uninterested. Wilding smiled sadly down at his wife, kissed her, then they parted. A day or so later, Elizabeth herself was airborne, flying to Kentucky for work on the resumed *Raintree County*.

Mike Todd now pressed urgently ahead with his courtship. Its pattern was instructive. Instead of surrendering to her, he kept her in suspense. For several days running, he would call her after she finished shooting. Then one day the telephone wouldn't ring, and she would unsuccessfully pursue him through the long list of numbers he had given her. He'd deliberately made himself unavailable, keeping her on tenterhooks, observing the extent to which she would go in order to track him down. This ploy was followed by the special delivery of two hundred roses, by air, packed in crushed ice to retain their freshness in the 101-degree heat on location. A grandiloquent gesture like this restored communications.

Clift was used as an emissary, too. On Elizabeth's arrival at Danville, Kentucky, he had passed her a pearl ring from Todd, along with the message that she would get 'the real engagement ring' later on, and Todd hoped 'later' didn't mean too long. Then Todd himself arrived in a chartered twin-engine silver aircraft and spirited her off to Chicago, just for lunch. The bill for that day's jaunt came to $820.75. Such conspicuous extravagance dazzled her and gave him publicity; that was to be the pattern.

On the Labor Day weekend, they took off for Atlantic City, where Todd gave her a gold ring set with garnets. She wore it when it wasn't visible in the shot, but had to remove it when Clift's ability to speak his lines ran into a block when she was wearing it.

Whatever her co-star thought of her marriage prospects, he was in no fit state to issue the warnings he had done on earlier pre-nuptial occasions. Though his injuries had healed sufficiently well, but not invisibly enough to prevent people trying to spot the close-ups taken before and after his appalling accident, Clift's emotional balance was precarious. He was still heavily into drugs and drink. When they moved to Natchez, Tennessee, a strait-laced place with little to do after shooting, time was filled with partying – as was evident from the claims submitted later for alleged damage to the accommodation rented for the stars. The claim on Elizabeth's place referred to 'liquor spilled all over the house. The walls are full of grease; her make-up is all over the bedspreads; imprints of her hands on the shower curtains; ditto on windowsills and, during a party, the back end of a couch was broken'. The claim for this totted up to between $700 and $800, later reduced to $385.25 'chargeable to her', as the ever precise studio accounts put it.

Two months after the cast and crew returned to Hollywood, on 4 October 1956, the studio announced that Elizabeth Taylor Wilding was suing for divorce.

'I hope and pray that after her divorce she will take some time to consider her next move,' Hedda Hopper wrote sanctimoniously. 'But knowing her as well as I do, I doubt if she will.'

Hopper was half-right. Elizabeth did consider her next move, but she did not wait until after the divorce before she made it.

Early in October, she flew to New York, then motored to Connecticut, where Clift had arranged for her and Todd to stay for a few days with yet another of those mother-figures he cultivated, Libby Holman. There Todd gave her a third ring, one with a diamond an inch across and five-eighths of an inch thick. The value: $92,000. She wasn't able to get her glove over it. Libby Holman found the glove she'd removed and left behind; she had it framed and labelled: 'Elizabeth Taylor, 1956'.

'A friendship thing,' said Elizabeth, when the press noticed this addition to her finger.

'An engagement ring,' Todd corrected her, signifying the intention if not the fact, as she was still a married woman. She soon showed her loyalty by preferring to go to the premiere of his *Around the World in Eighty Days*, rather than the simultaneous opening of George Stevens's *Giant*. Love transcended duty. She even sat with her new 'fiancé' in the projection booth, as Todd barked orders, checked the gate of the lens for specks of dirt and operated the sound volume. Despite his public flamboyance, Todd was a 'control freak'. The grand gestures he was known for were often made by a pernickety tyrant.

Another aspect of Todd began to show up even in these early stages: his impresario's need to be seen to be in charge. It reflected his male vanity, but also his proprietorial attitude to marriage.

Well before they were married, and all through their life together, Todd showed a disposition to cut Elizabeth down to size in public. He usually did it by way of an acerbic remark. The one-line quip that came so quickly to his tongue enhanced his own custodial indulgence of her whims and tastes, yet at the same time diminished her as someone who could exist independently of him. A Hollywood producer would not have made his star submit, in public at least, to the barrage of cracks about her temperament and appearance that Todd kept up, even when they were among friends, but especially when the press was present to record and report his self-aggrandizing banter. Of course there is a long and honourable show-business tradition of the 'roast', which every celebrity has to endure, some time or another, at the hands of his or her peers; it is usually enhanced if the person on the sharp end of the wisecrack is someone of beauty and uniqueness. But Todd adopted this attitude so compulsively that it embarrassed people who met him and Elizabeth, and made them wonder why she took it with such enjoyment. 'Lizzie Schwartzkopf', was how he'd introduce her in the early days of their 'engagement', slapping her on the rump and telling her she'd have to slim. He made it plain he would be the master. Nor was he complimentary about her stardom. 'To stay married to an actress,' he said, 'you gotta be able to worry about her hair style.' He added: 'In the case of Elizabeth, my son approves, so I have some mature judgement to guide me.' Accompanying Mike Todd anywhere meant assenting to be the stooge in a perpetual stage act. Even his compliments could be back-handed. 'We met and she told me I was wonderful – what more brains and discrimination can you ask for than that? She's an egg-head.' And when he barked at reporters that Elizabeth was 'loyal' and 'devoted' and 'compulsively honest', he made it sound as if all such virtues reflected well on his own discrimination, the way a host glows in the compliments of guests for whom he has selected a vintage wine, even though he has been guided by the price as well as the year.

All these public slights were accepted by Elizabeth as if they were love-bites. Maybe she felt it humanized someone like herself, praised so excessively for her beauty, to have this man treat her with irreverence. It was sexy, too; to be dominated by a man who professed his love in more reassuring currency than words. Mike Todd was going to be the most public – and publicized – experience of Elizabeth's life to date. 'A new kind of man, a new kind of world,' she could have murmured, echoing Norma Shearer in *A Free Soul*.

Once again, Elizabeth professed a total commitment to her man. For her, that meant abandoning everything that had made her who she was – it was a kind of professional death-wish. 'A career wasn't my idea,' she said. 'I am far more interested in being Mrs Michael Todd than in being an actress.' This was a virtual reprise of what she promised herself at the time of her first marriage: 'If my career interferes with my marriage, my career can fly out of the window,' and of her second: 'I've learnt not to dedicate myself to my career. It's just a job which I enjoy while I have it.' But there ensued a significant variation in this theme. She might want to give it all up for the love of Todd; but her retirement didn't suit Todd's book at all. Her celebrity contributed a great deal to his own ego. Her comments were quickly revised: 'Retirement? Quitting films? I've never said I'd retire or quit. It's just a job which I enjoy while I have it.' That was more like it ... For better or worse, for richer or poorer, in sickness and in health, Elizabeth was a part of Todd's showmanship. It was a marriage built on the secular altar of supply and demand.

She was generous in her divorce terms; as she always would be. When romance went out of marriage, there was no consolation – except another romance. In the divorce papers filed at Santa Monica on 14 November 1956, she waived all alimony, asked for custody of her sons and requested that Wilding pay $250 a month for their support and education.

Later that month, Todd and Elizabeth were returning to Miami from a weekend visit to Lord Beaverbrook in the Bahamas when Elizabeth lost her grip on a companionway she was trying to climb up in heavy seas. She fell and landed on her coccyx. She couldn't rise off her knees because of the pain. Todd carried her to bed and ordered their cruiser to radio ahead for an ambulance to meet them. Later, in the Harkness Pavilion of the Columbia-Presbyterian Medical Center, New York, tests confirmed an impacted series of spinal discs, the new injury probably aggravated by the old ones incurred while filming *National Velvet* and *The Conspirator*. Immediate surgery was advised; the discs would have to be cut out and replaced with ones purpose-built from a bone bank, supplemented with bonding tissue taken from Elizabeth's hip and pelvis. A five-hour operation followed, then a couple of weeks being turned 'like a pig on a spit', as she described it, so that the 'reconstructions' were given equal tension, otherwise it might have affected her balance, or even her ability to walk.

But if pain was one pole of her life, she now had a man who supplied pleasure at the other. Todd's solicitude was bounteous, but, as always, expressed through publicly advertised extravagance. The meals sent in from an exclusive restaurant were only the beginning. He transformed an austerely functional hospital suite into a millionaire's art gallery by hanging on the walls a Renoir, a Pissarro, a Monet and a Frans Hals, though this last was surely the present from Elizabeth's father on her marriage to Nick Hilton. Todd also cabled a car showroom in Berkeley Square, London, for the most costly British automobile on the market, a Rolls-Royce Silver Cloud, which he intended to have waiting for her when she came out of hospital.

The man who handled money and rare possessions so confidently had assuredly not been born to them. Avrom Hirsh Goldbogen was how Mike Todd had come into the world, in Minneapolis, in 1907, one of several children in a poor immigrant family that moved to Chicago. But after making a fortune and losing it in the construction business, he found his talent lay in showmanship; and the New York World's Fair, in 1939–40, allowed him to exercise it spectacularly with an act that consisted in burning the fairy wings off a dancer with gas jets and leaving her looking naked. Twice married – Joan Blondell became his second wife – and several times bankrupt, he had a flair for publicity, self-promotion and getting his way with people, especially rich women, that was coupled with enormous self-confidence and disregard for consequences. He had struck lucky with some ventures, but usually let his financial excesses plunge him again into the life of turbulent insecurity – some said self-destructiveness – in which he thrived. But now, to all appearances, he was 'in the money'.

It is worth pausing to ask where all Todd's money came from. American taxes on the rich were not all that lenient. Tax shelter deals hadn't then reached the dizzying degree of sophistication that later saved (or, at least, hid) money for their users, although the Bahamas trip may have been undertaken for this purpose. Todd's expenses were huge, even by millionaire's standards. Where did he get it all? The most likely answer may seem the unlikeliest to ordinary folk who live within their incomes. Todd always lived outside, well outside his immediate income, but created the impression through each new and conspicuous extravagance that he had the money to match it – match it, not pay for it. It is always a surprise to people to learn how generously credit is supplied to a big spender, provided his public image is sustained by the gullible media, who have a vested interest in supporting a colourful character who gives good quotes and even better hospitality. Media collusion can be a licence to print credit notes. The publicity generated seems to be collateral for one's financial worthiness. The emperor can have as many new suits of clothes as he likes, and in this case they will be tangible enough; they will not be concealing his own nudity so much as the nakedness of his bank account.

But Todd had also more solid collateral in the form of *Around the World in Eighty Days*. It had opened strongly and seemed likely to build into one of the blockbusters of its day – which it did. This gave him credibility – and something even more valuable, ready cash. For it is one of the attractive aspects of the film business that it permits money to be raised before it is earned. The process called hypothecating, whereby a movie's future receipts will be hypothetically calculated and then converted into real money by creative accountancy, served Todd well and his bank account better. The system in which the movie was shot – Todd-AO-

Scope: a joint venture between him and the American Optical Company – gave him additional investment collateral. And since it had to be shown in cinemas equipped with special projectors, it was the custom to 'buy' the cinema for the duration of the run on the basis of a 'four-wall deal'. The distributors in effect became the exhibitors as well, allowing the cash flow to proceed rapidly, and without fear of diversion, into their bank accounts – and, of course, enabling the producer to cut himself into the box-office receipts at a much earlier stage, more directly and more generously, than if he were waiting well down the line with his hand out. That way one can get slapped.

For Mike Todd, being rich was a state of mind: it didn't need money in the bank to sustain it. He had made and lost several fortunes as a fairground showman, Broadway impresario, inventor and promoter. 'I've often been broke, but I've never been poor,' is a litany that he sang at a multitude of press conferences. He meant it, too. And it was one that Elizabeth could adopt, and did, with the bonus of knowing that she had never been broke. She believed in the fatefulness of life; Todd put his trust in the luck of existence. True: she didn't believe in gambling, whereas Todd didn't believe in anything else. But there was gambling and gambling; one where you threw it all away on the tables in the casino, the other where you cast your bread on the waters and might find it coming back to you. Todd and Elizabeth: each could accommodate the other. She loved Todd's contagious energy, curiosity and impatience.

So impatient was he, in fact, that he could not wait for the slow-moving process of the California divorce laws. Two days after Elizabeth's discharge from hospital, he whipped her off to Acapulco for a quickie Mexican divorce.

21

HEY, BIG SPENDER!

'Are you hoping for a reconciliation?' Michael Wilding was asked, when he flew to Acapulco on 24 January 1957. 'Good God, no!' he answered; he was only there to help, if there were any snags over the divorce. Few husbands can have been more obliging.

Snags there were not. Instead, a major obstacle appeared: the local elections. No politician wished to take a favourable view of quickie divorce because of the Roman Catholic church's attitude, and its power to help or hurt a candidate for office. The divorce petition was tossed out of court. Todd raged. Here was this important 'business deal', as he put it, and a couple of minor legal flunkeys were frustrating it. The city was scoured for a judge who was retiring from office, not running for one; eventually, before nightfall on 31 January 1957, one such nodded through the mutual consent decree – and made Elizabeth Taylor a free woman again. That obstacle out of the way, the guests were summoned: a restrained (for Todd) thirty-four in number. They included Elizabeth's parents ('I hope that this time her dreams will come true,' said Francis Taylor on cue at the airport); Eddie Fisher, who was best man, and his wife Debbie Reynolds, matron of honour. Debbie's friendship with Elizabeth went back to their MGM days together when Elizabeth, jaded by her star's diet of filet mignon, had once swapped her order for the starlet's cheese sandwich on Debbie's plate.

Eddie Fisher, then twenty-seven, at the peak of his bobby-soxer popularity as a crooner, and often at the top of the Hit Parade, was Mike Todd's closest friend and protégé, and had been his go-between in Todd's wooing of Elizabeth. Eddie had been almost a proxy Mike Todd, telling Elizabeth all his stories about the man he adored as a father-figure, generally warming up the heart for the big romance. His own feelings about his role had been mixed, as he later revealed. He had had to stand by and watch Todd and Elizabeth fall passionately for each other, all the while aware that his own marriage was coming apart. He still felt envious of Todd for seizing this beautiful woman's love and person.

The wedding was to take place on 2 February in the clifftop residence owned by a business partner of a former Mexican president. The government assigned sixty bodyguards from the presidential corps to keep out the swarms of 'gringos' from the foreign press trying to slip through the gates or even scale the steep rocky paths dropping from the gardens to the Pacific. Helen Rose had designed this, the third wedding dress Elizabeth had worn inside five years. Cocktail length, it was in hydrangea blue – to match the eyes – worn without a tiara this time, simply a chiffon kerchief tied over her hair, peasant-style – a gesture perhaps to the country of the nuptials. However, lest she needed identification, Todd presented her with a magnificent matching set of diamond pendant earrings, ring and bracelet valued at $250,000. As an additional token of his affections, he also purchased two cinemas in Chicago and renamed them after himself and his bride – 'His' and 'Liz'. The wedding wear issued to male guests consisted of shirts in an Indian print, monogrammed 'MT' and 'ET'. It was less easy to keep tabs on the essentials, such as the Protestant pastor and the Jewish rabbi, churchmen symbolizing the respective faiths of the bride and groom. They stayed away on orders from their superiors. The civil authorities were again appealed to, and came up with the mayor of Acapulco – he was not due for re-election. He conducted the ceremony in brisk Spanish, not a word of which Elizabeth understood, though she was once or twice heard to exclaim, 'How interesting.'

Despite the passion with which she embraced Todd as they were pronounced man and wife, her appearance still reflected weeks of pain in hospital. Todd and Cantinflas, Mexico's leading screen comic, who had played David Niven's valet Passepartout in Todd's film, took turns in carrying her from room to room and out on to the terrace where a buffet reception was illuminated by flaming kerosene torches. Her spine still hurt her greatly. Strolling violinists in gaucho costume serenaded the party. Tables were laden with hot tamales, tortillas, tacos, avocados, greenboned fish, giant hams, suckling pigs on the spit and lemon-and-peach chiffon pie. Those preferring something less regional could dig their spoons into a dozen two-pound tins of Beluga caviar packed in ice-filled silver bowls. Indian boys shinned up the palm trees, sliced the green fruit open and topped up the coconuts with champagne.

African drums added a jungle pulse to the festivities and rose in a crescendo as suddenly, at a signal, the skies turned to a sheet of tequila-coloured flame: it was Cantinflas's wedding gift, a fireworks display whose burning, fizzing nebulae gradually resolved themselves into the familiar twin set of initials, 'MT' and 'ETT' (Elizabeth Taylor Todd), which turned molten red, faded, separated and fell to earth. As they exploded, Elizabeth gave a cry. 'Mike ... Mike ... don't leave me.' He sprang to her side and smothered her in kisses. A year later she was to explain why the fiery sky had alarmed her. It touched off a fleeting premonition of tragedy, the nature of which was then unknown to her, except that it somehow involved the two sets of blazing initials now lying in ashes on the earth.

A Mexican orchestra struck up a romantic melody as she and Mike cut their cake: 'Only once does love come in a lifetime / Only once and never more.' It was thought by some to be not the most appropriate of ballads.

'"Don't spoil her," I told him again and again. "She's impossible enough already."' It was an impossible demand, though, and Hedda Hopper knew it even as she said it. Mike Todd saw the world as a place for him to plunder and Elizabeth as someone on whom to display the loot. Spoiling her was only a means of sating himself. A man who sent champagne to his wife whenever she went to the hairdresser's, lest she be thirsty under the drier, could put that extravagance down to an act of love; it was also part of his own overwhelming ego. His congenital restlessness now became a peripatetic life-style they shared – a style that Elizabeth was to maintain for the rest of her life. They were never still. 'I might as well be married to a roulette wheel,' she once said. The honeymoon was brief; Todd couldn't stand inactivity. To keep themselves amused while Mexican soldiery with loaded rifles guarded the hacienda in the village of Puerto Marquez, Todd hired the entire Ballet Africain from a floorshow in Acapulco. He was starting married life as he meant to go on – he was 'producing' it.

But Elizabeth almost certainly didn't feel herself to be the victim of Todd's male chauvinism. Not servitude, but synergy: that was probably how she viewed their relationship. She had – and has – a very conventional view of where the woman fitted into marriage. She believed that marriages began to go wrong when the partners developed separate interests – and separate ways. She took a vow that had the characteristic Todd-like flavour of a Biblical injunction turning into a wisecrack: 'Whither thou goest, I will go – buster'. Todd set the pace; she followed a half-step behind. The agenda and itinerary of their life together over the year was set by *Around the World in Eighty Days*, which was opening globally in a staggered schedule, allowing them to attend its premieres on all continents, if they wished, and, of course, charge the expenses to the film.

Another thing that kept them close was Todd's fidelity. It might be thought that having achieved the sexual conquest of the most beautiful woman in Hollywood, his vanity would compel him to exploit other women's curiosity about what he had that the rest of mankind apparently hadn't. He did not. There is not a single anecdote of his infidelity to Elizabeth. He was as continuously close to her as her mother had once been, caring for her, reassuring her of his love with a never-ending stream of presents. Todd, too, was a man of convention: totally faithful to one woman – one at a time, anyhow. Interesting proof of his propriety occurred when he insisted that the press statement that Michael Wilding issued about his separation should assert that 'Elizabeth and Mike Todd did not see one another alone until we were separated, and I wish to say that Todd's conduct in this whole thing has been above reproach.' True, as far as it went, though 'reproach' has to be defined by the subjective Hollywood dictionary.

She began to look, as well as behave, like her husband as they embarked on their circumnavigation of the globe. One of Elizabeth's biographers has noted the 'rich, contented opulence' that she soon began manifesting. Almost every time they went to a premiere of the film, Elizabeth received a major piece of jewellery from her husband. Homage and chutzpah were inextricably linked in their minds. When Elizabeth had come out of the anaesthetic after her spinal discs were renewed, she cried, 'Where is my diamond ring?' Another woman might have called for her husband. But Elizabeth, in a sense, was asking for both in the same breath. Todd was the sum of his presents.

Not everyone, of course, enjoyed his largesse: mainly those he wanted to impress. Those who worked for him – a very different matter – were paid in power, not coin. When his employees were with him and Elizabeth, they felt like 'family', sharing the boss's life-style, sustaining it night and day, experiencing the pleasures of a perpetual shopping trip, only realizing after they had left his service just how much energy had been extracted from them by Todd's commandeering manner, and how little tangible compensation they had to show for it. The months with Todd got Elizabeth into the habit of travelling with a troupe of employees who were always on tap for the company she needed as well as the errands she sent them on. The entourage of later years, the praetorian guard that ultimately shut out the world like Roman centurions with their shields, became her modus vivendi in this period. Elizabeth felt that where the Todds went, the world went – buster.

On 26 March 1957, the MGM publicity department announced that she was pregnant again and expecting a baby at the end of the year.

In April, they embarked on the *Queen Elizabeth* for the European premiere of *Around the World in Eighty Days* at the Cannes Film Festival: Elizabeth, Mike, her sons Michael and Christopher, a nurse, a Japanese secretary (his), twenty pieces of luggage (mostly hers) and three white poodles. At Cherbourg, wearing a champagne mink against the chilly spring, she added something else to the impedimenta: the Rolls-Royce Silver Cloud that Todd had bought her to cheer her up after her operation. It was sent on ahead to Nice, while the Todd party piled into a chartered aircraft for the same destination, diverting for an hour or so to Jersey, in the Channel Islands, after they were seized by the need for afternoon tea. The island's anomalous independent status in the British Isles made it one of the few bits of Anglo-Saxon soil where three white poodles could enjoy the same privileges as their mistress, unaffected by quarantine restrictions.

Todd had taken a three-month lease on Lady Kenmare's house, the Villa Fiorentina, near St Jean–Cap Ferrat. It had such essentials as pine woods, extensive gardens, an aviary with three hundred canaries fluttering ceaselessly up and down, and a swimming pool filled twice daily with fresh seawater. Just the place for Elizabeth to have seclusion while waiting for her child. For the premiere of his film, he commandeered the elegant Edwardian winter casino on the Croisette in Cannes, invited one thousand guests and the entire press corps covering the festival, and flew a circus down from Paris. As lions and tigers prowled around inside a bell-shaped cage in the midst of supper guests tucking into caviar and smoked sturgeon ('After the babies, we eat the mother,' said someone), a few of those present surveyed the glitz and gluttony and felt it would be justice if the wild beasts made their breakfast of the guests.

Over the casino floated a huge hot-air balloon, a replica of the one in the film. Todd himself added to the hot air the next morning, with a press conference that lasted two hours. At one point he clapped his hands and ordered lunch for the three hundred journalists, so that they could sit and eat while he continued talking. At least one of them, attempting to keep pace with Todd's verbal shorthand, found a familiar woman materializing beside him saying, sotto voce, so as not to distract her lord and master, 'Can I freshen your drink?'

'Honey, honey,' Todd would cry, when he saw Elizabeth making herself useful, 'don't scintillate ... you got one husband already.' The newsmen loved it – as they were intended to do.

The casino must have recalled painful memories of the humiliation and rough treatment Nick Hilton had made her suffer. But when the Todds appeared at the tables, and she dipped into Mike's dinner jacket and came up with a wad of notes, he disclaimed any intention of gambling.

'There must be $10,000 here,' she exclaimed, after a quick scan.

'Pocket money,' snapped Todd, chewing a champagne swizzle stick, 'put it back. And don't count – it's vulgar to count money.'

It wouldn't have been in character for him to count the cost of the next few weeks, either; but it was considerable, even by his standards. Elizabeth sometimes took a private plane to Paris, to shop at Dior or Balenciaga; while she did the haute couture rounds, Todd shopped for paintings. He paid $71,428 for three pictures – by Degas, Utrillo and Vuillard – from the collection that Aly Khan was selling, and quipped in the characteristic manner of a philistine with taste, which he was adept at assuming, 'Hollywood'll think me crazy, paying that much for coloured stills, pictures that don't even move.' Wilding flew over to stay with them, causing the conventional to comment about the propriety of the ex-husband cohabiting with the current couple. And all the time, Todd's cornucopia of presents showered down on Elizabeth. He found excuses for inventing anniversaries – 'I've had so many anniversaries, I'll soon be as old as Mike,' she said. Pressed for details of his gifts, she said they were simply 'little' ones – 'You know, little diamonds, little rubies, little emeralds.' She was developing as deft a line in wisecracks as her husband-mentor. She appeared in a new tiara: 'Oh, that's just a Saturday night present,' was the airy explanation.

The scale of Todd's gifts suggests his generosity had a pathological coloration. And even their rows acquired an exhibitionist character – the kind that needed an audience to enjoy the show. Like a situation comedy, it was not for real, but it sounded good; it relieved the undoubted tensions of two stubborn temperaments; and it led to a profligate display of affection when they made things up again. 'The gal's been looking for trouble all her life,' he said. 'When she flies into a tantrum, I fly into a bigger one. She's been on a milk-toast diet until me: but me, I'm red meat.'

They flew to London for the *Around the World in Eighty Days* premiere on 2 July 1957. It is safe to say the capital hadn't seen a night of jubilation like it since Princess Elizabeth's coronation four years earlier. It is even safer to say that no more vulgar event has taken place since. 'Dad,' Mike Todd Jr cabled from New York, 'the film is doing fine. We are making almost as much money as you are spending.' But it must have taken the box office a few days to recoup what Todd spent on that one night.

The event was in aid of the Newspaper Press Fund – a canny choice, assuring maximum media coverage. Some 1,500 people had been invited. The Duchess of Kent and her daughter Princess Alexandra were patrons and, for once, Elizabeth was on time to receive them in the cinema foyer. Visibly pregnant, she wore a Dior gown in ruby-red chiffon and Todd's 'premiere present', a ruby and diamond necklace and earrings costing $350,000. Seeing the Duchess's jewellery, Todd fingered his wife's. 'I'm in trouble – she'll be throwing these away tomorrow.'

'What are you hoping for?' the Duchess asked Elizabeth.

'A girl,' her husband chipped in, 'the world's not ready for a second Mike Todd.'

For the post-premiere party, he had taken over Battersea Gardens, a Thamesside park with a permanent fun-fair. Guests were ferried there in riverboats or red London buses whose destination plates showed Hong Kong, Yokohama, San Francisco and half a dozen other round-the-world staging posts. The Duchess of Argyll was glimpsed holding up her gown as she climbed the stairs to – appropriately – the top deck. It had begun to rain: but Todd had second-guessed God. Minions passed out two thousand black plastic raincoats stamped with Todd's monogram in even bigger letters than the film's title. Six bands played a cacophony of different tunes as the guests arrived. Waiters circulated in Victorian costume. Some two hundred Methuselah-sized bottles of champagne were drunk. Cigarette girls were got up as can-can dancers. All the sideshows were doing a roaring business – for free. Todd even positioned galvanized buckets filled with copper pennies, shillings and florins around the slot machines so that no guest needed to dig into his pocket to try his luck.

Turn in any direction and one ran into the rich and famous. Laurence Olivier and Vivien Leigh rode the carousel; Douglas Fairbanks Jr and his wife behaved like kamikaze pilots bumping into everyone in kiddy cars; Sir Hartley Shawcross, the socialist attorney-general, danced a tango with Debbie Reynolds; Lord Dalkeith played on a swing like a five-year-old child; Mrs Gerald Legge blazed away at a sharp-shooting booth like Annie Oakley. Michael Wilding even met the woman who was to become his next wife, Mrs Susan Nell, then married to a dairy magnate. And somehow, everyone – including the Thames river police, whom Todd invited ashore – found a breathing space to consume huge quantities of food. This was 'typical' London fare (or what passed for it): whelks, toffee apples, fish-and-chips in specially printed copies of The Times dated 1893, the year of Phileas Fogg's global circumnavigation. From further afield came egg rolls (China), giant prawns (Hong Kong), sweet potatoes (Virginia), curry (India), pasta (Italy), strawberries and cream (England).

Seven bars had been granted special one-night liquor licences: beer, wine and champagne were dispensed until dawn.

Todd sat holding Elizabeth's hand. He counted this the pinnacle of his success. At one point, he had shouted at an inebriated guest who bumped into the expectant Elizabeth, and threatened to throw him into the Thames. Elizabeth restrained him. 'Please behave like a gentleman,' said Todd to the fellow, varying the punishment.

Yet this brash American showman somehow acted as a catalyst for the still stiffly 'correct' London society. He turned them into children again – the choice of a fun-fair was inspired. As the Todds left at dawn, stepping into their Rolls-Royce Silver Cloud, he suddenly smacked himself on the forehead.

'What's the matter?' asked Elizabeth.

'Holy cow! I knew there was something I forgot – the headache powders.'

He forgot something else, too; his passport and Elizabeth's. The American consul opened up his country's embassy on Independence Day to supply new travel documents. That was how 'important' Mike Todd was.

They left for America the same day, 4 July 1957, sailing across an ocean of irreproachable calm. 'It knows Elizabeth is having her baby,' said Todd. At that time, he had little more than eight months of life left to him.

22

THE FALL OF A TYCOON

By now, Elizabeth was appreciating that being 'Mrs Mike Todd' was a vicarious kind of stardom, in some ways preferable to the traditional kind. She didn't need to make a film to be the centre of attention. She didn't have to spend weeks on sets or uncomfortable locations: boring hours of doing nothing; repeating a few seconds of dialogue or a tedious bit of business until someone called 'cut'; getting up at an hour that a barnyard rooster would consider on the early side of sunrise; going to bed without a social life so as to be fresh for the camera the next morning. As Todd's wife, she enjoyed stardom's privileges and power, without its constraints. She benefited from the media's collusive friendship with Todd, liked for his accessibility, his fund of quotes, his irreverent attitude to the stars, his endless news value. Elizabeth got the best of both worlds: her own and her husband's. He gave her a persona outside pictures, and amplified it.

But he also had plans for her inside pictures. He was preparing a spectacular version of *Don Quixote*, scripted by S. J. Perelman (who had taken screen credit for *Around the World in Eighty Days*), with Fernandel as the Don, Cantinflas as Sancho Panza – 'and', he added, 'Liz'll probably play Thérèse.' Characteristically, Todd was cocksure he could improve on the book. 'That guy who wrote it. He was a once-around Willie. He never wrote anything else in the same class. We got a new concept for it.'

MGM monitored Todd's announcement carefully. Elizabeth owed the studio two more films; unless summoned to a European throne, like Grace Kelly, she was very unlikely to get MGM's waiver to appear in a Todd film until its own plans for her were announced. One was, quickly. She would play Maggie the Cat in a film version of Tennessee Williams's *Cat on a Hot Tin Roof*.

Despite Todd's commendation for the Atlantic Ocean's considerateness on their recent crossing, Elizabeth's baby had been less obliging. A kick from it against her reconstructed spine had made her cry out in pain. A check-up in New York disclosed it was growing up under her ribcage, pushing against her heart, and needed remedial repositioning. It wasn't due until October. But in August, she collapsed, clutching her abdomen, during dinner at the Westport mansion that Todd had rented for the summer. By nine o'clock, in terrible pain, she was in the Harkness Pavilion. And at 12.03 p.m., on 6 August 1957, a baby girl, to be named 'Elizabeth Frances' and known as 'Liza', was delivered by Caesarean section after Elizabeth, fearing the consequence to the child of such premature birth, had pleaded in vain, 'Please don't take her – she's not cooked yet.' Attending her were two doctors – one of whom worked for fifteen minutes to give the kiss-of-life to the infant – an obstetrician, a pediatrician, a diagnostician, a resuscitationist and two neurologists. Todd was leaving nothing to chance. He exulted: 'I have the picture of the year, the bride of the year and now the baby of the year. What more could a man want?' As if to offer a hint to the new father, a cable was received which said simply, but sufficiently: 'Congratulations – Cartier.' Reverting to the show-business habit of delivering a back-hander at someone else's celebrity, he added: 'Compared with the kid, her mother looks like Frankenstein.' (Reporters assumed he meant the monster.) Would he be helping with all the little things a father had to do? Business came first: 'All I know about kids is that they get in for half-price.'

The photographs taken of the family group show Elizabeth looking more 'Earth Mother' than ever, reclining in bed, cradling her baby like a chipmunk on her shoulder, while Todd for once yields the top spot on the bill to mother and child. To mark the birth, he wired Annigoni, the Italian portrait artist who had recently done what became the definitive iconographic image of Queen Elizabeth II, and commissioned him to paint the other Elizabeth. But having had royalty sit for him, Annigoni knew where commoners came in. He cabled back that Mrs Todd must come to Florence. Years later, Andy Warhol, more obliging and, in terms of work, more economical, 'did' Elizabeth from her photograph for a famous series of her in multicoloured guises.

Elizabeth had joined the board of Mike Todd Pictures Inc. Her husband had contracted her to appear in *Don Quixote* – a bit of 'hype', MGM concluded, albeit nervously – and announced he was 'renting Spain' for filming. Picasso was hired to do a 'concept' drawing for the film's advertising, and Vincent Korda the production design. Keeping his name in headlines, by whatever means best served his mood or project of the moment, was one of the engines that fired Todd with energy. But from this moment on, the techniques he used began to be counter-productive.

There is a media phenomenon that afflicts most celebrities from time to time, often for no reason other than that news editors believe that their readership is becoming sated by overkill. Quite quickly, the coverage assumes a more abrasive tone or shifts to unflattering angles. If readers respond – favourably or unfavourably doesn't really matter: it all sells papers – then the celebrity feels a sharpness in the hitherto caressing wind, and great can be the bewilderment and rage.

Todd began to feel these unaccustomed sensations when the first anniversary of his blockbuster film approached, and he planned a spectacular event that would relaunch it on to the front pages and so lengthen the lines outside the box office. He would take over Madison Square Garden – 'one of the few places Liz and I have never fought' – and throw an immense birthday party.

He publicized it as 'an intimate little party for a few chums'. The invitations numbered eighteen thousand. The huge hall was trimmed in blue and pink by Vincent Korda – ordered to quit his drawing board in England where he was sketching *Don Quixote*, and come post-haste to design a greater folly than tilting at windmills. A forty-foot-tall reproduction of the Oscar won by Todd was built of golden chrysanthemums and dominated one end of the hall. In the centre was a cake, thirty feet in diameter and fourteen feet tall, weighing over a ton, made of two thousand eggs and $15,000 of cake mix. Delivered in sections and fitted together, it was covered with 150 pounds of pale-blue icing-sugar. A single candle was arranged to spring up out of the centre when it was cut.

There were fourteen thousand free gifts to be won by guests, ranging from a Cessna aircraft, four cars, half a dozen Vespa scooters, mink stoles and a hundred pelts of lesser degree, to Olivetti typewriters, Decca LPs, soft toys by the hamperful, tins of Scottish shortbread, 260 bottles of Smirnoff vodka, ten thousand Havana cigars – all brand items, all donated, costing Todd nothing, but allowing him to pose as the king of cornucopiae.

The whole show was to be televised by CBS, which put up $300,000 for the privilege of giving Todd more airtime than even he could have afforded to pay for. All the food and drink was likewise donated by the makers or franchise holders: two hundred gallons of vichyssoise, a ton of baked beans, fifteen thousand doughnuts, as many hot dogs, ten thousand egg rolls, thirty gallons of ice cream. Qantas flew in kangaroos from Australia; TWA, not to be outdone, flew in Tony Curtis, Bea Lillie, Janet Gaynor, Ginger Rogers, Shelley Winters ... The cost of the bash, estimated at $250,000, was more than defrayed by these freebies. It was virtually eliminated. Todd's only sizeable expense was for hiring the hall, the decorations and the huge sign outside on which two thousand lights spelled out the sardonic information: 'Private Little Party'. This might have cost him $5,000, but one reporter who suggested Todd might actually be in pocket was met with an indignant: 'Who should have that much fun and make a buck, too!'

On 17 October 1957, at a signal from Todd, George Jessel, host for the evening, stepped on to a rostrum the height and size of those from which ocean-going ships are usually launched down the slipway. From that moment, everything that could go wrong, did. 'Anarchy raged,' was how *Variety* put it.

The build-up was colossal, but the party was a débâcle. The prizes were 'openly and boldly hijacked Chicago-style, or broken open and pilfered waterfront-style'. Waiters hired to dispense free champagne began slapping prices on the bottles. Guests struggling through to the food found themselves behind a heaving human wall of professional performers who had been hired to entertain them, but who, finding themselves within privileged reach of the buffet tables in the main arena, and probably not yet having been fed (unlike the wild animals Todd had freighted down to Cannes), wasted no time on party tricks but began stuffing themselves. Fights broke out. Pizzas were rammed into people's faces, ice cream skidded underfoot. Even the cops brought in to keep order proved 'the most outspoken rude set of moujiks'. The celebrities began pushing and shoving to get out. Women were particularly vocal in decrying Todd for telling them to dress up to the eyes, only to have their finery torn and mangled in the crush. 'The manner of dispensing the dubious free drink was beyond alibi' said *Variety*'s 'obituary' of the event. As the bonbon wagon rolled by, guests were pelted with candies. That was not so bad as when some idiot on the hot-dog wagon started throwing franks and buns. Gowns were stained: 'About the only thing the hot-dog dolt failed to do was put mustard on 'em before he started pitching. Let's be grateful.' No happier were the celebrities chosen to take part in a procession which included a live elephant topped by Sir Cedric Hardwicke. He almost became 'the first indoor elephant-trampling casualty this side of Sabu country'. The TV commentators could not see their monitor screens. Sponsors were left out of commercial breaks. Arthur Fiedler and Duke Ellington, booked to provide dance music, found themselves with orchestras, but no dancers – there was no room.

Amidst the chaos, Elizabeth somehow mounted the red-carpeted rostrum and cut the cake, having first scooped up a handful of the still wet icing with an appreciative 'mmm ...' She looked blithely happy, as if totally unaware of the seething multitude below her resembling the evacuation of some Vandals-invaded city.

Todd's great night collected the blackest headlines imaginable from the media he had been used to manipulating so smoothly. '[He] gave the public bread-crumbs and a circus,' said the *New York Daily News*. That was mild. The *Herald Tribune* thundered: 'The United States ... can well imagine how the Soviets will present a picture to the rest of the world of New York fiddling while the country burns.' The party and all connected with it, including Elizabeth, were taken to be a symptom of decadence, an omen of worse to come. 'In the days of the fabulous banquets which preceded the fall of the Roman empire, the participants used to purge themselves, retire to a specially named room and empty their stomachs so that they could return to stuff themselves anew.'

It was left to George Jessel to bestow, instead of a toastmaster's tribute, what sounded like a coroner's verdict: 'Such an evening will not happen again. Nobody could stand it.'

Todd did his brash best to pick up the pieces, even asking Price Waterhouse – the firm of accountants that supervised voting for the Academy Awards, and was therefore above suspicion – to supervise the lotteries that hadn't taken place. 'Liz who is honest will pick the numbers,' he added. But he could not conceal that the tide of approbation he and Elizabeth had ridden was now turning against him. The flak continued as the couple set off once more around the world on 1 November 1957, to promote the film that now paid the bills.

They ran into trouble in Sydney, where, as Frank Sinatra could have ruefully told them, a sabre-toothed species of journalist was bred, the kind who bit, not licked, visiting VIPs. 'The rudest personality ever to hit [town],' Todd was called in the press. It was noticeable that he and Elizabeth, when under pressure like this, demonstrated an unusual amount of conspicuous public affection for each other, kissing and embracing for the cameras, as though they feared to lose the attention of the media, having already lost its uncritical approval.

After Hong Kong – and a rush home to have Elizabeth's gnawing appendix treated – they set out for Moscow. Todd announced he wanted to film *War and Peace* and proposed hiring as much of the Soviet army as could be spared from Cold War duties. 'I [also] thought it might be a good idea to show off Liz to the Russians. She's the best secret weapon we've got. It may undermine their whole structure.' Not surprisingly, the Soviet Minister of Culture gave them the brushoff.

Before leaving for Moscow, Elizabeth made a friend of someone who was to stand by her again and again in future years, alternately beautifier and comforter: Alexandre, the Paris hairdresser, whom Todd had cabled at his salon in the capital: 'Please reserve appointment for Elizabeth Taylor. Set aside whole day.' In Moscow, the inevitable joke was on Todd's lips as Western reporters thronged round the aircraft steps: 'This is the only place in the world where Mike Todd is not Mr Elizabeth Taylor.' With equal truth, he might have said that the Soviet Union was one of the few places in the world where Elizabeth was relatively unknown as either herself or as Mrs Mike Todd. She was gratified when a girl rushed up to her in Red Square demanding an autograph: but it turned out she'd been mistaken for Marilyn Monroe.

When Nikita Khrushchev, then the Soviet leader, attended a reception at the Indian Embassy celebrating the republic's tenth anniversary, Elizabeth was already installed as the centrepiece. She wore a black cocktail suit trimmed with broadtail fur, and glistening with sequins and diamond buttons. After signing autographs for the diplomats, she approached the main table to shake hands with Krishna Menon, Indian Ambassador to the UN and one of the guests who had been liberally bespattered by Todd's hospitality at the Madison Square Garden débâcle. Mr Khrushchev was seen to give her a casual glance. There was a second's uneasy pause; then the Soviet leader diverted his attention to a more urgent attraction, the Norwegian ambassador. Mrs Khrushchev threw Elizabeth a kindly look, and asked: 'Who is the pretty young lady?'

The Todds retreated to Paris, if not in rout, then somewhat depressed. Todd had tried to regain attention by telling a radio interviewer that since he had failed to hire the Russian army for *War and Peace*, he would select another Tolstoy book that would do the Russian people justice. Elizabeth chimed in and said she hankered to play Anna Karenina. At least that only required the loan of non-aggressive items like railway trains.

Todd was now well-placed to do what he liked doing best – making a deal. He had two positions of strength: his wife's readiness to give up her career for marriage, and the continuing success of his blockbuster film, now spoken of as likely to be the first to gross $100 million. It was time to move in on MGM. He was reluctant, though, to make an enemy of a major studio. And he may have sensed that the synergy which served their two careers so well might turn into frustration if Elizabeth was more or less forcibly 'retired' by protracted lawsuits aimed at preventing her working for anyone, if she wouldn't work at MGM.

So he opened negotiations by telling the studio that *Cat on a Hot Tin Roof* would be Elizabeth's last film for MGM, unless ... Then Kurt Frings, Elizabeth's new agent, began the talks about that 'unless'. He began the bargaining in February 1958, by insisting that MGM reimburse his client at her agreed weekly rate up to the time of making *Cat on a Hot Tin Roof*, then she would do that film for a flat fee of $125,000 (plus per diems and pro rata overages). Then she would do a second film for the same price.

He also asked for her to have the right to appear in *Don Quixote*, or any other production Todd nominated, before she made the second film for

MGM. It was agreed, with the proviso that Todd would not have the right to assign her services to any other producer, should he not have a production of his own ready. She was to begin her second MGM picture within three years of completing Todd's. Elizabeth's MGM contract had still another year on it. It was to be terminated on 1 June 1958, and a new one on the above lines would come into force the next day. She was to get $4,850 a week (forty weeks guaranteed). Her mother was to continue to be paid $300 a week by MGM. The contract was written out. It only awaited signature.

The extent of Todd's influence on MGM can be gauged from the way he determined costly decisions about the new MGM movie starring Elizabeth. It was budgeted at $2 million – Tennessee Williams had been paid $450,000 for the rights. It would begin shooting on 5 March 1958, with a thirty-four-day schedule. But Richard Brooks, its director, was downcast over the penny-pinching attitude that dictated his shooting the film in black and white.

'I told them it was crazy,' Brooks says. 'It had one of the world's most beautiful women in the leading role. For Christ's sake, when you get a chance to shoot the violet eyes of Elizabeth Taylor and the blue ones of Paul Newman' – who had been loaned out from Fox for the role of Brick at $25,000 – 'do you use black and white? I told Mike. He said, "I see ..." and wandered off. A little later the same day, three black crows' – Brooks-speak for front-office men in suits – 'visit me on the set: Benny Thau, Eddie Mannix [an MGM vice-president] and [the producer] Laurence Weingarten. "Why are you shooting this picture in black and white? We'd like you to use colour." "Okay," I said, "you got colour." "What'll it cost," they then said, "to redo the sets and wardrobe in colour?" "Look," I said, "the wardrobe and the sets are already in colour: it's the film stock that's in black and white."'

Brooks had been shooting for several days when Todd re-appeared. 'I've got a great idea,' he said, 'we all fly to New York this weekend, you, me and Elizabeth, and have dinner at 21.' Todd was being given a roast by the Friars Club at the Waldorf-Astoria that Saturday. He couldn't bear to be alone; he was like Elizabeth in that way. Any company was better than his own, and Brooks knew he was dying to have Elizabeth at his roast. But he told Todd that Elizabeth was already running a temperature – confirmed by her doctor Rex Kennamer – and a thirty-four-day schedule didn't leave leeway for mishaps. After calling around town for companions – Warren Cowan the publicist, Kurt Frings and the director Joseph L. Mankiewicz all had other engagements – Todd resigned himself to flying east with just his crony and current biographer Art Cohn for company.

Before he left Elizabeth for the airport, on an afternoon of heavy rain and intermittent lightning flashes, he ran back several times to embrace and kiss her. 'Without you, honey,' he repeated, 'I'd feel like half a pair of scissors.' He then left to board his chartered aircraft, *The Lucky Liz*.

He had often cracked that half-joke, but his reiterated insistence this time so worried her that she remained feverishly awake, unable to sleep, and as night passed into 23 March 1958, she had still not heard from Todd at any of the stops from which he had promised to call her.

It was Jim Bacon, Associated Press's West Coast reporter and a friend of Todd's, who got a 6.00 a.m. call from an AP stringer near Albuquerque, New Mexico. Bacon's name had been found on the passenger list of a Lockheed Lodestone aircraft that had crashed in appalling weather – its wings had iced up – into a mountain. Bacon remembered he had hoped to go with Todd but had cancelled.

'Is anyone injured?' he cried.

'Everyone's dead,' came the reply.

Richard Brooks was preparing brunch when Todd's secretary, Dick Hanley, called him from his employer's home on Schuyler Drive. 'I got to the house. All I could hear was this terrible shrieking coming from the upper storey. Shrieking and epithets … interminable cursing … uncontrollable grief.' Hanley, on receiving the news, had enlisted Dr Kennamer's help and both had driven over to Elizabeth, hoping to reach her before the wire services began calling. As soon as she saw them both enter her bedroom, before a word was spoken, she shrieked 'No!' and, leaping out of bed, her hands to her ears, rushed past them, determined not to have the news confirmed in words that she already knew in her heart. 'Her first instinct,' Dick Hanley said later, 'was not to listen, like if she didn't hear it, it hadn't happened. Keeping reality at bay. Running from your own nightmare while still in it.'

The two men chased after her down the staircase, and caught her as she wrenched open the front door. Neighbours had come to their own front yards, alarmed by that great cry, appalled yet attracted by the screams following it. Hanley feared she might do herself some harm – 'like throw herself out of a window'. With Kennamer's help, he carried her, still struggling, up to bed again. There she was sedated. But it proved impossible to make her totally unconscious. 'Then the black crows came calling,' says Richard Brooks. 'Benny Thau and Eddie Mannix walk in and Elizabeth thinks, "My God! Mike's hardly cold and all they're thinking of is: what'll happen to the picture? When will you be able to come back to it, Elizabeth?" so she starts screaming her head off again, cursing them and MGM and the whole movie industry. That's when I walk in. "You, too!" she shrieked at me. "Look," I said, "forget the picture. I don't care when it's made. I don't care if you're in it or not in it when it's made. I don't give a fuck if it's never made." It didn't do any good. I left her screaming.'

Debbie Reynolds arrived to take the Wilding children into her temporary care. Police and police cars guarded the house. Only her parents and intimate friends were let past the barriers. Telephone calls in and out were impossible. The lines were jammed continuously by calls from all over the country – from all over the world.

Todd's body had had to be identified by its jewellery; it was charred beyond recognition. A ring blackened by the heat was eventually returned to Elizabeth, who swore to wear it for the rest of her life. Over 3,500 telegrams were delivered to the house or to MGM, including one from Mamie Eisenhower. Elizabeth asked for donations, in lieu of flowers, to be sent to the Children's Hospital. It was nearly three days before she could hold down food. Mostly she lay in bed, clasping Liza to her, comforted in turn by her ex-husband Michael Wilding, or Helen Rose, or Sidney Guilaroff. Guilaroff spent a whole night stretched out on the floor by her bed, as sleepless as she, taking her hand and lightly squeezing it whenever he heard her shaken by sobs. Someone had to be always with her: the risk of suicide was still real.

Now she knew why she had shivered and cried out in alarm on her wedding night when she had seen the two sets of flaming initials, 'MT' and 'ETT', fall to earth in the fireworks show. She felt now that she wanted to fall to earth with Mike. Possibly only the existence of her children deterred her from some rash act. As sanity returned, her will to go on living proved the stronger. What few knew then was that barely a month before, she and Mike Todd had taken the resolve to enlarge their family yet again. Elizabeth had been advised not to attempt to give birth to another child. But there was still a way. In great secrecy, Kurt Frings was sent to New York on 13 February to see Maria Schell, the Austrian actress then enjoying some celebrity in American-made movies. The purpose of the visit was to find a German child to adopt. Years were to go by before Maria Schell came up with the crippled orphan girl who was to be named 'Maria' after her and adopted by Elizabeth and her then husband – Richard Burton. In the middle of death, it was the thought of life for others that pulled Elizabeth through.

23

A FUNERAL IN CHICAGO

The remains of Mike Todd arrived in a large grey packing case aboard a Santa Fe mail train from Albuquerque, shunted into the goods yard at the almost deserted Dearborn Station, Chicago, at 4.20 a.m. Besides the funeral arrangers, a cop, a few station workers and a reporter on the aptly-named graveyard shift were the only people there to greet the box as it was carried across the tracks to a waiting hearse. Even faced with the grisly reality of his death, those present still found it hard to believe in the instantaneous metamorphosis of the voluble, energizing, flamboyant, Barnumesque Mike Todd into the charred bits and pieces that were later tipped into the ornate bronze coffin.

Todd and Elizabeth had several times discussed death. Todd had been against cremation. Elizabeth now stood by his wish, though Mike Todd Jr argued that having his father cremated at Albuquerque would avoid the enormous emotional strain, and even physical risks, of a funeral, which would attract thousands to the Jewish Waldheim Cemetery just outside Chicago, Todd's native city. Mike was to have his way to the end, she insisted.

Helen Rose, who had done all Elizabeth's bridal gowns, now prepared her widow's trousseau. Howard Hughes, once her unlucky suitor, had put one of the airliners from his TWA fleet at her disposal. Heavily sedated and leaning on an MGM man's arm, Elizabeth climbed slowly into it to join, among others, Dr Kennamer, her brother Howard, Eddie Fisher, Helen Rose and Dick Hanley. She refused to lie down, but dozed fitfully, sitting upright. Gradually, the oppressive atmosphere of the flight relaxed. Someone remarked, with black humour, that the Super Constellation they were flying in had been made by the same company that had built Todd's death plane. Someone else began opening champagne. As Elizabeth floated in and out of consciousness, she could hear what sounded almost like merrymaking in the forward lounge: it seemed to be all part of the surrealist nightmare she was trapped in.

She was half-carried down the ramp into the limousine that Mike Todd Jr had waiting. Before it gained the freeway, its windows were smeared to the point of obscurity by the sweaty hands and lipsticked graffiti of the pressing spectators. The funeral party occupied a whole floor of the Drake Hotel. Eight security agents took turns to mount a day-and-night guard on Elizabeth.

The next morning, 25 March 1958, the cortège set off, escorted by two Chicago police cars. Helen Rose had helped dress Elizabeth in mourning: a black suit trimmed with broadtail fur, a black cloche hat in velvet, black leather gloves, a black mink wrap and a veil that left only her lips visible. What had been intended as a quiet family affair had, of course, got as wildly out of hand as Todd's Madison Square Garden mêlée. It was a 'spectacular' with no one to direct it. Movie resemblances had been highlighted by the plan to place a nine-foot, two-ton marble replica of the Oscar statuette at the gravehead. Fortunately, this idea was vetoed, after Mike Todd Jr's unavailing protests at such vulgarity, by a threat from the Academy of Motion Picture Arts and Sciences to sue if its 'Oscar' symbol were pirated. An estimated 21,600 sightseers had come, the biggest turnout since the rites for the St Valentine's Day massacre victims in 1929. They climbed on gravestones, shinned up trees, opened lunchboxes, spread picnics on the burial turf, strewing beer cans and litter all over the place. It was like a movie premiere, but with a body, not a film, to draw the crowds.

Elizabeth's limousine came to a halt half a dozen times as it neared the cemetery. Crowds pressed around it like a black-fly plague. Women held their babies up to the smoked-glass windows. Photoflashes penetrated the gloom within, showing eerie outlines of the occupants. Gypsy violinists – Todd's distant family was rumoured to have Romany roots – had been working the waiting crowds and, with the widow's approach, their dance tunes turned to dirges as they perambulated alongside the slow limousine. Even more ghoulish, an Eddie Fisher fan club, regardless of the mournful purpose of the day, chanted messages of calf-love to the passing crooner. Like some show-business Calvary, every ritualistic element of star-worship was converted into its cannibalistic extreme. Elizabeth thought of these scenes when she was called on, a year or so later in the film *Suddenly, Last Summer*, to imagine a brother being eaten alive by human predators. She, too, felt consumed.

A large tent erected over the opened grave mercifully offered her a refuge. Petals pulled from two thousand red roses brightened the freshly turned clay. A purple strip of carpet pointed VIP mourners towards

Todd's final resting place. As Elizabeth set foot on it, she collapsed. Her burly brother caught her. 'Oh, God! Oh, God! Oh, God! Oh, God!' she shrieked.

As her eyes fell on Todd's coffin, she cried out, 'It can't be!' She attempted to embrace it, before Dr Kennamer dissuaded her and helped her to a nearby chair. Outside, the crowds could be heard chanting not for the dead, but for the living: 'Liz! Liz! Liz! Liz!'

The Jewish prayer for the dead was recited. There was no eulogy, as the burial fell within the Passover period. Mike Todd Jr spoke a mere three-sentence response. Then Elizabeth was left alone for a few minutes.

The journey back to Chicago was an even worse nightmare. The crowds at one point began to climb on the car roof. It reminded Eddie Fisher of the funeral scene in *A Star Is Born*. They began thumping on the metal. The chauffeur feared to drive on. Elizabeth suddenly jerked herself into an upright, commanding stance and shouted an order that couldn't be disobeyed: 'For God's sake, get this thing moving!'

Back in Hollywood, George Jessel, who would have hosted the Friars Club roast for Todd in New York, was pronouncing an elegy for him. Its mix of bathos and chutzpah deserves recording. 'His voice heard a long time ago at Chicago's World's Fair spoke, "Step right up, see the little girl in the fish bowl – only a dime." And within two decades he was softly purring, "Picasso, wrap up those pictures. It will be a nice Sunday present for Elizabeth."'

The MGM executives were harassed men during these days. When was their picture going to get moving again? Richard Brooks had run out of covering scenes to shoot in the absence of his star. 'Mike would have wanted you to finish this movie,' they appealed to her. 'You *owe* it to him.'

'Owe' was truer in a more tangible sense. The truth was, Elizabeth had little choice but to go to work. Todd had left a meagre estate – hardly $250,000 in cash in the bank. The rest of his 'fortune' was either tied up, mortgaged or nonexistent. Virtually all his property was rented: the Hollywood home, the Palm Springs hacienda, the Connecticut mansion, the penthouse on Park Avenue were all on short leases: his automobiles likewise. The $3 million insurance he had boasted having, when trying to inveigle friends aboard *The Lucky Liz* for that last fatal flight, was heavily borrowed against. Barely $13,000 was eventually paid to Elizabeth after his debts had been cleared. A $3 million claim for alleged negligence against the company leasing the aircraft took years to settle and yielded a nugatory sum. Taxes were years behind. His principal asset was his interest in the Todd-AO photographic system and the film *Around the World in Eighty Days*. Exploitation of the former would prove disappointing. The film had grossed $35 million at the time of his death, but the cost of prints, advertising and publicity (as well as the jaunts of Todd and his wife around the world) had reduced the net take to $3.5 million. He had borrowed heavily against the expectation of future profits. Though Elizabeth's own assets were considerable, clearly they wouldn't enable her to live in the style set by her late spouse's manic indulgence. As it was, her $4,750 weekly MGM salary had halted immediately she absented herself from the production: though the MGM executives felt deeply for Elizabeth, mourning has no meaning for a film studio's accounts department. In short, the luxury of retirement she had toyed with over the years was now something barely affordable.

In addition, she felt terribly lonely once the momentum of the funeral was spent. Even her children – apart from Liza who had her nanny – were away from her; the boys were at the Todd home in Palm Springs, being cared for by their father and Susan Nell, the English heiress he had recently married.

Richard Brooks had just returned to MGM after taking Paul Newman, the co-star in the film, to a nearby campus to pick up some shots of him for an athletics scene, 'when this Japanese woman arrives on the set' – Mike Todd's assistant – 'and says to me, "Elizabeth wants to talk to you." – "Tell her to call," I say. "She's outside." So I leave the stage and outside is this long black limo with the curtains drawn. The chauffeur opens the back door and in I climb – beside Elizabeth. "What should I do, Dick?" "It's up to you, Elizabeth." "Mike said I looked wonderful in the rushes. I think I should come back. I owe it to him." "Okay, when?" Then she really surprised me: "Why not now?" So she got out of the car and into costume and make-up and played the scene there and then. And it was the worst possible one in the circumstances, the one where Big Mama tells her that Big Daddy has got cancer and is going to die. One of the lines she had to speak was "I know what it's like to lose someone you love." She did it on the first take, perfectly.'

Her loss of about twelve pounds actually made Elizabeth look more beautiful than ever. All Brooks had to worry about was, would she have enough energy to see her through? He ordered a low-key atmosphere for her official return to work on 14 April. Her own anxieties are reflected in an MGM memorandum about a call from her attorneys on 11 April to alert the studio 'to the possibility that she may not be able to get through the day. She is going to do her best and says she thinks she'll at least be able to get started, and she is anxious to, but ... it's entirely possible she may wear down as she gets into the day and may not be able to finish up.' Her dressing room was banked with red roses from the cast and bunches of violets from the crew, some of whom had worked with her on films since she was a ten-year-old. Such love tokens raised her spirits. She got going after lunch, but all she did was a reaction shot to a family feud, wearing the low-cut white chiffon gown that was to highlight the movie's tremendously successful advertising campaign. Brooks was worried and the next day, at the birthday party scene, he had real food replace the more customary props and kept repeating Elizabeth's takes, forcing her to consume the much-needed nourishment of ham, turkey and fresh fruit. As he'd hoped, her appetite grew with her intake. As if starvation had sharpened the edge of her sexuality, and her experience of grief had added a spark or two of private hellfire to Maggie the Cat's frustrations in the film, the performance Elizabeth gave was one of her best. Brooks noted she was slightly sleepy in the mornings – probably she was still on her sedatives – and re-arranged the shooting schedule so as to catch her on the 'up' curve of her medication. The tensions thus engendered between uppers and downers may have entered into her intuitive grasp of Maggie. 'She is Maggie with all her little ways,' wrote the English critic Isabel Quigly; 'beautiful and brittle, endlessly talking, mostly unpleasant, occasionally touching, even humorous, above all intensely alive.' Alive, yes: but also something almost as useful to a star – tragic. The public saw her now as a woman whose world had been sundered by the gods: widowed in the prime of life, almost in the moment of motherhood, vulnerable despite her fame, beauty and apparent riches to the fateful consequence of her husband's arrogance and pride. She had everyone's sympathy.

It was not enough; she needed someone's love. Elizabeth's brave return to the job in hand didn't signify a cure. Quite the reverse: acting, she admitted later, was a refuge from a reality she couldn't face. Unable to tolerate what she was – the widow who had survived and felt guilty – she grasped with gratitude the chance to become someone else. 'When I was Maggie, I could function. The rest of the time I was a robot.' In fact, without being able to diagnose what was occurring, she was undergoing a slow decline into nervous breakdown. At night, sleeping in one of Todd's shirts, she would dream that he was still alive, that she would wake in the morning with the balance of her world restored and find him by her side. There were plenty of witnesses to the dysfunctional way she was behaving. One of them, Eddie Fisher, visited her almost daily, to find that 'one moment [she] would be talking rationally, and the next crying hysterically'. In shoeboxes by her bed, she kept dozens and dozens of letters and cables of condolence; and she and Fisher would read and reread them. He grew increasingly uneasy as he realized the widow was keeping the dead man's grave moist with her tears. As she herself put it: 'I was married to a ghost and the ghost was more alive to me than any human being.'

She tried to make a break. She moved out of 1330 Schuyler Drive – Todd had intended it to be only a temporary home, until he could find something more in keeping with his grandiose style – and into a bungalow on the grounds of the Beverly Hills Hotel, and spent the summer trying to surface from the undertow of memory by visiting relatives and friends: her brother, a family man now, living in La Jolla and engrossed in work as an oceanographer; or Arthur Loew Jr, of the theatre-circuit family, with an estate at Tucson, where stable doors emitted a smell of horses and fresh straw that took her back to childhood days at Little Swallows ... But then she would find herself back in Todd's home at Palm Springs, sorting through memorabilia, inviting grief to rise up and exert its apparently unbreakable hold on her. She tried sending things off to charities: but how could she part with a tiny frock in pink organdy edged with lace and wrapped in gold paper? A dress for Liza, she said. It struck a witness as distinctly odd. A baby doesn't need dresses, just a diaper. It was more a memento of Mike Todd's choice of what Liza would one day wear.

She decided she must get away, and perhaps escape lay in travelling. After all, travelling by sea or air gives one the illusion of being insulated from worldly cares. She went to New York to embark for the Côte d'Azur and the Hotel du Cap at Eden Roc.

But then she discovered her passport was in the joint names of 'Mr and Mrs Mike Todd'. She would need a new one. She cancelled her flight to Paris on 29 August – eight tapestry-embroidered suitcases went on ahead and awaited her for ten days at Orly Airport. She never caught up with them. She stayed in America. It was more than a simple switch of holiday plans. The real reason for it was a man who had been her late husband's closest admirer and who was currently married to one of her own dearest friends: Eddie Fisher.

Some weeks earlier, Elizabeth had called Eddie Fisher in Las Vegas. It was the night he opened his new act. She asked him to come to Los Angeles to see her. When he got to Beverly Hills the following day, he found her in good spirits, playing with Liza. She gave him a wallet that had belonged to Mike Todd for his birthday. He had the impression that, to her, he was now something closer than a best friend. With the baby in her arms and himself by her side, it was as if she was re-assembling a family group. Before he returned to Las Vegas, he had made up his mind to marry her. When or how, he didn't exactly know; but he had taken the decision.

Born Edwin Jack Fisher in Philadelphia, in 1928, he was a child of the Depression brought up in the continuous disruption of a family that moved twenty times in his early years. From a young age, he was in awe of 'strong' men – even a father who beat him got his dutiful attention, though he knew there must be better, kinder ways of earning love and making people feel good. He discovered how when he opened his mouth, in school and the synagogue, and a beautiful voice came floating out. Soon radio was offering him a home from home and shows on the vacation and honeymoon hotel circuit provided him with another 'family'. In Mike Todd – who auditioned him for the Winter Garden Theater, New York, which he was then managing – he found a hero.

Eddie Fisher came into prominence exactly when the big band was being displaced in the charts by the big voice: and the bobby-soxers, having taken their cue from the near riots that greeted Sinatra, were in search of even younger, cuter, cuddlier crooners to scream at and swoon over.

Eddie craved acceptance, security, power, money, love – and sex, too, if that didn't contradict his mother's advice to be a good boy. Mike Todd had achieved all these things: escaped, flourished, married and, additionally, was everything Eddie admired without actually attempting to emulate – 'flamboyant, impetuous, totally unconventional'. The impresario virtually adopted Fisher; they were more father–son than buddy-buddy. Todd liked Eddie's youth: he admired Todd's maturity.

The girl that Eddie Fisher met when she was 'more than a starlet, not quite a star' was almost a junior edition of Elizabeth. Debbie Reynolds came out of the same studio (MGM), possessed the same air of being (or needing to be) the centre of attention, had the same sort of mother bent on living her own career vicariously through her talented child's. Her first affair paralleled Elizabeth's, too, in the sense that her romance with Eddie was promoted by stories planted in the newspapers and built into a national preoccupation. But unlike Elizabeth's first, disastrous step into matrimony, Debbie Reynolds's marriage appeared to be a successful union of sweethearts. To Fisher, though, it was less than that. 'We were married to the fan magazines, not to each other,' he admitted later. His Jewish delight in getting and spending was not matched by his wife's Protestant ethic of saving and economizing. In this respect, he was much more like what Elizabeth had become in her year or so as Mrs Mike Todd. Once Fisher knew he could always earn money, he got an additional thrill out of spreading it around – the way Todd did. Once Elizabeth got to view money as secondary in importance to getting her way, she treated it almost with disdain. And Mike Todd, who had often been 'broke but never poor', fitted in like the triangle's third angle.

Mike Todd, too, had liked to think that the Reynolds–Fisher union was perfect, and Eddie hadn't wished to disillusion him while he was alive. Both men found vicarious satisfaction in each other's careers, life-styles and marriages. Eddie was quick to spot Todd's fascination with

Elizabeth – how she was 'a little too subdued' on the occasion he had
entertained them all at his home, how Todd's then girlfriend, Evelyn
Keyes, was, in significant contrast, 'a little too animated'. Fisher subsequently wrote: "'Wait a minute," I said [to Todd] with a big grin,
"you're in love.'" He watched the progress of the affair 'with envy' – his
own marriage held 'so little love'.

Elizabeth's widowhood came at exactly the moment when Eddie Fisher's desire to get a release from his constricting marriage had reached its
pitch. Todd's death brought them together, shocked by the loss, feeling
lonely, one of them now free to marry again, the other not yet free but now
making no secret of his wish to be so. They had a shared companionship, a
common need, a mutual opportunity – and Mike. In her often sedated
and sometimes distracted state, Elizabeth may have felt that Eddie Fisher
somehow represented Mike Todd's bequest to her; in his unsatisfying
marital state, Eddie Fisher seems to have found it natural that the woman
whom Mike Todd had made into 'the other half of the scissors' was a
temptation he was almost obliged to give in to out of loyalty to the buddy
he had lost. He stepped into Todd's shoes, and ultimately into his bed.

24

THE MATING GAME

It was a scandal waiting to happen; which, although not connived at by either party, was certainly not concealed. The way that the press – most influential of the media in those days – manipulated the three principal players over the weeks following the 1958 Labor Day holiday weekend is a phenomenon that can best be appreciated with hindsight. It would make a classic case-study of how people interact with 'news', and vice versa, so that the people are encouraged to take the steps that the media almost 'will' them to take, which, if left to themselves and their saner judgement, they might possibly not have taken.

At first no one thought it odd that Elizabeth and Eddie Fisher should be together in New York. After all, they had often been seen in each other's company. Anyhow, the notion of a romance between Mike Todd's widow of less than six months and Debbie Reynolds's 'happily married' young husband was unthinkable, wasn't it? It was – for a few editions of the papers, anyhow. The two of them had gone dancing at The Blue Angel, a New York supper club; then they set off to Grossinger's, the hotel resort in the Catskill Mountains in upper New York state much favoured by honeymooners; it was where Eddie Fisher had got his first substantial break. This trip proved their undoing. A night out was one thing; a weekend together meant quite another. By the time they returned to New York, the 'unthinkable' had been printed. Over the next few days, while Elizabeth shopped, saw Monty Clift and dined with Fisher again, the pair of them were trailed by newsmen and photographers keyed up for the moment when their expectations would turn into evidence. After Elizabeth's Los Angeles-bound aircraft was turned back by engine failure on 8 September – considerably alarming Elizabeth, as may be imagined – she was 'doorstepped' by the press at her overnight airport hotel. She woke up to find the papers running what was then known in journalists' parlance as a 'flyer', but, more accurately, should be called a 'tryer'. The hope is that the reaction to the story will elicit more information than one dares print at the time. It was headlined: 'Eddie Fisher Romance with Liz Taylor Denied'.

Elizabeth took the bait and backed up her denial with the kind of quotes that bring joy to a news desk. 'It's much too soon to forget all Mike meant to me.' They were, she added, 'just good friends – everyone knows that'. Everyone did; and everyone had heard that before. Over in Hollywood, Debbie Reynolds did the hoped-for thing, too. She wouldn't dignify the story with a comment, she said, thereby enabling it to be repeated, if not dignified, at even greater length. It was a game of journalistic ping-pong in which the papers put the ball into play, then eagerly report the strokes as each of the parties tries to get it back over the net.

Elizabeth returned to Los Angeles, cuddling a Yorkshire terrier and wearing an exotic turban whose femme fatale associations were denied by the innocence of the Peter Pan collar on her dress. 'I have nothing to say but hello,' she said to the mob of reporters. She instinctively knew when dialogue was a handicap in a scene, and silence much more effective. Eddie – more naive where the media were concerned – was taken off guard in New York. He pushed the story a useful stage further by admitting to 'having a misunderstanding' with his wife. 'She's in Holly-wood, looking after the kids,' he added, imprudently drawing attention to the children whose fate would soon sway public sympathy against one side and for the other. But it was Hedda Hopper who really dished everyone.

'Elizabeth, level with me': Hedda's favourite (and much feared) opening gambit. 'What's this Eddie Fisher business all about? You're being blamed for taking Eddie away from Debbie. What have you got to say?'

What Elizabeth had to say was impenitent. She made it plain that she regarded Hopper's intervention as impertinent. It was: but only to someone who didn't know that the rites of stardom include the sacrificial ceremony, as well as the crowning one.

'Well, you can't hurt Debbie like this without hurting yourself more, because she loves him.'

The immediate denial this elicited told Hopper more about the affair than any amount of speculation. 'He's not in love with her and never has been,' she reported Elizabeth saying.

Hopper thundered: 'What would Mike Todd say to this?'

'"Well," Elizabeth said calmly, "Mike's dead and I'm alive."'

Such a quote was then transmuted into the sort of gold that makes a lifetime's grubbing in the Hollywood foothills worthwhile: this was the big strike. According to the columnist, Elizabeth continued: '"Ask [Eddie] to go back to [her]? He can't ... they'd destroy each other ... I'm not taking away anything from her because she never really had [anything]."' Then, said Hopper, she made a statement that was 'unprintable'.

At least it was in that exclusive interview, syndicated and reprinted across America and the world. But in her memoirs, Hopper observed no such inhibitions. Elizabeth, she alleged, asked rhetorically: 'What do you expect me to do? Sleep alone?'

'What you've just said to me,' Hopper responded, dabbing at eyes made moist by this slur on the beloved Mike Todd's memory, 'bears not the slightest resemblance to [the girl who used to call me at 2 a.m. and talk her heart out]. Where, oh where, has she gone?'

The story from then on would have been best done as a Hollywood scenario featuring such scenes as: 'Eddie returns home'; 'Debbie sobs uncontrollably'; 'A marriage counsellor arrives'; 'The lawyers move in'. It was greatly enlivened when Debbie Reynolds herself appeared on the doorstep, her hair in curlers, her child in her arms – the very picture of sinned-against motherhood. A large safety pin was stuck in her blouse, symbol of maternal and domestic virtue. An MGM publicist, who had been feeding the encampment of photo-journalists hot-dogs and quotes, then made room for a studio messenger delivering the script of Debbie Reynolds's next MGM picture; no doubt it was felt she would have plenty of time to study her role. The press were given an opportunity to read and transcribe its title: *The Mating Game*. *Life* magazine reflected the way that real events were being simultaneously processed into the stuff of soap opera (or was it the other way round?) when it reported in its 22 September issue: 'Last week Hollywood was caught with its make-believe down when the Fisher romance got stuck on the point of a triangle, the point being the Widow Todd.'

Elizabeth's explanation for the apparently damning 'quote' from Hedda Hopper was to claim that the words were correct, but out of context. 'What I really said to [her] was, "Oh, God, you know how much I loved Mike. I loved him more than my life. But Mike is dead and I'm alive and the one person who would want me to try and be happy is Mike."' This has the ring of truth about it. But it was too late. By then, the Hopper version was reverberating throughout the heartland of American populist prejudice. The weather-vane did a total about-turn, from sympathy for a grieving widow to outrage against a selfish bitch. As the public perceived it, however inaccurately, Elizabeth had become a home-wrecker, Eddie Fisher a weakling husband and Debbie Reynolds a wronged innocent. Now Hedda Hopper reaped a rich harvest of the crop she had sown.

In the Hopper archives at the Academy library, Beverly Hills, is a large cardboard box labelled: 'Widow Todd: Fisher and Debbie Letters'. It is stuffed with scores of communications addressed to Hopper at the *Los Angeles Times* or her home, 1708 Tropical Avenue, Beverly Hills, all showing how her huge constituency of readers felt Elizabeth and Eddie had betrayed them – and must get punished. Generally, Fisher comes in for the angriest denunciation, but Elizabeth catches it hot and strong, too. Some representative samples:

Laurette C., Silver Spring, Maryland (5 November 1958): 'Eddie Fisher and Liz Taylor deserve each other. I haven't seen one [TV] program of his this fall, nor do I intend to. I haven't spent a dime on seeing *Cat* something, nor do I intend to. It's a matter of principle – a word neither Miss Taylor nor Mr Fisher seem to have heard about.'

Mrs G. M. H., Lompoc, California (11 September 1958): 'It is to [*sic*] bad Mr Fisher is so weak minded as to be swayed by such a woman. I sincerely hope that he will see the light before it is to [*sic*] late and return to his sweet wife and family.'

Mrs E. H., Chicago, Illinois (26 September 1958): 'All of Fischer's [*sic*] records they are on the trash heap where he belongs. All members of our families have decided not to see any programs or movies wherein these two appear.'

Mary G., Hollywood, California (12 September 1958), who also carbon-copied the letter to the commercial sponsors of Eddie Fisher's TV show: 'I am more than a little shocked to find you could allow a man of such moral turpitude to represent a supposedly reliable product such as Chesterfield [cigarettes].'

Over the ensuing months, no fan magazine worth its newsstand space let its readers forget the scandal of a single issue. Sensing the moral anger at Elizabeth, the magazines' editors put the accent of sympathy on Debbie Reynolds. *Photoplay*'s January 1959 issue had an up-front picture of domestic heartbreak: Debbie and her two children (one a baby) and even a forlorn-looking dog. Caption: 'Can't daddy be with us all the time?' Even upmarket publications were not immune to the nation's prurience. A cartoon in *The New Yorker* featured an outraged wife wielding a rolling pin. It is 4 a.m. and her husband has just staggered home. His excuse: 'I got to thinking about Debbie and Eddie.' The strength of public feeling was so universally manifest that even a few years later President Kennedy's widow could warn her husband's official biographer, William Manchester, when they clashed over his view of Kennedy: 'Anyone who is against me will look like a rat, unless I run off with Eddie Fisher.'

Yet the surprising and significant thing was that virtually none of this indignation had any adverse impact on the box-office sales of *Cat on a Hot Tin Roof*, which MGM released in September, just as the scandal broke. Advertised with what was, for then, a most provocative shot of Elizabeth, the very picture of carnal come-hither in a white silk slip, it grossed nearly $10 million in America alone, pushing her into the list of 1958's top money-making stars (at number two, just behind Glenn Ford). And despite an orchestrated siege of Hollywood's censors and studios by church leaders and moralizers, she won a 1959 Oscar nomination. It was powerful evidence of how the line between celebrity and notoriety, which had once been so strictly drawn, was ceasing to count in the public's view: now everything was becoming 'good' publicity.

Hollywood producers were not slow to perceive this. And they were emboldened to undertake increasingly controversial subjects once banned outright by their own Morality Code or abandoned after boycott threats by the Roman Catholic Legion of Decency. The 'Eddie-Debbie-Liz biz', as the tabloids labelled it, was a catalyst in Hollywood's search for a more contemporary identity. As the biographer Brenda Maddox has pointed out, 1957 was the peak year for the American birth-rate. And from 1958 on, the divorce rate rose, then soared. Not only was the scandal good media copy; it was like a morality play 'for all the American families who were just beginning to go through the same thing'.

As it happens, the British papers proved even worse vilifiers than the American. 'It would be a splendid thing for the marriage prospects of our daughters,' thundered the *People* about Elizabeth, 'if this nauseating woman could now be barred from the screen.'

It is true that Eddie Fisher suffered a sizeable, if transient, loss of public esteem and personal income. His records were banned by some radio stations; his sponsors did not renew his TV show. But he was more vulnerably placed than Elizabeth. He had lived a self-confessed lie as the happy husband of a wife who had her own image as the simple, innocent, waif-like 'Tammy' to protect: as the Hollywood wit Oscar Levant once said to her, 'Did anyone ever tell you, Debbie, you dominate wistfully?' The public felt misled, deceived – as it had felt insulted by Ingrid Bergman's elopement with Roberto Rossellini – and took it out on Fisher. But Elizabeth was already perceived, in life and on screen, as a woman with few, if any, inhibitions about her desires – and she certainly didn't sell innocence. Maggie the Cat's sexuality, dammed up in the film by her homosexual husband's impotence, was as understandable as the Widow Todd's compulsive need not to sleep alone. Elizabeth now went to work to make it forgivable, too.

She went into purdah in a house rented from Linda Christian on Copa de Oro Road, Bel Air: guarded, disdainful and under the strain of not knowing which of her friends would cut her dead if she ventured out. (When she *did* make a public appearance at Chasen's with Eddie, it was in order to deny a tabloid lie that she was languishing in a mental hospital.) Fisher spent most of his time with her, though officially living in a Sunset Boulevard apartment. A reporter got close enough to the rose-red Spanish-style stucco house to observe the Rolls-Royce Silver Cloud standing in the driveway and looking as if it had been used to sneak her and the children out for a day on the beach, its coachwork stained with dust and sand, its windows dirty with the paw-marks of dogs. While he was there, a van from I. Magnin on Wilshire Boulevard delivered a whole rack of new dresses for her to choose from at home, rather than in the store.

Elizabeth's sharpest concern was the protection of her growing children. She was quite right to be concerned. The fan magazines were relentless in their attack on her for 'the official destruction of a marriage that had brought two children into the world', as *Photoplay* put it, sanctimoniously, in its June 1959 issue – the one with contrasting pictures of Debbie *en famille* and Elizabeth and Eddie Fisher taking her children to Disneyland. The affair, said the magazine, 'should be marked in silence and in sorrow, not in public revels'. The sins of Hollywood parents had been brought to lurid prominence barely a year earlier when Lana Turner's daughter Cheryl gave her mother's lover, Johnny Stompanato, a fatal knife thrust. Show-business morals had become the stuff of serious or salacious comment just prior to 'the Eddie-Debbie-Liz biz'. Elizabeth caught the backlash of a more savage debate than her own fall from grace had deserved.

All of it only strengthened her determination to marry Eddie Fisher. There was a logic besides stubbornness in this, or so she thought. If they were married, they would cease to be news, she told Louella Parsons, now her mother confessor since Hedda had excommunicated her. In this, she showed a total and unaccustomed naiveté. Marrying Eddie would only legitimize speculation, not dismiss it.

However, she prepared herself to be his bride as far as she could, considering he wasn't yet free to marry her. For a start, she converted to Fisher's Jewish faith. Besides betokening what appears to be a genuine sympathy for Judaism, this was in line with the way she embraced the attractive strengths of each man she took as her husband. Todd had discouraged her wish to become Jewish. Not that he doubted her sincerity, but the satisfaction he had got from marrying a Gentile princess might have been diminished had Elizabeth converted to his own religion. Tension had helped keep them together, not harmony. Eddie Fisher had no such reservations. To convert would be a way of honouring Mike, he told her. He remembered that during Elizabeth's collapse after Todd's death, he and his mother had read to her – not only love poems, but books of Jewish celebration that had seemed to bring her late husband closer in spirit. She also pledged $100,000 to Israeli charities – a most generous sum considering her straitened finances. In this respect, her reported enquiry to Eugene Black, the president of the World Bank, is piquant. How much could she borrow, she asked him, and at what rate of interest? That humourless man replied soberly, 'We only lend to under-developed people.'

Fortunately, financial pressure was soon relieved. An offer came through from the producer Sam Spiegel – one that would eventually gross her half a million dollars.

It was for another Tennessee Williams project, a film version of *Suddenly, Last Summer* to be made on loan-out from MGM. Plenty of voices warned her off this mix of madness, incest, homosexuality and cannibalism. It was too raw, too off-putting and, not the least consideration, only too likely to be bad box-office. It both attracted and repelled her – for it was also about psychoanalysis, to be personified by Monty Clift as the doctor who pushes the girl Elizabeth would play to the cathartic recital of her gay brother Sebastian's horrifying death by flesh-eating urchins. Eddie Fisher had once suggested analysis might help Elizabeth get over Todd's death. According to him, she leaped out of bed and tried to flee from the house, the idea of self-exposure terrified her so much. She told Fisher it was *he* who needed a psychiatrist.

But converting to a new faith may have given Elizabeth a new identity, or, at least, a new resolution. Public purgation toughened her private will. She said yes to Spiegel's film.

But first there was the question of marriage. Word arrived that, having won a substantial settlement, Debbie Reynolds would consent to a Nevada divorce. And on 29 March 1959, Elizabeth drove to Las Vegas where Eddie was to open at the La Tropicana on 1 April: that night had to be a vindication of their relationship.

It was also to be a demonstration of family togetherness. She confessed 'shamelessly' that she was 'terribly happy'. The quote won the approval of a newspaper columnist and Brandeis University professor three thousand miles away. Max Lerner, in the *New York Post*, praised Elizabeth's 'forthright life of the senses' and his support was to be warmly repaid, not many months later. Elizabeth's confession was timely. America had begun converting itself into a sensate society with the proselytizing success of Hugh Hefner's Playboy Club and its so-called 'philosophy'. Elizabeth's candour hit the same note. A generation of young, aggressively ambitious, self-obsessed, high-spending Americans – mostly male, and chauvinist, it must be said – was being taught that gratification was what life was all about. Thus Elizabeth found herself going with the flow of the times, and Max Lerner's public approval of her gave her valuable buoyancy in the newspapers.

Unblushingly, she confronted the pickets outside the La Tropicana who waved placards saying 'Liz Leave Town' – Eddie Fisher was carrying a gun for protection – and, in white chiffon and diamonds, with her young sons by her side to show solidarity with their future stepfather, she milked the words of Eddie Fisher's act ('Another bride, another June / Another sunny honeymoon') by tapping out the rhythm with her nails, nodding her head in time to the beat and generally making more of a meal of it than she did of the crabmeat cocktail and champagne which was all she consumed. 'It's a double act – she's part of it,' said the columnist Sydney Skolsky.

12 May 1959, was a busy day in Las Vegas. Since occupation of a house near the third hole of the Desert Inn Golf Club, plus acquisition of a Nevada licence plate, allowed him to claim residence in the state, Eddie Fisher now proceeded to claim his divorce. A judge, who had promised in advance that the petitioner would not go away disappointed, awarded him one inside ten minutes. Not many more minutes later, with Elizabeth beside him, he was asking jokingly if he could pay for the marriage licence in gambling chips. 'No, cash please,' said the registrar. 'Now sign here. You first, Mr Fisher. It will be the last time you are first for a long time to come.'

Then on to Temple Beth Shalom, Las Vegas's year-old synagogue. In a moss green chiffon gown and hood of the same hue, created this time round by Jean Louis, before two rabbis – one local, one from Hollywood – and a modest fourteen guests including Elizabeth's mother (beige lace) and Eddie's (navy lace), as well as the head of production at the bride's film studio, her hair stylist, her doctor, her secretary, her press agent, her lawyer and his wife, Elizabeth became Mrs Eddie Fisher. Eddie was so flustered that he forgot to remove his white yarmulka when it was all over. The local rabbi took it off his head, folded it up and placed it in the singer's pocket. 'You may need this some day,' he said.

That same evening they flew to Los Angeles and then on to New York, bound for a honeymoon in Europe. Eddie confessed himself 'drugged with love'. Elizabeth took with her the conviction that marrying him made Mike Todd feel more alive than ever. That it might not necessarily be a good thing for newlyweds to be travelling with a third party, albeit only the memory of one, was something that did not cross their minds, yet.

25

SIC TRANSIT GLORIA

Even before they started their honeymoon in Europe, Eddie Fisher had had a taste of what life with Elizabeth would be like.

She needed a lot of looking after. Problems, small in themselves, had a way of turning into major crises. With servants, aides, children and a small menagerie of animals living and travelling with them, there was plenty of chance for confusion – 'chaos', he called it later. Mustering people and their possessions for even the simplest move from 'A' to 'B' meant a fever-pitch of activity. Elizabeth was her own master; nobody ordered her around. If she felt pushed one way, she would shove in the other. In a Hollywood studio, with each move a power ploy, this might be good thinking. But the compliant Fisher felt no compulsion to stand up to her the way Mike Todd had done. From that marriage, she had acquired the habit of living at full stretch. Todd thrived on nervous energy; so did Elizabeth. Eddie thought it was a means of mutual arousal – their fights ended in love-making. His own metabolism worked at a different rhythm. He found that 'fighting was a part of living with Elizabeth', but he hadn't the stomach to go the distance with her. Consequently, they both relied heavily on presenting each other with a never-ending stream of costly gifts. Their love was essentially gift-based. Elizabeth's generosity to him included a Cartier watch inscribed with the romantic reminder 'When time began . . .', a Piaget platinum watch appositely inscribed 'You ain't seen nuthin' yet', diamond and emerald cufflinks for dress wear and, for run-of-the-mill daily functions, cabochon emerald and gold links. No wonder every day seemed to him like Christmas.

Then there was the question of her health. Like others before – and after – Eddie discovered how alarmingly a minor upset could flare up into an emergency requiring frantic calls to Dr Kennamer. Debbie Reynolds, in contrast, always enjoyed good health. In addition to being 'father, brother, friend and lover', he had to be a nurse. Was there a psychosomatic factor at work? he wondered. Did her illness appear when she needed love and attention? He was devoted to her. But living with someone is not the same as looking after someone.

Reconciling each other's work schedules proved troublesome. In their naîveté, they had simply decided that when Eddie was performing, she would be with him; when she was filming, he would always be around. The unreality of this was soon apparent. Elizabeth often had long stretches of inactivity between making movies, and even during them; Eddie's recording and performance dates required him to keep fully trained. And attending to Elizabeth's needs, whether or not he was working, soon became full-time.

Eddie Fisher would probably have been a perfect partner for Elizabeth in her first marriage. But now her nature had been formed by her turbulent experiences. He was simply three marriages too late.

On arrival at Barcelona, they boarded the *Orinoco*, Sam Spiegel's yacht, which the producer of *Suddenly, Last Summer* was lending them for a Mediterranean cruise before shooting began. It was a two-hundred-ton converted minesweeper, staffed by six servants, a French maid, a full crew and a Belgian chef. It also had a canopied four-poster bed said to be modelled on Christopher Columbus's; its foot-deep mattresses and brocades suggested that the discovery of America must have been a comfortable enterprise. Despite all this, bad weather made for a rainy, sodden voyage, and eventually they took a taxi to Nice airport and so to London. They had nine hundred pounds of overweight baggage. For the first time, Elizabeth looked a shade overweight, too. There was a hint of a double chin, though she attributed her plumpness to water retention. One or two of the English press asserted that this entirely pardonable, and transient, gain in weight by a post-honeymoon bride was responsible for delaying the start of *Suddenly, Last Summer*. Her lawyers later extracted an apology and a sum for charity from at least one national daily paper; Elizabeth was showing she had claws. Unfortunately, claws were also used by the mass media at the press conference she held on arrival. She was asked what her greatest ambition was and replied, 'To be a good wife and mother.'

'But haven't you said all that before?' the reporter asked. 'Didn't you say it just eighteen months ago with Mike Todd?'

Still smarting from the American media's attacks, Elizabeth tightened her lips. 'Certain things happened, you may remember?' she said in the tones of venomous sweetness that were to become her standard put-down in public. The press conference was abruptly ended.

She had faced the press wearing white beaver; she walked out on them looking as grim as if she were in a suit of armour. Thereafter, she hand-picked the few journalists to whom she granted access. Barbed wire surrounded the Surrey mansion that Spiegel had rented for her; and police were hired as supplementary guards – which again made the media show their claws. Perhaps they didn't know that 3,500 letters of spite, threats and criticism of her and Eddie had been received at the film studios.

Shooting *Suddenly, Last Summer* was an unhappy experience for everyone. Monty Clift was being treated for alcohol and drug abuse, and additionally reverted to a chronic infantilism at mealtimes, stuffing food into his mouth with his hands. Spiegel had been unable to get him insured for the film. Katharine Hepburn, playing Elizabeth's vengeful aunt, was missing her lover Spencer Tracy. Even Joseph L. Mankiewicz, the director, was afflicted with a painful skin rash that compelled him to wear gloves throughout the shoot.

But such discomforts probably contributed to the edgy, neurotic mood in which Mankiewicz cloaked the film's Gothic monologues. Elizabeth's crash diet restored her to the peak of physical beauty; she actually looked ten years younger than her twenty-seven years. Mankiewicz gave her more 'direction' than she was used to; and his sense of theatre stimulated her to let the suggestions about the character that he insinuated into her mind show up more immediately in her face. She emits vibrations of evil, not just words. Even her voice has changed; Mankiewicz told her to lower it. 'She tended to be shrill and I wanted a sense of masculine will,' he says. Where Hepburn drawls, Elizabeth growls; their voices are like a sinister counterpoint. The soliloquies were tough on an actress with no dramatic training and a director unwilling to cut away to accommodate her. 'But she had a tremendous primitive talent on which very few demands had been made. You feel she sees what she thinks.'

Tennessee Williams at first thought her miscast – 'too wised up' a girl not to realize the nature of her brother and his homosexual death. 'Tennessee giggled when embarrassed,' the director said, 'but he saw Elizabeth's last big speech out in total silence.' It was the hardest sequence by far to shoot. Mankiewicz wanted to do it in one unbroken take of agonized recall by Elizabeth, rising to hysteria, then restored to the calm after the storm as the catharsis clears the girl's mind and her madness is transferred, retributively, on to her aunt. 'It tore Elizabeth's gut out. I must have done five takes without getting what I wanted. So I said, "Let's break." A few minutes later, my assistant director said, "Joe, look at this." There was Elizabeth behind some scenery, lying full-length on the floor. I thought at first she'd fallen and hurt herself. Then I heard her sobbing. I wanted to spare her more distress. As it was nearly five o'clock – when the English film unions pull the plug for the day – I said, "Okay, everyone – fresh start in the morning." Suddenly Elizabeth was there.

"Fresh start, my ass," she says. Over to the camera and we go for take six. When the rushes were run for Tennessee, he said, "Jesus, what a moment!"' Elizabeth's face fills the screen while, unfocused in the background, shapes and scenes from her overwrought mind form and re-form as her voice rises and falls in what her director calls 'an aria'. She finishes up tranquil and sane again, being led off on Monty Clift's comforting arm – an ironic reversal of the services she was used to performing off-screen for him.

For days after she filmed the scene, Elizabeth was in a visible state of tension. And it was then that, according to her director, she confessed that her marriage was in serious trouble. It had been a terrible mistake in the first place. She had been propelled into it by the explosion of public hostility against her. But within weeks, she had found that the strongest bond between her and Fisher was the dead man who had been her husband. She couldn't face up to another divorce, she said. It would 'tear me apart' – a phrase that had a mordant appropriateness, considering she had just done an agonized commentary on a scene of cannibalism.

The exposed and lonely position Elizabeth still occupied in much of the media in 1959 was reflected graphically in the poster used to advertise *Suddenly, Last Summer*. It showed her in a white, low-cut, one-piece bathing suit – a shot taken on a Costa Brava beach which, by Elizabeth's edict, had been cleared of anyone not connected with the film. 'Suddenly, last summer Cathy knew she was being used for evil,' said the slogan. Considering the beating her reputation was taking at the time, the words had an effrontery not lost on the public. They suggested she was an innocent party. But could a girl in that pose, in that swimsuit, ever be really innocent?

Elizabeth and Katharine Hepburn were both nominated in the Academy Awards for best actress – 'but,' as Mankiewicz said, 'it was a foregone conclusion they would knock each other out.'

While Elizabeth was still shooting the film on a closed set at Shepperton Studios, two projects were taking shape in Hollywood that would prove to be turning points in her life and career: *Butterfield 8* and *Cleopatra*. The way each took shape, separately yet influenced by the other, is instructive and ironical. Both were destined to affect the way that the public viewed Elizabeth – the star roles in each film, a nymphomaniac who makes promiscuous conquests and a queen who throws her enchantment over men, seemed to confirm the view of her that the media projected.

The *Cleopatra* project had been conceived by Walter Wanger, the veteran producer of such classics as *Queen Christina* and *Stagecoach* as well as recent hits like *Riot in Cell Block Eleven* and *Invasion of the Body Snatchers*. Spyros Skouras, president of Twentieth Century–Fox, proposed that Wanger remake the silent version of *Cleopatra* starring Theda Bara in 1917. 'All this needs is a leetle rewriting,' the Greek-born mogul said, handing him a brittle ten pages or so retrieved from Fox's storeroom. Wanger felt it needed a 'leetle' more than that – for example, Elizabeth Taylor.

'Too unmanageable,' said Skouras. A Skouras aide clarified his master's thought. 'Who needs Elizabeth Taylor? Any hundred-dollar-a-week girl can play Cleopatra.'

Wanger had nevertheless approached Elizabeth when she was married to Todd. She deferred to her husband's opinion. Maybe Todd saw the advantage of his wife starring in a subject that would be ideal for the Todd-AO-Scope process he part-owned: but he also knew Wanger to be a formidably self-willed producer, as ruthless as he himself was in protecting his own investment. Todd was in no hurry; maybe Wanger's interest would lapse. But Todd was deceased when Wanger again approached Elizabeth, this time through her lawyers, in November 1958, and sent her a script that Nigel Balchin had produced. She wanted to do it – but not from that script. It was 'terrible'. Wanger agreed; it was just a rough treatment that he had commissioned in a hurry to keep interest simmering at Fox. It would be much improved if she agreed to do the project. Eddie Fisher believed it could be improved even more if the price for Elizabeth were right. She was brushing her teeth and laughed when he said to her, 'You ought to do it for a million dollars.'

On 1 September 1959, Eddie Fisher took a call to Elizabeth placed by Wanger, who wanted to find out if she'd changed her mind. Elizabeth came on the line. 'I'll do it for a million dollars,' she said. Later, she insisted it was spoken as a jokey turn-down, although her recollection that she added a demand for 10 per cent of the box-office gross suggests that the joke, if it was one, was on the borderline of bargaining. Wanger said he would call back. He did. They had a deal, he said.

How Walter Wanger ever got Fox to pay this (then) astronomical sum has never been fully disclosed. The notoriety of Elizabeth's recent marital affairs had certainly distanced her from her rivals for the role – Jennifer Jones, Audrey Hepburn, Kim Novak and the Italian beauties Loren and Lollobrigida – both in terms of public curiosity and personal worth. Still, it was the highest fee ever offered to an actress for a single picture. The likelihood is that the blow to Fox's exchequer was softened by the proposed method of payment: not as a lump sum, but in instalments paid to her children from a trust fund. That way, Fox would be able to buy her services 'on time', or by 'hire purchase', and the fee would be protected from the taxman's axe. If the movie turned out to be a success on the scale that Wanger envisaged, Fox would be paying the star out of profits that had already earned it fat interest. William Holden had made such an arrangement with Columbia Pictures for *The Bridge on the River Kwai*. The film generated such profits that Columbia was able to pay Holden his annuity out of the interest alone.

Elizabeth made another demand, however; the film had to be shot abroad. She wasn't prepared to live and work in Hollywood while the Debbie Reynolds pack was pursuing her.

MGM had monitored Fox's deal closely and jealously. The studio contended that Elizabeth's services were still its property, to dispose of as it determined. The new contract that Todd negotiated for Elizabeth had never been signed and was regarded as being lapsed after his death. Elizabeth owed MGM one more picture. Delay in enforcing that obligation might invite the legal defence that she had not been unwilling to perform it, but MGM had been dilatory in employing her. A film must therefore be offered to her quickly and, if need be, she must be enjoined to make it – or to make no other film for anyone until dispensatory relief was granted her by the courts, which might well take years. *Butterfield 8* was the film that MGM wanted her to make. She immediately resisted it.

While money – and big money, too – was involved, as she might have to forfeit the million-dollar fee for *Cleopatra* if Fox couldn't wait for her, Elizabeth's opposition wasn't based solely on cash considerations. She objected to the morality of the role in *Butterfield 8*. 'The leading lady is almost a prostitute,' she declared. 'The whole thing is so unpalatable, I wouldn't do it for anything – under any conditions.'

Butterfield 8 was based on a John O'Hara novel, inspired in turn by the true story of Starr Faithful, a professional call-girl who was murdered in 1931 at Palm Beach. MGM had its own corporate worries about such a story. How could it get round the censorship prohibition on prostitution being depicted in films? What kind of retribution could be meted out to the flagrant girl that would be a moral *quid pro quo* for her sinful life? It was no secret that a substantial part of the public perceived Elizabeth in a way that didn't much differ from O'Hara's heroine. This was totally unfounded, but it was a box-office plus. Then again Elizabeth's disdain for public opinion reflected Starr Faithful's disregard for her own reputation. Neither felt that she owed the public an explanation for her life-style, never mind an apology. What the studio had to remove from the story as a sop to the censors would be compensated by the notoriety attaching to Elizabeth's name – so MGM saw it. Hence it was preferable to cast her, and not some more publicly approved screen actress, in the role. She had moral right on her side in resisting it, but morality in Hollywood is rarely a match for contractual sanctions.

At first, though, it looked as if MGM had an impossible task. Geoffrey M. Shurlock, the Production Code administrator, hated the story of

'Gloria Wandrous', as Starr Faithful had been renamed in the script. The story was unacceptable, he informed MGM on 12 October 1958, because it portrayed an undisguised nymphomaniac and rejected the view of marriage as an institution whose sanctity must be 'upheld at all times'. The sex was too detailed: there was too much emphasis on adultery. Though this verdict seemed final, it was simply the start of a long process of plea bargaining, morality trimming and inbuilt hypocrisy.

Pandro Berman, the producer of four earlier films of Elizabeth's, believed she could play the part well, if only she would. 'She said she'd be damned if she'd do the film,' he says, 'then she turned on the tears to Sol Siegel who was in charge of production. Was this any way to treat someone who had served MGM well for nearly twenty years? Mr Siegel said, "Fortunately or unfortunately, Elizabeth, sentiment went out of this business a long time ago."'

After he had assigned her to the role, Siegel sent Berman a memo on 4 July 1959: they must build sympathy for the character, he said. 'Gloria is a woman who knows that the solution [to nymphomania] doesn't lie in marriage. She's never found a man with whom she can couple love and sex – love of the spiritual order with her physical needs ... Remorse sets in, but only for a short time.' Being raped as a child might offer an explanation which would encourage sympathy, not blame. But sympathy by itself wasn't enough; retribution had to follow. 'Perhaps the best way to dispose of Gloria would be to have her running across the road to her bar when she is hit by a speeding car,' ran a story department memo. Yes, came the reply: but should it be accidental death or voluntary suicide? Such were the moral niceties that film studios still had to decide, with almost Jesuitical hair-splitting, in 1959.

Gloria's motivation continued to worry MGM. A Sol Siegel memo succinctly encapsulated the producers' more acceptable reasons for casting Elizabeth. 'There is another factor which the screenplay does not take advantage of. The girl will be played by Elizabeth Taylor who is unquestionably one of the most beautiful women in the world. A good deal of her obsession is that she remains the most beautiful woman in the world. Her only way of knowing this is adulation and conquest on the part of any man she meets.' What seems explicit here is an admission that Elizabeth's own need for love would illuminate Gloria's obsessive pursuit of it in bed after bed – as a sort of female Casanova, in fact.

Yet even having Elizabeth in the role did not give the cautious Sol Siegel the feeling that all would be well, unless the script were able to clarify Gloria's character. 'I think the premise that we have Elizabeth Taylor, who is a big star and will therefore protect us against loss, is a false one. We have seen too many pictures go down the drain with big stars in the last few years.' At this point, Elizabeth had not even seen the script of the picture she had been ordered to do. Pandro Berman, disappointed by what he felt was MGM's waning enthusiasm, did the one thing that would immediately restore the studio's faith in the project. He offered to buy it and make it for his own company. MGM suddenly decided to put *Butterfield 8* into production with all speed.

While Elizabeth still fretted and fumed, John Michael Hayes was put to work on a quick rewrite. Hayes had a well-earned reputation for censor-proof screenplays; he had adapted the 'unacceptable' *Peyton Place* for the screen, had slipped a long passage of sexual innuendo in *To Catch a Thief* past the code watchdogs – and he would later bring lesbian love to the Hollywood screen in his version of Lillian Hellman's play *The Children's Hour*.

Elizabeth's anxiety at being forced to act a nymphomaniac may, in retrospect, seem exaggerated. This was not so in 1959. The American censor's fine-combing through the final version of the script mirrored the star's own angry distaste for a role that, unless she went through with it, would keep her away from the million-dollar fee to come for *Cleopatra*. In a letter to Robert Vogel, dated 27 October 1959, Shurlock indicated his approval, provided the following points were attended to: 1) when Gloria was first shown, she shouldn't be seen in bed in her lover's bedroom (he was to be played by Laurence Harvey); 2) the 'casual and repeated use of profanities' was still unacceptable; 3) the 'admissibility' of featuring Gloria pulling on silk stockings was questioned; 4) Gloria's line 'Love is a four-letter word' was unacceptable; 5) her lover's line 'You walked up to me without moving your feet' was to be eliminated; 6) her lover's complete disregard for violating his marriage must be 'corrected'; 7) Gloria's line 'They use, for drunk, the past tense of a verb for a liquid body function' must be eliminated; and lastly, 8) 'it must be clearly established that Gloria is wearing a slip under her gown when [her lover] rips it.' All was 'attended to'. Elizabeth and her lawyers now had no hope of getting her released from her obligation to make the picture. The pressure on her had carried the day; possibly she felt more violated by that than by the public image of her that such a movie might create.

If Elizabeth were racked by private doubts about the wisdom of her marriage to Eddie Fisher, they were not yet apparent to others. Publicly, she and Eddie seemed inseparable. If they were to part, it would be conceding defeat and acknowledging how right Debbie Reynolds's defenders were. At the 'Night of a Hundred Stars', a charity benefit at the London Pavilion on 23 July 1959, Eddie looked at Elizabeth in a stage box and, choosing the ballad 'They All Said We Could Never Be Happy', truculently belted out the lines: 'But oh, ho, ho, hee, hee, hee / Who has the last laugh now?' The Fishers did, of course; they had to have. Privately, though, Eddie Fisher was far from feeling blissful. He had got used to the slighting references to 'Mr Elizabeth Taylor', but he still had to reckon with the public's demand to see his more celebrated wife participating peripherally in his act wherever he was performing. People didn't think they got their money's worth unless she was visible in a theatre seat or, better still, at a nightclub table near the stage while he sang to them, and to her. At first it had been an exhilarating experience for him, a form of public love-bonding, linked all the more firmly by an apposite choice of lyrics. What he didn't grasp at first was how necessary such a declaration of love was to a woman for whom each moment of romance had to be superseded by an even more intense one.

They flew back to Los Angeles (and two bungalows in the Beverly Hills Hotel grounds) on 7 September. Having conceded defeat to MGM over *Butterfield 8*, Elizabeth won a series of small victories when she presented her demands to the studio: they must shoot the film in New York, employ Helen Rose to design her outfits, use Sidney Guilaroff for her hair, and add Eddie Fisher to the cast.

On 19 October, before leaving Hollywood to start the film in New York, Elizabeth initialled an agreement to make *Cleopatra*. Feeling even more moneyed than usual, she went straight out and bought her husband solid gold cufflinks with kisses picked out on each in a couple of diamond X's. Not to be (much) outdone, he gave her a mink sweater, adding vaguely, 'You wear it with slacks, or something casual.'

'How do I love thee? Let me count the ways,' goes Mrs Browning's poem. By the Fishers' reckoning, the ways were infinite, provided the chequebook had matching funds to draw on. It was beginning to look as if it had.

But Elizabeth's fury was rekindled when it came to learning her part. 'I hate the girl I play,' she raged. 'I don't like what she stands for – the men, the sleeping around.' Though there were plenty, including the offended John O'Hara, who pointedly drew what they considered to be a parallel between fact and fiction in the matter of men and beds, it was clear that Gloria Wandrous violated Elizabeth's self-image. The studio was profiting from her and, at the same time, punishing her – or so she felt. It was as if they wanted to brand her a whore before flinging her out. She took the script to a trusted friend, Joseph L. Mankiewicz, and pleaded with him to rewrite her part. He read it and agreed; it was 'shit'. But changing a line here and there would neither improve it nor sanitize it. Laurence Harvey felt as miscast as Elizabeth, but that was because he knew it was going to be her picture. 'The bitch is where the money is,' he said, meaning it was Elizabeth who would be favoured in the shots, not he. He recalled her remark, before shooting began on 1 January 1960, that 'this is going to be one rough picture.' By which he took her to mean that she would assert every right she possessed, and maybe some she didn't, to compensate for her humiliation.

Harvey remained a friend of Elizabeth's, though never an intimate one like Clift or McDowall, until his death from cancer in 1973. Like her, he was a battler, a survivor; he admired her grit and acknowledged her beauty, but was not awed by it. Although bisexual, Harvey didn't offer himself, like Clift, for mothering. He rejected pity, lest it get the upper hand. He once said to her, 'We certainly live dramatically, you and I, Fat Ass. But we must never complain. There's no living, if there's no rage, no sting. The likes of you and me would be done for without a little torment in our lives.'

The fact that Pandro Berman, the producer, had made some of her best films didn't soften Elizabeth's attitude to him. 'She reminded me I'd helped get her the present of the horse she raced in *National Velvet*,' Berman says, 'then snapped at me for what it cost her to keep him eating his head off.' He believed she might feel tempted to make MGM 'pay' for casting her in the film – the budget was $2.5 million and delays would obviously push it higher. But he didn't believe she'd ever actually do this. 'I always thought her professionalism would get the better of any personal animosity. "Elizabeth, you'll have all these other professionals playing the scene with you," I said. "You mean to tell me you'll screw things up for them, too, just to get your own back? I don't believe it. You play this part – which you *know* you can do – and you'll get an Oscar. You can say, 'Fuck it!' But when you're with the others in the film, you won't have the guts to say, 'Fuck them!' "' Elizabeth left, he claims, banging the door.

Berman did relent – at Benny Thau's urging – and let Eddie Fisher play the part intended for David Janssen, that of a young composer who acted as Elizabeth's best friend and voice of conscience, forever urging her to get herself together, as 'I'm sick of opening that door every other day and finding you burned out, boozed up and ugly.'

Because Fisher knew he was no actor, he asked Monty Clift to do what he'd done for Elizabeth in their first film together – hear him read his part and offer advice. The result was discouraging when he looked up in the middle of a reading and found Clift had fallen asleep – overcome by the drugs he was on. Fisher, too, was taking vitamin injections generously laced with amphetamines. The depth charge effect of this mix was ill understood in the era when 'Dr Feelgood' physicians used 'speed' to treat celebrities who wanted to experience the rush of confidence that they were on top of things. He later feared that during her spells in hospital, Elizabeth may well have been made an involuntary victim of habit-forming medication administered for benign motives, as insulation against pain and depression.

Elizabeth prevailed on a couple of screenwriters to do a quick rewrite job on Eddie's dialogue, reckoning the character he played could do with some humour to lighten the downbeat drama.

'She presented me with the revised script,' Berman recalls. 'I took it from her, I didn't even glance at it. I walked straight across the room to where the wastebasket was. I held the script over it, let it go, and it fell in. "That's what I think of this lousy crap," I told her. She flew at me.' In short, everyone suffered on *Butterfield 8*.

Amusingly, the early rushes brought the studio out in a nervous lather for the same old reasons. A cable to New York reached Berman on 7 January 1960, from Robert Vogel in Hollywood. 'If you share my concern that excessive Taylor cleavage on shot at piano you may want to protect for safety sake. Shot of her at door near end of sequence is even worse. But for this one assumed you can use close-up which only goes down to her shoulders.'

Shooting, under the direction of Daniel Mann, lasted throughout the exceptionally cold first quarter of 1960. And as Pandro Berman had predicted, Elizabeth's professionalism got the better of her distaste for the film. She certainly complained often enough – her clothes, the tint of her lipstick, the temperature of her dressing room – although a bout of double pneumonia showed it wasn't all temper. She sometimes openly disdained the more fanciful suggestions made by Daniel Mann. Shooting a bathtub scene, Eddie Fisher recalled, Mann told Elizabeth, 'Make believe you're fucking the faucet. That's the expression I want.' The expression he got was one of withering contempt.

Yet although Elizabeth thought the movie was trash, the role reached out and absorbed her imaginatively. A friend of Fisher's briefed her fully on the sub-culture of New York call-girls. As a result, Elizabeth's own talent transfused and made vividly realistic one tragic representative of a profession that was changing with the mores of the new decade. The kept woman was becoming practically indistinguishable from the free-living playgirl of the *Playboy* philosophy that Hugh Hefner and his editor, Auguste Comte Spectosky, were articulating monthly: economic self-indulgence, freedom from constraints, tasting a vast range of experience, using the body as a source of guilt-free enjoyment. These were the very characteristics that Elizabeth's own life-style exemplified throughout the 1960s, and later. Shed of its tragic ending, Gloria's death in a car crash, the film looks like a firing-pin that was soon to explode its star into the centre of the 'most public adultery in history' – the *Cleopatra* scandal.

The script specifically mentions *Playboy* magazine as a buzz-word for the times in which the film is set. Yet if the project is itself a product of those liberated times, the screenplay is ultimately a victim of the Hollywood morality code, which had almost another decade to run before it was abandoned. It establishes Elizabeth in the Gloria Wandrous situation, and extracts the maximum permissible amount of titillation from Gloria's nymphomania, then it devotes the rest of the running time to backtracking scenes that allow the character to abandon reality for the sort of moral retribution which leaves her dead in the wreck of her sports car. The crash is precipitated, to some extent, by Harvey's pursuit of her – and her death is used to recall him to a sense of self-respect and decency. The story thus sustains the pre-liberation moral of the man's redemption through the woman's sacrifice.

Elizabeth's looks always belie the words on her lips. She is in perfect tune with the character until she has to utter the dialogue that MGM used to protect itself from the censors. This is why the sinning Gloria of the early reels is far more effectively rendered than the contrite woman of the later sequences. But the way that Elizabeth uses her looks and body to define a life-style (almost without words, for the long opening sequence), is what keeps her performance from looking dated or diluted. It is one of the best performances she has ever given.

This ten-minute sequence begins with Gloria waking up in the married man's apartment after he has left the bed for his office. All alone in the luxurious rooms, Elizabeth shows a confident resourcefulness combined with a detailed accuracy to fill us in on the sort of woman Gloria is beneath the skin. The phone that's off the cradle indicates the way that the night has been passed. Her discovery that the packet of cigarettes she automatically reaches for is empty causes her to toss it over her shoulder in a gesture of instinctive moral casualness. She lights up one of Harvey's cigarillos – more evidence of her meeting the male on equal terms. She pours a slug of whisky into a tumbler for a wake-up thirst-quencher and then uses the rest of it to rinse her teeth. She finds her dress on the floor where it fell the night before, ripped apart by the heavy sex that an American film could now imply, but not yet show. She pulls on her petticoat – Elizabeth in that shimmering garment is far sexier than another actress totally naked. Over it, she tugs a mink coat 'borrowed' from Harvey's wife. This 'Venus in furs', with only her underwear beneath, is the limit of the film's eroticism. But the cool effrontery with which Elizabeth carries it off is masterly. Thus robed, she sallies into the morning to hail a cab and speak her first line of dialogue to the driver: 'Double your tip for a cigarette.'

Every man – and every woman, too – who saw Elizabeth 'assemble' Gloria Wandrous could recognize precisely that type of woman.

Gloria's attitude to life is exactly what one has come to expect of Elizabeth. She goes her own way defiantly, whatever the cost. When Gloria scrawls 'No Sale' on the mirror in Harvey's apartment, after she has found his present of $250 for the night, it echoes Elizabeth's own belligerently independent stance. Money is a reminder of an unacceptable state of dependency. After this movie, she was never again to tolerate being caught in the commercial grip of a film industry which dictated the terms for her remuneration and held her to contract. Henceforth, it was she who would set the terms for the sort of woman that they could have.

Despite the cumulative hypocrisies of the dialogue, Elizabeth almost manages to subvert the studio-made morality. Lines sound as if they are communiqués she herself has sent. 'You're all alike,' Harvey snaps. – 'I'm not like anyone,' she blazes back, 'I'm me.'

Well before the women's movement got the parade going, Elizabeth Taylor was out there in *Butterfield 8* striking a blow for the sisterhood – appropriately enough with her stiletto heel on the instep of Harvey's glossy pumps. He grips her wrist ever more tightly to force her to abandon the excruciating pressure. He loses.

Yet her attitude to the film shows the depth of her hurt at being compelled to make it: she hates it to this day. Nevertheless, there are certain inconsistencies in accounts of her reactions to it at the time. According to her own account, she walked up to the screen after she'd seen a rough cut and scrawled an obscenity on it in lipstick. According to Eddie Fisher, they both stood up and dashed the contents of their glasses at the screen. As he remembers it, she then stormed through the corridors of MGM until she reached Sol Siegel's office and on the door of the studio boss, she wrote in lipstick Gloria's damning rejection of male ownership: 'No Sale'. Quite likely, she performed all three acts of rebelliousness.

From now on, Elizabeth would have the upper hand. Even a 'hateful' film can stiffen one's resolve. Even a character who is 'practically a prostitute' can offer one a lesson in survival. Henceforth, Elizabeth would set the price and conditions for the sale.

26

BETWEEN LIFE AND DEATH

‛The question was asked in a whisper, but the words seemed to grow louder and louder and more insistent – "Does God always punish?"' So began a *Photoplay* cover story on Elizabeth. Even the articles now gave the impression of being premature obituaries. The star had been wicked; the star must pay for it. What was God waiting for? The fan magazines purveyed a petulant moralizing. The trouble was, the star refused to comply. On the contrary, she seemed to be flourishing.

By now, in her new mood of toughness, Elizabeth knew what brought respect in Hollywood. It was certainly not rushing to put a signature on a contract. Mike Todd had acquainted her with the rules of the game; now she was in a position to play it herself. Having signed the agreement to make *Cleopatra*, she was in no hurry to sign the actual contract. She enjoyed the luxury of watching her lawyers add one golden clause after another to her demands. She was to get $1 million; overage at $50,000 a week; per diem living expenses at $3,000 weekly; 10 per cent of the film's gross box-office take; first-class round-trip transportation for herself and three children; economy-class tickets for four employees; first-class round-trip for her lawyer-agent during the pre-production period and each time the film moved to a new location or studio; and finally one 16 mm print of the finished film. Eddie Fisher was to receive $150,000 to do a job whose purpose eluded even him – 'some kind of production assistant,' he termed it, though, put bluntly, it meant he had to supervise Elizabeth and produce her in a happy state of mind whenever she was needed. Her services were contracted to Fox by a new corporation called MCL Films SA, registered in Zürich, its initials standing for the chief beneficiaries, her children Michael, Christopher and Liza. The tax break this would give her was the strongest reason for shooting the film abroad.

But the original plan to shoot *Cleopatra* in Rome had foundered on what were called 'budgetary anomalies' – which meant that the Italian film people employed by Fox were likely to rob the company blind. The box-office subsidy that was then available to British films decided Fox in favour of turning Pinewood Studios' back lot into the sun-struck desert of Egypt, though the approach of a wet, cold autumn gave Walter Wanger and his director, Rouben Mamoulian, anticipatory shivers of the financial kind. A star just recovered from double pneumonia would be vulnerable to England's damp, clinging climate. The film's budget fluctuated, sometimes daily, according to how exhilarated or depressed the Fox chairman, Spyros Skouras, happened to be. The cost in September 1959 was between $4.6 million and $5 million, which included $1.8 million for the stars: Elizabeth as Cleopatra, Peter Finch as Caesar, Stephen Boyd as Antony. An extra half a million was soon to be added to the budget, although it would never show on the screen – it was the price paid for an Italian version of the story, bought up and shelved to keep the market uncluttered for Fox's film.

If the augurs had taken the omens on 8 September 1960, the day Elizabeth and her retinue arrived at Heathrow Airport, they would not have been reassuring.

They all moved into the Dorchester Hotel's two penthouse suites: the Terrace suite (for Elizabeth and her husband, at £300 a week) and the Harlequin (for the children, nanny, etc., at £200). Elizabeth had become, in effect, a rich nomad, sustained by her entourage, travelling with her husband and children, working to a routine determined by a film that was starting to slip out of control, vulnerable to her own restlessness, her low threshold of boredom, her extreme susceptibility to infection, and a growing, if as yet unacknowledged, discontent with the marriage she had made.

As the first day of shooting approached – it was scheduled for 30 September – Elizabeth's temperature rose, and the outside temperature fell. The palm trees transplanted to eight and a half acres of the film studio withered in the overnight rain and cold, and fresh fronds had to be flown in daily from North Africa. In the Dorchester, afflicted with a growing fever, Elizabeth took to her bed and vapour inhalations. Yet to delay or cancel the production at this point would have affected far more than the budget. *Cleopatra* had become a hostage to Twentieth Century–Fox's boardroom politics. Skouras was an embattled president, facing accusations of waste, folly and even insanity. He had to keep his foes at bay, if not rout them, by exhibiting every outward sign of confidence in the grandiosity of his enterprise. Elizabeth and the huge volume of publicity generated by her mere presence in the movie were the only things that lent credibility to Skouras's folly. Her most recent films were all exceptionally high earners. Preview opinion cards were indicating that *Butterfield 8* would follow that pattern; in fact, it grossed an amazing $9 million domestically, as much again overseas, all for a basic outlay of $2.5 million. Skouras clicked his worry beads and sweated it out.

The strain was also starting to tell on Eddie Fisher. He had begun to hanker for a few moments of the day that he could call his own. His career had virtually ground to a halt. The future he now saw for himself lay in developing and producing his wife's future films, using her star power as collateral to get finance and attract other bankable co-stars. Mike Todd had made it all look so easy. But 'what I didn't know,' Fisher later confessed with creditable candour, 'was that movie deals were just as complex, and could be just as venal, as anything I had ever encountered in the record business or television.' He took off for Los Angeles on 19 October 1960, to try and get these business deals rolling. In his heart, he felt his wife would respect him more if he were the wheeler-dealer, not the gofer. But her state was akin to panic as she realized she would now be left alone in London. She behaved, as Walter Wanger saw it, the way she had just prior to Mike Todd's departure on his fatal air journey. And her fever grew worse. Even after an abscessed tooth had been extracted, all was not well. She developed an irritation of the spine that kept her in her suite. *Cleopatra* came to an almost complete halt, reflecting Elizabeth's similarly immobilized state. Her day was empty of purpose, yet filled with diversions: throwing poker parties, eating junk food, playing records, constantly telephoning Eddie and hearing up-to-the-minute reports of near-freezing conditions at Pinewood from Peter Finch, who would drop in on her at the end of a wasted day, spend hours drinking, convivially at first, then growing more exasperated and boisterous until he finally passed out and had to be carried down to his car and driven home. Truman Capote also stopped by and found the luxury suite a mess of shedding cats, stray dogs, Paris dresses and the occasional animal turd.

On 18 November 1960, production was shut down – the insurance company actually offered Fox $1.74 million to halt, promising to reinsure Elizabeth when work resumed in the new year. But for her presence in it, the film would have been abandoned for good there and then. But because she was there, though so far not on a foot of exposed film, it remained alive still. Her star-power was like an artificial heart.

The Fishers spent Christmas 1960 in Palm Springs. They returned to London before New Year's Eve to meet the movie's new director, Joseph L. Mankiewicz. Eddie Fisher claims to have had the inspiration to replace Mamoulian with Mankiewicz, largely in the hope that the last man with whom Elizabeth had been in harmony, when they made *Suddenly, Last Summer* together, would be able to work the miracle anew.

'I'm here to do whatever you want, Elizabeth,' Eddie reported him saying. Elizabeth melted and Mankiewicz went to work.

Elizabeth gave Mankiewicz her respect, and he, in turn, devoted all his professional attention to her. He was too cool, too rational, too analytical a filmmaker to indulge in an affair with his leading lady, as some directors did – incurring a sort of marriage that lasted for the duration of the production. What Mankiewicz was able to offer her was a sense of security – and that came as close to love as possible for someone in Elizabeth's current state of mind and body. But Mankiewicz made an analysis of her that was both professional and profound. He guessed that 'what knowledge she'd acquired in life came out of her own experience of it or the "experiences" created for her in films. And for someone like Elizabeth, that added up to a helluva lot of experience. She was the reverse of other stars. She didn't need to be acting in order to prove something about herself. She's often said that she puts acting into second place in life, and that's true. But for her, living life was a kind of acting. And being cast in a star role, or assuming the characteristics of roles written with her in mind, heightened her sensation of living.'

Mankiewicz's own original screenplays – in particular *A Letter to Three Wives*, *The Barefoot Contessa* and, of course, *All About Eve* – illustrate his preoccupation with feminine power and the female psyche. Now he had the opportunity to watch Elizabeth in close-up, so to speak, and create the title role in *Cleopatra* in part out of his own observation of her personality and the way she used it to gain the ascendancy, at whatever cost to herself.

It would be going too far to say that Mankiewicz saw the outline of his *Cleopatra* screenplay in the recent events of Elizabeth's life – in which a Caesar figure like Mike Todd, destroyed by pride and the gods, was succeeded by a protégé who was accepted into his widow's bed, but otherwise was ill-equipped to follow in the footsteps of the man he aspired to emulate. But as he watched Elizabeth's marriage deteriorate, the role of a woman like Cleopatra who wants it all and receives the homage of two lovers in rapid succession must have gained coloration and substance from contemporary events. As Mankiewicz went home from one day's shooting to sit down and write the script for the next day's scenes, the drama of love, power and infidelity that was soon to unfold all around him certainly guided his pen. Even Elizabeth was conscious of this phenomenon. In her published recollections of this time, she was to employ the sort of terms that Cleopatra herself might have used for Antony: 'Since I was a little girl, I believed I was a child of destiny, and if this is true Richard Burton was surely my fate.'

Work on indoor scenes was due to resume on 4 April 1961; exteriors would be shot in Egypt. Elizabeth was still on pain-killers, which were much more powerful than her usual sedatives. Fisher tried one and 'suddenly everything began swimming in front of my eyes' and he had to lie down so as to 'ride it out'. He protested at what she might be doing to herself. There was no point; Elizabeth just kept taking the pills prescribed for her. Now the hopelessness of his situation really hit him. 'I was giving up my life for the pleasure of standing by helplessly while the woman I loved seemed to care so little for her own.' They flew over to Munich for the annual carnival and there, as Fisher recollects it, a terrifying incident took place. He remonstrated with Elizabeth for being so tardy in coming to bed. The row turned ugly. He yelled that he had had enough and was leaving in the morning.

'You're leaving in the morning,' she said. 'Well, I'm leaving now' – and she swallowed a handful of Seconal pills. A doctor, hastily summoned and paid in an envelope stuffed with marks, as much for his discretion as for his services, gave her emergency treatment, then sedated her. Eighteen hours later, or so it seemed to her husband sitting beside her and reflecting on what had gone wrong in their marriage, she woke up, and protestations of remorse and mutual affection followed. But Eddie Fisher felt he couldn't stay the course much longer. Elizabeth now frightened him.

Suffering from exhaustion, he checked into hospital on their return to London and, to prolong his rest, pretended to feel a twinge of appendicitis. He recalls Elizabeth saying that there was no need for anyone to be in pain in this day and age – which he interpreted as a compliant acceptance of medical drugs as a normal part of life. He might have tarried longer in hospital – in sanctuary, as it were – while his marriage remained in a state of partial paralysis, had it not been for the much greater calamity that suddenly overwhelmed Elizabeth.

Just after midnight on 4 March 1961, the desk clerk at the Dorchester took a call from the Terrace suite. A doctor was needed urgently. The nurse who had been caring for Elizabeth – the Munich trip had been followed by Asiatic flu – had observed that she was worsening. Suddenly, she began gasping for breath, turning blue in the face and purplish under her fingernails. A physician who happened to be at a colleague's stag party in a nearby room and who, by the grace of God, was also one of the capital's leading anaesthetists and respiration specialists, rushed to the suite. 'By the time I arrived, she had stopped breathing,' he says. 'She might have survived fifteen minutes without attention, but no more.' He shook her vigorously by her heels, tilting her upside-down to dislodge the congestion in her lungs, pummelled her chest for the same purpose, and, failing to 'thump-start' her into conscious breathing, thrust his fingers down her throat to make her gag, then pushed at her eyeballs. That pain jerked Elizabeth back to life. She was rushed to hospital.

Eddie Fisher sat slumped outside the operating theatre, not knowing if the next person he saw would tell him his wife was dead or still fighting for her life. In fact, the next person was a woman with that universal English remedy for all crises, a cup of tea. Then came a surgeon with a document he asked Eddie to sign – authorization for a tracheotomy, a 'hole in the throat' operation that would allow Elizabeth to breathe. The surgeon added that it might leave a scar. Even at death's door, a star's beauty counted. Within minutes, Elizabeth was having a two-inch incision made in her throat and a large tube inserted into it connected to a Barnet ventilator which kept her lungs pumping on borrowed air. She had often called MGM's front office 'the Iron Lung', because you only breathed when it said so. Now she was dependent for her very life on just such a machine.

Later, she was to recall that, although deprived of speech, she was mentally screaming for help. But she was also angry. 'I was fierce.' Several times, she was sucked back into unconsciousness. 'I died four times. You feel yourself falling, falling into a horrible black pit. You hear a screaming jet noise. Your skin is falling off. But even when I was unconscious, I had my fists clenched ... I fought so hard to live.' The first thing she saw on regaining consciousness was 'a bright shining light'. Then a nurse held up a looking-glass and she saw herself without recognizing herself. The image she saw was like a dissociated entity, floating there in space. The natural rhythms of her body were subsumed into the pumping of the suction machine. Then she recognized Eddie's face hovering above her. Eventually, a grease crayon of the sort used to mark the place for the knife to enter a patient's body was put in her hand. Understanding, she scrawled 'Am I going to die because I feel I am?' on a piece of paper. Eddie shook his head. A few minutes later, with the aid of a stethoscope, he could just about interpret the words her lips were forming from the vibrations that the tube amplified. Elizabeth recalled: 'I began to feel a sense of calm, gratitude and tranquillity.' She had always had a religious sense, of course – 'but I never had the feeling before that I had been in close touch with God'.

Mankiewicz, already almost resigned to seeing *Cleopatra* expire with its star, had noted much of this with the acuity of a journalist – the crowded operating theatre, the surgeons' robes like a green glade, Elizabeth's deathly pale face above her own green sheet, and directly overhead the many-bulbed central light. Some months later it was he who wrote the speech she gave at a fund-raising dinner for Los Angeles hospitals, and heard her infuse his text with the dramatic tenseness she had evoked when he guided her through her 'aria' at the end of *Suddenly, Last Summer*. This time, too, art had preceded life, or, perhaps, even 'death'.

On 6 March, though, her recovery suffered a near-fatal setback when anaemia complicated the double pneumonia. Word went round the world that Elizabeth Taylor was dying: some papers even printed her obituary. Skouras called Wanger in London: 'My God! How did it happen?' Wanger told him grimly it wasn't true – yet.

As she was being fed intravenously with fresh blood – even her palms were pierced with the stigmata of the tube – the London Clinic became an embattled castle. Reporters, photographers and TV trucks choked the surrounding streets, checking everyone who entered or left, hourly expecting a death announcement to be pinned up. Bystanders were weeping openly. People made detours to the hospital on their way back from work, leaving flower posies on the steps as at a shrine. 'Miracle cures' arrived with every mail sack. Merle Oberon called from Rome with an 'elixir', which she offered to fly over by private plane; it was tactfully declined. Elizabeth's brother and parents arrived. 'Two years before,' Eddie reflected, 'Elizabeth had been "the biggest slut in Hollywood" ... Now all was forgiven.' Religious sects the world over held services of intercession. At a US Army base in West Germany, the men prayed for her. At West Point, the cadets included her name in their chapel prayers. Bottles of holy water were left like milk on the hospital doorstep. During the days ahead, more than twelve thousand messages were received and stacked in laundry baskets. One cable was signed on behalf of six thousand Boeing aircraft workers; another was from a US destroyer at sea. A clinic in the Soviet Union offered rare drugs; an American government agency even allowed drugs still in the testing stage to be flown to London.

By 7 March, with six physicians in attendance, including the Queen's, Elizabeth was pronounced much improved, though not yet out of danger. By 11 March, her chest, ankle, leg and hand infusion tubes were removed, the tracheotomy tube came out for short periods, and she was fed nasally. 'She has made a very, very rare recovery,' said a medical bulletin.

Modern life lacks clear-cut tragedies. But the dying star is still one that focuses people's imaginations like an old-time morality play. For some, perhaps for the majority of those who followed events, Elizabeth Taylor's agony was simply a morbid form of pseudo-intimacy. But for millions more, it confirmed that film stars were as vulnerable as they were themselves. Her crisis brought Elizabeth back to life-size, restored her to a state of sympathy for ordinary folk. The wave of identification with her that built up could easily have turned into an orgy of grief, had she died. But a near-miraculous recovery having taken place, Elizabeth was also restored to her fantasy dimension – only now she was left that little bit more immortal.

Overlapping with the coverage of the drama was the Academy Awards voting period. Hollywood was thus provided with an irresistible opportunity both to do penance for the way it had treated Elizabeth and to honour her – to bracket the recovery of the woman who had so recently been sent into exile and had now been recalled to life with its own gold-plated token of movie immortality, the Oscar for her performance in *Butterfield 8*. In this film, of course, she *had* died suddenly, tragically and needlessly. That she had skirted death in reality again contributed to the power of watching her suffer it in fantasy.

Her recovery followed a now well-established pattern; it was unusually quick and apparently complete. She felt that she had been born again. Sara Taylor took some credit for that and related how she had prayed at the bedside, urging her all-but-mute daughter not to dwell on past or present, but face the fortified spiritual life of future days. A scene was enacted that seems to have been much like one in *The Secret Garden*. Like that novel's stricken child, Elizabeth 'believed' – and was cured.

The black humour which she now displayed to visitors was very much her own, however. The doctors had temporarily plugged the tracheotomy hole in her neck. Sometimes she deliberately pulled the plug and, to the consternation of visitors, let her voice 'vanish' through the hole – a prank she accompanied with howls of glee, like a witch whose spell has worked.

Work on *Cleopatra* was not scheduled to begin before the autumn. Then it was to take place in Rome, out of deference to the star's need for a warm climate. She spent the intervening months in California, convalescing and reading many of the get-well messages – love by the hundredweight now. She refused plastic surgery for the tracheotomy scar; it was to be her 'badge of life' and make-up would hide it from the camera. This, in itself a small sign, was a symptom of the larger change that manifested itself during the months after the crisis. 'I knew that I wanted more in my life than what I had,' she announced. That should have warned Eddie Fisher. The fact that she insisted she had 'talked' to Mike Todd 'on the other side' during one of the periods when she had departed this life was an even clearer alert. A woman who claimed she had been in touch with God was one thing; that could prefigure a changed life. But a woman who had been in touch with her last husband might adopt a changed attitude to her present one. Fisher felt the difference in her, as she now renewed acquaintance with a man who had been her mentor, and became her lover.

She had already met Max Lerner in 1959, in London, where the Brandeis professor and *New York Post* columnist was covering the summit meeting between President Eisenhower and Prime Minister Macmillan. She thanked him for the support he had shown her in his column when the rest of the media were baring their teeth at the 'home-wrecker' and 'husband-stealer'. Lerner was then fifty-nine, Elizabeth just twenty-seven. He was naturally flattered to have her attention, but not entirely a stranger to the attention of film stars. He had been close to Marilyn Monroe, too. Having a man of intellect in love with them, rather than a man who used his body or looks to distinguish himself, reinforced the feeling of both stars that they were accepted in a world different from (and superior to) that of movie-making. 'It strengthened Elizabeth's self-respect, her index of self-worth,' Lerner was to say. The lover in the worldly academic, however, had not extinguished the sociologist. Monroe, to him, was a 'myth': Elizabeth, a 'legend'. The former he saw as a victim of the system; the latter would probably beat it. Monroe was the stuff of every actress who aspired to stardom; Elizabeth was a rare quantity, but of a particular type, not universal. This did not entirely please her, according to Lerner. 'Both of you are forces,' he told her. That went down better.

When they met again in California, in the summer of 1961, it was plain to Lerner that Elizabeth's marriage was 'very shaky'. They went around under the complaisant eye of Eddie Fisher, now almost relieved to have the strain taken off him by another man. 'She has a great capacity for seeming very dependent on you when you are with her,' Lerner recalls. 'She seemed to defer to my wishes in all manner of ways.' But this attitude he judged to stem from her need for a man: 'It's very difficult to visualize Elizabeth without a man.

'I think it's fair to say that I saw Elizabeth as fitting a very old, universal pattern – she is a romantic who keeps rushing into marriage and swearing she will be faithful for eternity. But it is really a self-referring wish rather than a full partnership. She is impelled to it by the desire to postpone her own mortality. Marriage is a reaffirmation of life and love – a means of holding death at bay, the idea of *l'éternel retour*. If death cannot be avoided, then at least the lovers will be re-united in the hereafter.'

She and Lerner decided to write a book together. 'She said to me, "I'll do the recalling, you do the heavy thinking."' She even proposed a title: *Elizabeth Taylor: Between Life and Death*. Later, Lerner wrote that during their tape-recorded 'collaboration', Elizabeth had remarked, 'There is this thing I have about death. The people I love . . . get killed, like Mike. Or they come close to it, like Monty Clift.'

Eddie Fisher, who was in due course to publish his own surprisingly articulate and perceptive account of these years, read the situation correctly and acted accordingly. Neither jealous nor yet indifferent, he preferred not to be caught between two formidable people, his wife and Max Lerner. He would let the situation pass. And pass it did. A book appeared, some three years later, though Lerner's name was nowhere mentioned in or on it. It was called *Elizabeth Taylor: An Informal Memoir by Elizabeth Taylor*.

Self-referral, indeed! As for her professor, he has since had no regrets. '[My relationship] has given me the delightful feeling of becoming a legend myself without having to pay the price.' A legend, note; not a myth.

PART THREE

. . .

The Burtons

27

'LE SCANDALE'

Part of Elizabeth's need to love and be loved involved, as some saw it, a reluctance to discard the old before she had acquired the new. It was as if the romantic temperament were always glancing out of the castle window to see if another prince was on the way. One now was. Into the saddle climbed Richard Burton, declaring, as he signed the contract for *Cleopatra* in the summer of 1961, 'I must don my armour once more to play against Miss Tits.'

Burton replaced Stephen Boyd as Mark Antony. To buy him out of the stage musical *Camelot* cost Fox $50,000 – not a cent of which needed to have been spent, since he did not begin *Cleopatra* until January 1962. By that time, his guaranteed fee of $250,000 for three months' work had spectacularly escalated through overtime payments: he would eventually make nearly $1 million. Elizabeth's contract had been renegotiated, too: all in all, with her percentage of the film, she would eventually make about $7 million. 'It wasn't a flop for me,' she could say with justice – and did – in later years.

The absurdity of filmmaking has seldom more forcibly, or profitably, been impressed on the participating beneficiaries. This wasn't anything new to Burton. Aged thirty-six and a star of fluctuating fortunes and status for the last ten years, he was already a hardened cynic about committing his talents to filmmaking. He considered it an unworthy activity, which nevertheless made him a fortune.

Richard Burton was in many ways a male mirror-image of Elizabeth. Both were adventurers, in the sense that they were people who took risks to please themselves, and damn the consequences. Both had disdain – often well-founded – for 'the industry'. Both had developed a brazen disregard for public opinion. Burton bragged openly of his mistresses, his self-esteem bolstered by the tolerance of a hard-headed wife whose own

practical sense of reality enabled her to put up with her husband's phil-
andering. Elizabeth, too, defiantly defended her romances and remarriages,
sometimes successfully in the libel courts. Unlike Burton, however, she
did not need to play to an audience of media people; quite the reverse. In
this respect, Burton was more like her late husband Mike Todd. Like him,
Burton felt entirely at home with the press – indeed, he felt deprived if
they weren't to hand. His Celtic hunger for convivial company (i.e.
boozing) and impromptu performance (i.e. narcissism) resembled the
abstemious Jewish showman's adroitness with the wisecrack and the self-
advertising extravagance. The language of both men was, in Max Lerner's
words, 'often stormy and always salty'.

Burton, like Todd, loved hearing his own voice; but for an actor, that
could be a drawback. If bored, he fell easily into a mildly self-enraptured
trance. There was a curse as well as a blessing laid on his lips. Throughout
his career, he retained an actor's voice; his phrasing remained theatrical.
Some actors hated appearing with him; it got on their nerves, they said,
anticipating the way he would draw breath before speaking his lines.
Elizabeth was by far the more naturalistic player – something which he
sensed from the beginning, and for a long time was defensive about.
Skouras hadn't wanted him in the film. 'No one will be able to understand
you,' he said. Burton shot back, 'Like I can't you.' But Mankiewicz had
carried the day, for a fine speaking voice would do justice to the dialogue
written by a director who had a deep respect for words and knew how an
actor could fine-tune a script. As he also had Rex Harrison to replace Peter
Finch as Caesar, Mankiewicz had no worries about elocution.

There was another important difference between the stars. Unlike
Burton, Elizabeth hadn't ever felt poor. Burton never really freed himself
from a fear that he would be poor again – as poor, anyhow, as he suggested
when he used to exaggerate and embellish the circumstances of his birth
as one of a Welsh miner's large brood of eleven children in a family called
Jenkins. Actually, he had been plucked from his siblings while still a
teenager and reared, like a changeling child, by a local schoolteacher,
Philip Burton, who made himself his legal guardian, changed the boy's
surname to his own, and set about turning him into an actor to replace
another Welsh schoolboy whom he had successfully groomed to play
opposite Gielgud in the West End, and who had been killed in the war.

Burton was already comfortably off, with a villa in Switzerland and the
tax advantages of an expatriate. For Elizabeth, possessions were simply
for extravagance and display; for him, they were for display and reassurance. Mike Todd had taught Elizabeth how to get; she was now to teach
Richard Burton how to spend.

Both of them had a sublime capacity to ignore any trouble they landed themselves in. Like Elizabeth, Burton could 'leap into the next frame' of the action, and kill all thought of consequences as he pursued fresh ambitions. Both conceived of life as theatre – they saw it in terms of each day's infinite variety of dramatic possibilities. Elizabeth was more committed to living the parts she played, carrying over her roles into life and reacting accordingly. Burton was very easily bored. He saw the day in terms of the empty space that needed to be filled satisfyingly by dramatizing himself, becoming the character who fits the scene and then transforming the scene so that the character can dominate it. Most of his endless press interviews have to be read with this in mind.

Burton's biographer Melvyn Bragg has compared him to an Elizabethan poet who, without embarrassment, would compose an ode in public to his mistress. Elizabeth may have lacked the lyrical talent, but her observations on love and marriage were conducted, in prose, with just as much bravado. They both had a gypsy-like disregard for convention which was Elizabethan in the historical as well as the histrionic sense. Both of them were people of passionate parts. Elizabeth had already told one husband, Michael Wilding, that starring in a film obliged her to fall in love to some degree with her co-star. Burton was to remark to his brother, Graham Jenkins, 'You can't act falling in love without really falling in love – if just a little. There's no harm in it.' Maybe not; but there was, for him, more than a little guilt. The puritan side of his Welshness, as distinct from the carnal side, always felt guilty about the betrayals, especially the pain caused to his wife Sybil and his children – he already carried a burden of self-reproach for the mentally retarded condition of his daughter Jessica. He would attempt to mitigate this by buying presents for the people he hurt – and then do the same for the person he had made his mistress. Presents were his form of buying off guilt, just as, to Elizabeth, spending was a display of love. Self-reproach was appeased in Burton's case; in Elizabeth's self-love was reinforced.

Max Lerner said about Elizabeth: '[She is] a romantic, yet with some solid investments in her portfolio.' He could have said exactly the same about Burton.

That these two extraordinary people fell in love with each other when *Cleopatra* called them to Rome should surprise no one. One would have been surprised had they not done so. Even before they met, they were primed by temperamental affinity to explode into the love affair that needed no other identification except the sardonic nickame Burton gave it – '*le scandale*'.

It had been decided to shoot *Cleopatra* entirely in Rome – not just the outdoor scenes – because George Stevens's Biblical spectacle, *The Greatest Story Ever Told*, was monopolizing so much space on the Fox lot in

Hollywood. ('*Le scandale*' was soon to be known as Fox's 'Second Greatest Story'.) The shift of location worried Elizabeth. She expressed fears for the safety of herself and her family. She knew how hard the Italian paparazzi were to avoid, how difficult security would be in Rome, how many surcharges would be added to the bills simply because she was who she was. She was soon proved right. An expensive villa was rented – at $3,000 a month – on the Via Appia Antica, a few minutes' drive by Cadillac or Rolls-Royce – her two studio cars on twenty-four-hour call – from Cinecittà Studios. But it had high trees round it in which the paparazzi clustered like monkeys. And although the villa looked luxurious, its plumbing fell somewhat short of Beverly Hills efficiency. Otherwise, she was given all the appurtenances of a queen: her personal physician (at $25,000 retainer for the seven weeks for which Wanger still thought her services would be needed), a script bound in purple Moroccan leather, a special chair to sit in made of California redwood and Russian leather, and a whole studio building converted into a personal facility for work and relaxation and named the 'Casa Taylor'. 'Isn't that overdoing it a bit?' she asked, her only reported protest at extravagance, ever.

She was impressed, too, by the staggering scale of the epic, which was now visible. An army of 2,500 men was being daily drilled for the great land battles. At Anzio, a fleet was being constructed for the Battle of Actium. Cleopatra's royal barge was being outfitted with purple sails of pure silk and real gold-leafed figureheads. A 'Forum' was rising half a mile from the actual Forum, and twice as big, for Cleopatra's ceremonial entry into Rome. Skouras pleaded with Wanger to hold the budget to $10 million and, on being told that $15 million might not be enough, nervously enquired if *Cleopatra* couldn't end with Caesar's death. The parallel with the Roman emperor's assassination oppressed Skouras: he was aware that his own executives were plotting to oust him from control of Fox.

By now, Eddie Fisher had learned to forecast his wife's moods with some precision. He never gave Elizabeth orders, or contradicted the impression that she was the boss. He infiltrated his suggestions into her thoughts, feigned immediate acceptance of her objections, left her with nothing to oppose and then, by seeming to yield, was rewarded by the response he'd been after all along. Thus on the first day of shooting, 25 September 1961, he had her on the set fifteen minutes early, in make-up (she and she alone did her eyes), costumed in heavy gold robes and jewellery, her hair regally styled by Sidney Guilaroff. All this was only for a test, but it was the vision that Fox had waited a year and shelled out a fortune to see materialize.

She saw very little of Burton at this time. Before his wife arrived, on 1 October, all his spare hours were spent with a young woman from the

New York cast of *Camelot* who had left the show when he did and accompanied him to Rome.

Burton was still treating Elizabeth's star-power as something of a Hollywood joke. And she seemed more amused than ensnared by him. He had come up to her on the set and made a standard pass – 'Has anyone told you that you're a very pretty girl?' It was intended to be self-mocking, uttered as it was in Shakespearean cadences. It misfired; she had been anticipating eloquence and instead got a platitude. Eddie Fisher, who was no fool, didn't think Burton much of a threat. To Elizabeth's husband, he cut an unimpressive figure, his head a shade too large for his body, his legs manifestly too short for his broad shoulders, his face so pitted with acne that it required a special foundation make-up to fill in the imperfections. When he had a hangover, he looked worse: dirty, unkempt and smelly. One night at a party, Elizabeth called Eddie over: 'Come look, Richard doesn't really have orchids growing under his fingernails.' No rival here, Eddie decided.

Eddie Fisher's confidence that all was well could only have been strengthened by the decision that he and Elizabeth had made to buy property in Switzerland. It had clear tax advantages for them both to be domiciled there. He found a chalet in the Bernese Oberland ski resort of Gstaad. It had been built for a Texas millionaire, but was unfinished. The price: $280,000. He thought it perfect. If that's how he felt, Elizabeth said, buy it. She thus acquired the Chalet Ariel, the one place that was to become a home for her and her family over the years – the place where, each Christmas, she would try to regroup her children, animals and husband, or, as it happened, current lover. The international set had already begun to make Gstaad their 'village', though the film colony of Blake Edwards and Julie Andrews, Peter Sellers and his wife Lynne Frederick, Robert Wagner and Natalie Wood, and Roger Moore and his wife was still some years away. Elizabeth could already count among her neighbours Henry Ford II, the Aga Khan and ex-King Umberto of Italy.

What began to draw Burton and Elizabeth together was a common delight in ribald humour. He soon had her laughing uproariously at the indelicate stories he told or, rather, performed. He was a skilful raconteur with a large repertoire. Although Mike Todd had made more use of one-liners and wisecracks than extended monologues, there was a lot of Todd's insolence in Burton's anecdotes. They were a means of dominating the company as much as entertaining it; invariably they went with drinking and late hours. Both indulgences broke the rules of abstinence and early nights that Eddie Fisher had guilefully established for Elizabeth; but he was powerless. He saw his wife making use of Burton's act as an excuse to put off her bedtime. He even detected Burton topping up her wine glass, as if both of them were conspirators against his fussy nursemaiding. Burton clearly saw he was intriguing Elizabeth by playing the licensed buffoon, the virile Welshman, the professional actor. He was egged on by another womanizer, braggart and Welsh compatriot, Stanley Baker; both of them, as Rex Harrison's actress wife Rachel Roberts noted in her diary, 'consumed by their need to be men'. There was no physical relationship between Burton and Elizabeth, as yet. Burton was imposing his personality on her, not his body, drawing her into his own arrogantly self-confident spell. He was a romancer as well as a stalker. He wanted to make sure both of them enjoyed themselves. He was, in short, fun. That is what made him dangerous; that is what Eddie Fisher failed to see.

Fisher resented being left out of things, of course, though that was commonplace when Burton took over the party. One evening, Eddie put on a record of his own and turned up the hi-fi to a deafening volume. But if it was a distress signal, it was a cry for attention, not one of alarm.

Then a scene in the film made things more dangerous. It was Cleopatra's bath scene, which Elizabeth, against her usually implacable opposition to nude scenes, had agreed to do out of trust in Mankiewicz. Burton jokingly threatened to sneak on to the closed set disguised as a veiled handmaiden. Instead, he watched the rushes, and was impressed. That glimpse seems to have given his sexual bravado its edge of concupiscence. The pleasure of captivating Elizabeth, which he was already enjoying, became charged with the thought of possessing her.

He was very nervous when he came to shoot his first scene with Elizabeth, scheduled for 22 January 1962. The night before, he went on a colossal binge and showed up red-eyed, unshaven and shaking. Elizabeth said afterwards that she had never in her life seen anyone so hung-over. She giggled as he sat down beside her, painfully massaging his head. Coffee was brought. His trembling hand threatened to spill it down his Roman tunic. She steadied the cup, as if administering refreshment to an invalid. The man who could command Shakespeare's verse at supper now looked as if he were about to be sick on Jack Daniel's whisky at breakfast. His vulnerability endeared him to her.

It was an important scene – a 'love at first sight' encounter, set in Cleopatra's villa, where the queen's girlish flirtation with Caesar begins to turn into a story of womanly infatuation with Antony. Elizabeth looked cool and beautiful in yellow silk. Only the week before, she and her husband had announced they were going to adopt the little orphan baby with a malformed hip whom Maria Schell had at last located for them in a German orphanage. Elizabeth was probably still feeling protectively maternal when she looked on the sickly-faced Burton. 'He was so sweet and shaky ... that with my heart I "cwtched" him,' she wrote later, adding, 'that's Welsh for "hug".' And when he then went and blew his lines, her heart went out to him even more.

Walter Wanger, watching from the edge of the set, wrote in the diary he was keeping: 'There comes a time during a movie when the actors become the characters they play. That happened today ... you could almost feel the electricity between Liz and Burton.' This scene was the one that cued its players into a romance that their lives were soon to duplicate sensationally. Yet one of the most curious aspects of the whole affair is the way that the wish-fulfilling media had already begun to write the story as they wanted it to come out. There sat Mankiewicz every night, after he had returned from the day's shooting, labouring till midnight on the script, wearing white gloves to stop himself biting his nails to the quick, taking the historical facts and, consciously or not, infiltrating them with his own shrewd analysis of the grandeur and destructiveness of the star personality. And at the same time, journalists, TV reporters and paparazzi, numbering over a thousand, left with precious little hard news and consequently forced to invent their own, were using any and every circumstantial report of what happened on the set and off it to suggest that the same sort of great romance was taking place between Burton and Elizabeth. The director's screenplay and the media's scenario had a common source in the conduct of the stars. When the two players themselves decided that they wanted the story to 'happen', then it was as if everyone was giving them their cues – as if events outside them, as well as their director and their own volition, were sanctioning and directing them.

A week earlier, on 14 January 1962, Louella Parsons had published a front-page story in Los Angeles claiming that the Fisher marriage was foundering. She quoted no source for this news; but none was needed. 'Planting' an item like this was a traditional Hollywood way of hyping interest in a movie; if *Cleopatra* was that movie, it was never too soon to start work. If it was to do box-office business commensurate with its vast cost, a feverish public desire to see it would need to be stimulated. A Burton–Taylor romance was the best publicity it could have. The Italian and foreign press seized on the Parsons story. Fiction was soon being fed into what was not quite fictional and helping it on its way to becoming corroborated fact.

Eddie Fisher heard (and read) all the rumours. But it still seemed to him that he possessed many proofs of Elizabeth's continuing love for him. Surely, if his marriage were at risk, his friends would tell him – friends like Dr Kennamer, Roddy McDowall (playing Octavius Caesar in the film), Irene Sharaff (the wardrobe designer), Sidney Guilaroff (the hairdresser). What he failed to take in was that these friends were actually her friends. They had belonged to Elizabeth's world long before Eddie Fisher entered it. To them, it was he who appeared the outsider, almost an intruder, compared to a man like Richard Burton, a star who was cut from their own kind of material.

On 26 January, Mankiewicz called in Walter Wanger. 'I've been sitting on a volcano all alone for too long,' he told him. 'I want to give you some facts you ought to know. Liz and Burton are not just "playing" Antony and Cleopatra.' There it was – official, no longer rumour – from the man who was daily creating in text and film the passionate affair that the couple were playing, under different names, in more elegant phrases no doubt, before the Todd-AO-Scope cameras. Wanger's first reaction was: 'Do you think it will help the movie?'

'Walter . . . ' said Mankiewicz, and spread his hands out wide in a 'How should I know?' sweep.

Wanger decided to keep quiet about this revelation – not turn it into anything worse by provoking a confrontation. If Eddie Fisher suspected it, then he was adopting the same tactics as he had done during Max Lerner's flirtation with his wife. Mankiewicz, too, feigned imperturbability. 'When you are in a cage with two tigers, you don't let them know you are terrified.'

Burton, however, seems at times to have been more than a little terrified of what he was involved in. Between the end of February and the first week of March 1961, he lost touch with reality. Though still living in his rented villa with his wife Sybil, he was seeing his showgirl from *Camelot* almost daily and, at the same time, was bringing all the power of a lover to bear on the bewitching woman whom he had sarcastically referred to only a few months earlier as 'Miss Tits'. To a man of his colossal sexual vanity, it was all highly flattering; but it was also frightening to a man with a sense of guilt at the hurt he was doing to others.

To all the parties involved, the movie began to seem like a refuge. There, at least, actions were written, passion was openly displayed, consequences were predestined and predictable.

A love affair of this nature, though, doesn't run smoothly, particularly when the lovers are still dissimulating, hiding their feelings from others and sometimes even from themselves. Burton and Elizabeth agreed to stay away from each other for a few days, perhaps in the hope that their passion would abate, perhaps to test how strong it was. The Fishers went off to Paris. The Burtons stayed behind in their villa. Richard had confided his affair to at least one of his brothers, Graham, and perhaps even to his wife. Every kind of pressure was now put on him. His conscience was appealed to: think how many people would be hurt, how his children in particular would suffer. Yes, he agreed; he had thought of it and he didn't want to hurt anyone. But if he agreed to this, surely he would hurt Elizabeth, the woman he loved.

In short, he was asking for two things that lovers down the ages have demanded, but have seldom been able to reconcile. He wanted to enjoy the adventure of adultery without forfeiting the security of monogamy. 'I have been faithful to thee, Cynara, in my fashion.' The line from Ernest Dowson's poem, which he was fond of reciting, may have occurred to him. He asked himself, could he not be faithful to both women, in his fashion?

28

L'AMOUR FOU

The two helpless spouses, Sybil Burton and Eddie Fisher, could do little for the moment but keep their dignity and their public silence and hope that things would blow over. The two lovers, on the other hand, considered themselves helpless victims of their own irresistible impulses. Burton's brother, Graham Jenkins, has recalled that 'many years afterwards Rich told me that he and Elizabeth had been thrown together.' When Richard was in trouble, Jenkins reflected wryly, his first inclination was to ignore it. Elizabeth's attitude was not to dwell on it, either. Such reactions make for poor communications.

Every day, they were immersed in fantasy, playing great lovers of history. The ever-present attentions of the pestilential paparazzi constituted an audience that was both resented and needed by egotistical natures that abhorred a vacuum. Such was the aphrodisiac that resisted a return to sanity and pushed the pair towards ever greater indiscretions.

Meanwhile, *Cleopatra* rocked and swayed on the financial uncertainties that the rumours about its two stars engendered. Fox executives tried to compute whether scandal would blight their box-office or enhance it.

Fear of family catastrophe – hurting Sybil and the children – periodically chastened Burton. On 5 February, he offered to quit the picture. Wanger closed his eyes at this glimpse of apocalypse, then, dry-lipped, he advised Burton that there was an easier way – just don't do anything more to cause speculation. But that apparently was too difficult a commandment to follow.

The impression created is one of people making promises to be good in the hope that they may never need to keep them.

Eddie Fisher's account remains the most clear-headed, even though he was scarcely a disinterested party. (Sybil Burton has never published what went on in her head or home.) 'Is it true that something is going on between you and Burton?' Fisher says he asked his wife in bed one night, and she whispered, 'Yes.' He then packed a bag and left to stay with some business friends in a Rome villa, only to have Mankiewicz on the phone later in the day ordering him 'to get the hell back to [Elizabeth's] villa before [he] was charged with desertion'. Mankiewicz, a skilled chess-player, obviously saw the moves available in this game of mating and mismating. Fisher attributed the blame to Burton, not his wife. If Elizabeth had fallen for the Welshman, it was due to his baleful seduction; it was not a voluntary surrender by her. Up to a point, this was confirmed by Elizabeth, who later told the world how strongly she had fought against temptation, how it had hurt her to give in, what heartache it had caused her thinking of the innocent people involved: 'but I couldn't help loving Richard.' On 10 February, Wanger arrived on the set to find her in tears, weeping because Burton had been kept waiting by her unpunctuality. He felt he had seen everything now. Eddie Fisher had been advised to 'have it out' with Burton, and his friends had even given him a gun to make his point stick. But Fisher wasn't a trouble-seeking – much less a gun-toting – type; he kept the weapon in the glove compartment of the green Rolls-Royce that had been Elizabeth's Christmas present to him, rather as another motorist might keep a lucky rabbit's foot dangling from the mirror – something to ward off harm, rather than cause it. To get away from the strain of it all, he gave out that the refurbishment of the chalet in Gstaad needed supervising. But he couldn't resist calling Sybil Burton first. Sybil had just been reassured by her husband that the affair was over, but that he would have to 'play along' with Elizabeth until they were through with the film. Sybil had believed him. After all, he had had other affairs, but had always returned to the mooring post she offered. Fisher now disabused her; it wasn't over and Richard was still seeing Elizabeth. It was serious.

On 14 February, according to a Fox publicist, Jack Brodsky, Roddy McDowall, who was sharing the Burtons' villa, came on the set and told Burton, 'Sybil is about to blow the joint.' Burton became agitated. '[Elizabeth] turned white ... when Burton took her into his dressing room to tell her the news.' Fisher had got as far as the city of Florence when he could no longer resist calling his wife, tracing her eventually to Dick Hanley's villa. In tears, she taxed him with what he had told Sybil Burton. Then Burton came on the telephone, drunk, bawling obscenities, threatening to kill the singer if he ever came within arm's length of him. A shaken Fisher re-routed his journey to Milan, meaning to fly back to New York. But his agent there, whom he telephoned, dissuaded him – he would fly over to Europe to bring Eddie aid and comfort. Let them meet in Lisbon. So, abandoning the Rolls-Royce in a parking-lot at the airport –

he says he never saw it again – Fisher embarked for the Ritz Hotel, Lisbon, from where, of course, he called Elizabeth's villa. She wasn't there. Then he called Dick Hanley's: not there, either. In fact, she had been rushed to hospital.

What had apparently happened was that Mankiewicz and Hanley had found her in bed at her villa, being treated by doctors for prostration caused by the upset with Sybil. Sybil had left for New York: some said, to see her lawyers. As Walter Wanger and Hanley were lunching downstairs, they saw a vision of Elizabeth, pale yet lovely, descending the staircase in a blue-grey Dior nightgown to join them. They prevailed on her to go back to bed while they laid emergency plans in the salon. Around 5.15 p.m. Wanger went upstairs to see her. She was sleepy, but hungry. When food was taken up to her a few minutes later, she was seen to have lapsed into a deep sleep. The alarm was sounded. Soon an ambulance sped her to the Salvator Mundi Hospital.

With the Italian press bursting with unconfirmed stories of a suicide attempt, the telephones of Fox executives never stopped ringing. 'The whole world is in front of the hospital,' said Jack Brodsky. A communiqué was issued; nothing but a little food poisoning, it said.

Thoroughly alarmed at the account of all this, Fisher booked a flight back to Rome. On it he encountered none other than Francis, Cardinal Spellman. The prelate, totally ignorant that such dramas were going on, praised the singer and his wife for overcoming so many obstacles to true happiness. As Eddie Fisher said in his memoirs, 'No writer could get away with a script as absurd as this one.'

As was the case in every crisis to date, Elizabeth emerged from hospital looking as if she had crammed a week's rest cure into a single night. 'She'd got her nerve back,' said one observer.

Her first question for her husband, when he entered her room, was why he had broken the bad news to Sybil Burton. He had the answer that the script needed: 'I love you and would do anything to keep you.' She faced the press the following morning as if it were the springtime of a new marriage.

But this left Burton out of the reckoning. He, too, had experienced something of a rebirth during his brief visit to Paris, in connection with his scheduled appearance in the film about the Normandy invasion, *The Longest Day*, which Darryl F. Zanuck had in pre-production. Burton found '*le scandale*' had made him a superstar: no longer just an international actor, but a world-famous star and one that was linked with a legend. 'Burton and Taylor . . . Taylor and Burton.' To his ears, ever tuned to the wavelength of self-interest, it sounded like a mantra. A celebrity chant. Now *he* was of as much interest as *she*. Pursued, photographed, besieged by the media:

his self-image swelled as confidently as his fee soon would. Ironically, it was being separated from Elizabeth for a few days that caused him to realize what his romantic links with her had done for him. Laurence Olivier would very soon send Burton an anxious cable asking him whether he wanted to be a great actor or a household name. 'Both,' Burton replied. It was reminiscent of Mike Todd showing Elizabeth two expensive fur coats on their first anniversary and asking her which she would choose. 'I'll choose both,' he reported she said. The fact that Sybil Burton was far away from her husband in New York increased his conceit by removing the source of guilt from the immediate vicinity. To retain this new-found aura of superstardom meant he must continue to link his fortunes to Elizabeth's. For the moment, that was easy. Both of them still had half of the world's most expensive celluloid epic to finish; its cost was over $20 million already, and still climbing. But what would happen then? Max Lerner had characterized Elizabeth as 'a plunger', someone who would leap off the deep end and take her chance. Burton was a plunger too. He shut his eyes and dived in.

He had helped write a statement that was issued to the press on his return to Rome, denying there was anything between himself and Elizabeth and saying his fidelity to his wife was unaltered and unalterable. Now he denied he had authorized its release – and so avoided actually denying its substance. It possibly struck him as too level-headed – even dangerous, as it might be interpreted as a token of his real intentions. But what were these? Wanger felt that Burton didn't yet know, though he showed no stress or strain on his return, but appeared on the set 'very gay, very cocky, with a glass of beer in his hand'. Elizabeth, too, seemed to observers to be trusting to instinct and biding her time. They had tiny tiffs on the set – he flirted with his girlfriend until Wanger asked her to leave – but these seemed only to incite their interest in each other: an augury, perhaps, of the cohesive tensions of the stormy later years. Burton's promiscuous nature simply gave Elizabeth's determination the backing of steel.

As before, it was the press that moved the game on to the next stage of reward or punishment. 'Row Over Actor [sic] Ends Liz, Eddie Marriage', said a headline over Louella Parsons's by-line on 9 March 1962. Though less than definite on that point – if one read on – this was the distress rocket that the international media had been scanning the heavens to see. Now the legally hedged rumours were out in the open. 'This time she's done it all on her own,' crowed Hedda Hopper, recalling how Elizabeth had blamed her for breaking confidences a year or so earlier.

By coincidence, Elizabeth had just played a scene where Cleopatra finds Antony has left her to marry Octavius Caesar's sister. With a dagger, she rips the royal bedchamber to shreds. The joke spread round the studio –

never confirmed – that she had cried, 'Sybil! Sybil' while she dug the knife into the furnishings.

Spyros Skouras arrived in Rome post-haste following the Parsons story and sent Burton a letter of reprimand, telling him to behave. The Welshman exploded. Elizabeth declared indignantly that if she received a similar telling-off, the film would need a new Cleopatra. The letter to her was hastily cancelled. As if to defy the paymasters who had had the nerve to rebuke them, they were demonstrably affectionate on the set, 'so close you'd have to pour hot water on them to get them apart,' as the film's Rome publicist confided to his opposite number in Hollywood. What Eddie Fisher called 'craziness' had all the classic constituents of *amour fou*.

Looking back on that era and to that affair, one is amazed that a couple of people, mesmerized by their own egos, should have monopolized for so many months the attention of the world. But the 1960s was the decade when permissiveness became the media message. Famous people could misbehave with impunity, and celebrity of the right strength could dilute the hitherto toxic effects of any scandal. The coincidental location of '*le scandale*' in Rome, the city that had been placed on the new map of sensate extravagance by the film *La Dolce Vita*, also made the illicit romance seem pardonable. Undeserved, of course: but celebrity was already the negotiable currency of the age. The importance of those who possessed it was subject to the same inflation as the consumer economies of the time. Publicity had trampled on taste as well as inhibitions: the photojournalist, one of the icons of the decade, had become the arbiter and the artificer of events, just as the chat-show host, alas, was to do a decade or so later. 'A private glimpse of the great becomes the alchemy of the media,' Norman Mailer says, 'the fools' gold of the century of communication.' There was plenty such gold to be mined in the Seven Hills of Rome that spring and summer.

One also has to reckon with the isolation of all the principal players. The movie schedule, depending on production imponderables rather than fixed flowcharts, stretched weeks into months, separating wives from husbands, imposing strains on marriages, causing babies to be born without fathers present at the glad event, creating homesickness, loneliness, idleness. In such conditions, the Burton–Taylor affair was viewed as a monstrous distraction, a play-within-a-play. The privileged audience of cast and crew was able to see only some of it, but avidly filled in the rest and felt as if it was present at some masque of lust being enacted inside a well-walled city-state called Cinecittà. Time was measured only by the progress of the *Cleopatra* epic: all other events were heard about faintly. They belonged to the outside world.

Despite his humiliation, Eddie Fisher remained convinced that Burton did not want to marry Elizabeth, but was only interested in borrowing her stardom to increase his own fame and fee. Burton, he recalled, had once said to him that he, Eddie, didn't need Elizabeth – he was famous already. A case, then, of 'Please, may I borrow your wife?' Perhaps; but Fisher also knew that Elizabeth understood no half-measures. When she went after something, no second thoughts restrained her; no rational counsels prevailed. Her pleasure lay in the desire and pursuit of the whole.

He was left with the tiny consolation that as long as she came to bed at night, then whatever she might be getting up to during the day could be put down to the rumour mills. One night, though, as he recalls it, she didn't come to bed until around 6 a.m. His sense of abandonment and jealousy – particularly acute in that darkest hour before dawn – provoked him to say the words that he maintained he ought to have uttered much earlier: 'Elizabeth, I'm leaving.' It was the moment when the chipmunk turned, looked at its mistress … but this time didn't come back. Eddie Fisher left for New York on 19 March 1962, and didn't see his wife again for two years.

'Everyone believes that Elizabeth kicked Eddie Fisher out,' Richard Burton said to the columnist Sheilah Graham some time later. 'But it was quite the other way round. Elizabeth and I were doing a very difficult scene in *Cleopatra* when she received a note that Eddie had taken off twenty-five minutes before for America. She turned ashen. Imagine that happening to her in the middle of a scene.'

But with Fisher gone, the tension dropped. Burton and Elizabeth were seen – and snapped by a paparazzo – kissing quite openly on the set in their bathrobes. For once, they laughed it off when the photo appeared in the newspapers. Burton's London agent, Hugh French, arrived and said he wanted to make a deal for another picture starring them both. Everyone was eager to cash in before the ball had even come to rest in its slot on the roulette wheel. Notoriety had to be converted into as many dollars as it would buy before the exchange rate dropped. They were now a team – two stars whose individual fame could be made to yield compound interest.

Though now 'at liberty', Eddie Fisher was still to be subjected to a final indignity. Fox had desperately – and successfully – prevailed on him to hold his tongue up to now. But when the newspapers printed unfounded stories that he had had a breakdown and was in a New York mental hospital, he felt compelled to hold a press conference. Even then, he insisted that if there was a separation, it was only a trial one. While he was speaking, a telephone call suddenly came through from Rome. He took it in an anteroom. The photo of Elizabeth and Burton in their bathrobes had appeared that very morning in the Rome papers. It soon became clear to Fisher that his wife wasn't going along with the story he had just given the press. Hurt, baffled, angry and feeling like the fall guy, he had no option but to go back to the couple of hundred media people, restively waiting for the communiqué, and confess lamely, 'You know, you can ask a woman to do something and she doesn't always do it.' There was a stampede for the exit.

A terse, coolly worded statement from Louis Nizer's law firm was issued in New York on 2 April: 'Elizabeth and Eddie Fisher announce that they have mutually agreed to part. Divorce proceedings will be instituted soon.'

The fallout scattered an unexpectedly poignant atom of hope and happiness on the one person who deserved it most. Eddie Fisher was tracked down to a Broadway theatre, where he was watching a play, and asked to comment. 'That's it . . . that's it!' he snapped: what more could he add? Then, as he left by the stage door, to his surprise he found himself being . . . well, if not exactly mobbed, then encircled by a crowd of people, mainly teenage girls. And gradually it sank in that he, who had once been the callow cad who abandoned his wife and then the devoted husband of a stricken star, was once again being viewed and indeed revered as the romantic loner of the bobby-soxers. Eddie perked up and announced that he was off to California to see his children.

'The appearance of their father may come as a shock to the wee ones,' said the unforgiving Hedda Hopper. 'I do hope they'll recognize him.'

29

O MISTRESS MINE!

Elizabeth's first concern was to protect her family. Herself, she could defend very well, legally at least, if not physically – one paparazzo, hiding in the shrubbery, had once punched her in the stomach simply to snap her naturally shocked expression. But she feared for the future of the child she was adopting. The process wasn't quite complete. The Munich orphanage had already contacted the German Embassy in Rome to verify that the child was happy and in good hands. Dick Hanley recalled his employer's alarm. '"They mustn't take her back, Dick," she said to me, "I won't let them. Maria's mine. She's my family now." She got me out of bed at 5 a.m. to get a cable off there and then. She was scared the adoption agency would not consider her a fit and proper person. Eddie, she'd almost forgotten about – the lawyers could take care of that. But when it was about kids, Elizabeth was like a she-wolf.'

Hanley cabled in her name: 'You may rest assured that I love little Maria Petra [the child's family name] and will take care of the child my whole life.' She was to be as good as her word.

Then she braced herself for the media attack. From all quarters of the world, it came. Mainly, and most woundingly, it represented her as a wilful child – i.e., a person unfit to have care of other children. Vatican Radio, without naming her, condemned 'the caprices of wilful children'; *Il Tempo*, not mincing words, termed her 'an avaricious vamp who destroys families and devours husbands'; the British columnist Cassandra bellowed in the *Daily Mirror*, 'The lady is one long eruption of matrimonial agitation'; and cruellest of all was the very magazine that had so recently offered up prayers of thanksgiving for her recovery. Please ... who's my daddy now?' asked *Life*, in a photo-feature suggesting the confusion of identity being caused to the children of several families by her 'headlong rush from one love to the next'. Dick Hanley said, 'She was red-eyed over that story.' The most sensational of the attacks came from the Vatican's own newspaper, *Osservatore della Domenica*, which printed an anonymous, clearly 'inspired' reader's letter. 'Dear Madam,' it began, and went on, 'Children count little to illustrious ladies like you when there is nothing for them to hold together.' Where, it asked, would such a rootless life end, and answered, 'in erotic vagrancy'. Elizabeth, reportedly, was overheard to ask, mockingly, 'Can I sue the Pope?'

Some Fox executives were shocked by events. They belonged to the older generation who feared a pulpit-led boycott of their epic even before it finished shooting. Others, the younger crowd in the boardroom, urged that Burton be signed to a six-picture deal, and a new movie offered to Elizabeth. The manner in which the vox populi differed from the ex cathedra condemnation was made manifest almost the very next day, the one on which Cleopatra entered Rome on a huge mobile sphinx, fifty feet high, hauled by three hundred slaves, preceded by a mammoth cavalcade of bands, horsemen, dancers and acrobats, the whole watched in well-feigned amazement by a crowd of four thousand Roman citizens. Guards armed with pistols but in costume surrounded Elizabeth; an attack was feared on her person, even an assassination attempt. The crowds had been instructed to chant 'Cleopatra! Cleopatra! Cleopatra! Cleopatra!' Instead, as a pale Elizabeth clung to a hidden handrail and wondered if brickbats (or indeed bullets) would be coming her way, she heard a mighty swell of noise and then made out one reiterated syllable: 'Leez! Leez! Leez!' Her mouth dropped open in gratitude. The people were with her, at least the section of them earning a Cinecittà crust. '*Grazie . . . grazie*,' she murmured through the director's bullhorn. 'One of the sweetest, wildest moments I've ever had,' she recalled.

Sybil Burton spent these days in London, at the large, white-painted mansion, Squire's Mount, Hampstead, that she and her husband had bought for their own use and that of the Jenkins clan when they were in town. She tried to get friends to intercede. One who did – and regretted it – was the actor-playwright Emlyn Williams. 'I made a most inappropriate remark within Elizabeth's hearing. I said to Richard that she reminded me of an importunate chorus girl. When I got home from Rome, my wife recalled to me I'd met *her* in the chorus. So there – a proper fuck-up, if you will excuse the Welsh.'

Burton was 'nervous, irritable, drinking', according to Jack Brodsky. His biographer, Melvyn Bragg, has said that the actor 'could have had no idea then of [the] future joint earning power [of himself and Elizabeth]'. This is debatable. On his visit to Rome, en route to Hollywood, his agent Hugh French had told him and Elizabeth of a new screenplay that Terence Rattigan was writing, tentatively entitled *International Hotel* in order to appeal to MGM's nostalgia for a star-packed past and movies like *Grand Hotel*. It was set largely in the VIP lounge at Heathrow Airport, where a mixed bag of celebrities, each with a personal drama to cope with, are grounded by fog. Rattigan had got the idea from just such a contretemps when Vivien Leigh, in one of her manic phases, had tried eloping to New York with Peter Finch. Before they could take off, the fog came down; by the time it lifted, Vivien had recovered her mental balance and was no longer seized by the idea of leaving Olivier. If such an episode could be mutated to fit Burton and Elizabeth, in parts like the Oliviers, would they be interested? They would! Burton's fee would be adjusted to his current status, French assured him, and that was based on his continuing notoriety. Elizabeth showed herself eager, too, since she badly wanted to set up trust funds for the children. Eddie Fisher's current work with Warner Bros., which her illness had interrupted, had been directed to just that end. If all had gone well, she would have made four films for Warners over four years. Work was to have begun on the first three months after *Cleopatra* finished shooting. The Fishers had asked for 40 per cent of the gross, but accepted Warners's counter-offer of 50 per cent of the net – the sum returned to the producers after the distributors and exhibitors had taken their cut. Projects earmarked included Harold Robbins's novel *The Carpetbaggers*, J. D. Salinger's *The Catcher in the Rye*, and a French drama, *The Gouffre Case*, based on a real crime. Eddie Fisher had flown to Switzerland to enlist Charlie Chaplin in playing the detective who tracks down Elizabeth's femme fatale. (The sixty-two-year-old Chaplin was interested, but could not be pinned down.) The first film would be made by The Fisher Corporation, each of the other three would be produced by a company in the name of Elizabeth's three children. Warners also agreed that in any additional picture they starred her in, Elizabeth would take 8 per cent of the first $10 million gross and 10 per cent after that; they guaranteed the gross would amount to at least $10 million within two years of release.

Of course, this stupendously advantageous deal collapsed with the marriage break-up. Instead of a fortune, Eddie Fisher got a bill – for the Warner Bros. office space that he had occupied while deal-making.

The result was that Elizabeth was very keen indeed – as keen as Burton – to see her earning power reflected in another film as soon as possible. Yet of the two, Elizabeth pinned much less importance to money as money. It always had to represent something else: love, family, power ... As Melvyn Bragg states, this time more authoritatively, Elizabeth believed in obsessive love, but Burton didn't. 'He had never totally "lost himself" in anyone else. Nor had he experienced the battery of assault that Taylor brought to bear.' The smart money at Cinecittà was on Elizabeth 'getting him'. The more cautious punters wagered that once he had hoisted his asking price into a higher bracket, he would be back with his wife and family.

Much depended on Sybil and the harmonizing refrain she had adopted every time her marriage had looked in peril in the past. She was an endlessly forgiving wife, putting their unity before pride, and enclosing her husband in a family circle which made him feel wretched and guilty every time he thought of breaking out of it. 'There is no question of a divorce between Rich and me,' said this 'tough and cheerful woman', as Bragg termed her, when she came to Rome at Easter. Her husband nodded and said, 'Absolutely not.' He looked, however, like a man grappling with the problem of two women, two families and two worlds – Sybil's and Elizabeth's. The two had almost collided that Easter, when Sybil's unexpected arrival had surprised him and Elizabeth hiding out incognito – Elizabeth had given the press the slip by putting on a blonde, Marilyn Monroe-type wig – at the coast resort of Campo San Stefano. Burton, alerted by Wanger, hurried back to Rome. Elizabeth returned alone in her car, and arrived sporting a black eye and other facial injuries – attributed variously to a sudden braking of her chauffeured car or to a lovers' tiff. She stayed in hospital, off the picture, during much of Sybil's visit.

To heal the breach, at least, gifts were distributed and Burton had his earliest experience of what a heartless wit called 'crying all the way to the jeweller's'. He left Bulgari's in Rome with a $150,000 emerald brooch that Elizabeth had admired, and a somewhat less costly piece for his wife.

On 28 May 1962, the asp – or, rather, its substitute, a warm-fleshed and wholly innocuous Sardinian garden snake – bit Elizabeth in the palm, not the bosom, as apocryphal wisdom, a.k.a. Shakespeare, had it. (Fox had already heard of all the censorship flutters that MGM had had over the years with that part of Elizabeth's anatomy: they were taking no chances.) 'We have it. Stop. She is dead,' Jack Brodsky cabled Hollywood. The next day, Fox stock plummeted to its lowest level in thirty-three years. It was clear that production was within sight of its end and the film would soon have to be shown.

Elizabeth worked her last day at Cinecittà on 29 May, redoing a scene – the original takes had been damaged in transit to Technicolor in Hollywood – in which Cleopatra and Antony fling reproaches at each other over the latter's new wife. It came too close for comfort to their present predicament. Even worse, Burton continually fluffed his lines in a later scene of Antony divorcing his wife in the formal Roman way by repeating her name thrice before the crowd. Finally, he swore, made a rude gesture and had the set cleared of the press who, as luck would have it, had been allocated one of their few visits on that very day. They left drawing the obvious inference of a husband's guilt, and they weren't thinking of Antony.

On 11 June, the company moved to Ischia – the stars, who had been told to keep a low profile, arrived by helicopter – and Elizabeth played her last scene in Cleopatra's $277,000 barge. It was about two years since she had begun the film. She ended it looking every inch a queen, seated on the prow, purple sails billowing behind her, incense clouds rising from the deck burners, flowers garlanding the masts and strong young male swimmers escorting the barge through the water while handmaidens showered rose petals down on them.

An ambulance was kept on stand-by, lest Elizabeth collapse as the shock of post-production reality set in. Fox need not have worried. She made that transition smoothly. Sixty of Cleopatra's costumes accompanied her and her mother and children back to the Chalet Ariel, Gstaad, a 'home' she had hardly seen since Eddie Fisher purchased it. They would make 'fabulous evening gowns', she said. Later, however, they were returned.

Soon afterwards, after surviving the last of the movie's battle sequences, Burton, too, arrived in Switzerland to recuperate on the one bit of foreign ground that he considered forever Wales – his bungalow haven named Pays de Galles. Sybil and the children joined him. He and Elizabeth were less than two hours' drive apart.

The weeks following were the hardest for Elizabeth, as withdrawal symptoms set in. Without Burton beside her on the set, in her arms before the camera, or across a night-club table on the Via Veneto, she had the sensation – according to Dick Hanley – of 'scenes missing', a technical term meaning the intertitle that editors insert in the film's rough cut to denote what is still to come. Burton had reverted, for the moment, to playing the role of Sybil's husband. Love of wife and children was as strong as a guilty conscience could make it. Would love of self and Elizabeth prove stronger?

But while they waited in this 'dead, flat' state, to quote Burton's diaries, the money deals were being made on their behalf, pushing them ahead into the future together.

Taylor Productions Inc. was now to lend Elizabeth's services to perform in *The VIPs*, as the Rattigan film was eventually called, for $500,000, with overage at $50,000 weekly, and a guaranteed $250,000 extra against a percentage of the receipts. Burton's company, Bushell Productions Inc., did a deal for him at $500,000 likewise, with $25,000 a week in overage compensation. Both companies were Bermuda-registered. With per diem expenses, the stars' combined remuneration was $1,530,000 – some $300,000 more than the budget for all the rest of the cast. Although the performance of such contracts was in no way legally dependent on the stars' romantic hold on each other, it would have been hard for them to appear together if they had already rejected each other. The strain of playing estranged lovers, coming on top of an actual estrangement, would have carried too violent a negative charge. The contract spelled the message out to Burton ever more clearly: Elizabeth was still the senior partner. She was the one whose charisma had helped him double his *Cleopatra* fee. If they broke up now, Elizabeth might suffer a severe emotional loss. His loss might be more calculable in terms of remuneration. Besides, he was still desperately in love with her.

The next move came from him. He asked her to meet him at a hotel on Lake Geneva; they would have lunch. She drove down with her mother and father. He turned up alone, in a convertible, the hood down, his face tanned, his eyes 'like bright blue bulbs'. But not happy-looking – nervous. Both of them, over lunch, assumed the roles of a shy couple on a date in one of those movies where a kiss is not exchanged at the first encounter, but seals the romantic commitment at the fade-out. That, anyhow, is how Elizabeth later recalled it. It left her with a feeling of self-abnegation. She wanted Burton more than ever. But now she conceived a way of having him without the pain that a break-up would cause everyone.

She would become his mistress. It went against the grain of her upbringing and her nature. To be someone's mistress was, to her, to become a secretive, slightly shameful figure: a woman kept, not necessarily by money, but by arrangement. Hitherto she had lived her life openly and in public, and taken what knocks it had given her in full sight of the world. There had been calamities; of course there had been. But the remarriage that followed the divorce had always sanctified the relationship and endorsed her sincerity. Now, if she followed her heart, there would be no resolution – only a relationship. It was no longer the clear-cut 'love me or leave me' dilemma of the storybook about her pets that she'd written as a child.

'By making myself so readily available, I lowered my stature in everybody's eyes but mine – and, as it turned out ... Richard's,' she wrote in a later judgement on herself. Ironically, the words echo the ones that had been on her lips so recently on the set of *Cleopatra*, when the Queen of Egypt, shocked by a premonition of Caesar's assassination, goes down on her knees before the flickering flames that contain her vision. As Elizabeth did so, she had cast a rueful glance at her director. 'You didn't think I could sink this low,' she said.

30

FROM PURGATORY TO PUERTO VALLARTA

On 6 December 1962, a cold, misty morning, Burton and Elizabeth arrived at Victoria Station, London, on the overnight boat-train from Paris. They left in separate cars – blue stationwagon for him, navy Jaguar for her – for the same destination, the Dorchester Hotel, where they moved into separate suites – Terrace for her, Harlequin for him. Sybil Burton made her way alone a little later to the Hampstead house, Squire's Mount. There all parties remained for the next two months: the patient wife up on the hill, the persistent mistress down in the town, the husband-lover still grappling with conscience versus ambition.

'He was in purgatory,' said Stanley Baker; 'in limbo,' said Elizabeth; 'on the bottle,' said his brother Graham (who, resembling him physically, was acting as his stand-in on *The VIPs*). He was 'close to a breakdown'.

Burton's chronic indecisiveness emerged in its most muddled and humiliating form in a *Playboy* magazine interview by Kenneth Tynan. In this, he swore allegiance to monogamy, then insisted that he had 'moved outside' convention 'without investing the other party with anything that makes me feel guilty'. Perhaps so: but in so saying, he failed to mention his wife – she made him feel guilty as hell.

The Jenkins clan at first disapproved of Elizabeth, the interloper, who had broken their unity and might yet destroy their brother Rich. This attitude gradually changed, as she made it her business to get to know Burton's relations. Graham Jenkins, prejudiced in advance, found himself conceding that she was indeed 'a natural woman ... [who] demanded attention and respect'. He took her out to dinner several times; Burton was too drunk on each occasion to accompany them. To his question 'Will you marry Richard?' she avoided giving a straight answer. He needed someone to look after him, she said.

'Isn't Sybil supposed to do that?'

He recalled receiving a reply as curt as the one allegedly made to Hedda Hopper ('Do you expect me to sleep alone?'): 'Sybil was yesterday.'

Burton took every chance before filming began to involve her in his own robustly macho world of rugby football, pub drinking and male cronies who had her joining in the choruses of saloon-bar songs. 'She could look men in the eye,' said Emlyn Williams. 'She also looked as if she could spit in their eye. She was becoming Rich's other half – Oh, poor Sybil!'

Time magazine thought she was playing for high stakes. 'If he should ever marry her,' it said, 'he will be the Oxford boy who became the fifth husband of the Wife of Bath. If she loses him, she loses her reputation as a fatal beauty, an all-consuming man-eater, the Cleopatra of the twentieth century.'

It is again hard to appreciate just how preoccupied the world was with the outcome. But some indication comes from the experience of the Hollywood publicist Warren Cowan, who visited the White House with Kirk Douglas, a client of his, early in 1963, and ran unexpectedly into Jacqueline Kennedy. The President's wife wasted no time on polite protocol, but came immediately to what was on her mind. 'Warren, do you think Elizabeth Taylor will marry Richard Burton?' A few years later, of course, people were asking the same of Kennedy's widow and Aristotle Onassis; the Taylor–Burton affair was of that order. Mankiewicz, even then struggling to retain directorial control of *Cleopatra* in the post-production stages, discerned a death wish in Burton's continued hesitation much like Antony's. 'Show a Welshman a dozen exits, one of which is marked "Self-Destruction", and he will go right through that door.'

Sybil had her supporters' club, too: but without the war cry from her, they were reluctant to enter the fray. And she belonged to the stoic Welsh, not the fighting Welsh; she bore suffering better than she inflicted it. Even so, her pride could show its teeth. With Christmas approaching and his bad conscience sharpened by desire to see his children, Burton slipped up to Hampstead one day. He was obliged to announce himself through the letter-box of the big white hall door. It did not yield an inch. He returned to the Dorchester, got blind drunk and was found by Stanley Baker hunched up in a chair, nearly insensible with remorse. It took three pots of black coffee to sober him up and he slept for twenty-four hours, with Baker guarding the door and not admitting anyone. Sybil was softened by this episode and consented to accompany Burton to the Bakers' for dinner. 'Now it was Elizabeth's turn to worry,' said Baker. 'The phone kept on ringing at intervals through the evening. The first time, I told Rich who it was. The other times, he didn't need to be told. He was one hunted boyo.'

It seemed as if it could not go on ... yet it did. One evening, early in January 1963, Burton was sent up to Hampstead again – this time to ask for a divorce. He set out with a half bottle of cognac to stiffen his resolve. But once inside the family home,'his courage deserted him.

'Have you come to stay?' Sybil asked.

'Yes,' said Burton, in tears.

They settled down in front of the fire with red wine and crème de menthe and he fell asleep. When he awoke, it was after four o'clock and he was in his other mood. He made his way back to the Dorchester, to be asked if he'd told Sybil. No, he hadn't. Well, there's the telephone ... With four-o'clock-in-the-morning courage, he picked it up – and made the break.

No sooner was this done than he began to mend relationships. As he wasn't needed in the early weeks of *The VIPs*, except for a few long shots in which his brother Graham stood in for him, Burton took time off, went to Wales, made it up with his adored sister Cis and mollified the other family members with a mixture of little-boy charm, genuine contriteness and a vow of how much Elizabeth meant to him. 'It was like a cry for help,' said his brother Tom. Astutely, he left it to their compassion – and curiosity – to decide whether to meet Elizabeth or not. How could they deny their favourite brother anything? He brought her down to Wales like a bride, not a mistress, and she was soon acting like one of the family. Down-to-earth (to show she hadn't been spoiled) and yet recognizably a star (to show she was his equal), she was compared by Graham Jenkins to a politician in an election campaign. She wanted their votes. As Burton had once sung in *Camelot*, they did what 'the simple folk' did: walked the cobbled streets, slept in Hilda Jenkins's cramped spare room, got wet in fine Welsh rain, argued the toss over rugby matches long past but still disputed. Emlyn Williams saw the ironic humour of it. It reminded him of Friedrich Durrenmatt's play *The Visit*, rewritten as a family comedy. Instead of the world's richest woman bribing the villagers to cut off the head of the man who done her wrong, here was Elizabeth, the highest paid female star, winning over her lover's suspicious kinfolk to bless their union. Williams later suggested they do *The Visit* as a film. The idea appealed to them – no wonder! There was an element of prophecy as well as psychology in the suggestion. Almost all the roles that the Burtons were to play together on the screen involved the destructive pressures that a strong woman brings to bear on a weak-willed man.

His family's approval of Elizabeth salved a little of Burton's guilt; she got accepted, he got absolved. When they returned to London, feeling like newly-weds, she also got a gold and ruby necklace. They could afford to celebrate. Between them, they would make $3.2 million out of *The*

VIPs; and Elizabeth had already been hired, at half a million dollars, to narrate and appear in a CBS-TV show about London, thus fusing, in *Variety*'s words, 'the world's most distracting foreground with its most illustrious background'. She passed a morning at a Sotheby's auction of the Alfred Woolf collection, spent £92,000 and came back with Van Gogh's painting of *The Lunatic Asylum, St Remy* under her arm. (The world record price for Van Gogh was then £132,000.) Her father bought her a 'little' Utrillo as a delayed birthday gift. Five weeks into the shooting of *The VIPs*, around the first or second week in February 1963, Burton asked her to marry him and she walked on to the set wearing his engagement present, a £50,000 diamond and emerald brooch. She was already wearing jewellery of her own in the film; continuity wouldn't allow her to switch the pieces. Some things money can't buy.

There were now two divorces under way – his and hers. A million dollars is the sum quoted as paid to Sybil Burton for her agreement; it is probably an accurate estimate, though it fails to take account of the fact that it was not a full settlement, but a 'token of intent' – more was to follow. Eddie Fisher was pressing Elizabeth for a similar sum, as well as claiming a half share in their production company, MCL Films. This was currently in dispute. She resisted even more hotly any claim he might make to custody of his step-children. Burton was not to see his own children for a full two years after the separation. 'It was a nightmare time,' he said. His drinking worsened, probably as a consequence: 'In 1963, Rich was an alcoholic,' Graham Jenkins said. He got into pub punch-ups if allowed out on his own, though Elizabeth's presence was protection, as she would behave like a saloon queen and charm the boys in the back room into tolerating Burton's masochistic binges.

In the period immediately following his separation from Sybil, it was Elizabeth who nursed Burton through what amounted to a nervous breakdown. She was the tougher of the two by far. She had been through it all several times; each time the reactor of scandal, widowhood or almost fatal illness had produced a power beyond the materials it fed upon. In retrospect, one can see that her impulsive marriage to Eddie Fisher and her almost immediate regret were uncharacteristic actions entered into on the recoil from Mike Todd's sudden death. Her illness in London had the character of a 'kill or cure' phenomenon; when she emerged from its agonies, it was as if she had been purged and resuscitated in more than physical terms. She had climbed back into command of things with that 'destined' love affair in Rome. Now she felt more alive than ever – whereas her partner, on the contrary, frequently wished himself dead.

The characters they played in *The VIPs* reflected these very tensions. Rattigan had literally written *them* into the screenplay. Elizabeth played a worldly sophisticated woman dissatisfied with chequebook love from her millionaire husband, played by Burton. In the end, however, she gives up her young lover (Louis Jourdan) because she sees that her husband's need for her is the greater (and nobler) impulse; it is also the theme of Bernard Shaw's *Candida*, a play that Burton and Elizabeth ought to have done together.

Burton, too, wanted to start a new life, or thought he did. Even at this early stage in their partnership, he talked about 'redeeming' himself by pursuing the vision he had of Richard Burton as an academic – a university professor. He took Elizabeth to Oxford in May to lunch at Merton College with Professor Nevill Coghill, who had tutored him when he had studied briefly at Exeter College on a Royal Air Force scholarship in the closing months of the war. He told Coghill that he fancied himself in the title role of Marlowe's play *Dr Faustus* – 'Elizabeth wants to carry a spear,' he added, in what was to become a casual, sometimes downright churlish attitude towards any pretensions she might have.

She did not seem to mind the implied put-down that he repeated in many forms, in many interviews, over many years. This puzzled people who did not realize that what Elizabeth wanted from Burton was something besides sex. As Max Lerner had lent his intellect to their relationship, so Burton lent her the glory of a stage tradition that made film stardom look pale and cheap. Burton represented classical training, literary respectability, theatrical achievement, all the accomplishments in which Elizabeth felt deficient. His ability to remember and recite soliloquies, sonnets and anthologies of English verse impressed her and made her proud to have such a man love her. At least, it did at first. Later on, when she had sat 'the show' round many times and seen inebriation take its toll and the literary polymath turn into the party bore, she was probably not so sure. At such times she would throw her arms out wide in a gesture of mock-deprecation and announce: 'I don't know anything about the theatre, but then I don't need to – I'm a star.'

On his thirty-eighth birthday, she gave him every single volume of the Everyman library of classics, each one bound in calf. It was as if she had made the library fit for her lover's intellect by adding to it the only gift in her possession: its binding. One volume she singled out for the special care and attention of the bookbinder: Robert Burton's *Anatomy of Melancholy*.

Once he had officially separated from Sybil, Burton, who liked order in his home life, had no one who could organize things for him as she used to do. Instead, Elizabeth's entourage closed around him: his isolation from friends and associates was beginning. The central support of Elizabeth's working life was Richard Hanley, the secretary she had inherited from Mike Todd; and he protected her loyally. Her attitude to the outside world had been hardened by experience. The few interviewers to whom she now granted audience often had to prove their worth by putting up with endless delays, inconveniences and frustrations before they reached her. She would let her children be photographed – but no interviews with them. All employees had to sign an undertaking not to breach her confidence. She had come out of *Cleopatra* more regal than when she went in, and now she had a queen's treasury to enforce her rule.

Yet, even here, there was a difference between her and Burton. The latter was still astonished by the swift rise in his market worth. But after twenty years in the business, Elizabeth knew that no matter how much she was paid, it was never enough. Not because she was unnaturally greedy; simply because someone else could still turn a profit on her. For her, the real victory lay in minimizing the amount of money that her stardom made for other people. Mike Todd had been a good tutor in this respect. Hence her increasingly stubborn stance on terms: up-front money, per diems, gross-profit participation and all the tangible and intangible vanities that boost a star's ego at the expense of a producer's budget. Her trump card was that, basically, she didn't like and didn't need the work. 'A call to the set,' wrote Peter Glenville, one of her directors, 'draws a reaction as if from someone disenchanted by her trade whose patience has worn thin.' Once there, she earned her money, but it was for the money she worked. 'Richard is still full of wonder at the magical apparition that emerges from their mutual Aladdin's lamp,' said Glenville, 'whereas Elizabeth would rather know the market value of the lamp itself.'

She did not need acting the way Burton did; and if she had married any other man but an actor at this stage of things, she might well have given up working and just settled for living. But Burton had become an indissoluble part of her life, and the fact that he was wholly and pre-eminently the actor is what gave Elizabeth the incentive to continue her own career. However, not just yet: for the next year or more, she did not make a single film. Burton would quip that when he was back on stage, Elizabeth would be in the wings, knitting. A dedicated actress, hearing this put-down from her man, might have rung the curtain down on their affair. Not Elizabeth: it coincided exactly with how the future Mrs Burton saw herself. 'I love not working. I have never felt so alive before ... If I get fat enough, they will not ask me to do any more films.' What would Burton and she do? '[We] will read together, but different books, everything from the sublime to the ridiculous, from Shakespeare to the comic strips.'

The VIPs was finished at top speed and reached the screen soon after *Cleopatra*'s New York premiere; at one point, it was outgrossing that $37 million film. Suddenly scripts started arriving. Among the few that weren't bent on using Burton as bait to hook Elizabeth was Hal Wallis's production of *Becket*. He decided to do it, even though his fee was only $300,000, much less than he received for *The VIPs*. After all, this was 'quality'. Elizabeth, sensing that the conscience-tortured prelate was the better part, persuaded him to take it and let Peter O'Toole play the king. Her intuition was good; she knew the conflict of loyalties Burton had been through. Just as she had found that playing Maggie the Cat gave her the outlet she needed for the loss of her man, so Burton found in Thomas à Becket a catharsis for his own moral dilemma.

Making *Becket* at Shepperton Studios in the summer of 1963 was a happy time for both of them. Burton had the kind of 'theatrical' part that tested him, a co-star in O'Toole who kept him up to wary pitch, and the joy of seeing Elizabeth on almost daily visits – once she hid herself in a prop laundry basket on the set and an astounded Peter O'Toole found her grinning up at him when, as Henry II, he wrenched off the lid in his pursuit of a serving wench. O'Toole suggested she continue her 'performance' in The King's Head, the local pub, and she promptly tied a barmaid's apron round her couture dress, slipped behind the bar and pulled beers for him and the regulars. Her accent became noticeably more English in this period. She brought Michael and Christopher down to Shepperton village for shopping, ice-cream and kite-flying on the green. She saw little Maria through the third of what were to be five operations to re-align the child's malformed hip. So infected was she by her own family happiness that she extended it wherever she thought she could do good. Thus a talented thirteen-year-old child who was having to give up ballet school because the tuition was too expensive for her parents had her fees paid by Elizabeth. This was only one of her many small, impulsive charitable acts, most of them unpublicized.

One day in mid-June, however, Elizabeth appeared at the studios with eyes red from weeping. *Cleopatra* had just had its New York premiere; the reviews varied from mixed to downright savage. She was weeping for Joseph Mankiewicz, not for herself, though she had every cause. 'Overweight, over-bosomed, overpaid and under-talented, she sets the acting profession back a decade,' said David Susskind in a TV judgement. *Newsweek* paid her a stinging backhander: 'Miss Taylor is not the worst actress in the world.' Her 'shrill, rasping voice' was mentioned in nearly every notice. A balanced judgement, though, would have to concede that the film itself suffers from the conditions under which it was made – and then unmade by the new regime at Fox. Darryl F. Zanuck had staged a successful coup d'état against Skouras. The film had undergone severe cutting and re-editing. Elizabeth handles the tight-knit first half well, as a kittenish co-ed of a queen seducing her professorial Caesar; but in the second half, her womanly passion deteriorates into a prolonged argy-bargy with Antony, petulant and disdainful by turn. The two of them are totally at variance with the public's expectation of great lovers – though their relationship is curiously prophetic of the Burtons in their final stages of disenchantment with each other, nearly twenty years later.

Advance reports suggested *Becket* would be a sizeable hit, and it was. Burton was 'hot', and was immediately signed up for *The Night of the Iguana*, a version of the Tennessee Williams play which John Huston was to direct in Mexico. His co-stars included Sue Lyon, fresh from playing the nymphet in *Lolita*, Deborah Kerr, and Ava Gardner playing the warmly sensual woman who brings carnal comfort to Burton's spiritually burnt-out priest. It was a project that must have sent a distant early-warning signal to Elizabeth. She knew from her own experience on *Giant* and *Raintree County* just how a lonely location loosened one's inhibitions. She also knew how dangerous a rival Ava Gardner might be – after all, she and Burton weren't actually married yet. There was time – and temptation, too – for another woman to turn Burton's head. To 'steal' him from Elizabeth Taylor: what a reverse takeover that would be! Packing her children off to school or into the care of a nurse, Elizabeth boarded the Mexico-bound jet with Burton.

They flew via Montreal and made a detour to Toronto, where Burton confirmed plans for John Gielgud to direct him on stage in *Hamlet* the following year. At each stopover, they experienced a physical battering from pressmen and fans that gave them no quarter and had Richard Hanley and Jim Benton, Burton's secretary, forming a kind of human airlock around them to get them from one form of transport to another. Six-year-old Liza, who accompanied them, got her first terrifying view of stardom as she was held in safety by Burton above his head in a storm of camera flashes like sheet lightning, while microphones thrust against her mother's grim, tight-lipped face looked as if they were sucking the breath out of her.

No wonder Puerto Vallarta seemed a haven of tranquillity – a tiny fishing community some three hundred miles to the north of Acapulco. To them, the homeless ones, this was to be the place where they first sank their roots. There were no modern fitments to speak of, plenty of flies and a mañana attitude to life. But like great personages who wanted to escape their court – for a day or two anyhow – it was a simplicity on which they could throw themselves with relief. It was like taking the honeymoon before the marriage that they couldn't yet have.

They rented a house that was in two parts, straddling an alleyway – later joined by a connecting 'Bridge of Sighs'. It had a tiled roof, secluded patios, stucco walls, four floors and six bedrooms. It resembled a peasant dwelling only in the absence of window glazing. Shutters allowed the air to circulate, Caribbean-style, through every room in the building. It made the occupants feel outdoors, whilst heavy wrought-iron gates made sure that the outdoors didn't come inside uninvited. Thick, voluptuous-looking tropical foliage fenced the courtyard; banana and papaya plants, lemon trees and coconut palms shaded the upstairs terrace. It reminded Elizabeth of a lusher version of Little Swallows and she fell instantly in love with it. There was room for all the children, most of the entourage, and their expanding menagerie of cats, dogs and cockatiels. Built for a foreigner and sited in the quarter of Puerto Vallarta nicknamed 'Gringo Gulch', the house was known as the Casa Kimberley, after the ex-owner. Locals knew it, less romantically, but probably more in line with the Tennessee Williams scenario that Burton was here to enact, as '*la casa de los zopilotes*' or 'the house of the buzzards': a reference to a nearby garbage tip frequently covered with the scavenging birds. Burton and Elizabeth kept the other name when they bought it three months later for $40,000 – and ignored the local one that seemed to symbolize film stardom in its untreated state.

'I can live here,' said Elizabeth simply.

'I can write here,' said Burton.

Both of them felt that this extraordinary and turbulent year had at last brought them to the quieter shores of love. For once, they were content not to seek the wilder ones.

31

A LIFE IN THE THEATRE

Burton's fee for *The Night of the Iguana* was half a million dollars and a percentage of the gross. The money was immediately pledged, along with the £25,000 fee he earned for a walk-through appearance in *What's New, Pussycat?*, to the total cost of his divorce settlement. This reportedly totalled $1.5 million, the last half-million to be paid in annual alimony instalments. He showed no resentment, however. It was as if surrendering his money staunched his guilt. A poor Richard had nothing but himself to offer to a rich Elizabeth: what she saw was what she got. It was a romantic gesture on his part, as well as a financial penalty – 'the groom stripped bare', rather than the bride. Yet Burton could not stop talking of money, the tangible collateral of what he called his 'diabolical fame'. That phrase crops up in interviews again and again – interesting in view of his declared intention to play Faustus. Endlessly, he talked of the things money could buy. Elizabeth was far more casual about these, and indeed was notoriously careless about her possessions.

John Huston was aware that he had assembled a combustible cast of talents, and mischievously gave every star a pre-production present of a gold-plated Derringer pistol – there was one for Elizabeth, too, even though she was not in the film – as well as five bullets. Each was engraved with the name of one of the other stars. Huston clearly hoped for 'action'.

Elizabeth's daily routine spared her most of the tensions generated on location. She would rise early, spend an hour or so tutoring little Liza in reading, then hand the child over to a nanny and change into one or other of the forty outfits she had brought to this fishing village. She was seldom seen twice in the same one. Then she stepped into *The Taffy*, a motor-launch that Burton had rented (and, inevitably, renamed to signify his Welshness). Like the Egyptian queen in her barge, Elizabeth was ferried six miles along the coast to a dramatically rugged promontory called

Mismaloya, approachable only by sea, where the film was shooting. Huston's assistant Thelma Victor kept a diary during the production and chronicled some of the resplendent entrées that Elizabeth made. One day she appeared in 'a Mexican-made green and white shift over a bikini bathing suit, beaded thongs of turquoise and gold on her feet and huge black flowers on her head – made of human hair and bought from an elegant Paris couturier's collection of accessories'. On another occasion, she chose a loose, sack-like outfit in white batiste, trimmed in red, but semi-transparent in strong sunlight, which suggested that she was bra-less. Her jewellery, however, compensated for any undue exposure. Her current taste ran to gold chains looped across her bosom to the navel. The sun also caught 'a magnificent gold ring loaded with pearls and what looked like either pink diamonds or rubies'. Burton took a look at this ensemble and quipped, 'She's seducing me again.'

If so, Elizabeth seemed intent on ensuring that no one else did. She ate lunch with Burton, at a table apart from the others. She was friendliest with Deborah Kerr, who was accompanied by her husband, the novelist Peter Viertel. Towards Ava Gardner, she was polite but distant. But to Sue Lyon, she and Burton hardly said a word. Sometimes their lunch came by hamper from the boat. Burton had an assumed, or genuine, sense of intimidation in Elizabeth's presence and was heard to ask her permission before he photographed the other female stars.

After lunch, Elizabeth would sunbathe on a rock. She was observed reading a copy of the newly published Denning Report on the Profumo affair – the scandal which was currently unsettling the Macmillan government whose War Minister, John Profumo, had admitted lying to Parliament about his relationship with a call-girl, Christine Keeler, and her friend Mandy Rice-Davies. A few months earlier, Elizabeth's lawyers had protested to the London *Daily Express* about a drawing by Giles, the paper's celebrated cartoonist, which, she alleged, had suggested that she herself was no better than those girls. A sum in settlement was paid to charity. Memories of the Gloria Wandrous role she had been forced to play probably still rankled.

Her companions noticed she had put on weight. She didn't seem to mind this at all; it could be easily burned off by a few days' dieting and exercise. Besides, not having to worry about her camera image was part of the sabbatical she was taking.

Once John Huston called a halt to the day's shooting, Elizabeth collected her husband-to-be and they both headed for the launch. Ava Gardner used to return to Puerto Vallarta on water skis, with beach boys as her escorts; but Elizabeth already looked settled into the ways of marriage. As they chugged through waters reddened by the Mexican sunset, the white wine was opened and Elizabeth could be seen in silhouette apparently tipping the bottle to her lips, then passing it to Burton. Once back in the Casa Kimberley, they showered and dined by candlelight as insects blackened the mosquito nets veiling the ever-open windows. Sometimes they drove down to Playa de Oro, sipped beer, and watched the white surf against the black, black waves. Once, Burton stripped off to his jockey shorts and ran into the sea, declaiming a verse of Swinburne.

'This is the life,' he bawled.

'If you don't come out,' Elizabeth yelled back, 'it'll be the death of you, too.'

Old Indian women slapped clothes against the rocks of the stream to get them clean; naked children ran around everywhere and mongrel dogs with the enlarged eyes of starvation victims lapped up the beer slops in the local cantinas. It was a strange place for the world's most talked-about film stars to call home, but, for a spell, they were like happy bohemians.

All the same, signs of disintegration were already apparent to some of their companions. When not being chaperoned, Burton became a trial to his co-stars. A certain semblance of dissipation fitted his role in the film. But to the women who were his co-stars, he was a headache of another kind – a bore. He never flirted with them, was never in the least unfaithful to the absent Elizabeth. But he moved among them, his trail marked by empty bottles, declaiming stanzas of Shakespeare in ringing tones, switching to music-hall songs, then to a Lorca poem, a passage of Dylan Thomas ... and gradually slipping over the edge of intoxication into justification for his illicit romances, his 'great love' for Elizabeth, the trashiness of Hollywood, the dishonesty of the film business.

'After a time,' said one of the crew, 'you'd say to yourself, "This guy is having a breakdown."'

Emboldened by drink, yet not daring to overstep the mark and draw Elizabeth's wrath upon himself, Burton would mock his own fidelity by proposing to greet his beloved's arrival with a tableau of himself and the female stars in orgiastic postures on the barroom floor. But defiant raillery quickly subsided into prudence. When she entered the cantina he'd had erected at the location so as to have somewhere to drink, Elizabeth would spy him sitting next to the plainest girl he could find, chatting her up with mock-romantic spiel. Elizabeth sensed when it was time to call 'Cut' to this performance.

'I've been sitting here for half an hour, just waiting for you to say hello to me, you boozed-up, burned-out Welshman.'

'Oh, hello, darling,' Burton would say weakly, as if spotting her for the first time.

The best present that Elizabeth received that Christmas was the arrival

Maggie, the sexually frustrated wife in Cat on a Hot Tin Roof, *with Paul Newman as her impotent husband,* *Elizabeth found a new style in edgy hysteria. Being tragically widowed seemed to give her performance an additional* *cutting edge.*

Poster for the film of Tennessee Willia[m's]
play: the poster was daring for its day.

A famous pose in Suddenly, Last
Summer. The beach in Spain was
cleared of people while the scene was
shooting.

*(right) The Wilding children, Christopher (left) and
Michael, with their mother and step-father Eddie Fisher
living in England in 1960.*

(below) Montgomery Clift, on the set of Suddenly, Last
Summer, *takes a walk with little Liza Todd.*

(Above) *What Twentieth Century-Fox paid a million dollars (and more) to get: the 'official' photograph of Elizabeth made up for her role as the Queen of the Nile.*

(Above right) *Elizabeth is solicitous, Burton is hung-over: their first scene together in* Cleopatra *generated a sympathy that quickly turned to love.*

(Below right) *Director Joseph L. Mankiewicz (extreme left) supervises Cleopatra's nude bath scene. Years later, advertisements for Elizabeth's perfume, 'Passion', adopted a similar setting of Roman hedonism.*

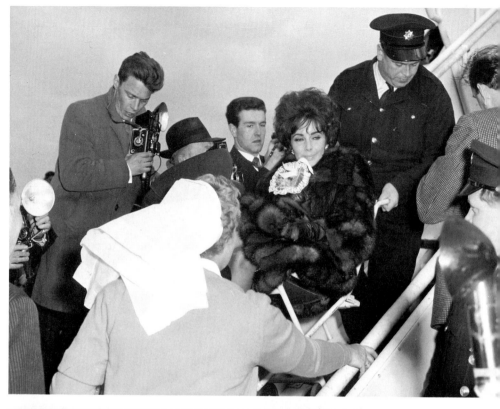

(Above) *Just one of the me[...] crowded exits from hospita[...] this time being carried aboa[...] the aircraft at London airport following her 'mira[...] recovery from pneumonia in March 1961.*

(Left) *Convalescing with Bobby Kennedy following he[...] 1961 illness. The throat sca[...] from her tracheotomy operation is still visible.*

(Above) *December, 1961. The Fishers entertain Richard Burton on the set of* Cleopatra *at Cinecittà. Before long, Eddie would find his marriage under threat.*

(Left) *March, 1964: 'The Burtons' at last, just married in Suite 810 at the Ritz-Carlton, Montreal.*

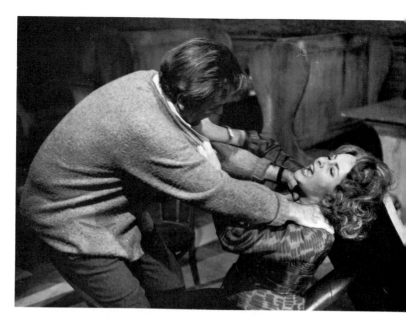

The Burtons at war ... and
peace – The two extremes of
their performances in
Who's Afraid of
Virginia Woolf?
Audiences thought they saw
their own married life
mirrored in the stormily
wedlocked couple on screen.

Showing off some of her jewellery collection. This emerald and diamond set was given her by Burton and became her favourite.

(Right) *Knockabout comedy was something the Burtons also knew how to play.* The Taming of the Shrew *provided non-stop evidence.*

(Opposite above) *A day out with the family: Left to right, Beth Clutter Wilding (Michael's wife), Maria Burton (Elizabeth's adopted orphan child), Michael Wilding Jr., Liza Todd, Elizabeth with her grand-daughter Leyla on her knee, Richard Burton, Christopher Wilding.*

(Opposite below) *With Burton and Clint Eastwood, his co-star in* Where Eagles Dare, *Elizabeth shows off some of the pets that caused the yacht they were quarantined on in the Thames to be nicknamed 'the world's most expensive dog kennel'.*

(Below) *Elizabeth and Men. John Huston's* Reflections in a Golden Eye *teamed her with Marlon Brando as a mismated couple on a US army base. Her hair-style was also thought to be rather mismated.*

(Left) *Director Joseph Losey orchestrates a row between Elizabeth and Mia Farrow in* Secret Ceremony. *It was an over-decorated disaster.*

(Left) Grand guignol *in* Night Watch. *The future didn't look too attractive, either.*

(Opposite above) *The glamour of being 'The Burtons'. Richard and Elizabeth at the height of their joint stardom.*

(Opposite below) *December, 1976: The farmer takes a wife. John Warner and Elizabeth announce their engagement.*

(Right) *Elizabeth takes to the stage for* The Little Foxes: *the fashions in period villainy helpfully concealed her thickening figure.*

The other men in her life: Aristotle Onassis (above), then married to Jacqueline Kennedy, willingly came to her side when she needed advice and comfort ...

... Henry Wynberg escorted her between marriages, but she left him with a gold watch for remembrance ...

. . . Malcolm Forbes, the millionaire publisher, was closer than a business adviser, but his sudden death soon after she had been the guest of honour at his Moroccan party in 1989 left her lonelier than ever.

(Left) *Just one of the family: Elizabeth meets some of Richard's brothers and sisters on a visit to Pontrhydyfen.*

(Right) *Before Elizabeth took off: on her launch tour for her perfume 'Passion', fat reflected her unhappiness as the wife of Senator John Warner.*

Even the grave proves not to be a private place. Elizabeth's bodyguards open umbrellas to shield her from the paparazzi waiting to catch her pre-dawn visit to the Swiss cemetery where Burton was buried.

of little Maria. The hitherto disabled child was able to walk unaccompanied down the ramp of the airplane and into her adoptive mother's arms. On 25 December, all the poor children of Puerto Vallarta found Elizabeth and Richard paying visits to the wood and tin shacks with sackfuls of toys. On their way back to a Taylor family reunion, a newspaper man asked her about Eddie Fisher. 'Please,' said the châtelaine of Casa Kimberley, 'do not spoil my Christmas.'

But things were moving. By the turn of the year, the matrimonial bindings began to be loosened, if only in preparation for them to be tied again. First, Sybil Burton filed for a Mexican divorce. Immediately, Elizabeth ordered her wedding dress. Then, after a rapid-fire exchange of insults and an obstinate and noisy resistance by lawyers for both sides, the Taylor–Fisher divorce petition was filed in Puerto Vallarta under a Mexican law that allowed one party to do so without the other entering an appearance. Those whose heads were swimming, trying to follow what *Time* magazine called 'the not-quite-polygamous marriage ritual that has been called, "serial monogomy"', could take comfort from Burton's acidulous comment. 'If you come down to it,' he said, 'Elizabeth may not even have been legally married to Mike Todd [in Acapulco, Mexico] after the Wilding divorce. So that means no one was ever married to anyone really, and we might just as well start again and get married and divorced on the Koran.'

On 25 January 1964, giving the media the slip by flying to Toronto direct from Los Angeles under the assumed names of 'Walter Rule' and 'Rosemond Sutherland' (Elizabeth's middle name and a variant of her mother's stage name), they gained the sanctuary of the Royal Suite at the Ritz-Carlton Hotel, and waited for their baggage to arrive by train – all one hundred pieces of it.

There was still a backlash against them from organized lobbies of moralists – and one Congressman tried to darken the lights on Broadway in advance of *Hamlet*'s opening there by seeking to have Burton's US entry visa revoked on the grounds that his presence would be 'detrimental to America's morals'.

All this might have put a sizeable dent in their careers ten years earlier. But the 1960s had already manifested a youthful disdain for conventional morality. Beatlemania was currently rife. The Fab Four were set to make their first US trip that August. *Time* magazine hadn't yet dubbed it the 'swinging' era – it didn't do so until 1967, later than most people think – but anything of English provenance was in fashion. The future Mr and Mrs Burton found that this Anglophilia took the sting out of their notoriety. They were on the right side of the trendy date-line: famous, youngish, rich, talented, peripatetic, quotable and outrageous. In fact, they were adopting that heady, if precarious attitude that it didn't matter what they did, so long as they did it brazenly and unapologetically. They themselves were of more interest than the category of their sins.

There was a physical side to all this celebrity, however, and it was not so pleasant to live with. The fear of assault, or worse, was omnipresent. The perils of media exposure had collected around Elizabeth in particular. Taunts, curses, spittle occasionally flew her way, even from 'respectable' people. The couple now engaged a burly bodyguard called Bob LaSalle; soon Elizabeth would have a chauffeur, Gaston, with a black belt in judo. It was easy to sneer at the numbers of people who served the Burtons in one capacity or another, and to consider them as ostentatious symbols of their employers' grandeur. In fact, so far from ornamenting the totems around which the entourage danced, they were the taboos that the king and queen had to endure by reason of their own pre-eminence. The time would come when the Burtons could not make a move without them. Just when celebrity had given them the key to the city and the world, they were discovering that the one lock it did not fit was the doorway to their own freedom.

This phenomenon of celebrity incarceration, familiar to the rich and famous in other countries and careers, was visited with particular ferocity on the two film stars over the next few months. Everywhere was their kingdom, yet nowhere was safe. Hisses, faint at first but growing in volume, greeted Elizabeth's appearance at a charity preview of Burton's *Hamlet* in the O'Keefe Center – it happened to be her thirty-second birthday. She sat tight in the second row, biting her lip, while people started a slow hand-clap that was only stopped by the curtain rising. At the first interval, on Burton's orders, ushers sprinted down the aisle and formed a human wall of bodyguards, shouldering aside people in front of her as she made for the directors' suite. This had to be repeated at the second interval. Burton took only two curtain calls, as if to show his resentment of the way Elizabeth had been treated. 'She put twenty-eight minutes on the play,' he joked sourly.

They had nourished the hope that once they were married, this aggressive voyeurism would end or at least tail off. On 6 March 1964, Elizabeth's divorce became final. Nine days later, the new wedding ring was slipped on to her finger in Suite 810 of the Ritz-Carlton Hotel, Montreal. They had had to leave Ontario, which didn't recognize the validity of Mexican divorces, and get married in Quebec province, which was less picky. Elizabeth wore an Irene Sharaff yellow gown, inspired by the one she wore when she and Burton had done their first scene together on the *Cleopatra* set: a proof that if journeys end in lovers meeting, then hangovers sometimes end in their marrying. Other mementoes of Rome adorned her:

the thirty-four-inch switch of Italian hair augmenting her own headdress, and the white Roman hyacinths entwined in it. There were eleven guests including her parents, six of them from the entourage. Burton had given her diamond and emerald drop earrings for her birthday; his wedding present was a matching necklace. (This set was to become her favourite jewellery, notwithstanding other items of greater carat and celebrity. She wears them to this day at events she patronizes – the AIDS charities, in particular.) The wedding service was on Unitarian lines. They hoped to repeat their vows in a synagogue in New York, but in fact never got around to it.

Far from diminishing public attention, their marriage only increased it. They now possessed the dynamic appeal of an official duo – 'the Burtons'. This denoted more than a union of celebrities. It was to become a label for a life-style. Elizabeth and Richard were not just loving consorts; they were inordinate consumers. They ordered without reflection, wolfed down the fare, signed the bill without a glance at the total. The Burtons were extravagant by nature and arrogant by inclination. They lived life on a scale few hereditary rulers except the despots of Africa or Arabia would have thought prudent for either their people to witness or their treasury to support. On screen, under a succession of different names, in different films, they played characters who were in many respects representations of themselves. Time was past when Elizabeth drew on the fiction of her films for what she hoped would be her experience of life. Now her life was lived on a grand scale. Her activities were publicly reported (whether truthfully or not) and intensely followed (whether approved of or not). It was more tempting than ever to surrender to the lure of a screenplay which invited her and Burton to bring their public images into its plot, characters and incidents.

But she did not doubt, either, that the teaming of herself and Richard Burton was basically sexual in its fascination for the public. Together, they suggested love. What kind of love? she was asked, and candidly admitted, 'illicit love, at first; now, married love', although 'there's still a suggestion of rampant sex on the wild.'

This impression would have been confirmed by anyone who had followed the progress of Burton's *Hamlet* from Toronto to Boston and Broadway. Love sometimes took a battering. In Boston, a crowd of over one thousand people packed the Ritz-Carlton Hotel lobby, and in scrambling through them Elizabeth sprained her shoulder and had a strand or two of hair wrenched out by people crying, 'See if it's a wig.' But when they reached New York, the mauling ended. Replacing it was an altogether stranger event; a nightly rite of semi-mystical worship outside the Lunt-Fontanne Theater on 46th Street. Prurient, sceptical, hopeful, nervously wisecracking or unashamedly adoring, hundreds and sometimes thousands of people surrounded the stage door. Stanley Elkin, an *Esquire* magazine writer, mingled with them one night and left a graphic report of the phenomenon.

'All stood there, holding their ground, rooted to the spot by some strange, felt presence of history, some current event. They might have been people at an accident, across the road from a fire, a wreck, or people come to watch a demonstration – a wedding, a riot, a famous Star come to pick up her husband, another famous Star.' At least three times a week she came, wearing a different outfit each time, waiting in her chauffeured car until the mounted police were in line before her driver unlocked the passenger door and she crossed the few feet of sidewalk, swiftly, radiantly, head poised and turning this way and that just enough to allow anyone with a camera to snap her before the stage door was whipped open and she slipped inside. On the trip back to the Regency Hotel, it might take the Cadillac carrying her and Burton ten minutes to inch half a block through the crowd. Burton loved it all. He raved about 'the crowds, the enthusiasm'. Elizabeth, however, agreed with Truman Capote, who had witnessed with anxiety – for a Cadillac was a fragile defence between them and the mob – what he called 'an exalted condition of libidinous excitement'.

'For God's sake, Richard,' she snapped, 'don't you realize the only reason all this is happening is because they think we're sinners and freaks?'

What she *did* love was the feeling of being part of the theatrical company, if not in the cast of the play. She saw *Hamlet* some forty times: seated in the stalls, standing in the wings, often a champagne glass in hand to plight a love-troth with her man between scenes. Audiences sensed the running romance kept up tantalizingly off-stage, but which they might glimpse if they waited, craning their necks, applauding at the end, louder, louder ... Elizabeth was a part of Richard's stage world now – by marriage, if not by art.

Burton had legitimized this the day after their marriage in Montreal. After taking several curtain calls, he had stepped up to the footlights, silenced the applause and said, 'Ladies and gentlemen, I should like to quote from the play you have just seen – from Act Three, Scene One. "We will have no more marriages."' Now it was he who was reciting the standard vow that Elizabeth had made whenever she had married each of her four previous husbands.

Before *Hamlet*'s run ended on Broadway, she was up there beside him, sharing an evening of poetry and prose in a charity benefit for Philip Burton's drama school, steeling herself to do what she had never done before – face a live audience. At first she sweated so much that the armpits of her midnight-blue silk dress turned black. She 'screwed up' a few lines. Sadistic titters were heard. She later related how she felt Burton's body heat rise in embarrassment and sympathy. Then professional discipline steadied her; adrenalin energized her; she got the sense of 'theatre'; and she raised her eyes and looked at the audience. Wonder of wonders, her eyes didn't drop out of their sockets.

Hamlet grossed over $400,000 in Toronto. In Boston, in a fortnight it made $140,000. The Broadway run (and a TV film made of it) accounted for takings of nearly $6 million. Burton's personal earnings were put at well over $900,000. He had paid off over half the cost of his divorce. Elizabeth must have felt it was worth losing a hank of hair for that.

32

'FOR THE MONEY, WE WILL DANCE'

The mid-1960s were their years of prodigious earnings. Film companies rushed to throw money at the Burtons. Sign up one or other, or best of all both; pay them what their advance party of lawyers, agents and accountants demand as their market worth; comply with their requirements as to how the money should be paid, where on the earth's surface it should be banked, to which company, trust or account it should be credited. That was all there was to it, or so it seemed. 'For the money, we will dance,' said Burton.

Though Elizabeth hadn't made a film since *The VIPs*, she had been in the news so continuously that she had gained more exposure than many stars who went from film to film. But she was anxious to do a joint project. *The Sandpiper* seemed perfect. It had emerged from Dalton Trumbo's typewriter as a 'taut little drama about a poor young woman living on a beach with her four-year-old illegitimate kid who becomes involved with a minister' – to quote its author. For a million-dollar fee, plus percentages, etc., etc., etc., Elizabeth consented to play the, by now not too poor, reasonably young 'young woman'.

'It is a potboiler,' Burton said bluntly.

'It is a moneymaker,' she insisted.

She was right. What he evaluated in his head, she felt in her bones. Illicit lovers, a morally weak man, a determined woman, love and concern for a child, a bohemian life-style proving stronger than bourgeois conventions, happiness redeeming sin, love conquering opposition: *The Sandpiper*, by the time Vincente Minnelli finished directing it, was the Burtons' own story in another guise. Even the reverend's wife in the film is a Sybil Burton-like figure: stoic, suffering, losing, retiring hurt, but setting two lovers free to find each other. The 'guilty parties' were washed whiter than white at the end. Of course it was all self-indulgence, not art; a public flirtation, not creativity. But there couldn't have been a better honeymoon picture.

Moreover, Burton, who was to be paid $500,000, needed a film he could coast through. Though *Hamlet* had enriched him, in other ways it had taken its toll on his health; his performances had become ragged, unpredictably quixotic, probably due to the pain-killing drugs he was taking for his arthritis: all this was a strain on his temper.

Elizabeth got him away to California for a rest – they travelled by train and read each other the parts of George and Martha in a playscript by Edward Albee called *Who's Afraid of Virginia Woolf?* to see if they were interested in filming it. Burton wasn't; Elizabeth couldn't make up her mind. Burton told her she should do it, if only to stop someone else making a sensation out of it. Decision postponed. At Los Angeles airport, where they were embarking for a holiday at the Casa Kimberley in Puerto Vallarta, an over-familiar sound made their hearts sink: the sound of squealing, like hundreds of pigs being simultaneously slaughtered in an abattoir. The fans had caught up with them. But they were wrong. The crowd wasn't there for them, but for the incoming Beatles. 'We never had such a wonderfully quiet departure,' said Elizabeth later. Their ears should have been more sensitively tuned to the times. For the high-decibel welcome accorded the Beatles was the sound of a generational change – a tumultuous reception by youth and for youth – that boded ill for the fortunes of the ageing Burtons. But off they flew to their own kingdom by the sea, leaving the Beatles to possess the future.

Except for a few outdoor locations in northern California, the bulk of *The Sandpiper* was shot in Paris so as to facilitate the tax status of the stars. Star-power indeed! Nevertheless, it was sensible, too. The weakness of the French franc made it attractive to MGM to spend its dollars abroad. Then, too, Elizabeth's health needed working conditions that were to be obtained more easily on the Continent: no shooting before 10 a.m., a five-day week, no evening work. As usual, her menstrual periods were catered to; and if Burton finished work before her, the director must use 'his best efforts' to see she wasn't needlessly detained at the studio. Insurance was still a problem. Elizabeth had insured herself on *The VIPs*, as the two dozen syndicates who had had to share the cost of her illness on *Cleopatra* were reluctant to start writing another policy on such an ill-fated star. The premium on her for *The Sandpiper* was a whopping $180,000; the amount payable had a ceiling of $3 million, and MGM had to meet the first $250,000 of any claim. No risks were to be taken at that price.

It was unfortunate that she decided at this time to change her nationality – back to British, having given it up some years earlier out of deference to Mike Todd. 'It is not true that I love America less, but I love my husband more,' she said. The nosey-parkers in the press suspected she loved tax breaks more still. While it was true that Britain's Labour Government at this time levied rates of tax in excess of those in America, it was also true that, unlike the American fiscal laws, British subjects domiciled abroad paid tax only on what income they remitted to Britain. The Burtons had formed two corporations, Interplanet Productions (hers) and Atlantic Programmes (his), both registered outside British jurisdiction. All of this was perfectly legal and had been resorted to by many others in their high-earning bracket. Nonetheless, some eight years later it became known that the US Internal Revenue Service was making claims against Elizabeth for monies earned abroad. Out of sentiment, she had found herself compelled to delete the phrase on the document of nationality that said she undertook to 'abjure all allegiance and loyalty' to the USA. The Internal Revenue Service is no softie in such matters of the heart, preferring to concentrate on the harder currency of the purse.

The film went well, however. Burton's ordained headmaster in the film is the 'sandpiper' of its title: the man with a broken wing who yearns to fly free of the domestic nest. All the attention of Elizabeth's single-parent artist in the film – a 'wild spirit' like Rima in the novel *Green Mansions* – is lavished on healing him so that he can join her in her free-living style of life. 'There is mercy for the sinner,' the school choir choruses on the day Burton resigns, after preaching a sermon of reconciliation to the two women he loved, his mistress and his wife. It is an ending that, to Richard Burton, was devoutly to be wished – repenting of one sin but not having to resist the other. However, he goes through his part with the emotions of a zombie. Maybe it was too painful still; more likely, his look was due to the mask-like make-up he had to wear to hide his acne'd face. (Its recipe began, dauntingly, according to the written instruction he carried around: 'Fill in the holes on the right side of [his] face with Plasto No. 1 Firm.') His brother states that '[He and Elizabeth] both kept alive the hope that the dross would turn to gold.' It didn't, but it made gold – a world-wide gross of $28 million, providing them with lucrative percentages and rentals from television later.

Although the producer, Martin Ransohoff, had tried to persuade Elizabeth to let her own son, Michael Wilding Jr, play her son in the film, she firmly refused to consider it because of her memories of being a child star herself. 'I didn't have an unhappy childhood,' she remarked. 'I just didn't have a childhood.'

Working on dross frees the mind, though, to enjoy the more civilized things of life. There was no better place to do this than in Paris. They used to be driven daily to the studio in their green Rolls-Royce convertible, on whose door Burton had had enamelled the tiny red dragon of Wales, rampant of course. Not for them lunch in the commissary. Instead, the car whisked them to a rendezvous that matched their mood that day: sometimes a small nondescript café where their entry would startle the working-class patrons, sometimes an exclusive restaurant in the Bois. 'In the post-prandial glow of their return,' wrote Jack Hamilton, a *Look* magazine correspondent who observed them often and tellingly, 'she may be heard skipping through the cold corridors, cackling her bloodcurdling Woody Woodpecker imitation and singing her own defiant version of "I'm Sitting On Top Of The World". He's doing his act, too. He is in the middle of a rolling, beautifully nuanced discourse on the agony in the Welsh [coal] mines.'

The signals for their future seemed permanently set on green. Burton told his brother Graham, rather shamefully, that he had agreed to do *The Sandpiper* only because it had been Elizabeth's turn to earn a million after he had starred in *Becket*: 'She can't just go on following me around.'

But after this film she followed him to Dublin, where he had been signed to play John Le Carré's burnt-out espionage agent in *The Spy Who Came in from the Cold*. He received $750,000 plus percentages. There was a part for Elizabeth in the story – as Burton's girlfriend – but Claire Bloom had already been cast. To put 'the Burtons' into the film would have risked turning a bleak story predicated in all respects on a lack of glamour into a 'vehicle' made for two stars. The presence of Bloom must have been a worry to Elizabeth. Bloom went right back to Burton's beginnings on stage and in the film *Look Back in Anger*. His lack of ease in her presence showed an anxiety not to kindle Elizabeth's suspicion that they were now anything other than old acquaintances.

For other reasons, too, it was not a happy time for Elizabeth. A series of misfortunes afflicted her: a burglary in Dublin which cost her £17,000 in jewels; then a road accident in which her chauffeured car was in collision with a woman pedestrian who later died; then, in March 1965, a stroke suffered by her father; and then Burton began drinking heavily again. He was complaining he was heartily fed up with living in hotels. He spoke of being willing to come back to England, even if it meant paying taxes at the then swingeing rate of 19s. 6d. in the pound. 'We want to buy a house,' said Elizabeth to an interviewer, 'somewhere in Kent, where I lived as a child.'

One good piece of news: Sybil Burton remarried in June 1965, forming what was to be a long, happy union with a man fourteen years her junior, twenty-four-year-old Jordan Christopher of The Wild Ones, a rock-pop group. This saved Burton $50,000 alimony a year.

The Spy Who Came in from the Cold turned out well – even if not half as profitable as *The Sandpiper* – and re-established Burton as an actor, not just a star. When they sailed for New York on 25 June 1965, it was to undertake the most exciting and daunting project either of them had ever contemplated – the film version of *Who's Afraid of Virginia Woolf?*

Elizabeth's urge to act, really *act*, had been revived by marriage to a man who was still regarded – admittedly by a diminishing number of his peers – as the once and future star of the British theatre. Another influence was her identification with Vivien Leigh: a tragic heroine, admired for her tenacity in inviting calamity and surviving it. Vivien, who had only another few years to live at this time, had also been a stage actress of limited but incisive range, partner on occasion to her husband, Laurence Olivier, and, like Elizabeth, a woman who didn't flinch from the hazards of seemingly unsuitable and daunting roles. She had played in her first Broadway musical, *Tovarich*, two years earlier, at the age of fifty. Elizabeth knew that took guts. Vivien had also been asked to play in the Paris production of *Who's Afraid of Virginia Woolf?* but had backed out because, as she wrote to her lover Jack Merivale after seeing it on Broadway, it was 'such a v.v.v. long play'.

Elizabeth, therefore, had every encouragement to emulate Vivien's example and live up to her own husband's reputation as an actor; she only needed the opportunity. A film of the Albee play provided that.

At first thought, it might seem wildly unlikely: Elizabeth Taylor as a lumpen, sluttish, dishevelled, foul-mouthed, middle-aged matron, a campus-land mantis whose nights are spent in devouring her self-pitying failure of a husband. Burton hadn't thought Elizabeth old enough or harridan enough when they had read each other the roles of George and Martha on the train to Pasadena. He still had no thought of playing George – or, rather, he had, but the truth was that he feared the producer-adapter Ernest Lehman might turn down the proposal on the grounds of money and, maybe, competence. Anyhow, to cast the Burtons as a married couple locked in mutual cruelty and mutual dependence from one brawling midnight to the next day's whimpering dawn might confuse life with fiction and sensationalize a play that, for all its volatile recrimination, needed to be held in delicate balance. Such were his reservations. And of course, they were ignored by Elizabeth. With her talent for projecting herself into a new role (or a new marriage) in advance of achieving it, she was already seeing herself as Martha.

There is no doubt that she pushed Burton into the role of George. Ernest Lehman's correspondence makes this clear. On 16 December 1964, he wrote to Jack L. Warner: 'Elizabeth Taylor told me at our last meeting that she wanted very much to have Richard play the role. I told her, and Richard, that I had certain reservations: a) we probably couldn't afford him, b) he might be too "strong" for the role, c) a Taylor and Burton picture might appear to be too [rich]. She disagreed with me on all counts, said the picture needs a great actor, which he is, a man who suggests great intellectual depth, which he has, an actor who can belt out great dialogue like no one else can ... My impression was that he was itching to have the role, but a bit over-proud to make a proposal to me.' Lehman added that Burton would have certain advantages: 'an important steadying influence on Miss T. during the making of the picture. (She would not have to be wondering and worrying where he is.)' He recommended doing a deal with Burton 'if we can live with it'. Jack Warner knew what the last phrase meant. His laconic reply read: '$750,000 – yes.' Elizabeth's agent, Hugh French, had already got her $1.1 million, the $100,000 being a sweetener for not taking per diems. She also got 10 per cent of the gross, plus her usual powers plenipotentiary over cast and crew. She approved George Segal and Sandy Dennis as the young couple who come to dinner and discover that they themselves are part of the meal. After John Frankenheimer had been considered as director, she approved Mike Nichols.

Nichols, thirty-four at the time and 'hot' as a Broadway stage director, had been in love with Elizabeth since seeing her in *Cynthia* some sixteen years earlier. He was an inspired choice: jokey, affectionate, an ex-actor who understood actors' traumas and a satirist from his days with Elaine May, who, like Elizabeth, took no one's pretensions seriously. Elizabeth felt she could work with him.

Even so, the Burtons were apprehensive. In their previous films together, they'd let the public see how love overcame all obstacles, or at least made the sacrifice worthwhile. Now with anti-romantic tempers at full throttle, they were set to land blow after blow on each other's weaknesses. The roles were in some ways a bit too close for comfort. Like George and Martha, they drank liquor to excess; they played games with each other in front of friends or strangers; they fed each other's fantasies, slipping in and out of the roles they had manufactured for themselves: as adulterous lovers, as husband and wife, as movie stars, as a theatrical couple, as nomadic millionaires, as eternally newsworthy celebrities. They enjoyed the punishment George and Martha inflicted on each other. They heard in it an echo of their own temperaments. But where and with whom would the audience's sympathy lie? Burton was playing an academic nerd; Elizabeth, a domestic monster with only the pathetic cadenza of Martha's rambling delusion about her imaginary 'lost' child to win her pity.

Elizabeth worried that she didn't look old enough. Martha was fifty-two, Elizabeth about twenty years younger. It was decided she should try to pass for forty-five. Well, grey hairs she didn't mind. 'My best feature is my grey hairs,' she was to write about this period, validating her love by embracing every little thing her marriage had brought her. 'I have them all named: they're all called Burton.'

She had once imagined herself 'the housewife Mrs Schwartz', now she had to convince herself that she was also 'the monster Medusa'.

The solution, as Elizabeth saw it, was to transform herself so physically and vocally that she no longer had an image she recognized on looking in her mirror. It was a reversal of the ordeal she would have to steel herself to face twenty years later when the mirror showed that the self she recognized had vanished into chronic obesity. This time she deliberately hid herself in someone else's shell – the marine metaphor of the sea-turtles in *Suddenly, Last Summer* occurred to her. Yes, she would put a shell around Martha but let the cracks in it show the woman's inner pain and loneliness.

So she stuffed junk food into herself until the scales quivered on the 155-pound line. After tests with five different wigs, she and Nichols selected one resembling Medusa's snake-locks, crowning her head in continuous agitation. She puffed up her cheeks until jowls depended from each side of her chin. She lowered her voice to a boozy, raucous rasp. She put into reverse all her own rules about make-up – keep it to the minimum – and larded her eyes with mascara, adding smudgy bags beneath them. And she suggested wearing one particular blouse she owned and always hated, because its tendency to ride up made her look middle-aged. Burton, too, had put on 'full-length drab'.

The entire cast rehearsed for two weeks, without pay, achieving such ensemble proficiency that, as Burton said, they could have taken the play across the nation on one-night stands. When shooting overran by thirty-five days, due to location problems at Smith College, Massachusetts, where the few outdoor scenes were set, the Burtons declined to claim overage which would have added a million dollars to their fees. Dedication, however, had to be its own reward. Warners, like MGM, knew the risks of showing gratitude to stars. When it was suggested to Jack L. Warner that a brooch would acknowledge her generosity, he snapped, 'I'm paying her a million dollars plus ten percent, aren't I? So screw her.'

The Burtons protested that their marriage was unaffected by the vehemence with which they sprayed each other over the months of shooting until the film wound up on 13 December 1965. 'A fantastic feeling, cathartic, purgative,' Burton called it. Not quite true. As one of his biographers, Paul Ferris, noted, 'change was creeping over Burton, the penumbra of a new dissatisfaction'. To an extent, *Who's Afraid of Virginia Woolf?* had put him in touch with arts he really hankered after. He had passed his fortieth birthday during the exhausting shooting. More and more, he talked of writing and the stage as the goals in his life: ones that Elizabeth couldn't so easily share. It was Mike Nichols's opinion that the marriage may have been 'a necessary stage'; but 'she was already wearing him down.' 'My only concern,' Burton told an interviewer, 'is that my quality is not exactly this American college professor [that I play] going to seed. He's not me, that moon-faced chap beaten down by a woman.' As Ferris noted, Burton seems to protest too much. 'Why should anyone think he was anything but an actor playing a part?' Why indeed, except that he feared he might end up like George?

About this time, he published a book – no, hardly that, a short story, a mere twenty-four pages including pictures. It originated in a *Vogue* article entitled 'Burton Writes of Taylor', and was retitled for hard covers *Meeting Mrs Jenkins*. A prose poem, it was cast in his by now characteristic style, in which he alternately praised Elizabeth's imperishable spirit, then did her down for her imperfect figure. Moonstruck and macho: a coarse blend, but one he thought poetic, although in truth it recalled the rodomontade of the pub bore who dares anyone to contradict his opinions. Melvyn Bragg, as has been noted, has said that the main distinction between the Burtons is that 'she was prone to obsessive love, he was not.' True: but he *was* prone to obsessive celebration of their love. It became the burden that many a journalist interviewing him had to bear – hearing him laud Elizabeth to the skies, but in a way that implied how high his own stock stood as a lover. What he was really celebrating was celebrity itself. *Meeting Mrs Jenkins* was a bit like hiding celebrity under a deliberately plain bushel, while ensuring that it could be found by the light of his authorship.

If *Who's Afraid of Virginia Woolf?* represented a coming of age for Elizabeth in more than one sense, the experience of playing in it did not leave Burton unscathed. In him, it sowed a seed of discontent with their relationship. Playing an unfulfilled man touched a guilty dread that all the star appurtenances, all the getting and spending in the world couldn't extirpate. He needed to succeed as himself, on his own terms, and not as someone else's husband – be it Martha's or Elizabeth's.

33

WORK, WORK, WORK — SPEND, SPEND, SPEND

Just 'for fun', they drove an Oldsmobile over the Swiss Alps and down to Rome in March 1966, with their Rolls-Royce bringing up the rear. 'The Rolls holds bags better,' Elizabeth said. Their purpose: a film of *The Taming of the Shrew* to be directed by Franco Zeffirelli. It was a 'reconciliation film'. They could exploit the same stormy temperaments that had served them well in *Who's Afraid of Virginia Woolf?* but this time end with a marriage ceremony, more than ever committed to each other. Burton saw it as a way of rehabilitating his classical reputation without having to drop his Hollywood standard of living.

Both of them were nervous, however. They had just received a drubbing for the *Dr Faustus* that Nevill Coghill had directed for the Oxford University Dramatic Society. Their patronage had backfired. Burton could remember the main speeches, but he had barely troubled himself to learn the connecting lines, so that he was forever sidling to the prompt corner of the stage, then returning centre stage for bursts of what one critic called 'solo acting fortissimo'. Elizabeth, in the 'walking through' role of Helen of Troy, floated speechlessly and resplendently on stage. But she evoked titters when, after Faustus implored, 'Sweet Helen, make me immortal with a kiss,' she obliged, giving him not one, but four – just to make sure of the immortality, perhaps.

They didn't want similarly rough notices falling on their heads again for the hubris of thinking that film stars, having failed at Marlowe, could now play Shakespeare. Yet the urge to do the *Shrew* was strong enough to abate that other perennial itch for up-front money. They agreed to waive their fees and take a percentage of the gross. Trouble struck early, however. Burton was drinking heavily and not at his best after lunch; Elizabeth needed hours of costuming and make-up and didn't look her best before lunch. They feared 'another *Cleopatra*', whose cost would this time come indirectly out of their purse. A *modus vivendi* was reached: no lunch.

Zeffirelli's pared-down set turned the *Shrew* into a *Tom and Jerry* cartoon in costume. Crude, yet surprisingly effective, it was pictorially well conceived, active, physical, visceral. If *Who's Afraid of Virginia Woolf?* was an all-night tongue-lashing with few blows struck, *The Taming of the Shrew* cut the cackle to the irreducible minimum and piled on the rough-housing in a broad, bawdy manner. The Burtons had flung insults at each other in the earlier film; in this one, they flung the furniture. Burton pursued Elizabeth, caught her, put her over his knee, spanked her and wrestled with her on a tile roof that collapsed and plunged them twenty feet on to a pile of raw wool. The tables were well and truly turned in Burton's favour. Now it was he who had the fight in his pocket or, more accurately, his codpiece. The movie was like therapy to him, after withstanding his wife's vicious vocal pummelling in the other film.

Shakespeare's ending, though, was changed slightly but significantly to accord with Elizabeth's views on marriage. She had always affirmed her faith in the vow itself, whatever construction might have been placed on her conduct leading up to or away from it. Accordingly, she pronounced Kate's act of submission to her lord Petruchio as if she meant it: 'Thy husband is thy lord, thy life, thy keeper / Thy head, thy sovereign, one that cares for thee.' It was like the communiqués she had been issuing to the press over four marriages, though perhaps better put.

The Burtons had picked Zeffirelli after seeing his Rome production of *Who's Afraid of Virginia Woolf?* but the inventive young Italian soon found, as others had, that handling the Burtons was a privilege accompanied by an entrance fee. He had flattered Elizabeth by complimenting her on her diamond earrings.

'They were a present from a director,' she said. 'It was *his* first film, too.'

Zeffirelli hedged. Such beautiful jewels would be hard to top.

'No, there's a little shop called Bulgari on the Via Condotti ...'

Zeffirelli pretended not to understand her English accent – but he took care to present her with a bracelet in enamel and precious stones that had belonged to Napoleon's sister. Zeffirelli, like Elizabeth, was a quick study.

In the middle of shooting, news arrived that Monty Clift had died of a drug overdose. It cannot have been a surprise, but all the same, Elizabeth was deeply shocked. And it created a professional problem. She had tried to bolster Clift's self-confidence by insisting that he play her husband in her next but one American film, *Reflections in a Golden Eye*, which John Huston was to direct in Rome. Playing an army officer on a lonely outpost, racked by homosexual guilt, attracted to one of his men and unable to love his wife: this was a part that Elizabeth's instinct told her Clift could align with his own self-loathing and craving for affection. Warners pressed her about recasting the film, for she had approval of her co-star. She would have preferred not to make the film now, and she may have used her 'contract-breaker' power to nominate Marlon Brando as the only acceptable actor, confident that he couldn't be coaxed into doing the film. To everyone's surprise, Brando said yes, though only after huge persuasion by John Huston.

Meantime, the Burtons had two films to make: a version of their *Dr Faustus* stage production funded by a million dollars of Burton's money as an act of piety to his old tutor Dr Coghill and his alma mater (for a term, anyhow), Oxford University. Then they would do an adaptation of Graham Greene's tragicomic novel *The Comedians*, set in Haiti in the time of the 'Papa Doc' regime.

Why on earth did they do so much work? What force drove them? They called themselves bone-idle, but it looks as if they were in overdrive. Perhaps the adrenalin released by the sheer number of projects they undertook provided the fuel. Perhaps it was the fear of having to run on empty and discovering that they came to a stop when the momentum died. Perhaps the projects were a means of distracting them from dwelling on themselves and each other during the long emptiness of days not filled by work, though overstocked with other intoxicants. Whatever the reason – and perhaps it was all three – these were the months when the Burtons went feverishly from film to film to film, as if no one would ever offer them work again.

Their spirits received a boost when the American reviews of *Who's Afraid of Virginia Woolf?* broke in June 1966. Never had praise been so lavish for them both – never would it be again. Elizabeth's performance could have been termed 'the triumph of the shrew'. People had never suspected that she could, or would, lay claim to such a radical alteration in style and appearance.

She makes an entrance with a fatted face, her slip strap betraying a casual sluttishness, with a braying voice, hair greying and threshing around in moments of temper. Even her body looks hard enough to take knocks, and rubbery enough to bounce them back. With intuitive, unnerving strokes, she constructs Martha's vulgarity out of physical details, like the cheap drag at a cigarette snatched off her husband's lips or the messy demonstration of wifely sensuality – 'I want a big sloppy kiss' – that can switch into bitchy harassment. *Time*'s critic found her moments of tenderness 'astonishing', too – and that was astonishing, coming from her old enemy *Time*. Her finest stroke, though, comes at the end when she mutes her termagant's trumpetings and blows a lament for the child Martha never had, except in fantasy.

What critics didn't know was that Elizabeth had undergone examination while in Dublin to see if she could bear Burton a child. The prospects had appeared bleak. So the scene at the end of the film may possess a more poignant and personal truth than the mere words suggest.

At the Academy Awards the following year, the Oscar for Best Actress went to Elizabeth Taylor: her second win. Burton lost to Paul Scofield in *A Man for All Seasons*.

A year and a half later, they were reading some of the worst notices they had ever received in their lives – either of them. These were for the film version of *Dr Faustus*, shot that summer in Rome with student actors from Oxford. The Burtons had taken the same £18-a-day rate as the rest of the cast. The critics had not appreciated their sacrifice – or anything else, it seemed. 'When [Elizabeth Taylor] welcomes Burton to an eternity of damnation,' *Time* magazine wrote on this occasion, 'her eyeballs and teeth are dripping pink in what seems to be a hellish combination of conjunctivitis and trench mouth.' Hell hath no fury like a woman scorned; she reportedly cancelled her subscription.

Soon after its showcase opening, the film foundered: the first small straw to show that the wind of public fascination with the Burtons was veering round against them. The world gross barely came to $600,000. Burton had lost a million of his own money. Still, not many stars are prepared to do that.

Reflections in a Golden Eye was being filmed in Rome – though its setting was the Deep South of Carson McCullers's gothic imagination – because of tax advantages. There was precious little other advantage in it for Elizabeth. Her role as a spurned wife was a shrill one that defied all efforts to make it sensuous. Though she and Brando share scenes, they act as if neither has even been introduced to the other. It is not a cold alienation – simply a matter of two entirely different kinds of concentration not being aligned in performance. Elizabeth, economical as always in gesture and movement, fits into Huston's traditional style of directing; Brando immerses himself so deeply in his tortured pondering as to appear independent of direction.

Not counting the deliberate coarsening of herself as Martha, Elizabeth shows for the first time the portliness of incipient middle-age. Perhaps putting on the pounds for *Who's Afraid of Virginia Woolf?* was easier than taking them off. Her hair-style, too, introduced her to the 'pineapple' look, an unflattering mode that doesn't become her as well as when her hair is left hanging at shoulder length. Critics viewed the film with more a jaundiced eye than a golden one.

Burton had begun to keep a diary around this time – perhaps because, as Melvyn Bragg guesses, he needed some intelligent conversation, even if it was with himself. It certainly wasn't supplied by their now huge 'palace guard' of aides. The entries show he was desperate for him and Elizabeth to root their wanderlust in a little settled domesticity. But always the lust for money and the fear of inactivity made it hard for soil to gather around the roots. The lawyers, the agents and the accountants seemed to be lashing them with a three-tailed whip – on, on, on, faster, faster, faster. So they packed their bags and set off for the African republic of Dahomey – of all forsaken places to make a film – which would double for Haiti in *The Comedians*.

For the first time, Elizabeth's fee fell below her husband's. He got $750,000; she, only half a million. But then her role was a supporting player's one – the German wife of Peter Ustinov's American ambassador, who starts an affair with Burton's self-loathing anti-hero. She later said she had been conned into the part. Translated, this meant she'd heard it was earmarked for Sophia Loren. So was the role Elizabeth had played in *The VIPs*. At this rate, Loren must have wondered if she would ever get to play opposite Richard Burton.

They were left relatively undisturbed in Dahomey, except by monstrous clouds of tiny mosquitoes. The arch-enemy was boredom, once Burton perceived the script was a dud and failed to find inspiration in what *Newsweek* was to call '[the character] he is in every picture he makes these days, The Man Who Has Lost Faith'. Champagne had been flown in by the crate – what else was there on which to spend per diems in Dahomey? When Burton was drunk – which was often, and loudly – he became more argumentative and abrupt with Elizabeth than even the entourage could remember. Elizabeth still hankered after expanding the family in some way or other – procreation obviously wasn't an option – so as to give her and Burton a 'child of their own'. She looked wistfully at all the small black babies around them, their wretched condition touching her maternal instinct. One of the benign ways in which she knew she could exercise the tremendous power that wealth gave was by magically transforming someone's fortunes. Plucking a child out of Third World poverty to join the charmed circle of the Burtons' family appealed to Elizabeth's conviction that life could be changed by strength of will. Maria's successful adoption had proved it. But Burton didn't care much for the idea; they travelled so much, he said, that another child would be a problem.

Their next film – yes, they were well and truly on the golden treadmill – was made by a man who had become, like themselves, something of a displaced person. Joseph Losey had been forced to leave America, where he had been enjoying increasing success as a director, by the Hollywood witch-hunt for current or former Communists. He had settled himself physically in England, though spiritually he remained a restless man, and intellectually a devious one. Films like *The Servant, King and Country* and *Accident* had won him an appreciative audience in Britain, though not a 'cash' reputation. He was an auteur who put his own style and stamp on films, including the actors who appeared in them. The common link between him and people like the Burtons, who rather fancied the notion of putting *their* stamp on the product, was Elizabeth's friend John Heyman, an Englishman and a one-time agent whose talent for finding budgets as well as projects naturally turned him into a producer. Elizabeth, he mentioned to Losey, had always been drawn towards Tennessee Williams; he'd been 'lucky' for her. He was now about to be 'lucky' for Losey.

A year or so earlier, Losey had tried to interest Simone Signoret and Sean Connery in a script called *Boom*, a conflation of two works by Williams: a failed Broadway play called *The Milk Train Doesn't Stop Here Any More* and a short story, *Man Take This Up Road*. More lucrative projects for the stars had intervened. Personally, Losey thought Elizabeth too young at thirty-seven for Flora Goforth, the world's richest woman, a cruel, heartless but fascinating monster who is dying in her white palace above the Mediterranean when she is visited by an angel of death, in the shape of a personable beach boy, who assists her rite of passage into the next world. But if Elizabeth and Burton, who was rather too advanced in age to be an angel, said yes, that meant he had a budget – and a picture. Losey persuaded himself that 'it would be more interesting [a film] if the heroine wasn't so old.' So, with Heyman he journeyed to Portofino in mid-May 1967 to 'audition' for the Burtons. He was just in time to see the two of them, never people to relish making quick decisions over new film projects, sailing off into the Tyrrhenian Sea in their expensive new toy – a yacht that soon became as notorious as themselves for extravagance.

A 279-ton, 130-meter vessel finished in solid Edwardian mahogany and chrome, it cost the Burtons £75,000 to buy, and more than twice that to refit and refurbish. They immediately renamed it the *Kaliẓma*, after Burton's daughter Kate and Elizabeth's two girls Liza and Maria. She had seven cabins and two staterooms, could sleep fourteen, and needed a crew of five. The Burtons had been told it would cost only twenty-five to thirty thousand dollars a year to run. This proved a huge underestimate. The Burtons felt the same way about living out of rented houses as other people do about living out of suitcases; there must be a better life. The yacht, they hoped, would be it. Though they owned two houses, at Gstaad and Puerto Vallarta, this way they would have a hull to shelter them and a gangplank to repel boarders, and not be moored in one place. They told themselves it was a solid investment; more important, perhaps, it was a symptom of their now chronic restlessness and need to escape from the entanglement of deals, obligations and projects, not to mention litigation – Fox had tried to hit them with a $50 million suit for allegedly causing the ruinous overrun on *Cleopatra*. (The suit was withdrawn.)

On 1 June, they committed themselves to *Boom*, their eighth film together, at a million dollars each. Overage would give them another half a million. Burton agreed with those who felt he was a bit old; but with $1.25 million at stake, he was not going to quibble over an angel's age. Both of them were now more and more drawn to the freakish and eccentric; it broke the monotony of a celebrity existence.

Shooting began in October. Elizabeth was immediately seduced by the pleasure dome that the designer, Richard MacDonald, had created for Mrs Goforth's residence on a Sardinian clifftop. A white marble palace-cum-mausoleum, it jutted dizzyingly out into space two hundred feet above the foam that seethed constantly around the foot of the sheer rock walls. Losey wanted the fierce music of the sea to echo Tennessee Williams's cruel poetry. Elizabeth tried to buy the land it stood on, to make a more permanent sanctuary for herself. It was not for sale. A withdrawal from the world had to exist in fantasy, or not at all. There was a moral there, somewhere.

Once Elizabeth committed to the role, Losey persuaded Williams to rewrite parts of his scenario with her in mind. This emerged even more clearly as shooting progressed and Losey's feelings for his players began to shape his direction of them. He and Elizabeth seemed of a similar mind when it came to testing people to breaking-point, so as to crack them open for inspection and see what they were made of. They gradually developed a mutual respect.

With one aspect of Flora Goforth, Elizabeth identified very strongly – not her wealth, but her health. The character's physical condition deteriorated throughout the film until she died in regal splendour. Losey had a Wimpole Street physician write a detailed report on Mrs Goforth's fictional malady, so that Elizabeth could graduate her performance like the graph of a fever. The doctor 'diagnosed' her illness as a form of leukemia, resulting in violent extremes of euphoria followed by depression. 'The states can linger for a long time and death can be very sudden.' Losey has said that Elizabeth remarked on how similar this progress was to Vivien Leigh's own manic-depressive end – Vivien had died, with unexpected suddenness, the year before, after suffering from tuberculosis and possibly leukemia complications. Elizabeth seems to have played Flora Goforth with Vivien in mind.

An incident occurred that recalled the inspiration Elizabeth had passed on to Richard Brooks when they were shooting *The Last Time I Saw Paris*.

Losey wanted, as far as possible, to eliminate colour from the film. 'Wear one colour,' he advised her. She trumped that. 'I'll wear no colour at all.' She gave her approval to an all-white look for Mrs Goforth's wardrobe of sack-like shifts. 'They looked like shrouds in waiting for their occupant,' said Losey, delightedly.

However, the first scene Elizabeth shot, when she was still nervous and edgy, nearly caused a rift with Losey. It was the one where Mrs Goforth is dictating her memoirs to her secretary over the intercom, enumerating the ex-husbands she has had, who are all commemorated in larger-than-life statues on the terrace. 'Married to five industrial kings ... my name in lights since I was a child ...' Like every other element in the film – the physical luxury, retinue of servants, ostentatious wealth, physical pain and personal loneliness – the dialogue echoes the public Taylor.

'It's a funny scene, Elizabeth,' Losey said, 'but not as you're playing it.'

She looked him full in the eye and snapped, 'I do not find such a life funny.'

Another passage about the death of one of her husbands, she recited quite tonelessly, like a sleepwalking Lady Macbeth. 'She was thinking all the time of Mike,' Burton later told Losey.

As it takes nearly fifty minutes into the film before Elizabeth and Burton meet, the interest was concentrated on her alone for an unusual length of screen time. It is as if the camera is making an inventory of possessions and describing a way of life. This becalmed, indeed at times stagnant state isn't lightened by an iota of warmth or sympathy for the character – things that were commercially hurtful to the film.

'They say she's a bitch to approach,' says the burly, bearded skipper of the motor launch who throws Burton into the sea at the start of the film on discovering he is one of Mrs Goforth's uninvited guests. The mariner is played by Elizabeth's own brother, Howard Taylor, making his first – and, to date, only – film appearance some twenty-five years after he had so successfully aborted his mother's attempt to set up a screen test for him by cutting his hair off. Elizabeth had pressed him into the role when the actor supposed to play it hadn't turned up. Howard was now a professor of oceanography at the University of Hawaii, a happily married family man. There was a flurry of memos between Losey and Elizabeth about having to cut him out of the film when it was being trimmed for length. Is it necessary to add that Howard Taylor stayed in?

It is impossible to look at the film other than as Tennessee Williams's commentary on some of Elizabeth's well-known characteristics. 'If you have a world-famous figure, why be selfish with it?' is the most pertinent comment, and one she enunciated with pride.

The miscasting, as well as the real-life nature of their relationship, reduces Burton to the status of a houseguest in the film rather than a high priest. He recovers his function only at the end, when he solemnly prepares Mrs Goforth for her passage into the next world: removing her regalia, positioning her head on the pillow, stripping off her jewellery, holding her in death like a lover who never embraced her in life, and finally relieving her of the glittering jewelled ring, the so-called 'Aurora' stone, soon to be associated with Burton's purchase of the real Krupp diamond for his wife. He places the ring in a wine glass like a libation and offers it to the gods of the sea as if an earthly empress was going to her wedding, not her burial, in its restless depths.

During the making of *Boom*, they begged time off to visit Venice and be fêted at the carnival. They also flew to Paris, where *The Taming of the Shrew* received a gala premiere on 29 September at the Opéra. Five members of the French government received them at the opening, one bearing a welcoming message from President de Gaulle. Elizabeth wore a tiara specially created for her by Van Cleef and Arpels, which Alexandre incorporated in a hair-style that also included a wild rose made of nine-carat gold with diamond petals. Burton estimated that all this jewellery was worth $1.5 million. It was on loan for the occasion and escorted by eight guards, two of them armed. The night before, they had dined with the Windsors and the Rothschilds. It was all 'sweet revenge on the social ostracism we endured such a relatively little time ago,' Burton wrote in his diary.

If indeed living well *was* the best revenge, he sweetened it even a little more by laying out $960,000 on the morning of the premiere to buy the jet aircraft they had chartered to fly them to the French capital.

'Boom – the shock of each moment of still being alive,' was a line that recurred several times in their new film. But they could hardly have heard the pulse-beat of time, they were living so furiously already.

34

BARQUES AND BITES

No one wanted to cross them. Anyhow, their moods were unpredictable. Their fierce arguments with each other helped stabilize them because they were equally matched in invective. Burton called it the 'status quo'. All the same, the tensions in their marriage were accumulating like calcified tissue round a once-flexible joint.

Burton now immersed himself in an action thriller, *Where Eagles Dare*, because, he said with a backswipe at Losey, 'I don't want the kids to associate me with the more highbrow things.' Though he and Elizabeth revelled in extravagance, he was afflicted with retrospective guilt. Intellectually, he could see the vanity of the world they both enjoyed and he would turn in on himself, plunge into his 'black dog' mood and, assailed by the deeper trauma of his own divorce, take to the bottle for oblivion and his study for consolation. Elizabeth was probably the more honest of the two of them in her comments on their up-and-down relationship. 'Sometimes it's not easy to be with Richard, especially when he's angry. Then I think he's capable of almost anything.'

Yet they continued to wrap themselves in the sort of security that satiety brings, and allowed themselves the luxury of reflecting that if it all vanished overnight, they could do without it. But it wasn't about to vanish, was it? Was it?

Not suddenly, certainly not overnight. But change came like the wind imperceptibly veering round to another quarter. Gradually they became aware that it was blowing with chastening force on two vulnerable people. The flattering attentions paid them, the huge fees offered them, the very awe they generated by their semi-regal life-style, were to be transformed into scorn, resentment, failure and, worst of all, indifference.

The blows began falling in a minor way – after all, it was only a minor picture – as soon as *Dr Faustus* had been seen and damned. But then *The*

Comedians opened late in October 1967; and common to the mixed-to-bad reviews was the ominous refrain that they had outworn their welcome as stars in tandem. Business for the film was only respectable; the public sensed something wrong. Self-publicized Great Lovers they might be off. screen, but how seldom did they generate on screen what could be called a spark of passion. Elizabeth's urge to play the dominant partner precluded her from making a successful pitch for sympathy. It was not the power of love, but the love of power that gazed out of her violet eyes.

Earlier films had looked like illustrated gossip columns to audiences that were eager to identify the Burtons with their roles. That had worked strongly in their favour when the movie was *Who's Afraid of Virginia Woolf?* But there simply wasn't enough of 'them' – of themselves – in the roles they played in *The Comedians* to satisfy such voyeurism. Audiences dropped away. Immediately that happened, a seed of doubt was sown among the people who had the privilege of paying their million-dollar fees. The Burtons could play themselves – right. But could they play other people? The faith that a film, *any* film starring the Burtons would show a profit began to falter.

They could still undoubtedly command the attention of the media. But even this type of attention changed in kind if not quantity. The media couldn't deny their glamour – how could they, when the New York premiere of *Dr Faustus* made the night swing till daybreak and collected the likes of the Robert Kennedys, the Peter Lawfords, even Mrs Johnson, the president's wife. Why, even their old foe Spyros Skouras rose to toast the demi-royal couple. Unable to deny them their centrepiece status among the 'Beautiful People', the media took it out on what was deemed to be egoism and disdain. Jacqueline Kennedy's marriage to Aristotle Onassis in October 1969 was to be viewed by many Americans as a betrayal rather than a betrothal – 'The president's widow marrying that evil old man just for his money!' Although the storm of shock and anger helped Elizabeth's transgressions recede into the diminishing perspective of memory, the Burtons were caught under the harsher scrutiny to which celebrities were now subjected by the media.

In short, the public perception of them began to change because the media felt it was timely. They were not unimportant enough to be dropped into the unfashionable pages. But the media were tired of having to compose (or invent) the same stories about them as had been appearing week after week for what now seemed years – and was. The media thrive on change, much as do the appetites they stimulate. But the only way that the Burtons were changing was by getting richer and more flamboyant. They were overdue for a come-uppance.

It was not a concerted strategy: no master-plan was involved. But columnists, critics, reporters, photographers, news and feature editors sense a need for change – and if it doesn't come readily enough of its own accord, they possess the power to change the direction of the wind and see how the public likes the effect. That was what began to happen to the Burtons' public image from 1968 onwards. Their failure to deliver the goods in terms of hard cash was simply the corollary of it. Once the box office confirmed the media's feelings about them, a change in the way they were regarded was inevitable.

Their bank manager wouldn't necessarily have noticed any of this. The money kept on rolling in. They backed a bid by the newly formed Harlech Television consortium for a broadcasting franchise for Wales and the West of England. Their prestige – and a promise to appear on the network – carried the day. 'A television station, that's all we want,' whooped Elizabeth. They owned a substantial shareholding in the new station, in the days when commercial television in Britain was still a 'licence to print money'. It gave them, the absentee landlords, power in their 'own' land, cultural credibility and a nationalist solidarity with the Jenkinses and all the other Welsh clans. Burton's reputation crossed frontiers. That was a bonus in the arrangement – he himself didn't need to cross them, otherwise he might have had to start paying British taxes.

Elizabeth, at thirty-six, was putting on a brave face above what photographs suggested was a double chin. She shrewdly implied that though dieting made a slim woman, eating made a desirable one, provided you 'keep the fat firm'. Her plumpness was more useful to her than one might imagine. It brought her down nearer to the earth most ordinary women walked on – or at least the bathroom scales most of them stood on – and her candour about fat and wrinkles made for the reflection that if she had earned these as well as her fabulous fees, then God showed no favouritism in the distribution of basic things like double chins.

The Burtons arrived in London in mid-February 1968, to work on two films: his was *Where Eagles Dare*, which had been on winter location in the Austrian snows and was now to move into the studio, and hers was a new Joseph Losey film, *Secret Ceremony*, co-starring Mia Farrow and Robert Mitchum. She got her now customary million dollars; Mitchum and Mia Farrow got $150,000 and $75,000 respectively. The star fee hadn't been shaken down yet; but then *Boom* hadn't opened yet.

To say the Burtons merely 'arrived' in the capital is to understate the stir their entry made. They came by yacht. No, not the *Kalizma*: it was having a half-million dollar refit, so they chartered another boat from a tin millionaire, at $20,000 a month. Since they themselves had engaged their usual Dorchester suite, the sole purpose of the vessel, it appeared, was to allow their dogs to beat the anti-rabies law that required all animals touching British soil to be put in quarantine for six months. So long as the pets, four in number, didn't put a paw over the landward side of the gunwale, they would not incur the penalties inflicted on the less pampered of their breed. The boat was immediately dubbed 'the world's most expensive dog kennel'. Cruelty to dogs is the surest thing to inflame the British public. But this time, the indignation of the country was roused by the indulgence shown to dogs. Even the then Home Secretary, James Callaghan, had to reassure Parliament that the British taxpayer wasn't stumping up for the policemen and the animal welfare officers stationed at the foot of the gangplank to stop a pet Peke running amok on the Embankment. (Mr Callaghan: 'The cost falls entirely on Mr and Mrs Burton.')

Trivial though the fuss may now seem, it had one important consequence not known at the time. A knighthood for Richard Burton was under active consideration by the Prime Minister, Harold Wilson, in response to a discreetly circulated petition from distinguished Oxford dons. Wilson was sympathetic to the idea. He felt the criticism of Burton for avoiding British taxes had been overdone. Burton was popular; he and Elizabeth were heavy contributors to charities; he was Welsh, and next year would see Prince Charles's installation as Prince of Wales. But the furore over the floating dog kennel quashed the Prime Minister's enthusiasm to have Burton honoured with a knighthood. Instead, he was given the lesser distinction of a CBE two years later. It was the first serious stumble that he and Elizabeth had made on their seemingly unstoppable advance to honours and fortune. A CBE for him was very nice and well deserved. But a knighthood would have changed Elizabeth's rank – to Lady Burton.

Work began on *Secret Ceremony* in bitterly raw March weather. It was not a pleasurable experience, although Elizabeth, who retained her childhood fascination with houses and secret gardens shut away from the world, was intrigued by the bizarre example found for the film in Kensington. An Edwardian mansion that had been built by an eccentric architect for a millionaire draper, it was clad inside and out with acres of glazed wall tiles, leftovers from the great sea-going liners of the nineteenth century. It also boasted a Byzantine gold cupola, *art nouveau* doorways, rooms stacked with period bric-a-brac, a towering white bathroom that needed a coal fire to heat it and wardrobes big enough for Elizabeth to walk into as well as a bed large enough for her and Mia Farrow to nestle in together. Everywhere the gloom was perversely lightened by the gay twitter and tinkling of dozens of music-boxes.

Into this sealed world, Mia Farrow brings Elizabeth, a London prostitute, whom the fey little rich girl insists is her own long-lost mother.

Elizabeth loses a trade and gains a surrogate daughter – until the step-father (Mitchum) comes nosing around. The film ends with a fatal stabbing. *Secret Ceremony* had pretensions to being an updating of Shelley's verse drama *The Cenci*, which deals with Renaissance lust and incest. Actually it was nearer in tone and content to the 1960s' obsession with dressing-up and playing roles – becoming one's own fantasy, or someone else's.

To keep herself warm throughout the location shoot, Elizabeth wore two sets of long johns bought at an army surplus store in Victoria. Still, she crouched over the open braziers positioned in the tiled corridors that were as cold as a refrigerator. Little joy was brought into the inhospitable location by Mitchum. For some reason, Losey felt the American star was hostile to his ideas, and even his person. 'He did nothing with pleasure,' said Losey later. 'It was impossible to make any contact with him.'

One day, they received a visit from Burton, who had finished shooting *Where Eagles Dare*. He may have come at Elizabeth's behest – Losey thought he did, but the evidence is contradictory. Anyhow, strong hints were dropped by him that the film might be helped if there were a switch of cast – if Mitchum left and Burton stepped into the role. Burton had a few weeks free before he began his next film, a version of Nabokov's *Laughter in the Dark*, which Tony Richardson was to direct in London. Burton eventually had to be taken aside and told that although some people might think Mitchum was not behaving well, he was a very popular, if no longer a front-rank, star back in Hollywood. For it to get around that he had been sacked at Burton's instigation would create a bad scene – for Burton. He let the idea drop.

Boom opened in New York at the end of May 1968 – to devastatingly bad reviews. But worse, much worse, was the opportunity that the film gave for attacking the Burtons. *Life*'s comments may not have been a death sentence, but what the then influential magazine wrote was picked up by the rest of the media, and it helped to adjust the tone and volume of their own dissatisfaction with the Burtons. It deserves quoting at length, for it exactly marks the turn-down in their public fortunes:

'When people reach a certain status in show-biz – have plenty of "clout" as they like to say – a kind of arrogance seems to set in. They get to thinking, perhaps unconsciously, that they can dare us to reject anything they feel like shovelling out. The Burtons are particularly afflicted with this malaise ... There is a slack, tired quality in most of their work that is, by now, a form of insult. They don't so much act as deign to appear before us and there is neither dignity nor discipline in what they do. She is fat and will do nothing about her most glaring defect, an unpleasant voice which she cannot adequately control. He, conversely, acts with nothing but his voice, rolling out his lines with much elegance, but with no feeling at all. Perhaps the Burtons are doing the very best they can, laden as they are by their celebrity. But if they are not cynics, over-estimating their charisma and under-estimating our intelligence, then they are guilty of a lack of aesthetic judgement and self-awareness that is just as disheartening.'

The film died everywhere it was shown. Dirk Bogarde was in Rome that summer and wrote to Losey about the 'ghastly advertising' all over the capital. The film wasn't even being called *Boom*, he said, but something he could only roughly translate as 'A Widow Filled with Disease'. John Heyman admitted that he knew of this but didn't feel justified in doing anything in view of the 'massive loss' being suffered by the Italian distributors.

'Thus,' said Losey, 'I became the first director to make an Elizabeth Taylor picture that lost money.'

In fact, *Boom* did not cover its cost until twenty years after it was made. Worse was on the way for *Secret Ceremony*. The latest available figures, for March 1974, show a deficiency of $3.5 million, and it is probably still in the red.

Maybe the Burtons felt their credit slipping. Their extravagance did not slow up, but changed tack. They switched from investing in gold to investing in diamonds. Just before *Boom* blew up in their faces, Burton bought one of the world's biggest stones, the Krupp diamond, a 33.19 carat oblong jewel originally the property of the German armaments king and his wife. He paid $305,000 for it. As well as an investment, ownership being vested in one of their tax-shelter companies, it was a masterly publicity stroke. The reviews of *Boom* might be bad, but they were on the inside pages. There on the front page was Elizabeth wearing the Krupp diamond: a breath-catching union of beauty and rarity. It was delivered to its new owner in time for the Burtons to attend the opening of their television station in Bristol. They travelled in a special railway carriage reserved for themselves and other celebrities and board members. Graham Jenkins was among them. He recalls seeing his brother, high on champagne, dredging handfuls of brooches and necklaces out of Elizabeth's jewel box and draping them playfully round the necks of the other women present. 'Isn't it nice,' asked Elizabeth at the reception, 'that a diamond owned by a German arms king should finish up on the nice little Jewish finger of a girl like me?' It was also useful for catching the auctioneer's eye a little later when she paid £50,000 for Monet's *Le Val de la Falaise* at Sotheby's. Burton managed to secure a Degas for £145,000 without any sparkler on his hand.

A few weeks later, though, he was out of a job – sacked on the spot by Tony Richardson for turning up late and allegedly incapable of playing his role of an English art dealer in *Laughter in the Dark*.

He retired to the Dorchester in deep despondency and took to the bottle. His mood was further darkened by Elizabeth's having to undergo a hysterectomy. Her uterus was removed on 21 July, after a three-and-a-half-hour operation that left her in great pain and hallucinating from the drugs administered to her. Burton took a room next to her hospital suite and recorded in his diary how alarmed he was to find her, suddenly, standing at his bedside when she wasn't even supposed to walk, staring at him with what he took to be a look of pure malevolence. Yet when the fever passed, she was affection itself. The nightmare experience revived for a time their mutual dependency. Fear of losing Elizabeth always sharpened anew Burton's need of her. By an awful irony, Elizabeth had just finished shooting a scene in *Secret Ceremony* where she ruthlessly destroys Mia Farrow's fantasy of her own imaginary pregnancy.

The summer hadn't ended before his beloved brother Ifor was paralysed in an accident at Burton's chalet in Switzerland and had to be confined to a wheelchair, waiting to die.

Illness, humiliation, accidents, addiction: the sky was darkening over the bright couple. They returned to America in August for a rest before beginning yet more film projects. Such now were the logistics of moving themselves, the family and the entourage that the thirty luggage labels Cunard sent them had to be supplemented by a hundred more. Their three stateroom suites and a private dining room cost £4,000. Burton drank heavily on the voyage. Elizabeth kept mostly to her cabin, where twenty-seven beautiful new caftan-style dresses, created for her by Tiziani of Rome, hung in the closet, ready to meet the demand of any mood that seized her on the Atlantic crossing. For the moment, however, peace of mind was more precious than possessions – and harder to acquire.

Over a year before, she had agreed to make a romantic comedy set in Las Vegas called *The Only Game in Town*, with Frank Sinatra as co-star. Her fee of $1.25 million was 25 per cent up on what she usually commanded. 'The price of bread is going up,' she quipped, adding, 'and diamonds, too.' The film was to be made by Fox, the company that not long ago had been suing the Burtons for $50 million over *Cleopatra*. Was she surprised at their newfound generosity? 'They must be out of their tiny Chinese minds.' Fox was also paying Burton the same fee to make *Staircase*, in which he and Rex Harrison played gay hairdressers. The Burtons wanted the two movies to be made at the same time, in the same place, and for tax reasons not in America or Britain. Each feared that a lengthy separation might be the unmaking of a marriage now held together by tension as much as by love. So the East End of London and the Las Vegas casinos were recreated in two Paris studios. The cost was enormous, but having chosen the pipers, Fox had to pay for the tune. Ironically, such 'aid' to the French film industry gained Darryl F. Zanuck a government honour.

Elizabeth's hysterectomy had put back the date of the film, which caused Sinatra to withdraw and Warren Beatty, fresh from his triumph in *Bonnie and Clyde*, to step in. Burton knew of Beatty's reputation with women. And as often as possible, the green Rolls-Royce ferried Burton from the bitchy argy-bargy with Rex Harrison in the barber's shop in one film studio across town to the parking space in another beside Elizabeth's white Rolls-Royce that, in its turn, was opposite the space occupied by Beatty's black Rolls-Royce. Burton need not have worried. A fan club of the French female aristocracy grouped itself around Beatty, often so densely that Elizabeth could not even see him. She finished the film in great pain, wearing a surgical corset because of sciatica and renewed disc trouble, sometimes discovering that her feet had no feeling in them and fearing she might turn into a hobbling old woman. At such moments, Burton was at his most admirable. 'She asked if I would stop loving her if she had to spend the rest of her life in a wheelchair,' he wrote in his diary. The answer was clear from his compassionate care of her, though he worried about the build-up of pain-killing drugs. How could they be good for her long-term health?

But although their life was still packed and golden, and the deals done months or years before still kept the money supply flowing, there is evidence that the Burtons were attempting to withdraw from the world they were locked into – a sort of *huis clos*, with a gilded entrance but no visible exits, furnished with all material comforts but devoid of most spiritually satisfying ones. They now spent a lot of time hobnobbing with the French aristocracy and moneyed classes by whom, they recognized, they had been taken up. They seem to have been motivated not only by their understandable love of conquering an exclusive fan club, but also by a desire to divert themselves, with constant socializing, from an existence whose glamour had turned into hard labour.

They veered from high society – the Rothschilds, the Windsors, 'marred royalty' and 'nameless nobles', as Burton put it – to severe depression unleavened even by a weekend aboard the *Kalizma*, freshly decorated and as cosy as a floating home could be with the new Monet in the salon, the Picasso and the Van Gogh in the dining room, Epstein's bust of Churchill, and a Vlaminck hanging inconveniently in the stairwell. Occasionally they calculated how much money they would need to quit work altogether and decided that, with all the children now provided for in trust funds, their capital of $10 million would soon, if untouched and 'short of a war', double itself. 'If E. and I have the strength of mind to give up being famous,' Burton set down in his diary, 'we can at least live in more than lavish comfort. I might even be able to buy her the odd jewel or two ... There are many worlds elsewhere, Coriolanus.'

But had they the strength of mind? With *The Only Game in Town* not yet finished, Fox were nevertheless so sure they had a hit that they were willing to pay Elizabeth 1.5 million to play the title role in Gore Vidal's transsexual satire *Myra Breckinridge*. Then again, would the film companies ever let them off the contractual hook? Burton tried to get out of playing Henry VIII in the project he had signed for months before, a costume potboiler with pretensions called *Anne of the Thousand Days*. Elizabeth had hoped to play Anne Boleyn, but had been adjudged too old. Universal threatened to sue him to the end of his days if he didn't appear. He had once spoken airily of dancing for money. Now he felt hobbled in golden leg-irons.

'As a result of this half-life we're leading,' he wrote on New Year's Eve, 'I am drinking twice as much. The upshot will be that I'll die of drink and she'll go blithely on in her half-world.'

35

DIAMOND LIZ

'I've been re-reading [*Myra Breckinridge*] and it's marvellous,' Joseph Losey wrote to Elizabeth at Gstaad on 26 December 1968. 'Done properly, neither of us need ever work again, but you could afford that and I don't care – or, rather, we should put it the other way round. I could afford it (!) and *you* don't care.'

Actually, at the time she received Losey's letter, Elizabeth was almost past caring if she never saw another movie set again. *The Only Game in Town* had overrun its schedule. Work remained to be done on it in Paris early in the new year; then she would have to drag her tired, suffering self, her husband, her entourage and her pets off to a godforsaken place like Las Vegas for the location sequences. Her spine was giving her hell and causing her physicians concern. She was receiving daily injections of pain-killing drugs; they eased her condition, but their side effects were devastating. Burton was horrified to see her 'incoherent' – sometimes she was rendered speechless from the severe reaction. As an extra pain-killer, she had turned to alcohol, which sometimes left her, in his words, 'sloshed as a Cossack'. One night in the Plaza-Athenée Hotel in Paris, he became aware of her beside him in bed, leaning forward but immobilized, a cigarette in one hand, a book of matches – empty! – in the other. It was as if the pain in her back had cranked her up and then left her stuck in that posture. Both he and Elizabeth were worrying about their weight and were on special diets. Typically, he was embracing something called 'The Drinking Man's Diet'. Elizabeth lacked the persistence to stick to her routine. Her face was vacant. She couldn't finish even the lightest of lightweight fiction. She showed no interest in any project suggested to her.

At first, Burton thought it was the after-effects of having her uterus removed. Now he recorded that he took it to be the symptoms of some deeper malaise.

So in a ghastly reversal of the last scene in *Boom*, where Burton as the angel of death had stripped Mrs Goforth of her bejewelled regalia to send her humbly into that dark night, he now went out and bought Elizabeth another of the world's rare stones. It was as if he hoped it would have a talismanic effect on her drained spirits and pain-wracked body, which had to go through the daily masquerade of filmmaking and then be returned to him, 'crocked as a sock', at the end of the exhausting day. The jewel he went after this time was called 'La Peregrina', or 'The Wanderer', after its restless historical provenance. A lustrous, milky white pearl pendant, it had been discovered by the explorer Bilbao in 1520, subsequently given by Philip II of Spain to Henry VIII's daughter, Mary Tudor, in 1554, and from this queen it had passed to the next-in-line and greater monarch, Queen Elizabeth I. 'It used to belong to the Welsh,' Burton boasted, unable to resist the strain of nationalist braggadocio in any anecdote touching his ancestry. 'I thought it time they got it back.' He had a New York auctioneer buy it for $37,000, intending to give it to Elizabeth on her thirty-seventh birthday. But the day after he took delivery of it, it was mislaid and only recovered when Elizabeth noticed one of her Pekes playing with what looked like a gleaming white bone. She picked it up. 'La Peregrina' had almost finished its wandering down a dog's gullet.

Burton hesitated over whether to buy at auction a sixteenth-century portrait of Queen Mary wearing the pearl. To the vast relief of Sir Hugh Leggatt and the National Art Collections Fund, who were holding their collective breath at having to bid against him, he decided magnanimously to let the nation keep some of its heritage. He even contributed to the cost of its purchase.

But more than a bauble was needed to restore Elizabeth's mind and body to a fit state for the six-thousand-mile journey to Las Vegas in early February. Before she got there – mercifully, perhaps – a death occurred in California. It was that of Nick Hilton, her first husband, who succumbed to cardiac failure at the age of forty-two. Prior to his decease, three male nurses had been needed – and sometimes a strait-jacket – in order to stop him doing injury to himself and others with his household armoury of guns. At times, he was sufficiently disturbed to warrant removal to a hospital. His oil heiress wife had already separated from him charging him with threats and actual physical abuse, and he had fallen under the influence of one of the fashionable mystics who, in the 1960s, began attaching themselves to the wealthy freaks and dropouts of Beverly Hills society. Whatever pity Elizabeth may still have felt for her ex-husband, she must have reflected that she had had a fortunate escape and got off lightly – and early.

By bizarre coincidence, she was not to be spared a minor memento of another of her marriages. While she was being made up to do a location shot in front of one of the hotels on the Strip, a technician spotted a sign winking on and off to advertise the resident attraction in the place. It said: 'EDDIE FISHER'.

Even the house they had bought at Puerto Vallarta, and to which they went after filming – both exhausted, in pain, and consequently in a bad temper with each other – no longer gave them any real seclusion. Thanks to their own well-advertised presence, this mere speck of a fishing village, as it had been when they first discovered it, was now a package-holiday resort of twenty thousand and more in the tourist season. Days passed without their being able to venture outside Casa Kimberley. Elizabeth looked forward to having the children visit them – both boys were now at Millfield, an English public school, although she would soon have to remove them at the request of a headmaster who feared that the constant flux of their parents' lives was having an unhelpful effect on the children's concentration. But Burton was now finding that children bored him. He wanted to concentrate on creative writing. Instead he was stuck with appearing in a bore of a film like the upcoming *Anne of the Thousand Days* – and without Elizabeth.

'Is there any interest on the part of either of you in [Edward Albee's] *A Delicate Balance*?' Losey cabled in March. There was not.

What was she to do in London while Richard was playing Henry VIII to Genevieve Bujold's Anne Boleyn? Besides keeping her eye on him, that is, since he had taken to calling his co-star nicknames like 'Gin' and 'Ginny'. Their own affair on *Cleopatra* had grown more intimate as he playfully plied her with names he had invented like 'Ocean' or 'Gutsy'. An ominous sign.

What could she do to occupy herself? Well, there was her obligation to contribute to the programmes of Harlech Television. She proposed to the Welsh TV station that they do a version of Antoine de Saint Exupéry's fairy-tale *The Little Prince*, with herself narrating, a Welsh composer scoring the music and Joseph Losey directing. After that, they might do *The Wind in the Willows*. It would need judicious editing, she warned Lord Harlech, and she implored him not to think of making it into a series, as she might want to do another film sometime. It was not the contribution that Harlech had foreseen his superstar board member coming up with. Even Losey felt it lacked, well, 'juice'.

But if Burton had been minded to try to seduce the delectable Bujold, ten years Elizabeth's junior, an alarming deterioration in his wife's health would have deterred him. They were staying on the *Kalizma*, moored near Princess Steps, on the Thames, with a twenty-four-hour police guard. It was not the most convenient place to be afflicted with severe bouts of bleeding as they were about to make love. Elizabeth had to undergo painful treatment. The only saving grace was the fact that other people's suffering brought out the best in Burton – and took him off the bottle for a time.

As he held her hand one day, that curiously caustic side of his natural affection – as if he had to keep his male supremacy even while lavishing tender loving care on another – compelled him to tell Elizabeth that her hands were ludicrously large and red as beetroots. 'Nobody can turn insults to her advantage more swiftly or more cleverly than Lady Elizabeth,' he later noted ruefully. Both of them had recently heard of a huge sixty-nine-carat diamond coming on the market, the possession of a sister of Walter Annenberg, the US envoy to Britain, who was now terrified of wearing it in a place like New York. Elizabeth rounded on Burton. If her hands were so large, then he could distract people's attention from them by buying her the immense diamond.

On 25 October 1969, Burton's agent just missed securing it at the Parke-Bernet sale. It went to Cartier, who bid $50,000 above the million-dollar reserve that the agent was authorized to go up to. Elizabeth and he got the bad news while having dinner at an inn, The Bell at Aston Clinton in rural Buckinghamshire, near the hospital where Burton's paralysed brother Ifor was slowly dying.

From a public phone box in the bar, with Elizabeth giggling her encouragement, Burton called Aaron Frosch, his lawyer in New York, to make a deal with Cartier. Phrases like 'Fuck the million ... offer them what it takes ... a million one ... a million two ... For Christ's sake, Aaron, don't be stingy,' were barked peremptorily over the line to America while the English locals sank their own modest orders and listened to the Big Deal. Burton got the stone for $1.1 million. It was immediately renamed the 'Cartier–Burton diamond', and put on view in the window of the New York jeweller's before being delivered to the new owner. The 69.42-carat stone is possibly the only one to have inspired a biting editorial in the *New York Times*, although the brunt of the sarcasm fell not on the flawless jewel, but on the rather less than perfect couple who now possessed it: 'In this age of vulgarity marked by such minor matters as war and poverty, it gets harder every day to scale the heights of vulgarity. But given some loose millions, it can be done – and worse, admired.'

Elizabeth spent another £40,000 on a diamond necklace from which her monster diamond could be hung. A jeweller flew from New York to measure her neck for it, so that the new pear-shaped jewel would exactly cover what remained of the scar from her tracheotomy operation.

Three men with identical briefcases, only one of which contained the massive diamond, left New York by air for Nice escorted by an armed security man. From Nice, they proceeded across the frontier of Monaco to where the *Kalizma* was now riding at anchor in Monte Carlo harbour. At this point, the Monegasque police added a man with a sub-machine gun to the picket. After the jewel had been handed over to Elizabeth, a small package was fished out of the same briefcase. Inside it were three pairs of Palmer tights that the owner of the world's most costly jewel had asked to be sent over from New York. They cost fifty cents a pair.

Ironically, the insurance coverage for the diamond only tightened the screw on Elizabeth's freedom of movement. No American insurance company would touch it. She had to pay a premium of $75,000 for a $1.2 million cover placed at Lloyd's of London, which immediately laid it off with over a dozen other British firms. They specified it must be kept in a vault when not on her neck, that she could wear it publicly only thirty days in any single year, and that armed guards must be in attendance when she did so. It was more of a millstone round her neck than an ornament. Eventually, she had a replica made at a cost of £1,400 and was sometimes suspected of wearing it in public; she, after all, was the setting that gave the stone its credibility.

For all that, there were one or two compensations that only money of this amount could have bought.

When Elizabeth had been given the Krupp diamond, no less a person than Her Royal Highness Princess Margaret had declared it the most vulgar thing she had ever seen.

'Like to try it on?' said Elizabeth. The ring changed hands and the princess flexed her now flashing finger. 'Doesn't look so vulgar now, does it?' asked Elizabeth sweetly.

One finger besides its owner's on which the Cartier–Burton diamond figured was Lucille Ball's. The Burtons made a guest appearance in one of her *The Lucy Show* segments. The diamond got stuck on Lucy's finger. Champagne was tried as a lubricant. '[It's] good for everything,' Elizabeth chipped in. The Burtons' appearance in this sit-com was regarded by themselves as an amusing distraction, but their eagerness to display themselves in public could be interpreted as an act of defiance to those who said that their marriage was on the rocks – and that didn't mean diamonds.

Burton's diaries record that he had been warned off drink because of an enlarged liver. The withdrawal from alcohol possibly contributed to a diminished interest in sex. Whether or not this was so, his diary entries reveal what he considered a marked increase in Elizabeth's impatience with him. His published journals record his fear that she might 'be going to take off one of these days ... I have known it deep down for some time, but have never allowed it to surface'.

Their stay in Hollywood – Burton had been nominated for an Oscar for his *Anne of the Thousand Days* performance, but lost to John Wayne from *True Grit*, just as he had lost to Lee Marvin from *Cat Ballou* when nominated for *The Spy Who Came in from the Cold*: these cowboys were a curse – convinced them of one thing. 'Our world has changed,' Burton commented. 'Nobody, but *nobody* will pay us a million dollars a picture again for a long time ... I am afraid we are temporarily (I hope that it is only temporary) out in the cold and fallen stars. We haven't of course fallen very far – we could doubtless still pick up $750,000 a picture, which ain't chickenfeed. What is remarkable is that we've stayed up there so long.' While they'd been away, a revolution had happened.

For the film industry that gave the Burtons their living, the turn of the decade was the worst of times and the best of times. The old-established and the safely conventional were being ruthlessly and swiftly decimated by youth, boldness and, above all, economy. Studio inventories were crowded with unreleased films. Expensive blockbusters like the Julie Andrews vehicle *Star!* had been unexpected disasters. *The Only Game in Town* was doomed to suffer that fate, too, for despite Elizabeth and Warren Beatty, it was to gross under two million dollars domestically. Movies costing more than four million dollars were now regarded as suicidal folly. The truth was that a generational change in moviemaking and moviegoing had taken place while the Burtons were dancing to the old tunes of the Hollywood band. The youth audience, its appetite whetted by films like *Easy Rider, Bonnie and Clyde, The Graduate* and *Midnight Cowboy*, were passing up self-consciously 'big' movies, and ageing stars and conventional stories. They wanted movies that were sexually franker, more explicitly violent, with newcomers cast in the liberated life-styles of their audiences: Faye Dunaway, Dustin Hoffman, Jack Nicholson, Dennis Hopper, Jane Fonda. 'We can't make a picture with Burt Lancaster and Deborah Kerr groping each other any more,' said James Aubrey, for the moment MGM's new chief executive. The Burtons felt the chill. If Burt and Deborah had the curse laid on them, could Richard and Elizabeth escape it?

A cable arrived from the indefatigable Joseph Losey. He had a script about Leonardo da Vinci, Cesare Borgia and Niccolo Machiavelli which was 'not without merit'. There might even be a part in it for Elizabeth – 'Lucrezia Borgia, I should think'. Elizabeth, according to the filmmaker, responded with one of her wild Woody Woodpecker laughs.

As if to demonstrate their togetherness in the face of this cold wind, they went out and bought something appropriate: a $125,000 fur coat. Turning from stones to skins, Burton had ordered the coat made out of forty-two specially-bred Kojah mink, three times the girth of the ordinary rodents, and, as Jonah Roddy, one of the Burtons' most acidulous critics, wrote in *Look*, 'just dying to be the world's costliest coat for a fading movie queen who has much and wants more'. A picture showed what purported to be Elizabeth in the fur, striding along beside the Pacific, while it shielded her 'from the tropical sun and the diamond glare'. Yes, the hounds were after them now, teeth bared, dripping with unfriendly prose.

Extravagance was probably a necessary distraction from the messy reality of life in the 1970s, much of which now had to do with Elizabeth's health. A particularly painful kind of illness erupted – anal bleeding – and then her doctors had to wean her off the pain-killing medication. No photographers were there when she left hospital in May in a wheelchair. Burton sighed with relief; pictures could have been considered as evidence that she might not be able to perform in films. Her convalescence coincided with his periods of alcoholism: bad timing. But she grew well again, attended by her mother Sara, a widow now after Francis Taylor's death on 20 November 1968. Elizabeth's obligations to care for her adolescent children brought out her best qualities as a mother – the ones she had seldom been able to exhibit on screen with such an authentic sense of fulfilment.

'Here Comes the Mother of the Groom' was the banner headline on 7 October 1970, when she attended her son Michael's wedding in London, at Caxton Hall, where Elizabeth had married his father in 1952. After his withdrawal from Millfield, young Michael had spent a year or so with Howard Taylor's family in Hawaii. Burton's own Welsh reverence for education made him furious that the boy had no degree and no job, but Elizabeth viewed it all rather as her character in *The Sandpiper* had done – seeing her son as the embodiment of her own free spirit, whatever the mortifications she had had to endure from the flesh. The actual ceremony conformed as much to the dying era of hippies and flower children as it did to the form of civil weddings. Michael wore his hair almost as long as his mother's, his toes peeped out of his sandals, he had on a Tudor tunic of maroon velvet and bellbottom trousers. His bride, an American girl named Beth Clutter, wore white butter muslin and had an Afro hair-do. Elizabeth was in a knitted trouser suit and a maxi-coat. Burton, as the best man, looked discordantly conventional. Elizabeth's gift to the newlyweds was a Jaguar, a £35,000 cheque and a house right next door to hers and Burton's in Hampstead. Within a few weeks, a pregnancy was announced and a diamond ring and designer layettes somewhat overwhelmed Mrs Michael Wilding Jr.

To be made a grandmother didn't trouble Elizabeth the Earth Mother in the slightest. Such proxy parentage put her in fighting form for her new film. For against the odds, there was a new one ready – and one for Richard, too. His was *Villain*, a low-budget but well-made British gangster thriller in which his debilitated appearance helped him give one of the best performances of his career, as a menacing racketeer. Hers was in a film variously called *X, Y and Zee* or *Zee and Co.*, which she was doing for expenses and a percentage, rather than her usually munificent up-front fee.

Though based on an original screenplay by the novelist Edna O'Brien, the film was to contain abundant resemblances to the current state of the Burtons' marriage, with Michael Caine as a suitably coarsened Burton-figure enacting with Elizabeth the blood-thirsty rows that sustain a marriage which otherwise might expire from mutual boredom. Pauline Kael called the film Elizabeth's 'coming-out' picture. 'The ageing beauty has discovered in herself a gutsy, unrestrained spirit ... and, for the first time that I can recall, she appears to be having a roaring good time on camera.' In her published version of the script, Edna O'Brien describes Zee in a way that suggests she was itemizing Elizabeth Taylor: 'Her aura is crimson ... her manner a trifle raucous, her face masked with mechanical joy, her wardrobe of clothes vast; her energy, ruthlessness and will-power are prodigious. Perhaps she is a monster. Zee is a ruthless survivor.'

Elizabeth's weight gain was now unconcealable: not 'gracefully voluptuous', said Kael, 'she's too hard-bodied to be Rubenesque. [It] seems to have brought out her coarseness and now she basks in vulgarity.' She uses language in the film like a knife-thrower, but cries with triumph when one hits home and her target bleeds. Dependency and disengagement, endlessly repeated, are the twin motors that keep her and Caine locked in a masochistic marriage that sounds and looks pretty much like what the Burton diaries record of his furious rows with Elizabeth, in which he feared he would put her into hospital, or do worse to her. 'You bloody bitch, I'll kill you,' yells Caine in the film, raining blows on her as she spits defiance and goads him into worse brutalities. They are characters who need such aggression for the sake of mutual sexual arousal, so that they can later nurse their wounds in each other's arms. Thanks to Elizabeth's faithful representation of relentless masochism, the pathology of *Zee and Co.* is powerful.

After this, the Burtons at last buckled down to work for Harlech Television, which they had promised to support with plays, films and programmes ever since they had joined the consortium bidding for the franchise and seen their investment multiply 110 per cent.

They graciously used some of the days allowed them for a tax-free stay in Britain to appear in Andrew Sinclair's film of the Dylan Thomas 'play for voices' in verse, *Under Milk Wood*. Peter O'Toole was already cast, so Burton appeared as 'First Voice', the narrator, and Elizabeth as the town harlot Rosie Probert. Their impatience with each other occasionally flared up in what Sinclair put down to sheer exhaustion. They had lived off each other's energy. Now, after all the illness, alcoholism, medication and withdrawal symptoms, their energy was running down and they lived off each other's nerves.

The interviews they gave at this time are instructive and rather eerie to read. They spoke like players who had been coached in their lines for one play and had refused to depart from them when they found themselves in a completely different one. It is the chill of the zombie life that the reported opinions give off: the 'sunshine' that strikes cold, the 'freshness' that tastes stale. As far as they were concerned, speaking for the public record, nothing had changed. 'He is the ocean. He is the sunset ... He is such a vast person. He has such a huge personality. He is capable of being so many people, of doing so much. How can I describe him in words?' Thus Elizabeth babbling about Burton to the *Ladies' Home Journal* in April 1971. It was pardonable to think she had been infected by a poetic virus caught from Dylan Thomas. Burton, interviewed about Elizabeth for a back-to-back article in the same magazine, came on like an episode entitled *I Love Liz*. What had become a tragic impasse was still being presented by the partners as if it were a sentimental romance or a situation comedy. Whom were they deceiving?

36

'OH, WHERE ARE THE WRITERS TO RESCUE US?'

'The trouble with actors,' said Joseph L. Mankiewicz, 'is that unless you give them the lines, they don't know how to leave the stage.'

The marriage was obviously nearing its painful end, yet neither of them could separate from the other. They began 1971 still locked into a film contract. This was their lowest ebb. Gone were the great film companies of Hollywood, now too busy adjusting to their own painful shake-out to have time to consider projects for pensioners like the generation of stars to which the Burtons belonged. Their sponsor this time round, for a film called *Hammersmith Is Out*, written and to be directed by Peter Ustinov, was a manufacturer of mobile homes, J. Cornelius Crean. He had found some advantage in financing it; no one else would. Again the Burtons worked for expenses and a percentage; at least they didn't have to travel far, as it was to be shot almost on their own doorstep, in Cuernavaca, Mexico, masquerading as the American southwest. This was their only bonus. Had their instincts not been blunted by illness and alcohol, they would have been warned off the project from the start. Neither of them was a natural comedian. Moreover, the story was intended to be an updated parody of the Faust legend, about selling one's soul to the Devil, and they'd come to expensive grief on that in the past, God knows! Burton played a lunatic who promises the world and the flesh to a young hospital intern in return for his release. (Robert Redford had been considered for the role, but rejected, and Beau Bridges inherited it.) Elizabeth played a hash-slinger in a diner with whom the Devil fornicates after he has been released from his strait-jacket and has overthrown his disciple.

Burton was in appalling health. He adopted what Elizabeth loyally characterized as 'that terrible mad stare', except that it was the only expression he owned in the film. He had not only begun another bout of drinking, but he was snorting cocaine. He had been introduced to the drug in London, while shooting *Villain*. Mercifully, he never became habituated to it. But he resorted to it at times when stress, work and the bottle needed additional thrust. A *Los Angeles Times* reporter, Don Knapp, conveyed the shock that his appearance now presented: the pot belly, the puffy and bloodshot eyes, the mouse-coloured hair brushed forward to hide his balding crown, his pitted and pockmarked face additionally blotched by booze. He rambled bibulously to himself between takes. Though he turned up to watch Elizabeth perform her scenes, it was noticeable that she rarely did the same for him. To spectators, it appeared that he had become unendurably boring to her. Even the lip service he paid their relationship in interviews had the repetitive grind of the needle stuck in the groove: 'We were offered everything ... Elizabeth one of the greatest enduring stars ... despite the money problem [*sic*] things are smashing ... but everyone goes down for a bit, luv ... that's over now.' The contrast his appearance made with Elizabeth's was breath-catching. She who had seemed worn and wasted by pain only a few months earlier, now glowed with renewed health, or at least remission. 'Forty next year, she is in better shape than at any time within recent memory,' the man from the *Times* concluded. But he drew a cruelly just lesson from his visit. 'What does it matter ... that they have become an anachronistic king and queen whose domain has shrunk to the dimensions of two deferment contracts? ... They have each other ... Only the power and the magic are gone. But that doesn't matter either, you see, luv – for it will probably be years before they know it.'

Burton tried to pass off as a joke a film that was called 'a tasteless and tedious little atrocity'. 'I don't have to do this for a living. As a longtime employee of MGM, Elizabeth gets a pension ... That's why I married her, really – for the pension.'

They were recovering from this fiasco and cruising the Mediterranean in the *Kalizma* when Elizabeth heard, in August 1971, that she had become a grandmother. Immediately she rushed back to London, pausing only long enough to buy more baby clothes from Christian Dior. Her son Michael's life-style was a source of worry to her. The boy's laid-back existence had turned the grand Hampstead house that had been a wedding present into something resembling a squat for his friends, with sleeping bags and blankets on bare boards. Next door, security men stood guard over Elizabeth's house. It was as if Michael were making a point about his mother's privileged mode of living. Soon he and his wife took off for a commune in Wales, ironically near his step-father's birthplace, where they lived until Beth found conditions too severe for the child, whom they had named Leyla. She arrived on the Dorchester doorstep and was taken in by Elizabeth with open arms. But a tug-of-love appeared to develop between Beth and her mother-in-law over who could be kinder to little Leyla. Eventually, Beth Clutter Wilding went home to her own mother in Oregon, taking Elizabeth's grandchild with her, and divorce proceedings began.

Burton had stuffed two more films under his belt by the year's end: one a highly selective account of Marshal Tito's heroic war in Yugoslavia, the other a romanticized enactment of Trotsky's murder. And now he signed to make the life of Bluebeard, a film he knew would be rubbish – but it had the advantage of giving him and Elizabeth a rest in Budapest – 'a little lightness after Tit and Trot,' as he noted.

A rest! No sooner were they installed in the Duna-Intercontinental hotel, on 7 February 1972, than they started organizing a party to celebrate Elizabeth's fortieth birthday. Already they'd considered and rejected grandiose schemes to mark the date. One had involved borrowing two of France's Concordes for a concurrent birthday party aboard while each exceeded the speed of sound. Amazing how few guests had accepted. Then they thought of a non-stop party aboard a European super-train. But as well as the security risks, there was the humiliation that might ensue from the VIPs being shunted into a siding to let some proletarian express have the right of way. So in spite of still stringent rationing in Hungary, and food and fuel shortages – not to mention constraints on liberty – the party at the Intercontinental was arranged– not one single party, but three of them graded to the status of the guests. 'The hotel is very Hilton,' they telexed the two hundred guests, 'but there are some fun places to go. Stop. Dress slacks for Saturday night in the dark cellar and something gay and pretty for Sunday night. Stop. Dark glasses for hangovers.'

Burton had wanted to add 'No Presents'. But the invitations had gone out: it was too late. Anyhow, with people like Bulgari coming ...

Elizabeth worked feverishly through most of February. Part of the time, however, she spent on the *Bluebeard* set, watching her husband acting with eight of Europe's most beautiful women, including Raquel Welch, Virna Lisi and Nathalie Delon. Bluebeard's tastes, unfortunately, had run to women who hadn't yet celebrated their fortieth birthdays. The rest of her time was devoted to the logistics of the party. Private homes in Budapest were visited; their long-hoarded silver, fine pre-war furnishings and family paintings were borrowed or rented in order to transform the 'very Hilton' look of the hotel suites into something more in line with what a guest like Princess Grace of Monaco would feel at home with. The capital of Hungary had never seen so many VIPs descending on it all at once. A chartered British Airways Trident was needed to convey the British contingent, which included a dozen members of Burton's family, Elizabeth's mother and brother, Michael Caine and his girlfriend (and later wife) Shakira Baaksh, Susannah York, Ringo Starr and his wife, Victor Spinetti, Liza Todd (released from Heathfield, her English boarding school, for her mother's birthday), Chris Wilding (now at the University of Hawaii), the poet Stephen Spender and the Oxford don Francis Warner. From Los Angeles came Michael Wilding and his new wife Margaret Leighton; from Paris, Joseph and Patricia Losey, the Cartiers, the Bulgaris and, of course, Alexandre the hairdresser.

Elizabeth's presents ranged from the campy to the costly (received with what appeared equal delight): a tin of diamond polish (from Victor Spinetti); a coal scuttle filled with Welsh coal; a rose fashioned from stainless steel and a box of laver bread made from seaweed (the Jenkins clan); paintings (the Caines and the Starrs); a copy of Sir Walter Raleigh's *Historie of the World*, written by him while awaiting execution in the Tower (Francis Warner).

From Richard came – but what else? – yet another jewel, one of the most exotic in Elizabeth's now sizeable collection: a £350,00 heart-shaped yellow diamond cut in 1621 for Shah Jahan, the Indian mogul who built the Taj Mahal. Held up to candlelight, it revealed an inscription in Parsee incised into the jewel: 'Love Is Everlasting'. Later, that seemed to be the final irony.

The only fly in the goulash was an outburst by Alan Williams, novelist son of Emlyn, who publicly scolded all of them for such capitalist high jinks in a city that still bore traces of the revolt so cruelly crushed by Russian tanks a bare twelve years earlier. Embarrassment spread until Burton offered to match the cost of the party by a contribution to a charity. Thus the United Nations fund for children, Unicef, became the richer by £50,000. Guilt subsided, appetite was re-whetted.

Over two hundred sat down to the birthday supper. Elizabeth wore white cyclamen blossom in her hair and a white Grecian-style dress, the Krupp diamond on her finger, her new jewel suspended from a gold chain on her bosom. On one side of her sat Caine; on the other, the American ambassador, one of eight envoys present. The Ringo Starrs were opposite. Burton was flanked by Princess Grace, his sister Cis, the British envoy and Stephen Spender. Some 3,500 helium-filled gold balloons hovered above them; a Hungarian pop group played throughout a dinner of chicken Kiev and fruit salad, and an iced chocolate cake with forty candles was cut and devoured. Dancing went on until 4 a.m. As the band played (gamely if hardly appropriately) 'I Left My Heart In San Francisco', Elizabeth bent down, scooped off her white satin shoes and cried 'Let's go' – and the party was over.

Not just the party. The Burtons seemed to have decided the event marked not only a new decade for Elizabeth, but a complete change of life for them. They had resolved to tunnel out of the compound in which the entourage held them virtual prisoners, and retreat to a home base – at last! – in the place where Elizabeth said she had had her happiest years: England. Her friend Sheran Cazalet, now married to Simon (soon to be Sir Simon) Hornby, heir to the W. H. Smith fortune, was asked if she and her husband could find them a house in the country with a paddock, a stable and easy access to Oxford where Francis Warner had invited Burton to give lectures.

Such a vision comfortably accommodated their daydreams of a life that was the very opposite of the one they'd just celebrated – a life of quietness, seclusion, horses and scholarship. How realistic their resolve might have been, one will never know. Barely two weeks later, news arrived that brought their good intentions and indeed their marriage itself tumbling down around them. It wasn't due to any infidelity on Burton's part: guilt still kept him in bonds of chastity to Elizabeth. It was grief that shattered him. His beloved brother Ifor died. He had been a paraplegic since the fall at Pays de Galles that broke his neck. Now for the first time, Burton was brought face to face with the finiteness of life – and all his perspectives altered. 'Ifor's death unhinged him,' Melvyn Bragg wrote, after reading the diary passages recording it – the last entries for the next eight years. 'His deep and furious affair with self-destruction was under way ... he was adrift.' So, too, was his marriage. Elizabeth realized in the months ahead that it was beyond her strength to pull it back to any safe anchorage. That was surely the moment when she saw that her fortieth birthday had indeed been a turning-point, a signpost on a road she was going to have to travel alone.

She watched helplessly as her husband went physically and emotionally to pieces. He hit the bottle from breakfast-time onwards. He had to be carried into his car at the hotel, out of it at the film studios, sobered up for his costuming and make-up, coached in learning his lines. Faithfulness was the first casualty. He began to play Bluebeard for real at the studio, and, at last, unable to stand his drunken pursuit of one actress, Elizabeth flew off to Rome. There she had supper with Aristotle Onassis. For the paparazzi, it was like the old days again. Was it a deliberate dare to provoke Burton's jealousy? Or a need to reassert her own power as a woman who could summon one of the world's richest men, and the husband of the ex-Mrs Kennedy, to console her in public? Probably both. The vigilant entourage she left back in Budapest reported round the clock. From her suite at the Hotel de Paris, in Rome, she called Burton.

'Get that woman out of my bed,' she snapped when he answered.

'How did she know?' he asked lamely.

Another marriage might have ended right there. But although their grand passion was now in public tatters, the Burtons were still yoked together by apprehension of what life would be like for them if apart. It was as if they were totally dependent on the agenda being set for them: a day without it would be a terrifying void. Work was what plugged the void – and work for them meant filming. Their public personae as 'the Burtons' had denied them the chance to develop separate and private identities. They could not bring themselves to split up; they could only go on.

The Hornbys' estate at Pusey, Oxfordshire, became their temporary home; Burton commuted to lectures at Oxford University, while Elizabeth prepared for a new film, *Night Watch*, in which she played a woman being driven out of her mind amid the luxury of an extensive Valentino wardrobe, Van Cleef and Arpels jewellery and even a Westinghouse fitted kitchen.

One day during location shooting she ate lunch at a Wimbledon hotel. She had lamb and avocado, and then asked for a sandwich to be made out of what she had left. The woman who packaged the snack thought that she looked 'a little like a rather forlorn schoolgirl being sent off to school with her dinner pail'.

She revived her plan to adopt another baby. She tried Jewish agencies in New York, but learned very few children born into that faith were in need of adoption. Even Marshal Tito's wife – Burton was finishing his film of her husband's life – failed to locate an orphaned child. She thought of going to Asia where there were Vietnamese children born to American fathers and abandoned. She devoted more and more time to Unicef. Such aid was to her credit, though it also recalled how the domestic rows of *Who's Afraid of Virginia Woolf?* had ended in the whimpering of a woman for a child.

Had the Burtons' lives not run in and out of their movies so insistently, it would have seemed cold-blooded in the extreme to write two films especially for them with the titles *Divorce His* and *Divorce Hers*. But there they were in Munich, in the autumn of 1972, shooting them for Harlech Television – at last they were delivering to Lord Harlech the promised payload, just when the gold mine was exhausted.

Burton played a high-powered executive devoting all his time to office politics; Elizabeth was his left-at-home wife. This time, the roles were not even close to those they played in life. But what was too real for comfort was the nagging unhappiness of the couple in the films. Not for them the royal rows of *Who's Afraid of Virginia Woolf?*, which had been like workout exercises on the marital trampoline when their own marriage was fresh and vigorous. Now they had fought each other to an exhausted standstill.

Elizabeth broke off in the middle of one scene, her eyes filling with real tears. 'For a moment it seemed as if we were really quarrelling,' she said to director Waris Hussein.

'We can't just go on playing ourselves,' Burton said, and in a line that recalled Joseph L. Mankiewicz's observation on actors, he added, 'Oh, where are the writers to rescue us?'

The actress Carrie Nye, playing Burton's mistress in the films, which were designed to examine the same situation from the husband's viewpoint and then from the wife's, gave *Time* magazine an inside view of both performers that suggested how time (without a capital letter) was running out for them. Burton occupied himself over long liquid lunches that reduced Hussein to anguish to know 'when, if ever, work could be resumed'. But Elizabeth showed little of the old stoic patience. Catching his eye in mid-account of some oft-told tale, she snapped, 'Come on, Richard, just finish the story.'

Waris Hussein commented that they were best in the scenes of remorse, when they were at their quietest, regretting lost opportunities and past mistakes, wishing it were possible to do things differently. In other films they had played people in love, or people discovering that love was what mattered most. Now the words they were commissioned to utter spelled the end of love. John Heyman said later, 'We wanted the theme explored [in] three ways: the husband's story and then the wife's and then "the truth".' As things turned out, they never wrote 'the truth'. They didn't need to. The truth was, they had really nothing left to give each other – except a divorce.

Maybe so: but as the saint's prayer for the strength of will to remain chaste put it – not just yet, O Lord.

The seductive power of confession, Burton's brother Graham always thought, was one of the reasons why he accepted some roles: which is possibly why he decided to play a penitent German officer in a film based on the killing of wartime hostages entitled *Massacre in Rome*. It helped cleanse his own sins. He didn't show such understanding, though, to the film Elizabeth embarked on around the same time. *Ash Wednesday* was the story of a rich woman who has a face-lift and forms a relationship with a gigolo. Vulgar and unworthy of her, Burton piously called it. One is tempted to think the appeal of youth reflected her own state of mind at forty. But as Dominick Dunne, its producer, discovered when he sold her on the idea, it wasn't any increasing concern about losing her looks, and hence her sex appeal, that predisposed her to accept yet one more movie done for expenses and percentages. 'She was dying to do another "dress-up" movie. The wardrobe had been designed specially for her by Edith Head.' Invited by Elizabeth to a party for twenty-four of her 'friends',

Dunne was surprised to discover that nearly all of them were her hired employees – a sycophantic bunch, he decided, whose gifts she 'received with pleasure and opened with a flurry of gesticulation'.

That relations between the Burtons were soured was plain for all to see. Even physical pleasure, according to some observers, had gone out of the marriage. One day after shooting at the Italian ski resort of Cortina D'Ampezzo, Dunne was summoned to Elizabeth's suite at the Hotel Miramonte. He found her sitting there, regal-looking, impeccably made up and wearing a turban head-dress with a large ultramarine clip in its front folds. Burton was drunk. 'My husband,' Elizabeth began in measured tones, 'claims that I held up shooting today and cost the studio many thousands of dollars. Is that true, Dominick?' Dunne saw she was barely suppressing her rage and suspected Burton had been taunting her in front of Liza and Maria. 'No, it's not, Elizabeth, we got all our footage.' She glared in triumph at Burton, who filled the room with expletives. The children began to cry.

They moved back to Rome for the summer of 1973: Burton to finish the *Massacre* film there and then begin another film for Carlo Ponti, *The Voyage*, with Sophia Loren (Mrs Ponti) as his co-star, and Elizabeth to start work on a film of Muriel Spark's novella *The Driver's Seat*. In this her character's state of mind again matched her own with startling, indeed ominous, appropriateness – and this time her wardrobe was restricted to two or three changes. She was to play a woman alone, travelling toward a fatal destiny that she had helped to arrange, as if her own extinction will bring a meaningless existence to its wished-for end. Elizabeth's life, in more disarray than ever, looked like a mirror reflection of the character's premeditated search for someone, anyone, with whom she could form a dangerous liaison. The part suited Elizabeth's talent for assuming a tremulous sanity on screen: her performance was to be acclaimed as one of her best, though ironically the film was such a commercial failure that even today copies of it are hard to find under the various would-be sensational titles (*Identikit* and *Blood Games*) it was eventually given.

Burton was now, in the opinion of observers like Franco Zeffirelli, dangerously uncontrollable. Just as he had been whipsawed between Sybil and Elizabeth when it came to choosing which woman to make his life with, so he now veered wildly between regarding Elizabeth as the object of all his desires or the agent of most of his misfortunes.

In this mood, they made an uneasy couple when they arrived in New York in late June before the work started on their films in Italy. For once, Elizabeth flew on to California unaccompanied; Burton went to a cottage owned by his lawyer, Aaron Frosch, on Long Island. Elizabeth's mother had been ill – but soon reports of dates around town with acquaintances began seeping back to Burton. Some people felt she was deliberately creating a disaster to test him. A call from him arrived one night in the middle of a dinner party at Laurence Harvey's. She refused the offer to take it in another room. 'Fat Ass adores an audience,' said Harvey sardonically. If the report is accurate, the conversation that followed sounded like something out of *Who's Afraid of Virginia Woolf?* It was at times scathingly frank, mirthful, rebarbative, whisperingly pathetic, finally firm yet hopeful. But Burton was still in an ugly mood when Elizabeth returned to the East Coast, and they had no sooner reached Aaron Frosch's cottage than she ordered the Rolls-Royce back to New York and checked into the Regency Hotel. Burton's vanity clearly couldn't endure a scene that looked as if Elizabeth had walked out on him. 'I told her to go – and she's gone,' he said.

But just as characteristically, it was Elizabeth who wrested back the initiative. The next day, which happened to be 4 July, Independence Day, a coincidence missed in no report, the wire services received a communication from Elizabeth written in her own hand. In childish block capitals, sometimes scored through and dramatically peppered with exclamation marks, she wrote: 'I am convinced it would be a good and constructive idea if Richard and I were separated for a while. Maybe we loved each other too much – I never believed such a thing was possible. But we have been in each other's pockets constantly, never being apart but for matters of life and death ... I believe with all my heart that the separation will ultimately bring us back to where we should be – and that's together! ... Wish us well during this difficult time. Pray for us.' Not so much a press statement, more a personal confidence that the troubled star wished to share with millions; it had all the lachrymose drama of a fan magazine. Yet it also held the eccentric grandeur of its own egoism, as if a sovereign were invoking her people's sympathy in a moment of constitutional crisis.

Burton professed amusement. He missed the point. The open letter had all the earnestness of the little girl that Elizabeth had once been – the child who had promised her parents that she wanted to be a star and would never, never do anything to spoil her mother's happiness.

37

A CHIPMUNK RETURNS

On 20 July 1973, Burton sat in the back of a Geneva-registered Rolls-Royce at Rome airport. Though it was hot, he wore a red blazer and a white polo neck. Two hundred *carabinieri* held back at least twice as many photographers and reporters. Everyone was waiting for 'her' to arrive. It was like Cleopatra's entry into the Forum in miniature. Elizabeth had taken off from London in a Mystère aircraft leased to speed her to the expected reconciliation without delay after she had arrived overnight from Los Angeles.

Yet when her aircraft taxied in, Burton didn't alight from the car. To some observers, he seemed sunk in reflection; to others, more unkind, he just seemed drunk. Maybe he was expecting Elizabeth to come bounding down the aircraft steps for a lovers' embrace. Maybe she wanted him to come bounding up them for a homecoming kiss. It was soon clear that neither wanted to make the first move. Half an hour passed, then out she came, followed by nine cases, two dogs and a cat. Still Burton didn't get out of the car. He stayed there, crouched, purgatorial, silent, shaking. Face set, she vanished into Customs. She was in comfortable worn blue jeans and a sloppy orange T-shirt, but jewellery made points of light on this drab attire, reminding people of the wealth behind a plain cotton outfit. Security guards forced a passage through the massed media folk and propelled her towards the car. And still Burton did not emerge. Now his ungallantry was like a gauntlet thrown down in front of her. Elizabeth's eyes hardened; she looked cold and offended. A sudden heave from the paparazzi, fearful of missing the great encounter, had the effect of impelling her through the open rear door, almost across her husband's knees. That galvanized him. He kissed her on one cheek, then the other, as flashlights flooded through the smoked glass windows, lending the interior a promiscuous brightness. Burton could be seen burying his head on her shoulder. The car inched forward, picked up speed, hit the *autostrada* and then, pursued by a fleet of photographers, raced for the sixteenth-century villa owned by the Pontis in the Alban Hills, about thirteen miles away. Through the photocell-controlled gates, up the drive bordered by elec- trified fencing, past the armed guards and the fierce Alsatians, and up to the door of the fifty-room mansion they went. Sophia Loren stood waiting to welcome them. They had drinks with her and Ponti, then were shown to the guest house in the grounds. Lunch followed on the terrace: risotto, roasted Palumbo fish, fruit, white wine. The separation had lasted two weeks. The reconciliation would last just half that time.

Loneliness was what had made them each try to patch things up, but now their attempt at togetherness showed the folly of it. The old pernicious pattern of attraction and repulsion repeated itself. Their marriage was no longer elastic enough to expand and make room for their changed attitudes. Even presents palled now. Burton gave her a Cartier-designed bit of exotica costing £80,000, made of oriental pearls, diamonds and rubies and designed to be worn with the famous La Peregrina pendant. But now she treated it as a collectible, not a pledge; into the bank with it. By the end of the week, Burton mentioned the hitherto unmentionable and, on 30 July, each of them separately called Aaron Frosch to prepare the divorce papers. Elizabeth checked into the Grand Hotel in Rome. Burton stayed behind with Sophia Loren, a woman with a reputation for earth-motherliness which resembled Elizabeth's when it came to com- forting the hurt child in a grown man.

While Burton lay low, waiting to resume filming, Elizabeth went through the public rites of fortitude expected of a star under pressure: she started a film, she arrived late, and she took a lover – in that order. The film was *The Driver's Seat*. Begging the morning off, she turned up for the first shot – coincidentally at Fiumicino Airport, where hope had been so recently kindled – and announced, 'It takes one day to die and another day to start living again.' By rights, someone should have called 'Cut' at that point. One had to hand it to Elizabeth; she knew what to give the people.

Loneliness was again her great problem. She took up Andy Warhol, who had a bit part playing himself in the film, and poured out her heart to him – until her hand fell on Warhol's black leather blouson, which he'd placed on the restaurant banquette beside her. Instantly, she knew she was being taped. She hauled out the mini-recorder – the usual way that Andy's *Interview* magazine filled its pages – and subjected the albino-toned American to a tirade that turned his face red. Then her long fingernail hooked the tape, and all her confidences recorded thereon, out of the machine and dumped it in a ball on Andy's side plate. Later, they were reconciled.

But as Max Lerner said, 'Elizabeth never abandons one man until another is there to offer his arm.' This time the man was Henry Wynberg. Henry *who?* people asked.

She had met this young, half-Jewish Dutchman, a used-car dealer and Beverly Hills playboy of the gold-chains-and-Gucci-loafers variety, just a few weeks earlier. A story, which he denied – and which certainly seems inconsistent with his conduct – had it that a group of Playboy Club pals had banded together to send him off to Europe to romance Elizabeth when the break-up of her marriage was announced. What did she see in him? He was not a star; he was divorced; he was conventionally handsome; he was not given to declaiming Shakespeare drunk or sober. But he was gentle-mannered and soft-spoken, yet hard-headed and quick-witted. Max Lerner, writing of new romance, believed that 'in the case of many marriage break-ups, the choice of the next mate may contain elements of nostalgia, self-reassurance and revenge'. Wynberg reminded some people of a convenient cross between Eddie Fisher (the soft side of him) and Mike Todd (the hard-man image). Lerner also added a third quality to Elizabeth's mixture of romantic abandon and womanly strength – her motherly love. 'My child's just come in,' he reported her saying to him on the phone; he concluded she meant Wynberg.

Burton was predictably sarcastic about the liaison and probably thought Elizabeth had taken a lover so as not to seem left in the lurch. Well, that too may have counted a little. 'No name can be all bad if it has "wine" in it,' Burton said self-deprecatingly. He also observed that, as in the used-car trade, a vital part of Wynberg might drop off at the moment it was most needed. Such quips, forced though they were, at least lightened the solemnity with which the players usually took themselves.

Although it may have seemed unlikely in the extreme that a reconciliation could emerge from this impasse, one did occur at the turn of the year, due to alarm over a medical check-up Elizabeth had had that suggested the possibility of a malignant tumour. Burton was still filming *The Voyage*, and was in Palermo, when he heard the news. He was immediately concerned, but without a beckoning gesture from the woman who was still his wife, he was unready to risk turning up at the UCLA Medical Center, Los Angeles, to find Wynberg, his rival, ensconced in a suite next to Elizabeth's. 'Maybe that's what she's playing at,' he said. 'Remember how she humiliated Eddie Fisher when he begged her to deny their break-up?' Fortunately Elizabeth's cyst proved benign. Burton at last got the 'come hither' signal and, paying $45,000 a day compensation to Ponti for the privilege of being granted leave from the film, he showed up in Elizabeth's suite in Los Angeles. It was as if thunderclouds had never rained on them.

'Hello, Lumpy,' he said to her.

'Hello, Pockmark.'

He turned to a medical attendant: 'I'm the husband. I want a bed.' Exit Henry Wynberg.

Newscaster John Chancellor announced on NBC TV: 'Elizabeth Taylor and Richard Burton are reconciling permanently, as opposed to temporarily.' In London, Madame Tussaud's wax museum acted on the news; the Burtons' effigies were moved back together again.

It was not to last. And when it ended, finally, it was in the unlikeliest of places – no, not strictly true. Oroville, as the name suggests, was a worked-out goldmine town in northern California, selected as the location for Burton's latest film, *The Klansman*, a sorry tale of racial hatred leavened with violence, sex, rape and castration. His co-star was another 'hard man', Lee Marvin, cast in the expectation that the two of them would produce aggressive performances. They did, in a way, but it was to see who could drink most. By the time that Burton was lagging several bottles behind, Elizabeth knew she had lost him again. He was drunk, despairing and so unsteady that he clutched at whatever was available, be it his co-star or the seventeen-year-old waitress who had borne well his recitations from Shakespeare and the Welsh bards. They got him through the film; then they got him into hospital. He emerged after six weeks' drying out older, whiter, feebler. Irreversible damage had been inflicted on his constitution. In the meantime, once again, Aaron Frosch shuffled the divorce papers. This time, it went through.

The Burtons were divorced in just forty minutes, in a wooden-frame courthouse in the Swiss town of Saarinen, on 26 June 1974. Dressed in cream and brown silk and wearing dark glasses, Elizabeth sat in the third row and heard the small-town judge ask, 'Is it true that to live with your husband was intolerable?'

'Yes, life with Richard became intolerable.'

The suit was uncontested. Burton sent a doctor's certificate from California; he was too ill to attend. Together they had gone through ten years of marriage, eleven movies and thirty million dollars.

Over the next eighteen months, they found their pleasure with others: Burton taking his with various women, including Princess Elizabeth of Yugoslavia, the other Elizabeth sticking to a re-activated Henry Wynberg, and helped by friends who formed what they called 'The Elizabeth Taylor Life Support Group'. Max Lerner was a welcome caller. 'She had gotten rid of most of the staff who had hedged her and Richard off from the world. I told her that was an improvement at least. She was down to a secretary, a chauffeur, a butler and Henry.' She rented an Italianate mansion in Bel Air, whose master bedroom was papered in silver foil which threw her reflection back at her from every wall, as well as the ceiling. Because the walls weren't quite flat, the reflections were often distorted – it was like living in a fun-fair hall of mirrors. 'Henry had a lot of patience,' said a friend, 'that was the secret. He'd work hard at business deals. He could organize her life.' He was probably the man who gave Elizabeth a taste for the corporate life in other occupations besides moviemaking. Not that their business ventures were markedly successful: a cosmetics company was short-lived and Elizabeth's later association with a diamond-selling firm ended in litigation. But she went with Wynberg on business trips, her presence giving an aura of glamour and magnitude to projects one would not have associated with such adjectives had Wynberg been pursuing them alone. Whether they were in love is a matter for dispute. Certainly they were good partners.

'Elizabeth often spoke with Richard,' Max Lerner recalled, 'but intimacy was "on hold" for the time being, anyhow.' Burton, though not cured and still drinking, was working furiously; he once again discovered how relatively 'poor' he was after a divorce settlement that awarded Elizabeth the houses, the *Kalizma*, the jewellery and much else. Max Lerner said to her, 'Elizabeth, he's a changed man, now you're not around.' That bucked her up, he reported.

Later on, Burton would be fond of saying, 'Elizabeth will surprise us all yet.' He spoke with irony. But it *was* a surprise when she announced she was off to film in Russia, in May 1975, to play four roles in a musical version of Maeterlinck's *The Blue Bird*, with seventy-six-year-old George Cukor directing, and Ava Gardner, Jane Fonda and Cicely Tyson as her co-stars. It was described as the first Russo-American co-production, budgeted at $15 million and financed by Fox, Mosfilm and the millionaire mobile-home manufacturer J. Cornelius Crean, who thought it would be good for peace, friendship and big business. Elizabeth got $3,000 a week expenses, most of which it was impossible to spend in Moscow, and a lot of which she ploughed back into the production by paying for her own costumes to be remade on more effective lines. She turned up her nose at the paste jewellery supplied by the Russians for one of her roles, the Blue Fairy, and decided to use what she had brought with her of her own. After checking in at her hotel, she had called the Russian concierge to enquire about strongroom facilities. He told her to bring her jewellery down. When she said how much it was worth, he said, 'Stop in your room, we'll bring the safe up.' Conditions were spartan. Her name was hand-lettered on her dressing-room door. She learned to carry her own toilet paper. Food was the main difficulty. In addition to herself and Henry, she had to feed the pets she had bought in Moscow: a Siamese cat called Cleo, a Yorkie called Sally, a half-Papillon half-Shih Tzu called

Daisy and two puppies which she hadn't got round to naming. When Henry wasn't on hand, she had to get down on her knees to do her own cleaning up of 'the doggie doo'.

In Leningrad, she caught amoebic dysentery from infected ice cubes, lost eighteen pounds, and admitted to the columnist Rex Reed that she'd never looked so good – 'but what a hell of a way to diet – flush it all down the toilet'. The illness put her into hospital, always a decisive step in Elizabeth's life, since it was in the 'rebirthing' atmosphere of treatment and healing that the past slackened its grip on her. Reed queried if even a silver bullet would drop her in her resilient tracks, and doubted it.

Some friends wondered if Russian wedding bells wouldn't ring out for her and Wynberg. She had domesticated him so successfully that each morning, with the phlegmatic patience of an old hand at caring for women's whims, he fried her rashers of bacon cut from a joint that Fortnum and Mason's had sent from London, then sat quietly by in his blue blazer, Gucci loafers and Cancer the Crab belt buckle while she wolfed them down. But Liz Smith, the New York social columnist, noticed on a visit that they were 'correct' with each other, but nothing more – 'she never did call him "darling" or "sweetnose" or "dearest" or "fuckface", as she had called Richard Burton.' As for calling him 'my child', that signified his dependence, Liz Smith thought, not her devotion. It was as if she were saving herself – as if she had her ear cocked for a faint chastened voice from far away.

Her calls to Burton increased after his break-up with Princess Elizabeth of Yugoslavia, ostensibly over his simultaneously dallying with a model who had achieved fame as a *Playboy* centrefold. Was it time for him to come in from the cold, he wondered, as he and Elizabeth talked for hours. Then again, the lure of the familiar was comforting. Better still, a reconciliation was flattering. It meant that *he* was the one, the only one she cared enough about to remarry. She, of course, may well have been thinking that *she* and she alone was the only one he would marry again. Vanity is sometimes the stronger part of love. Burton's brother Graham thought he was trying desperately to revive his career and believed Elizabeth offered the best chance for 'self-control and stability'. But he can't have been that much of a fool. Boredom probably played its part, too, the feeling that their joint role as man and wife was more exciting and charged them with more power than the separate identities they'd had to get used to while apart. It was a gamble, all right. But then, as Max Lerner had said, both of them were 'plungers'.

Elizabeth returned to London from Moscow in mid-July 1974, and summoned a jeweller to the Dorchester. Out of his samples, she picked a man's gold wrist-watch. A birthday present for Henry Wynberg? Perhaps so. But it also proved to be a retirement present. A month later she checked into the Hotel Beau Rivage in Lausanne, and Burton joined her. Her chipmunk had come back to her.

In Israel the following week, for a benefit concert at which she read the Story of Ruth and he the twenty-third Psalm, they precipitated a gratifying riot. Another Henry was staying at the King David Hotel – Henry Kissinger – and offered them some of his own protective cordon of seventy US Marines and one thousand Israeli troops. But in their daze of restored happiness, they declined such worldly safeguards. Fate had united them again; fate would look after them. It always had done.

38

THE FARMER TAKES A WIFE

Elizabeth kept pressing him to do the romantic thing – propose to her. Rationally – that's to say, in his sober state – Burton knew he wasn't re-entering any holy state of matrimony; but with gout, sciatica and arthritis attacks disabling him at times, he needed nursing. His hands shook so much now that he couldn't raise a coffee cup to his lips without Elizabeth's help. They set off for Johannesburg – another charity event – and there he lowered himself painfully on to his knees and asked, 'Will you marry me?'

'Sure, honey bunny.'

Actually, the proposal had come in the first breath of relief he had drawn on hearing that Elizabeth had received the all-clear after undergoing X-rays for suspected cancer; it was only old pneumonia scar tissue. The proposal was a gesture of thanksgiving. And now for the remarriage.

In her 'back to basics' mood, Elizabeth wrote him a note, as Sara had taught her to do when something profoundly personal needed affirming, and asked, 'I know we will be together forever in the Biblical sense, so why are we afraid of that legal piece of paper which the missionaries made necessary?' Burton replied that the paper could be torn up; true promises couldn't. Whereupon she wrote him – and later published – the purest concentrate of the romantic argument she always used to convince herself – and others, too, she hoped – that her pursuit of men could not be considered promiscuous or immoral, so long as it was deeply and honestly felt. She agreed to stay 'as we is' for the moment, but added: 'Maybe I'll carry you off on a white charger, but I'd prefer it to be the other way round ... someday, something will make you realize you cannot live without me and you have to marry.'

It sounds like the patient availability that had worked so well when she and Burton were separated from their respective spouses in the months immediately after *Cleopatra*. It had been successful before, this Tristan and Iseult appeal to Burton's Celtic soul.

What finally brought them to their vows was the primitive spell which Africa sometimes casts over people in their receptive state. Elizabeth's published account of the wedding makes extraordinary reading. Borrowing the style that Burton cultivated, one of lyrical floribunda, she wrote of the 'earth gut' from which they and all their 'kind' had been wrenched. Marriage would be like going back to the womb and being reborn – it was, when seen through her eyes, a mixture of Darwinian philosophy and Erich Segal's *Love Story* taking place in the Africa of Le Douanier Rousseau, or a sort of Woodstock Festival for two, with peace, love and promises. The pledges, symbols and nature imagery of the *Song of Solomon* are scattered throughout her account. She seems to hear a voice – the voice of her beloved – asking her for her hand in marriage. Burton, who used to wear an old green blazer out of vanity to match the colour of his eyes, has now acquired 'green, cheetah-like eyes'. Her own heart is 'salty and bloodied through'. They seek the 'magical place' for the marriage ceremony and find it in the Chobe Game Reserve. And they hug each other until their ribs crack.

Elizabeth's Gauguinesque daze was only slightly dispersed on discovering that her beloved had woken up on his wedding day with pink eyes this time, and a hell of a hangover – 'Booze day on our wedding day.' She also noted that he was 'as stout as a Welsh chicken'. For her sixth wedding outfit, she chose a long green robe with pastel-coloured birds blending into each other, ribbed with multicoloured wooden beads threaded on chiffon cords and ending in guinea-fowl feathers. She must have looked like an exotic bird herself. Actually, it was an outfit that had a heart-wrenching significance for Burton; it had been a present to Elizabeth from Ifor, the brother whose death he still blamed on himself. It was as if his guilt was being incorporated into the marriage rites. The date was 10 October 1975.

This time the groom wore white slacks and a red silk turtleneck sweater. Their wedding limousine was a Range Rover. The place was a one-room cabin owned by the district commissioner of Kasane. The ceremony lasted twenty minutes. Both were asked if they understood the consequence of marriage; both replied they did. Afterwards, at the 'magical place' on the riverbank, champagne was opened and, under the watchful gaze of a rhinoceros and two hippos that kept a safe distance, they solemnly repeated their wedding vows. Elizabeth's written account refers to trees like 'Epstein sculptures'. She may have had that artist's well-known statue of Rima at Hyde Park Gate in London in her thoughts. But there are connotations, too, of *The Secret Garden* – though no longer an English country garden, but one that was primitive and exotic.

They went off for a honeymoon safari. Then Burton suddenly came down with severe malaria. Deeply alarmed, Elizabeth had a qualified pharmacist helicoptered in to attend to him, and also to an ailing bush policeman. The pharmacist was a woman of about Elizabeth's age called Chen Sam, Egyptian-born with an Italian Catholic mother and a Muslim father. She had married a Spaniard rather than submit to an arranged marriage. She was clearly a good organizer. She got rid of Burton's fever and was touched to see the trouble that Elizabeth – despite her understandable concern for Burton – took for the policeman who was a total stranger to her. The two women quickly felt an affinity with each other, and when the Burtons left Africa for London, Chen Sam went with them as part of their 'extended family'. She soon became indispensable, the more so since Dick Hanley had died a year or so earlier, and Elizabeth's affairs and public relations badly needed organizing. Chen Sam became her New York-based chief of staff. It was typical of the way destiny, in Elizabeth's eyes, provided for her when she was in need.

Burton looked terribly ill to many people at the fiftieth birthday party she threw for him at the Dorchester, and it wasn't just the malaria bout he had been through. He began to drink heavily again. Within a few weeks, it was clear to both of them that the promises they had made by the river hadn't really been in the nature of a remarriage, only a short-lived remission.

They spent Christmas 1975 in Gstaad. Burton took every chance to get out on the slopes. Not that he was a skier, but it offered him escape from the problems that he was locked into with Elizabeth. One day he was riding in a cable car when he caught the eye of a girl who looked in every respect the opposite of Elizabeth. Suzy Hunt, the estranged wife of the racing driver James Hunt, was tall, blonde, not at all big-bosomed, and only twenty-seven. As Burton said later, Elizabeth was a jealous woman, and such women have an instinct about the real rival when she arrives on the scene.

But as the new year, 1976, arrived with its flurry of parties, a fourth member became attached to the trio – this time, at Elizabeth's invitation. Peter Darmanin was thirty-seven, an advertising executive from Malta, a tall, athletic-looking fellow younger in appearance than age through keeping himself in trim by skiing and cycling. He was in Gstaad with well-connected friends, including the Prime Minister of Malta's son.

The pattern of a year or so before repeated itself within a week or two at Gstaad. As Burton drifted from her and towards Suzy Hunt, Elizabeth reached out for an available man. It had been Henry Wynberg before; now it was this youthful-looking stranger in ski-pants and sweater who came into the Olden Hotel's disco bar. Darmanin recalled, 'She was dancing with a man' – probably Brook Williams, Burton's close friend and factotum – 'and as she turned to go back to her table, she caught my eye and said, "Good to see you." I thought she'd mistaken me for someone else. Then, as I nursed my drink and looked in her direction, I became convinced she was introducing herself. When the band began playing another dance number, I made a sign that said, "Shall we ...?" And we did. And after that we danced every number. I said to her, "You look exactly as I remember you in your first movie – the one with the horse." She laughed and said, "My first movie was the one with the dog ... Give me your number and I'll call you."'

Darmanin became as frequent a guest as Suzy Hunt at the Chalet Ariel. When Burton left for New York, where he was to take the sizeable (but successful) risk of going on stage again in the play *Equus*, the young man's visits became of longer duration. 'We tended to fight a lot. To make her happy, you have to stand up to her. She has to have someone to test her constantly. And she needs company desperately. Sometimes, she'd call me over the intercom and order me into the bedroom, even while she was having her hair done.' Darmanin found Elizabeth emotionally possessive, demanding that he didn't let his attention waver, even when she was taking phone calls. She could also be mischievous in order to keep him close to her. She would send him on a wild goose chase for a dog that had gone missing when, he suspected, she knew where it was all the time. One time, he found himself outside in sub-zero temperatures, whistling for one of the pet dogs, and himself dressed only in a fur coat he had snatched on the way out.

Not having the means to match the bounty of earlier husbands and admirers, Darmanin gave her what he could afford in the way of presents. One such was a Maltese cross, the simplicity of which brought a smile to her lips. In return, she selected a trinket from a boxful; it had the message, 'I need you' engraved on it in Italian. 'Who had given it to her first, I don't know,' Darmanin says.

What did Darmanin and other occasional friends and lovers find so fascinating about Elizabeth? 'She cares for you. She remembers all the little things that give pleasure. She has the power to make you feel you have never left her, however long the parting has been. She knows something about a man that flatters him. She lends you her glamour. And when she takes it back again, it's as if the light's gone out.'

The light went out, temporarily anyhow, when Elizabeth was summoned to New York by an appeal from Burton. Imagining him ill, she found him resolute, with Suzy Hunt helping him face the terrors of sobriety again. He immediately asked for a divorce. It was said that the hotel executives had to apologize to other guests for the row that followed. Once again, Aaron Frosch prepared the severance papers.

Elizabeth now made her 'home' in one of the bungalows at the Beverly Hills Hotel; but like Tennessee Williams's heroine, Mrs Stone, she found herself 'drifting'. Being Elizabeth, however, she 'drifted' wherever the eddies seemed to promise most fun. Henry Kissinger and his wife, whom she had met in Jerusalem in 1975, introduced her to social Washington in the spring of 1976. Just as she had always done, she quickly adapted to the life-style of the place. The new routine steadied her; it gave her restlessness a purpose. She used New York and its 'Beautiful People' to kill the boredom of Hollywood and its movie people; and then she used Washington and its political movers and shapers to kill the boredom of the other two pleasure capitals. Politicians as well as diplomats were intrigued to find such a famous face at their dinner-tables, and took advantage of the approachability that her need for stimulation and variety had opened up. Once virtually inaccessible, she was now saying yes to invitations from people she wouldn't have wanted to know about a year or so earlier, or who wouldn't have thought they stood a chance of inviting her.

Elizabeth was soon part of the political scene, without being in politics. She endorsed Jimmy Carter's presidential ambitions, however, by attending a fund-raising dinner for him wearing a golden peanut, the symbol of his farming background. She dined with Vice-President Nelson Rockefeller; she endorsed Democratic Congresswoman Bella Abzug in New York. And on 8 July 1976, she was back again in Washington, this time for a dinner in honour of the bicentenary of American independence that Queen Elizabeth II was giving at the British Embassy. The only trouble was, she had no one to escort her. She suggested her Hollywood hairdresser. Sir Peter Ramsbotham, the British ambassador, felt that the event would be somewhat more formal than, say, Oscar night in Hollywood, and promised to find someone suitable.

She saw the man who was to become her next husband from the rear. John Warner had his back to her as he awaited her in the lobby of the Madison Hotel, Washington DC. As she later described it, it was like a camera set-up on a Hollywood shooting stage. First, there was 'that marvellous silver hair'. Then the forty-nine-year-old Virginian turned to face her. He was in evening dress and white tie, the only man in the lobby in formal dress. 'I thought "wow!"' said Elizabeth. Truth to tell, she had sent Chen Sam downstairs in advance, and her impression had been a 'wow!' too. If a Hollywood studio had sent to Central Casting for 'a politician-figure, powerful, dignified, sexy', Warner would have been among the first to be picked.

At this time in his political career, he possessed status without reputation; that is to say, he had done two political jobs very well, as President Nixon's Secretary of the Navy, then as co-ordinating chairman of the bicentenary ceremonies. In neither capacity did he gain much public recognition or acquire any real power. That was about to change; and the woman whom Warner was due to escort to the Queen of England's ball was the one who was going to change it.

It was not a meeting of minds that took place in the lobby of the Madison Hotel that evening, but rather a matching of opportunities that would have done credit to a dating agency.

John Warner was then as respectably divorced as it was possible to be. A bare three years before, he had parted from Catherine Mellon, daughter of one of America's richest philanthropists. It had been so friendly a divorce that his ex-wife now lived next door, so that they could more easily share the care of the children. It had been a generous divorce as well, accompanied by handsome compensation from his former father-in-law which included a mansion in fashionable Georgetown and a six-figure trust fund whose interest was Warner's for life. He was politically free, too. He had resigned from his bicentennial duties, the better, it was said, to take up 'real' politics by running for a state governorship or a Senate seat. In other words, he and Elizabeth were both free from 'obligations' at the very moment of their meeting, when both were on the lookout for a new direction in their lives and careers. As well as eligible, Warner was experienced. His post-divorce years had been spent in the social company of women like Barbara Walters, the television interviewer. His girlfriends were usually well disposed to partner a man who checked off such pursuits as canoeing, skiing, tennis and horseback riding. He was more in the mode of Ralph Lauren than Hugh Hefner – except for the Hef-like pipe that lent a philosophic cast to a face that might otherwise have been considered a little too handsome, a little too 'arranged' to fit into the class and circumstances he had acquired by marriage. Warner came from old Washington stock – he was the son of an Episcopalian rector – but he had spent the same sort of restless, rebellious boyhood that quite a few film stars had found of use in the roles they later played. He had dropped out of school and joined the navy, but had been just too late to get 'blooded' in World War II. After graduating from university with a degree in engineering, he had a second try and joined the marines; this time he saw service in Korea. He found it hard to settle into civilian life and on discharge he hiked to California, landed a bartender's job and was only jerked back to family obligation and convention by his father's death. He enrolled in law school at the University of Virginia and then quickly found his feet as a trial lawyer in the state prosecutor's office.

Warner's career, in short, suggested the sort of impulsive quest that might just as easily have turned him towards a movie career and developed a talent for role playing. He was a striver in the Nixonian mould, a late developer. He was not on the 'inside' of either politics or society – after their divorce, his wife remained in the Social Register, but he was dropped from its pages. Yet just because of his semi-detached status, he was a freer agent. For a man like John Warner, marriage to one of the most famous and beautiful women in the world would be an ambitious gamble, rather than a risk to existing achievement.

He had been born in the same month as Elizabeth, though five years earlier, and shared her star sign. Sceptics may smile; but such astral conjunctions do count for a lot with those who look for omens to bless their decisions.

Warner believed strongly in the value of family life, even if his own experience of marriage – in some ways similar to Elizabeth's, though not so ritually repeated – hadn't been entirely successful. Like her, he believed children needed stability, notwithstanding their parents' own failure to achieve it. He was devoted to his elderly mother – and Elizabeth could certainly understand that sentiment. He embraced the social conventions that Elizabeth's behaviour had often broken, though it has to be remembered that Elizabeth had always maintained that her honesty was what redeemed her, in her eyes at least. In his turn, John Warner could understand that, though he probably wouldn't have come out publicly and endorsed it. He didn't seem at all interested in movies: he had never seen *National Velvet*. He did love horses, though. He had a stable on his 2,600-acre farm in Middleburg, Virginia, and, as Elizabeth said later, 'John's farm ... reminds me of the countryside in England.' She could have added that, instead of playing at rustic living in a make-believe cottage like Little Swallows, she was now up at the Big House itself, as its mistress. Elizabeth's nostalgia for her childhood years made the prospect of marriage to John Warner even more attractive. It gave her the role that she used to say would probably have been hers had there been no war, no evacuation to America and no Hollywood career. It made her a lady of the manor. Elizabeth's heroine, Scarlett O'Hara, had a strong attachment to places: and John Warner, with his Virginia acres, his manly good looks, his reputation for being a ladies' man if not exactly a playboy, all lent him the superficial but sufficient appearance of a Rhett Butler to a woman whose marrying inclinations already matched those of Margaret Mitchell's impulsive heroine.

Elizabeth had a knowledge of the world and its personalities that hadn't come Warner's way, with his sober but humdrum life in Washington. He was a provincial; she was the cosmopolitan. Though the show-business

side of her life didn't appeal to him, Warner recognized and was impressed
by her experience of the world and acquaintance with its rich and powerful
connections, the kind a politician could use, the kind that could raise a
politician's profile. 'She is so exciting and stimulating,' he confided.
'People say she wants to come to Washington to get into the power
structure, but that's wrong.' At the time, maybe – but whether in Washington or Hollywood, power structures have an inherent similarity. If
Elizabeth didn't want to get into Washington's inner circle of movers and
shakers, it was maybe because she already felt at home. This was yet
another company town like Hollywood, where gossip and glamour and
celebrity and power exercised their seductive appeal (until you had to live
with them for long periods of time), and where the rivalry of the office-
seekers recalled the struggles she herself had fought for the best scripts,
the best directors, the best pictures. She assumed it was easy to fit into
political Washington, and for a time she was right. The mystique of
stardom that had ceased to work its magic on her film career could return
in the political context of fund-raising, celebrity endorsement and the
diplomatic round: all things she had been enjoying before the man with
the marvellous silver hair turned round and said, 'Hello, I'm your date
for tonight.'

Elizabeth danced the night away with John Warner at the British
Embassy ball, and a few hours before dawn they moved on to a private
club in Georgetown and saw the sunrise while breakfasting on scrambled
eggs and champagne. A change and a shower, then they drove to Atoka,
his farm at Middleburg, a little over an hour away. The grey fieldstone
house recalled the great mansion in *Giant*. It sat at the end of a mile-long
drive, amid spacious fields where a herd of six hundred pedigree Hereford
cattle grazed, with coppices dotted around. In one of the barns Warner
had built a swimming pool – a discreet compromise with what he maintained was his real life as a working farmer. Elizabeth was enchanted by
the duck ponds, even more by a five-hundred-acre wildlife preserve: a
more spacious version of 'The Wilderness', where she'd played as a child
in Hampstead.

The farm won her heart. She married John Warner for his roots, not
his money. Money she had herself, and plenty of it, more than he, much
more: but she had no roots at all. 'She turned to me at sunset,' Warner
recalled, 'and I knew the farm had won her over.'

Some time later, when she had become Mrs John Warner, Elizabeth
did a television interview with Barbara Walters on the farm, and made
the pull of the land plain. Wasn't it very different from cruising the high
seas in a film star's yacht? Barbara Walters prompted the woman who was
now the wife of the man she herself had dated. 'The yacht, in a sense, was

my farm,' Elizabeth replied, as they all sat round the kitchen table, she in a loose-fitting smock that a milkmaid might have worn a century before, her husband drawing reflectively on a pipe, his shearling coat thrown carelessly over a chair-back as if he had just come in from wood-chopping. The scene spelled rural simplicity – as it was intended to do.

That was what she tasted on this first visit, which grew from an overnight stay into one of a few days. Warner had a reputation as a workaholic who used to cat-nap in an eye-mask when he was an attorney at the Justice Department; he had taken only four days off in the past eighteen months. Despite this, he now called his Washington office and told them to cancel all his appointments for the next couple of days. Elizabeth very quickly projected herself into a picture of life down on the farm that resembled a rural idyll blessed by a Hollywood screenwriter. 'If he wants to be the patriarch,' she said, 'I am willing to be the matriarch,' and then, as if to show she had a sisterly sympathy for the women's movement as well as a wifely loyalty to her future husband, she added, 'as long as it's fifty-fifty'. A landowner, a farm, family, horses and politics: MGM could not have visualized a better sequel to *National Velvet* – 'Velvet Grows Up', say.

Though Warner also spoke rhapsodically of rural bliss with Elizabeth down on the farm, he didn't deny that even earthier sentiments brought them together. These he was careful to couch in the metaphors that came more easily to the lips of a cautious politician than those of a bold lover. He was fond of interpreting his relationship with Elizabeth in a way that reflected Ben Franklin's similar experience. 'Franklin was born in Boston. Moved to Philadelphia. Met a lady on the street. She laughed at him. They got engaged. And then he discovered electricity.' This always got approving applause and knowing laughter. Elizabeth's account of their betrothal also harboured something of the elemental. 'We had gone in a Jeep to watch the sunset and have a picnic on the hill. There was a rainstorm all around us. We sat there surrounded by thunder and lightning ... Finally the skies opened in a torrential downpour. We just lay back in the grass, hugged each other, soaked by the rain but in love.' A sign that passion didn't altogether extinguish one's political instinct, or ambitions, came when she mentioned that the picnic consisted of a bottle of Paul Masson wine – and caviar. The wine was all right: good American stuff, whose time to be opened had clearly come. But Warner was sensitive on the caviar issue, since the then Shah of Iran rated poor marks from the American electorate, or the part of it that was currently protesting against the styles in torture favoured by his Savak secret police. No, surely not caviar, said Warner; that would have been blasphemous. Elizabeth persisted. Well, not Iranian caviar, then. All right, said Elizabeth, Virginia caviar. It was felt that a sensitive issue had been successfully skirted. The politician's romantic temperament was more smoothly translated into patriotic colours when he produced an engagement ring made of rubies, diamonds and sapphires in bicentennial bands of red, white and blue.

But it was an appropriate symbol in another sense. Warner's marriage to Elizabeth had to be seen through the prism of politics. It was a calculated risk. Would conservative Virginians accept a woman who had been married to six men and gone through five divorces, who was a Hollywood star, a Jewish convert and – worst sin of all, perhaps – a self-proclaimed Democrat? A straw poll produced a divided answer. But Elizabeth showed a certainty that should have shamed the waverers. Declaring that she felt she had come to rest at last, she added, with the finality of someone planning the last rite before she is over the first hurdle, 'We've even chosen our burial site – next to each other.' 'Roots' could scarcely be more firmly settled in Virginia's soil than that.

The formal engagement ceremony was planned for Vienna, where Elizabeth would be at work on the film of Stephen Sondheim's *A Little Night Music*. She left for Austria in August. 'Travel light,' her future husband advised her, perhaps getting her in training for his own star role in campaigning for the Republican nomination to the Senate. With an effort, she got her freight down to fifty pieces of luggage.

Before filming started, news reached her of Burton's marriage to Suzy Hunt at Arlington, Virginia. She telephoned her congratulations and then asked whether he'd consider playing her husband in the film – Robert Stephens had just quit the part. It was evidence, perhaps, of ties lying deeper than marriage that Burton almost said yes. Even his public congratulations on her engagement betrayed how hard he also found it to give up the idea of 'Richard and Elizabeth' – of 'the Burtons'. 'I want her to be happy; to have success with marriage and her work. That will take any guilt off my shoulders.'

On 4 December 1976, fortunately a mild winter's day, Burton's wish for Elizabeth came to pass. John Warner, accompanied by his son and friends, walked from a day's fox-hunting to the top of Engagement Hill, as he and Elizabeth had now named the place where he had asked her to marry him. The service was ecumenical, to say the least. It combined the Twenty-Third Psalm – whose reference to 'green pastures' was considered to be particularly appropriate to the occasion – with the Book of Ruth. There was no music, but just before the ceremony, Warner called to his Herefords and the cows obliged by wandering up the hill to serenade the little wedding party with deep lows of confidence: a contrast to the doubting hippos that had mutely surveyed the Taylor–Burton rematch in Botswana. Elizabeth walked up the hill just before sunset, attired in a dress of lavender-grey cashmere, grey suede boots and a matching coat trimmed with silver fox. She wore a lavender turban to tone with her violet eyes and carried a bouquet of lilac-coloured heather. On one of her gloved fingers already rested a plain gold band, which she had had made from a trinket she had given her father just before his death. John Warner slipped on to another of her fingers a ring that his mother had received from her husband fifty years earlier.

After they had made their vows, Warner kissed her gently, then whooped, 'We did it! We finally did it!' The cows bellowed even louder, no doubt imagining that hay or something even more succulent was on the way. The sun touched the neighbouring line of bare trees. Scarlett O'Hara could hardly have arranged a more bucolic mixture of romantic yearning and belonging. For wedding presents, diamonds were avoided in favour of a farm silo (him to her) and two cows and a pedigree bull (her to him).

Like all the weddings Elizabeth had been through, this one reflected the sort of man she had married. Nick Hilton had been an alliance with big business; Michael Wilding had been a low-key English union; Mike Todd had been a sky filled with fireworks over Mexico; Eddie Fisher had been a Las Vegas show-business match; Richard Burton had been (the first time) a rehearsal for a double act that spared no expense and then (the second time) a ceremony of innocence regained in the aftermath of the fall. And now came the Warner marriage, smelling of the good earth in which the newly-weds hoped to root their affections more securely than ever before.

No sooner were they man and wife than Elizabeth remarked in an interview that they intended to construct a log cabin on the site of their nuptials. It did not escape comment that this was the traditional beginning for all American boys who wanted to become president. If you weren't born in one, build one.

39

ISSUES OF WEIGHT

No sooner had they returned from a Christmas honeymoon in Gstaad than Warner set about wooing the Republican Party elders. He wanted to be selected as the party's nominee for senator: but as yet he didn't declare it openly. His strategy required humility – and at the same time celebrity. A difficult double to bring off, unless one was married to a star like Elizabeth. It was essential that she became an asset, attracting attention to him and influencing opinion on his behalf. She threw herself into his campaign with a will as they criss-crossed the country, raising funds.

It was totally the opposite of the sort of life she had led in movies. Now she was without any of the protection that a star enjoyed. She had to be willingly accessible, submit with a smile to importuning by strangers, put up with the snatched and unflattering photo, endure unrehearsed and even prurient questioning. No Alexandre trailed her to comb her hair out at every stop and thread diamonds into her newly styled coiffure. There were no diamonds on view, in any case; the Cartier–Burton stone languished in the vaults. The Krupp diamond was never incised into any of the two thousand palms she pressed over one three-day stint. She learned a new discipline: punctuality. Her husband had the ex-Navy man's strict code of 'watches' and would be up and stirring even before the 5 a.m. alarm shrilled for them both. Nevertheless, she made a success of her new role. She drew record crowds, many times larger than Warner alone could have done. She was an active auxiliary, too. Whenever they visited a campus that had a drama department, Elizabeth held a brief seminar and handled questions like an old pro – no wonder, of course, for the questions were often the old favourites: the film of hers she liked best ('*Virginia Woolf*'), how she learned to act ('by osmosis'), her biggest thrill ('riding my horse in *National Velvet* aged twelve'), her favourite actress ('Vivien Leigh . . .

she represented innocence on the edge of decadence'), her favourite actor (Aha! But she took this jump without hesitation: 'Richard Burton ... perfectly marvellous to work with'). Her candour gained her applause – and applause might earn her husband votes one day.

Then her shoulder began hurting with bursitis from all that hand-shaking, and she needed cortisone injections. Her hand became so swollen that it had to be protected with an elastic bandage. Yet she didn't slacken her pace. She and her husband sometimes engaged in mock spats: there was a touch of Mike Todd about John Warner's willingness to tell a story against his wife – with her complicity. Nick Thimmisch, a writer for *McCall's* magazine detailed to accompany the couple, reported one such piece of populist wife-baiting, when Warner told the story of how Elizabeth had left him to visit the ladies' room at an airport. 'He saw her waving at him from inside, and he waved back. At the next stop, a short while later, Liz again took off for the ladies' room, and John stopped her, saying, "But Liz, you went at the last airport ..." She replied, "Oh no, you damn fool. I waved at you for a dime, but you didn't bring it."'

Warner continually stressed his famous wife's 'orneriness' and 'contrariness'. She'd occasionally reprimand him with a playful tap on the jaw. Theirs looked to be a loving, punchy relationship – *Who's Afraid of Virginia Woolf?* with the fangs extracted. To some, however, it looked as if they were deliberately creating a politically advantageous image. When their private plane was grounded by bad weather, they switched to a beat-up local bus. She changed outfits in toilets at filling stations. Sometimes her show-business candour grated on staid Virginian sensibilities: she could do anything she wanted for John, she said with wifely pride, 'except become pregnant – I haven't the tubes'. The emphasis all the time was on 'the natural' – natural people, natural opinions, natural functions.

Only a few intimates glimpsed the change she was making in Warner's style of life. A disco floor had been installed at the farm; a screening room at the townhouse. Elizabeth's art collection – paintings by Monet, Vlaminck, Utrillo, Picasso and Renoir, among others – hung in the room they used for entertaining. Its walls were scarlet – to match the screenprint of her by Andy Warhol that was sandwiched into the window glass. Otherwise, the place was surprisingly bare of show or even comfort. 'You can tell we use it to change our clothes in,' she joked. Warner used it as a private office: the farm was really where they lived.

With her husband's approval, she took cameo roles in several cinema and television films. One was *Winter Kills*, a political thriller in which she appears at the side of a fictional presidential candidate, though only his arm is seen – it was John Warner's. Another was *Victory at Entebbe*, though this was less a role than a tribute to the Israeli commando raid: it was said, though never confirmed, that at the time of the Uganda crisis, she had called the Israeli ambassador in Washington to offer herself as an exchange hostage.

Elizabeth now spoke of politics much as she used to speak about film acting – a game in which conviction was everything. 'If you lapse for one second, the people can feel it. If you aren't sincere, people can sense it. You cannot allow yourself to get tired. When you shake someone's hand, look into his eyes. You have to be absolutely there.' It was the same technique she had used before the camera.

One person she called frequently – or so he claimed – to report her progress in helping raise Warner's political profile was Richard Burton. He told her that once he was finished with a slew of profitable potboilers – he still got $750,00 a film – he intended to return to the stage.

But as the novelty of it all faded, the strain began to tell – on both of the Warners. Arnold Latham, seconded from *Esquire* magazine to keep tabs on their double act, saw tempers starting to fray. When Elizabeth at some dressy function was delayed in the powder room by a broken pin in her diamond and emerald clasp, Warner barely heard her out – 'I'm not interested in jewellery,' he snapped. In an off moment, Elizabeth compared her role in the campaign to that of 'a bird of paradise in a chicken coop'. Latham sensed how hungry the film star and the senatorial aspirant both were for love and approbation from the mass audiences they addressed. Warner had had the good luck, or shrewdness, to marry money with his first wife; now he had married celebrity. What would happen when he attained it in his own right? Already, for those with an ear cocked, a definite competitiveness had begun to obtrude between him and Elizabeth, as if each were leery of letting the other hog the limelight completely. According to Latham, Warner would ask Elizabeth to excuse him while he composed his speech. It was his habit to wear a flying suit with a US flag appliqued on to it: a relic of his days in the navy and the marines. 'You're a male chauvinist!' she tossed over her shoulder, as she left his study. His explanation for the flying suit seemed to bear this out: 'It doesn't grab you by the balls and it's so seedy a woman won't touch you. You can work.' Work, Latham concluded, was really Warner's first love – and an obsession like that could outlast love itself.

The pattern of a marriage held together by tension was re-asserting itself – the sort that had kept Elizabeth and Burton together for over a decade. But how long could the Warner–Taylor marriage stand the strain?

As 1977 wore on, Warner stepped up the pace for his nomination as senatorial candidate. But already an unforeseen factor had entered the calculation. This was Elizabeth's increasing weight. As early as April, newspapers were unkindly referring to her 'rolling around the US political circuit on her spare tire'. Although she was channelling all her energies into her husband's politicking, this didn't mean she used up the extra calories she took aboard. Just the reverse. 'Like many other political spouses I knew, I was gaining weight and didn't really care,' she later wrote. 'The only thing that counted was winning ... and since I wasn't working as an actress, I felt there was no reason for me to look any particular way or weigh any particular amount.' Her emotional loyalties were her dietary downfall. At the end of an exhausting day, she was usually too tired to eat sensibly. And while on the stump, she was too full of bloating carbohydrates. Even Chen Sam, who gamely shared her chores, began to balloon.

As her weight increased, so did the jokes about it. John Belushi, the corpulent comedian of *Saturday Night Live*, put on a frock and lampooned her. 'She has more chins than the Hong Kong phone book' was a gag that turned up everywhere. Arnold Latham suggested she was turning into the trademark of Mike Todd's *Around the World in Eighty Days* – a hot-air balloon. Even Debbie Reynolds in far-away California was credited with a sly crack at her ex-husband's ex-wife: 'Got to watch the weight, girls. On my refrigerator door, I've pasted a picture of Liz Taylor.'

Elizabeth protested, 'It's happy fat. I eat because I'm so happy.'

But only the excuses wore thin. Not coincidentally, perhaps, the playful differences of opinion between Warner and his wife began to assume a sour note. One of their most public clashes on the difficulty of reconciling male chauvinist ambitions and feminist issues was sharpened by the relevance of a feminist issue like fat to Elizabeth's sad condition. She chided her husband for not supporting the Equal Rights Amendment. 'I've been working since I was ten. I have supported my family and a couple of husbands [a pardonable scaling down] and I feel absolutely equal.' Such differences with her husband increased with her poundage. It was clear that people were coming to John Warner's rallies to verify how obese his wife was. Warner seemed to adopt a typically male viewpoint on her plight. There was really no problem, he said. 'She's enjoying life more. She's not so concerned with vanity.' Some of the other things associated with Elizabeth were bothering him more – like the post-forty-sixth birthday party thrown for her by Halston, the couturier, and about two thousand people at New York's Studio 54, the nightclub notorious for its coke-sniffing celebrities: not a place that a senatorial candidate would wish to be seen in or near by a million miles. The politician hung back as various kids, naked except for sequinned jockstraps, danced attention on Elizabeth, forty-six white gardenias were strewn in her path, and a cake with her portrait iced on it was wheeled in. She cut off one of her confectionery breasts and handed it to Andy Warhol to eat. She was wearing a mauve sequin-covered trouser-suit and matching cape. 'Liz looked like a belly-button – like a fat little Kewpie doll,' Warhol recorded in his secret diary. At 1.30 a.m., as Bianca Jagger was kicking her shoes off, Warner announced testily, 'I'm a politician. I've got to get up in the morning and work.' He left with a clearly reluctant Elizabeth. Earlier, they had attended the New York premiere of *A Little Night Music* – a painful experience. Since making the film, her weight had visibly increased. Now when Len Cariou sang, 'If only she'd been faded / If only she'd been fat,' the next line of the lyric was drowned out by laughter.

Warner made his candidacy official in February 1978, and almost at the same time rumours circulated on the international jewellery market that Elizabeth was selling the great Cartier–Burton jewel to provide funds for her husband's campaign. Some diamonds, it seemed, were not forever. In fact, it was not sold until June 1979, for a reported three million dollars, roughly twice what Richard Burton had paid for it. If invested in securities, the same money would have tripled itself. Warner lost narrowly, and gamely, to his rival Richard Obenshain at the Republican nominating convention at Richmond that June. Elizabeth looked visibly deflated. This was not how the script was supposed to end – surely the film had another reel? Indeed it had. The very title of the television film she now went off to California to make, *Return Engagement*, was prophetic. On 2 August 1979, Obenshain was killed in a plane crash that had striking resemblances with the one that had killed Mike Todd. In the immediate aftermath of this tragedy the Republican state committee made John Warner their official nominee for the Senate by universal acclamation. Elizabeth's presentiment had been right. The story wasn't over yet, there was still a reel to go.

Like it or not, Elizabeth now became, in *People* magazine's words, 'the focus of the race [between her husband and his Democrat rival Andrew P. Miller] and perhaps its most volatile issue'. 'Volatility' was, perhaps, not the best-chosen word. She weighed more than ever. But thousands who came to gawk found that although her figure was, well, 'Splat!' it was nevertheless the authentic Elizabeth Taylor above the chin (or chins). If the glamour wasn't as visible as it had once been, she set out to prove that her genuineness was still there. She visited churches, synagogues, fairs, retirement homes; she shook hands relentlessly, hurled cream pies in charity events; she ate her way through a 'hen pen' of fried-chicken legs, which unfortunately for her calories carried political clout for Southern voters; and she exposed herself to all manner of indignities to testify to her husband's integrity, compassion, simplicity and earthiness (in the agricultural sense). She was frank about her numerous husbands, yet found that the fickle voters reproached her most for leaving a man like Richard Burton, twice: 'What kind of good sense could that woman have?' John Warner, it was noted, referred to only one of her previous five husbands, Mike Todd, who had been removed from his wife's side by an act of God, rather than a decision of the divorce courts.

Almost on the eve of the election, Elizabeth had another of those seemingly fateful accidents of hers: a chicken bone got stuck in her throat. It could have been fatal – or so the headlines suggested – but the effect of the daily bulletins was to bring her sympathy, and, perhaps, sympathy votes to her husband. It removed her from the contentious centre of the election, yet guaranteed him an aura of husbandly concern. She was well enough to see John Warner win on 7 November 1978, by the narrowest of margins: 4,720 votes out of approximately 1.2 million. His opponent could not raise the $125,000 required for a recount.

On 16 January 1979, Elizabeth sat with her eighty-four-year-old mother in the gallery of the US Senate and saw her husband sworn in as a member. As the new senator turned his triumphant face up to her, she jumped to her feet and blew him a full-size Hollywood film-star kiss. It was the start of his career – and the end of their marriage. For it was brought gradually home to Elizabeth that the man she had successfully helped to achieve high office was a man who saw politics as she had always seen films – in terms of stardom. Only this time it was to be a stardom that she couldn't share.

She already knew what it was like to serve a cause; she now discovered what it was like to serve an institution. It was not nearly so exhilarating. The burden of a US senator's duties suited John Warner's workaholic temperament, but they included no place, or function, that Elizabeth found it easy to fit into or adopt. Just as Hollywood had failed to prepare her for the reality of life, the life she had led up to then as a candidate's wife failed to prepare her for what she later called 'the domestic Siberia' of a senator's lady. The chores of attending the Tuesday meetings of senators' spouses soon failed to grip her. She had none of the alternative uses for her energy that these women enjoyed. Yes, she had the home that she and her husband lived in, but no place they had really made their own together. Her children were grown up. She was never a person for routine engagements. And though charitable causes were to consume more and more of her time, making glove-puppets with the Red Cross group of senators' wives was a come-down from jetting to the world's capitals for a charity tribute or concert with other bill-topping stars. Waiting at home while Warner attended to late-night business on Capitol Hill was torture for someone of her restless disposition. 'John was up and out early in the morning,' she later described these days. 'He ate breakfast on the run, jamming most of it into a brown paper bag and sticking it in his briefcase.

I'd say goodbye, and then go back to sleep. There was no reason for me to get up. I had nowhere to go. Later in the day I'd rise, get dressed, and then maybe read or watch television, or look at the walls, or do nothing.' In short, she, the former star, had ironically become that object of Hollywood pity, the star's wife.

The split wasn't long in showing itself publicly. The senator was addressing a policy forum of Republican VIPs and saying that women should be exempt from the draft, when Elizabeth gave vent to a dissenting mutter and then, to the surprise of many, a prolonged boo. Warner, in what was interpreted as an attempt to placate her, succeeded in looking as if he were slapping her down. Women, he claimed, were volunteering for jobs in the services. Elizabeth's hard-edged voice split the tense atmosphere building up. 'What kind of jobs – "Rosie the Riveter" jobs?' Laughter broke out. Emboldened by feeling that the audience was with her, she backed up her position. 'Women have been in active control since Year One.' Look at Margaret Thatcher, she said; look at Cleopatra. Warner, now flushed, appeared to try and subdue her with a wave of his hand – a gesture that brought her leaping to her feet. 'Don't you steady me with that all-dominating hand of yours.'

Once, her increase in weight had signified her zeal on her husband's behalf; now it reflected her unhappiness with the life his success had brought them. She had the sense to know that many people were sorry for her; but mixed with their pity was often a peculiarly cruel compensation. 'My God, we've spent half our lives wishing we could look like Elizabeth Taylor – and my God, now we do,' was how one fat Washington matron put it, and she was not the only one. Elizabeth now weighed over 150 pounds – she was obese, there was no other word for it. When at last she forced herself to strip to the buff and look at herself in a full-length mirror, she didn't even recognize herself. 'I had literally thrown my gift away,' she recorded.

Her husband was growing more and more concerned as well. Warner took pains to keep himself in shape: he did the Canadian Air Force exercises daily. He didn't feel himself flattered by the figure his wife now cut; it didn't fit his own image of what a senator's wife should look like. He therefore urged her to diet, which only made her feel more guilty. She entered a health spa at Pompano Beach, Florida. 'Unlike Scarlett O'Hara,' she told herself, 'you can't think in terms of tomorrow when it comes to dieting.' At first she kept to the guarded privacy of her room, ashamed to come out, but gradually she relaxed enough to take meals – such as they were – with other guests, to do three hours of daily exercise, to abstain from all alcohol and to go jogging with a hairdresser friend from Washington pacing her on roller-skates. She lost twenty pounds, and would have lost more had sad news not interrupted the discipline. She learned that her second husband, Michael Wilding, had died after a fall in his home in Chichester, England. He was sixty-six years old. His funeral, in mid-July 1979, brought her and her children flying to England.

Elizabeth's wreath of white roses topped the coffin. 'Dearest Michael,' read the card, 'God bless you. I love you, Elizabeth.'

But checking in and out of a health spa could not be a permanent solution. And when that embarrassing rat-tat-tat exchange with her husband occurred, the worn nerves of their marriage were exposed to everyone's sight and hearing. When she declared that she had been working since the age of ten – and meant it as a boast, not a complaint – John Warner recognized that it was better that she continue working now that she was his wife – or he might not have a wife much longer, and he was barely half-way through his four-year term. He showed an unwonted cheerfulness about her going back to films.

Natalie Wood had just turned down the role of a murderess in an Agatha Christie film, *The Mirror Crack'd*, which was to be made in England, and, for a fee of $250,000, Elizabeth joined the cast of stars whose thinning hair and thickening waists made her own imperfections less noticeable or blameworthy. They included Rock Hudson, Tony Curtis and Kim Novak; if the mirror crack'd, then, as one critic said, the movie creak'd. But for Elizabeth, perhaps, there was a compensating sentiment in the English location. 'I was delighted to have the chance of going back to Kent, a part of England I knew very well when I was a child. Kent,' she added, 'is so like Virginia. [It] could be an adjoining state.'

The shooting finished just in time for her to dash back to Detroit in July 1980, and preserve the appearance of a secure marriage by joining her husband at the Republican National Convention – the one that nominated Ronald Reagan as the party's presidential candidate. Yet appearances also damned her. For she was escorted to the seat of honour beside Nancy Reagan who, as Nancy Davis, had been an MGM actress like herself. The pair of them made a cruel contrast, a stick insect beside the Michelin Man. Once the pressure of film work had dropped off, Elizabeth had relaxed her self-discipline. The calories had conquered. And now, as she conceded later, she looked like a drag queen. The make-up coating those celebrated eyes had spread like a highwayman's mask from ear to ear; the cheeks were hillocks of fat; and the hair-do resembled the coiffure that the *fin de siècle* artist Aubrey Beardsley had taken a perverse pleasure in designing for the decadent Messalina.

The campaign conducted by the Warners on behalf of Ronald Reagan was dutiful, but perfunctory compared with their campaign two years earlier on Warner's own behalf. One contributory factor was Elizabeth's comparative lack of zeal.

Elizabeth and her husband did not separate: at least, not yet. They gradually drifted apart. John Warner's energies were assimilated into the presidential election campaign. His wife's desperation to regain her looks and self-respect not only took her back to the health spa – but also in another, totally unanticipated direction. Elizabeth fell back on the old will-power that had served her so well. She would set herself the most exacting test she could devise. She would make her first appearance on the stage in a leading role in a legitimate play. It would discipline her. It would do more than that. As a senator's wife, there was no role for her, no prescribed way for her to behave, other than not affront convention. But as an actress, as the star of a play, she would have to win an audience's respect – and appearing live in front of them was the most merciless test she knew. It would require her to recover her dignity. But if she succeeded, how sweet the reward! It would restore her to a position of power and as the centre of interest. It would give her a renewed sense of worth. It would be her passage back to being needed – to being loved.

40

POSITIVELY THEIR LAST
APPEARANCE

Mike Nichols pleaded with her to take voice lessons, but the advice was wasted on her. She'd never had them, and to start now would upset her settled confidence in the rightness of her instincts. She quoted Ethel Merman, who'd once been asked if she was ever afraid of losing her voice: 'Let the audience worry, they paid good money to hear me.' Elizabeth was absolutely right, except that her audience were going to pay good money to see her.

But to see her in *what*? She enjoyed the luxury of choosing her own vehicle; and now she went about it the way she would shortly go about choosing a new Rolls-Royce – by having several models driven round to her doorstep for inspection. She had allied herself with a shrewd business partner, Zev Bufman, a Broadway impresario, who brought in a 'Sunday afternoon' cast of professional players, sworn to secrecy, so that she could 'read' the possible plays with them in a rehearsal hall. One obvious choice had already been rejected. To do *Who's Afraid of Virginia Woolf?* would have brought her into competition with her younger screen self, and her acknowledged excellence as Martha. But they considered Tennessee Williams's *Sweet Bird of Youth*, James Goldman's *The Lion in Winter*, and Noël Coward's *Hay Fever* before settling on *The Little Foxes*, Lillian Hellman's melodrama of a rabidly avaricious Southern clan. Not only was Elizabeth at ease with a Southern accent, but she claimed that Regina Giddens was more like her own role model, Scarlett O'Hara, than the villainess whom Tallulah Bankhead and Bette Davis had already portrayed on stage and screen. 'She was more vulnerable than she knew or would have admitted. When I talked over *The Little Foxes* with John [Warner], he said, "If you're going to plunge, plunge."' That had been Warner's political philosophy, too; look where it had got him.

But perhaps it is not just a coincidence that Elizabeth's conversion to the stage occurred around the same time that her ex-husband, Richard Burton, had embarked on a 'kill or cure' adventure with his debilitated body and damaged reputation by starring in a revival of *Camelot*, the musical he was in when the fateful call had come to join the cast of *Cleopatra*. Thus both ex-spouses were about to submit themselves to a test of potential destruction in front of an audience, rather like invalids who've been told they'll not know if they can walk until they try. By the time he opened on Broadway in August 1980, Burton knew he had a smash hit. But it was a Pyrrhic victory: the pain-killing drugs he needed to sustain his performance eventually did him in, and soon after the post-Broadway tour reached San Francisco he had to check into the Santa Monica hospital where he had been dried out in the last stages of his marriage to Elizabeth. By the time he emerged again, his marriage to Suzy Hunt was more or less over. As soon as this was made public, his journals record that the telephone started ringing again – Elizabeth on the line. She had never quite cut the ties with her ex-husband. Now he was at liberty, her marriage was failing, and a sequel may well have seemed within sight for both of them. First, though, Elizabeth had to reassert the faith that Burton had once instilled in her, that she was no mere Hollywood star, but could hold her own as a legitimate stage actress. Scoring a hit would do more than generate adrenalin. Incredible though it seemed to some, it might revive their union.

First, though, she attended to her weight. Here, too, she was indulged by Bufman, who decided to open the play out of town in Fort Lauderdale, Florida, because of its proximity to the fat-farm where Elizabeth went for weekend dietary workouts.

There had been some apprehension that Lillian Hellman might veto the idea of her play being mounted around Elizabeth: she had rejected other actresses. In fact, Hellman warmly endorsed her. 'Each of them recognized a lot of herself in the other,' said one observer. 'There's a line in the play that Elizabeth speaks – "There are people who can never go back, who must finish what they start" – and that described both Lillian and Elizabeth perfectly.'

Moreover, Elizabeth's instinct for timeliness was working again. In the 1980s, a play about treachery and avarice had ceased to seem a story of deep-dyed villainy; it looked more and more as if these were defensible responses for women to make if they were to survive in a man's world. 'Elizabeth pitched that idea to Lillian. It was like an extension of what was by now her own well-publicized stance vis-à-vis her husband's brand of right-wing chauvinism. She found Lillian had already "bought" it.' Hellman's own quoted remark confirms this: 'I like [Elizabeth Taylor's] approach. Regina has frequently been played too much as a villainess.'

Elizabeth saw her as a victim she could understand, a woman forced by the times and circumstance to do ugly things. 'She's a killer,' she acknowledged, 'but she's saying "Sorry, fellas, you put me in this position."' As motivations go, it might not have gained high marks in an Actors Studio exam. For Elizabeth, it was analysis enough.

By the opening night on Broadway, 7 May 1981, her weight was down to 125 pounds. Maybe not yet enough: but enough to raise her morale. Anyhow, period fashions were sympathetic to well-upholstered ladies. At her first entrance in a full-blown gown that seemed to consist only of blood-red beads, the entire audience rose in ovation – 'an *a priori* bravo,' as the *Wall Street Journal*'s critic, Edwin Wilson, commented caustically, yet justly. It was true, too, as John Simon pointed out in *New York* magazine, that 'at forty-nine, Miss Taylor is not yet ready for the legitimate theater', but it was a redundant observation. The audiences were ready for her, impatiently ready, and there was a grudging undercurrent that style could go hang itself, so long as she made her appearance. (Bufman had taken out a $125,000 insurance premium against her non-appearance.) '[Regina's role] doesn't require great acting,' Frank Rich said; then, placing his finger on the dramatic pulse of the evening, he added, 'but it does require the tidal force of pure personality . . . we never question that this is one woman who gets what she wants, when she wants it, at any price. Taylor makes us hate her guts . . . God bless her!' But it was the *Village Voice*'s Michael Feingold who pointed out the irony of '[a] leftist attack on American materialism and greed being used to bolster the reputation of a graceless woman whose whole career has been a walking exhibit of them and who takes an active role in a political party that is now openly made up of people who share the Hubbard clan's ideals'. True, true . . . but when Elizabeth joined Lillian Hellman, her husband and others after the curtain fell, she knew that hers was the triumph of a woman who had looked the adversary full in the eye and turned aside judgement by her display of effrontery, if not talent. She took the success of the evening and anointed herself with it. 'I was overwhelmed with waves of love which nourished me long after the curtain fell.' She was like the little girl doing an impromptu dance before Royalty forty-five years before, and feeling the same waves of affection for such impudence lap round her. Elizabeth had regained her ego.

Affection didn't blunt business sense. Before the play had ended its run, the Elizabeth Taylor Repertory Co. had been formed, a fifty-fifty venture with Bufman intended to draw together stars like Jane Fonda and Robert De Niro as well as herself in limited-run stage productions in New York, Washington and Los Angeles. They would later be filmed and sold to the burgeoning video and cable market. One ticket (at ninety-nine dollars) would be valid for all three plays. Television would finance 40 per cent of the filming budgets. 'There is no way we can fail to make money,' said Bufman. Regina Giddens herself couldn't have wished to hear better news. Elizabeth's nine months' work in The Little Foxes enabled her to bank over $1.5 million. She was back in the money and back in the public eye – and there was the London opening still to come.

What did not appear to lie ahead was any future for the Taylor–Warner marriage. It had served its turn and run its term. Barely a week before Christmas, on 21 December 1981, the couple formally announced their separation after five years of marriage. The statement said: 'They have agreed [to part] with sadness, but no bitterness. Neither party presently intends to seek a divorce.' The senator behaved the way he had done before – like a gentleman. They had signed prenuptial agreements, but, really, each was so comfortably off that neither needed a compensatory share of the other's wealth. A few months before, in an interview with the English journalist David Lewin, Elizabeth had said, 'I have always thought that love was synonymous with marriage. The difference with marriage is that it is not just a 50–50, but a 51–51 relationship.' What precipitated the separation at the end of 1981 was not an act of infidelity, but rather one of thoughtlessness. Warner wanted to sell his Washington home and proposed that they move into an apartment in the Watergate building. In doing so, he inadvertently struck at one of his wife's strongest attachments. The new residence had a firm rule against keeping pets; the dogs and the cats would have to go. From childhood days at Little Swallows, Elizabeth had protected virtually everything that moved; one visitor to the Washington house even saw her tenderly tipping up a cardboard carton in the living room, and out scuttled a newly hatched chick she'd 'rescued' from the duck pond at the farm after a severe rainstorm had engulfed the little ball of gristle and fluff. She wouldn't be separated from her pets. She chose instead to be separated from her husband.

As soon as the Warners' marriage was seen to be breaking up, rumour once again linked her with other men. Zev Bufman was one, but Andy Warhol noticed the impresario at a New Year's Eve dinner with his wife, 'who, I could see, would never let him have an affair with Elizabeth Taylor'. Warhol was right; they remained just good business partners. And there were various young actors, nicknamed 'Saturday-night specials' for their limited-purpose availability as escorts with the right combination of good looks and eager attentiveness to Elizabeth's wishes. Gradually, however, the one man with whom her name always would be linked began to be spoken of as her next husband – and for the third time.

Richard Burton was by then so ill that any other man would have been frightened into retirement by the doctor's prognosis. He could barely raise his arms above his shoulders; he was partially blind in one eye. Consultant after consultant advised him not to accept the dreadful burden of his latest project, in which he was to play the title role in a miniseries about the composer Wagner that would take seven months of whatever span of life he had left. Yet he accepted it. Like Elizabeth, inactivity for him was the kind of death that was worse than death itself. He spent a lot of time telephoning Elizabeth. 'I can't live without her,' he confessed. Soon what the papers had once called 'the grand affair' was being refurbished for fresh occupancy – and being renamed 'the grand addiction'.

She arrived in London on 23 February 1982, quite the film star again, a mink coat over her jeans, the Rolls-Royce in from the airport making an unscheduled stop at The Feathers pub, Chiswick, where Zev Bufman got a lesson from her in sinking a pint of bitter in one go. A few days later, arriving in a private jet, a haggard but still handsome Burton gratefully sank into the chocolate-coloured limousine she had sent for him, to be whisked to her London address, a house in Cheyne Walk, Chelsea, owned by the producer Norma Heyman, where four round-the-clock security men, Chen Sam and an Italian hairdresser had made Elizabeth safe and presentable. She greeted him with 'Where's my present?' But it was more an affectionate catch-phrase than a query. She'd invited Burton to her fiftieth birthday party. He was also there to give a poetry reading for charity. *The Little Foxes* was scheduled to open on 11 March.

But although the pair of them had enough excuses to be together in the same place at the same time, close friends felt Elizabeth's real desire was to have Burton witness the way she took the London stage by storm. 'She is always saying that Richard never made it in the West End,' Bufman let slip out. The inference was that she could. His presence was, in a very real sense, her present. Otherwise, there was really very little money in bringing an expensively mounted play – production costs were at least £180,000 – to a West End theatre where the cost before profit began was nearly £100,000 a week, even with the sellout business expected (and obtained). 'She really does desperately want to have a success here,' Bufman admitted. 'She feels it is her first home.'

Her marriage break-up had intensified that feeling. One day she decided to visit the house where she was born. She took along with her a thirty-four-year-old actor, Anthony Geary, star of the American soap opera *General Hospital*, which was one of her favourite programmes back home. She had actually filmed a guest appearance in the 'soap' the previous year, and she and Geary continued their relationship intermittently over the months. She had it in mind to cast him opposite her in a revival of *Sweet Bird of Youth*, which Bufman was hoping to present on Broadway as one of the Elizabeth Taylor Repertory Company productions. The present owners of Elizabeth's old home, Steven and Susan Licht, opened the door, 'and there Elizabeth Taylor stood with this American gentleman'. The Lichts showed them around – or, rather, followed her while she conducted them on a memory tour. She asked if the house might be for sale. The owners indicated that it was not. Soon afterwards, tickets for the play arrived for them.

The birthday party, at that month's 'in' restaurant, Legends, tried to recreate the old Mike Todd mix of 'pauper and prince': sausage-and-mash was served (to some), caviar and poached salmon (to many more). Nureyev, Tony Bennett, Ringo Starr, all Elizabeth's children, Burton: the guest list had a curiously left-over look from another, lusher era. Photo blow-ups of Elizabeth covered the walls; silver balloons, on which a pair of eyes was thought to be the only necessary identification, were released. Burton looked tired, lined and drained – and asked for the music to be turned down.

The next night, 28 February, as he was preparing to read *Under Milk Wood* at the charity recital, a figure glided on stage – Elizabeth! Recovering from the surprise, he tried to kiss her as she walked past. But the sight in that eye was now so uncertain that he missed. Flustered, it took him time to find his ease among the pages of his text, which he turned with shaking hands. But back at the house, if he is to be believed (which is not at all certain), he apparently made a complete recovery and did not emerge until the early hours, wrapped in a short mink top-coat and looking exhausted but pleased with himself. 'Marriage?' he was asked by the inevitable waiting reporter. 'Oh come on ... we don't need another one. We love each other with a passion so furious that we burn each other out.' According to him, Elizabeth had begged him to remarry her. According to her, she had done nothing of the sort. Burton's embellishments on the night's entertainment – if that is all it was – upset her all the more because he appeared to have used the occasion and the papers as a way of saying publicly 'Thanks – but no thanks.' There was no use saying he always had done – and that old habits die hard or not at all. Later, the blame for the mixed reactions her first night got from the critics was attributed to the way she had been 'psyched up' by Burton's apparent public brush-off.

Within weeks, he was talking of marriage – but it was not to Elizabeth. He had met a woman who satisfied his needs as well as his affections. Sally Hay was a television assistant on the multi-part film he was making about Wagner. Several friends noticed a resemblance between her and Burton's first wife Sybil. Both women were devoted homemakers. He had reached the age and condition when a home was as necessary to him as a marriage bed.

Elizabeth was savaged by most of the London critics. 'As grisly as an undertakers' picnic,' said Robert Cushman in the *Observer*. 'For the most part, as an actress she teeters on the brink of competence,' wrote the *Daily Mail*'s Jack Tinker. 'Her reactions . . . are signalled with a machete. "The rich don't have to be subtle," she squeals at one point. And on this philosophy, she has clearly based her entire performance.' And again, it hardly mattered. People didn't come to see her act; they came to see her – period. They were spending their money on mythology. She saw her eighty-five-year-old mother Sara witnessing her daughter holding the stage in the capital city of her own success fifty-six years before; somehow, a wheel had come full circle. And eventually, in July, she saw Burton and Sally Hay sitting out front. She asked afterwards what he intended to do next and, before he could answer, said, 'What do you say to having some fun and making a pile of money on Broadway?'

According to Sally Hay, Burton agreed to star with Elizabeth in Noël Coward's *Private Lives*, believing that after a respectable Broadway run and a lucrative taping for television, that would be that. 'Had the deal been: "Do you want seven months on tour with *Private Lives?*" Richard would have fled,' said Sally Hay. 'But it only came to that when he was too far in.'

Rehearsals were not scheduled to begin until March 1983. Well before then, she was again a single woman; John Warner and she were divorced on 7 November 1982, after the failure of what appeared to be several attempts at reconciliation. Elizabeth had now a great many months to fill before she was reunited with Burton in *Private Lives*. She filled them partly at the health spa – for she had ended the London run of *The Little Foxes* overweight and in bad shape – and partly with a new man-friend, one Victor Gonzalez Luna, who had emerged seemingly out of nowhere and was the most unlikely escort she had ever had. A fifty-five-year-old Mexican lawyer, divorced, he had two young children and a brace of maiden aunts already deeply shocked by the divorce and quite incredulous at the prospect of their nephew becoming Elizabeth Taylor's seventh. Luna seems to have fulfilled Elizabeth's current need for a fatherly figure rather than a passionate lover. He was politically well-connected, had handled the Burtons' holdings in Mexico, and may well have entertained hopes that forming a liaison with a famous figure would help him to gain government office as successfully as it had done the last man she had married north of the border.

As she'd done with *The Little Foxes*, Elizabeth again re-interpreted the play she was set to do in terms of her current feelings. Playgoers of several generations may have thought *Private Lives* was a self-consciously mannered but witty comedy about the reunion of a couple who had once been married to each other and now, through boredom with their present spouses, decided to give love another try. But to Elizabeth, it was far more personal. It was a play about 'two middle-aged people who, though miles down the road from their once all-consuming passion, still care deeply for each other'. In other words, it was a meditation on age and weariness, on herself and Richard. Later, in the light of what followed, she admitted they should have done a drama, 'not an English drawing-room comedy [sic]'.

By the time she and Burton began rehearsals in March 1983, her divorce from John Warner had come through and Burton had gone to Haiti for one of those almost 'do it yourself' divorces from Suzy Hunt. On returning to New York, he found Elizabeth in a worse physical state than even he was: 'Face okay, but figure splop!' She had trouble even reading her lines – which signified to him that she was 'on something or other'. She lacked energy and kept on telling him how lonely she was. Earlier in the year, she had been to Israel and tried to adopt a twelve-month-old baby girl found for her in a Tel Aviv orphanage. Her hopes were frustrated at the last moment by the reluctance of the child's father.

The pain-killing drugs she had been prescribed seemed to be contributing to her bloated appearance. Moreover, Burton's diary suggests that the sight of Sally Hay now running her lover's daily life efficiently and compassionately, shopping for his health foods and supervising his daily rest, was lowering Elizabeth's vitality and self-confidence. Burton was having his energies conserved by being weaned off alcohol; Elizabeth was seeking energy from the drugs she had been prescribed. Or so it seemed to him. Actually, as Melvyn Bragg speculates, her hesitancy may simply have been a film actress's approach to the play – treating it as a film script, learning it in parts, only bringing it together when she'd been through all the 'shots'. As ever, she relied on intuition; as ever, he was a conscious seeker-and-shaper. Their rehearsal tactics and their conflicting metabolisms simply didn't match or meet until the very end of the rehearsals. All too often, Burton was left feeling out of temper.

The play proved a humiliating experience, and it was no consolation to know they had brought it on themselves. With players like themselves, Coward's play was bound to resemble an animated gossip-column. Though the characters' names might be Amanda and Elyot, to all who came to see them they were Elizabeth and Richard, now admitting the public to their own 'private lives'. The painful relevance of some of the dialogue to their real lives – and, conversely, the visible irrelevance of some of their remarks to their own well-known natures – was a bonus to the prurient playgoer. The Burtons – for it was impossible to think of them otherwise – were putting themselves on show in something which resembled a psychodrama of the kind that the mentally disturbed were encouraged to do in order to exorcise their demons. Only in this case, the stars were indulging theirs.

The first night was doomed. The curtain rose thirty-five minutes late and the interval after the first act lasted longer than the act itself. Burton, in platform shoes to make himself look taller on stage, looked a sick man and sounded like someone about to be buried. Elizabeth was still fat enough for her to have developed what one critic called 'dorsal cleavage', where her backless evening gown cruelly compressed her flesh. Both were twenty years older than the play indicated. Burton, said Frank Rich, resembled 'a tired millionaire steeling himself for an obligatory annual visit to the accountant'. Even the lines so prudently pruned from the text had been noted by critics who heartlessly quoted them nonetheless. Thus John Simon noted the disappearance of the reference to Amanda's 'running like a deer', and commented that with Elizabeth in the role 'anything faster than a sumo wrestler is inconceivable'. Burton, the same critic surmised, viewed the play as a weekly paycheck; Elizabeth, looking at the audience, saw a crowded house. For him, it represented money; for her, love. *Variety* spoke the requiem verdict: '*The Dance of Death* would have been a more appropriate choice.'

There was a bizarre irony in all this. While their performances were sending out the message to the theatre critics that this couple, now parted, should never have met again, the gossip columnists were playing up the reports that their partnership on stage might precede their rematch at the altar.

Burton was depressed by more than bad notices. Soon after the play's opening, John Huston had asked him to play the British consul in the film version of Malcolm Lowry's *Under the Volcano*. Burton might have been in training for the part all his life: the desperate man's chronic alcoholism, his tattered rags of literate self-disgust drawn round his ravaged frame, his pathetic relationship with his ex-wife. What a temptation this was for the actor, compared with the present exhibition he was making of himself! But try as he might, Burton couldn't win his contractual release from *Private Lives* and Elizabeth. The consul's role went to Albert Finney, and Burton soldiered on through a six-month ordeal on Broadway.

It was an odd experience for their intimates, who went backstage to see the stars and discovered their respective lovers, Victor Luna and Sally Hay, waiting, so to speak, in the wings. The set-up was less like a quartet from Coward's brittle comedy than the foursome who had been locked into the love-hate traumas of Albee's bitter play.

At the end of June, Elizabeth's health collapsed and she dropped out temporarily. Bufman closed the play until she recovered. And Burton profited from this unexpected parole to slip off to Las Vegas, where he and Sally Hay were married on 3 July.

Everyone held their breath to see what Elizabeth would do or say. She did not disappoint. Like a prima donna who knows the show isn't over till the fat lady sings, she sent flowers, congratulations – and news of her own engagement to Victor Luna. For once, one felt, Coward had been trumped.

The bewilderment of their friends was now such that those who flew into Philadelphia in August, in response to an invitation to the first-night party at the start of the play's cross-country tour, were uncertain whether they had been summoned to celebrate Burton's secret marriage to Sally Hay or Elizabeth's short-notice engagement to Victor Luna.

As usual, Elizabeth had risen from her sick-bed in fighting form. In the whimsical mood of a *grande dame du théâtre*, she had made a few additions of her own to Coward's play. One of these was a brightly coloured parrot named Alvin which she brought on stage in the last act. Alvin took his bow with her, and sometimes she ostentatiously effaced herself and diverted the applause towards her feathered co-star. Malevolent whispers had it that it was her oblique comment on Richard Burton.

The party after the show was identified as 'hers', rather than 'his', by the lilac colour scheme, by a huge cake that the menu called Gâteau Elizabeth et Victor', and by a positively massive sapphire-and-diamond Cartier ring. But if the guests anticipated hearing an announcement of the wedding date, they left disappointed. Alvin the parrot was kissed good-night and sent upstairs to his suite with the invocation 'Good night, sweet prince,' that had once been addressed to Burton's mortally wounded Hamlet. The Spanish guitarist and the exotic singers packed up and went home. Any Taittinger champagne rosé (1973) that had been left unconsumed was sent to Elizabeth's suite. Victor Luna kept smiling, but said nothing. As Burton was presumed to have an interest in his ex-wife's wedding plans, he was discreetly pumped for information. For once, he was circumspect: 'I have no idea ... we have touring commitments.'

The tour ended in Los Angeles some three months later. Well before the end of the line, Elizabeth cracked up. Her weight was on the upward march again. The medication had distressing side-effects. She was taking pills constantly, gorging herself before the show, gasping for a Jack Daniel's after it – she was too professional ever to risk a drink beforehand – and sometimes she didn't see bed until 4 a.m.

It was left to her family to mount a painful rescue – her brother, her children and a few of her oldest friends like Roddy McDowall. She sat there in the family circle, hearing them tell her of their deepest concern for her health and welfare. It was like a prayer meeting at which all present lay hands on the afflicted victim in an attempt to expel the demon. They urged her, under pain of collapse or worse, to enter a clinic where her alcohol and drug abuse could get attention and the related problems of her obesity and self-respect could be treated with the self-awareness that only comes with complete and utter seclusion. She listened in shock. This was no congregation of professional consultants. She was on trial, as it were, at a court of love. Her distressed accusers were friends, children, blood relatives. It was the harm she was doing to them – not just to herself – that brought her to the decision she reached after an hour's solitary reflection.

On 5 December 1983, she entered the Betty Ford Clinic at Rancho Mirage, an exclusive suburb adjoining the slightly less tony Palm Springs. It was a rehabilitation centre sponsored by the wife of the ex-president, dedicated to breaking the self-destructive will of its patients and resetting it in a self-supportive cast of mind. It was, in fact, very much like the positive philosophy she had absorbed from her mother in her childhood. Sara Taylor, now in her late eighties, was living close by in a luxury colony of retirement homes. It was like going back to mother.

A stern 'mother', though. Humility was needed before recuperation could do its job. She had the protective scar tissue stripped off her star's ego. She had to share a spartan bedroom, make her own bed, wait her turn for the shower, forgo phone privileges, take part in emptying the wastebaskets and cleaning and sweeping the living space she shared with folk who were total strangers – or almost. A little later, an ailing Peter Lawford arrived at the clinic in the advanced (and, as it turned out, terminal) stages of alcohol and drug addiction. Thus the two child stars of MGM, who had played young lovers in *Julia Misbehaves* and got married in *Little Women* thirty-five years earlier, now found themselves in the same clinic, salvaging their lives.

The clinic's first rule was to obliterate any idea a patient had that he or she was unique. For someone like Elizabeth, that amounted to a course in anti-stardom. But only then, with abasement before confession, could the therapy work. And for her, it worked. When she discharged herself in January 1984, what she had seen as loneliness and loss of identity had been transformed into self-support and freedom of expression. She set out to remake herself physically. She dieted down to 122 pounds; she had a modest but effective bit of surgery to sharpen her jawline and put some of the iron back into her sagging jowls.

And with that missionary sense of helping others, which ran alongside her own epic binges of self-indulgence, she found time to get out a book, *Elizabeth Takes Off*, containing charts, philosophical as well as dietary, of how to reach her new-found land of peace and contentment. 'You can be anything you like, if you set your mind to it'; now it wasn't 'Tell mama', but 'Let mama tell you.' She wrote of the new home she had bought in Bel Air and the sense of roots and revival conveyed by one particular tree in the garden – one that recalled, again, those woods of her Hampstead childhood. She found reassurance in witnessing its annual miracle of flowering every spring and the firm grip on the soil which it had used the years to secure.

The marriage to Victor Luna did not take place. It was called off in August 1984. 'Since we can't be together, we can't get married,' he said sensibly, confirming the view that the men in her life generally came out of it more happily than the husbands. His family held a celebration party in Guadalajara.

As for Burton, who was living in Switzerland, though Elizabeth was far off she was not beyond call or report. According to Sally Burton, her husband would read some news item about her and say, with a kind of disabused amusement, 'You'll never guess what she's doing now, the old girl. She'll surprise us all, that one.'

The last time he met her was in May 1984, in a London pub; he was with Sally, she still had Victor Luna squiring her around. Burton was amazed at how well – and slim – she looked. She now weighed under 112 pounds. Eerie, some called the effect.

Burton was still in demand for films; more than ever, it seemed. Nor had his price sunk much, though the fees he was paid were based on past successes like *Where Eagles Dare* rather than on his less profitable efforts. There was always the hope he would deliver a new moneymaker to his producers. The gathering years and their ravages worked in his favour, too: his scarred and scuffed looks lent him a battered romanticism. Unlike Elizabeth, he didn't have to remove the evidence of misspent years and self-indulgence; he accumulated their 'interesting' additions, like poker chips. A remake of Graham Greene's novel *The Quiet American* was offered him, but it was the classic status of another simultaneous project, George Orwell's *1984*, that seduced him into acceptance. It was being rushed into production so as not to miss the date in its title. His part was that of O'Brien, the State inquisitor and torturer. It was to be one of the best, least self-conscious of all his film performances. The erosion the years had made on his face and figure showed up to advantage in his fined-down characterization of dispassionate ruthlessness.

Elizabeth was commuting between Bel Air and Gstaad that summer. When in Switzerland, she was not far from the Burtons. Sally half suspected her of meaning to have 'another go' at involving Burton in a fresh stage or film project. Burton said he couldn't ever see himself living with her again; he needed a nurse as much as a wife now, in fact more so. But he admitted that the old hold was not entirely broken – Elizabeth and he always knew they were there 'when we need each other'.

On the night of 4 August 1984, Burton suffered a cerebral haemorrhage when he was in bed, alone. He was rushed to the hospital in Celigny, then to Geneva when the seriousness of the stroke was diagnosed. Sally Burton then returned to the chalet to await the outcome of what the doctors had told her would be a lengthy operation. Hardly had she entered Pays de Galles than the telephone summoned her back to Geneva, urgently.

She was just too late to see her husband before he died. He was aged fifty-eight when life left him, a bare two years short of the span he had once grimly allocated himself. Valerie Douglas, his American agent, relayed the news to family and friends. Chen Sam, in turn, called California to let Elizabeth know. On hearing the news, she collapsed from shock.

PART FOUR

Surviving

41

'I HAVE NO PLAN TO SUCCUMB'

Elizabeth had hoped to attend Burton's burial in one of Celigny's two small churchyards. In the event, she did not. His widow, family and friends, it was made clear to her, might be unable to cope with the scenes that her arrival would have precipitated among the media crammed into the burial ground. She took it hard, but probably decided it was sensible if cruel advice. Being together in life had presented enough logistical and security problems for her and Burton; being near each other in death, however briefly, carried unacceptable risks. That was the unsentimental sum of it.

Burton's bones would have to lie in Swiss soil, otherwise British taxes could be levied on his estate. Domicile, in the strict legal sense of the word, in the end came down to matters of fiscal advantage, despite the ringing declarations of his Welshness that he had made in his lifetime.

Even so, the paparazzi kept watch day and night long after the flowers on the grave had wilted, and they were rewarded – though the word signifies a wholly undeserved bonus – at the unlikely hour of 6 a.m. on 14 August. Elizabeth's hope of finding privacy in a graveyard at that time of the morning was shattered as soon as she saw them running towards her between the burial plots, flash bulbs going off palely in the dawn. Her four bodyguards interposed themselves. Umbrellas of incongruously bright colours were snapped open to improvise a makeshift screen, and she knelt behind it, in prayer or thought, for some ten minutes before picking her way back – on the supporting arm of her daughter Liza – to the waiting grey Mercedes. 'It was one of the few occasions Richard and I were alone,' Graham Jenkins reported her saying to him later, 'almost wistfully'. It must have taken sensitivities well-proofed against the world's intrusiveness to have felt alone at the centre of that morbid pack.

There was a warmer welcome from Burton's family and relatives when she arrived in Pontrhydyfen about a week later, descending from a private executive jet at Swansea airport, dressed in pink, the Krupp diamond he'd bought her flashing its old message of defiance at what the world might think. She slept that night in the two-bed front room in the home of Burton's married sister, just thirty yards from the grey and sandstone Baptist chapel where five hundred Welsh voices had been raised in song and prayer at the memorial service eight days earlier.

On 30 August, she again sat among the Welsh clan and hundreds of other acquaintances and fellow professionals of theatre and cinema at the thanksgiving service for Burton's life and work which was held at St Martin-in-the-Fields, Trafalgar Square. Burton's widow Sally and his third wife, Suzy Hunt, were present, too; Sybil Burton Christopher had observed the memory of her first husband privately in Los Angeles. Elizabeth had by now recovered from the shock and humiliations. Dressed and beturbanned in black, she looked, said one guest, 'like a queen in mourning'.

Burton's probated estate totalled some £2.7 million, including £700,000 in assets in Britain, but was certainly more – much more if all the assets registered in Bermuda and elsewhere had been included. It made no provision for Elizabeth; but none was needed and none expected. A tenth share of it went to Maria Burton, the adopted child to whom he had always felt so close, being himself a child who had been adopted by his mentor Philip Burton. A token memento was left to Liza Todd – all Elizabeth's children, in any case, had already been made rich by trust funds.

Elizabeth returned to Los Angeles with the resolve to turn her 'loneliness' into 'independence'. The old iron determination, supplemented by the dietary and detoxifying treatment she was receiving at the Ford clinic, helped her seize control. Men friends helped, too. She confessed that it felt 'pretty strange' to be dating men at an age when many women are involved in the duties of being a grandmother. Escorts were not scarce – quite the contrary. But she was aware of the sizeable inhibitions that her previous six marriages – and especially those to Todd and Burton – must present to any man sincere enough to want to become her seventh husband. The men who simply wanted to share her celebrity, not her life, were the ones who were easy to spot – and just as easy to do without, once they had served their time. The media, however, were ever ready to link her romantically with friends with whom she was seen making the social round.

One of these was Dennis Stein, an entrepreneur, who had at least made her laugh by gaining admittance to her Bel Air home while she was out, then springing out from behind the door when she walked in and popping a 20-carat ring on her finger. For a moment, an engagement looked imminent; but they ended up friends, not newly-weds, and he took away another of the gold watches that came the way of her sometime beaux. This one had 'Forget me not' inscribed on its case. If Stein took this as encouragement, he was disappointed; 'almost a mistake', Elizabeth said later in an exceptionally candid interview in *Vanity Fair*. Then there were Carl Bernstein, the investigative journalist, and Sir Gordon Reece, the public relations consultant and image-maker to Margaret Thatcher and the Tory party. And there were friends who went way back, and were close and valued: Roddy McDowall headed that list. Malcolm Forbes had not yet figured prominently among her dates.

Then there were other old friends, to whom she discovered she owed compassion, not love, since they were not likely to be part of her world for much longer. One was Peter Lawford, now losing the fight against liver and kidney failure; she kept vigil by his bed that December in what turned out to be a death watch. So, too, was her hospital visit to Rock Hudson, her co-star in *Giant*, when news that he was the first celebrity victim of AIDS was made public in the summer of 1985. Undeterred by rumours current at the time of the virus's contagiousness, Elizabeth sat and comforted him as best she could. When Hudson died eight weeks later, among his possessions auctioned for AIDS charities was a white bathroom stool on which had been written in indelible pink letters: 'Elizabeth Taylor stood here. I had to in order to reach the sink.' That was when she had used the actor's New York flat while rehearsing *Private Lives*. Now she had seen the mighty six-foot-four-inch star reduced to a wasted husk weighing under ninety pounds.

Hudson's death, and the prurient picking-over of such a public favourite as Liberace, another AIDS victim, revealed how vulnerable even riches and celebrity were to the ravages of the disease, and gave her a new resolve. She subsequently became national chairwoman of the American Foundation for AIDS Research, which has raised over $14 million to date. Spearheading such a campaign represented, in part, a battle against the indecencies of invasive publicity which she had had to fight all her life – death should at least spare one that. It was predictable that her well-publicized work would be viewed by some as just one more way of providing herself with a platform and an audience. But this would be to deny the consistency of Elizabeth's reaction throughout her life to all kinds of suffering, whether self-inflicted or God-sent. 'In each century since the beginning of the world, wonderful things have been discovered,' wrote Frances Hodgson Burnett in *The Secret Garden*, the story that moulded so much of Elizabeth's outlook. And though it is unlikely she could have recalled those words of hope, the Victorian sentiment of her own mother's favourite children's writer supported Elizabeth's growing participation in the search for a cure for AIDS.

Her characteristic outspokenness served her cause well. She used words that cut through the evasiveness and prejudice of the establishment. 'It's going to take a famous heterosexual woman dying before AIDS gets the attention of the heterosexual community,' she said. She personalized her appeal in a way few stars would have dared. Congressmen who were more accustomed to hearing pleas from the virtuous rather than the admissions of the worldly (if prudent) people who testified before them were astonished to hear her tell them during one fund-raising submission that she would take an HIV test before beginning any new affair, and that she hoped her prospective partner would do so, too.

Indeed the sale of the late Duchess of Windsor's jewel collection in the spring of 1987 allowed her to reconcile private indulgence and public health strikingly well. Bidding over a pool-side telephone from her home in California to the auction in Geneva, she paid $449,625 (£349,792) for a piece fashioned in the shape of the Prince of Wales's plumed crest in diamonds – a memento, too, of Richard Burton's ancestry. The money raised by the auction went to the Paris-based Pasteur Institute, a leading clinic for AIDS research. 'The first time I've ever had to buy myself a piece of jewellery,' Elizabeth said laconically.

Inevitably, though, her own health continued to preoccupy her. That tortured spine of hers had to be continually soothed; which meant recourse to the full range of pain-killing drugs such as Demerol, Percodan, Xanax, Zantac, Acturvan and others that sound like spells from medicine's cabinet of black magic. Toxins unavoidably built up in her body. In 1988, she tumbled back into the nightmare of pain, pills and excess pounds and was admitted once more to the Betty Ford Clinic. By coincidence, her ninety-two-year-old mother was at the Eisenhower Clinic next door, suffering from bleeding ulcers. Elizabeth was allowed the privilege of a daily call on her parent. Typically, she arranged it like a state visit, getting freshly coiffed, groomed and manicured, even having her eyebrows pencilled in, and, in her incapacitated condition, being carried through the hospital corridors like a queen in a royal litter to Mrs Taylor's bedside. 'Sara Taylor's a tough old bird,' an orderly was quoted as saying. 'Elizabeth's her daughter, they're two of a kind.' Even so, Elizabeth was also described as 'a female Elvis Presley'. 'You know what happened to him,' said the medical attendant darkly.

Not to her, though, not this time. Mother and daughter did well and recovered. And the confessional sessions at the Ford clinic, and later at Alcoholics Anonymous meetings, brought Elizabeth unexpected support in the impressive shape of a husky thirty-five-year-old fellow patient, one

Larry Fortensky, a truck driver serving a term of probation after a drunk-driving conviction, whose medical fees had been paid by his Teamsters Union insurance policy. If death was the great leveller, then clearly medication at the Ford clinic was no bad advertisement for democracy, either. To some, the sight of Elizabeth and Larry Fortensky offering each other mutual sympathy and support recalled the set-up in her film *Boom*, where Flora Goforth, the world's richest woman, welcomes a passing beach bum with the gifts of life and death into her world of affluence and illness. But their relationship appears to have been only a friendly interlude, based on her old 'damn the world' defiance – if it thinks ill of me, so what? Let it! Fortensky, in due course, joined the list of 'escorts', rather than 'eligibles'.

There are some who still insist that a woman of Elizabeth's impulsive nature could never have given her children the time and devotion that they need. But based on the available evidence, a jury would acquit her without even needing to retire. Some of her four children have certainly made bad judgements in their own marriages – separations, custody cases and other painful allegations have figured in stories that gain the headlines because of the family ties to Elizabeth Taylor. But such things are not unusual in many non-celebrity marriages. The Wilding children, now in their mid-thirties, had an unsettled education as a result of the Burtons' own peripatetic years. But in the late 1980s, Michael Wilding Jr had become an actor, and had married Brooke Palance, daughter of the film star Jack Palance. When his mother couldn't go to New York to see him in an off-Broadway play, she had the cast fly out to her home in California and put on the show for her there. Maternal indulgence, maybe: but scarcely more reprehensible than commanding an order of chili con carne to be flown out from the Chasen's kitchens in Hollywood to Cinecittà, as she once did when she was consumed with ravenous homesickness while making *Cleopatra*. All things are relative.

Christopher Wilding, after a troubled marriage to the oil heiress Aileen Getty, is an artist and photographer with a bent towards film editing. Liza Todd and Maria Burton are also married and practise sculpture and clothes designing respectively. Their mother admits that her family might have benefitted from a little of the discipline that constrained her own moments of childhood rebellion. But more significantly, in view of the way that mother-love shaped her every waking moment, she insists she did not force her own love on her offspring. Rich now, the children will be even richer one day. As none of them has a passion for buying jewellery or collecting paintings, their mother's substantial holdings will be sold after her death to benefit them and their families.

Elizabeth continued her acting career in the years following Burton's death, but in the more accommodating medium of telefilms or miniseries. The quicker pace of shooting such movies suited her fluctuating health (and the companies that would have to insure it). It was better, too, to accept a cameo role with other prestigious stars, or a leading role in a smaller-budget telefilm, than try and adjust to the more painful demotion to a supporting role in a large-budget feature film whose stars might possibly be younger than her own children.

There has usually been something of an autobiographical link between her life and many of these movies. Illness prevented her from starring in an inspirational movie entitled *From This Day On*, based on her own battle against alcohol abuse.

But in the telefilm *Malice in Wonderland*, she settled the score with one of her oldest tormentors by playing Louella Parsons, the gossip columnist, to Jane Alexander's Hedda Hopper, though the film was only a mildly bitchy skit that turned the two old dragons of filmland into beauty-parlour matrons. In the Civil War miniseries *North and South*, she played a managerial madam, co-starring with Robert Mitchum, Gene Kelly, Jean Simmons and Johnny Cash, and picked up $200,000. Rather more was paid her for *Poker Alice*, a burlesque Western in which she played a travelling lady gambler with her then escort in real life, George Hamilton, squiring her in gentlemanly fashion through the pros and cons of the saloon belt. Needless to say, she held a winning hand. It suited Elizabeth's 'plunger' disposition and her refusal to be even remotely associated with a losing streak.

The custom of smoothing the shooting by anticipating her delight in little baubles had now been regularized and the budget of *Poker Alice*, according to the producers, contained an allowance of $100,000 for daily douceurs: twenty-four days was her shooting schedule and twenty-four gifts were reported to have been tendered. The old names were well represented: a stick pin from Cartier, a Van Cleef and Arpels travel clock ... But such acts of tribute and propitiation had by now acquired an element of self-satire – almost comic comfits. She was able to join in the joke when she made the feature film, *Young Toscanini*, in Rome in 1987, directed by the steadying and flattering hand of Franco Zeffirelli. In this romantically padded but historically threadbare biopic of the cub-like musician, played by the brat-pack ministar C. Thomas Howell, Elizabeth was cast as the conductor's muse, a famous opera diva called 'the divine Nadina Bulycova', who was also the Emperor of Brazil's mistress, a more comfortable role for the star. When Toscanini is dispatched to her country estate to plead with the diva to return to Rio and rehearse at least the high notes for the gala performance of *Aida*, he is confronted by a ravishing, imperious Elizabeth who demands tribute before toil: 'Where are the flowers? Where are the jewels?' The film owed more to its star's life-style than to Toscanini's life.

The script gave her the chance to espouse another unimpeachable, if unlikely, 'good cause': the abolition of slavery. A new landmark in camp cinema was set when Elizabeth, in dusky-skinned make-up, halts the performance of *Aida* in mid-aria to glide up to the footlights and implore the celebrity audience, which includes the Emperor, to emancipate their slaves, promising instant freedom for her own seven. ('The transition period may be a little difficult.')

For all its unintentional risibility, the film provided her with a splendid showcase for her own restored looks and reduced poundage – both well illuminated by the wattage of the jewellery she wore.

A companion for part of the filming in Rome was Malcolm Forbes, the multi-millionaire business-magazine publisher, balloonist, biker, collector of Fabergé eggs and toy soldiers, and party-giver. Then in his sixty-eighth year, he unashamedly hungered for publicity as much as she remained wary of it; that she was able to take the heat at so many of his media-manipulating events signifies a bond between them of more-than-usual closeness and flexibility. Marriage was inevitably bruited, particularly when they were photographed together in a church near his French château.

Max Lerner's observation, already quoted, seems to explain this liaison: there is usually something of the previous marriage in each new relationship. This time it was surely Forbes's resemblance to Mike Todd – both men, probably coincidentally, made hot-air balloons into a personal trademark. Forbes had Todd's love of flamboyance, gregariousness, high spending and a persistent courtship of the media. Both Forbes and Elizabeth enjoyed spending – it was often more satisfying than the act of getting. It gave them an aura of power. But because he generally spent his money on others, it gave him a halo of good-fellowship. For all her charity work, Elizabeth could not completely break out of the isolation ward of stardom. Forbes, by contrast, remained eminently sociable for all his financial power. She recognized this enviable gift and was drawn to him by it. He borrowed her fabulous life; she regained, through his lavish parties, the position of power and centrality that was no longer available through the fantasy life of the screen. Julie Baumgold, assigned by *New York* magazine to cover Forbes's Arabian Nights-like fête in Morocco in October 1989, spotted the way that 'the weekend [was] a study in fame . . . the minor New York-bound fame of Blaine [Trump] and Carolyne [Roehme] . . . the television fame of Henry [Kissinger] and Barbara [Walters]. And, at a whole other level, the sick, desperate, movie-star-freak fame, the merciless charge, the centipede movement of camera and crews pushing to the center, where Elizabeth Taylor stands like the defendant at a big trial.'

Forbes's death, a mere five months later, came with the same suddenness as the deaths of Todd and Burton. Unsurprisingly, perhaps, it was followed by Elizabeth's own collapse from a virus complaint and the shockingly swift escalation of her illness into a reportedly life-or-death battle against pneumonia. As she lay in a California hospital in April 1990, being kept breathing by a ventilator, it looked to many like a replay of her battle for life in London nearly thirty years earlier. This time, though, there was the unpleasant rumour of an AIDS-related cause in her illness. Medical bulletins issued on Elizabeth's behalf authoritatively quashed this speculation.

To some observers, her crisis seemed to fit more plausibly into the life pattern of a born survivor, not a fateful loser. It is the possibly intuitive strategy of collapse, retreat, revival, recuperation, renewal and re-emergence at her fighting weight that has underpinned her existence at such times of stress. 'She knows more about suffering than Charles Dickens and Saint Augustine put together,' Laurence Harvey once said of her. And she herself could have quoted another authority on the human condition. 'Not to change is to die,' says Alexandra del Lago, the ailing movie queen in Tennessee Williams's *Sweet Bird of Youth*, who breathes borrowed life into every minute of her waking day when free of the oxygen mask that periodically revives her. Elizabeth had played the part in a telefilm as recently as July 1989, though it was now Mark Harmon, not Anthony Geary, who was cast as her young lover. She herself has never feared death. If she has had any fear, it is of living too long. 'She once remarked that longevity ran in her family and that it terrified her,' a close acquaintance recalled at a time when Elizabeth's mother was in her ninety-fifth year. And she has changed her being, her looks, her interests, her ambitions so compulsively with each new lover, husband or phase of her career that, as John Leonard said in reviewing her performance in *Sweet Bird of Youth*, 'it's difficult . . . to look at Elizabeth Taylor, even when she's supposed to be someone else. She's a palimpsest of all the revisions we've made of our fantasies about her over the decades.'

'I have no plan to succumb,' she has said. 'I am a survivor.' Not only did she succeed in demonstrating her passion for living, but she was even able to bottle it and sell it – in the amethyst-coloured flagons of perfume with that very name, 'Passion', which she began promoting in mid-1987. As an illustration of how to convert the philosophy of life into an instant commercial success, no wonder it drew the admiring endorsement of Malcolm Forbes. He even presented her with one of his own sources of energy, a Harley-Davidson bike sprayed in matching amethyst with the fuel tank proclaiming, 'Elizabeth Taylor's Passion'. The aura of Big

Business was the celebrity fragrance they both wore.

She once said to Truman Capote: 'What do you suppose will become of us? I suppose when you find out what you've always wanted, that's not where the beginning begins, that's where the end starts.'

Maybe Elizabeth's salvation lies in the fact that she has never quite found out what she wants, and thus never reached the place where 'the end starts'. In an existence crowded with enough events for three lifetimes, her attitude has always been to let fate embrace her. 'I take things as they come, usually with a great deal of relish. I just lie back and wait for it to happen, and it usually does.'

This is the voice of someone who doesn't analyse experience, but simply accumulates it. It is the quantity of experience in her life, rather than the quality of any particular achievement, that explains the public's fascination with her. In this, she resembles an earlier generation of movie queens who gave the public what they most expected. 'In those days,' said Gloria Swanson, 'they wanted us to live like kings' – and, she might have added, like queens. 'So we did – and why not. We were in love with life. We were making more money than we ever dreamed existed, and there was no reason to believe that it would ever stop.'

Elizabeth has behaved with the grand indifference of the rebel, even when she has conformed most closely to the pattern of stardom. Cocooned by mother-love from her earliest years, and constrained by the paternal discipline of a studio that pushed her into womanhood without letting her pass through the phase of childhood, her rebellion against these parents gave her an impulsion that has carried her imperiously through the vicissitudes of life, always the survivor, never the victim – or not for long.

By following where the heart leads, as she once summed up the 'philosophy' of her directionless desires, she has ensured that her life will have the constant fascination of a miniseries. Not for nothing has she been called 'a one-woman soap-opera'. She contains within herself all the multitudinous twists and turns of those convoluted plots. Like the fictional stars of such serials, she has been viewed as a mass of inherent contradictions, which are simply the means of survival that instinct puts at her disposal: manipulative and romantic, forever seeking love and endlessly doomed to be deprived of it, a hostage to sudden climactic tragedies that threaten life itself, yet always escaping terminal extinction to appear in the next episode.

But if such a life can do without an ending, it still needs the means to support it. These she has had in abundance. Great beauty, great power, above all great wealth. Her huge fees gave her, early on in her career, the incitement for unrestraint in every part of her life. She was endowed with the power that comes from spending as well as getting. Yet, to her, money has simply seemed the means to intangibles – to status, uniqueness, fantasy, love. For all her extravagance, there is a kind of Calvinism about her that comes, perhaps, from her acceptance of suffering – some would say her search for it – as a concomitant of her self-indulgence. She has seemed to use experience to punish as much as to exalt herself.

At first knowing next to nothing of life outside her films and the studios where they were made, she was cruelly unprepared for the real world when she went into it as a bride; it seemed infinitely safer to divorce herself from it, as she quickly divorced herself from that first mismatched husband, and live life in terms of the fictions on the screen. Stardom is one of the few ways that provide the means to live out that dream. Love has remained the great imperative in Elizabeth's life – not just the love of individual men, though that is clear enough in all conscience, but the wider love of the public. For all the indifference to public opinion that she affects, her consciousness of people's vicarious involvement with her is the ventilator that keeps her breathing. Some of those who have grown up with her have been her unofficial biographers from the start; others have come late to her unfolding story, but have been absorbed into its episodes with painless addiction. Her very star status ought, as Richard Schickel has suggested, to put her 'out of touch with common mortality'. Paradoxically, instead of viewing her from afar as a remote and exotic being, 'common mortality' involves itself intensely and personally in her life and fate. And when it has looked as if she is dying, as has happened on at least two occasions, there has been a spontaneous, genuine, world-wide expression of concern lest the epochal life she has led should at last be slipping from her, leaving people feeling the poorer.

It scarcely matters that there were – that there are – greater actresses. As Elizabeth herself used to remind one of her husbands, she didn't need to act – *she* was a star. A star does not require a great part, a great script, a great film. A star is a star is a star, on or off screen, in and out of character. 'I have decided that when I am a star,' said Gloria Swanson, 'I will be every inch and every moment the star.' That resolution has been Elizabeth's, too. The parts she has played in films good, bad and indifferent have taken her through the whole life experience, and quite a few of the fantasies that outstrip experience, from childhood to middle age. People feel closer to Elizabeth Taylor than they do to any other star. But then few other stars have created so vivid an image of what a particular kind of woman can achieve and suffer, and still survive as well as she has done over such a long span of years.

Does she ever look back and ask herself why? Why it has happened to *her*. She says not. To her, the past is a film that has been shot and released and there's nothing she can do about it – the future is the script she is writing in her head. So why look back? But surely there were times when even she was forced to break her vow and look back at her life. She's half-admitted there were – when she was in the rehabilitation clinic and recalling the past was part of the cure, if one was to have a future at all.

What does she see when she contemplates in flashback the light and dark forces, the happy moments and the tragic ones that have shaped her life and image? A woman in a Swiss graveyard trying to be alone in the false dawn of flashbulbs. A fat lady in front of a mirror plucking up the courage to strip and look at the damage she has done to her figure and fortunes. A bride getting married like a latter-day Scarlett O'Hara to her farmer-politician as the December sun sets on 'Engagement Hill'. Another wedding, on an African riverbank, coloured like a child's painting book in the primary hues of hope rather than the dark tones of experience. The power and excesses of their joint reign as The Burtons. Martha the shrike-wife in *Who's Afraid of Virginia Woolf?*, nailing her husband on the thorn of a lacerating tongue. Rome, *Cleopatra* and the '*scandale*' of the most public adultery in history. A girl's face anguished with trauma in *Suddenly, Last Summer*. A Las Vegas wedding. Gloria Wandrous scrawling 'No Sale' on the mirror in *Butterfield 8*, and then going out into the New York morning wearing a look that says, 'Is the world ready to face me?' Widowhood sudden and brutal. The roller-coaster ride around the world with Mike Todd. The initials of two newly-weds falling ominously to earth in letters of fire over Acapulco. Being happy, broke and pregnant with her first child. The shock and shame of the first divorce. 'Tell mama', whispered to a lover to comfort him in *A Place in the Sun*. A childhood that was all work and no play. Nibbles and the test of love. A girl in jockey's silks winning the Grand National by will-power as much as by horseflesh. The new life for a wartime family in California. Wild woods, cottage flowers, an English paradise. Applause for a little miss who breaks the rules and pirouettes before Royalty in a patch of unscheduled stardom. A podgy child on a pony's back. An unsteady toddler in the enchanted garden. The baby with black hair suddenly snapping open those violet eyes and fastening them for the first time on her mother's face.

ELIZABETH TAYLOR: A CHRONOLOGY

Author's note: In some cases it has proved hard, or impossible, to establish precisely when work began on a Taylor film. The dates below are approximate ones. The date given for the first public performance of her main films is usually that of the New York premiere. For more recent films, which did not obtain conventional release, it is that of the first major screening in other cities or at film festivals.

1932 . 27 February: Born at Heathwood, 8 Wildwood Road, London.

1933 . Winter: Taken to the United States to be shown to grandparents.

1936 . Date unknown: First (unscheduled) public appearance in charity concert before Royalty.
Date unknown (probably early summer): Taylor family acquire Little Swallows cottage on Cazalet estate.

1937 . Easter: Given first pony, Betty, by godfather Victor Cazalet.
September: Begins school at Byron House, Highgate.

1938 . Winter/spring: Pays short visit to grandparents in US, briefly attends American school.

1939 . Easter: Family warned by Cazalet of coming war.
Mid-April: Leaves for America with mother and brother.
1 May: Arrives in California, stays temporarily with grandfather in Pasadena.
September: Enrolled at Willard Elementary School.
December: Joined by father. Family move to Pacific Palisades.

1941 . March/April: Auditions informally at MGM and Universal.
21 April: Signs contract with Universal.
Summer: Filming B-movie *There's One Born Every Minute*.
29 September: Suspended indefinitely by studio.

Autumn: Moves with family to 307 North Elm Drive, Beverly Hills. Enrolled at Hawthorne School.

1942 . 24 February: Option on services not taken up by Universal.
23 March: Employment terminated.
September/October: Interviewed for film role by MGM.
15 October: Signs test option at MGM for *Lassie Come Home*.

1943 . 5 January: Signs seven-year MGM contract.
March/April: Loaned out to Twentieth Century-Fox for minor role in *Jane Eyre*.
June: Filming *The White Cliffs of Dover*.
7 October: *Lassie Come Home* premiere (New York).
November: Begins rigorous horseback training for *National Velvet*. Injures spine in riding fall.

1944 . January: Filming *National Velvet*.
3 February: *Jane Eyre* premiere (New York).
11 May: *The White Cliffs of Dover* premiere (New York).
Spring: Enrolled in school at MGM studios.
July: Filming *The Courage of Lassie*.
15 December: *National Velvet* premiere (New York).

1945 . Date unknown: Writes children's book *Nibbles and Me*, published late spring/early summer, 1946.

1946 . 18 January: Signs new MGM contract.
April: Loaned out to Warner Bros. for *Life With Father*.
24 July: *Courage of Lassie* premiere (New York).
September: Visits England with mother during parents' temporary separation.
October: Filming *Cynthia*.

1947 . 15 August: *Life With Father* premiere (New York).
18 September: *Cynthia* premiere (New York).
October: Filming *A Date With Judy*.

1948 . February: Filming *Julia Misbehaves*.
June: Filming *Little Women*.
6 August: *A Date With Judy* premiere (New York).
Summer: Meets first boyfriend, Glenn Davis, and begins romance.
7 October: *Julia Misbehaves* premiere (New York).
October: Sails for England with mother to make *The Conspirator*.
November: Filming *The Conspirator*. Meets Michael Wilding for first time.

1949 . February: *Life* magazine birthday photo-spread emphasizes burgeoning sexuality. Catches attention of Howard Hughes, but not attracted to him.
27 February: Meets William Pawley, Jr at birthday party in Florida.
10 March: *Little Women* premiere (New York).
5 June: Engagement to Pawley announced.
8 August: Filming *The Big Hangover*.
22 August: Appears on cover of *Time* magazine.
20 September: Engagement to Pawley broken off.

October: Loaned out to Paramount for *A Place in the Sun.*
November: Meets Nicholas Hilton, falls in love with him.

1950 . January: Filming *Father of the Bride.*
26 January: Graduates from high school. Formal education ends.
20 February: Engagement to Nicholas Hilton announced.
27 April: *The Conspirator* premiere (New York).
6 May: Marries Nicholas Hilton in Beverly Hills.
19 May: *Father of the Bride* premiere (New York).
23 May: Hiltons leave for three-month European honeymoon.
25 May: *The Big Hangover* premiere (New York).
September: Returns to Los Angeles. Marriage in a bad way. Filming *Father's Little Dividend.*
17 December: Hiltons separate.
December: Filming *Love is Better Than Ever.* Starts seeing Stanley Donen.

1951 . January: Hospitalized after viral infection and nervous collapse.
29 January: Divorced from Nicholas Hilton.
February: Moves into apartment with secretary-companion and resists Hilton reconciliation attempts.
12 April: *Father's Little Dividend* premiere (New York).
15 June: Leaves for England to make *Ivanhoe.*
Summer: Meets Michael Wilding again and falls in love with him.
18 August: *A Place in the Sun* premiere (New York).
October: Returns to America without proposal from Michael Wilding.
December: Renews acquaintance with Wilding in Los Angeles.

1952 . 1 January: Engagement to Wilding announced.
17 February: Returns to London with Wilding.
21 February: Marries Michael Wilding in London.
March: Returns to America to negotiate new MGM contract and look for house.
3 March: *Love Is Better Than Ever* premiere (New York).
21 June: Announces she is expecting baby.
July: Signs new MGM contract.
Summer: Buys house at 1771 Summitridge Drive, Beverly Hills.
June: Filming *The Girl Who Had Everything.*
31 July: *Ivanhoe* premiere (New York).
5 August: Suspended with reduced pay until after birth of child.

1953 . 6 January: Gives birth to first child, Michael Howard Wilding, Jr.
19 March: Restored to full pay and loaned out to Paramount as Vivien Leigh's replacement in *Elephant Walk.*
April/May: Suffers post-production injury to eye.
19 April: *The Girl Who Had Everything* premiere (New York).
June: Filming *Rhapsody.*
September: Wildings leave for delayed honeymoon in Europe. Contracts severe viral illness in Denmark. Recovers and leaves for England to make *Beau Brummell.*

1954 . 11 March: *Rhapsody* premiere (New York).
21 March: *Elephant Walk* premiere (New York).
April: Filming *The Last Time I Saw Paris.*
May/June: Discovers she is pregnant again. Agrees to extra year being added to contract in lieu of suspension and pay cut.
July: Wildings move to new home at 1375 Beverly Estate Drive, Beverly Hills.
20 October: *Beau Brummell* premiere (New York).
19 November: *The Last Time I Saw Paris* premiere (New York).

1955 . 27 February: Gives birth to second child, Christopher Edward Wilding.
May/June: Loaned out to Warner Bros. for *Giant.*

1956 . April: Filming *Raintree County.*
13 May: Comforts Montgomery Clift, badly mutilated in car accident.
30 June: Accepts invitation from Mike Todd for weekend family cruise.
19 July: Wildings separate.
20 July: Receives impulsive proposal from Mike Todd.
21 July: Resumes filming *Raintree County* while Todd continues courtship.
4 October: Files for divorce from Wilding.
10 October: *Giant* premiere (New York).
November: Suffers severe spinal injury in cabin-cruiser fall. Hospitalized in New York for operation on back.

1957 . 31 January: Divorced from Michael Wilding.
2 February: Marries Mike Todd in Acapulco, Mexico.
26 March: Announces she is expecting a baby.
2 May: Todds attend Cannes Film Festival for European premiere of *Around the World in Eighty Days*
2 July: Attends London premiere of film followed by huge gala party.
4 July: Todds return to America to await birth of baby.
6 August: Gives birth prematurely to third child, Elizabeth Frances (Liza) Todd.
September: Todds move into temporary home at 1330 Schuyler Drive, Beverly Hills.
17 October: Todds attend disastrous anniversary party in New York for *Around the World in Eighty Days.*
1 November: Todds leave on round-the-world tour (Australia, Hong Kong, France, Russia).
20 December: *Raintree County* premiere (New York).

1958 . March: Filming *Cat on a Hot Tin Roof.*
22/23 March: Widowed by Todd's death in air crash.
25 March: Mobbed at Todd's funeral in Chicago.
14 April: Resumes filming on *Cat on a Hot Tin Roof* after seclusion and depression.
August: Flies to New York intending to go on to South of France for rest. During stop-over, meets and begins affair with Eddie Fisher.
September: Beginning of Taylor–Fisher–Reynolds marital troubles. Moves to Copa de Oro Road, Bel-Air.
18 September: *Cat on a Hot Tin Roof* premiere (New York).

1959 . 29 March: Joins Eddie Fisher in Las Vegas for opening of new show.

12 May: Marries Eddie Fisher in Jewish service in Las Vegas. Fishers leave for European honeymoon.

June: Filming *Suddenly, Last Summer* in England.

1 September: Agrees (jokingly) to star in *Cleopatra* for a million-dollar fee. Twentieth Century-Fox agrees to deal.

7 September: Forced to make *Butterfield 8* before starting *Cleopatra*.

19 October: Leaves for New York to make *Butterfield 8*.

22 December: *Suddenly, Last Summer* premiere (New York).

1960 . 8 September: Arrives in London to make *Cleopatra*.

16 November: *Butterfield 8* premiere (New York).

18 November: Illness contributes to *Cleopatra* shut down.

29 December: Returns to London, after recuperation in Palm Springs, to resume work on *Cleopatra*.

1961 . 4 March: Taken ill suddenly in London. Emergency tracheotomy performed as she hovers between life and death. World-wide concern, prayers offered.

6 March: Suffers severe relapse.

11 March: Makes 'miracle' recovery. Speedy recuperation in California.

17 April: Named 'Best Actress' in Academy Awards for performance as Gloria Wandrous in *Butterfield 8*.

1 September: Arrives in Rome to resume work on *Cleopatra*. Meets Richard Burton and romance quickly develops.

21 December: Formally adopts German child, later known as Maria Burton.

1962 . 22 January: Shoots first scene in *Cleopatra* with Richard Burton. Both now deeply in love.

26 January: *Cleopatra* director Joseph L. Mankiewicz tells producer Walter Wanger, 'Liz and Burton are not just *playing* Antony and Cleopatra.' Beginning of '*le scandale*'.

13 February: Eddie Fisher leaves Rome, then changes mind and returns. Sybil Burton reproaches husband. Crisis grows.

14 February: Hospitalized after 'illness' scare.

9 March: End of marriage publicly forecast.

19 March: Fisher leaves for New York, Sybil Burton leaves for London, lovers left in Rome.

30 March: Publicly repudiates Fisher's plea to deny marriage rift.

2 April: Fishers agree to divorce.

Summer: Romance with Burton now unconcealed amid world-wide outrage. Attacked by Vatican for 'loose morals'.

11 June: Moves to Ischia for *Cleopatra* barge scene.

July: Returns to Gstaad to await developments. Has meeting with Burton at Lake Geneva hotel.

6 December: arrives in London with Burton to make *The VIPs*.

1963 . January: Burton tells wife he wants divorce.

February: Asked by Burton to marry him.
Summer: Relaxes in London with family while Burton makes *Becket* and lawyers work out double divorce.
12 June: *Cleopatra* premiere (New York).
20 September: *The VIPs* premiere (New York).
October: Accompanies Burton to Puerto Vallarta, Mexico, where he is to make *The Night of the Iguana*.
December: Sybil Burton files for divorce.

1964 . 24 January: Files for divorce from Eddie Fisher.
25 January: Flies with Burton to Toronto where he begins *Hamlet* rehearsals.
6 March: Divorce from Fisher finalized.
15 March: Marries Richard Burton in Montreal.
Summer: Accompanies Burton to US for out-of-town opening of *Hamlet*. Attracts huge crowds during New York run.
21 June: Faces live audience for first time in poetry recital with Burton.
October: Burtons leave for France to make *The Sandpiper*.

1965 . 9 February: Accompanies Burton to Dublin where he makes *The Spy Who Came in from the Cold*.
June: Burtons return to Hollywood to prepare for *Who's Afraid of Virginia Woolf?*
15 July: *The Sandpiper* premiere (New York).
September: Burtons filming *Who's Afraid of Virginia Woolf?*

1966 . February: Appears on stage as non-speaking Helen of Troy in Oxford University Dramatic Society production of *Dr Faustus*.
March: Burtons filming *The Taming of the Shrew* in Rome.
29 June: *Who's Afraid of Virginia Woolf?* premiere (New York).
July: Burtons filming *Dr Faustus* with student cast in Rome.
October: Filming *Reflections in a Golden Eye* in Rome.

1967 . January: Burtons filming *The Comedians* in Dahomey.
8 March: *The Taming of the Shrew* premiere (New York).
10 April: Wins second 'Best Actress' Academy Award as Martha in *Who's Afraid of Virginia Woolf?*
May: Burtons buy luxury yacht, the *Kalizma*.
29 September: Fêted by Paris society at French premiere of *The Taming of the Shrew*.
October: Burtons filming *Boom* in Sardinia.
11 October: *Reflections in a Golden Eye* premiere (New York).
15 October: *Doctor Faustus* premiere (Oxford).
31 October: *The Comedians* premiere (New York).

1968 . 6 February: *Doctor Faustus* premiere (New York).
Mid-February: Burtons cause scandal by using *Kalizma* as 'floating dog-kennel' during visit to London to make *Secret Ceremony* and *Where Eagles Dare*.
10 March: Burtons make combined profit of £55,000 as shareholders in Harlech Television.
17 May: Burton buys Krupp diamond at New York auction for $305,000.

20 May: Burtons attend opening ceremonies of Harlech Television. Show stolen by Krupp diamond.

26 May: *Boom* premiere (New York).

8 July: Burton fired from new film *Laughter in the Dark*, goes on drinking binge.

21 July: Has hysterectomy operation in London.

15 August: Burtons return, exhausted, for rest in America before beginning new films in France for Twentieth Century-Fox.

September: Burtons in Paris to film *The Only Game in Town* and *Staircase*. Fêted by Rothschilds, Windsors.

20 November: Death of Francis Taylor, at age of seventy.

1969 . 26 January: Given historic pearl, 'La Peregrina', bought by Burton for $37,000.

5 February: Hears news of death of her first husband, Nicholas Hilton.

February: Resumes filming *The Only Game in Town* on location in Las Vegas.

5 May: Accompanies Burton to London for *Anne of the Thousand Days*.

June: Suffers severe bleeding spasms.

19 June: *Secret Ceremony* premiere (London).

25 October: Burton buys Cartier–Burton diamond for $1.1 million.

1970 . 1 March: *The Only Game in Town* premiere (New York).

May: Recurrence of bleeding spasms.

Mid-May: Burtons film segment of *The Lucy Show* in Hollywood for a joke.

July: Visits Burton on location of *Rommel* in Mexico.

September: Accompanies Burton to England where he makes *Villain*.

October: Filming *Zee and Co.* in London.

6 October: Burtons attend wedding in London of Michael Wilding, Jr.

1971 . January: Burtons film *Under Milk Wood* in Wales.

May: Burtons film *Hammersmith Is Out* in Mexico.

25 August: Becomes grandmother for first time with birth of Leyla, daughter of Michael Wilding, Jr and Beth Clutter.

26 August: *Under Milk Wood* premiere (New York).

September: Accompanies Burton to Yugoslavia and stays with Tito while making *The Battle of Satjeska*.

October: Accompanies Burton to Paris where he makes *The Assassination of Trotsky*.

2 December: Burtons attend 'Ball of the Century' held by Rothschilds at Ferriers.

1972 . 26 January: *Zee and Co.* premiere (New York).

27 February: Gives extravagant (and much criticized) fortieth birthday party in Budapest. Receives Burton's present of $900,000 Shah Jahan yellow diamond.

21 March: Burtons' marriage begins to break up following shock of his brother Ifor's death.

6 May: Meets Aristotle Onassis in Rome, strengthening divorce speculation.

24 May: *Hammersmith Is Out* premiere (New York).

June: Filming *Night Watch* in England while Burton gives lectures at Oxford University.

November: Burtons filming *Divorce His/Divorce Hers* in Munich.

1973 . February: Filming *Ash Wednesday* on location in Italy.

June: Accompanies Burton to Rome in pre-production preparation for *Massacre in Rome* and *The Driver's Seat* (a.k.a. *Identikit* and *Blood Games*).

20 June: Burtons fly to America. He remains on Long Island while she goes on to California, ostensibly to visit ailing mother. Rumours of split.

4 July: Burtons' separation announced.

20 July: Temporary reconciliation attempted in Rome, almost immediate separation again.

August: Filming *The Driver's Seat* in Rome. Begins affair with Henry Wynberg.

9 August: *Night Watch* premiere (New York).

21 November: *Ash Wednesday* premiere (New York).

1974 . January: 'Permanently, as opposed to temporarily, reconciled' with Burton.

February: Accompanies Burton to California while he makes *The Klansman*. Fight and final separation.

26 June: Burtons are divorced at Saarinen, Switzerland. Resumes liaison with Henry Wynberg.

1975 . May: Filming *The Blue Bird* in Russia, accompanied by Wynberg. Taken ill with viral infection.

August: Reconciliation with Burton in Lausanne.

10 October: Burtons remarry in Botswana, Africa.

1976 . January/February: Burtons' marriage disintegrating. Burton meets Suzy Hunt. Elizabeth meets Peter Darmanin, goes to New York at Burton's request. He asks for divorce.

23 February: Burtons' separation announced.

13 May: *The Blue Bird* premiere (New York).

Summer: Takes increasing interest in political/diplomatic events in New York and Washington.

8 July: Meets John Warner for Bicentennial Ball, Washington DC. Instant romance.

August: Leaves for Austria to make *A Little Night Music*.

1 August: Burtons divorced in Haiti.

22 August: Receives news of Burton's marriage to Suzy Hunt in Vienna when in Arlington, Virginia.

4 December: Marries John Warner in Middleburg, Virginia.

1977 . February: Campaigns with husband to raise funds for Republican Party and burnish his senatorial nominee hopes.

April: First early comments on increase in weight.

May: Filming cameo role in *Winter Kills*.

Summer: Filming cameo role in TV film *Victory at Entebbe*.

1978 . 6 January: Embarks on campaign to help husband win Republican nomination for US Senate.

7 March: *A Little Night Music* premiere (New York).
3 June: Sees husband narrowly lose nomination in Republican Party vote.
Summer: Making TV film *Return Engagement* (a.k.a. *Repeat Performance*).
12 August: Sees husband adopted as Republican candidate due to death in air crash of former nominee.
7 November: Sees husband win US Senate seat.

1979 . 16 January: Attends husband's swearing-in as US Senator.
18 May: *Winter Kills* premiere (New York).
10 July: Begins visits to health farm for obesity problem.
16 July: Attends funeral in England of former husband Michael Wilding.

1980 . Spring: Resumes visits to Florida health farm.
May: Filming *The Mirror Crack'd* in England.
July: Appears with Ronald and Nancy Reagan at Republican Party's presidential nomination convention in Detroit. Suffers comment on obesity.
September: Denies reports of rift in marriage.
October: Announces plans for appearance in stage play.
17 December: *The Mirror Crack'd* premiere (New York).

1981 . February: Reports current of split in Warners' marriage.
7 May: Opens on Broadway in *The Little Foxes*.
21 December: Warners' legal separation announced.
24 December: Admitted to California hospital with chest pains, but discharged after twenty-four hours.

1982 . 19 January: Returns to Washington for first time since separation in apparent attempt at reconciliation.
27 February: Reunion with Burton in London encourages remarriage rumour.
11 March: Opens in London in *The Little Foxes*.
September: Announces that she and Burton will appear together in *Private Lives*.
October: Filming *Between Friends* for television.
7 November: Divorced from John Warner.
November: Name linked with Mexican lawyer Victor Gonzalez Luna.

1983 . 28 February: Burton and Suzy Hunt divorced in Haiti.
March: Begins rehearsals with Burton for *Private Lives*.
8 May: Opens on Broadway with Burton in *Private Lives*.
3 July: Learns of Burton's marriage to Sally Hay in Las Vegas. Announces own engagement to Victor Gonzalez Luna.
9 August: Gives party during *Private Lives* tour in Philadelphia, but expected announcement of forthcoming marriage to Victor Gonzalez Luna does not materialize.
5 December: Checks into Betty Ford Clinic, Rancho Mirage, for rehabilitation after alcohol and medication abuse, following family conference.

1984 . Spring: Visits Japan and China with Victor Gonzalez Luna.
May: Meets Burton in London for what is to be the last time.
July: Breaks off engagement to Victor Gonzalez Luna.

4/5 August: Burton dies of cerebral haemmorhage in Celigny, Switzerland.
5 August: Collapses in Bel Air home on receiving news of Burton's death.
14 August: Visits Burton's grave at Celigny before dawn, harassed by paparazzi.
19 August: Pays visit to Burton's relatives in Wales.
30 August: Attends thanksgiving service for Burton in London.
September: Name linked with entrepreneur Dennis Stein.
November: Filming TV movie *Malice in Wonderland.*

1985 . February: Breaks off relationship with Dennis Stein.
March: Filming TV movie *North and South.*
6 August: Makes bedside visit to AIDS-stricken Rock Hudson.
August: Joins other Hollywood stars, shocked by Hudson's illness, to raise funds
for fight against AIDS.

1986 . March: Name linked with George Hamilton.
9 May: Addresses Congressional subcommittee to plead for more AIDS research
funding.
May: Filming TV movie *There Must Be a Pony.*
December: Rumours of forthcoming marriage to George Hamilton intensify
when they spend Christmas at Gstaad.

1987 . 3 March: Becomes national chairwoman of American Federation for AIDS
Research.
March: Filming TV movie *Poker Alice* with George Hamilton. Both deny intention of marrying.
6 May: Pays £349,792 for jewellery from late Duchess of Windsor's collection.
14 May: Receives Legion d'Honneur decoration from French president.
June: Launches 'Passion' brand of perfume.
23 September: Tells Congressional subcommittee she would take AIDS test before
beginning affair.
September: Name linked with Malcolm Forbes.
October: Filming *Young Toscanini* in Rome.

1988 . January: Publishes memoirs-diet book *Elizabeth Takes Off.*
1 September: *Young Toscanini* premiere (Venice Film Festival).
October: Has relapse and returns to Betty Ford Clinic for further treatment for
medication abuse. Meets and befriends ex-trucker and fellow patient Larry
Fortensky.

1989 . Spring/summer: Continues AIDS work and 'Passion' publicity while main-
taining close friendship with Malcolm Forbes.
July: Filming TV movie *Sweet Bird of Youth.*
October: Attends lavish Malcolm Forbes party in Morocco.

1990 . March: Receives news of Malcolm Forbes's sudden death.
April: Suffers collapse from viral pneumonia. Life endangered, but makes slow
recovery in California hospital.
May: Suffers relapse and re-enters hospital. Concern for her life, but later discharged.

ELIZABETH TAYLOR'S MARRIAGE WEB

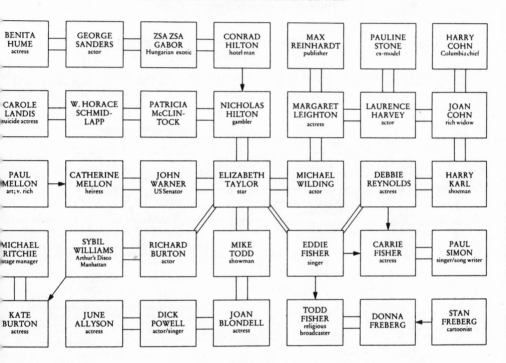

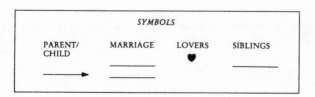

THE MARRIAGES OF ELIZABETH TAYLOR

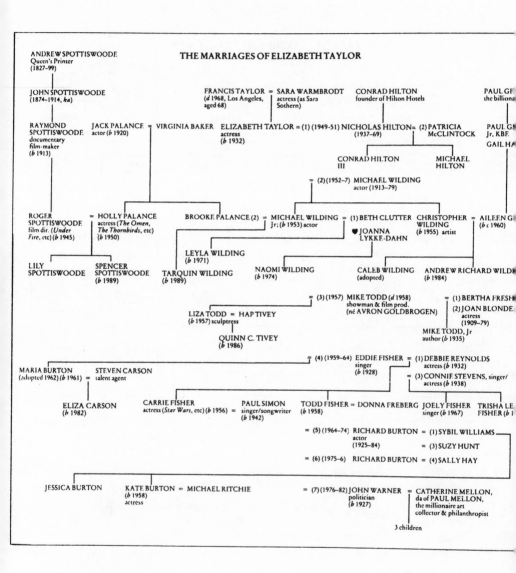

ANDREW SPOTTISWOODE Queen's Printer (1827-99)

JOHN SPOTTISWOODE (1874-1914, *ka*)

RAYMOND SPOTTISWOODE documentary film-maker (*b* 1913)

JACK PALANCE actor (*b* 1920) = VIRGINIA BAKER

FRANCIS TAYLOR (*d* 1968, Los Angeles, aged 68) = SARA WARMBRODT actress (as Sara Sothern)

CONRAD HILTON founder of Hilton Hotels

PAUL GE... the billiona...

ELIZABETH TAYLOR actress (*b* 1932) = (1) (1949-51) NICHOLAS HILTON (1937-69) = (2) PATRICIA McCLINTOCK

PAUL G... Jr, KBE

GAIL HA...

CONRAD HILTON III

MICHAEL HILTON

= (2) (1952-7) MICHAEL WILDING actor (1913-79)

ROGER SPOTTISWOODE film dir. (*Under Fire*, etc) (*b* 1945)

= HOLLY PALANCE actress (*The Omen*, *The Thornbirds*, etc) (*b* 1950)

BROOKE PALANCE (2) = MICHAEL WILDING Jr; (*b* 1953) actor = (1) BETH CLUTTER ♥ JOANNA LYKKE-DAHN

CHRISTOPHER WILDING (*b* 1955) artist = AILEEN G... (*b c* 1960)

LEYLA WILDING (*b* 1971)

LILY SPOTTISWOODE

SPENCER SPOTTISWOODE (*b* 1989)

TARQUIN WILDING (*b* 1989)

NAOMI WILDING (*b* 1974)

CALEB WILDING (adopted)

ANDREW RICHARD WILD... (*b* 1984)

= (3) (1957) MIKE TODD (*d* 1958) showman & film prod. (né AVRON GOLDBROGEN)

= (1) BERTHA FRESH...
(2) JOAN BLONDE... actress (1909-79)

LIZA TODD = HAP TIVEY (*b* 1957) sculptress

MIKE TODD, Jr author (*b* 1935)

QUINN C. TIVEY (*b* 1986)

= (4) (1959-64) EDDIE FISHER singer (*b* 1928) = (1) DEBBIE REYNOLDS actress (*b* 1932)

= (3) CONNIE STEVENS, singer/actress (*b* 1938)

MARIA BURTON (adopted 1962) (*b* 1961) = STEVEN CARSON talent agent

ELIZA CARSON (*b* 1982)

CARRIE FISHER actress (*Star Wars*, etc) (*b* 1956) = PAUL SIMON singer/songwriter (*b* 1942)

TODD FISHER (*b* 1958) = DONNA FREBERG

JOELY FISHER singer (*b* 1967)

TRISHA LE... FISHER (*b* ...)

= (5) (1964-74) RICHARD BURTON actor (1925-84) = (1) SYBIL WILLIAMS

= (3) SUZY HUNT

= (6) (1975-6) RICHARD BURTON = (4) SALLY HAY

JESSICA BURTON

KATE BURTON (*b* 1958) actress = MICHAEL RITCHIE

= (7) (1976-82) JOHN WARNER politician (*b* 1927) = CATHERINE MELLON, da of PAUL MELLON, the millionaire art collector & philanthropist

3 children

ACKNOWLEDGEMENTS AND
BIBLIOGRAPHY
. . .

A great many people contributed to this book by providing me with interviews or information: friends, associates, directors, fellow players and others who have known Elizabeth Taylor at various stages in her life and career. Some asked for anonymity, and, regrettably, cannot be thanked here except in general terms. Others again spoke to me during their lifetime and their views are quoted with posthumous acknowledgement.

This is in no sense an 'authorized biography'. It was written without Elizabeth Taylor's collaboration – a rule she has followed throughout life – but I have drawn on my interviews with her and social hours spent in her company since 1958.

For their time, knowledge and friendship, all of which they have extended generously to me in writing other biographies and film-industry studies, I thank most warmly Herbert S. Nusbaum and Florence Warner, two of the longest serving, devoted and most scrupulous employees of MGM.

I am indebted to Barbra Paskin and Sandra Archer for their help in arranging interviews and locating documentary evidence in Hollywood.

Much research was done in American archives. Among their curators and staff who led me to material I did not know existed, I must thank in particular Sam Gill at the Margaret Herrick Library, Academy of Motion Picture Arts and Sciences, Beverly Hills; and Leith Adams and Ned Comstock, of the University of Southern California, Cinema and Television Library, Los Angeles. Without their creative suggestions, much motion-picture research today would be the poorer.

I thank the following for responding so generously to my requests for interviews or information:

Pandro Berman, Richard Brooks, Kevin Brownlow, Jeremy Campbell, Charles Champlin, Warren Cowan, Peter Darmanin, Glenn Davis, Lord Deedes, Dominick Dunne, Dr Geoffrey Dymond, Susan Endacott, Roland Flamini, Margaret Gardner, Sandra Goodman, John Heyman, Elliott Kastner, Gavin Lambert, Sir Hugh Leggatt, Max Lerner, Susan and Steven Licht, Ben Lightman, William Mader, Rosemary and Joseph L. Mankiewicz, Patricia Marand, Robert Morley,

Sheridan Morley, Dorothy Mullen, Carolyn Murphy, Ben Presser, St Clair Pugh, Rex Reed, Sidney Sabin, Richard Schickel, Rose Tobias Shaw, Ronald Shedlo, Dick Sheppard, Andrew Sinclair, Liz Smith, Golda and Nathan Weiss, Shirley Williams MP, Jane Withers.

Information and opinions offered to me in interviews and conversation with the following during their lifetime have been drawn on:

Sir Stanley Baker, Richard Burton, Dick Hanley, Laurence Harvey, Rock Hudson, Ernest Lehman, Joseph Losey, Dame Anna Neagle, Victor Saville, Mike Todd, Walter Wanger, Andy Warhol, Herbert Wilcox, Michael Wilding, Emlyn Williams, James Woolf.

My gratitude is expressed to the following archives and libraries for the access they afforded me to relevant material in their possession. Over the 25 years that I have been writing books about movies and the film industry, the most heartening thing has been the increasing willingness of corporate sources to make material available for serious study and scholarship.

The former Metro-Goldwyn-Mayer studio archives, now part of the Turner Entertainment Group, Los Angeles.

Time-Life archives and library, New York.

The Hedda Hopper Collection in the Margaret Herrick Library, Academy of Motion Picture Arts and Sciences, Beverly Hills.

The Warner Brothers and Universal Pictures Collections in the Cinema and Television Library, University of Southern California, Los Angeles.

The Museum of Broadcasting, New York.

The Billy Rose Theater Collection in the Library of the Performing Arts, Lincoln Center, New York.

The New York Public Library.

The Joseph Losey Collection in the British Film Institute Information Library, London.

The National Film Archive Stills Library, London.

The British Theatre Association Library, London.

I gratefully acknowledge the help of the National Film Archive and Rex Reed in obtaining prints and videos of Elizabeth Taylor's films.

Finally I would like to thank the editors of this book, David Roberts and Allegra Huston; the copy-editor, Shunil Roy-Chaudhuri; the picture researcher, Tom Graves; and for her patience and encouragement, my agent Carol Smith.

The following books were consulted for this biography and quotations from them are fully acknowledged in the source notes:

James Agee, *Agee on Film* (Grosset and Dunlap),1969.

Mary Astor, *A Life in Films* (Delacorte Press), 1979.

Patricia Bosworth, *Montgomery Clift* (Bantam Books), 1979.

Melvyn Bragg, *Rich: The Life of Richard Burton* (Little, Brown), 1989.

Jack Brodsky and Nathan Weiss, *The Cleopatra Papers* (Simon and Schuster), 1963.

Frances Hodgson Burnett, *The Secret Garden* (Collins/Armada), 1987.

Richard Burton, *Meeting Mrs Jenkins* (William Morrow), 1964.
Michel Ciment, *Le Livre de Losey* (Stock), 1979.
Art Cohn, *The Nine Lives of Mike Todd* (Random House), 1958.
John Cottrell and Fergus Cashin, *Richard Burton* (Prentice Hall), 1972.
George Eells, *Hedda and Louella* (Putnam), 1972.
Paul Ferris, *Richard Burton* (Coward McCann), 1981.
Eddie Fisher, *My Life, My Loves* (Harper and Row),1981.
Sheilah Graham, *Hollywood Revisited* (St Martin's Press), 1985.
Hedda Hopper with James Brough, *The Whole Truth and Nothing But* (Pyramid Books/Doubleday), 1963.
Rock Hudson and Sara Davidson, *Rock Hudson* (Morrow), 1986.
Graham Jenkins with Barry Turner, *Richard Burton, My Brother* (Harper and Row), 1988.
Elia Kazan, *A Life* (Knopf), 1988.
Kitty Kelley, *Elizabeth Taylor: The Last Star* (Simon and Schuster), 1981.
Robert LaGuardia, *Monty* (Arbor House), 1977.
Brenda Maddox, *Who's Afraid of Elizabeth Taylor?* (M. Evans), 1977.
Joseph L. Mankiewicz and Gary Carey, *More About 'All About Eve'* (Random House), 1972.
Sheridan Morley, *Elizabeth Taylor* (Pavilion), 1988.
Christopher Nickens, *Elizabeth Taylor* (Doubleday), 1984.
Rex Reed, *Valentines and Vitriol* (Delacorte Press), 1977.
Debbie Reynolds and David Patrick Columbhia, *Debbie, My Life* (Morrow), 1988.
Marjorie Rosen, *Popcorn Venus* (Coward McCann), 1973.
Lillian Ross, *Picture* (Rinehart), 1953.
Richard Schickel, *Common Fame* (Pavilion), 1985.
Dick Sheppard, *Elizabeth* (Doubleday), 1974.
Paulene Stone with Peter Evans, *One Tear Is Enough: My Life with Laurence Harvey* (Michael Joseph), 1975.
Elizabeth Taylor, *Nibbles and Me* (Duell, Sloan and Pearce), 1946.
Elizabeth Taylor, *Elizabeth Taylor* (Harper & Row), 1965.
Elizabeth Taylor, *Elizabeth Takes Off* (Putnam), 1988.
Andy Warhol, *The Andy Warhol Diaries* ed. Pat Hackett (Warner Books), 1989.
Herbert Wilcox, *Twenty-Five Thousand Sunsets* (Bodley Head), 1967.
Michael Wilding with Pamela Wilcox, *Apple Sauce* (Allen and Unwin), 1987.
Shelley Winters, *Shelley, also known as Shirley* (Morrow), 1980.
Donald Zec, *Marvin* (St. Martin's Press), 1980.
Franco Zeffirelli, *Autobiography* (Weidenfeld), 1986.

SOURCE NOTES

. . .

1. Like Father, Like Mother

3: 'Probably if there hadn't been ...'
Elizabeth Taylor, interviewed by
David Wigg, *Good Housekeeping*,
February 1977.

4: 'He dressed like ...' Sir Hugh Leggatt
to author, London, 2 May 1988.

4: 'She spoke with ...' Max Lerner to
author, New York, 6 December
1988.

4: 'He was a gentleman ...' Sir Hugh
Leggatt, letter to author, 28 April
1988.

5: 'Not long after cars ...' Hedda
Hopper Collection, Academy of
Motion Pictures Arts and Sciences
(AMPAS), Margaret Herrick
Library, Beverly Hills. Letter from
Mrs Mona Smith, 27 January 1964.

6: 'He married a girl ...' *ibid.*

6: 'Once I set my mind ...' Elizabeth
Taylor to author, Cannes, May 1957.

7: 'A religious orgy ...' *The Times*, 19
September 1924.

8: 'We knew that when the time ...' Sara
Taylor, *Ladies' Home Journal*,
February 1954.

9: 'Tulips almost three feet ...' *ibid.*

9: 'It was a wonderful ...' *ibid.*

10: 'Just pink skin' Elizabeth Taylor,
Elizabeth Taylor (Harper & Row,
1965), p. 3.

2. 'A Marvellous Feeling'

11: 'First we put up ...' Sara Taylor, *op.
cit.*

12: 'He was a great bear ...' Sir Hugh
Leggatt to author.

12: 'It shows you ...' Sidney Sabin to
author, London, 14 June 1988.

14: 'Mother, please call Victor ...' Sara
Taylor, *op. cit.*

15: 'Thoughts ... just mere thoughts ...'
Frances Hodgson Burnett, *The Secret
Garden* (Collins/Armada, 1987),
pp. 243–4.

15: 'He makes them perfect ...' Sara
Taylor, *op. cit.*

16: 'Oh, mummy, do look ...' Sara
Taylor, *ibid.*

16: 'To the point ...' Sara Taylor, *ibid.*

18: 'It was a marvellous ...' Elizabeth
Taylor, *op. cit.*, p. 4.

18: 'A reputedly staid ...' Sara Taylor,
op. cit.

19: 'It was almost like being shut out ...'
Sara Taylor, *ibid.*

3. Trouble in Eden

20: 'But they made me...' Elizabeth
Taylor, *op. cit.*, p. 3.

20: 'Betty ... I'm your new mistress ...'
Sara Taylor, *op. cit.*

21: 'A rather posh little place ...' Susan
Endacott (née Ritchie) to author, 29
October 1988.

21: 'Very 1930s ...' *ibid.*

22: 'Careful writing ... communicative
and friendly ...' Private information.

23: 'Decided English ...' Sara Taylor, *op.
cit.*

23: 'A wholesome, unhurried . . .' Sara Taylor, *ibid.*
23: 'Breathing in the clean . . .' Sara Taylor, *ibid.*
24: 'It was a bombshell . . .' Sara Taylor, *ibid.*
24: 'A lady with coronets . . .' Bosley Crowther, *The New York Times*, 11 March 1939.
24: 'A baby Bernhardt . . .' Bosley Crowther, *ibid.*
25: 'The children very quickly lost . . .' Sara Taylor, *op. cit.*

4. *'Sing for Miss Hopper'*

29: 'Better than a prize fight . . .' Hedda Hopper, *From Under My Hat* (Muller, 1953), p. 203.
29: 'That's what the family . . .' Hedda Hopper Collection, AMPAS, note dated 19 March 1965.
30: 'When we said goodbye . . .' Sara Taylor, *Ladies' Home Journal*, March 1954.
31: 'Sign her up . . .' Sara Taylor, *ibid.*
31: 'Now sing for Miss Hopper . . .' Hedda Hopper, *The Whole Truth and Nothing But* (Doubleday, 1963), p. 9.
31: 'A competent music teacher . . .' Universal Pictures Collection, Archives of the Performing Arts, University of Southern California, Los Angeles.
32: 'The kid has nothing . . .' Secondary source only, quoted variously, consensus attribution to Kelly.
32: 'What's the matter, honey. . .' Sara Taylor, *op. cit.*
33: 'Imagine excitement . . . Victor Cazalet, quoted by Brenda Maddox, *Who's Afraid of Elizabeth Taylor?* (M. Evans, 1977), p. 33.
33: 'Run around firing . . .' Elizabeth Taylor, *op. cit.*, p. 7.
33: 'If there's anything . . .' Hedda

Hopper, *Los Angeles Times*, April 17 1941.
33: 'The above artist . . .' Universal Pictures Collection, USC.
33: '[The contract] will therefore . . .' *ibid.*
35: 'Please photocable close-up . . .' MGM Archives.
35: 'Would like to see animals . . .' *ibid.*

5. *National Idol*

37: 'On a freelance basis . . .' MGM Archives.
37: 'Her last salary . . .' *ibid.*
37: 'She is to be paid . . .' *ibid.*
38: 'A pretty moppet . . .' *Variety*, 3 October 1943.
38: 'Elizabeth Taylor looks . . .' *Hollywood Reporter*, 4 October 1943.
38: 'Little Elizabeth Taylor . . .' Hedda Hopper, *Los Angeles Times*, 27 September 1943.
38: 'She was the least troublesome . . .' Secondary source only, quoted variously, consensus attribution to Wilcox.
38: 'Perfect, an exquisite . . .' Roddy McDowall, *Photoplay*, August 1951.
38: 'There sat my daughter . . .' Sara Taylor, *op. cit.*
40: 'It'll be good business . . .' Private information.
40: 'The little girl . . .' *Hollywood Reporter*, 1 February 1944.
40: 'She strikes me . . .' James Agee, *The Nation*, 23 December 1944.
42: 'Please have Harold Huth . . .' MGM Archives.
42: 'Get what info . . .' *ibid.*
42: 'By section 25 . . .' *ibid.*
42: 'Kindly appreciate . . .' *ibid.*
42: 'We understand . . .' *ibid.*
42: 'I was ten or eleven . . .' Shirley Williams, letter to author, 7 June 1988.
43: 'It had more to do . . .' Pandro Berman to author, Beverly Hills, 21 April 1988.

43: 'I measured her progress ...' *ibid.*
43: 'I ate a lot ...' Sara Taylor, *op. cit.*
44: 'She landed very hard ...' *ibid.*
44: 'Elizabeth and I ...' *Time*, 22 August 1949.
45: 'Hold familiar conversations ...' *Los Angeles Times*, 3 January 1965.
45: 'The studio were afraid ...' Sara Taylor, *op. cit.*
45: 'But he loves me ...' *ibid.*
46: 'It is ... an interesting ...' *Time*, 10 January 1944.
46: 'Two or three speeds ...' James Agee, *op. cit.*
46: 'A mania ...' Campbell Dixon, *The Daily Telegraph and Morning Post*, 25 June 1945.
47: 'Mr Thau stated ...' MGM Archives.

6. Love and the Lonely Child

48: '[We] would give her ...' MGM Archives.
48: 'Don't you dare ...' Elizabeth Taylor, *op. cit.*, p. 16.
48: A 'gross thick' person ... *ibid.*, p. 15.
49: 'You and your studio ...' *ibid.*, p. 16.
49: 'She had an artificial ...' George Stevens, quoted in *Elizabeth* by Dick Sheppard (Doubleday, 1974), p. 44.
49: 'For me to quit ...' *ibid.*, p. 48.
49: 'She was a fair student ...' Dorothy Mullen, letter to author, 10 May 1990.
50: 'Those in regular schools ...' Paramount Pictures publicity release, *circa* October 1949.
50: 'Two big boys ...' *American Magazine*, July 1948.
51: 'Boys ... they are silly ...' *ibid.*
51: 'Spurned ...' Louella Parsons radio interview, 13 July 1947. Transcription in USC Archives.
51: 'You do not like boys ...' *American Magazine, op. cit.*
51: 'A mistake ...' Sara Taylor, *op. cit.*
52: 'There is a quality ...' Letter from D.

Halliwell Duell to MGM, 31 October 1945.
52: 'The toothmarks ...' *Time, op. cit.*
52: 'It seemed as if I was right ...' Elizabeth Taylor, *Nibbles and Me* (Duell, Sloan and Pearce, 1946), p. 9.
52: 'Flew down from his tree ...' Frances Hodgson Burnett, *The Secret Garden* (Collins/Armada, 1987), p. 74.
53: 'Oh! to think ...' *ibid.*, p. 74.
53: 'I held Nibbles ...' Elizabeth Taylor, *op. cit.*, p. 64.
53: '[Nibbles] stretches himself ...' *ibid.*, p. 20.
53: 'He was *too* good ...' *ibid.*, p. 32.
53: 'Mr Louis B. Mayer ...' *ibid.*, p. 47.
54: 'Would come to me ...' *ibid.*, p. 66.
54: 'As long as you love ...' *ibid.*, p. 56.
54: 'He ran to the edge ...' *ibid.*, pp. 64–5.
55: 'Tumbling out so fast ...' *ibid.*, p. 3.

7. 'Why, She Is a Woman!'

56: 'Sophisticated fortyishness ...' *Time*, 22 August 1949.
56: 'Well-preserved charm ...' *ibid.*
56: 'One studio ...' *ibid.*
56: 'Billy Grady ...' *ibid.*
56: 'She whinnies ...' Louis Berg, *Los Angeles Times*, 25 July 1948.
56: 'Let's hear you whinny ...' *ibid.*
56: 'The studio doesn't want ...' *ibid.*
57: 'A touching story ...' Publicity release, *circa* October 1948. MGM Archives.
57: 'Why, she is a woman! ...' Hedda Hopper, *op. cit.*, p. 8.
57: 'The eyes still have it ...' Hedda Hopper, *Los Angeles Times*, 29 August 1948.
60: 'It was no special loss ...' Kitty Kelley, *Elizabeth Taylor* (Simon and Schuster, 1981), p. 15.
60: 'Maybe they loved me ...' Hedda Hopper, *Los Angeles Times*, 10 October 1957.

60: 'Rather the worse ...' Sara Taylor, *op. cit.*

61: 'We wore some of the pretty ...' *ibid.*

62: 'Do you want to hear ...' Diane Scott, *Photoplay*, September 1947.

62: 'Wait till that lassie ...' Private information.

62: 'But Elizabeth, you never ...' *ibid.*

62: 'They talked to me ...' *ibid.*

62: 'What did they call you?' *ibid.*

63: 'Perfectly miserable ...' Elizabeth Taylor, *op. cit.*, p. 22.

64: 'Oh, mother ...' Sara Taylor, *op. cit.*

64: 'Another milestone' *ibid.*

8. ... And a 'Dangerous' Woman

65: 'The boys were smooth ...' *Photoplay*, October 1948.

66: 'Dress with real care ...' *Modern Screen*, *cit.* Marjorie Rosen, *Popcorn Venus* (Coward McCann, 1973), p. 238.

66: 'Elizabeth Taylor will portray ...' Publicity release, *circa* September 1946, MGM Archives.

67: 'That buss was more ...' Elizabeth Taylor, *Elizabeth Takes Off* (Putnam, 1988), p. 56.

68: 'I had seen ...' Mary Astor, *A Life in Films* (Delacorte, 1969), p. 192.

68: 'Just a little ole peek ...' Louella Parsons radio interview, 13 July 1947. Transcription in USC Archives.

69: 'Elizabeth Taylor has suddenly ...' *Life*, 15 September 1947.

70: 'That was the beginning ...' Sara Taylor, *op. cit.*

70: 'There's nothing wrong ...' *Modern Screen*, *cit.* Marjorie Rosen, *op. cit.*, p. 238.

70: 'Oh, Ritchie ...' Secondary source only, quoted variously.

71: 'The time, the clichés ...' Archer Winston, *New York Post*, 6 August 1948.

71: 'Wits, courage, determination ...'

Sheilah Graham, *Photoplay*, November 1948.

72: 'Why doesn't someone ...' *Photoplay*, December 1948.

73: 'When I saw that frank ...' Sara Taylor, *op. cit.*

74: 'I have no idea ...' Glenn Davis to author, Palm Springs, 12 January 1990.

9. Conspiracies and Suitors

76: 'A potential younger [Ingrid] Bergman ...' Hedda Hopper, *op. cit.*

77: 'You are looking through ...' *Picture Post*, 29 January 1949.

77: 'Rested vigilantly ...' *ibid.*

77: 'Elizabeth gave me ...' Victor Saville to author, *circa* 1965.

77: 'She did as she was told ...' *ibid.*

78: 'The diplomatic situation ...' MGM Archives.

78: 'While these people ...' *ibid.*

79: 'Tipped me into madness ...' Vivien Leigh *cit.* Alexander Walker, *Vivien* (Weidenfeld and Nicolson, 1987), p. 198.

80: 'How can I concentrate ...' Private information.

80: 'But ... the tricks ...' Elizabeth Taylor, *op. cit. (Elizabeth Takes Off)*, p. 60.

81: 'It feels so strange ...' Elizabeth Taylor to author, Cannes, May 1957.

81: 'You have bosoms ...' Secondary source only, variously quoted including Elizabeth Taylor (*Elizabeth Takes Off*), p. 58.

81: 'But he left her cold ...' Richard Brooks to author, Beverly Hills, 22 April 1988.

82: 'Maybe I should have fallen ...' *Los Angeles Times*, 21 March 1949.

83: 'Suddenly it was all over ...' *Time*, *op. cit.*

83: 'Like any young girl ...' Unsourced news report, dateline Miami Beach, Florida, 7 June 1949.

10. The First Dent

84: 'What I'd really like ...' *Time*, 29 August 1949.

85: 'He hustled [Elizabeth] into his car ...' Hedda Hopper, *Photoplay*, December 1949.

86: 'We talked it over ...' Hedda Hopper, *Los Angeles Times*, 21 September 1949.

86: 'The thing between Elizabeth ...' *ibid.*

87: 'It brought me my first ...' Ruth Brigham, *Photoplay*, October 1949.

87: 'If I'd known ...' *Los Angeles Times*, 28 September 1949.

87: 'If I were the kind ...' *ibid.*

87: 'Somebody should administer ...' Geoffrey Carr, *Sunday Pictorial*, 25 September 1949.

87: '[Elizabeth Taylor] is a living argument ...' *ibid.*

11. The Sun and the Stars

92: 'Not so much a real girl ...' George Stevens, *cit.* Dick Sheppard, *op. cit.*, p. 90.

92: 'Who the hell ...' Private information.

94: 'I'm so awful ...' Patricia Bosworth, *Montgomery Clift* (Bantam, 1979), p. 180.

94: 'She'll never be able ...' Private information.

94: 'She was longing ...' Shelley Winters, *Shelley, Also Known as Shirley* (Morrow, 1980), p. 284.

94: 'Instead she thought ...' *ibid.*, p. 284.

94: 'It'll open your eyes ...' *ibid.*, p. 283.

95: 'When [Monty] would start ...' Elizabeth Taylor, *op. cit.* (*Elizabeth Taylor*), p. 49.

96: 'It was the first time ...' *ibid.*, p. 48.

96: 'A tremendous believer ...' George Stevens, *Dialogue on Film* (American Film Institute, May–June 1975).

96: 'The little lady said ...' *ibid.*

97: 'Wasn't just some meeting ...' *ibid.*

97: 'I explained that I'd like ...' *ibid.*

97: 'I tried to thrust them ...' *ibid.*

97: 'Always beautiful ...' *Look*, 1 September 1951.

97: 'A shaded, tender ...' *The New York Times*, 29 August 1951.

97: '[George] Stevens's skilled hands ...' *Variety*, 27 August 1951.

98: 'Look, Monty ...' Robert LaGuardia, *Monty* (Arbor House, 1977), p. 82.

98: 'I never saw a girl ...' Hedda Hopper, *Modern Screen*, July 1950.

98: 'When somebody comes along ...' *Los Angeles Daily News*, 26 January 1950.

12. A Movie Romance

100: 'To bring back the Sun – Nick ...' Private information.

101: 'Are you sure ...' Michael Wilding to author, *circa* 1962.

101: 'Being eighteen won't make ...' Aline Mosby, *Los Angeles Daily News*, 26 January 1950.

101: 'I'd like something besides ...' *ibid.*

101: 'Serious? Of course ...' New York *Daily News*, 15 February 1950.

101: 'Elizabeth would be motored ...' Private information.

103: 'We both love ...' *Los Angeles Citizen-News*, 15 February 1950.

103: 'I keep thinking ...' *Photoplay*, August 1950.

103: 'First ... you'll make ...' Hedda Hopper, *Modern Screen*, July 1950.

103: 'Esther, that's enough ...' *ibid.*

103: 'Bet you never learned ...' *ibid.*

103: 'Blonde or brunette ...' *Photoplay*, August 1950.

103: 'Jules ... that's not a Hilton ...' *ibid.*

103: 'May I keep it? ...' Secondary sources, *cit.* variously including Dick Sheppard, *op. cit.*, p. 66.

104: 'Liz, you'd better marry someone ...'
Betty Sullivan, *Photoplay*, September
1950.
104: 'It was Nick this ...' Private
information.
105: 'Elizabeth loves and respects ...'
Photoplay, August 1950.

13. 'Wedding of Weddings'

106: 'Elizabeth, when you walk ...' Hedda
Hopper, *Modern Screen*, August 1950.
106: 'Cocktail dresses ...' *Los Angeles
Citizen–News*, 5 May 1950.
106: 'About twenty yards ... doesn't even
count ... crown-like halo ... It's
about as plunging ...' *ibid.*
107: 'It's not half as revealing ...' *Los
Angeles Examiner*, 6 May 1950.
108: 'I won't have cold fish ...' *Photoplay*,
August 1950.
108: 'Keep her on salary ...' MGM
Archives.
110: 'Let's hear it ...' Private information.
110: 'Seeing it's you ...' *ibid.*
111: 'Every time ...' Elsa Maxwell,
Photoplay, September 1950.
111: 'No scene that Elizabeth ...' Hedda
Hopper, *Modern Screen*, August 1950.
111: 'Not if she turns into ...' *ibid.*
112: 'Wedding of weddings ...' *ibid.*

14. A Clash of Dynasties

114: 'But Nick ran ...' Private
information.
114: 'Elizabeth and I ...' *Los Angeles
Examiner*, 17 May 1950.
115: 'My mother packed them ...' *ibid.*
115: 'Travelling with a film star ...'
Private information.
115: 'You would never have imagined ...'
Queen Mary purser to author, *circa*
August 1952.
115: 'You'd have thought ...' Michael
Wilding to author, Nice, *circa* April
1968.

116: 'Now you have the whole world ...'
Elsa Maxwell, *Photoplay*, September
1950.
117: 'Let's leave that one ...' *Daily
Express*, 11 June 1950.
117: 'To wear around home ...' *ibid.*
118: 'All her life ...' Shelley Winters *cit.*
Dick Sheppard, *op. cit.*, p. 79.
118: 'I really did think ...' Christopher
Nickens, *Elizabeth Taylor*
(Doubleday, 1984), p. 26.
119: 'To stay married ...' Private
information.

15. Divorce – Hollywood Style

120: 'And I bought him ...' *Daily Mail*, 22
August 1950.
120: 'What the hell's ...' Divorce court
evidence, 29 January 1951.
121: 'Would you please carry ...' *ibid.*
121: 'Get the bellboy ...' *ibid.*
121: 'Very tired ...' *ibid.*
121: 'I understand he threw ...' Hedda
Hopper, *cit.* Dick Sheppard, *op. cit.*,
p. 78.
121: 'Other young people ...' Louella
Parsons, *Los Angeles Examiner*, 8
December 1950.
123: 'There is no denying ...' *ibid.*
123: 'They both have a temper ...' *ibid.*
123: 'Nick and I ...' MGM Press release,
17 December 1950.
124: 'Stanley is a little boy ...' Private
information.
125: 'Was indifferent to ...' Divorce court
evidence.
125: 'Mrs Hilton ...' *ibid.*
127: 'I can't talk ...' Unsourced article,
1951.
127: 'The main thing is ...' Hedda
Hopper, *Photoplay*, August 1951.
127: 'This is your Aunt Hedda ...' *ibid.*
127: 'I had to spend ...' *ibid.*
128: 'I am trying ...' *ibid.*
128: 'A fountain to be tapped ...'
Elizabeth Taylor to author, London
1984.

16. 'Give the Girl Anything She Wants!'

130: 'It weighs two pounds ...' *Daily Herald*, 15 August 1951.

130: 'We wear long dresses ...' *ibid.*

130: 'Stay home ...' *ibid.*

130: 'A piece of cachou ...' Elizabeth Taylor, *op. cit.* (*Elizabeth Taylor*), p. 33.

131: 'I told him ...' Pandro Berman to author.

132: 'There is only one man ...' Sara Taylor, *Motion Picture*, October 1952.

133: 'Courage ... undismayed by disaster ... strength of character ...' Michael Wilding, *Apple Sauce* (Allen and Unwin, 1987), p. 75.

134: 'What made the biggest ...' Anna Neagle to author, London 1983.

134: 'I had never seen ...' Michael Wilding, *op. cit.*, p. 75.

134: 'I was cured ...' *Daily Mirror*, 12 November 1951.

134: 'Michael was nearly forty ...' Anna Neagle to author.

135: 'If only I was older ...' Michael Wilding, *op. cit.*, p. 76.

135: 'I'm running after ...' Anna Neagle to author.

135: 'I do believe ...' *ibid.*

135: 'Mentally equipped ...' *New York Post*, 23 September 1951.

135: 'Goodbye, Mr Shilly Shally ...' Michael Wilding, *op. cit.*, p. 76.

135: 'Well, not too close ...' *Los Angeles Examiner*, 16 October 1951.

136: 'This is one occasion ...' Anna Neagle to author.

136: 'Michael, it'll be the end ...' Michael Wilding, *op. cit.*, p. 134.

136: 'We were all concerned ...' Anna Neagle to author.

137: 'I was twenty years younger ...' Elizabeth Taylor, *op. cit.* (*Elizabeth Takes Off*), pp. 65–6.

137: 'I think that's the finger ...' Michael Wilding, *op. cit.*, p. 77.

137: 'That makes it official ...' *ibid.*

137: 'It's leap year ...' *Los Angeles Examiner*, undated clipping, January 1952.

137: 'He's gone and done it ...' Anna Neagle to author.

137: 'But of course ...' *ibid.*

137: 'Let's just say ...' *cit.* variously and in Herbert Wilcox, *Twenty-Five Thousand Sunsets* (Bodley Head, 1967), p. 150.

138: 'I had thought ...' *Photoplay*, May 1952.

138: 'I couldn't ...' *New York Post*, 20 October 1951.

138: 'I just want to be ...' *Daily Express*, 17 February 1952.

138: 'To the day she left it ...' Sara Taylor, *Photoplay*, 1951.

139: 'I never put ...' *Daily Express*, 5 March 1952.

139: 'Schary asked ...' Lillian Ross, *Picture* (Rinehart, 1952), p. 218.

17. Big Mama

141: 'Great difficulties ... new demands ...' MGM Archives.

142: 'If they stand pat ...' *ibid.*

142: 'I am one hundred per cent ...' *ibid.*

142: 'I re-signed because ...' Eleanor Harris, *Look*, 24 July 1956.

142: 'But mainly it was because ...' *ibid*, p. 119.

143: 'I vowed then ...' *ibid.*, p. 122.

143: 'We will have the outside ...' Martha Buckley, *Motion Picture*, November 1952.

144: 'She is very clever ...' Sara Taylor, *Photoplay*, September 1951.

147: 'The happiest days ...' Michael Wilding to author, April 1968.

147: 'Michael Wilding joins Lana Turner ...' MGM Archives.

148: 'Terrible ... ' Michael Wilding to author, April 1968.

148: 'Michael, Michael, Michael ...' *ibid.*
148: 'She is to come ...' MGM Archives.

18. Fame and Frustration

151: 'Anybody I know? ...' Elizabeth Taylor, *op. cit.* (*Elizabeth Taylor*), p. 45.
151: 'Eating a watermelon ...' *ibid.*, p. 45.
151: 'Thoughts – just mere thoughts ...' Frances Hodgson Burnett, *op. cit.*, p. 243.
151: 'She is incapable of worry ...' Herb Howe, *Photoplay*, June 1954.
151: 'I didn't think ...' Ralph Edwards, *Photoplay*, December 1954.
152: 'Poor miner's son ...' Melvyn Bragg, *Rich* (Little, Brown, 1988), p. 90.
152: 'A girl sitting ...' *ibid.*, p. 90.
152: 'Coarse and self-important ...' Rachel Roberts, unpublished diaries.
152: 'I used to watch ...' Eleanor Harris, *Look*, 24 July 1956.
152: 'Don't make yourself ...' *ibid.*
153: 'Please be sweet ...' MGM Archives.
154: 'I hate to bother ...' *ibid.*
154: 'It was on television ...' Elizabeth Taylor to author, 1984.
155: 'She met me in Rome ...' Joseph L. Mankiewicz to author, Venice, 4 September 1987.
155: 'I did enjoy ...' Elizabeth Taylor, *op. cit.* (*Elizabeth Taylor*), p. 47.
156: 'What's pneumonia ...' Richard Brooks to author, 1988.
156: 'If she opens a beer can ...' Eleanor Harris, *Look*, 24 July 1956.
157: 'She was a ravenous mother ...' Michael Wilding, *op. cit.*, p. 87.
157: 'Fabulous-looking kids ...' *ibid.*, p. 87.

19. The Crack-Up

158: 'Write me a cheque ...' Eleanor Harris, *Look,* 26 June 1956.

158: 'Then she became a pirate ...' *ibid.*
159: 'In sharp contrast ...' Rick Williams, *Photoplay*, November 1956.
159: 'Our home is like ...' Herb Howe, *Photoplay*, June 1954.
160: 'You're always surrounded ...' Michael Wilding, *op. cit.*, p. 111.
160: 'I'm your wife ...' Eleanor Harris, *Look*, 24 July 1956.
161: 'Like a lesbian ...' Elizabeth Taylor, *op. cit.* (*Elizabeth Taylor*), p. 51.
161: 'He wanted to create ...' Rock Hudson to author, Cannes, *circa* 1976.
162: 'Like brother and sister ...' *ibid.*
162: 'Beautiful ...' Rock Hudson, *Rock Hudson, His Story* (Morrow, 1986), p. 59.
162: 'It was true ...' *ibid.*
162: 'Cut ...' George Stevens to author, Beverly Hills, *circa* 1963.
163: 'She would cry ...' Eleanor Harris, *Look*, 24 July 1956.
163: 'You'd better know ...' Michael Wilding, *op. cit.*, p. 114.
163: 'I can't help it ...' *ibid.*, p. 113.
163: 'I have never two-timed ...' *ibid.*
163: 'I can't believe it ...' Elizabeth Taylor, *op. cit.* (*Elizabeth Taylor*), p. 57
164: 'Whether it's true or not ...' Eleanor Harris, *Look,* 24 July 1956.
165: 'Such a goddamn ...' Eleanor Harris, *Look,* 24 July 1956.
165: 'A displaced person ...' Michael Wilding, *op. cit.*, p. 118.

20. 'A New Kind of Man, a New Kind of World'

167: '[Monty] acted as interpreter ...' Michael Wilding, *op. cit.*, p. 116.
167: 'One breast is clearly ...' MGM Archives.
167: 'There is no possibility ...' *ibid.*
168: 'There's been a terrible ...' Secondary source only, quoted variously, consensus attribution to McCarthy.

168: 'We all ran ...' Elizabeth Taylor, *op. cit.* (*Elizabeth Taylor*), p. 57.

168: 'Suffering terribly ...' *ibid.*

168: 'I may need it ...' Rock Hudson to author, *circa* 1976.

168: 'I'd never seen her ...' *ibid.*

168: 'If you take as much ...' *ibid.*

168: 'That shook them ...' *ibid.*

168: 'By the time ...' Elizabeth Taylor, *op. cit.* (*Elizabeth Taylor*), p. 58.

169: '[Elizabeth] seemed moody ...' Hedda Hopper, *cit.* Dick Sheppard, *op. cit.*, p. 167.

169: 'All actresses ...' Michael Wilding to author, April 1968.

170: 'She admired men ...' *ibid.*

170: 'Thanks, but I'd rather ...' Michael Wilding, *op. cit.*, p. 122.

170: 'Too bossy ...' Frank Lard, *Los Angeles Mirror–News*, 26 July 1956.

170: 'I see you have ...' Private information: cf. Hedda Hopper, *op. cit.* (*The Whole Truth and Nothing But*), p. 11.

170: 'He didn't ask me ...' Private information.

171: 'Set the pattern ...' Aline Mosby, *Photoplay*, January 1957.

171: '[It] points to the fact ...' *ibid.*

173: 'Liquor spilled ...' MGM Archives.

173: 'I hope and pray ...' Hedda Hopper, *Los Angeles Herald–Examiner*, 5 October 1956.

173: 'But knowing her ...' *ibid.*

173: 'Elizabeth Taylor, 1956 ...' Patricia Bosworth, *op. cit.*, p. 309.

173: 'A friendship ...' 'an engagement ...' Unsourced news clipping, 17 October 1956.

174: 'To stay married ...' *Daily Express,* 7 September 1956.

174: 'In the case of Elizabeth ...' *ibid.*

174: 'We met ...' *ibid.*

174: 'A career wasn't ...' *Daily Mail,* 1 November 1956.

174: 'If my career ...' *News Chronicle,* 10 April 1950.

174: 'I've learnt not to dedicate ...' *Daily Express,* 5 March 1952.

175: 'Retirement? ...' *Daily Express,* 18 November 1956.

21. Hey, Big Spender!

178: 'Are you hoping ...' Maurice Smith, *Photoplay*, May 1957.

178: 'Good God, no!' *ibid.*

179: 'How interesting ...' *ibid.*

180: 'Mike ... Mike ...' *ibid.*

180: 'Don't spoil her ...' Hedda Hopper, *op. cit.* (*The Whole Truth and Nothing But*), p. 11.

180: 'I might as well ...' Logan Gourlay, *Sunday Express,* 5 May 1957.

180: 'Whither thou goest ...' Logan Gourlay, *Sunday Express,* 28 April 1957.

181: 'Elizabeth and Mike Todd ...' *Photoplay*, May 1957.

181: 'Rich, contented opulence ...' Brenda Maddox, *op. cit.*, p. 128.

182: 'Can I freshen ...' Elizabeth Taylor to author, April 1957.

182: 'Honey, honey ...' Mike Todd, Cannes, April 1957.

182: 'Pocket money ...' Private information.

183: 'A philistine with taste ...' Richard Schickel to author, London, April 1988.

183: 'Hollywood'll think me crazy ...' Sam White, *Evening Standard*, 4 June 1957.

183: 'I've had so many ...' Elizabeth Taylor to author, April 1957.

183: 'You know, little diamonds ...' Earl Wilson, *Photoplay*, October 1957.

183: 'Oh, that's just ...' Earl Wilson, *Photoplay*, March 1958.

183: 'The gal's been looking ...' Marilyn Kruse, *Chicago Sun–Times*, 10 November 1957.

183: 'Dad, the film ...' *Daily Express,* 1 July 1957.

183: 'I'm in trouble ...' *Daily Express*, 3 July 1957.
183: 'What are you hoping for? ...' *ibid.*
184: 'A girl ...' *ibid.*
184: 'Please behave like ...' Mike Todd, *cit.* Dick Sheppard, *op. cit.*, p. 187.
185: 'What's the matter? ...' Private information.
185: 'I forgot ...' *ibid.*
185: 'It knows Elizabeth ...' *ibid.*

22. The Fall of a Tycoon

186: 'And Liz'll probably play ...' Logan Gourlay, *Sunday Express*, 28 April 1957.
186 'That guy who wrote it ...' *ibid.*
187: 'Please don't take her ...' Elizabeth Taylor, *op. cit. (Elizabeth Taylor)*, p. 79.
187: 'I have the picture ...' *Photoplay*, October 1957.
187: 'Congratulations – Cartier ...' *Daily Mail*, 17 October 1957.
187: 'All I know about kids ...' Earl Wilson, *Photoplay*, March 1958.
187: 'Renting Spain ...' *ibid.*
188: 'One of the few places ...' *Los Angeles Examiner*, 18 October 1957.
189: 'Who should have ...' *New York Herald–Express*, 18 October 1957.
189: 'Anarchy raged ...' *Variety*, 23 October 1957.
189: 'The build-up was colossal ...' *ibid.*
189: 'Openly and boldly ...' *ibid.*
189: 'The most outspoken ...' *ibid.*
189: 'The manner of dispensing ...' *ibid.*
189: 'About the only thing ...' *ibid.*
189: 'The first indoor ...' *ibid.*
190: '[He] gave the public ...' *New York Daily News*, 18 October 1957.
190: 'The United States ...' *New York Herald Tribune*, 18 October 1957.
190: 'Such an evening ...' *Variety*, 23 October 1957.
190: 'The rudest personality ...' Sydney *Sunday Truth*, 7 November 1957.

190: 'I [also] thought it ...' Mike Todd, *cit.* Dick Sheppard *op. cit. (Elizabeth)*, p. 195.
190: 'Please reserve ...' *Daily Mail*, 18 January 1958.
190: 'This is the only place ...' *Daily Mirror*, 28 January 1958.
191: 'Who is the pretty ...' *Daily Mail*, 28 January 1958.
192: 'I told them it was crazy ...' Richard Brooks to author, April 1988.
192: 'I've got a great idea ...' *ibid.*
193: 'Without you, honey ...' Warren Cowan to author, London, 30 March 1988.
193: 'I got to the house ...' Richard Brooks to author.
193: 'Her first instinct ...' Dick Hanley *cit.* Richard Burton to author, Oxford, 15 October 1967.
193: 'Like throw herself ...' *ibid.*
193: 'Then the black crows ...' Richard Brooks to author.

23. A Funeral in Chicago

197: 'Oh God! ...' Private information.
197: 'It can't be ...' *ibid.*
197: 'For God's sake ...' *ibid.*
197: 'His voice ...' Richard Kline, *Los Angeles Examiner*, 26 March 1953.
197: 'Mike would have wanted ...' Richard Brooks to author, April 1988.
198: 'When this Japanese woman ...' *ibid.*
198: 'To the possibility ...' MGM Archives.
199: 'She is Maggie ...' Isabel Quigly, *The Spectator*, 17 October 1968.
199: 'When I was Maggie ...' Elizabeth Taylor, *op. cit. (Elizabeth Taylor)*, p. 86.
199: 'One moment ...' Eddie Fisher, *My Life, My Loves* (Harper and Row, 1981), p. 149.
199: 'I was married ...' Elizabeth Taylor, *op. cit. (Elizabeth Taylor)*, p. 88.

201: 'Flamboyant, impetuous ...' Eddie Fisher, *Photoplay*, p. 93.
201 'More than a starlet ...' *ibid.*, p. 106.
201: 'We were married ...' *ibid.*, p. 126.
202: 'A little too animated ...' *ibid.*, p. 131.
202: 'Wait a minute ...' *ibid.*, p. 131.
202: 'With envy ...' *ibid.*, p. 132.

24. The Mating Game

204: 'Eddie Fisher Romance ...' *Los Angeles Examiner*, 9 September 1958.
204: 'It's much too soon ...' *New York Daily News*, 9 September 1958.
204: 'I have nothing to say ...' *Los Angeles Examiner*, 10 September 1958.
204: 'Having a misunderstanding ...' Unsourced clipping, 10 September 1958.
204: 'Elizabeth, level with me ...' Hedda Hopper, *op. cit. (The Whole Truth and Nothing But)*, p. 16.
204: 'Well, you can't hurt ...' *ibid.*
204: 'He's not in love ...' *ibid.*, p. 17.
204: 'What would Mike Todd ...' *ibid.*
204: 'Ask [Eddie] to go back ...' *ibid.*
205: 'What do you expect ...' *ibid.*
205: 'Bears not the slightest ...' *ibid.*
205: 'Last week Hollywood ...' *Life*, 22 September 1958.
205: 'What I really said ...' *Cosmopolitan*, August 1961.
206: 'Eddie Fisher and Liz Taylor ...' Hedda Hopper Archives, AMPAS, Beverly Hills.
206: 'It is to [*sic*] bad ...' *ibid.*
206: 'All of Fischer's [*sic*] ...' *ibid.*
206: 'I am more ...' *ibid.*
206: 'Won't daddy be ...' *Photoplay*, January 1959.
206: 'I got to thinking ...' *The New Yorker*, undated clipping.
206: 'Anyone who is against me ...' Uncorroborated quote, *cit.* variously, consensus attribution to Mrs Jacqueline Kennedy.

207: 'For all the American families ...' Brenda Maddox, *op. cit.*, p. 143.
207: 'If this nauseating woman ...' *The People*, 5 April 1959.
207: 'Did anyone ever tell you ...' Anecdotal, source unknown, consensus attribution to Oscar Levant.
208: 'The official destruction ...' *Photoplay*, June 1959.
208: '[The affair] should be marked ...' *ibid.*
209: 'We only lend ...' *Daily Telegraph*, 15 March 1959.
209: 'Shamelessly ... terribly happy ...' *Los Angeles Examiner*, 2 April 1959.
209: 'Forthright life ...' Max Lerner, *New York Post, circa* April 1959.
210: 'It's a double act ...' Sidney Skolsky, *Photoplay*, August 1959.
210: 'No, cash please ...' Rene MacColl, *Daily Express*, 13 May 1959.
210: 'You may need this ...' Jonah Ruddy, *Daily Mail*, 14 May 1959.
210: 'Drugged with love ...' Eddie Fisher, *op. cit.*, p. 163.

25. Sic Transit Gloria

211: 'Chaos ...' Eddie Fisher, *op. cit.*, p. 166.
211: 'Fighting was a part ...' *ibid.*, p. 168.
211: 'When time began ...' *ibid.*, p. 162.
213: 'She tended to be shrill ...' Joseph L. Mankiewicz to author, 4 September 1987.
213: 'But she had a tremendous ...' *ibid.*
213: 'Too wised up ...' *ibid.*
213: 'Tennessee giggles ...' *ibid.*
213: 'It tore Elizabeth's gut out ...' *ibid.*
214: 'Tear me apart ...' *ibid.*
214: 'But it was a foregone ...' *ibid.*
215: 'All this needs ...' Walter Wanger and Joe Hyams, 'Cleopatra', *Saturday Evening Post*, 1 June 1963.
215: 'Too unmanageable ...' *ibid.*
215: 'Who needs ...' *ibid.*

215: 'You ought to do it ...' Eddie Fisher, *op. cit.*, p. 173.

215: 'I'll do it ...' Walter Wanger and Joe Hyams, *op. cit.*

216: 'The leading lady ...' *Los Angeles Examiner,* 13 October 1958.

217: 'Unacceptable ... upheld at all times ...' MGM Archives.

217: 'She said she'd be damned ...' Pandro Berman to author, 21 April 1988.

217: 'Gloria is a woman ...' MGM Archives.

217: 'Perhaps the best way ...' *ibid.*

217: 'There is another factor ...' *ibid.*

217: 'I think the premise ...' *ibid.*

218: 'Casual and repeated ... admissibility ... corrected ...' *ibid.*

218: 'It must be clearly ...' *ibid.*

219: 'Mr Elizabeth Taylor ...' Eddie Fisher, *op. cit.*, p. 194.

219: 'You wear it with slacks ...' Earl Wilson, *New York Mirror News,* 18 November 1959.

219: 'I hate the girl ...' *Photoplay,* January 1960.

219: 'The bitch is where ...' Laurence Harvey to author, London, 15 November 1960.

220: 'This is going ...' *ibid.*

220: 'We certainly live dramatically ...' Paulene Stone, *One Tear Is Enough* (Michael Joseph, 1975), pp. 153–4.

220: 'She reminded me ...' Pandro Berman to author, 21 April 1988.

220: 'I always thought ...' *ibid.*

221: 'She presented me ...' *ibid.*

221: 'If you share my concern ...' MGM Archives.

221: 'Make believe ...' Eddie Fisher, *op. cit.*, p. 176.

221: 'The most public adultery ...' Variously attributed without consensus agreement.

26. *Between Life and Death*

224: 'Does God always punish? ...' *Photoplay,* April 1960.

224: 'Some kind of production assistant ...' Eddie Fisher, *op. cit.*, p. 179.

226: 'What I didn't know ...' *ibid.*, p. 180.

227: 'I'm here to do ...' *ibid.*, p. 180.

227: 'What knowledge she'd acquired ...' Joseph L. Mankiewicz to author, Bedford, NY, 9 April 1988.

227: 'Since I was a little girl ...' Elizabeth Taylor, *op. cit.* (*Elizabeth Takes Off*), p. 83.

228: 'Suddenly everything began ...' Eddie Fisher, *op. cit.*, p. 186.

228: 'I was giving up my life ...' *ibid.*, p. 187.

228: 'You're leaving ...' *ibid.*, p. 199.

228: 'By the time ...' Private information.

229: 'I was fierce ...' Jack Hamilton, *Look,* 15 August 1961.

229: 'I died four times ...' *ibid.*

229: 'A bright shining light ...' *ibid.*

229: 'Am I dying ...' Eddie Fisher, *op. cit.*, p. 192.

229: 'I began to feel ...' *Look,* 15 August 1961.

230: 'My God, how did it happen? ...' Walter Wanger and Joe Hyams, *op. cit.*

230: 'Two years before ...' Eddie Fisher, *op. cit.*, p. 192.

231: 'I knew that I wanted ...' Elizabeth Taylor, *op. cit.* (*Elizabeth Taylor*), p. 100.

232: 'It strengthened Elizabeth's self-respect ...' Max Lerner, *McCall's,* September 1974.

232: 'Myth ... legend ...' *ibid.*

232: 'Both of you are forces ...' *ibid.*

232: 'Very shaky ...' Max Lerner to author, New York, 6 December 1988.

232: 'She has a great capacity ...' *ibid.*

232: 'It's very difficult ...' *ibid.*

232: 'I think it's fair to say ...' *ibid.*

232: 'She said to me ...' *ibid.*

232: 'There is this thing ...' Max Lerner, *McCall's*, September 1974.

233: '[My relationship] has given me ...' Max Lerner to author, 6 September 1988.

27. *'Le Scandale'*

237: 'I must don my armour ...' Richard Burton *cit.* Melvyn Bragg, *op. cit.*, p. 145.

237: 'It wasn't a flop ...' *Cosmopolitan*, August 1961.

238: 'Often stormy ...' Max Lerner, *McCall's*, June 1975.

238: 'No one will be able ...' Variously attributed without consensus agreement.

239: 'You can't act falling ...' Graham Jenkins, *Richard Burton, My Brother* (Harper and Row, 1988), p. 79.

239: '[She is] a romantic ...' Max Lerner, *McCall's*, September 1974.

239: '*Le scandale* ...' Variously attributed without consensus agreement.

241: 'Has anyone ever told you ...' Elizabeth Taylor, *op. cit.* (*Elizabeth Taylor*), p. 102.

241: 'Come look ...' Eddie Fisher, *op. cit.*, p. 213.

242: 'Consumed by their need ...' Rachel Roberts, unpublished diaries.

242: 'He was so sweet ...' Elizabeth Taylor, *op. cit.* (*Elizabeth Taylor*), p. 103.

243: 'There comes a time ...' Walter Wanger and Joe Hyams, *op. cit.*

244: 'I've been sitting ...' *ibid.*

244: 'Do you think ...' Joseph L. Mankiewicz to author, 9 April 1988.

244: 'Walter ...' *ibid.*

244: 'When you are in a cage ...' *ibid.*

28. *L'Amour Fou*

246: 'Many years afterwards ...' Graham Jenkins, *op. cit.*, p. 124.

246: 'Is it true ...' Eddie Fisher, *op. cit.*, p. 215.

247: 'To get the hell back ...' *ibid.*, p. 215.

247: 'But I couldn't help ...' Elizabeth Taylor, *op. cit.* (*Elizabeth Taylor*), p. 106.

247: 'Have it out ...' Eddie Fisher, *op. cit.*, p. 218.

247: 'Sybil is about ...' Jack Brodsky and Nathan Weiss, *The Cleopatra Papers* (Simon and Schuster, 1963), p. 47.

247: '[Elizabeth] turned white ...' *ibid.*, p. 37.

248: 'The whole world is in front ...' *ibid.*, p. 38.

248: 'No writer could get away ...' Eddie Fisher, *op. cit.*, p. 218.

248: 'She'd got her nerve back ...' Rachel Roberts, unpublished diaries.

248: 'I love you ...' Eddie Fisher, *op. cit.*, p. 221.

249: 'Both ...' Emlyn Williams to author, London, 4 August 1986.

249: 'I'll choose both ...' *Daily Mail*, 4 May 1958.

249: 'A plunger ...' Max Lerner, *McCall's*, June 1976.

249: 'Very gay, very cocky ...' Walter Wanger and Joe Hyams, *op. cit.*

249: 'Row Over Actor ...' Louella Parsons, *Los Angeles Examiner*, 9 March 1963.

250: 'Sybil! ...' Jack Brodsky and Nathan Weiss, *op. cit.*, p. 132.

250: 'So close ...' *ibid.*, p. 46.

250: 'Craziness ...' Eddie Fisher, *op. cit.*, p. 218.

251: 'Elizabeth, I'm leaving ...' *ibid.*, p. 224.

251: 'Everyone believes ...' Sheilah Graham, *cit.* Dick Sheppard, *op. cit.*, p. 303.

252: 'You know, you can ask a woman ...' *Los Angeles Herald–Examiner*, 30 March 1962.

252: 'Elizabeth and Eddie Fisher ...' *Los*

Angeles Herald–Examiner, 3 April 1962.

252: 'That's it ...' *ibid.*

252: 'The appearance ...' Hedda Hopper, *Los Angeles Times*, 5 April 1962.

29. *O Mistress Mine!*

253: 'They mustn't take her back ...' Dick Hanley to author, London, *circa* April 1963.

253: 'You may rest assured ...' *ibid.*

253: 'The caprices ...' Vatican Radio broadcast, 3 April 1962.

253: 'An avaricious vamp ...' *Il Tempo*, 4 April 1962.

253: 'The lady is one long ...' Cassandra, *Daily Mirror*, 3 April 1962.

253: 'Please ... who's my daddy' *Life*, 13 April 1962.

253: 'She was red-eyed ...' Dick Hanley to author, *circa* April 1963.

254: 'Dear Madam ...' *Osservatore della Domenica*, April 1962.

254: 'Can I sue the Pope? ...' *Cit.* variously, no consensus attribution, possibly anecdotal.

254: 'Leez! ... Grazie ...' Walter Wanger and Joe Hyams, *op. cit.*

254: 'One of the sweetest ...' Elizabeth Taylor to author, Oxford, 15 October 1967.

254: 'I made a most ...' Emlyn Williams to author, 4 August 1986.

254: 'Nervous, irritable ...' Jack Brodsky and Nathan Weiss, *op. cit.*, p. 59.

254: 'Could have had no idea ...' Melvyn Bragg, *op. cit.*, p. 158.

255: 'Interested? ...' Warner Bros Collection, USC.

255: 'He had never totally ...' Melvyn Bragg, *op. cit.*, p. 158.

256: 'There is no question ...' David Lewin, *Daily Express*, 2 May 1962.

256: 'This tough and cheerful ...' Melvyn Bragg, *op. cit.*, p. 64.

256: 'Absolutely not ...' David Lewin, *Daily Express*, 2 May 1962.

256: 'Crying all the way ...' Private information.

256: 'We have it ...' Jack Brodsky and Nathan Weiss, *op. cit.*, p. 110.

257: 'Dead, flat ...' Melvyn Bragg, *op. cit.*, p. 155.

258: 'Like bright blue ...' Elizabeth Taylor, *op. cit.* (*Elizabeth Taylor*), p. 119.

258: 'By making myself ...' *ibid.*, p. 122.

258: 'You didn't think ...' Joseph L. Mankiewicz to author, 9 April 1988.

30. *From Purgatory to Puerto Vallarta*

259: 'He was in purgatory ...' Stanley Baker to author, London, *circa* 1970.

259: 'In limbo ...' Elizabeth Taylor, *op. cit.* (*Elizabeth Taylor*), p. 122.

259: 'On the bottle ...' Graham Jenkins, *op. cit.*, p. 131.

259: 'Moved outside ... without investing ...' Kenneth Tynan, *Playboy*, April 1963.

259: 'A natural woman ...' Graham Jenkins, *op. cit.*, p. 133.

259: 'Will you marry ...' *ibid.*, p. 133.

259: 'Isn't Sybil supposed ...' *ibid.*, p. 133.

260: 'Sybil was yesterday ...' *ibid.*, p. 133.

260: 'She could look ...' Emlyn Williams to author, 4 August 1986.

260: 'If he should ever marry ...' *Time*, 26 April 1964.

260: 'Warren, do you think...' Warren Cowan to author, London, 27 March 1988.

260: 'Show a Welshman ...' Joseph L. Mankiewicz to author, 9 April 1988.

260: 'Now it was Elizabeth's turn ...' Stanley Baker to author, *circa* 1970.

261: 'Have you come ...' Private information.

261: 'It was like a cry ...' Graham Jenkins, *op. cit.*, p. 133.

262: 'The world's most distracting ...'
Variety, undated clipping.

262: 'It was a nightmare time ...' Fergus
Cashin, Daily Sketch, 6 March 1968.

262: 'In 1963, Rich ...' Graham Jenkins,
op. cit., p. 139.

263: 'I don't know anything ...' Elizabeth
Taylor to author et al., 15 October
1967.

264: 'A call to the set ...' Peter Glenville,
Vogue, September 1967.

264: 'Richard is still full ...' ibid.

264: 'I love not working ...' Stanley Elkin,
Esquire, November 1964.

265: 'Overweight, overbosomed ...'
David Susskind, television review,
date not identifiable.

265: 'Miss Taylor is not ...' Newsweek, 17
June 1963.

267: 'I can live here ... I can write here
...' Richard Burton to author, 15
October 1967.

31. A Life in the Theatre

269: 'A Mexican-made green ...' Thelma
Victor, Saturday Evening Post, 11 July
1964.

269: 'A magnificent gold ring ...' ibid.

269: 'She's seducing me ...' ibid.

270: 'This is the life ...' ibid.

270: 'After a time ...' ibid.

270: 'I've been sitting here ...' ibid.

270: 'Oh, hello, darling ...' ibid.

271: 'Please ... do not spoil ...' Time, 3
January 1964.

271: 'The not-quite-polygamous ...' John
Cottrell and Fergus Cashin, Richard
Burton (Prentice Hall, 1972), p. 195.

271: 'If you come down to it ...' ibid., p.
295.

272: '[She] put twenty-eight ...' Cit. Dick
Sheppard, op. cit., p. 350.

273: 'Illicit love ...' Elizabeth Taylor, op.
cit. (Elizabeth Taylor), p. 172.

273: See if it's a wig ...' ibid., p. 125.

274: 'All stood there ...' Stanley Elkin,
Esquire, November 1964.

274: 'The crowds, the enthusiasm ... an
exalted condition ...' Truman
Capote, Ladies' Home Journal,
December 1974.

274: 'For God's sake ...' ibid.

275: 'Screwed up ...' Los Angeles Herald–
Examiner, 26 June 1964.

32. 'For the Money, We Will Dance'

276: 'For the money ...' Melvyn Bragg,
op. cit., p. 199.

276: 'Taut little drama ...' Variety, 15
October 1971.

276: 'It's a potboiler ... it's a moneymaker
...' Elizabeth Taylor and Richard
Burton to author, Oxford, 15
October 1967.

277: 'We never had ...' Daily Express, 19
August 1964.

277: 'It's not true ...' Daily Express, 10
January 1965.

278: 'Fill in the holes ...' MGM Archives.

278: '[He and Elizabeth] both kept alive
...' Graham Jenkins, op. cit., p. 153.

278: 'I didn't have an unhappy ...' Evening
Standard, 12 October 1964.

279: 'In the post-prandial glow ...' Jack
Hamilton, Look, 8 March 1965.

279: 'She can't just go on ...' Graham
Jenkins, op. cit., p. 153.

279: 'We want to buy ...' Roderick Mann,
Sunday Express, 7 February 1965.

280: 'Such a v.v.v. long play ...'
Alexander Walker, op. cit., p. 276.

280: 'Elizabeth Taylor told me ...' Warner
Brothers Archives, USC.

281: 'An important steadying ...' ibid.

281: 'If we can live with it ...' ibid.

281: '$750,000, yes ...' ibid.

281: 'My best feature ...' Elizabeth
Taylor, op. cit. (Elizabeth Taylor), p.
170.

282: 'Full-length drab ...' Joseph Roddy,
Look, 8 February 1966.

282: 'I'm paying her ...' Anecdotal evidence, no consensus attribution.

282: 'A fantastic feeling ...' Sheilah Graham, *Citizen–News*, 12 August 1965.

282: 'Change was creeping ...' Paul Ferris, *op. cit.*, p. 127.

283: 'A necessary stage ...' Melvyn Bragg, *op. cit.*, p. 205.

283: 'She was already ...' *ibid.*

283: 'My only concern ...' Robert Jennings, *Saturday Evening Post*, 9 October 1965.

283: 'Why should anyone ...' Paul Ferris, *op. cit.*, p. 128.

283: 'She was prone ...' Melvyn Bragg, *op. cit.*, p. 158.

33. Work, Work, Work—Spend, Spend, Spend

284: 'The Rolls holds bags ...' Elizabeth Taylor to author, 15 October 1967.

284: 'Solo acting ...' Terry Coleman, *Manchester Guardian/Los Angeles Times*, 16 February 1966.

285: 'They were a present ...' Russell Braddon, *Saturday Evening Post*, 3 December 1966

285: 'No, there's a little ...' *ibid.*

286: 'Astonishing ...' *Time*, 30 June 1966.

287: 'When [Elizabeth Taylor] welcomes ...' *Time*, 7 February 1968.

288: '[The character] he is ...' *Newsweek*, 2 November 1967.

289: 'It would be more interesting ...' Michel Ciment, *Le livre de Losey* (Editions Stock, 1979), p. 316 (translation: Walker).

290: 'The states can linger ...' Joseph Losey Collection, British Film Institute, London.

291: 'Wear one colour ...' *Evening Standard*, 17 June 1968.

291: 'I'll wear no colour ...' *ibid.*

291: 'They looked like shrouds ...' Joseph Losey to author, 15 June 1968.

291: 'It's a funny scene ...' *Evening Standard*, 17 June 1968.

291: 'I do not find ...' *ibid.*

291: 'She was thinking ...' Joseph Losey to author, 15 June 1968.

292: 'Sweet revenge ...' Melvyn Bragg, *op. cit.*, p. 246.

34. Barques and Bites

293: 'I don't want the kids ...' Roderick Mann, *Sunday Express*, 17 September 1967.

293: 'Sometimes it's not easy ...' *Daily Express*, 11 October 1967.

295: 'A television station ...' Stanley Baker to author, *circa* 1970.

295: 'Keep the fat firm ...' *McCall's*, 22 December 1967.

296: 'The world's most expensive ...' *Daily Mail*, 21 February 1968.

296: 'The cost falls ...' *Daily Telegraph*, 22 February 1968.

297: 'He did nothing ...' Michel Ciment, *op. cit.*, p. 335 (translation: Walker).

297: 'When people reach ...' *Life*, 29 May 1968.

298: 'Ghastly advertising ...' Joseph Losey Collection, British Film Institute, London.

298: 'Massive loss ...' *ibid.*

298: 'Thus I became ...' Joseph Losey to author, *circa* December 1968.

298: 'It was pandemonium ...' Private information.

298: 'Isn't it nice ...' *ibid.*

299: 'The price of bread ...' John Cottrell and Fergus Cashin, *op. cit.*, p. 366.

299: 'They must be out ...' Tommy Thompson, *Life*, 17 January 1969.

300: 'She asked ...' Melvyn Bragg, *op. cit.*, p. 264.

300: 'Marred royalty ...' *ibid.*, p. 272.

300: 'Short of a war ...' *ibid.*, p. 313.

301: 'We can at least live ...' *ibid.*, p. 313.

301: 'There are many worlds ...' *ibid.*, p. 314.

301: 'As a result ...' *ibid.*, p. 280.

35. Diamond Liz

302: 'I've been re-reading ...' Joseph Losey Collection, British Film Institute, London.

302: 'Sloshed as a Cossack ...' Melvyn Bragg, *op. cit.*, p. 289.

303: 'Crocked as a sock ...' *ibid.*, p. 289.

303: 'It used to belong ...' *Daily Express*, 27 January 1969.

304: 'Is there any interest ...' Joseph Losey Collection, British Film Institute, London.

305: 'Nobody can turn ...' Melvyn Bragg, *op. cit.*, p. 318.

305: 'Fuck the million ...' Fergus Cashin to author, *circa* 1970.

305: 'In this age of vulgarity ...' *New York Times*, undated clipping.

306: 'The most vulgar thing ...' Anecdotal source only.

306: 'Be going to take off ...' Melvyn Bragg, *op. cit.*, p. 326.

307: '[Our world] has changed ...' *ibid.*, p. 324.

307: 'Not without merit ... Lucrezia Borgia ...' Joseph Losey Collection, British Film Institute, London.

308: 'Just dying ...' Jonah Roddy, *Look*, 10 June 1970.

308: 'From the tropical sun ...' *ibid.*

309: 'The ageing beauty ...' Pauline Kael, *The New Yorker*, 12 February 1972.

309: 'Her aura is crimson ...' Edna O'Brien, *Zee & Co.* (Weidenfeld and Nicolson, 1970).

309: 'Gracefully voluptuous ...' Pauline Kael, *The New Yorker*, 12 February 1972.

310: 'He is the ocean ...' *Ladies' Home Journal*, April 1971.

36. 'Oh, Where Are the Writers to Rescue Us?'

311: 'The trouble with actors ...' Joseph L. Mankiewicz to author, 9 April 1988.

311: 'That terrible mad ...' Don Knapp, *Los Angeles Times Magazine*, 5 December 1971.

312: 'We were offered ...' *ibid.*

312: 'What does it matter ...' *ibid.*

312: 'I don't have to ...' *Los Angeles Times*, 13 May 1972.

313: 'A little lightness ...' Melvyn Bragg, *op. cit.*, p. 384.

315: 'Ifor's death ...' *ibid.*, p. 512.

315: 'Get that woman ...' Kitty Kelley, *op. cit.*, p. 219.

316: 'A little like a rather forlorn ...' Private information.

317: 'For a moment it seemed ...' Keith Botsford, *New York Times*, 25 March 1973.

317: 'We can't just go on ...' *ibid.*

317: 'When, if ever ...' *Time, cit.* Paul Ferris, *op. cit.*, p. 153.

317: 'We wanted the theme ...' John Heyman to author, New York, 5 December 1988.

317: 'She was dying to do another ...' Dominick Dunne to author, New York, 6 December 1988.

318: 'Received with pleasure ...' *ibid.*

318: 'My husband ...' *ibid.*

319: 'I told her to go ...' Peter Evans, *Cosmopolitan*, November 1974.

319: 'I am convinced ...' *Los Angeles Herald–Examiner*, 4 July 1973.

37. A Chipmunk Returns

321: 'It takes one day ...' *National Enquirer*, 8 August 1973.

322: 'Elizabeth never ...' Max Lerner to author, 6 September 1988.

322: 'In the case of ...' Max Lerner, *McCall's*, June 1975.

322: 'My child's ...' *ibid.*
322: 'No name ...' Roger Falke, *Ladies'
Home Journal,* December 1974.
322: 'Maybe that's what she's playing at
...' Sydney Edwards to author, *circa*
September 1973.
323: 'Hello, Lumpy ...' Sydney Edwards
to author, *circa* October 1973.
323: 'Is it true ...' *Daily Telegraph,* 27 June
1974.
323: 'She had gotten rid of ...' Max Lerner
to author, 6 September 1988.
324: 'Henry had a lot of patience ...'
Private information.
324: 'Elizabeth often spoke ...' Max
Lerner to author, 5 September 1988.
324: 'Elizabeth, he's ...' *ibid.*
324: 'Elizabeth will ...' Melvyn Bragg, *op.
cit.,* p. 480.
324: 'Stop in your room ...' Robert
Morley to author, 24 May 1988.
325: 'But what a hell ...' Rex Reed,
Valentines and Vitriol (Delacorte,
1977), p. 21.
325: 'She never did ...' Liz Smith,
Cosmopolitan, May 1976.
325: 'Self-control ...' Graham Jenkins, *op.
cit.,* p. 212.

38. The Farmer Takes a Wife

327: 'Will you marry ...' Elizabeth Taylor,
Ladies' Home Journal, February 1976.
327: 'I know we will ...' *ibid.*
327: 'Maybe I'll carry you off ...' *ibid.*
328: 'Green ... salty ... magical ...' *ibid.*
328: 'Booze day ...' *ibid.*
328: 'As stout as ...' *ibid.*
328: 'Epstein sculptures ...' *ibid.*
330: 'She was dancing with a man ...'
Peter Darmanin to author, London,
3 October 1988.
330: 'We tended to fight ...' *ibid.*
330: 'Who had given it ...' *ibid.*
330: 'She cares for you ...' *ibid.*
331: 'That marvellous silver ...' Arnold
Latham, *Esquire,* November 1977.

334: 'She is so exciting ...' Nick
Thimmisch, *McCall's,* January 1977.
334: 'Hello, I'm your date ...' *ibid.*
334: 'She turned to me ...' *ibid.*
334: 'The yacht ...' Barbara Walters
Special, ABC–TV, 6 April 1977,
Archives of the Museum of
Broadcasting, New York.
335: 'If he wants ...' *ibid.*
335: 'Franklin was born ...' *McCall's,*
January 1977.
335: 'We had gone ...' *cit.* Kitty Kelley,
op. cit., p. 259.
336: 'We've even chosen ...' *Esquire,*
November 1977.
336: 'I want her ...' Roderick Mann,
Sunday Express, 29 May 1977.
337: 'We did it ...' *The Washington Post,* 5
December 1976.

39. Issues of Weight

338: '(*Virginia Woolf*) ...' Nick
Thimmisch, *McCall's,* July 1977.
339: 'He saw her waving ...' *ibid.*
339: 'Except become pregnant ...' Robin
Leach, *People,* 14 February 1977.
339: 'You can tell we use it ...' Elizabeth
Taylor to author, Washington DC,
May 1977.
340: 'If you lapse ...' *McCall's,* July 1977.
340: 'I'm not interested ...' *Esquire,*
November 1977.
340: 'A bird of paradise ...' *ibid.*
340: 'You're a male chauvinist ...' *ibid.*
340: 'It doesn't grab you ...' *ibid.*
340: 'Rolling around ...' *Daily Express,* 27
April 1977.
341: 'Like many other ...' Elizabeth
Taylor, *op. cit.* (*Elizabeth Takes Off*),
p. 38.
341: 'Got to watch ...' Secondary source
only, *cit.* Kitty Kelley, *op. cit.,* p. 273.
341: 'It's happy fat ...' *Daily Express,* 22
October 1977.
341: 'I've been working ...' David Wigg,
Daily Express, 14 January 1978.

341: 'She's enjoying life . . .' *ibid.*

342: 'Liz looked like . . .' Andy Warhol and Pat Hackett, *The Andy Warhol Diaries* (Warner Books, 1989), p. 115.

342: 'I'm a politician . . .' *ibid.*

342: 'The focus of the race . . .' Garry Clifford, *People*, 23 October 1978.

343: 'What kind of . . .' *ibid.*

343: 'John was up and out . . .' Elizabeth Taylor, *op. cit.* (*Elizabeth Takes Off*), p. 43.

344: 'What kind of jobs . . .' *Sunday Express*, 4 February 1980.

344: 'Women have been . . .' *ibid.*

344: 'Don't you steady . . .' *ibid.*

344: 'My God, we've spent . . .' Source unknown, possibly anecdotal.

344: 'I had literally . . .' Elizabeth Taylor, *op. cit.* (*Elizabeth Takes Off*), p. 48.

344: 'Unlike Scarlett O'Hara . . .' *ibid.*, p. 114.

345: 'I was delighted . . .' John Higgins, *The Times*, 18 February 1981.

40. *Positively Their Last Appearance*

347: 'Let the audience . . .' Elizabeth Taylor, *op. cit.* (*Elizabeth Takes Off*), p. 94.

347: 'When I talked over . . .' *The Times*, 18 February 1981.

348: 'Each of them recognized . . .' Private information.

348: 'There's a line . . .' *ibid.*

348: 'Elizabeth pitched . . .' *ibid.*

348: 'I like . . .' *Time*, 30 March 1981.

349: 'She's a killer . . .' *Washington Post*, undated clipping.

349: 'An *a priori* bravo . . .' Edwin Wilson, *Wall Street Journal*, 12 May 1981.

349: 'At forty-nine . . .' John Simon, *New York*, 18 May 1981.

349: '[Regina's role] doesn't require . . .' Frank Rich, *New York Times*, 8 May 1981.

349: '[A] leftist attack . . .' Michael Feingold, *Village Voice*, 13 May 1981.

349: 'I was overwhelmed . . .' Elizabeth Taylor, *op. cit.* (*Elizabeth Takes Off*), p. 94.

350: 'Who I could see . . .' Andy Warhol and Pat Hackett, *op. cit.*, p. 424.

351: 'I can't live . . .' *Daily Express*, 21 February 1982.

351: 'The grand addiction . . .' *Daily Mail*, 4 October 1982.

351: 'She is always saying . . .' *Evening Standard*, 25 February 1982.

351: 'She really does . . .' *ibid.*

352: 'Opened the door . . .' Susan and Steven Licht to author, London, 24 May 1988.

352: 'Oh, come on . . .' Peter Archer, *Evening Standard*, 1 March 1982.

353: 'As grisly . . .' Robert Cushman, *Observer*, 14 March 1982.

353: 'For the most part . . .' Jack Tinker, *Daily Mail*, 12 March 1982.

353: 'What do you say . . .' Graham Jenkins, *op. cit.*, p. 236.

353: 'Had the deal been . . .' Melvyn Bragg, *op. cit.*, p. 470.

354: 'Two middle-aged people . . .' Elizabeth Taylor, *op. cit.* (*Elizabeth Takes Off*), p. 97.

354: 'Face OK . . .' Melvyn Bragg, *op. cit.*, p. 472.

354: 'On something . . .' *ibid.*, p. 473.

355: 'A tired millionaire . . .' Frank Rich, *New York Times*, 9 May 1983.

355: 'Running like a deer . . . anything faster . . .' John Simon, *New York*, 25 May 1983.

355: '*The Dance of Death* would . . .' *Variety*, 11 May 1983.

356: 'I have no idea . . .' *Daily Express*, 11 August 1983.

358: 'Since we can't . . .' *Sun*, 14 July 1984.

358: 'You'll never guess . . .' Melvyn Bragg, *op. cit.*, p. 480.

358: 'Another go . . .' *ibid.*, p. 484.

359: 'When we need . . .' Graham Jenkins, *op. cit.*, p. 242.

41. 'I Have No Plan to Succumb'

363: 'It was one of the few ...' Graham
Jenkins, *op. cit.*, p. 245.

363: 'Almost wistfully ...' *ibid.*

364: 'Like a queen ...' Private
information.

364: 'Pretty strange ...' Elizabeth Taylor,
op. cit. (*Elizabeth Takes Off*), p. 104.

365: 'Almost a mistake ...' *Vanity Fair,*
December 1985.

365: 'Elizabeth Taylor stood ...' *Daily
Mail,* 20 April 1986.

365: 'In each century ...' Frances
Hodgson Burnett, *op. cit.*, p. 243.

366: 'It's going to take ...' *Daily Express,*
17 April 1987.

366: 'The first time ...' *Los Angeles Herald–
Examiner,* 3 April 1987.

366: 'Sara Taylor's a tough ...' *People,* 6
November 1989.

366: 'A female Elvis Presley ...' *ibid.,* 13
March 1989.

366: 'You know what happened ...' *ibid.*

368: 'For the first time ...' *Daily Mirror,* 1
December 1985.

369: 'The weekend [was] ...' Julie
Baumgold, *New York,* 2 October
1989.

370: She knows more ...' Paulene Stone,
op. cit., p. 154.

370: 'It's difficult ...' John Leonard, *New
York,* 2 October 1989.

370: 'I have no plan ...' Myrna Blyth,
Ladies' Home Journal, November
1987.

371: 'What do you suppose ...' Truman
Capote, *Ladies' Home Journal,*
December 1974.

371: 'I take things ...' James Grant, *Los
Angeles Times,* 1 October 1989.

371: 'In those days ...' DeWitt Bodeen,
Films in Review, April 1965.

371: 'A one-woman ...' *cit.* Mike Bygrave,
Sunday Correspondent, 29 April 1990.

372: 'Out of touch ...' Richard Schickel,
The Stars (Crown/Bonanza, 1962), p.
280.

372: 'I have decided ...' *Films in Review,*
April 1965.

INDEX

. . .

E. stands for Elizabeth Taylor.